Prince Henry 'the Navigator'

Christmas, 2000

Good Reading, Tom,
for Portugal and Spain,
2001. Love,
Mary

Prince Henry 'the Navigator'

A Life

The Lusitanian prince, who, Heaven-inspired,
To love of useful glory raised mankind
And in unbounded commerce mixed the world

James Thomson, *The Seasons*, Summer, 11.1010–12

Peter Russell

Yale University Press
New Haven and London

For Anthony Pagden – despertador de almas
durmientes – with gratitude and affection

CALOUSTE
GULBENKIAN
FOUNDATION

FUNDAÇÃO
ORIENTE

We are grateful to the Calouste Gulbenkian Foundation
(UK) and the Fundação Oriente for their generous
financial support of this publication, and also to the
Portuguese Arts Trust for its additional assistance.

Designed by Adam Freudenheim

Set in Sabon by Best-set Typesetter Ltd, Hong Kong
Printed in Singapore

Library of Congress Cataloging-in-Publication Data
Russell, P. E. (Peter Edward), 1913–
Prince Henry 'the Navigator': a Life
p. cm.
Includes bibliographical references (p.).
ISBN 0-300-08233-9 (cloth)
1.   Henry, Infante of Portugal, 1394–1460. 2.   Explorers—Portugal—
Biography. 3.   Princes—Portugal—Biography. I.   Title.
G286.H5 R88 2000
946.9'02'092—dc21
[B]
99-049569

A Catalogue record for this book is available from the British Library

10 9 8 7 6 5 4 3 2 1

Endpapers: *The World Map of Mecià Viladestes* (detail of fig. 4).

Contents

List of Illustrations

Glossary

alferes mor	bearer of the royal standard and, until 1382, the commander-in-chief of a Portuguese army in the field (*see also* constable)
alvará	a decree usually but not always issued by the crown, often in the form of letters patent
almoxarife	the collector of the crown's taxes in a specified locality
arroba	variable measure of weight nominally the equivalent of 32 lbs (English)
barinel	a small square-rigged ship capable of being rowed
capitão	in addition to its normal military and maritime meanings, the term was also used from Henry's time to refer to the office of governor of one of the Atlantic islands on behalf of its territorial lord and to the representative of the king in Portuguese fortresses in North and West Africa and elsewhere overseas
Casa de Ceuta	literally 'House of Ceuta'; referred to in this book as the Ceuta Agency
Casa da Guiné	the Guinea Agency (see preceding note)
comenda	commandery; refers to a territorial property belonging to a military order whose name and revenues were assigned for the sustenance of a particular knight (*comendador*) of the order
comendador	see preceding entry
comuna	community; the Jewish community regarded as a separate administrative and ethnic group
constable	(Port.) *condestabre*; after the military reforms of 1382 the title of *condestabre* was given to the commander-in-chief of the army in the field
Cortes	parliament
cruzado	a 23¾ carat gold coin introduced by Afonso V in 1457 to rival the Florentine florin and the ducat

degredado	a banished person; name given in the fifteenth century and later to a convict ordered or allowed to commute his or her sentence to exile in one of the Portuguese overseas territories
dízima	tax of one-tenth payable to the crown on all imports by sea
dobra	Span. *dobla* – the generic name for gold coins minted in Muslim North Africa or in Granada and, in imitation of the gold coinage of those countries, in Castile. No gold coins were minted in Portugal in the reign of John I but the *dobra* was widely used there then and later as a money of account
donatory	Port. *donatório*; lord-proprietor; in this book normally refers to the beneficiary of a semi-feudal donation of crown land in the form of a lordship carrying with it devolved juridical authority
foro	charter
freire	'monk or friar'; in this book the term normally refers to a secular member of one of the military orders who by virtue of his membership held the rank of knight
haik	(Ar.) Port. *alquiçé* – a Moorish cloak or mantle manufactured in North Africa
hambel	(Ar.) coloured striped blanket manufactured in North Africa
Infante	'Prince'; title held only by princes of the blood royal
Infanta	Princess
lente	a university professor or reader
libra	a pound – money of account used in Portugal from the thirteenth to the fifteenth century
madeira	timber, wood
malagueta	West African pepper – botanical name *Afromomum Melegueta* – often known as 'grains of Paradise'
marshal	(Port. *marechal*); after the reforms of 1382 the second most important military officer in a Portuguese army in the field

Mestre	Master; the title given to the head of any one of the Portuguese military orders
nascimento	horoscope
parecer	a written opinion on an important question of policy often intended for presentation to the king in council
pedido	special subsidy raised in the form of a property tax and granted by the Cortes for a particular and temporary purpose. Nobles, royal officials and serving soldiers were not required to pay it
qadi	(Ar.) judge; the principal officer of a town or city
quinto	the royal fifth; refers to the percentage due to the crown of any booty taken by force of arms
real branco	coin of silver and copper first launched in 1415 and then reckoned to be worth 35 *libras*
realengo	lands belonging to and administered by the crown
regimento	directive; in a Henrican context 'sailing orders'
resgate	any place on the coast of Guinea or up one of its great rivers where trading between the local people and the Portuguese was regularly carried on
sahel	the lands between the Sahara and the tropical forest
sesmaria	a system of rural leasing under which the lessee, to retain his lease, contracted to bring his land fully under cultivation within a fixed period of years
sub-donatory	in this book the term refers to a person whom the original donatory, unable to exercise in person the governorship of the territory granted to him by the crown, appoints as his deputy
vedor da fazenda	treasurer; the officer appointed by the king to be in charge of the kingdom's finances
vintena	tax of $\frac{1}{20}$ imposed by Prince Henry on imports from Guinea nominally because the Order of Christ had ecclesiastical jurisdiction in perpetuity over all the lands overseas discovered in his time or later

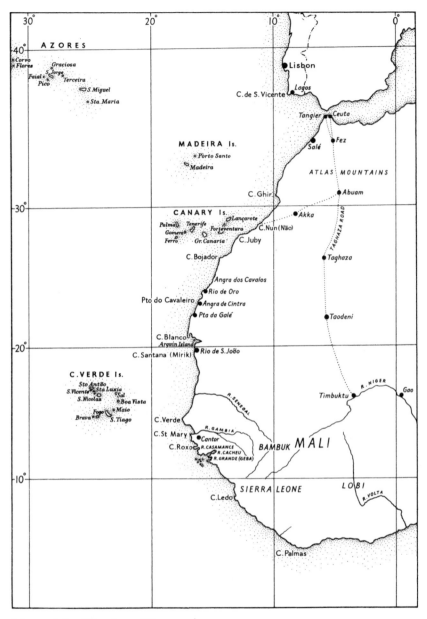

Map of the Henrican Discoveries

HOUSE OF AVIZ (from 1385)

PEDRO I (1357–67)
= (1) (1340) Constanza,
    daughter of Don Juan Manuel (d. 1345)
= (2) Inês de Castro
    (murdered 1355)
= Teresa Lourenço

María = (1354) Ferran, son of
(b. 1342)   Alfons III of Aragon
            (murdered 1363)

FERNANDO I (1367–83) = (1372) Leonor Teles
(b. 1345)   de Meneses (d. 1386)

Beatriz = (1383) Juan I of Castile
(b. 1372,
d. 1405)

Alfonso, count of Gijón, (1378) = Isabel (b. 1364)
illegitimate son of
Enrique II of Castile

Inês Peres = JOÃO I (1385–1433) = Philippa of Lancaster

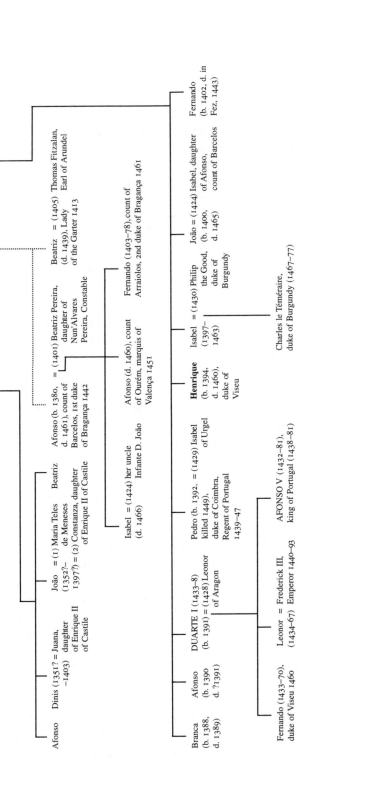

Afonso

Dinis (1351?, –1403) = Juana, daughter of Enrique II of Castile

João (1352?–1397?) = (1) Maria Teles de Meneses = (2) Constanza, daughter of Enrique II of Castile

Beatriz

Afonso (b. 1380, d. 1461), count of Barcelos, 1st duke of Bragança 1442 = (1401) Beatriz Pereira, daughter of Nun'Alvares Pereira, Constable

Beatriz = (1405) Thomas Fitzalan, Earl of Arundel (d. 1439), Lady of the Garter 1413

Fernando (1403–78), count of Arraiolos, 2nd duke of Bragança 1461

Fernando (b. 1402, d. in Fez, 1443)

Isabel = (1424) her uncle Infante D. João (d. 1466)

Afonso (d. 1460), count of Ourém, marquis of Valença 1451

João = (1424) Isabel, daughter of Afonso, count of Barcelos (b. 1400, d. 1465)

Branca (b. 1388, d. 1389)

Afonso (b. 1390, d. ?1391)

DUARTE I (1433–8) (b. 1391) = (1428) Leonor of Aragon

Pedro (b. 1392, killed 1449), duke of Coimbra, Regent of Portugal 1439–47 = (1429) Isabel of Urgel

Henrique (b. 1394, d. 1460), duke of Viseu

Isabel (1397–1463) = (1430) Philip the Good, duke of Burgundy

Fernando (1433–70), duke of Viseu 1460

Leonor = Frederick III, (1434–67) Emperor 1440–93

AFONSO V (1432–81), king of Portugal (1438–81)

Charles le Téméraire, duke of Burgundy (1467–77)

Acknowledgements

Since the start of my interest in Prince Henry goes back five decades or more there will inevitably be undeserved omissions from this register of those to whom I am indebted for their valued help in the making of this book. I specially have in mind those Portuguese colleagues and friends who, in the difficult 1950s and 1960s in Portugal, were willing to reveal in discussion with me their then heterodox conjectures about Prince Henry and his achievements when he was at the peak of his centuries-old mythical destiny to serve as a national icon.

Two figures from those days deserve my particular gratitude. It was the late Professor Virgínia Rau, long-time professor of economic history at the University of Lisbon, who first suggested to me that the time was ripe for a new study in English of Prince Henry. From her I received invaluable information, advice and practical help in the early stages of this undertaking. I also owe much to the constant support then and later of Professor Charles Boxer who pressed me to go ahead with a life of the Prince despite some disapproving official comments from Portugal about the way I had presented him in print. Professor Boxer has shown soldierly forbearance as the years passed without the promised volume reaching a publisher. Among contemporary colleagues in the United Kingdom and the United States I have another special debt to Professor Anthony Pagden of Johns Hopkins University who, in his writings and in many discussions I have had with him, helped me to find some much-needed new perspectives on matters in which the Prince was involved. Dr Nigel Griffin, in the infancy of electronic scanning, took away the daunting first draft of this book in typescript and returned it to me on disk ready for word-processing. The project might never have passed beyond the draft stage had it not been for his skill in information technology. Dr Bruce Taylor, from California, kindly devoted much time and patience to checking and improving the Bibliography and to pursuing successfully difficult entries in it.

Among the many others in the United Kingdom and the United States who have directly helped me in one way or another over the years, I must particularly mention Professor T. F. Earle, Professor P. E. H Hare, Professor David Hook, Dr Kristen Lippincott (now Director of the Old Royal Observatory, Greenwich), Professor Ian Michael, Professor Luís Rebelo, Professor John Russell-Wood, Mr Gregory Russell, Mr John

Wainwright of the Taylor Institution Library and Mrs Sara Rodger, Assistant Librarian of the Arundel Castle Library.

This project would, of course, have been in jeopardy without the generous help I have always received from Portuguese colleagues. I specially think of that I received from the doyen of Henrican scholarship in our times, the late António Joaquim Dias Dinis, OFM, who was always ready to give up his time to answering my queries. I have a unique debt, too, to Dr João Gouveia Monteiro of Coimbra University who, despite his own busy academic life there as a medieval historian, has never failed to find time to investigate and promptly to produce answers to questions or requests for information with which I have troubled him. Others who have always generously responded to my claims on their expertise are Professor A. H. de Oliveira Marques, Professor Humberto Baquero Moreno, Professor Aires Nascimento, the late General Luís da Câmara Pina and Professor Américo Costa Ramalho. I am also indebted to Dr Miguel Duarte of the University of Oporto – who, as well as opening the doors of the Seminário de História and the University Library to me, saw that I had access there to the latest articles relevant to Henrican studies. In Oporto too I owe a debt of gratitude to Senhora Natália Fauvrelle and her colleagues for their expert help with the teasing problems of iconography that lie in wait for those who would like to know what Prince Henry may have looked like.

The Gulbenkian Foundation generously funded two research visits I made to Portugal to work in archives and libraries while working on this book.

Ms Margaret Pinsent and Ms Jill Eagle of the Modern Languages Faculty office here in Oxford kindly made sure that the hard-copy version of this book reached the publishers in respectable form.

Now is also perhaps an appropriate time for me to acknowledge my debt to the RAF pilots who, in 1943 and early 1944, several times ferried me in stages up and down the coast of West Africa in DC3s flying at altitudes that made it easy to secure close bird's-eye views of many of the geographical features which are mentioned in this book and which Prince Henry's men first saw in the fifteenth century. Though I did not properly realize it at the time, the visual memories of those flights and of the months I then spent in various parts of West Africa long ago were to serve me well when I came to work on the Henrican discoveries.

Last but far from least, these Acknowledgements would be seriously incomplete if I did not end them with an expression of my gratitude to

Mr John Nicoll for his encouragement and many helpful suggestions and his patience while this book has been on the stocks, and to Mr Adam Freudenheim for the care, skill and insight with which he has copy-edited my text.

Introduction

And all the courses of my life do show
I am not in the roll of common men.

Shakespeare, *King Henry The Fourth, Part I*, Act 3 Scene 1

Prince Henry of Portugal, Knight of the Garter and universally but somewhat misleadingly known to all as 'the Navigator', has attracted the special attention of English-speaking writers ever since the beginnings of England's colonial expansion overseas in the sixteenth century. Indeed, because of his half-Plantagenet parentage, Henry was claimed in 1625 by the geographer Samuel Purchas to have been the first person to demonstrate the English genius for maritime exploration. Purchas wrote that Henry was 'The true foundation of the Greatnesse, not of Portugall alone, but of the whole Christian World, in Marine Affairs, and especially of these Heroike endeavours of the English (whose flesh and bloud hee was) . . .'[1] Those familiar with the history of the House of Plantagenet may find it a little difficult to believe that any urge to seek out new worlds across unknown seas could have emerged from that establishment but, as will be suggested in the course of this book, Purchas was on the right track, though not in the way he supposed. He, like Richard Hakluyt in the previous century, believed Henry to have been an outstanding mathematician whose mathematical theories, when turned to practical navigational purposes, had made oceanic discovery possible. Indeed he assured readers of *Hakluytus Posthumus* that Henry was so devoted to mathematics that he abjured matrimony to give himself up to it.

Purchas's assumption that mathematics was the foundation of the Prince's genius was to meet with the approval of a succession of other English-speaking biographers in the centuries that followed. Purchas, of course, took his cue from the Portuguese chroniclers of his own age who were keen to promote Henry's supposed scientific skills.[2]

It was left to British eighteenth-century rationalists to introduce a more sceptical note into their appraisals. The Scottish poet, James Thomson (1700–1748), from whose lines on Prince Henry the epigraph of the present book is taken, refused to allow that the commercial benefits exploration in the African Atlantic brought to Portugal during Henry's lifetime were merely the fortuitous consequences of the pursuit of more transcendental goals.

Later on in the eighteenth century Samuel Johnson, though praising Henry as 'the first encourager of remote navigation', thought the record of his dealings with the peoples of Africa far from unblemished and concluded, with his usual perceptivity, 'what mankind has lost and gained by the genius and designs of this Prince, it would be long to compare and very difficult to estimate'.[3] But these eighteenth-century doubts were not destined to prosper. Portuguese and foreign historians alike usually preferred to go along with the unproblematic interpretations of Henry's career now sanctified by tradition. William Robertson, the great eighteenth-century historian of America, evidently saw Henry as a mixture of bewigged general and Quaker do-gooder when he observed of him 'to the martial spirit, which was the characteristic of every man of noble birth at that time, he added all the accomplishments of a more enlightened and polished age'.[4] Following this up, Robertson charitably if improbably concluded that most Portuguese of the Prince's time must have considered that his projects were not inspired by ambition or any desire for wealth but flowed, as he put it, 'from the warm resolve of a heart eager to promote the happiness of mankind'.[5]

*   *   *

It was, of course, in Portugal, already in Henry's own lifetime and with his own active participation, that the Prince's personality and achievements first began to part company with reality and take on some of the lineaments of myth. The chronicles of his contemporary and devoted admirer, Zurara, moved Henry's biography strongly in that direction. It was Zurara who first contrived to portray Henry in the triple roles of exemplary prince, dedicated crusader against Islam and solitary savant specially chosen by destiny to uncover secrets previously hidden from men. However, Zurara's personal relationship with his hero meant that his portrayal of the Prince for the most part still depicted him as a recognizably historical personage. Before long, any attempt to take into account historical probability was abandoned as Henry was transformed, in narrative writings and in official documents, first into a vindicatory icon of the usurping dynasty of Aviz, and then into a national symbol representing the heroic destiny and imperial achievements of the Portuguese.

The cult surrounding the ever more mythical figure of Prince Henry has proved capable of continuous remodelling over the centuries to serve the purposes of succeeding ruling élites in Portugal. However, its day may well be nearly over, except as a tale to be told to tourists. At the end of the twentieth century invitations to give credit to alleged exemplars of human perfection from the past are more likely to meet with suspicion than with respect. In the present case there is no reason to regret this. The historical Prince, in so far as we can get near him, was plainly a far more interesting if also far more perplexing figure than the uncomplicated culture hero of the mythmakers.

What was the man, the history-making man behind the myth, like? To try to find out something about that is obviously the necessary starting-point today for any discussion of Henry's life and works. For a variety of reasons any such investigation is unlikely to be easy to carry through. Apart from the problems that usually confront historians attempting to get close to the life of any medieval grandee, fate in several guises has often intervened over the centuries to close off important sources of knowledge about Henry and his doings that we know once existed. Though it can easily be established that the Henry of myth often has little connection with everyday historical reality, that does not mean that a rereading of the sources will enable us to replace uncertainty with certainty. On the contrary, we soon find ourselves confronted by an obstinately enigmatic personality who seems, chameleon-like, to present a range of different images according to the various contexts in which we come across him. This characteristic is well illustrated by the problems that arise when we try to establish from surviving evidence what Prince Henry looked like. Generations have been taught to believe that Henry is the kneeling figure wearing the famous black Burgundian hat as big as a cartwheel, who appears on one of the six altarpiece panels belonging to the retable known as the *Veneration of São Vicente*. This painting was found in Lisbon in 1882 and is attributed to the fifteenth-century artist Nuno Gonçalves (*c*. 1425–*c*. 1491). Since then, it has been reproduced countless times as a true portrait of the Prince. Studies carried out by modern art historians have demonstrated that this work cannot have been painted in Henry's lifetime. They have also noted that it does not tally either with Zurara's description of his physical appearance or with the effigy on his tomb in Batalha. Some specialists have concluded that the figure was not intended to be that of Henry at all. The problem is too complex to examine here, but it seems quite possible that the famous portrait supposedly of Henry started life as a portrait of someone else.[6]

While it was his part in the history of oceanic navigation and discovery which, in the opinion of posterity, would assure the Prince of his place among the greats who have changed history, how he came to be involved in this process cannot be understood in isolation from the various other projects, purposes and obligations which, like a skilled prestigitator, Henry contrived simultaneously to juggle.

In the present study I have sought as far as possible to keep the Prince centre stage, despite the fact that quite often one is left to intuit his motivation and his intentions by peering in from outside at the events in which he was involved. It was by no means only as the inventor of organized oceanic discovery and the economic innovations this brought that, in his time, Henry was famous not only in Portugal but in Europe generally. The reputation he gained as a crusader at the capture of Ceuta secured him his place in the annals of fifteenth-century chivalry so that, when his intended enterprise in Guinea became known abroad, a number of European knights errant asked to be allowed to take part in it. Their quixotic attempts to practise chivalry in Black Africa were not successful.

In our own times impatience with traditional Henrican mythology's disregard for historical probability as well as with its exploitation for political purposes has led to the creation of something of an anti-Henrican backlash in some academic circles in Portugal. Beyond drawing attention to some of the less than heroic episodes that mark the Prince's career, it has even been suggested that, when presenting himself in his own day as the initiator of the Portuguese discoveries in the African Atlantic, Henry fraudulently sought to take the credit for an achievement that in reality belonged to his elder brother, the Regent D. Pedro, deposed in 1448. Contemporary writings, however, supply no evidence for an interpretation of events which even the words and actions of the Regent himself contradict.

For four centuries information about the Prince's personality and deeds was mainly dependent on what the chroniclers had to say about him. As already explained, the most important of these chronicle sources are the narratives written around the middle decades of the fifteenth century by Afonso V's chronicler-royal and keeper of the national archives, Gomes Eanes de Zurara. Zurara was no mere palace clerk but a person of consequence at court, a protegé of princes who were very much aware that it lay in the hands of chroniclers such as he to determine if and how posterity would remember them. Thanks to the patronage of Prince Henry, Zurara rose to the rank of *comendador* (commander) in the military Order of Christ, a promotion not calculated to increase his objectivity where Henry was concerned since the latter was the lay governor of that Order. But his relationship with the Prince directly involved his work as chronicler too. Zurara had known Henry well before the latter's death in 1460 and was an unconditional admirer of all the causes he stood for. For all that, or perhaps because of it, Zurara is for the modern historian a less satisfactory biographer than we might expect from someone who had been so close to his subject. Faithful to the traditional medieval view of what an official chronicler's duty was, he never supposed that he should present Henry objectively, warts and all. He believed that, as chronicler-royal, what was expected of him when he wrote his *Chronicle of the Capture of Ceuta* (c. 1450; revised after 1460)[7] and his *Chronicle of Guinea* (c. 1457–c. 1465)[8] – the latter's full title in Portuguese significantly translates as the *Chronicle of the Deeds of Arms Involved in the Conquest of Guinea* – was that, by dint of a selective approach to the facts when necessary, he should provide posterity with an exemplary prototype of a great Christian prince. In Henry's case this purpose received considerable impetus from the fact that the chronicler, as he himself emphasizes, frequently took advantage of his relationship with Henry to secure first-hand accounts of the historical events in which he had been involved, especially in North Africa. The consequence of this dependency is particularly evident in the *Chronicle of the Capture of Ceuta*, where Henry appears not only as the driving force behind the Portuguese decision to attack the Moroccan city, which he probably was, but also as the hero of the successful assault on it, a much less certain claim. The Prince, always very conscious of the fact that he was a star turn, was obsessively preoccupied with the problem of making sure that his fame w as transmitted to posterity in a form acceptable to him. Naturally, he made full use of the opportunities offered to him by Zurara's interest in his reminiscences.

The *Chronicle of Guinea*, mainly an account of the Henrican-controlled exploration of western Africa between 1434 and 1447 – was also partly written in Henry's lifetime on the orders of his nephew, Afonso V.[9] It contains some annexed panegyrical chapters which go well beyond even the demands of exemplary history when they set about establishing the Prince as a paragon of piety and Christian chivalry as well as the genius behind the discoveries whose foresight and determination alone had brought previously unimagined prosperity to Portugal. Only occasionally do the chronicler's personal criticisms of the actual man he knew slip unobtrusively into this narrative in the form of an occasional passing observation which hints that Henry's personality and conduct, when encountered at first-hand, were not always beyond criticism. Later writers, unaware of the exemplary and rhetorical conventions of chronicle writing in an earlier age, would draw largely on Zurara's panegyrics to build up what they supposed to be an objective account by an eyewitness of what Henry was like. Nineteenth- and early twentieth-century British biographers of Henry were by no means exempt from this error.

As has already been suggested, sixteenth-century Portuguese humanist historians added a new dimension to Zurara's quintessentially medieval portrait of the Prince. In their writings Sir Galahad now also acquired the skills of Merlin. Thus in the first part of the history of the Portuguese expansion he called *Ásia* (*c.* 1549), João de Barros presented Henry *inter alia* as a scholarly student of geography and the science of navigation,[10] while Damião de Góis, duly noting that he was an intrepid warrior knight, also assured his readers that the Prince had won fame in his time as a dedicated student of astrology and cosmography.[11] From his continuous study of ancient authors Henry, according to Góis, had already learnt that Africa was circumnavigable and that India could be reached by sailing eastwards from the Atlantic. The same author was responsible for lending his authority to the romantic canard – which still proves irresistible to many today – that, early in his career, Henry took up permanent residence at Sagres, near Cape St Vincent. He chose, so it was then said, to make his permanent home on those remote, wind-swept sea cliffs so that he could pursue his studies of cosmology and stellar navigation far away from the world's affairs. Though such assertions melt away when the Prince's itineraries and frequent kingdom-wide ambulations over the years are traced, it was but a step further from them to claiming, as an indispensable constituent part of the myths surrounding him, that this royal prince had set up on one of the Sagres capes a formal school where, acting as a domine himself, he personally taught the science of oceanic navigation to sea-captains and pilots.

With this post-medieval insistence on the scholarly attainments of the Prince went an assumption that his involvement in maritime exploration was, from the start, a carefully planned affair which, as we have just seen, had nothing less than the opening of the Atlantic sea route to India as its final goal. Science did not, however, wholly take over from religion as the motivator of the Henrican discoveries. Near the beginning of the sixteenth century another writer, the navigator, soldier and colonial administrator Duarte Pacheco Pereira, doubtless drawing on oral tradition, explained to readers of his well-stocked pilotage manual, *Esmeraldo de situ orbis*, that Henry's destiny to be the man who would disclose the existence of Black Africa to Europeans and who would bring that continent's peoples within the Christian fold had been revealed to him by the Holy Spirit in a visionary dream one night in bed.[12]

These encomiastic accounts of the Prince and his doings were, of course, never questioned in his own country or outside it at the time. There was one exception. At the time of the high tide of Henry's sixteenth-century fame in Portugal, the Spanish friar Bartolomé de Las Casas denounced him root and branch for having impiously brought war and violence to the newly discovered lands bordering on the African Atlantic.[13] Las Casas's voice was, however, a solitary one and his motives for singling out the Portuguese prince as a chief target for his invective are somewhat suspect.[14] Most European writers, particularly English ones anxious to make something out of Henry's half-English ancestry, were content to accept the received Portuguese accounts of the Prince and his work since these supplied useful material to justify the maritime expansion of Europe generally.

Nineteenth-century scholars in various fields brought to light bit by bit new documentary material and fresh ways of scrutinizing and explaining the Prince's achievements. One effect of their work was to remind students of his life that, as a great medieval warrior-magnate and politician, Henry was always deeply involved in projects and commitments that had little to do with oceanic exploration or even with crusading against Islam. It was now sometimes even cautiously admitted that there were some events in his career that seemed to lack the heroic touch. But the work of such scholars, whether originating in Portugal or in other countries, avoided casting any doubt on the essential validity of the traditional Henrican stereotype. In the heyday of Europe's imperial expansion, particularly in Africa, it was convenient to be able to follow Robertson's suggestion that the person who was credited with giving the initial impulse to that expansion had been driven by Christian zeal working hand-in-hand with the spirit of scientific enquiry.

It was the nineteenth century, too, with its love of attaching descriptive tags to important historical figures, which seems to have imposed on Henry the sobriquet 'The Navigator', a label which seemed to offer assurances that Henry's claim on the attention of scholars was not only for his work as a sponsor of oceanic exploration and student of navigational science but was also calculated to suggest that the Prince himself personally participated in the exploratory voyages he sponsored.[15] In fact, a feature of Henry's career that modern writers may find surprising is that, despite his undoubted interest in and preoccupation with the problems of oceanic navigation, his only known personal experience of seafaring remained limited to routine voyages along the Portuguese coast and the short sea journey from the Algarve to Ceuta. Nevertheless, because of the universal acceptance of the sobriquet, considerations of expediency make it necessary for this to form part of the title of the present book. For the reasons given I shall, however, avoid using it in my text.

In modern times Henry became a major cult figure of the political régime that ruled Portugal from 1926 to 1974, but this only represented a more overt manipulation by the state for its own purposes of a myth that, from the Prince's lifetime onwards, had always had marked political undertones. Nor was it only in Portugal that the traditional encomiastic presentation of him as a scholar–hero continued to prevail. Throughout the nineteenth century and much of the twentieth century too, foreign scholars and publicists, despite the increase in knowledge about various aspects of his biography, went on presenting him without serious reservation as a paragon of Christian and chivalric virtue and intellectual achievement. R. H. Major's much-read biography of the Prince in English, which first appeared in 1868, still accepted uncritically the account of his career supplied by Zurara and other fifteenth- and sixteenth-century Portuguese chroniclers. Major thus informed English-speaking readers that the Prince 'unweariedly devoted himself to the study of mathematics, navigation and cartography' and assured them that the Portuguese discoveries began as a consequence 'of the patience, wisdom, intellectual labour, and example of one man, backed by the pluck of a race of sailors'.[16] C. R. Beazley, in a study first published in 1895 but still reprinted in the second half of the twentieth century, while recognizing, perhaps for the first time, that reliable information about Henry was scanty, nevertheless concluded that there was enough to demonstrate that he was 'a hero, both of science and action'.[17] When it came to describing the Prince's personality, Beazley did not hesitate to offer his readers a more or less straight translation of a panegyrical passage from Zurara which makes Henry seem like an ideal District Officer of British colonial times.

The dominance of the chroniclers as sources for Prince Henry's biography nevertheless had begun to be undermined when, at the end of the nineteenth century, scholars started systematically to search Portuguese and foreign archives for documents directly or indirectly connected with his life and times. Deserving of special mention among the most recent collections of documents which have enlarged our knowledge in this way are the three massive volumes entitled *Descobrimentos Portugueses* edited by J. A. Silva Marques (1944–71)[18] and the fifteen volumes of *Monumenta Henricina* (1960–74).[19] The latter is a tour de force which, under the editorship of the late A. J. Dias Dinis, OFM. seeks to make available in annotated form all known documents, whether previously published or now discovered by the editorial research team, that had a bearing on any aspect of Henry's life and career. While one may criticize some of the editorial decisions, the publication of these works has put at the disposal of any biographer much material which has radically altered earlier perceptions of the Prince's biography by opening up whole tracts of his life about which little was previously known.

Unfortunately there are disappointingly few new documents in any of these collections that bear on any aspect of the way the exploration and commercial exploitation of Guinea was conducted in Prince Henry's time. This dearth is attributable to the fact that the monopoly over navigation and trade then granted by the Portuguese crown to the Prince for his lifetime was a personal one. As a consequence most everyday documents relating to Guinea did not pass through the royal chancery except on the rare occasions when prerogatives that remained reserved to the crown were involved. They were dealt with by Henry's personal chancery, the contents of which have been almost entirely lost. There are some grounds for believing that, after Henry's death in 1460, routine records relating to the operation of the Guinea monopoly may have been transferred from Lagos to the Casa da Guiné in Lisbon. This was the name given to the new crown agency responsible for the affairs of Guinea established in Lisbon by Afonso V after Henry's death. There they, or some of them, perhaps survived until the eighteenth century. If so, it was only a stay of execution since the archives of the Casa da Guiné and the other overseas agencies which later developed from it were destroyed in the fire which followed the great Lisbon earthquake of 1755.

Another potentially important archival source, particularly for information about the financing of Henry's Guinea enterprise, also disappoints. As he himself freely admitted, the Prince used his authority as lay governor of the military Order of Christ to divert substantial sums from the revenues of the Order to meet the expenses he incurred in connection with that enterprise. No documents bearing on the extent of the Order's forced monetary contributions to the Henrican voyages appear to have survived in what remains of the Order's archives for this period.

Fortunately, these losses can often be partly made good by an attentive reading of contemporary narrative sources. Zurara's addiction to indulging in rhetorical panegyrics in his *Chronicle of Guinea* is well known, as is his determination to present the first two decades of Portuguese exploration in West Africa as a chivalric enterprise carried out mainly by Henry's squires anxious to win their spurs by crusading against the infidel there. Nevertheless this chronicle does also offer a good deal of down-to-earth detail about the way the Henrican voyages up to 1446 were organized and the results they achieved and failed to achieve. Most of this reflects the fact, freely admitted by Zurara, that he borrowed extensively from the lost narrative about the Guinea voyages from the work of a so far unidentified but very well-informed predecessor whom he calls Afonso Cerveira.[20] Zurara sometimes expressed his impatience with Cerveira's pernickety historical methods and glossed his borrowings from him to make them fit his own prejudices, but, for the most part, he seems to have reproduced Cerveira's text largely as he found it.[21]

For the 1450s we have the extraordinarily detailed eyewitness account of Guinea and the way the Guinea trade monopoly functioned from the pen of the Venetian explorer Luigi da Mosto, known to Portuguese and other foreign scholars as Cadamosto. The latter's *Navigazioni* – one of the great autobiographical travel books of the fifteenth century – describes in detail two voyages devoted to exploration and trade in Guinea made by Cadamosto in 1455 and 1456 under Henry's direction, and one made shortly after the Prince's death by a Portuguese pilot.[22] Cadamosto had been personally recruited by the Prince for whom he continued to work for several years after 1456. His book was written after he had returned to Venice for good in the mid-1460s. In addition to its famous first-hand descriptions of Guinea – its peoples and its flora and fauna – as seen through the eyes of an intelligent, curious and unprejudiced fifteenth-century Italian traveller, the *Navigazioni* contain much information about how exploration in and trade with Saharan and Black Africa was organized and directed by Henry. Cadamosto is, therefore, a major source for the latter part of the present study.

Some useful if much less trustworthy data about the Henrican voyages can, with due caution, also be garnered from the often confused reminiscences dictated in his old age to a German interlocutor by one of Henry's former pilots, Diogo Gomes.[23] The *Registro del Sello* archives in the Archivo General de Simancas, in Spain, have proved to be a useful source of information about the details of the licensing system used by the Portuguese in the Prince's time to control voyages to Guinea. This is because, when the Catholic Monarchs broke the Portuguese Guinea monopoly during the Castilian–Portuguese war of 1474–9, they largely took over the bureaucratic controls introduced by Henry and carried on by Afonso V.[24]

It is probable that, judging by a few examples that have so far come to light, Italian commercial archives may contain new information about the Henrican voyages included in the reports sent to their parent houses in Italy by Italian merchants stationed in Portugal and in Andalusia.[25] I have not been able to undertake the daunting task involved in pursuing this line of enquiry.

Only one strictly private document written by the Prince survives. This is a letter written to his father, John I, in which Henry describes the nuptials in Coimbra in 1428 of the heir to the throne, D. Duarte, and Leonor of Aragon. The letter is remarkable for the well-observed descriptive details of the proceedings it contains and for the unpretentious liveliness of its style. More unexpectedly, Henry reveals a distinct appreciation of the comic side of life when he is describing the behaviour of his brother as a lover or the marriage ceremony itself and what happened afterwards.[26] In it Henry, unconcerned about protecting his official image because he is writing privately to his father, reveals himself, *inter alia*, as both a very different kind of person from the one who appears in official documents originating with him or in his name and intended for public record. The significance of Henry's letter, whose authenticity appears unassailable, seems not to have received the attention it deserves. I have therefore included an English translation as an appendix.

Since the present study approach is concerned with the life of Prince Henry, it limits itself to presenting the explorations in the African Atlantic and the opening up of the region to trade as they were known to and interpreted by Henry and his contemporaries. To avoid falling into possible anachronisms I have not usually attempted to advance beyond or correct their perceptions by taking into account the detailed ethnographical, political and economic information about the African scene that was set down in writing in Portugal by several authors some forty or fifty years after Henry's death. When the book deals with matters relating to Guinea, its concern is with the impact the new world (to use Cadamosto's description) discovered there had on fifteenth-century Europeans. It does not attempt to discuss what was, of course, also a cardinal event in the history of the peoples of West Africa. What it does attempt to do is to reclaim Prince Henry and his achievements for the Middle Ages. One of the consequences of looking only at his successes as sponsor and motivator of the opening up of the African Atlantic to navigation and trade is that the self-consciously medieval context within which he worked can easily be overlooked.

Chapter One

Matters of Nativity

In the science of astrology, a worthy branch of learning, the astrologers of old declare that, when a man is born, they take the [heavenly] sign that is dominant at the moment of his birth to lay down the path his life will take.

Juan Ruiz, *Libro de Buen Amor*[1]

Prince Henry, the third surviving son of John I and Philippa of Lancaster, was born in the northern Portuguese city of Oporto on Ash Wednesday, 4 March 1394. If that traditional day of mourning and penitence was thought to be an unpropitious one for a prince's birth, no one was ever tactless enough to say so, at least in writing. Zurara's report that the boy emerged from his mother's womb embracing a simulacrum of the Holy Cross, a piece of information that the chronicler seems to attribute to Henry himself, was seen as proof positive that the young prince's dedication to religion and to crusading against the infidel was prenatally arranged.[2]

As mentioned in the Introduction, Samuel Purchas, writing in 1625, patriotically attributed special significance to the fact that Henry was half-English by blood.[3] This suggestion that the Prince's English genes both contributed to his achievements as a sponsor of oceanic expansion and made him a kind of honorary English discoverer can hardly be sustained, at least in the sense that Purchas meant. Though Henry's consciousness of his Plantagenet descent may very well have provided a spur which would drive him to seek to emulate the chivalric fame of his English ancestors and cousins on the battlefield, a concern to seek out new horizons was hardly a characteristic of the House of Plantagenet. A more certain contributory cause of the Prince's future relentless pursuit of personal fame was his status as a third son; from an early age he seems to have made it plain to those around him that he was unlikely to turn out to be a man content to settle for the subordinate role that this accident of birth seemed to have assigned to him.

Documents in the municipal archives of Oporto record that, though it was the start of Lent, all the city's bells were pealed to celebrate the birth. A few days later Henry was baptized. The bishop of Viseu, an inland city with which he was later to have close connections, acted as godfather.[4] In the naming of their children Philippa and her husband seem to have agreed that traditional Portuguese baptismal names should alternate with ones used by her own family. The first-born daughter of the royal couple was thus called Blanca, presumably after Philippa's mother, the Duchess Blanche of Lancaster. If their first-born son (died in infancy) was called Afonso in deference to Portuguese tradition, the second was given the wholly English baptismal name of Edward (Port. 'Duarte') – doubtless in memory of both Edward III and the Black Prince. Prince Henry was perhaps named after his famous crusading maternal grandfather, Duke Henry of Lancaster (d. 1361), who had taken part in the epic siege of Moorish-held Algeciras in the time of Alfonso XI of Castile. Awareness that he bore Duke Henry's name may well have been among the various influences that confirmed the Prince's sense that he was born to be a crusader against Islam. This commitment seems, however, on a worldly level, to have been made for him by his mother before he was capable of self-awareness. Apart from the unusual symbol that he brought with him into the world when he was born, we also have the Prince's own word for it that his parents then chose as his patron saint the French crusader king, St Louis (d. 1270).[5]

It seems very likely, however, that Henry grew up believing that, thanks to the science of astrology, his destiny had been fixed for him at the moment of his birth. The chronicler Zurara, who was himself particularly interested in the influence of the stars on human affairs, supplies a detailed description of the horoscope or nativity (Port. *nacimento*) that, according to the custom of the times, was cast by a court astrologer on Henry's birth in order to discover what the stars foretold about his destiny.[6] This document, the chronicler claims, revealed that the main planetary influences on the child's life would be those of Mars and Saturn. Their exact position in the zodiac at the time of birth showed Henry, according to Zurara's interpretation, to be predestined to devote himself both to making 'great and noble conquests and to the uncovering of secrets previously hidden from men'. This latter power, the chronicler relates, was explained by the particular location of Saturn in his horoscope.

Zurara sets out and interprets the contents of Henry's horoscope in chapter seven of his *Chronicle of Guinea*. He first lists there five reasons which it was generally said in the Prince's time accounted for Henry's interest in oceanic discovery. These all involve the sort of everyday explanations any medieval or later writer might put forward as a reason for setting up voyages of exploration: e.g. curiosity about the African Atlantic coast beyond the traditional limits of navigation; concern to discover whether people might be found there with whom it would be possible and permissible to trade; a wish to learn the real strength of Islam in those remote regions and to learn of any Christian princes there who might be willing to ally themselves with Prince Henry in his unending crusade against the Moors. Referring to these last two points, the chronicler emphasizes Henry's abiding desire to spread the faith by converting to Christianity the lost souls of those who might be found to inhabit regions of Africa then unknown to Europeans.

This statement of Henry's motives as a patron of oceanic discovery was probably copied by Zurara from Afonso Cerveira's lost account of the voyages of exploration up to 1448. The chronicler, however, then goes on, before describing the Henrican horoscope and its predictions in astrological detail, to observe that the contents of the horoscope provide an explanation of Henry's career that completely outweighs in importance the five others he has just mentioned.[7]

Zurara's description of the horoscope takes a form that makes it plain that he probably had before him the original document cast in March 1394 or at least a copy of it. According to this information, Mars was in the eleventh House, the 'House of Secrets and Ambitions', at the time of the Prince's birth.[8] Zurara's description of the horoscope is credible and may be interpreted in this way. Horoscopes could however be used to 'predict the past' so that the possibility that the interpretation Zurara gives was made in the light of Henry's later career cannot be totally excluded.[9] However, it seems unlikely that the chronicler would have referred to the horoscope unless he was sure that Afonso V would not take exception to his comments. Henry's own approval of Zurara's observations cannot be taken for granted since it is not possible to determine whether or not the passage concerned was already in the version of the chronicle written before his death.

Henry's biographers have usually chosen to ignore the existence of the horoscope and the significance attributed to it by Zurara. If they mention the matter at all, it tends to be in order to ascribe its presence in the *Chronicle of Guinea* to the private superstitions of Zurara himself. An anachronistic desire to protect Henry from any suggestion that he can have had any time for astrology appears to be at work here. Such a notion is, of course, wholly untenable given the status of astrology and astrological prediction in his time. Indeed, it may well be that it was through an interest in what astrological prediction had to say about his future and that of other members of his family that Henry first began to take a serious interest in the stars. There was nothing in the least unusual about a fourteenth- or fifteenth-century prince or nobleman taking an active interest in astrology. Everywhere in Europe then (as well as long afterwards) astrological prediction was widely accepted as a proper science. The reason for its importance is given by Juan Ruiz, the fourteenth-century Spanish popular writer quoted in the epigraph at the beginning of this chapter. Similar opinions are found over and over again in medieval writings. Sometimes they were accompanied by the orthodox caveat that free will aided by divine grace could enable a Christian to escape his stellar destiny if he wished. Often they were not.

A work studied as a textbook in every European court and noble household in Henry's day, was Aegidius of Colonna's famous treatise on the education of princes, *De regimine principum*. One can therefore virtually take it for granted that the youthful Henry's preceptors had recourse to it. Aegidius's work specifically draws attention to the need for young princes and noblemen to study astrology. As a Castilian version of this work made in the middle of the fourteenth century has it when referring to the education of princes,

It is desirable for them to study astrology, which is the science of the heavenly bodies, showing the movements and the distances of the stars and of the influences which they have on earthly bodies. This science is of much value as far as the works of men are concerned since it discloses the kind of power the heavens have over them and over all corruptible things.[10]

Astrological prediction was certainly used routinely at the Portuguese court as in other European courts. The chief astrologer there at the time of Henry's father's declining years was a Jewish doctor, Mestre Abraham Guedelha[11] and the seriousness with which the astrologer's role was taken is illustrated by the fact that, after John I's death in 1433, Mestre Guedelha begged Duarte I, the new king, to delay the appointed time for his proclamation as king for a few hours until the heavenly bodies were in a less unfavourable position. Duarte, according to his chronicler, decided to ignore this advice, not because he doubted the influence of the planets on man's fate but because, since the day concerned was the Feast of the Assumption, he was bound, as a pious man, to suppose that God would, on such a day, take care to see that divine grace intervened to save him from any malign stellar destiny that might threaten him at the appointed time.[12] The disasters that marked Duarte's short reign, however, may well have served to reinforce the Portuguese court's respect for astrological prediction.

In the light of all this, the importance Zurara attributes to Henry's 'nativity' as a major influence on his career has to be taken very seriously. As already noted, the chronicler himself was something of an amateur expert on astrology and traces of personal correspondence between him and Afonso V about astrological matters survive.[13] Since Afonso was the king who had commissioned him to write an account of the Prince's life and deeds it is even possible that this correspondence arose out of Zurara's assertion in the *Chronicle of Guinea* that Henry's horoscope was the most important influence on his career.

There is, of course, no direct evidence that the young Prince himself, when he reached an age when he could understand such things, did attribute to his horoscope the same importance that Zurara does. All one can say is that he lived in an environment where belief in the predictions read from horoscopes belonged to the category of received ideas and no contemporary source suggests that, unusually, Henry did not share those beliefs. No doubt, as a pious son of the Church, he claimed to go along with the orthodox Christian doctrine that, thanks to the exercise of free will aided by divine grace, the faithful could always overcome whatever destiny the stars predicted for them. Contemporary evidence suggests, however, that, as far as most medieval

Christians were concerned, this reassuring doctrine failed to carry the day against a belief in astrological prediction without strings that dated from the earliest days of civil societies. Zurara does not even mention Christian teaching on the matter when discussing Henry's horoscope and its predictions.

There are other reasons for taking Zurara's claim seriously. Students of Henry's life in modern times have often been frustrated by the way in which the Prince insisted on partitioning his life between crusading and planning crusades against Islam in Morocco on the one hand and, on the other, in sponsoring oceanic exploration. Anxious to present this latter activity as the one which gave unique significance to his life, historians sometimes find it inconvenient to have to admit that he was always willing to set exploration aside when opportunities occurred for him to go crusading in the traditional sense. It is at least arguable that this apparently inconsistent behaviour owed something to the fact that, like other figures in history, Henry tried dutifully to live up to the particular twin destinies he believed had been predicted for him. One wonders, too, if it was not perhaps his trust in astrological prediction which gave him that obsessive certainty that success would be his, both as crusader and as sponsor of discovery, which is an abiding feature of his personality. Of course those who practised astrology accepted that no astrological predictions could successfully foretell the course of an individual's life unless the stars had seen to it that he or she was born with the mental and physical attributes necessary for them to measure up to their predicted destiny. Astrologers took it as axiomatic that the forces which determined human destiny made sure that this would always be the case. This was certainly true in the case of Henry. In the pages which follow it would be inappropriate to keep on returning to Zurara to remind readers of the predictions of the Prince's horoscope and their probable influence on his self-awareness and his career, but these should nevertheless always be thought of as an ever-present part of his mental furniture.

The Portuguese world into which the Prince was born in 1394 exhibited no features that could have caused anyone to suppose that, forty years on, Portugal would become Europe's first maritime empire. In Henry's boyhood this kingdom of some million inhabitants was still trying to recover from the economic and social devastation which two decades of armed resistance to Castilian expansionist ambitions and the collapse of a dynasty had brought upon it. Though John I had, in 1385, effectively won the war to secure Portuguese independence, Castile and Portugal were still technically at war with each other during

Henry's boyhood and the absence of further hostilities would remain dependent on a series of uneasy armed truces until a shaky peace was concluded in 1411. The Portuguese currency had been ruined by massive and seemingly unstoppable inflation caused by the war. Large sections of the community were impoverished, especially landowners, lay and ecclesiastical, who depended on rents and other fixed dues.[14] But if obvious economic and financial considerations suggested that the kingdom urgently needed a long period of peaceful recuperation, such a prospect was not welcome to the upstart nobility created by John I, all ranks of which had grown accustomed to regarding war as the means by which they expected to secure honour and an honourable livelihood and who therefore saw more war as a way out of the kingdom's problems.

After his baptism, almost total silence envelops the Prince's life for fourteen years. Medieval biographers did not, of course, know that the years of childhood are the formative ones and were inclined to pay scant attention to them. However, the fact that so dedicated a contemporary biographer as Zurara had evidently heard nothing worth the telling about Henry's boyhood perhaps entitles us to suppose that nothing of particular interest about him during these years was known to the chronicler. It is recorded that Henry and his two elder brothers, Duarte and Pedro, had, as preceptor (aio), a knight of the military Order of Aviz whose task was, no doubt, to see that they were brought up trained in the knightly virtues as befitted young princes.[15] Prominent among these was the chase, the chief diversion of princes and nobles. Henry's enthusiasm for the hunt is plainly to be seen in his 1428 letter to his father.

No direct information is available about the education the princes received at court though it seems likely that, as was the custom, Queen Philippa herself would have had much to do with arranging and supervising this. No doubt Henry and his brothers were schooled along with the sons of nobles serving in the royal palaces. The education they received there was plainly of good quality. The literary writings of Henry's brothers, Duarte and Pedro, show, as does their work as translators and political moralists, that they were quite well grounded in humane letters, though Pedro once confessed that his ability to understand Cicero's Latin was not all it might be.[16] These two princes were able, not only in their literary works but also in their written opinions about current political and military matters presented to the royal council, to define and set out in a well-organized way the arguments for and against a particular policy. The good reputation of the education provided at the Portuguese court in John I's time survived into the later fifteenth century when the Portuguese Cortes requested Afonso V to see to it that boys attached to the court were once again taught to read and write there as they had been in the time of John and his son, Duarte I.[17]

The quality and scope of the intellectual interests Henry acquired as a result of his schooling present the first of the many enigmas which confront the student of his life. If, like some of his brothers, he tried his hand at creative or instructive literary authorship, nothing of it survives. Zurara, always anxious to draw attention to the Prince's achievements in any field, does not ever mention any activity of this kind. The claims made already in his lifetime that he was an acknowledged expert in the sciences of astronomy, navigation and the like lack the authority that the survival of some formal writing by him in these fields would supply. Nevertheless, even after allowing for the element of flattery and exaggeration that inevitably accompanied contemporary references by others to his expertise in these matters, it seems plain that his contemporaries were satisfied that Henry had more than a commonplace knowledge of them. Thus, in 1443, his brother, D. Pedro, then Regent of Portugal, made much of Henry's interest in marine cartography and, in particular, of his concern to see to the charting of the coast of western Africa south of the traditional limit of navigation there.[18] The Franciscan, André do Prado, author of the imaginary theological dialogue called *Horologium fidei* (perhaps *c.* 1450) in which the Prince is a dummy interlocutor, spoke in his *Proem* to this work of Henry's studies of the stars and of his researches into matters concerning both the heavens and the earth.[19] Though the *Proem* is, as was usual, an overtly panegyrical piece of writing, the fact that these observations, made during the Prince's lifetime, were in no way called for by the strictly theological nature of the treatise, seems to confirm that Henry's status as a student of astrology-cum-astronomy and as a cosmologist in his own right was generally recognized then and was considered in learned circles to be perhaps the most remarkable thing about him.

There is nothing debatable about the extent of Henry's dedication to biblical and theological studies or his special interest in matters liturgical. In official documents he was never at a loss to quote the Bible (not always relevantly) to back up a position he was defending. His very real devotion to theology is attested by his decision to found a chair of theology at Lisbon Univerity. It is significant, too, that one of the very few non-liturgical books he is known to have had to hand when he died in 1460 was Peter Lombard's standard theological manual *Libri sententiarum quatuor*. His interest in liturgical matters, which would be fully displayed in his final testamentary instructions, may well have been one of the results of his mother's schooling. Portugal's English queen had turned out to be a determined liturgical reformer who introduced into Portugal the so-called 'New Use of Sarum' – an important modification of the Roman rite associated with Salisbury Cathedral – to replace the traditional Roman liturgy employed there. She is reported to have forced the chapter of Lisbon cathedral to adopt the Sarum usage and to have taught celebrants how to use it. She also insisted on its use at court and by her sons in their private chapels, according to a near-contemporary.[20]

Various papers survive in which Henry, as a member of the royal council, presents to the king and council in writing a defence of his position with regard to important matters of policy being debated there. These consultative statements do not do much to establish Henry's reputation as a person at ease with the task of setting up in writing properly argued defences of a political standpoint to which he had committed himself. Thus, when the advisability of an attack on Tangier was being discussed by the council in 1436, he submitted a formal written opinion (*parecer*) to the king ardently supporting the project. This document is notable for the lack of order in which its arguments are deployed, for its employment of traditional crusading rhetoric in place of reasoned exposition and its failure, in the end, to make any attempt to address seriously the pros and cons of the matter.[21] The document gives the impression that it was written by an impatient crusading zealot who, since he had long made up his mind that an attack on Tangier was obviously the right course for a nation of Christian crusaders to undertake, was not going to waste his time affecting to examine objectively a project to which he was emotionally wholly committed. But, though documents like this one supply insights into the way Henry's mind worked when his obsession with the idea of himself as a crusader-in-chief was dominant, it would be improper to conclude from an emotionally-driven *parecer* of this kind that, in other contexts, he was not perfectly capable of both formulating and setting out in writing in reasoned form his ideas and plans. Thus the various instructions he gave in later life in his role as Protector of the University of Lisbon are straightforward, innovative, and obviously the result of careful thought about even minor details concerning the running of the university. More importantly, as we shall see, the evidence is strong that Henry's management of the discovery and exploitation of Guinea

was, despite the crusading rhetoric that often accompanied it, both per-
cipient and well planned. Though there was always a strong streak of
religious zealotry in Henry's make-up, except where Portugal's crusading destiny in North Africa was concerned, it did not often blind him
to realities, even unwelcome ones.

If we have few factual details about Henry's boyhood years, it is not
too difficult to establish what were some of the influences at work upon
him then. He plainly was brought up to venerate the achievements of
his father as the hero of the wars against Castile and the man who
had saved Portuguese independence. There are a number of pointers to
suggest that he was, from an early date, John's favourite son.
According to Fernão Lopes – who uncharacteristically devotes a whole
hyperbolic chapter to the matter, all the princes, as long as the king
was alive, displayed an unfailing obedience to him and a determination never to do anything to displease him. The chronicler goes on to
assert that, even when he called upon them to do something of which
they themselves disapproved, they carried it out without showing a sign
of their inner feelings.[22] Lopes's account makes the sons of John I sound
like nothing so much as early practitioners of the rule of unlimited obedience imposed on Jesuit novices by Ignatius Loyola in the next century.
It is not clear, though, whether or not the chronicler's account of the
group hypocrisy practised by Henry and his brothers in their relations
with their father was really intended to be read as the praise it pur-
ports to be. Lopes, who was sometimes of an ironical turn of mind,
perhaps chose this roundabout way of indicating his opinion that
John's sons should have done more in the latter's later years to impede
the ageing monarch's tolerance of misgovernment and his support for
mistaken policies.[23] Certainly, as far as the Prince was concerned,
Lopes's picture of John I's children playing at happy families was far
from reality.

It is safe to presume that the young Prince Henry, like his brothers,
was much influenced in his formative years by his English mother and
the tales she told them of the military victories and the famous deeds
of chivalry performed by their Plantagenet ancestors. Philippa's special
interest in liturgical practices was also transmitted in full measure to
Henry and to his youngest brother, Fernando. Indeed, as will become
clear in due course, her piety perhaps proved to be more influential
in Henry's case than was altogether good for an ambitious and full-
blooded young man. However there was more to Philippa than the Portuguese chroniclers' accounts of her would lead one to suppose. Fernão
Lopes and Zurara depict Philippa, as the tradition of exemplary history

required, as a model Christian queen and little else. In their writings she appears as an icon-like figure, wholly given up to exceptional and finally heroic piety, whose only desire was to see her husband and sons living religiously in perfect family harmony and winning fame fighting for Christianity against the infidel. Zurara even has her delivering long and impeccably polished last-minute instructions on how to achieve this while she was dying of plague. There are, indeed, good grounds for supposing the chronicler's depiction of Philippa's piety to be true as far as it goes. But a number of surviving letters to the English court which she wrote from Portugal show that she was more than a symbol of queenly piety. We thus find her actively intervening in English politics on behalf of followers of the dethroned Richard II when they appealed for her help after her brother, Henry IV, had usurped the English throne. Another letter shows her successfully using her influence with the new English king to get him to force a reluctant earl of Arundel to marry the Portuguese king's bastard daughter Beatriz. Other letters have a more personal tone, as when she declares that she understands the homesickness which had led her English secretary to wish to return home after years in Portugal or asks to be sent a sample of the latest English fashion in purses.[24] One lesson Henry plainly did not learn from his mother was that piety required one to put aside active involvement in worldly affairs.

There are various signs, too, of the effectiveness of the queen in making her sons proud of their Plantagenet ancestry. Thus, when the time came for them to be knighted, they all adopted Anglo-Norman mottoes as if to proclaim to the world that, where chivalry was concerned, they intended particularly to invite comparison with their English relatives. Henry chose the motto *talant de bien fere* which, in the English court language of those times, meant 'a hunger to perform worthy deeds'. There is other evidence that the queen filled the minds of her sons with a sense of respect and admiration for the chivalrous deeds of their English royal relatives. The future king, Duarte I, when he turned his hand to writing moral literature, made a special point (in his *Leal Conselheiro*) of reminding his readers of the great victory of his cousin, Henry V, at Agincourt and of the chivalric bravery of the English king on that occasion.[25] In 1437, when Duarte instructed Prince Henry how to carry out his duties as commander-in-chief of the Portuguese army sent to capture Tangier, he would direct his brother to enforce the discipline, drill, self-restraint and strict compliance with orders that, he said, had been responsible for winning famous victories for the English, who had demonstrated to the world that prudence was not incompatible with chivalry.[26] Along with this respect for the chivalric preoccupations of the English court, Philippa, according to Zurara, was also responsible for communicating to her sons some rather heady notions about the blueness of their blood, at least on her side of the family. The chronicler thus makes the young princes, among them Henry, begin their announcement to her in 1415 of their intention to take part in the attack on Ceuta using the following words:

> Lady: you well know the nobility of blood by virtue of which we, by God's grace, enjoy the great position in which we have been placed. It is on that account that our quality continually presses us to equal in excellency those princes from whose lineage it has pleased God to bring us into the world.[27]

It is, of course, decidedly unlikely the actual words used by the Infantes to their mother on this occasion, if it ever happened at all, were anything like these, but they evidently represented the kind of language which Zurara thought Henry and his elder brother, Pedro – whose memories of the occasion he consulted in the 1440s – would be content to have attributed to them. This desire of John's sons to stress their blue-bloodedness on the English side was perhaps motivated by an uncomfortable awareness that their father, great though his reputation was as a warrior, was of tainted descent. What a problem bastardy always was in a court which exalted the values of chivalry is made clear by Zurara who, when discussing the very impressive career of John's illegitimate son, Afonso, count of Barcelos and founder of the great ducal house of Braganza, thought it necessary to say of him that 'though he lacked nobility of ancestry on his mother's side, God made him so virtuous and endowed him with so great a heart that, in all things pertaining to honour, he was able to hide the low blood he inherited from his mother'.[28]

The readiness with which Philippa's sons and the Portuguese nobility in general asserted their apparently very sincere devotion to such notions of ancestry and chivalry at a time when these were tending to become mere rhetorical gestures in the rest of Europe is, at first sight, unexpected. In the war of independence against Castile in the 1380s, the old Portuguese landed aristocracy had mostly sided with the Castilian invaders. In consequence it had seemed to have been been destroyed as a consequence of the Castilian defeat at Aljubarrota, though before too long it would contrive to recover much of its former power and possessions. The victor of Aljubarrota, John I, had tried to create a new aristocracy by lavish grants to his supporters of lands often confiscated from the dead or the exiled magnates and lesser nobles who had sided with the invaders. These *nouveaux nobles*, by a familiar social process, rapidly developed pretentions and aspirations far more exalted even than those of their rather provincial predecessors. These, indeed, earned them a satirical comment from Fernão Lopes, who, forgetful of his own humble circumstances, snobbishly wrote of the new nobility

> ... another and new world then arose and a new generation of men; for the sons of people of such low degree that it would not be fitting to name them were, at that time, made knights for their good services to the king, and for their courage. They then adopted new names and new lineages. Others, however, declared themselves to be descended from ancient noble houses of which no living memory had survived.[29]

Henry, indubitably kitted out on his mother's side with some of the bluest blood in Europe, was to find ready followers from among this upstart nobility anxious to prove its worth and to acquire booty by participating in any chivalric enterprise that could be staged. The pact was sealed when Henry, in 1415, proclaimed himself the defender of the rights and privileges of all ranks of the Portuguese nobility from great lords to squires, a duty that, according to Zurara, his mother had charged him with on her deathbed. It might be supposed that the existence of a prince officially dedicated to defending the rights of the nobility against the crown would be a recipe for the kind of political discord that had overtaken Castile and other European countries. In fact it was a skilled political move. Despite the political upheaval of the 1440s, Henry seems always to have used his position to ensure that the nobility usually did the crown's bidding.

The notions of chivalry that the Prince learnt as a boy at court taught him that fondness for theatrical display which characterized the chivalric ethos. From an early date, as Zurara records, Henry liked organizing displays of extravagant pageantry, dressing himself in expensive clothing and seeing that his retainers wore splendid liveries. He also liked to stage expensive festivities, either simply as entertainment or to lend chivalric splendour to the departure of Portuguese armies setting off to go crusading in Morocco. As the letter he wrote to his father in 1428 describing the wedding in Coimbra of D. Duarte to Leonor of Aragon shows, he was able to recall and depict in minute detail every aspect of the pageantry of the occasion. Unsurprisingly, given his much-publicized dedication to total chastity, there is no suggestion in Zurara that he had any time for the idolizing of women or for the amorous or pseudo-amorous games that, according to chivalric practice, were part and parcel of the lives of knights and squires as portrayed in the chivalric romances then much read at the Portuguese court.

There was, though, to be nothing ludic about actual war against the infidel as the young Henry conceived it. Relying on a simplistic reinterpretation of the Iberian tradition of Reconquista, he believed that war against an Islamic enemy was a deadly serious duty blessed by church and state and to be thought of in terms of the traditions, privileges and rhetoric characteristic of earlier crusades in the Holy Land. Henry was plainly quite untouched by the ambivalences which, by the fifteenth century, characterized Castilian and Aragonese attitudes to the kingdom of Granada and to Islam generally. The crusade was seen by him as the epitome of all chivalrous activity.[30] Chivalry, for all its ludic aspects, amounted to nothing unless it was fuelled by a determination to achieve honour on the battlefield. The Castilian Diego de Valera in his *Tratado de las armas*, dedicated to Henry's contemporary, John II of Castile, makes it clear that, for a nobleman, chivalric virtue is obtained only by prowess won in battle and must be earned afresh in war by each new generation.[31] Henry plainly took this latter precept very seriously.

It should be remembered, though, that behind all heady talk of heroic ancestors, crusading, chivalry, expensive pageantry and the cult of the blood that seems to have characterized the secular side of the adolescence of the Prince and his brothers, there lay the decidedly unpromising economic and social realities already mentioned. Henry and his brothers were first made to experience at first hand what these meant when, in 1408, the king decided that the time had come to set them up with their own households. The Portuguese Cortes, not without some grumbling because of the heavy new expense involved, agreed to supply the necessary finance. D. Duarte was already seventeen and, as heir to the throne, clearly now needed an establishment of his own. Pedro too, only a year younger, had also reached an age when it was customary for princes to enjoy some independence of status. It is less obvious why, in a time of extreme financial stringency, the king also now determined to give the fourteen-year-old Henry a household of his own. Had he already graduated to the status of John's favourite son, or was the Portuguese king perhaps aware that Henry, even at that age, would not tolerate any denial to him of the new status accorded to his elder brothers?

The establishment of independent households for the three princes involved not only supplying them with an annual budget paid for by the taxpayer but also providing them with territorial estates commensurate with their royal status. This latter need caused all John's sons first to come face-to-face with a problem which would always affect in different ways the lives of most of them. Since childhood they had been encouraged to think of themselves not only as the relatives of but also as the equals of the princes and great lords of England, France and Castile whose power and prestige rested, in the last resort, on the great estates they possessed. The Portuguese king's desire to supply his sons with patrimonies great enough to satisfy their ambitions in this respect immediately came up against the inescapable fact that Portugal was too small and too poor a kingdom ever to be able to supply five royal princes with lands or revenues on the scale each considered his due. Still less could this be done at the beginning of the fifteenth century when the wholesale alienation of royal demesnes to John's supporters in the War of Independence had eaten up the patrimony at the crown's disposal. It took three years of permutations and exchanges with these veteran beneficiaries before the king could put together sufficient territory to make what he regarded as adequate patrimonies for Pedro and Henry.[32] Eventually, by 1411, John I was able to repossess enough alienated land in the hilly region of north-central Portugal known as the Comarca da Beira, north of the Serra da Estrela range, to make a reasonably adequate lordship (senhorio) for Henry. Its chief city was Viseu. Care was taken to see that, in the east, to avoid any possibility of his involvement in border incidents, the Prince's domains stopped well short of the Castilian frontier.[33] Some years later the lordship of Covilhã, on the south-eastern approaches to the Serra da Estrela, was also conveyed to him by another royal grant.[34] How much Henry resided in his new lordship of Viseu before 1415 is uncertain but there are suggestions that, even at fourteen, he or his entourage wasted no time in consolidating his personal hold over his newly acquired patrimonial lands. Among these was a ducal residence, the Quinta de Silvares near Viseu, which John I bought for him in 1411 by exchange from the then holder of the office of Marshal, Gonçalo Vasques Coutinho. The Quinta is described in the document recording the exchange as a country estate of some size with twenty-three houses located round the main residence. In later times Henry seems to have been regarded in Viseu as an exploitative and neglectful lord but too much should not be read into that; it probably only means that he treated his possessions and his tenants as other territorial lords of the time did theirs. D. Pedro was also supplied in 1411 with as large a patrimony, mainly in the region of Coimbra, as his father could put together. D. João, D. Fernando and the illegitimate D. Afonso would have to wait for better days. Prince Henry, for his part, characteristically lost no time in looking around for ways of winning fame and improving his economic situation.

So it was that, in 1415, when he was twenty-one, he bounded cap-à-pie on to the national and international stage, agog to win his spurs as a crusader against Islam. Henry's career as a public figure really began then. He was to take good care thereafter to see that, for the next forty-five years, he was never out of the limelight.

~ Chapter Two ~

The Force of Destiny: Ceuta

War is a joyous thing for in its course many fine deeds are heard and seen and many good lessons are learnt from it ... When you see that your quarrel is just and your blood is fighting well, tears rise to your eyes. A great and sweet feeling of loyalty and of pity fills your heart on seeing your friend so valiantly exposing his body to execute and accomplish the command of our Creator and out of that there arises such a joy that he who has not experienced it is not fit to say what a delight it is.

Jean de Bueil, *Le Jouvencel, c.* 1466[1]

Many reliable historians have written about the knightly deeds of arms and about the tales of valour performed by many kings, dukes and princes, but it is certain that in none of these writings will be found another example of the seizure by force of arms in so short a time of such a large and famous city.

Zurara, *Crónica da Tomada de Ceuta*[2]

There was nothing improvised about what was to turn out to be the beginning of the Portuguese expansion overseas, nor was there anything fortuitous about the carefully self-orchestrated début of Prince Henry before the European and Arab worlds as a new age crusader against Islam. Notice that Portugal was on the move outside its traditional frontiers was given to a watching but somewhat mystified Europe on Friday, 26 July 1415, when, amid a blaze of publicity, the greatest fleet and perhaps the largest army ever assembled by a Portuguese king sailed out of the Tagus on a southerly tack. The odd thing was that, apart from a handful of commanders, no one had any idea about the expedition's destination.

The fleet was made up of about a hundred requisitioned or chartered merchant ships. Many of them were foreign vessels – Castilian, Flemish, German, Breton and English. They carried large quantities of timber and a number of siege machines, baffled observers noted, an indication that an attack on some fortress was in prospect. Other sources make it plain that the 'siege machines' included a number of cannon. A squadron of twenty royal galleys accompanied the troop-carrying merchant ships. A number of the galleys and the Portuguese merchant ships that sailed from Lisbon had originally been fitted out and assembled in Oporto under the direction of the young Prince Henry, who had then brought them south to Lisbon carrying the troops he had mustered in northern Portugal.

So large was the army assembling in Lisbon that it soon became plain that it could not, with its stores, be completely accommodated aboard the requisitioned or chartered merchant ships and the royal galleys. In consequence, considerable numbers of caravels as well as other types of fishing vessel and estuarine craft also had to be commandeered to transport some of the troops, a fact which ought to have suggested to some – but apparently did not – that the expedition's secret destination could not be all that far away.

Given the disastrous condition of Portugal's finances at this time, one has immediately to ask how a kingdom then so impoverished by past wars was able to meet the heavy expenditure involved in setting up a military expedition on this scale. The answer is a familiar one. In strict accountancy terms, the Portuguese crown obviously could not afford such an enterprise, but history shows that even desperate financial stringency rarely proved a serious impediment to a medieval ruler now determined, as John I was, to make war.

Until fairly recently our information about all stages of the military campaign now about to begin was largely dependent on Zurara's *Chronicle of the Capture of Ceuta*, a work not written until 1449–50 and, according to the chronicler, often based on the personal reminiscences of Henry himself regarding events thirty-five years earlier. The Prince, Zurara perhaps rather ingenuously observes, 'had a more reliable memory of these matters than any other person in the kingdom'.[3] In recent years, however, some important contemporary documentary evidence has come to light which, at least as far as the military and naval preparations for the expedition are concerned, removes the need to rely entirely on a chronicle composed more than three decades after the event. This new evidence takes the form of reports sent from Portugal to Fernando I of Aragon between April and July 1415 by a very competent secret agent. This was Ruy Díaz de Vega, a Castilian in the service of Fernando, who had been despatched to Lisbon in the spring to find out what was going on there.[4] Ruy Díaz informed Fernando as early as April that the planned size of the Portuguese expeditionary army was 5,400 men-at-arms, 1,900 mounted bowmen, 3,000 un-mounted bowmen and 9,000 footmen, a total of some 19,000 men. These figures, the agent assured the Aragonese king, did not represent mere street gossip; he had contrived, he explained, to secure a look at the details contained in the muster rolls and account books of the offi-cials responsible for assembling and paying the expeditionary force. This latter claim was certainly true, for Ruy Díaz was also able, when he wrote his first report, to supply exact information about the tonnage of and crew numbers aboard each of the foreign ships already under charter to the Portuguese crown. He could only have obtained this information in the way he claims. The size of the army, particularly the number of men-at-arms, was remarkably large given the kingdom's size and the crown's financial condition. Only as recently as 1411 it had been agreed that the crown could not afford to maintain a standing army larger than 3,200 men-at-arms all told, whereas now it was planned to raise and send overseas almost double that number. That Díaz de Vega's figures were not exaggerated is confirmed by a letter sent to Castile with John I's permission two days before the Portuguese fleet eventually sailed.[5]

Already as early as March 1413 Henry had been engaged in talks with John's veteran generals about a crusade against Islam and there are grounds for supposing that such a project had first been floated soon after the conclusion of the peace with Castile in 1411. Before the end of 1413 the Portuguese king had made it known to the knights of Europe that a great chivalric enterprise under Portuguese auspices was in the making and had issued an open invitation to them to take part in it without, however, disclosing what the intended scene of the oper-ation was to be.[6] He had originally expected his English in-laws to send a strong contingent to join him under the command of his son-in-law, Thomas, Earl of Arundel, but this project fell through when Henry V himself decided to undertake the Agincourt campaign.[7] In the event only a small number of Frenchmen, Flemings and Englishmen turned up to fight alongside the Portuguese in 1415. One of the French knights, Antoine de La Salle, was to write up his memories of the Ceuta cam-paign rather usefully some forty years later.[8] But, as already noted, the most extraordinary feature about the expedition was that, even when it set sail from Lisbon, no one except those in the innermost circle of the Portuguese king's advisers had been given any firm idea of where it was going. Given the habit medieval rulers and generals had of publicizing their campaigning and especially their crusading intentions, such security was remarkable.

Portuguese silence on this point had troubled various other European rulers during these preparations. The problem for them was that Portugal, now that a permanent peace with Castile had been concluded, had no identifiable enemies anywhere to account for such a major military effort as that now being prepared. The Portuguese king, realizing that the success of his planned attack on Ceuta might depend on catching his intended enemy unprepared, indulged for months in the dangerous but in the end efficacious ploy of spreading disinformation about his intentions so that Christian rulers from Holland to Italy were led to wonder if they were at risk from the Portuguese. The fact that the Portuguese king felt able, between 1413 and 1415, to play these strategic games against his two most powerful neighbours and various other European rulers besides, is evidence of the mood of national self-confidence which had come to dominate the Portuguese court at the time the overseas expansion began. Whether Prince Henry, just out of his teens, was really, as he seems to have persuaded Zurara, the key figure in bringing about this crusading mood among the ruling élite in Portugal we cannot know for certain, but later events in his life make it quite probable. He certainly seems to have had the king's ear when it was a question of persuading John I to ignore the warnings of opponents of the Ceuta project.

The sovereign most apprehensive about the Portuguese king's plans was the newly elected (1412) Trastámaran ruler of the Crown of Aragon, Fernando I. Díaz de Vega's efforts to discover the truth for his master were, in this respect, not reassuring. Early in January 1415, before the agent's arrival in Lisbon, the Aragonese king had been told that the probable destination of the Portuguese expedition was his Mediterranean island of Ibiza. In April Díaz de Vega informed him that the troubled kingdom of Sicily, then also part of the dominions of the Crown of Aragon, was now rumoured in Lisbon to be its goal; the Portuguese, it was said, had been secretly carrying out reconnaissances of Sicily's sea defences. But another rumour the agent passed on concerned a possible threat to Fernando's own position. Despite his election to the Aragonese throne, Fernando continued to hold the office of co-regent of Castile during the minority of John II with special responsibility for the government of Andalusia. The other Castilian regent was the Portuguese king's sister-in-law, John of Gaunt's daughter Catherine of Lancaster. John of Portugal, it was suggested, would, by agreement with Catherine, land with his army at Sanlúcar de Barrameda at the mouth of the Guadalquivir, seize Seville and proclaim himself co-regent instead of Fernando. As a quid pro quo for freeing Catherine from her uneasy condominium with Fernando, the Portuguese king would be given Castilian permission to conquer the Moorish kingdom of Granada and to instal Henry's second brother, Pedro, there as the first Christian ruler of the Nasrid sultanate. Madcap a project as this appeared to be, Fernando could not afford to dismiss it as totally implausible. It was a fact that Catherine of Lancaster was on very bad terms with him. It was also true that, some time after the peace of 1411, the Portuguese king had already sought from him, and been refused, Castilian permission to send a Portuguese army against Granada.

Díaz de Vega, in his report of April 1415, had also mentioned two other rumours then circulating in Lisbon. One was that, without any kind of understanding with Catherine or anyone else in Castile, the Portuguese intended to seize Málaga, the main port of Granada. He also noted in passing that some of his informants in Portugal had suggested that one of the ports in the Marinid kingdom of Fez (Morocco) was the expedition's real target. In support of these two rumours it was said – correctly as it eventually turned out – that John I had been negotiating with the antipope John XXIII to secure bulls of crusade against the infidel. The Aragonese king's agent did not, at this stage, attach much importance to either of these last rumours, evidently, in this, reflecting the general opinion in Portugal itself.[9]

The reasons for the spy's scepticism must have seemed sound enough. It had long been accepted by the other Christian states of the Peninsula, including Portugal, that Muslim Granada was within the Castilian sphere of influence. It was hardly to be supposed therefore that the Portuguese, having recently concluded a very difficult peace with Castile, would, four years later, by unilaterally attacking Granada, risk a reopening of hostilities on their only land frontier at a time when most of their army, if this rumour were true, would be far away overseas. As for the suggestion that a city on the Moroccan coast was the target, somewhat the same conditions applied. In pre-Islamic times what was now Morocco had been the Visigothic province of Mauretania Tingitana, ruled from Toledo. It had long been understood among the Christian rulers of the Peninsula that, if and when the moment for the reconquest of Tingitana arrived, Castile, as the successor kingdom to the Visigothic empire of Hispania, had exclusive rights there too. A hundred-year-old treaty (1291) between Aragon and Castile formally recognized this to be the position. The planned Portuguese military intervention in Morocco without Castilian consent thus represented, as in the case of Granada, a refusal by John I, probably egged on by Prince Henry, to admit the claims of Castile to be the successor state to the former Visigothic empire. The fact that Castile claimed the sole right to undertake operations of 'reconquest' in Morocco would certainly have cut no ice with Henry, whose subsequent career was often to reveal his contempt for and willingness to snub those who had tried to annex Portugal thirty years before. But offending Castile was only a minor concern of the Prince at this time. He planned to use the ensuing campaign, if all went well, to serve notice on Christians and Muslims alike that a new crusading celebrity – himself – had appeared on the European scene.

Despite the Portuguese king's misleading ploys in various directions, the general opinion in Portugal until a few months before the expedition sailed was that his plans involved an aggressive incursion into the Mediterranean and that the most probable goal was indeed Sicily. Contemporary sources provide no satisfactory reasons to explain why John I and his sons were thought likely to have fixed their attention on that distant and troubled Christian island. The truth behind all the deliberately spread disinformation did not finally become known in Lisbon until after the fleet had set sail. On 28 July 1415 Díaz de Vega, in what seems to have been his last report to Fernando of Aragon, said it was by then generally believed in the Portuguese capital that either the Nasrid fortress of Gibraltar or the Marinid fortress of Ceuta, on the opposite side of the Straits, was the chosen target.[10] In fact, just before the fleet sailed, John I himself had taken steps to reassure the Aragonese king by informing him that the expedition's goal was Morocco. Even then, however, he did not communicate directly with Fernando but, instead, directed one of his counsellors to transmit the news to the archbishop of Santiago in the latter's archepiscopal see. By the time the letter had reached the Galician capital and thence been forwarded to Aragon, the Portuguese, it was hoped, would already be in possession of Ceuta and it would be much too late for Fernando to interfere. Even so, John, in his letter to the Castilian archbishop, refrained from disclosing which particular Moroccan city was his objective. He merely wrote that the expedition was directed against the Marinid kingdom.[11] Its actual destination was only made known to the members of the expedition generally when the fleet put into the Algarve port of Lagos in the last days of July. The bulls of crusade were then published and an appropriately rousing sermon preached to the troops by the king's confessor.[12] Zurara claims, however, that even then many in the Portuguese army thought these hortatory formalities in Lagos merely represented another piece of disinformation practised by their king. They continued to suppose that Sicily was the army's real destination.

Modern scholars have often been unwilling to believe that the expedition against Ceuta can have been motivated simply by religious and crusading zealotry and by the wish of a new dynasty to make its mark on the European stage by embarking on a major military venture of that kind outside its frontiers. Assiduous efforts have been made to establish respectable economic and strategic reasons for the attack. The results have been something less than convincing. The failure of the Portuguese themselves (apart from the handful in the know) to identify Ceuta as even a possible target for these massive and expensive military and naval preparations suggests just how insignificant a role the Moroccan fortress, located 160 miles south-east of the nearest point on the Portuguese mainland, played in the everyday strategic or commercial thinking of John I's subjects before 1415. Indeed, if Zurara is to be believed, so unfamiliar was this major Moroccan trading port to the Portuguese that they had had to send agents there secretly to spy out its defences.[13] More significantly still, rumours of these military preparations, while they caused much anxiety in Granada, seem to have produced no apprehension at all in the Moroccan capital, Fez, or in Ceuta itself. It was certainly true that Moorish corsairs based on Ceuta were among the corsairs, Christian as well as Islamic, who from various shelters harried shipping passing through the Straits or sailing off the Spanish and Portuguese coasts. There seems to be no evidence, however, that the Portuguese particularly suffered from the depredations of corsairs based on Ceuta.

What sort of a place was the Moroccan stronghold in 1415? Ceuta (Ar. *Sabta*), though less prosperous than it had been in previous centuries, was still not only a major commercial port but also one of the strongest fortresses in the Mediterranean. Sited just within the western entrance to that sea and nearly opposite Gibraltar, the two keys on Ceuta's banner proclaimed its strategic importance, one symbolically illustrating the fortress's claim to control the entrance to the Mediterranean, the other its exit to the Atlantic. The main part of the city was sited on a narrow, mostly low-lying tongue of land running almost due eastwards out to sea for more about three miles from the point where it joined the mountainous mainland. In some places this peninsula was no more than 300 yards wide from sea to sea. At its eastern end, however, it terminates at the foot of a steep, almost circular, massif about three-quarters of a mile wide and some 650' high at its maximum elevation. After the Portuguese occupation this eminence was known to the Christians as Monte Almina (today Monte Hacho – 'Beacon Mountain'). On Monte Almina an elaborate system of both perimeter and cross-walls, with occasional towers, defended the slopes from beach level upwards. Other walls guarded the low-lying and partly urbanized peninsula itself against direct attack from the sea and also enclosed sections of the built-up area. From their fortress and observation posts on Monte Almina the Moroccans could keep the Straits of Gibraltar and the coast of Europe as far as Castilian-held Tarifa to the north-west under observation. To the north-east they had the coast of the Nasrid kingdom of Granada under surveillance from Gibraltar (still in Nasrid hands) nearly as far as Málaga. Monte Almina of course also completely dominated the main quarter of the Moroccan city established at its foot on the peninsula but some distance to the west. A separate quarter of the city was actually sited on the lower western slopes of Monte Almina. Beyond the westernmost defences of the city proper lay Aljazira, a suburb of villas, market gardens and pleasances established on the mainland. The Portuguese kept the Arabic name but in their time it referred only to the usually small area they held to the west of the castle and the accompanying outer fortifications that defended the peninsula of Ceuta against attack from the land. Near where the peninsula joined the mainland a dyke or moat had been dug across it from sea to sea. Behind the dyke rose the castle guarding the land approach to the city. Anchorages were available both on the north and south sides of the peninsula but a drawback to Ceuta as a port, as the Portuguese were soon to find, was that ships had to be ready to switch anchorages quickly should either the *levante* from the east or the *poniente* from the west start to blow strongly in the Straits, as often happened. Such was the formidable stronghold against which the Portuguese king now proposed to throw an army and navy, scarcely any of whose leaders had any experience of war outside the Iberian Peninsula.

In earlier centuries Ceuta had been an important naval base for the large fleet of galleys formerly maintained by the Marinid sultans. For reasons not fully explained, by the early fifteenth century the naval power of the sultanate was greatly diminished and naval defence was to play no part in the coming action. The Moorish corsairs who notoriously used the port as a base for their operations knew better in 1415 than to remain there to face the Portuguese fleet.

Though political relations between the ruling Marinid dynasty in Fez and and the Nasrids of Granada were often far from friendly, their common faith could always be relied on to arouse the Moroccans to support the Spanish Muslim kingdom against Castilian attacks. Through Ceuta troop reinforcements, arms, horses and essential food supplies were carried across the Straits in large numbers of small craft whenever the Castilians felt obliged to make one of their much trumpeted but traditionally indecisive onslaughts on Granada. This relationship between the two Muslim nations probably contributed to Henry's enthusiasm for the Ceuta enterprise. As was soon to become apparent, he regarded the fortress's capture as, among other things, a success which would open the way for him to raise again in Castile his demand that he be allowed to conquer the Nasrid kingdom.

Even more important than its role as a key Moroccan fortress was the fact that Ceuta was also a major Mediterranean commercial port, noted, among other things, for its export of the large quantities of wheat grown in the Atlantic region of the sultanate. The great public granaries in which the cereal was stored there while awaiting shipment to other parts of North Africa and to Christian Europe were famous in the Islamic world. But Ceuta's main commercial importance had always depended on its entrepôt traffic. It was one of the northern terminals of the trans-Saharan caravan trade and, through it, European silver as well as North African goods and artefacts as well as horses went southwards to be carried thence by caravan across the desert to the powerful Muslim kingdoms of the Sahel. The caravans returned north with gold, slaves, ivory and other luxury goods. At the time of the Portuguese attack Ceuta was still one of the main ports through which the gold that Europe needed so badly reached the Christian world from the distant and mysterious mines of Black Africa.[14]

Portugal's rulers, when referring to Ceuta, were always careful to imply that, prior to its conquest by John I, it, like the rest of Morocco, was a *terra clausa* for Christians. This was far from the truth. Jewish merchants based in the Balearic Islands, notably in Ibiza, as well as Catalan, Aragonese and Castilian merchants, had long traded freely in the city. But it was the Italians, and particularly the highly organized Genoese, who dominated Ceuta's maritime trade with Europe in 1415. Their *fonduk* or trading factory in the city was the most important of the various foreign commercial establishments which had long existed there. The Genoese in Ceuta had very close links with their compatriots established in the Andalusian ports of Seville, Sanlúcar de Barrameda and Cadiz.[15] Much of the gold brought from Black Africa by caravan ended up in the hands of the latter and was used in part by them to pay for the massive Genoese imports from the Iberian Peninsula.[16]

It will be seen that, in terms of economic and political realities, nothing could be further from the truth than to suppose that Ceuta (and, indeed, the whole of Morocco) represented a region closed to Christian Europe. It was true that occasional outbursts of Muslim fanaticism against unbelievers could make life difficult for the merchants and other Christians who lived and worked there. But these risks seem never to have deterred Christian merchants from seeking the lucrative profits the North African trade was able to provide, even in the state of near political anarchy into which Morocco seemed sometimes to have sunk by the early fifteenth century. Nor was it a question of the Moroccans simply tolerating the presence of the unbelievers for strictly commercial reasons only. Since the thirteenth century, the personal bodyguard of the Marinid sultans had routinely consisted of Christian troops who were considered, because of their religious and cultural isolation, less likely to be seduced from their loyalty than Muslim soldiers.[17] Christian merchants were allowed to practise their religion freely in their trading factories. While it is somewhat doubtful how far the titular Christian bishops of Morocco routinely nominated by the Roman curia actually were permitted to reside there, there is some evidence that the Franciscans were permitted to maintain in Ceuta a hermitage which was turned into a convent after the Portuguese conquest.[18] It was, then, this delicately balanced economic, political and religious structure, highly important to the trade of various Christian states bordering on the Mediterranean, that a Portuguese army, preaching a crusade *à l'outrance* against the infidel, would shatter in 1415. When reading what Zurara has to say about all this, one receives the impression that Portugal's rulers were extraordinarily ignorant of the real state of relations between Morocco and the Christian world at this time. Or did they perhaps choose to pretend to ignorance so that reality was not allowed to interfere with their crusading plans?

Zurara's *Chronicle of the Capture of Ceuta*, in addition to the main task referred to in its title, is also, in an important way, a biography of Prince Henry's early years as a public figure. In particular, it demonstrates how he considered eye-catching chivalric display to be inseparably associated with crusading enthusiasm. Thus, when the attack on the city had been decided on in 1413 and Henry, not yet out of his teens, returned to his lands in the north to raise an army there, his first act was to celebrate the decision by organizing in Viseu some extraordinarily lavish Christmas festivities for the entertainment of his brothers and the knights who resided on his patrimonial lands in Beira. Of these essentially ludic festivities Zurara remarks with evident approval that no expense was spared so that it seemed to those who saw the jousting, feasting, dancing and other forms of knightly and courtly diversions arranged by Henry that they were present at a king's court, not at that of a mere great magnate. Even if Zurara allowed his own imagination full play when writing up his description of these long past events in Viseu, it seems likely that, as so often in this chronicle, the original source of his information about them was the Prince himself. It is when describing these elaborate festivities too that the chronicler permits himself the revealing general observation that Henry was the most regal of all his royal brothers both because of the deeds he carried out and the state he maintained.[19] Henry plainly used the occasion of the festivities at Viseu to demonstrate on a grand scale that 'lordly liberality' as Zurara calls it – in other words his penchant for lavish and conspicuous expenditure – which the theory of chivalry, borrowing from the doctrines set out by Aristotle in the *Nichomachean Ethics*, regarded as an indispensable sign of true nobility of spirit. Henry, throughout his life, would always practise this form of noble magnificence with enthusiasm, showing, it seems, scant concern whether his treasury held the necessary resources to pay for such displays.

Zurara's chronicle presents the Ceuta expedition as entirely motivated by crusading and chivalric considerations. The Portuguese chronicler does not attempt to offer any real insights into the state of mind or deeper emotions that characterized those Portuguese who now sought a chance to make war. It can safely be assumed, however, that they were driven by the kind of feelings described by Jean de Bueil in the epigraph at the beginning of this chapter. The young princes and the nobles of the post-Aljubarrota generation, the chronicler explains, wished to win their spurs in a real battle and to show the world that Portugal in no way lagged behind other Christian lands in its hatred of Islam. To account for the warlike spirit of the nobility Zurara explains that, though the end of the long war with Castile had been greeted with intense satisfaction by much of the Portuguese population, and not least by the mercantile class, one social group was greatly disconcerted by the cessation of hostilities. The young nobles of

Portugal – brought up expecting to win reputation and fortune in action against the traditional enemy as their fathers had done – suddenly found this prospect taken from them. It was not that their hatred of Castile had diminished. As Duarte I could still tell the pope more than two decades later, 'after twenty years of bitter war between the two kingdoms treaties of peace cannot remove from the hearts of men so great a foundation of hatred and ill-will'.[20]

Now the younger knights of Portugal decried their elders for giving way to the war weariness which had led to a settlement with Castile at the very time when, so they believed, the prospect of a long and politically weakening royal minority there – John II, born 1405, had acceded in 1406 – offered Portugal ideal conditions in which to continue hostilities against the old foe. As things were, they would have to look outside the frontiers of their country to seek honour and material rewards in the only way acceptable for persons of their quality – by the sword. Their opinion was certainly shared by some of the royal princes. Several of them did indeed unambiguously complain that Portugal was too small and too poor a kingdom to supply them with the great estates, the impressive revenues and the opportunities for military glory appropriate to their rank and ancestry.[21]

Strictly crusading purposes apart, one may also see the Portuguese seizure of Ceuta as an attempt to set up a military frontier with Islam which would serve to give the knights of Portugal the kind of opportunities for battle, booty and the practice of chivalry with which history had provided their Castilian contemporaries on the frontier with Granada. A document survives in which Duarte I, twenty-two years later, sought to justify the disastrous attack on Tangier for exactly such reasons. He then wrote that he had judged a new campaign in Morocco necessary to give an opportunity for 'the excellent exercise of arms to be practised, for lack of which many peoples and kingdoms have been lost, and to draw our subjects away from an idle life lacking in [military] virtue.'[22]

Zurara's version of the reasons for the attack on the Moroccan fortress has often been seen by later twentieth-century scholars as a mere chivalric misrepresentation of the real reasons which, it is claimed, must have prompted the Portuguese action. A major military initiative of this kind could not have been undertaken, it is suggested, unless it had been propelled by important economic motives and forces.[23] According to this view, the chronicler's account as well as what contemporary documents have to say about motives should be viewed as reflecting the self-deception of an aristocracy unwilling to admit, or at worst naïvely unaware, that its real task at Ceuta was to fight on behalf of an expansionist bourgeoisie seeking new markets. The attempt to write off the validity of Zurara's account of the motives for the attack seems, however, not to rest on any alternate factual evidence that can be marshalled in support of this interpretation. It depends, instead, on some questionable a priori assumptions that we are invited to take for granted. Thus it is suggested that the doctrines of chivalry, by definition only influential among the nobility – the natural defenders of the existing order of things – cannot ever have supplied the kind of radical, innovative drive necessary to cause the Portuguese to break out of their traditional geopolitical environment. Such a fundamental change of direction could only have been instigated by a merchant class impelled by economic motives to look for new markets and new sources of profit. Moreover, evidence that this is what happened is to be found, it has been claimed, hidden away in Zurara's narrative. Attention has concentrated on the fact that, according to Zurara, the royal treasurer (*vedor da fazenda*), João Afonso de Alenquer, first put it to Prince Henry and his brothers that, if they could persuade their father to mount an expedition against Ceuta, then, instead of the elaborately staged festive tournament in Portugal John had in mind as a preliminary to knighting his sons, they would have a real-life chance of winning fame and honour by attacking and capturing an important and noble infidel city.[24] This reading has led to the claim that João Afonso was the true instigator of the Ceuta expedition and that, because of the nature of his office, he must have spoken for the merchant class.[25]

The latter deduction in particular seems decidedly dubious. The rank and career of John's treasurer show that, in fact, he was very much a member of the upper ranks of the nobility as a 'king's vassal' (*vassalo do rei*). Other documents describe him unambiguously as a knight (*cavaleiro*). João Afonso certainly behaved as his noble status required when the expedition reached Ceuta, since Zurara names him among the principal personages who distinguished themselves in the assault on the city.[26] It may be noted, moreover, that Zurara himself comments that, when João Afonso suggested to the princes that they should get their father to agree to attack Ceuta, the treasurer actually knew nothing about the place except what he had been told on their return by some men he had recently sent there to ransom some Portuguese prisoners – a piece of information which confirms other indications that, until about 1413, Ceuta was, for the Portuguese, more or less a *terra incognita*. It is likely, therefore, that the treasurer's suggestion does not carry the implications sometimes read into it but was simply an off-the-cuff remark made in the light of what he had just heard about Ceuta. There seems to be no reason to doubt that João Afonso, despite his titular position as the principal guardian of the royal finances, did not fully share the enthusiasm of Prince Henry for putting Portugal firmly on the map of European powers to be reckoned with by achieving a spectacular military victory for Christianity and chivalry in Morocco.

The Portuguese king, if we accept the chronicler's version of events, was at first by no means easily persuaded to give the go-ahead for the proposed expedition. He or some of his counsellors voiced a number of obvious objections. It was noted that, given the military strength of Ceuta, any preparations to attack it would have to be kept secret until the last possible moment so that its garrison was not alerted or reinforced. That would be difficult to achieve since, among other problems, the Cortes would have to be asked for a subsidy to finance the project and, before they would grant it, would inevitably demand to know what the subsidy was for. There was also a shipping problem: the Portuguese could not supply sufficient vessels of their own to transport to Ceuta an army of the size deemed essential for success. Foreign vessels would therefore need to be chartered. That would not only be very expensive: the foreign shipowners would also want to know where their vessels were going. Where, in any case, the critics asked, was the kingdom going to get sufficient men to raise an army capable of undertaking an attack on a fortress of Ceuta's strength? If they did succeed in capturing it, what was then to be done with the captured city? It would be very difficult for the Portuguese, with their limited manpower and resources, to garrison the place on the scale that would be needed. On the other hand, to capture the city, sack it and then abandon it again to the Moroccans would turn the whole thing into an empty gesture.

There were strategic problems to consider too. Bearing in mind the dependence of Granada on military support from Morocco, the fall of Ceuta to Portugal would, ironically, make it much easier for Castile to conquer Granada, thus increasing the military and political strength of Portugal's traditional enemy. Some of the counsellors suggested that the Castilians might be tempted to use the occasion offered by the absence overseas of most of Portugal's fighting men to strike a new blow against the land frontiers of the kingdom. Nor was this the only consequence to be feared. Whatever happened, a violently hostile anti-Portuguese response from all the Islamic kingdoms of North Africa would be inevitable and retaliatory Moorish raids on the exposed coasts of the Algarve from the Atlantic ports of Morocco would be certain.

These were, of course, hard-headed strategic and political objections which took no account of the pressure on the court of ideological commitments and religious and patriotic emotions. It is highly unlikely therefore that John I himself personally set them out as Zurara implies. No doubt the chronicler, anxious to display the king as a monarch who prudently weighed up the odds before taking decisions, here puts in his mouth the case against the expedition aired by those members of the royal council who opposed the whole idea that the Portuguese should intervene militarily or politically in North Africa. According to Zurara, the princes, led by Prince Henry, dismissed all these objections out-of-hand by resorting to the time-honoured (however often discredited) ploy used by crusaders when their exalted projects were opposed by those who insisted on assessing their viability as if it were a question of any run-of-the-mill campaign. They simply reminded the ageing king that, since making holy war against the infidel was known to be the will of God, He could be relied on to assure a Portuguese victory.

Zurara comments that Henry's success in overcoming all the objections to the Ceuta expedition put forward by some of the king's counsellors should be attributed to the unique strength of will the prince possessed. Zurara perhaps confuses strength of will with the obsessiveness with which Henry always went about pursuing those goals he had made his own. The chronicler himself comments that at times his hero could appear overcome by aboulia.

The Portuguese king, however, still had one remaining problem to which it may be presumed some of those at court had drawn his attention. Was it quite certain that he, as a Christian prince, had the right according to canon or civil law to invade and conquer lands long held by an infidel ruler who presented no direct threat to him and who did not forbid Christians to practice their religion in his dominions? John refused to give the final go-ahead for the expedition until he had secured professional assurances that a Portuguese campaign against the Moroccans would be 'in God's service', that is to say that it would fall within the category of a just war. A number of Portuguese churchmen and canon and civil lawyers were consulted. They, unsurprisingly, readily supplied the necessary assurances.[27] In fact, however, the question the king had put to them involved what had become since the thirteenth century a major matter of dispute among lawyers and theologians. The Portuguese always adhered to the traditional so-called 'papalist' view that Christian princes had an unrestricted right to make war on any infidel or pagan ruler simply because of the latter's infidel or pagan status. There was thus no legal or theological impediment to the Portuguese attack on Ceuta.

Fifteenth-century records estimated the total cost to the crown of the expedition that captured Ceuta in 1415 to have been 280,000 gold dobras, that is about 333,000 Florentine florins or, in new Portuguese money of the period, 33,600,000 *reais brancos*.[28] This figure probably only refers to actual payments made by the royal treasury, not to debts contracted but not yet settled by the crown. In reality, many debts contracted by the crown in connection with the Ceuta expedition were never repaid at all so that decades later royal creditors would still be trying to recover their money. Some of the measures introduced in the king's name by his treasurer to raise the large additional sums needed to finance the expedition can scarcely have endeared him to the merchant class whose spokesman some think him to have been. The royal order that all holdings of silver and copper must be surrendered to the crown can, for example, hardly have been well received in such quarters. Highly unpopular there too must have been the new, though surreptitious, devaluation of the currency introduced at this time.[29] Nor can the merchants have approved of the manoeuvre employed to pay the charter charges owed to the foreign shipowners whose vessels had been hired as troop transports. The king, acting on his treasurer's advice, forced the producers of one of the kingdom's major export commodities – salt – to sell their product to the crown at artificially low rates. The crown then sold the salt at European market rates to the shipowners in settlement of his debt to them.[30] João Afonso de Alenquer, whether or not he was personally responsible for thinking up such measures, seems, so far from acting as the mouthpiece of the merchant class's interests, to have acted in ways highly detrimental to it. It is difficult to avoid the conclusion, as Zurara asserts and contemporary documents confirm, that the attack on the Moorish city really was driven by the determination of powerful forces at court and among the nobility to experience the pleasures of war in the name of religion and chivalry. As Huizinga long ago pointed out, if chivalry was sometimes used in the Middle Ages to disguise well-adjusted calculations under the appearance of generous aspirations, it was certainly also sometimes responsible, as here, for the actual nature of political decisions.

Prince Henry's confidence that God would guarantee the success of the coming crusade began to look rather premature when July 1415 came. Chivalric display intended to excite the army's zeal for battle was the order of the day as the soldiers and seamen assembled in Lisbon. The captains of the army had all been fitted out by their respective lords with expensive and colourful new liveries bearing the latter's devices while the ordinary soldiery was issued with fresh clothing. The fleet itself was festooned with specially made flags, banners and pennants embroidered with cloth of gold. Rich new awnings had been woven to be placed over the decks of the galleys. The kingdom might be in severe financial straits but, in accord with the beliefs of its leaders, in military matters magnificent appearances mirrored, and served to stimulate, great intentions. Zurara again dutifully reflects this belief when he remarks, as proof of Prince Henry's chivalric commitment, that he had spent more lavishly on these exterior displays than anyone else.

But some depressing realities now began to undermine the effect of all these outward signs of a great military enterprise in the making. A serious outbreak of pestilence in Lisbon and the surrounting area was particularly alarming, for it was almost certain to spread to the waiting troops and to the fleet. More ominously still, Queen Philippa herself caught the disease and quickly died of it on 18 July. Given the nature of her illness it must be doubted whether her last hours and the manner of her death really can have been quite so ritually heroic, or, indeed, so loquacious as Zurara, always ready to rise to an exemplary occasion, paints them. However, it does seem probable that Philippa was indeed an enthusiastic supporter of the Ceuta venture and the chronicler's assurance that she had had swords specially made for each of her sons to use in the attack on the Moroccan city may not be a fiction.

Zurara attributes to Philippa a number of death-bed injunctions. Among them he describes her rather surprising charge to Henry that he should make it his special responsibility to watch over the interests of all the lords, knights, fidalgos and squires of the kingdom, making sure that their rights were defended and that the royal grants they were entitled to receive were duly made to them. The reason the nobles needed this protection, the dying queen is said to have explained, was that 'it often happens that kings, misled by false information and exaggerated assertions made by other people, do to some what they should not do'.[31] Was she thinking of England and the accusations of Richard II and his counsellors against her brother, Henry Bolingbroke or did she have in mind the regicide for which he had been responsible? Or was the reference to unchronicled happenings at the Portuguese court? Whether the dying queen's well-known piety can really have permitted her to express such politically contentious sentiments at such a time must be open to doubt. Maybe this is one of the occasions when Prince Henry used the chronicler for his own ends. At all events he never objected to the notion that his dying mother had appointed him to keep his father and the latter's successors up to the mark where the rights of the nobility were concerned.

The queen's death coincided with what was thought by many to be yet another ill-omen – a long eclipse of the sun. The latent opposition to the whole enterprise among some of the king's own counsellors once more came out into the open. They pointed out that the death of Queen Philippa created ceremonial and administrative problems that made it desirable to postpone the expedition's departure – already behind schedule – for at least a month. The delay would have the advantage, they stressed, that the danger of pestilence breaking out among the soldiers and sailors might have abated. Zurara claims that Prince Henry and his brothers rejected any idea of further postponement, doubtless insisting that their mother would not have wished her death to imperil the crusade. Their determination once again carried the day. The newly widowed king drastically curtailed the initial funeral ceremonies associated with a royal death, cutting the period of official mourning for Philippa to a barely decent minimum. On Friday, 26 July, eight days after her demise, the fleet set sail out of the Tagus estuary.

By the time it reached Lagos Bay, on the 28th, a new explanation and justification for the enterprise had been thought up. The king's chief confessor, Fr. João Xira, when he preached his crusading sermon there, informed the army that John I had long been troubled in his conscience about the amount of Christian blood that, however inevitably, he had spilt during the wars against Castile. Now, said the Franciscan friar, the time had come for the troubled king's conscience to be assuaged by an appropriate act of penitence involving the spilling of a compensatory amount of infidel blood.[32] Presumably, no one in the royal entourage thought it odd that John's moral discomfort was to be assuaged at huge expense to his people and by yet more spillage of their blood.

In the days which followed more mishaps made it seem to many that the expedition must be doomed to failure. First the fleet was becalmed for a week off the Algarve coast. It did not manage to enter the Straits of Gibraltar until 10 August, when it appeared off Algeciras, on the Castilian side of the Straits. The inexperience of the royal commanders of the fleet and their pilots' evident ignorance of the notoriously difficult navigational problems existing in the region of the Straits then became apparent. On the 12th an attempt to approach Ceuta led to the separation from the protection of the royal galleys of the troop-carrying merchant ships under the command of Henry's older brother Pedro. Though the galleys, commanded by the king himself, managed to enter the northern roadstead of Ceuta, the merchantmen were carried by tide and wind in the wrong direction northwards along the Andalusian coast towards Málaga, Granada's main port. John and his galleys could do no more than wait off Ceuta for their return. The element of surprise, so carefully striven for as essential to the success of the enterprise, was thus lost. The Marinid governor of the city, Salah ben Salah, wasted no time in calling in reinforcements from the Moroccan mainland.

It took two more days for the transports to beat their way back southwards towards Ceuta. While they were doing so, a sudden change from easterly to westerly wind conditions in the Straits forced the king to move his galleys round the eastern end of the Ceuta peninsula to the anchorage on its south side known as Bahr Bassul (the 'Barbaçote' of the Portuguese era). This change of anchorage and the failure of the rest of the fleet to show up had one advantage: it gave the Portuguese king plenty of time to look out for weak points in the complicated defences on Monte Almina and on the low-lying isthmus itself. He wisely decided as a consequence that his best hope of taking the by now fully alerted city was to concentrate his initial attack on the mountain fortress. If the heights of Almina fell, the city below it could hardly hold out, whereas, if the isthmus only was taken, the Portuguese would be left in a very dangerously exposed position – particularly when the inevitable counter-attack from the mainland began. While the ageing Portuguese king and his commanders might know little about manoeuvreing a large fleet or about naval warfare, long experience in the wars against Castile made them well able to decide on the appropriate tactics for their onslaught on Ceuta once they could see the city's defences for themselves. Prince Henry's reaction to all these delays is not recorded by Zurara, but we can be sure that a man of his impetuous instincts where military matters were concerned would have found them highly frustrating.

After two days the wandering transports under D. Pedro's command at last also reached Ceuta. They had hardly done so when a new storm blew up from the east threatening the whole fleet now anchored off the port. It had hastily to put to sea again, galleys and all. Once again the Portuguese vessels crossed the Straits to take shelter in Castilian waters in Algeciras Bay, where they anchored off Punta Carnero. Here the king and his commanders, apparently having come to some arrangement with the governor of nearby Tarifa, coolly landed on a nearby beach and proceeded to hold a council of war on Castilian soil. Since the Castilian regents had forbidden their subjects to give any sort of assistance to the Portuguese, this show of contempt for Castilian sovereignty can have done nothing to improve the endemic hostility between the two crowns. The Portuguese king doubtless took the view that, since his forces were engaged on a crusading campaign authorized by the pope, it was, under canon law, the duty of all Christian princes automatically to provide him with all the assistance they could.

There was considerable support at Punta Carnero for the view that the whole project should be abandoned on the grounds that the odds were now too great. Pestilence had, as expected, broken out in the fleet. Many soldiers, quite unused to the sea, had been badly affected by prolonged seasickness. It was plain, too, that summer had already given way in the Straits to the storms of autumn. The king was advised by some not to tempt providence by moving his massive fleet once more into the dangerous anchorages which those of Ceuta had already shown themselves to be. Others among his counsellors, wishing to make the best of a bad job, recommended that he should forget about Ceuta and content himself with an attack on Nasrid Gibraltar, just across the bay. Safe anchorage was at least sure there.

Zurara again claims that the ardour of the young princes, and especially the insistence of Prince Henry, persuaded the king to adhere to the original plan despite its risks. On the other hand Duarte I, in his moralising treatise, *O Leal Conselheiro* (c. 1430), attributed the decision to proceed with the attack entirely to his father who, he wrote, declared that, rather than abandon the enterprise, he would choose certain death doing his Christian duty in an attack on the Moorish city.[33] Since Duarte is the only eyewitness to have recorded in writing what actually transpired at the council of war at Punta Carnero, his assertion has to be treated with respect. It may even have been inspired by a desire to cut down to size what he regarded as the exaggerated role his younger brother had come to claim for himself as a dominant figure in the whole affair. In fact, a decision to proceed with the attack on Ceuta whatever the risks was inevitable. The Portuguese king had got himself into a position where he could not, without exposing himself to international ridicule, abandon an enterprise which he had been proclaiming to the world for many months would be something to remember in the annals of European chivalry.

In the event the Portuguese conquest of Ceuta was triumphantly carried out in a single day on 21 August 1415 after an assault lasting thirteen hours.[34] The capture of the famous Moroccan city and fortress in this way was by any standards a most remarkable victory in the annals of medieval warfare. It was carried out against formidable odds by attackers inflamed by religious and nationalistic passion who, despite their many days aboard crowded ships, displayed exceptional courage and dedication in the attack. This would, however, have availed them little had it not been for the tactical insight and determination of their leaders. Some factors had favoured the attackers. The total absence of any Marinid naval squadron in the area meant that the large and unwieldy Portuguese fleet could manoeuvre at will, investing Ceuta without any danger other than that provided by the weather. The qadi or governor of the city, Salah ben Salah, had also made a serious misjudgement. After the precipitate departure of the Portuguese fleet from Ceutan waters a week earlier, he had rashly decided that the threat of a Portuguese attack was over and had sent back some of the reinforcements he had then called in from the mainland when the fleet first appeared in the Straits. This had serious consequences for the Moroccans. As even the Portuguese king himself admitted at the time, the famine and pestilence which had lately been raging in the Marinid sultanate had diminished the normal garrison's active strength to a level which made it impossible for the defenders, without reinforcements, to man the city's complicated fixed defences adequately. When the governor saw that, after all, the Portuguese intended to attack he therefore took the fatal step of ordering part of the garrison to leave the shelter of the city's walled defences in an attempt to destroy the Portuguese army while it was landing on the various beaches. When the Moroccans proved unable to prevent the landing the odds markedly changed in favour of the Portuguese.

Neither Zurara nor Antoine de La Salle (who fought at Ceuta as a young squire) mention the use of artillery by the Portuguese. However, a contemporary account of the fall of the city, based on eyewitness reports and sent on 13 September to Fernando of Aragon by the treasurer (*battle general*) of the kingdom of Valencia, discloses that the attack in fact began with an intense bombardment of the fortifications by a large number of cannon carried by the Portuguese fleet.[35] Zurara's failure to mention the bombardment is hard to explain, since no early fifteenth-century attack on a fortified city would omit to soften up the defences by the use of artillery. Perhaps Henry chose not to tell the chronicler about a feature of the action that, he felt, had little place in a narrative whose purpose was to record human acts of bravery in battle.

The Prince, according to the chronicler, had asked his father to let him lead the first troops ashore but it seems that it was in fact the heir to the throne, D. Duarte, who began the landing operations by disembarking on a beach at the foot of Monte Almina and from there opening the critical assault on that eminence. Though the *Crónica do Condestabre*, which contains the earliest narrative account of the whole action, attributes no special role to Henry in the fighting, Antoine de La Salle (who had no particular axe to grind) recalled years later that the Prince did indeed behave with outstanding bravery at Ceuta. The Frenchman's admiration for Henry's display of chivalric prowess did not, however, make him attempt to disguise the fact (which can also be inferred from Zurara's version of events) that the Prince carried personal rashness to selfish extremes during the action. His insistence on rushing ahead of his immediate retinue caused problems for the latter. Thus, when the attackers broke through the gates of the city proper, Henry ran so far ahead of those with him that he found himself on his own and cut off in a side street by the enemy. The governor of his household, an old friend and mentor, lost his own life when rescuing the over-bold glory seeker from the danger into which he had thus put himself.[36] It was at Ceuta that Henry, in his very first battle, earned himself among his peers his lifelong reputation as an exceptionally brave but also impetuous and imprudent soldier who held the dangerous belief that, at least when fighting the infidel, brio and religious zealotry counted for more than careful strategic and tactical planning and attention to military discipline. It was a credo which, while it seemed to have worked at Ceuta, was, twenty-two years later, to lead him to disaster and personal humiliation on another Moroccan battlefield.

The capture of Ceuta certainly represented, as he had determined it should, a climacteric in Henry's career. In the action there he had established himself by ordeal of arms as a military figure of heroic stature and as a man who, when he moralized about the duty of the Portuguese to go crusading against the Moors in North Africa, had indubitably shown in battle that he was one who could be relied on to practise what he preached. If, as I have suggested, he accepted the prediction of his horoscope that it was his destiny to take part in great conquests, then that too had been shown to be true. For the moment, the other prediction – that he would uncover secrets previously hidden from men – had to bide its time.

The Portuguese victory astonished Christian Europe when the news spread through it.[37] Historians of later times, their thoughts centred on the maritime expansion of Portugal in the African Atlantic, have tended to treat the capture of Ceuta as a mere sideshow, so underplaying the extent to which this famous victory and its implications came to dominate the thinking not only of Prince Henry himself but of all the kingdom's fifteenth-century rulers. Not only in an ideological and political sense but also in an institutional and administrative one, too, the experience of ruling Ceuta would give birth to models which spread overseas in the wake of Portugal's maritime expansion.

In accordance with normal practice, the first concern of the crusading victors was to loot the city. The Portuguese knights and squires, aware that Ceuta was a centre of the gold trade with Black Africa and enthused by tales of the wealth of the city's merchants, plundered the place mercilessly. Much time was spent searching for the treasures they supposed must be hidden in the city. As Zurara observes, while wasting their time doing this they thoughtlessly destroyed the stores of spices, conserves, oil and other commodities that, in reality, represented the city's most tangible wealth. There were some protests about this wilful destruction of valuable commodities but the Portuguese commanders were unworried. Zurara expresses their disdain for what such commodities represented when he comments, 'this destruction caused much wailing among some of those of lowly origin but respectable and noble persons did not trouble themselves about such [insignificant] things'.[38] The victorious Portuguese knights did not confine their hostility only to the property of the Moorish inhabitants of Ceuta. The Genoese merchants resident there, once they realized a Portuguese victory was inevitable, had sought belatedly to ingratiate themselves by offering to help the conquerors. This proved of little avail to them.[39] The Portuguese, intoxicated by the spirit of crusade, were not disposed to show any consideration to co-religionaries whom they regarded as guilty of the crime of trading with the infidel. Telling light on the way the Portuguese knights behaved towards the Christian merchants they found in the city is disclosed in some correspondence Fernando I of Aragon had with the Portuguese king in December 1415. In it Fernando complains that a Sicilian merchant residing in the city when it was captured had been savagely treated by the Portuguese king's own nephew, Fernando de Bragança. It was perhaps understandable that the merchant's stores of wheat should have been seized. But the Portuguese knight, the merchant complained, had also tortured him to make him sign a document surrendering to his princely tormentor a quantity of gold coin and other property which he had left in Valencia for safe-keeping.[40] The episode is a useful reminder that the Portuguese princes and nobles had not come to Ceuta only for the sake of religion and glory. Like all medieval crusaders, they also considered that it was a natural right to reward themselves by seizing whatever booty they could and were not particular about whom they seized it from.

When the looting was over, the other requirements of the crusade and of chivalry received due attention. After their victory, many of the Portuguese soldiers had dossed down in the city's great mosque, famous throughout the Maghreb for the exceptional height of its central nave, its 180 marble columns and its painted glass. Some days later the mosque was ritually cleansed and consecrated to Christian use, as were a number of other mosques in the city. In one such, now dedicated to Santa Maria da Misericórdia, the king knighted his three eldest sons, using for the purpose, it is said, the swords the dying Philippa had presented to each. The princes then, in turn, knighted various members of their retinues. It is notable that Henry's list included Fernando de Bragança, the alleged torturer of the Sicilian merchant. According to Zurara, John I had been so impressed by his third son's prowess that he had wished to knight him in the field on the day of the victory, an honour that was apparently not offered to his elder brothers. The chronicler reports that Henry very wisely declined, insisting that he should not be knighted ahead of his brothers. Since the source of the story was probably Henry himself, the Prince's self-effacement on this occasion was, perhaps, something less than total.

When these ceremonies were over, John I formally announced his intention to annex the city to the Portuguese crown. In accordance with this act he, soon afterwards, added the title 'Lord of Ceuta' to the traditional Portuguese royal titles. The annexation did not, however, signify that the Portuguese king had become the Christian ruler of the large Moorish population resident in the city at the time of the Portuguese attack. Most of the city's civilian residents had already fled to the mainland by the time the qadi was forced to give the order to what remained of the Marinid garrison to do likewise. The rest of the city's population soon followed. As far as we can tell, almost the only Moroccans ever to be found in Portuguese Ceuta were knights and squires awaiting ransom or prisoners of war of lesser status held in conditions of slavery.

The announcement of the annexation was not greeted with universal enthusiasm even by some of the members of the royal council. Some had expected that, having achieved a great military victory and sacked the city, the thirst for glory of the king and his sons would be satisfied and they would be ready to abandon their conquest as, for example, Peter of Cyprus and his crusaders had done in 1365 after the sack of Alexandria. The objections, military, financial and political, to a permanent Portuguese occupation of Ceuta were again rehearsed by the opponents of military expansion in Morocco. Their arguments acquired additional force when the king announced that, to hold the city, he would need to keep a permanent garrison of no less than 2,500 men there. An indication that some of the most important participants in the capture of the city did not favour the decision to hold on to it was given when a distinguished old soldier chosen by the king to be the first Portuguese governor of the place, Martim Afonso de Melo, turned down the royal offer. Since, in the summer of 1415, the governorship of Ceuta was plainly the most honourable and distinguished military appointment then at the king's disposal, Martim Afonso's refusal and consequent public affront to the king at first sight seem inexplicable.[41] However, two hypothetical reasons for his action suggest themselves. One is that Henry himself wanted to be the first Portuguese governor of Ceuta but could not get his father to agree. Given his subsequent infatuation with the place and the curious responsibility for it that he was actually given at this time, this suggestion seems entirely plausible. Alternatively it is also possible that Martim Afonso de Melo already knew that it was the king's intention that the new governor of Ceuta, whoever he turned out to be, would, when it was a question of the handling of the fortress's affairs at the Portuguese end, have to deal Prince Henry and his officials, not as was normal, directly with the king. One can see that such an unusual arrangement with all its possibilities for creating jurisdictional ambiguities and consequent friction between prince and governor could well have seemed unattractive to the old soldier. It is likely that this arrangement was engineered by Henry, probably as compensation for his failure to secure the governorship for himself.

The king's second choice as governor was a man who enjoyed his confidence and, indeed, that of Henry. Pedro de Meneses, count of Viana and standard-bearer to the heir to the throne, D. Duarte, offered himself to John I as a candidate for the post.[42] Reading Zurara's account of these events, one has the impression that, in the summer and autumn of 1415, the prudent and clear-headed John I of earlier decades had been replaced by a ruler who, in his old age, was troubled by guilt about the amount of Christian blood he had spilt and now wholly shared his twenty-one-year-old third son's belief in the crusading and expansionist destiny of Portugal in Islamic North Africa. He certainly paid no attention to warnings that Ceuta's annexation would turn out to be an intolerable burden on his kingdom's resources.

The Portuguese lost no time in making sure that the rulers of Europe fully grasped the importance of their decision to set up a military base on Moroccan soil. At the Council of Constance, in 1416, the Portuguese envoys explained that, by the seizure of Ceuta, Portugal was now in possession of the 'gateway and key to all Africa' – a claim which has been held to prove that, already, plans were being worked on for a further drive in Morocco far beyond the narrow confines of the Ceuta peninsula.[43] Documents reveal, however, that, in the autumn of 1415, the Portuguese court's immediate concern was not with further expansion in Morocco but with another singularly impractical scheme for the immediate conquest of Granada. Though this was nominally made in John I's name, its hubristic tone and airy dismissal of political and military realities are characteristic of that disregard for the dictates of prudence or even common sense which always seemed to take hold of Prince Henry whenever he was in a crusading mode. The details of this project are contained in a letter which, shortly after his return to Portugal, John I wrote to Fernando of Aragon. In it he put forward a detailed plan for a joint Castilian, Aragonese and Portuguese assault on the Nasrid kingdom. The relevance of the capture of Ceuta to such an enterprise was, he correctly pointed out, that Granada had now lost its North African supply base while, on the other hand, the Portuguese now in occupation there were excellently placed to deliver a naval and military assault on the Granadine coast.[44]

The Portuguese king, assuming he meant this proposal to be taken seriously, could hardly have chosen a worse moment to propose a tripartite crusade against Islam's last outpost in the Iberian Peninsula. Fernando was already suffering from the fatal illness which would kill him in April 1416. Even if he had been in good health, his political position as the newly elected Trastámaran ruler of the Crown of Aragon was still too insecure for him to contemplate denuding any of its territories of loyal troops in order to lead them against Granada, even if he had wished to, which he did not. Times had changed since Fernando, then Regent of Castile, had made his name as a general a few years before in a famous campaign against the Moorish kingdom. Now, as ruler of the Crown of Aragon, he was beset by political problems at home and overseas and by the fact that, anyway, his new subjects had little reason to interest themselves in helping others to bring the centuries-old *Reconquista* to a close. Apart from these extrinsic factors, there were others which, at any time, would have made it impossible in the fifteenth century for any ruler of the Crown of Aragon to join Castile or Portugal in an attack on Granada or on Morocco itself. Fernando's new subjects enjoyed good relations with Granada and had no desire at all to see the strategic position of their country weakened as would be the case if the Moorish kingdom fell into the hands of Castile (or Portugal). Moreover, the maritime regions of the Crown of Aragon in the Peninsula had, as we have already seen, strong traditional trading and other links with Morocco as well as with Granada. Fernando himself at the time of the Portuguese attack on Ceuta was on excellent terms with the Marinid sultan Abu Sa'īd 'Utman. As for Castilian participation in the project proposed by the Portuguese king, this was untimely too. Castile's endemic political problems, recently made worse by the prospect of John II's lengthy minority, had now been exacerbated by the virtual removal from the Castilian scene – consequent upon his election to the Aragonese throne – of the most powerful and politically skilled of its two regents, Fernando himself. In any case, any plan that involved allowing the hated Portuguese to take part in an all-out assault on Granada was totally unacceptable to Castile's rulers.

The Portuguese king's approach to Fernando showed he had some awareness of the latter's political problems at this time. However, he, or more likely Prince Henry, airily dismissed these as mere 'mundane impediments' which Fernando should sweep aside so as to make himself free to do God's work by eliminating Islam from the Peninsula. He offered Fernando a simple recipe for making sure that political unrest at home did not hinder the Aragonese king's ability to go crusading with him. All Fernando needed to do to avoid this, he said, was for him to bring in garrisons from Castile to occupy any Aragonese or Catalan cities of whose loyalty he was doubtful. The native garrisons of these places could then be packed off to fight against Granada. Should the presence of Castilian garrisons not suffice to guarantee the loyalty of the cities of the Crown of Aragon, John suggested another solution; he himself would be willing to lead a Portuguese army into Castile to put down, on Fernando's behalf, any rebellions there!

It would thus be quite wrong to dismiss these Portuguese proposals for an attack on Granada as no more than a political gesture intended to make the rulers of Castile conscious that the days were now past when it could be taken for granted that, as a military power, Portugal's concerns were strictly defensive and intra-Peninsular. We know that a Portuguese envoy spent five months at the Aragonese court trying unsuccessfully to secure Fernando's approval of the plan put forward in the Portuguese king's name. Fernando wisely decided to leave the Portuguese king's proposition unanswered until the passage of time had, he hoped, caused John's crusading enthusiasm to cool. He did not reply in detail to the Portuguese suggestions until March 1416. His letter then, rather belatedly one might think, paid tribute to John's crusading zeal and to his great victory at Ceuta on behalf of the Faith. In a politically correct passage he declared that, apart from securing the salvation of his soul, no cause was dearer to him than the conquest of Granada. He went on, however, to make it plain that the times were such that the Crown of Aragon could not for the moment take part in any campaign against the Moorish kingdom. He also took the opportunity to remind the Portuguese king that the conquest of Granada was a matter for Castilian decision only. For this reason he promised to write to his co-regent in Castile, Queen Catherine, to inform her of the Portuguese offer.[45]

The Aragonese king's real views about the Portuguese capture of Ceuta are made plain in a correspondence he had had on the subject towards the end of 1415 with sultan Abu Sa'ïd himself. There being few or no Portuguese merchants in the Marinid kingdom, the Moroccan authorities had evidently reacted by taking out their fury at the city's loss on Castilian and Aragonese merchants established elsewhere on Moroccan territory. Fernando demanded an end to these punitive measures, declaring that the Portuguese invasion of Moroccan territory was in no way approved of or supported by either Castile or Aragon. As he put it in an attempt to placate the Moroccan ruler, 'It is completely contrary to all justice and sound reason to disturb and injure the innocent in order to punish the sinners who have inflicted damage on you or your kingdom.' He went on to assure his 'very dear and well-beloved brother and friend' Abu Sa'ïd of his desire that the existing peace between Morocco and the two Christian states mentioned should continue unimpaired by what had happened at Ceuta.[46] So much for the crusading solidarity of the Peninsular kingdoms.

Fernando's death in April 1416 put an end to any further negotiations with Portugal. But the conquest of Granada continued to be an obsession of Prince Henry. Not only in 1419–20 but again in 1434 and later, attempts in which Henry was always the prime mover were made to persuade the Castilian government to allow Portugal, either alone or with Castilian and Aragonese participation, to conquer the Nasrid kingdom. Among his other crusading projects, it is plain that Henry ardently wished to be known to posterity as a military chief who had, in the name of the *Reconquista*, played a leading role in the removal from the Iberian Peninsula of the last remnant of Islamic rule there.

Early in September 1415, the king and his sons returned to Portugal. They left behind them in Ceuta a Portuguese garrison of perhaps 3,000 men (including support services) to meet the inevitable Moroccan counterattack. Before embarking, the Portuguese king sought to show publicly that he regarded Henry as having won the right to be singled out for his contribution to the victory. Instead of performing the ceremony himself, as would have been usual, he delegated to the Prince the formal task of handing over the keys of the city's castle to the new governor, Pedro de Meneses. According to one contemporary source, Henry, together with the aged Constable of Portugal, Nun'Alvares Pereira, was also charged by the king with instructing the governor on the way he should carry out his task of defending the city.[47] If true, this information is further evidence of the extent of Henry's euphoric state of mind after the victory and of his now dominant influence over his ageing father. Just how Pedro de Meneses responded to the suggestion that he needed lessons on military tactics from a 21-year-old prince who had just had his first experience of real war is not recorded.

When the royal party landed at the port of Tavira, in the Algarve, the king once again made public his special regard for Henry by creating him on the spot Duke of Viseu and Lord of Covilhã.[48] It was the first time that the title of duke had been granted in Portugal. It would be a number of months before Henry's elder brother, Pedro, despite the fact that he had been a senior commander to Henry in the attack on Ceuta, was created Duke of Coimbra. These special distinctions conferred on the king's third son for his performance at Ceuta must have put some strain on that exemplary brotherly love for each other and for their father and mother which, Zurara would have us believe, always characterized the relationship of the princes to each other and to their parents.

Henry's return to Portugal in no way signalled that he was distancing himself from the affairs of Ceuta. On the contrary, as will appear in the next chapter, there now began for him a close involvement with those affairs which was by no means limited only to the more spectacular sides of military life or to the occasional performance of some routine administrative act. The ideological and spiritual significance for Henry of the capture of Ceuta by the Portuguese was also profound. He plainly always regarded his participation in this victory, predicted by his horoscope, as the event which had defined for ever who he was.

Afterwards, he would never cease to present himself to the world as a leader whose life was dedicated to crusading against infidels and pagans wherever they were to be found. This commitment would have two lasting consequences for Portuguese maritime expansion. The oceanic discoveries themselves would always have to be made ideologically acceptable by taking care to present them to the world as religious crusades, however far removed from that status they in fact were. Even more important was the fact that, arising from the conquest of Ceuta and the prestige he had won there, Henry was able for good or ill to make the progressive conquest or reconquest of the whole of Morocco an active aim of the Portuguese overseas expansion for nearly two centuries.

~ Chapter Three ~

The Crusader as Administrator: King's Lieutenant for the Affairs of Ceuta and Governor of the Order of Christ

On 18 February 1416 John I notified the officials of his kingdom that he had appointed Prince Henry to be responsible for 'all matters pertaining to our city of Ceuta and the defence thereof'.[1] It was an appointment which would turn out to have important consequences for Henry's life and career, perhaps most of all because it placed him in direct contact with a world that royal princes usually only saw from a distance. The document issued by the Portuguese king in 1416 notably failed to clear up the ambiguity he had created in 1415 concerning the division of responsibility between Pedro de Meneses and Henry for the security of Portugal's first overseas possession. The captured fortress, as we have seen, now had as its captain–governor a distinguished and politically influential soldier. It was regarded at the beginning as if it were simply a major frontier castle on the mainland of Portugal and, in accordance with traditional practice in such cases, Pedro de Meneses was directly responsible to the king for the fortress's defence. However, it soon became clear that the fact that it was far away across the ocean, on another continent and wholly dependent on the metropolis for supplies could not be ignored. Because of Ceuta's isolation, its governor had perforce to be given wider powers and more juridical independence than the crown ever normally delegated to the commanders of even frontier castles in metropolitan Portugal.[2] What then did the 1416 document's attribution of the responsibility for Ceuta's defence to Henry mean? It seems that the king, conscious that he had frustrated his son's wish to be made first governor of the place, preferred to leave this ambiguity unresolved. The uncertainty is reflected by Zurara who, when he came to refer to the matter in his *Chronicle of Guinea*, declared that the Prince 'governed Ceuta' for thirty-five years.[3] The assertion is unexpected since Zurara himself is the author of another chronicle about Pedro de Meneses which is mainly concerned with events during the latter's long tenancy as captain–governor of Ceuta.[4]

Despite the potential for trouble inherent in the ambiguities of their respective situations, the two men clearly worked out a satisfactory *modus vivendi* for themselves. Thus Zurara reports that, when Henry arrived in Ceuta with reinforcements in 1419, D. Pedro, kneeling, offered him the keys of the city. Henry refused the offer, a gesture presumably intended to act as a public assurance that he made no claim to outrank the governor within the precincts of his own bailiwick. Firmer proof that, despite these problems of status, the relations between the two men were close may be found in the fact that, during the course of his governorship, Meneses made large loans to the chronically over-spent Prince. As early as 1433 Henry described himself as already much in debt to the governor.[5]

What is undisputed is that in 1416 John I intended to delegate to his son most or all the crown's responsibility for whatever administrative or fiscal measures proved necessary to see that Ceuta, now surrounded on its land side by a bitterly hostile hinterland, was kept supplied from Portugal with everything it needed. Henry seems to have had carte blanche as far as expenditure for these purposes was concerned. The appointment was, of course, yet another illustration of the king's notable readiness to heap responsibility as well as honours on his third son.

The reasons why John I needed to make exceptional arrangements to ensure the regular flow of supplies to Ceuta were obvious enough. The occupation of the place had suddenly presented the Portuguese with logistical problems for which they were unprepared and of which they had no previous experience. Since the city was now wholly cut off from its Moroccan hinterland, all supplies for a garrison of some 2,500 men on an active war footing would have to be brought in by sea from Portugal. That task involved difficult shipping problems. The vagaries of wind and weather in the Straits as well as the presence of the corsairs who notoriously lurked there, Christian as well as Moorish, made it unwise to rely on square-rigged merchant ships to keep Ceuta regularly provisioned. It was early recognized that much reliance would have to be placed on the caravel, a type of sailing vessel originally designed for ocean-going fishing but latterly developed by the Portuguese for carrying cargo. These small, lateen-rigged craft had the speed, manoeuvrability and shallow draught calculated to make them much more able than square-rigged vessels to beat against contrary winds or to evade attacks by hostile vessels. A disadvantage was that their cargo-carrying capacity was limited so that a considerable number had to be kept available if Ceuta's needs were to be regularly met. It was probably in this way that Henry became acquainted with the special qualities of the caravel.

It was immediately obvious that the crown itself must assume total responsibility for organizing, funding and arranging for the flow of supplies to Ceuta. Large amounts of money from various different sources were therefore set aside annually for this purpose. Thus the crown revenues from a number of tax districts in the north of the kingdom were permanently allocated to the purchase of food for despatch to Ceuta. It was in the north that the large amounts of cereals consumed there could usually most easily be purchased. Meat for the garrison came from the Alentejo. Inevitably, a special tax for Ceuta was imposed on the Jewish *comunas*. Some ecclesiastical revenues, too, were diverted with papal consent to the cost of its defence. However the main and most unpopular measure introduced by the crown to pay for that cost was a general annual poll-tax of 10 *reais*, known throughout Portugal as the 'ten *reais* for Ceuta'.

It is difficult to estimate what the total annual cost of the new North African possession was in these early years because, until the 1430s, official accounts do not survive.[6] There are, however, some pointers to the sort of figures involved. A quittance relating to money destined for Ceuta and raised in the tax district of Guarda alone reveals that, between 1431 and 1434 inclusive, annual sums in the range of some 26,000,000 *libras* (perhaps about 743,000 *reais brancos* in the new Joanine money) had been assigned to Henry 'for the expenses of our city of Ceuta'.[7] In 1437 Duarte I informed the pope that Ceuta routinely cost the crown 28,500 ducats annually, a figure which, he explained, did not take account of the exceptional outgoings which the crown had to meet from time to time for its defence. Ceuta, according to the Portuguese king, did not produce a single ducat of revenue to set against these outgoings.[8] While the king, to impress the pope, doubtless pitched the financial cost of Ceuta to his crown as high as he could, the figures he cited were, perhaps, not too far from the truth. The expenditure referred to in John I's request to the pope for financial assistance no doubt included everything – the wages, allowances and rations for all the members of the garrison and the civilian craftsmen who supported it, not to mention the heavy expenditure on arms of every kind.

At first a warehouse belonging to the Lisbon municipality in the Rua da Ferreria was used to store goods awaiting shipment to Ceuta. It became known, for obvious reasons, as the 'Casa de Ceuta' – literally 'House of Ceuta'. 'The Ceuta Agency' would perhaps more meaningfully convey in English an idea of the various activities eventually carried out there. In the late 1430s the municipality of Lisbon asked for its warehouse back and suggested that a more suitable site was available adjacent to an unused royal dockyard. It seems to have got its way for we soon hear of the Casa de Ceuta as established near the river front.[9]

Until Duarte I succeeded to the throne in 1433, not a great deal is known about the internal organization of the new agency. The new king seems not to have been entirely happy with the way his brother had conducted the affairs of Ceuta from Portugal in his father's time. He now insisted, for instance, that proper annual accounts be presented to him for scrutiny.[10] It is not clear, though, whether this move reflected doubts that Duarte may have had about Henry's handling of the funds earmarked for Ceuta, or whether the changes were introduced simply because of the new king's desire, after the more insouciant days of his father, to see that the rules of the royal treasury were strictly followed. Duarte's bureaucratic instincts were to on show throughout his short reign. Duarte also implied in a document issued in 1433 that Henry, by attempting to make appointments of royal officials in Ceuta itself, had usurped powers reserved to the crown.[11] It was by no means the only occasion in his lifetime when the Prince would be warned not to presume to exercise authority reserved to the crown.

The Casa de Ceuta soon became the central office in Lisbon of a purchasing, distribution and shipping agency whose ramifications extended throughout the kingdom. Requisitioning in the name of the crown was employed to obtain cereals and other foods at less than market rates, a procedure which was much resented by the landowners and farmers concerned. Protests were also made to the crown that the high-handed requisitioning by the Casa of caravels normally employed to carry part of Portugal's seaborne trade was adversely affecting the availability of shipping for this purpose. A merchant described as 'treasurer for the affairs of our city of Ceuta [in Lisbon]' is found in a quittance of 1426. This is probably the earliest reference to an official who was the person in charge of the agency.[12] He was succeeded in this post by a squire attached to the prince's household. Before 1434 the existence of a post described as that of 'treasurer responsible for the affairs of Ceuta in Lisbon' was formally confirmed.[13]

The treasurer's office was in the Casa de Ceuta where he was supported by a small staff. It was he who was in day-to-day charge of the agency's operations under the authority of the Prince. Before Duarte I's death in 1438 the office had plainly grown in importance as signified by the fact that its head was now described as chief treasurer (*tesoureiro-mor*). The post was now held by one Gonçalo Pacheco, also a former squire of the Prince's household but now a wealthy merchant and ship owner in Lisbon and a close associate of Prince Henry.[14] Pacheco held the post for many years. After Henry's caravels had successfully made the passage of Cape Bojador, he sent some of his own ships, with Henry's approval, on voyages to the Saharan littoral. Later documents describe Pacheco as a knight of Henry's household. He may be regarded as a symbol of the easy rapport which Henry, despite his bluest of blue blood and his regal ambitions, came to have with merchants and sea-captains, making them senior members of his household because of their usefulness to him. It was a relationship without which the Henrican discoveries might not have prospered.

As a fully fledged department of state the Casa de Ceuta was probably Pacheco's creation. There are clear indications that during his treasurership, the agency itself, though the permanent members of its staff were few, began to undertake activities that went well beyond simply purchasing and despatching supplies intended for Ceuta. It came to have its own in-house coopers and its own potters, who made pottery intended for export there. Carpenters, sail-makers, caulkers and other specialist shipwrights were permanently attached to the Casa to service the caravels and merchant ships under charter to it.

Since the treasurer was of the right social rank to enjoy the Prince's confidence but was also a merchant of substance and a shipowner to boot, it seems highly probable that he was numbered among those specially influential counsellors, condemned by the chroniclers and by medieval protocol to anonymity, with whom the Prince discussed his many projects and whose advice he no doubt sometimes – perhaps often – followed.

Whenever political questions relating to Ceuta came up, Henry always reminded the court that his main wish in life was to devote himself to crusading for Christ against the infidel in Morocco. Nevertheless, his association with the Casa de Ceuta inevitably gave him a much greater experience of a wider world where buying and selling was a way of life than usually came the way of great territorial lords. It should be noted, too, that, under Henry's aegis, the Casa de Ceuta exercised total control over the movements of shipping to and from Ceuta. It was inevitable that, when the question of how to organize navigation and trade with Guinea had to be resolved in the 1440s, Henry, drawing on his experience of the Casa de Ceuta's operations, should demand and obtain for himself similar control over all sailings there. An agency modelled on the Casa de Ceuta was set up in Lagos to administer this new monopoly under his direction. Henry was thus the original founder of the various agencies through which, after his death, the crown monopoly over all trade in the African Atlantic or the Indian Ocean operated.[15]

A substantial picture of the many-sided operations of the Casa de Ceuta in the Henrican period can be built up by analysing the quittances submitted from time to time by its officials to the crown. There was an English involvement in the despatch of supplies to Ceuta. English merchants were sometimes involved in shipping wheat there, as were vessels of the Hansa.[16] In the mid-1450s Ceuta received some unwilling settlers from the British Isles when Welsh and English seamen found guilty of piracy in a Portuguese court were sentenced to deportation for ten years in the Moroccan fortress.[17]

Henry's close connection with Ceuta and his well-known hope that the city's capture would prove to be only a first step in a far-ranging Portuguese military expansion in Morocco can have done nothing for his popularity in the kingdom at large, though, of course, critics of this policy never mentioned him by name. The Portuguese occupation of Ceuta and the policy of further expansion in North Africa, of which he was regarded as the principal promoter, soon came to be regarded as recipes for disaster, even by some magnates within the court. As early as April 1418 the problems of provisioning the place had become so acute that, in an extraordinary volte-face, John I petitioned the pope for permission for the Portuguese in the Moroccan fortress to trade with Muslims, especially for food. He attempted to explain away the request by declaring that it was his intention to convert the Moroccan infidels 'either by love or by fear' and that trade would provide an occasion for the love method to be tried.[18] This unconvincing declaration from John I was no doubt intended to provide a solution to Ceuta's desperate provisioning problems as the armies of Morocco and Granada got ready to try to recover the lost city. It is quite possible that the approach to the pope originated with Prince Henry who, as he was later to reveal in the case of Guinea, was, for all his crusader's rhetoric, adept at finding casuistical reasons for justifying postures that seemed to contradict everything he stood for. The necessary permission was granted by the pope a few months later but cannot have been of much help to the Ceuta garrison then as the Marinids had no intention of helping the Portuguese garrison to survive in a city they themselves were then preparing to retake.

Despite all the talk of high-minded crusading against the infidel, there is ample evidence that military service in Ceuta had scant appeal for most Portuguese men. Knights and squires were usually keen to put in time there to fight for honour and booty because that was their chosen way of life. Booty in human form was specially sought after. The ransoming of Moorish knights captured in skirmishes could be very lucrative indeed. One of the captured commanders of the besieging army in 1419 offered 2,000 gold *dobras* for his ransom. In 1422 the Portuguese king paid 3 million *libras* for two Moorish knights captured at sea.[19] During his governorship Pedro de Meneses seems to have made large sums from his share of ransom money and from booty taken by Portuguese corsairs operating out of Ceuta.[20]

For lesser folk, life on the new frontier with Islam in North Africa had, however, no such compensations. Attempts to persuade Portuguese colonists to settle in Ceuta as artisans or to cultivate the gardens and orchards on the peninsula abandoned by the Moors met with scant success. Even the governor himself could not recruit locally a sufficient number of Portuguese to act as servants in the gubernatorial palace and had to ask the crown to compel men from his estates in

Portugal to go to Ceuta to serve him. The failure to attract Portuguese settlers was seen as a military danger as early as 1419 when the Portuguese king asked the pope to grant a series of special religious privileges to any colonists who decided to move there. He explained at the time that the city's area was so great that it needed a large civilian population which could be called on to help in its defence when necessary.[21] Such efforts were always unsuccessful. As late as 1456 Afonso V complained that the number of residents in Ceuta was so small that its ability to resist an enemy attack was seriously impaired.

It was not just civilians who rejected attempts to persuade them to move to Ceuta. The soldiers of the garrison, too, greatly disliked serving there. It was not uncommon for them to desert at night in small boats in a risky attempt to make their way across the Straits to the nearest landfall on Castilian territory. Another sign of the problem was that Pedro de Meneses and his successors were sometimes so short of troops that they refused to allow time-expired men to return to Portugal – a procedure that did nothing to increase the popularity of service in the city. Nor did the mockery they sometimes had to listen to from passing mariners. Zurara reports an occasion in the 1430s when the crews of some Castilian galleys came close inshore and shouted sneers at the soldiers of the Portuguese garrison whom they described as being like prisoners reduced to living on a diet of millet and vinegar.

To deal with the unwillingness of its free citizens to go to Ceuta, the crown now resorted to a practice that would become a feature of Portuguese colonization generally and that of later entrants to empire such as, notoriously, the British. Criminals convicted of capital and other serious offences could have their sentences commuted on condition that they served a period of forced exile in Ceuta, usually as bowmen or as labourers.[22] There was a precedent in the Portuguese legal system for allowing convicted criminals to commute their sentences to periods of internal exile. Now recourse to this procedure was greatly increased. At first, in order not to offend the purity of the crusading spirit that was supposed to prevail in the Moroccan city, John I decreed that those convicted of murder, rape, treason, coining, buggery or the practice of magic could not evade the death penalty by getting themselves transported there, and that commutation could only be granted to those who had committed their offences before the capture of the city. But circumstances soon forced the crown to be less finicky and the *degredados* or 'degraded ones' as the exiled criminals were known, must have come to form a noticeable proportion of the shifting Portuguese population of Ceuta in Prince Henry's time, and later. Debtors, too, could get themselves deported to the city to work as servants there instead of undergoing a term of detention in Portugal. In 1431 one year's service in Ceuta was calculated as working off 1,500 *reais* of debt. It will be seen that there was a wide disparity between the way Henry and those who thought like him viewed the occupation of Ceuta and the on-the-spot realities experienced by those who were obliged to serve there without the ideological enthusiasm of their betters or the hope of important material rewards that sustained the latter.

From the early days of the occupation, the Portuguese court set about making sure that Europe's rulers grasped the significance of the conversion of the North African stronghold of Islam into an outpost of Christianity. Early in 1417, Martin V had been asked to raise the former chief mosque to the status of a cathedral and to place it under the jurisdiction of the ecclesiastical authorities in Portugal. After some hesitation, the pope granted the request. In 1419, using authority delegated to them by the Curia, the archbishops of Braga and Lisbon declared that the new diocese of Ceuta included not only the entire kingdom of Morocco but also all the coastal regions of the kingdom of Granada![23] There is every reason to suspect the hand of Prince Henry behind a decision which embraced his dream of an eventual Portuguese domination of all Morocco. The ruling, by seeking to place part of the kingdom of Granada under the ecclesiastical juris-diction of a Portuguese bishop, also seems to reflect Henry's deter-mination that Portugal should have a stake in the future conquest of that kingdom.

After the chief mosque had been made fit to function as a Christian church, some of the city's smaller mosques were also 'cleansed' for Christian use. Among these was that dedicated to Santa Maria de Àfrica by the knights of Prince Henry's retinue who had remained behind in the city after its conquest. He placed in it the image of the Virgin of Africa who soon became the patroness of the city and, indeed, of the Portuguese expansion in Africa generally. Henry claimed before his death that the Virgin had performed many miracles since he had installed her image in her church. He later made Santa Maria de Àfrica the headquarters of what seems to have been a somewhat chimerical commandery (*comenda*) of the Order of Christ which he established in the city.

The religious and civil consequences of the conquest of Ceuta are naturally presented in triumphalist terms in documents exchanged between the Portuguese court and the Roman Curia and in other contemporary documents. Here too, however, there was a marked gap between the aspirations of Christian zeal and what actually happened on the ground. Thus, in 1444, we find the Curia admitting that the 'cathedral' of Ceuta still had no endowments and that, in consequence, the canons and other clergy nominally attached to it were unable to reside in the city at all. Unsurprisingly the pope lamented that this had evil consequences for Christian worship there.[24] As for the commandery of the Order of Christ which Henry claimed, with papal authority, to have established in the city, it seems that not even his determination or his authority could make the *freires* accept that they were under any institutional obligation to serve there or anywhere else outside metropolitan Portugal. The members of the other Portuguese military orders took the same view. In 1456 Calixtus III, at the request of Afonso V, ordered all three major orders to establish convents at their own expense in Ceuta and to keep one third of their members there to serve for a year at a time to assist in the city's defence. Any failure to serve would result in deprivation of status and other severe penalties.[25]

During the uneasy last years of his father's long reign and despite Henry's still overriding political influence at court at that time, the view that the Portuguese occupation of Ceuta was a piece of gratuitous folly was openly suggested even by his own brothers within ten years of the place's capture. In a famous letter from Bruges sent home at the end of 1425 or early in 1426 by D. Pedro, the future regent, we find remedies suggested for a list of serious shortcomings in the way Portugal was governed during John I's decline. When Pedro came to discuss Ceuta, he expressed it as his unambiguous opinion that, as long as the affairs of that place were conducted as they had been so far, it could only be likened to an efficient drain down which were pointlessly flushed away the kingdom's resources in men, arms and money. This opinion, he added, was not just a personal one. Men of understanding with whom he had discussed the subject during his travels in England and Flanders had stopped speaking of the honour and fame the Portuguese had won by its capture in 1415 and now talked instead of their folly in holding on to the fortress in Morocco when to do so was plainly to the great detriment of the kingdom.[26] Though Prince Henry's name is not mentioned in the letter, his policies for North Africa were obviously the real target of Pedro's criticisms. Some years later, in 1432, the king's influential illegitimate son and Henry's half-brother, the count of Barcelos, took up the same theme. In a memorandum to D. Duarte he openly referred to 'the damage which you can see Ceuta causes'.[27] On this occasion the count opposed policies which he attributed to Prince

Henry by name. As for the city of Ceuta itself, deprived now of its hinterland, its trade and its Moorish population, it naturally fell into a sharp decline. Some foreign visitors in the fifteenth century testify to this. Pedro Tafur, the Andalusian world traveller, called there in a Genoese ship in 1435 and recorded that it was plain to see that, both as city and as fortress, it was no longer the place it had once been.[28] What seems at first to be a contradictory appraisal of Portuguese Ceuta in mid-century is given in 1451 by Nicolaus Lanckmann von Falckenstein, one of the German chaplains sent to Portugal to escort Henry's niece, Leonor, to Germany where she was to marry the emperor Frederick III.[29] Lanckmann gives, it must be admitted, a much rosier picture than Pedro Tafur of Ceuta as he saw it when the ships carrying the bridal party put in there for three days. Nicolaus was impressed by the size of the city's fortifications and, indulging in a piece of travellers' one-upmanship, went so far as to describe the place as twice the size of Vienna. He marvelled, too, at the cathedral (ex-mosque) with its columns of many-coloured marble, at the city's communal fountain under its lofty cathedral-like roof, at the beauty of the former royal palace and the baths. He was particularly taken by the governor's garden with its trees and plants unknown to Europeans. The German chaplain, it is plain, was captivated by the surviving evidence of the Moorish epoch in Ceuta's history. His knowledge of comparative religions was surprisingly defective for an imperial chaplain, as when he described the Muslim inhabitants of the city when it was under Moroccan rule as pagan idol worshippers. Sixty years later, another German traveller, the famous Hieronymus Münzer, reported that, instead of the great city of Moorish times, Ceuta was now just a small town.[30] Woodcuts of as late as the sixteenth century suggest, however, that, even if part of it was ruinous, Ceuta's location and its fortifications after more than a century of Portuguese occupation still made it an impressive-looking place when seen from the sea.

It is one of the ironies of Prince Henry's role in history that he sought to foist a crusading and evangelizing role overseas on a Portuguese church which had been greatly weakened by war, schism and inflation. By the early fifteenth century few clergy at any level displayed much interest in spreading the Faith in dangerous places overseas. As we have seen, churchmen, while loudly paying lip service to Portugal's crusading and evangelizing mission in North Africa, did not exactly rush to reside in Ceuta. However assiduously Henry and his partisans promoted the impression that all Portuguese were enthusiastically behind the policy of expansion in Morocco, it is evident that such unanimity even within the royal council and among the ranks of the higher nobility was lacking. Opposition to it among those who were taxed or otherwise forced to support it seems to have been general. Complaints from the merchant class about the burdens the occupation of Ceuta placed on them were frequent. Thus the proctors of the city of Oporto protested to the king in the Lisbon Cortes of 1455 about the detentions of shipping for Ceuta made in that port by a senior official of the Casa de Ceuta resident there.[31] At the Cortes of Evora in 1444 the municipality of the Algarve port of Faro had already complained of the special burdens imposed on it because it served as the main port of embarcation for troops and royal officials going to Ceuta.[32] Nevertheless, despite the continuing opposition to all his projects in North Africa, Henry had no difficulty, as long as John I lived, in persuading him that the honour and reputation of the House of Aviz depended on retaining the place as a base from which, eventually, all Morocco might be conquered. It says something for Henry's extraordinary political and personal power in the land at this time that, even after John's death in 1433, this policy not only remained intact but was actively pursued on a military level. Though full of doubts about the retention of Ceuta and the policy of expansion in Morocco, neither Duarte I during his short reign nor D. Pedro during his ten-year regency were able, when it came to it, to cut the Gordian knot tied by Henry. In 1437, when the capture of the Infante D. Fernando at Tangier seemed to provide an excellent occasion for abandoning Ceuta as a quid pro quo for the young prince's release, it would prove to be Henry, the man directly responsible for the disaster, who would successfully insist that the place should be held even if it meant Fernando's death in a Moorish prison – as it did.

The sixteenth-century chronicler of the expansion, João de Barros, claimed that there was a close causal connection between the occupation of Ceuta and Henry's subsequent dedication to exploration in the African Atlantic. Both at the time of the capture of the city and on subsequent visits, Henry, according to Barros, devoted himself to enquiring of the Moors there about the distant interior of Africa. From them, said the Portuguese chronicler, he learnt about the Sahara and the trans-Saharan caravan trade, about the peoples of the desert and something about Black Africa – Guinea – itself. Having in this way found out what he needed to know, Henry, according to Barros, was then equipped to 'set about executing the project that was so dear to his heart' – the maritime exploration of the uncharted Atlantic coast of Africa.[33] All this sounds very plausible at first reading, but none of it is in the least bit likely. Barros is attempting to establish a rational relationship between two of Henry's major preoccupations – crusading in Morocco and oceanic exploration. But his attempt is based on a number of false premisses. As will be made apparent in the next chapter, there was not the slightest need for Henry to have recourse to Moorish informants in Ceuta to secure information which was readily, and far more reliably, available to him in Europe from the accounts contained in a number of sources, both oral and written. In any case, since the Portuguese had driven away from Ceuta in 1415 all that city's Moorish inhabitants, there cannot have been many potential informants around except prisoners-of-war or slaves. Zurara, no slouch when it is a question of his hero's talents and achievements, makes no claim in any of his chronicles that Henry set about acquiring any knowledge of African geography or the trans-Saharan caravan trades during his early postings to Ceuta. As the Prince himself was the source of much of what the chronicler has to say about Ceuta, his silence is telling.

A crucial date in the history of the Prince's involvement with Ceutan affairs is 1419. In that year the governor of Ceuta, Pedro de Meneses, found himself particularly hard-pressed by the long-awaited attempt of the allied armies of Morocco and Granada to retake the city. The attack was to come from the sea as well as the land and so a fleet of galleys and smaller craft mostly from Granada took part. Zurara's account indicates that two separate attempts were made to drive out the Portuguese in the late summer of 1419. In the second of these, Granadine troops succeeded in establishing positions on Monte Almina and it took all the courage and tactical skill of Pedro de Meneses to overcome them. Some reinforcements had been sent from Portugal at the time of the first siege but these were not needed. When it was clear that the Moors were preparing a new and even stronger attack, the governor once again urgently demanded reinforcements from Portugal. These were duly sent, naturally under Prince Henry's command. On this occasion he was accompanied by a younger brother, D. João (b. 1400), who had just been appointed administrator of the military order of Santiago and therefore was thought to be in need of a chance to prove his knightly worth. The reinforcements under Henry's command did not, to his chagrin, reach Ceuta until just after the besiegers had been finally defeated by the garrison's own efforts.

Zurara's account of what now occurred shows that Henry's obsession with the conquest of Granada was still undiminished. Moreover, he could now put forward a new reason for claiming that Portugal had a right to intervene there. During the recent attacks on Ceuta, troops and ships from Granada had played a major and what was, from the Portuguese viewpoint, perilously near to being a decisive role. Henry, instead of returning home as was expected now that the immediate threat was over, informed the governor that he had decided to use the men and the ships he had brought from Portugal to mount an attack on Nasrid Gibraltar. This announcement demonstrated once again that, when a prospect of making war on an Islamic enemy presented itself to Henry, no considerations of elementary military prudence or even ordinary common-sense counted for anything with him. In the autumn of 1419 he accordingly spent three months in Ceuta preparing to attack Gibraltar. He had no authority from his father to involve the troops and ships under his command in any such project and does not seem to have sought it. Reminders that the reconquest of Gibraltar from the Granadine Moors was reserved to Castile naturally left him unmoved, as did suggestions that the force he had at his disposal was too small for the enterprise he had in mind. Even when the winter storms arrived early, making it obvious to observers in Ceuta that it was no time to start naval or military operations in the Straits, he remained determined to do just that. Only the timely arrival of peremptory instructions from John I that he and the soldiers and ships he had taken to Ceuta in September must return to Portugal forthwith put a stop to the project. Presumably the king's orders were issued on the prompting of Pedro de Meneses. However friendly the governor may have been with the Prince, he had every reason not to want the Ceuta garrison to find itself involved willy-nilly in a winter rescue operation on the other side of the Straits as a result of Henry's ill-considered plans. As Zurara tactfully puts it, the king 'knowing the greatness of heart of both princes, and particularly that of Henry, feared that they might attempt some grandiose undertaking inappropriate both for the season of the year and the number of soldiers at their disposal'.[34]

The three months the Prince and his brother spent residing as the governor's guests in Ceuta at the end of 1419 were not entirely devoted to planning the abortive expedition against Gibraltar. Zurara contrived, when he was writing Pedro de Meneses's biography in 1458, to examine the household account-books of the governor for 1419. From these, he discovered that D. Pedro had taken advantage of the presence of the two princes in his palace to show his nobility of spirit by staging the kind of lavishly generous banquets and other entertainments that the age of chivalry expected from its grandees. Zurara refers with undisguised admiration to the great sums which the account-books showed that Pedro de Meneses had spent on the entertainment of his royal guests and their retinues. According to him the governor spent 6,756 gold *dobras* during these months on food and presents for his guests alone. So much flesh and wine was bought for all the banqueting that the price of food and drink, never over-plentiful in Ceuta, rose to what the chronicler forty years later regarded as extraordinary heights. Zurara, faithfully reflecting contemporary beliefs in the milieux he frequented that nobility of mind could be measured by a knightly willingness to spend lavishly, presents these facts as evidence of D. Pedro's aristocratic generosity and magnificence.[35] The governor may have come to wonder if he had been altogether wise to display his wealth to the Prince in this open-handed way when Henry, always on the look-out for potential ways of raising money, drew the conclusion that his friend was good for at least one large loan of 3,000 gold *dobras*. Henry had not paid this back eighteen years later when the governor died.

Where did Pedro de Meneses and later governors of Ceuta get their wealth from? Some, no doubt, came from ransoms of important Moorish knights whom the Portuguese had managed to capture during the sieges of the fortress or on raiding parties into Moroccan territory. But, judging by Zurara's biography of the governor, a more important source of booty came from naval operations carried out by ships based on the port which preyed on traffic between North Africa and Granada and on coastal traffic too. These corsairs did not necessarily always restrict their attentions to Moorish vessels; Christian ships engaged in trade with the Moors were also regarded by the Portuguese as fair game. Portuguese corsairs enjoyed, as elsewhere, marginal official status.[36] Henry now decided to enter the corsair business too. His seamen were evidently not always too particular about making sure that only Moorish vessels were subjected to their attentions. Thus, in 1426, a barinel belonging to the Prince and commanded by Frei Gonçalo Velho unsuccessfully attacked a Galician ship in the Mediterranean. Velho was a friar of the Order of Christ who had distinguished himself at Ceuta in action against the Moorish besiegers there in 1419 and a few years later would become famous as the colonizer and perhaps the rediscoverer of the Azores. In the action his barinel was captured by the Galicians who brought it into the port of Valencia where they denounced its captain and crew to the authorities as corsairs and evil-doers. Gonçalo Velho claimed that the Galicians had done the attacking but his defence does not ring true since he admitted that

Henry's ship was carrying a large number of men. A barinel (a small square-rigged ship capable of being rowed) would not have carried as large crew if it was only employed on a trading voyage. The new Aragonese king, Alfonso V, contented himself with reporting the matter to the Portuguese king and to Prince Henry, remarking that he was unfamiliar with the terms of the truces between Portugal and Castile and therefore did not want to get involved in trying the case in his courts.[37]

The episode is interesting for students of the Prince's biography. It confirms, as do other documents, that Henry was already a ship owner in his own right by the middle 1420s. It also reveals that it was not unknown for his captains, when he sent them to sea as corsairs, to attack supposedly friendly Christian vessels. Such behaviour, though far from unusual in those times where privateers and corsairs were concerned, must have been more difficult to explain away when the ship owner involved was a royal prince, the head of a religious military order and a self-proclaimed Christian crusader.

Henry held on to his job as the king's lieutenant for the affairs of Ceuta from 1416 onwards not only through the 1420s and 1430s but also throughout the 1440s when he was at the height of his fame as the discoverer of Guinea. As we have seen, there is good reason to suppose that Henry had hoped to be appointed to the governorship of the city on its capture in 1415. Now, thirty-five years later, in 1450, it seemed that he might have his wish, though only for a limited time. The third governor of Ceuta, Fernando, count of Arraiolos, had asked to be relieved of his post. Afonso V, instead of immediately nominating a successor, issued a document announcing that he had decided to send Prince Henry to the city. To him, as the king's representative, the count was directed to hand over the city, castle and all other royal properties there.[38] What lay behind this order to Henry is not recorded but surmises are possible. Thus we know that he was heavily in debt to the count. Arraiolos, for his part, was anxious to give up his governorship but was finding this difficult to do since few Portuguese wanted the job, or were deemed suitable for it. It is possible, therefore, that the count offered to cancel some of Henry's debt if the Prince agreed to take his place for a limited time until the king had found a permanent successor. Another possibility is that Henry, who always regarded Portuguese Ceuta as his special responsibility, volunteered to relieve the count without strings so as to ensure that what might be a dangerous interregnum between governors did not occur. Six months later, however, Henry was still in Portugal. A document then describes him as preparing to go to Ceuta with his retinue. In fact he never did make the journey. Since it is difficult to imagine Henry ever refusing a task that involved the safety or well-being of Ceuta, reasons for this abortive affair also need to be looked for. The most likely one is that his critics at court persuaded the king that it was too risky to turn Henry loose there. Such a case would not have been difficult to make. His disastrous track record in Morocco in the 1430s and his well-known propensity to involve himself in rash military acts whenever he found himself with troops under his command in or near territory under Islamic rule spoke for themselves.

By the 1450s Henry's active responsibility for organizing supplies for Ceuta had passed into other hands. Nevertheless, this small Portuguese outpost in Muslim North Africa always occupied a pivotal place in his future plans for Portugal and for himself. Strong emotional ties bound him to the city where he had literally as well as metaphorically won his spurs. For him, the occupation of Ceuta by the Portuguese represented an assurance of the kingdom's continuing commitment to the policy of expansion in Morocco of which he was the architect and chief defender.

No account of the many years during which Prince Henry had control over all the monies raised in Portugal for the maintenance of the Ceuta garrison can avoid considering the possibility that the large sums involved were not always used by the cash-strapped Prince strictly for that purpose. His remit to do what was necessary to ensure the defence of the city seems to have been interpreted by him as involving far more than just seeing to it that the supplies and equipment needed to keep the fortress on a war footing were always available. Anything that would weaken Moorish power anywhere was seen by Henry as part of his brief. In that context it was entirely proper for his corsairs operating against Moorish shipping or raiding the coasts of Morocco itself to make use of the port facilities of Ceuta and to be allowed access to the resources of the Casa. Later the Prince, whose personal definition of what constituted a Christian crusade grew ever more elastic after his caravels reached Guinea, would sometimes use the resources of the agency to prepare and provision caravels about to sail there.[39] There is, however, evidence which seems to show that, on at least one occasion, Henry was not above diverting the large sum of money allocated to him to pay for the maintenance of the Ceuta garrison in 1450 for his own uses. This was done with the connivance of the third governor of Ceuta, Fernando, count of Arraiolos. To give the transaction a formal air of legality, the amount concerned was documented as a loan to Henry from the count of some $2\frac{1}{4}$ million *reais brancos* (16,804 gold *escudos*).[40] The count then paid the garrison out of his own ample resources, leaving the Prince free to do as he wished with the money originally assigned to him by the crown for that purpose. The loser from this arrangement was, predictably, the count. When he asked for repayment of the loan early in 1451, Henry explained to him that, 'because of the great affairs he was currently involved in and the no less great expenses that they caused him', he could not make the agreed repayment. In the end the count had to accept an undertaking by Henry that he would pay off the sum owed in instalments spread over twenty years. Though, to guarantee his good faith, some of his patrimonial lands were designated as sureties, available evidence suggests that, in fact, Henry, when he died, had not repaid any part of this large debt incurred by him ten years previously.[41]

Large and small-scale indebtedness would characterize Henry's financial position throughout his life and after it. Even the opening of trade with Guinea and the remarkable prosperity of his new colony on the island of Madeira seem not to have improved matters. In the context of the society in which Henry lived, we may be sure that his peers – unless they themselves were numbered among Henry's creditors – admired rather than censured him for the size of his debts. Moreover, over-fastidious accounting was not much in fashion in medieval Europe where public funds were concerned. Though enormous care was taken to see that the prescribed forms were scrupulously adhered to when the accounts were submitted for approval, everywhere the opportunities for creative accounting were many.

After Henry returned to Portugal in 1419 from his three-month stay in Ceuta, his competence as an administrator was destined soon to be tested in quite another way. On 25 May 1420, at John I's request, the Prince was appointed by the pope to be administrator general of the military Order of Christ, the successor order to the Templars in Portugal.[42] This appointment would have a decisive influence on the subsequent shape of his life. The Portuguese king had already made his first move to bring the Portuguese military orders under the crown's control in 1418, when he secured the Curia's consent to the appointment of the Prince's younger brother, D. João, as lay administrator of the Order of Santiago. The king's petition to Martin V on Henry's behalf was couched in similar terms to that used in the petition concerning D. João's appointment. It stressed the wealth of the order and its prime duty to defend the Faith and implied that, despite the wealth, it was doing little to carry out the latter duty. The king also asserted in the case of the Order of Christ that past Masters *(Mestres)* of the Order had been using its revenues for 'illicit' purposes.[43] There is, in fact, no evidence that this was so.

The Portuguese crown's decision to bring the rich and powerful military orders under its control preceded a similar decision of the Catholic Monarchs in Castile by some sixty years. The Portuguese orders were ripe for a take-over by the crown. They were indeed wealthy, they had politically undesirable ecclesiastical ties with Castile and, most importantly, the crusading function for which they had been founded had long since ceased to exist with the disappearance, within in the Peninsula, of any Portuguese frontier with Islam. Their popularity with Portugal's rulers cannot have been improved when the original decision to invade Morocco was taken. All the Portuguese orders then explained that their crusading obligations as institutions were limited to the Iberian Peninsula itself.[44] The official reasons put forward by the three orders in defence of their surprisingly unbelligerent stance were alleged administrative and financial ones. The Prince's adopted son and heir, the Infante D. Fernando, later rather let the cat out of the bag by suggesting that problems of social hierarchy were involved: the knights of the Order of Christ considered that garrison duty in Morocco, he explained, would lower the Order's social tone. While the Prince made various attempts to use his authority and that of the Roman Curia to force the Order of Christ and the other orders to set up shop in North Africa, he seems to have had little success. Shortly after his death, the Curia was constrained to issue a bull accepting the claim of the Portuguese orders that they were under no obligation as institutions to serve outside the Iberian Peninsula.[45]

The Order which had come under Henry's rule in 1420 considered itself an élite institution. When it was founded in Portugal in 1319 it inherited all the lands and other properties that had belonged to the Templars. Its statutes then fixed the total number of *freires* (friars) at eighty-six, of whom at least seventy-one must be laymen and knights of the Order. The number of clerics must never exceed fifteen. The lay *freires* had to take vows of celibacy. Each was assigned a commandery from whose lands he derived his income. By Prince Henry's time the headquarters of the Order was in the great former convent of the Templars in Tomar.

Whether Prince Henry played a part in John I's decision to destroy the independence of the military orders is not attested. Given his obsessive preoccupation with the intended crusade against Islam in Morocco, it is likely that their unwillingness to commit themselves with alacrity to that policy made him decide that something should be done about them. What is certain is that he enthusiastically accepted the opportunity to become the first administrator general of the Order of Christ. To be the head of a famous military order fitted in very well with his picture of himself as a militant Christian knight. He would not be uncomfortable, either, in a society whose members had had to take vows of celibacy. But there were more important benefits than these. His new role brought with it a substantial new accretion of economic as well as political power, for it meant that he would in future have effective control over the Order's revenues and the purposes for which they were spent. Henry himself repeatedly declared throughout his life that his use of the Order's income to meet the costs of the voyages of exploration in the African Atlantic had made a crucial contribution to his ability to finance that enterprise. Unfortunately, the surviving archives of the Order supply no information about its income or disbursements during the Henrican period, so it is impossible to attach a valuation to the forced contributions it made. To make restitution to the Order for its forced financial contributions to his Guinea enterprise, Henry arranged that a standard levy on the value of all goods imported from Guinea or from the Atlantic Islands should be payable to the Order's treasury. Once again, no evidence is available to quantify the annual receipts the latter received from this source. Cynics might suggest that Henry was, in practice, being less grateful than it seemed when he introduced this levy. In fact if not in theory, the proceeds from it would themselves also be at the Prince's disposal.

Unsurprisingly, no information remains about the reaction of any of the Portuguese orders to the crown's take-over. Henry, of course, soon saw to it that the statutory officials working for him in the mother house of the Order in Tomar, where he himself was quite a frequent visitor, were persons who would do his bidding. A few of the *freires* took part in the Henrican voyages to the African Atlantic.

It would be entirely to misunderstand the Prince's mentality if we were to assume that he was mainly interested in becoming the ruler of the Order of Christ because of the access it gave him to the institution's wealth. All the evidence is that he had or soon developed a strong personal commitment to the Order and what it had stood for in Portugal's history. He certainly regarded his role as its lay governor as something which merited pride of place among his various posts. Whether the members of the Order always responded favourably to the doings of their royal administrator is not known. Confronted by a formidable personality accustomed to having his way and who was also certain of his mission as a militant Christian, no doubt there were some who, despite their knightly status, thought that Henry was a more zealous administrator than he needed to be and hankered after the quieter days when they were ruled by a member of their own community. In the 1440s he revised the fourteenth-century statutes so as to free the *freires* from the rule of chastity and, to a large extent, from their vows of poverty also. Some of his reforms, however, aimed at tightening up discipline and increasing his own powers. Nevertheless, in the main, his régime was an unexpectedly liberal one.[46] To increase the Order's income he set about extending its already large patrimonial lands and took steps to increase agricultural production on the traditional ones. As a result he was able to increase the number of the commanderies of the Order. It does seem that he had some difficulty, where territorial ownership was concerned, in distinguishing between his personal patrimony and that of the Order. Documents show that he was known on occasion to refer to the territories of the latter as if they were his. Even Tomar itself was described as 'my town'. Under his government, too, a great deal of new building work at its headquarters in the old Templar convent there was undertaken as part of his determination to make sure that, under his régime, the Order of Christ justified its reputation as the grandest of the Portuguese military orders. He was certainly active in defending and extending the traditional rights of the knights-friars. On one occasion, having heard that some of them had been charged by the civil authorities with criminal and civil offences, he issued orders to the relevant official in Tomar to forbid the knights to respond to any summons from lay justices, declaring that, though not in holy orders, they enjoyed immunity from the jurisdiction of the civil courts just as if they were.

There was, of course, no suggestion in 1420 that Henry himself should become a member of the Order of Christ. As a lay administrator he exercised all the powers, temporal and spiritual, that had formerly been associated with the now suppressed office of Master, but he was under no obligation to respect the vows of chastity and poverty taken by the Order's members under the original statutes. As far as chastity was concerned, he lived, as his fellow countrymen often remarked, as if he had taken a formal vow to remain celibate.[47] Rumour had it, too, that he continually wore a hair shirt, hardly drank wine and generally practised asceticism in his personal life. In the early 1440s Henry did, indeed, briefly talk of becoming a full member of the Order. Eugenius IV even issued a bull permitting him, should he do so, to retain his duchy of Viseu and all his other possessions and titles despite the Order's statutes forbidding any such thing.[48] If Henry was ever serious about becoming a *freire* he evidently soon thought better of it.

The practical experiences the Prince had of administering a large and powerful semi-religious institution and of supervising the work of the Casa de Ceuta both stood him in good stead when he turned to organizing exploration and trade in the hitherto unknown regions of the African Atlantic. It is easy to forget the number and complexity of the organizational problems which had to be solved to set the voyages of discovery on the way to success. The task of setting up and then operating the complicated system by which Henry later managed his monopoly of trade with Guinea made even greater calls on his administrative ability. Detailed first-hand accounts of the effective way Henry and his advisers had organized all aspects of the Guinea trade by the 1450s are to be found in Cadamosto's *Navigazioni*. These can be supplemented by information contained in Zurara's chronicles and by documents issued by the royal chancery. They serve to remind us that the obsessive determination and the financial resources which Henry brought to his Guinea enterprise would have availed him little had he not also had the ability to set up administrative structures capable of dealing with the many new problems that success there brought with it.

Chapter Four

Lord of the Isles

He [Henry] caused settlers to establish themselves in five islands in the great Ocean Sea which, at the time this book was being written, were all fairly well populated, especially the island of Madeira. From there as from the other islands the kingdom has received many benefits e.g. in the form of wheat and sugar and honey and wax and timber and many other things from which not only our land but also foreign ones have received and continue to receive great profit.

Zurara, *Crónica dos Feitos na Conquista de Guiné*[1]

A s far as his declared intentions and his actions were concerned, Prince Henry, up to the end of the second decade of the fifteenth century, seems to have given no particular sign that he was preparing to look for those secrets previously hidden from other men whose discovery, his horoscope predicted, would be one of the two major activities which would dominate his life. But, just when his insistent calls for further crusading by the Portuguese against Islam in North Africa made it seem that nothing occupied his mind more than further conquests there, Henry sprang a surprise. Suddenly, in the 1420s, he revealed that he had evidently been looking at such charts of 'the Ocean Sea' (the Atlantic) as he could get hold of and had been tapping other sources of information about that region. In particular he was interested in the two island archipelagos lying no great distance to the west of the Moroccan and Saharan coasts. These were the Canary Islands and the much smaller group of islands and islets centred round the island of Madeira. It should be noted that the impression of the Atlantic the Prince derived from the maps at his disposal was quite unlike that of the largely empty ocean that became known to mariners a hundred years later. Late medieval map-makers, when they ventured to depict the Ocean Sea at all, showed, scattered randomly over its surface, numbers of islands, some supposedly inhabited, that time would prove only existed in legend – St Brendan's Island, Antillia, Brazil, the Island of the Seven Cities and the like.[2] Later Henry would instruct some of his captains to look for these islands too with a view to their incorporation into the island territories he already held from the Portuguese crown. For the moment, though, it was the Canaries and the Madeiras which held his attention.

Henry was not, as is sometimes claimed, the first Iberian prince to show an interest in what was to be found in the remoter reaches of the Atlantic beyond the Straits of Gibraltar. The highly cultured Catalan royal family which ruled the Crown of Aragon had, especially in the last half of the fourteenth century, taken a keen intellectual interest in the wider, non-European, world and what it might be like. Kings and princes of Aragon like Peter IV and John I collected and studied for this purpose not only world maps and the well-known travellers' tales of their time but also treatises concerned with oceanic navigation and examples of the tools used by cosmographers and pilots – all in order to understand how they worked and how this wider world might perhaps be reached by sea. Their interest in these matters was not wholly confined to the East, the main focus of such attention in the fourteenth century. As early as 1373 the future John I of Aragon sent to Majorca to secure a chart which, he requested, would show as much as possible of what lay to the west beyond the Straits of Gibraltar.[3] Prince Henry was nevertheless the first royal prince of his time who had the determination and, even more importantly, the funds to follow up theoretical speculation by actually sending ships into the Atlantic to search for what the cartographers said was to be found there. It would, though, be stretching matters too far to suggest that the voyages sponsored by Henry were ever motivated solely by a spirit of scientific enquiry. The lure of new economic opportunities and the augmentation of his personal fame were probably what always drove the Henrican expansion.

The occupation of the Canaries was destined to become one of the major obsessions of Henry's life. In the early 1420s he made it plain to all that, though French and Castilian settlers under the auspices of the Castilian crown had occupied two or three of the smaller islands at the beginning of the century, and though the Castilians had consequently claimed sovereignty over the whole group, he intended to secure space for himself and the Portuguese there. The Canaries, it will be recalled, were not far to the north of the legendary Cape Bojador on the Saharan coast, beyond which promontory scholars and navigators, both Christian and Arab, had successfully persuaded mariners that further navigation southwards in the Ocean Sea was impossible.

It has often been suggested that Prince Henry was already in the early 1420s planning the exploration of the coast of Guinea beyond Cape Bojador. The only basis for this assertion is a presumption that his attempts to gain control of the Canaries from 1425 onwards must have been motivated by a desire to secure safe anchorages in the archipelago where his caravels could take on supplies or undergo repairs when on their way to, or returning from, projected future voyages to Guinea. There is in fact no reason to believe that Henry's life-long obsession with the conquest of both the pagan-held Canary Islands and those already settled by Europeans can be accounted for in such a way. He was plainly concerned to conquer all the islands of the archipelago as a prize worth winning for its own sake, not just to secure a safe haven there for his Guinea-bound caravels. Had the latter been his motive, his first move would have been to oust the Castilians from their precarious settlements on the small islands of Lanzarote, Fuerteventura and, perhaps, Hierro; an easy task. Instead he set about sending an army to conquer Grand Canary. Since the Canarians notoriously were totally without the means or knowledge to sail or otherwise move on the seas, Henry can hardly have supposed that this island or the other pagan-held islands represented, in 1424, a potential threat to his plans to explore the mainland, even if he had had such plans then.

Well before Henry's time, the Canaries were already firmly established as a distant southern frontier of the European world. Nearly all the islands had been reconnoitred and the complex Stone Age culture of their pagan inhabitants described in writing. This work had begun in the middle of the fourteenth century when a famous first-hand account of the island people made by two Italian merchant adventurers had circulated in Italy and attracted the attention of early humanists like Boccaccio. Slave raiding was what mainly brought European merchants and sailors from Italy and the Iberian Peninsula to the Canaries, then and later, though 'dragon's blood' – a valuable resin from the dragon tree (*Dracaena Draco*) – and orchil, obtained from a lichen (*Rocella Montagnei*) growing on rocks and trees near the sea, were also highly marketable products in Europe where they were used by the dyeing industry and in medicine. The larger islands of the group – Grand Canary, Tenerife, Gomera and La Palma – remained firmly in the hands of their aboriginal inhabitants who successfully drove off all would-be conquerors from Europe until the time of the Catholic Monarchs.

By Henry's time, navigation between the islands in European hands and the ports of Andalusia had become routine. Though the Castilian crown had shown little interest in the Canaries, it was generally accepted, except by Prince Henry, that by the law of nations the whole archipelago had been properly annexed to it. In a famous treatise of 1435 dismissing the Portuguese claims put forward at the Council of Basel on behalf of Henry, the great Castilian fifteenth-century theologian and jurist Alonso de Cartagena would successfully show that, by whatever different legal tests one applied, the crown of Castile had established its sovereignty over the unoccupied islands, as well as over those where Castilian settlers had established themselves.

Prince Henry, true to his habit of treating with contempt any Castilian claims that interfered with projects that he had made his own, sent against the island of Grand Canary in 1424 what seems to have been a substantial military force of several thousand mounted and unmounted soldiers under the command of the governor of his household, Fernando de Castro.[4] The logistical problems and the expense involved in transporting an army of this size with its horses and equipment to the Canaries must have been considerable. Playing the crusaders' card as he was prone to do, Henry claimed that the purpose of this expedition was to convert the large pagan population of the islands to Christianity. The claim was not necessarily as benign as it sounded. Events in Guinea were to reveal, a decade later, that, in Henryspeak, conversion and enslavement were interchangeable terms. The later history of Henrican interventions in the Canaries makes it quite clear that what the Prince really hoped to achieve in 1424 was the conquest of the island of Grand Canary.

The 1424 expedition was evidently a military disaster. It was all the more humiliating to Henry because he had had to accept that his crusading Christian soldiers had been kept at bay and finally driven off by pagan tribesmen in what may be seen as historically the first truly colonial war in which Portuguese soldiers were involved. Henry's panegyricist, Zurara, simply could not bring himself to refer to the matter at all except in a single sentence in which he talks of the expedition's religious purpose but contrives to say nothing about what happened to it.[5] It appears, however, judging by complaints that Henry later made to the pope about the uncivilized way the Canarians made war against the Christians, that the expedition of 1424 sailed for the archipelago wholly unbriefed about the kind of armed resistance which was likely to confront the troops on Grand Canary.

This was to be the first of many bids by Henry to establish himself in the Canaries at the expense both of the Christian colonists there and of the diverse pagan peoples in the larger islands. The Prince, whose temperament did not make him respectful towards the arguments of lawyers – especially if they were Castilians – would continue for decades to try, sometimes by diplomacy but more often by force, to drive the Castilians out of the islands where they had settled and to take on the inhabitants of the so far unconquered ones. Despite all the setbacks and the military humiliations he suffered in the Canaries, Henry doggedly pursued this goal at great expense for much of the rest of his life. One can only surmise how much further south the coast of Guinea might have been reconnnoitred in his lifetime had it not been for the way men, money and ships were used up in the service of this obsession, an obsession which, on several occasions, was to bring Castile and Portugal to the brink of war.

The story of the colonial wars Henry unsuccessfully fought in the Canaries extends over a period of some thirty years. It is unusually well documented in Castilian as well as Portuguese sources. The study in detail of this material reveals important aspects of Henry's personality and mindset which are not discussed anywhere else. The Prince's initiatives in the Canaries cannot, however, be usefully examined alongside his creative role as the highly successful sponsor of the colonization of Madeira and the man whose efforts brought the Azores into Portuguese possession. I propose therefore to defer until a later chapter a full account of the part the Canaries played in Henry's life.

The main island of the Madeiran archipelago (286 square miles) lies some 350 miles from the coast of Morocco and about 300 miles north of the nearest island (La Palma) in the Canaries. Twenty-eight miles to the north-east of it lies the much smaller island of Porto Santo. Two or three other now uninhabited islands complete the group.[6] Zurara states that Madeira and Porto Santo were first discovered in the 1420s by two of Henry's squires, João Gonçalves Zarco and Tristão Vaz, who were blown off course by a storm. In fact it was at best a rediscovery.

Madeira, Porto Santo and Deserta, with their names already attached, had appeared, more or less correctly located, on maps and seaman's charts from 1351 onwards.[7] Though somewhat to the west of the normal course taken by ships sailing between Europe and the Canaries, it is impossible to believe that these other islands, one of them clearly visible from a distance, had remained all this time unseen or unvisited by passing vessels. What is much more probable is that the discovery that, unlike the Canaries, they were uninhabited made them of little interest to Italian or Iberian traders whose prime interest in any Atlantic islands was to take slaves.

The two squires reported their discovery to John I and to the Prince about 1425 and expressed the opinion that both islands looked to be eminently worth colonizing, a task they offered to undertake themselves. Zurara claims that Henry accepted their offer and organized their return trip after supplying them with the men, tools and materials needed to start agricultural development. Though the Prince may well have organized this initial despatch of settlers to the islands as he claimed in his last will, he did not do so as their territorial lord. Officially, the first colonists on Madeira and Porto Santo were sent there by John I himself and Portugal's first overseas colony was, until the king's death, for a few years part of his personal patrimony. Significantly, though, John did not treat the new colony as a conquest to be added to his royal titles as he had done in the case of Ceuta. The Madeiran archipelago's legal status then was the same as that of any royal (realengo) territory in metropolitan Portugal.

It is not obvious why Henry refrained from asking for the lordship of the islands from the beginning. It may have been as an act of respect for his father or simply to avoid arousing the jealousy of his brothers. At all events, as soon as John died he contrived in September 1433 to obtain from the new king a lifetime donation of the lordship of Madeira, Porto Santo and Deserta. The only limit on his freedom of action was that he was not permitted to tamper with the rights and privileges granted by John to the first colonists in the original royal charter.[8]

Henry's squires and sailors, accustomed though they were to hearing stories of the wonders associated with the legendary islands of the Atlantic, can hardly have failed to be impressed by their first sight of Madeira as they drew near it. From the shoreline it rises steeply on all sides from the sea in a series of cliffs and ravines leading upwards to the summits of the high mountain ranges of the interior glimpsed from time to time through the clouds. But what had most struck mariners from the fourteenth century onwards was that the whole island right down to the water's edge was covered with virgin forest. Fourteenth-century Italian and Majorcan cartographers named it 'Timber Island' in their own vernaculars. The name was adopted by the Portuguese (*madeira*, 'wood'). This place name both recorded the natural feature about the island which had most impressed its earliest discoverers and also drew attention to the existence there of an abundant and varied natural resource that was notoriously scarce in Portugal – timber. When Zarco and Vaz found an anchorage they may or may not have been pleased to have confirmed their suspicion that, unlike the Canaries with their warlike aboriginal populations, there was not a sign of human presence to be found on Madeira. Nor was there on Porto Santo, an island which, mostly low-lying, largely treeless and short of water, presented a very different appearance. Unlike Madeira, though, it had many open beaches where landings were easy. It was noted, too, that the waters around Porto Santo teemed with fish. It was a suitable base from which to start exploring the main island.

The first settlers did not, of course, know the highly romantic legends about the supposed original discovery of Madeira by a fleeing Englishman, Machin, and his lady, which later on circulated in various forms in Portugal and on the island. This story was concocted in the course of the fifteenth century and is patently literary rather than folkloric in origin.[9]

As already suggested, the fact that Madeira was uninhabited paradoxically explains why it was so long left alone. The absence of any indigenous population made it of no interest either to European merchants expecting to pick up cargoes of slaves in the Canaries or to the French mercenaries-cum-colonists who made their way there disguised as crusaders and needed an enemy to kill or at least to turn into an unpaid servant or labourer.

The exact date when the Madeiras began to be colonized by the Portuguese is obscured by contradictions. It seems likely, however, that the first Portuguese settlers arrived there *c.* 1425, or perhaps a little before. Attention, as we have seen, was first directed towards colonizing Porto Santo. Here passing ships had doubtless noted the existence of the dragon trees later mentioned by the navigators Cadamosto and Diogo Gomes. The valuable red resin extracted from them was, after slaves, one of the chief reasons European merchants had been interested in the Canaries since the fourteenth century. Dragon's blood was used principally in the dyeing industry but also figured in medieval pharmaceutics. Porto Santo, moreover, had other attractions for the

Portuguese settlers. Unlike forest-covered Madeira, the island offered opportunities for establishing with the minimum delay herds and flocks of domestic animals brought from Portugal. Essential cereal crops were also planted. The Portuguese settlers, perhaps at Prince Henry's suggestion, made a serious ecological mistake when, seeking a quickly available source of meat, they released rabbits on the island. Since Porto Santo was without any natural predators it was soon overrun by these creatures whose presence eventually made it impossible to grow anything there successfully. The settlers were, therefore, forced to concentrate on cattle-raising, fishing and on the export of dragon's blood. The task of colonizing Porto Santo was undertaken in Prince Henry's time by Bartolomeo Pallastrelli, son of an Italian from Piacenza who had settled in Portugal towards the end of the fourteenth century. Pallastrelli, called in Portuguese fifteenth-century documents 'Bartolomeu Perestrelo', had the status of knight of the Prince's household. He was destined, though he never knew it, to achieve greater fame as the father-in-law of Christopher Columbus.

The colonization of the island of Madeira also began about 1425 when the original settlers' rights and obligations were set out in a royal charter. There is, however, no reason to doubt later claims made on Henry's behalf that both Madeira and Porto Santo were colonized at his suggestion and at his expense and that the initial settlement was carried out under the leadership of two squires of his household, João Gonçalves Zarco and Tristão Vaz. When Duarte I, in 1433, made Henry life donatory of Madeira, Porto Santo and Ilha Deserta – the third largest island of the archipelago – the new king rather strikingly did not, as a justification for the grant, make the usual declaration in such cases that the Prince was being rewarded for having been responsible for the original colonization.[10] The royal charter (foro) granted to the original settlers by John I unfortunately only survives in fragmentary form. The portion that remains confirms, however, that, in the 1420s, Zarco officially represented the king, not Prince Henry, on Madeira. In this capacity he was authorized to distribute land to the settlers. The same document also contained an unequivocal statement that John I himself as king of Portugal was also ipso facto territorial lord of Madeira and everything in it.[11] Technically at least, therefore, the first stage in the colonization of Madeira – and probably that of Porto Santo too – was a royal enterprise. Henry had to wait, or thought it only decent to wait, until his father's death before he could set about having himself made legally the lord of Portugal's first Atlantic colony.

The first settlement on Madeira was probably established by Zarco on the shores of a bay on the south of the island which the settlers called 'O Funchal' ('the fennel meadow') because of the quantity of this herb which they found growing there. Diogo Gomes has a passage describing how the first colonists lived for a time in huts made of logs thatched with hay and plants. Fish and wild birds, both of which were available in abundance, provided their main diet until cattle and cereal crops became available. The existence of the settlement in its early days was threatened by a great fire which apparently resulted from careless attempts to burn off part of the forest to clear land for farming. There is no reason to credit the stories current later in the century that, as a result of this episode, all the island's primeval forest was destroyed. Forest timber was, in fact, a staple Madeiran export within a few years of the foundation of the settlement at Funchal. Zurara, when elaborating on the material wealth which Prince Henry had brought to Portugal as a result of developing the Atlantic islands, particularly mentions the plentiful supplies of new kinds of timber specially suitable for ambitious kinds of building work which were imported from Madeira.

From the start Madeira was a success story. Its soil, enriched by age-old accumulations of leaf-humus, proved astonishingly fertile when it first passed under the plough, though, according to the Venetian explorer Cadamosto, by the mid-1450s it had ceased to yield the abnormally abundant crops it produced during the earliest years of cultivation.[12] Another favourable feature of the Madeiran scene referred to by early writers was the abundant supply of pure water which everywhere flowed down the *ribeiras* ('streams') and smaller water-courses from the mountains.

When the initial phase of setting themselves up with shelter was over, the first settlers set about clearing some of the forest to grow cereal crops, especially wheat – a commodity which the Portuguese had in the past all too frequently had to import from foreign parts. This venture proved highly successful and wheat remained the main crop of many of the island's farmers during the whole of the Henrican period. Cadamosto in 1455 put the annual production of wheat on Madeira at 30,000 Venetian *stara* (3,000 Portuguese *moios* or about 68,000 bushels). It was quite soon pointed out to Henry, however, that to use Madeira's rich soil and always temperate climate solely to grow cereals was a wasteful use of the island's agricultural potential. It is likely that the first colonists had brought local vine-stocks from Portugal with them but it was soon realized that the soil and climatic conditions on the island were very well suited to viniculture. According to Cadamosto, Henry himself arranged for vines to be imported from the Morea and other Mediterranean regions known for the excellence of their wines. The Venetian navigator remarked that, by the time he visited Madeira in 1455, 'very good wines considering how recent is the settlement' were already available there.

The main economic future of Madeira, however, lay in the production of sugar. This followed on the introduction of Sicilian and perhaps Cypriot canes under Prince Henry's personal supervision. The soil and climate were favourable and by 1454 sugar was already being produced on Madeira in significant amounts. About that time the Prince reckoned that the time had come to put Madeiran sugar on the European market. When his representatives visited the northbound Flanders galleys of Venice lying off Sagres in 1454 while awaiting a change in the wind, one of the purposes of their visit was to show the Venetian merchants travelling on the galleys samples of sugar grown on the island. The next year Cadamosto himself, when he visited the island, estimated the annual production there to be 1600 *arrobas* (perhaps 18,000 kg) and rapidly growing.[13] By the time of Henry's death in 1460 the island had in fact become a major exporter of sugar to Europe and, *a fortiori*, a major contributor to the Prince's treasury.[14]

Cadamosto also remarks on the flourishing state of the timber industry on Madeira. In addition to the export to Portugal of furniture and building materials made from indigenous trees as well as timber, he notes that bows made from the native red yew, and cross-bow shafts were also numbered among Madeiran exports to Europe in the 1450s.[15] Zurara, too, enumerates among the many benefits that Henry's achievements had brought to his fellow countrymen the fact that timber from the Atlantic islands had made it possible for the Portuguese for the first time to erect buildings several storeys high.[16]

Cadamosto's account of Madeira notes the vigour with which the settlement of the island had been pushed ahead since about 1425. According to the Venetian, there were about eight hundred male inhabitants on Madeira in 1455, among them some hundred who owned their own horses, that is to say were persons of some substance. These numbers are not necessarily at variance with the figure of 150 *moradores* given by Zurara. The main settlements at that time, apart from Funchal and Machico, were, Cadamosto notes, at Câmara de Lobos, west of Funchal, and at Santa Cruz, near Machico, in Tristão Vaz's sector of the island. Many of these colonists came from Henry's seigneurial lands.

Zurara, in one of his panegyrical comments on Prince Henry's achievements in the Atlantic islands, claimed prominently among these the fact that high-class Madeiran timber imported into Portugal in great quantities had made it possible to change the traditions of house-building in Portugal. Using Madeiran timber frames, Portuguese builders could now build high if their customers wanted that.

The existence of native Madeiran hardwoods made it possible, too, for the settlers to build the wooden hydraulic saw-mills and sugar-mills that were to play so large a part in making the island's development possible. As might be expected, the exploitation of Madeira's forest resources was carried out with no effective regard for conservation or replanting. It was not until 1515 that Manuel I issued a savage *regimento* prohibiting all timber-felling except by licence and imposing a public flogging, two years exile to Africa and a twenty *cruzado* fine on anyone who contravened this ordinance.[17] It may thus be said that had Henry never succeeded in exploring the coast of Guinea the remarkable economic benefits the colonization of Madeira had brought to Portugal would still have guaranteed him a place of fame in the kingdom's economic history.

The constitutional and institutional history of Madeira under Prince Henry's seigneurial rule merits examination since what was done there set a pattern which would be broadly followed in the other Portuguese island colonies which came into existence in the fifteenth century. The original royal charter of John I evidently gave considerable powers to João Gonçalves Zarco. In it he was authorized, in the king's name, to make free grants of land to the colonists, subject only to the condition that land so granted must be brought into cultivation within a period of ten years, a proviso intended to prevent the establishment of large undeveloped or underdeveloped estates. It represented the transfer to the Atlantic islands of the *sesmaria* system of land-tenure introduced in late-medieval Portugal to ensure that those who received grants of land rapidly brought them into production.[18] Only if the beneficiary complied with this condition did he secure a permanent title to the land. It was a system which naturally commended itself to a donatory or sub-donatory confronted with the task of developing virgin territory overseas.

John I's charter also prohibited private acquisition of forests, pastures, springs and streams, or the foreshore. These were to be held in common for all time and might never become the property of a private individual in any circumstances whatsoever. The charter explained that these privileges were granted to the settlers because they had left their own property and country to colonize the new lands for the Portuguese crown.[19] The régime of land tenure contemplated by the royal charter was one of medium and small holdings; it explicitly stated that grants were not only to be made to persons of quality but must be available to those who would live from the work of their own hands as farmers, woodcutters or by raising cattle. This pattern of land division was, despite subsequent changes in the juridical status of the island, broadly kept to so that Madeira, and particularly the southern half of the island, never became a place of great estates. Prince Henry's natural instincts must have been to favour the latter but he plainly realized that the quickest way to develop Madeiran agriculture was to continue the model introduced in his father's time.

As soon as John I died, the Madeiran archipelago ceased to be crown territory and at once fell *de jure* as well as *de facto* into the hands of Prince Henry. The donation of the islands for life that Duarte I made to his brother in 1433 involved the surrender to him of the customary taxes and imposts due to the crown. Most of the latter's civil and criminal jurisdiction was also transferred to Henry, though with the important exemption of the right to impose death sentences or sentences prescribing judicial mutilation. These were reserved to the king. Nor was Henry's own ducal court in Portugal allowed to handle appeals from the island courts. The 1433 grant explicitly stated that such appeals must be heard by the royal *Casa do Civel* – the court of final appeal which heard cases arising in Lisbon and the surrounding territory. Henry was, however, granted an absolute right to make grants of land at his discretion subject only to the provisions of the royal charter granted by his father. Even this restriction was effectively negated by another clause in the donation which permitted the Prince to make whatever modifications he wished to that charter, though these would be valid for his lifetime only.[20] Though this donation, in accordance with Portuguese practice, was far from being a full feudal grant, it left Henry in a strong position to make it very like one if he wished. Such a probability was increased when, two and a half years later, after he had formally adopted his nephew the Infante D. Fernando as his heir, Duarte I revised the terms of the donation to make it heritable.[21]

Characteristically, Henry was not content just to secure the revenues which went with the secular lordship of the Madeiras. On the same day that he received this grant from the crown he also obtained from it another one placing the archipelago under the spiritual jurisdiction of the Order of Christ. The practical effect of this was, of course, to ensure that he, as the Order's administrator, had control of the dues payable by the islanders to their spiritual overlord as well as those directly payable to him as their secular lord.[22] It is not obvious why Henry requested his brother to make a grant that, as he well knew, clearly fell within the jurisdiction of the Roman curia, not that of the crown. It perhaps reflects some further confusion in Henry's mind between what was legally his and what belonged to the Order.

The second of the two grants made to Henry in 1433 declares categorically that the Prince was, at that time, engaged, with royal authority, on the work of establishing colonists on the islands of the archipelago. As already mentioned, one would have expected these donations to have contained, as was usual, a reference to the Prince's part in the rediscovery and original colonization of the archipelago as a justification for alienating crown lands in his favour. The omission probably simply reflects the fact that, up to then, the archipelago had been *realengo* territory and, therefore, all these initiatives were presumed to emanate from the crown.

The donation of 1433 was made in the king's name but certainly in consultation with Henry and probably according to a draft prepared under his direction. It is a document of considerable importance in the history of Portuguese overseas institutions for, as already suggested, it marked the adoption by the crown of a form of overseas government that would become the norm in all the Atlantic islands. In it we see the crown, after the death of John I, relinquishing the task of itself attempting directly to colonize or administer any of them. Instead they were handed over, as semi-feudal fiefs, to a donatory who, it was assumed, would, for a variety of motives among which self-interest predominated, set about developing them as fast as he could. The assumption proved to be fully justified. Although, as already noted, Madeira and the Azores were always considered to be provinces of metropolitan Portugal, some modifications were introduced to take account of Madeira's remoteness from continental Portugal. The donatory system was to work well enough during the early years of the colony's development but experience would show that, specially after Henry's death, it came to be much resented by the colonists when, as successful producers, they acquired a sense of Madeiran identity, when local municipal institutions began to be strong and when the exactions of Henry's heir became ever greater.

The rediscovery and highly successful colonization of Madeira brought, of course, not only what was to be an important new source of wealth to the Prince. It also brought him new prestige and political power as a leader who, by once again ignoring the voices of the sceptics and following his hunches, had succeeded in moving the territorial frontier of Portugal far into the Ocean Sea. Those who had regarded him until now as a religious zealot dedicated to planning gratuitous and expensive wars against Islam were compelled to recognize that there was much more to him than that. Yet, when it was a question of justifying the occupation and colonization of Madeira to the outside world, Henry's ideological commitment took over. He not only claimed that the settlement of the archipelago formed part of his crusade against Islam: taking advantage of the papal curia's notorious ignorance of what exactly was happening in the African Atlantic, he had Eugenius IV informed that he had freed Madeira and its neighbouring islands from the Saracen yoke and returned their (then non-existent) inhabitants to the Christian faith.[23] The Prince, devout Christian though he certainly was, never considered that there was anything wrong with feeding successive popes misleading information if it would help them to help him.

Henry, as far as is known, never visited any of his territorial lordships in the Atlantic islands. Political caution, the difficulty of maintaining royal protocol aboard small ships and perhaps simply a distaste for sea travel ensured that he himself never sought to experience at first hand what oceanic exploration was like or to visit his Atlantic thalassocracy. It was therefore plainly necessary to make special arrangements for the everyday government and administration of Madeira on the assumption that its lord would be a permanent absentee. Henry did this by delegating most of his seigneurial powers to three subdonatories, one on Porto Santo and two on the island of Madeira itself. Two administrative acts preceded the appointment of the sub-donatories. One was the issue of a seigneurial charter to replace or to supplement the one originally granted by John I to the first settlers. This document has been lost.[24] The second important act of local sovereignty performed by Henry after 1433 was to divide the island of Madeira into two separate territories (*bandas*), each having its own local government. The two squires who claimed to have rediscovered the place were each granted the status of sub-donatories. All the territory on the south side of the high sierras remained in the hands of João Gonçalves Zarco; that to the north Henry granted, by a donation made in 1440, to Tristão Vaz Teixeira.[25]

This division of the island into two separate territories perhaps reflects some kind of personal and jurisdictional clash between Zarco, who was established in Funchal, and Vaz, who had settled in Machico, at the eastern end of the island and had colonized the surrounding territory. Whatever the motives, the division of the island in this way made good sense. The northern half of the island was less immediately attractive to settlers than the southern half. It was also difficult to access from the south because of the height and extent of the central ranges. Zarco was, therefore, not well placed to develop the north from his capital in Funchal.

The donation or sub-donation to Vaz is the first of the Henrican donations which has survived. It did not, as has sometimes been suggested, confer on him the title of 'captain' (*capitão*) but used, instead, a form of words indicating that he was placed in charge of the territory of Machico to act on the Prince's behalf there as his lieutenant (*regedor*). In routine documents emerging from Henry's chancery, however, the title of *capitão* begins to be used by the two island sub-donatories from 1452 onwards. In the donation to him Tristão Vaz was granted one-tenth of all the revenues due to the Prince in the territory now placed under his jurisdiction. He had, moreover, the right to exercise all the Prince's civil and criminal jurisdiction within it. Two notable and characteristic innovations appear in the Henrican sub-donation. Henry attempted to make it heritable through the male line despite the fact that his own tenure was for his lifetime only. The other was his direction that appeals from the sub-donatory's court were to be referred to Henry's own court in Portugal – a direct contravention of the restrictive provisions of the royal donation of 1433 which, as we have seen, had clearly stated that appeals from the Madeiran courts were to be heard by the royal *Casa do Civel* in Lisbon.[26] These particular attempts to move his overseas territories further in the direction of a full feudal tenure than the crown was willing to accept was of course entirely to be expected. The Prince was always on the look-out for a chance to assume powers beyond those granted to him by the crown and by Portuguese custom. Vaz was also authorized to make perpetual grants of land within his territory, subject only to the provision that the land must be brought into exploitation within five years – not the ten stipulated in John I's original charter to the settlers. Henry, concerned to boost his personal revenues, evidently wished by this change to make the colonists work even harder at the job of making the island's virgin land productive. A further incentive in that direction was that no restrictions were now placed on a colonist's rights to dispose of his developed lands by sale as he wished.[27]

This donation was followed in 1446 by a similar one appointing 'Bartolomeu Perestrelo' sub-donatory and regent for the Prince in Porto

Santo.[28] Unlike the 1446 donation to 'Bartolomeu Perestrelo' – which explicitly stated that the grant was made because he 'was the first who, at my command colonized the said island' – no such justification was given in the case of Tristao Vaz. Perhaps this indicated that Henry felt some need to justify the appointment of an Italian as his man on Porto Santo. Curiously enough, documents suggest that it was not until 1450 that Henry's chancery issued a similar donation to Zarco, though the latter was certainly the leader of the first Portuguese who had settled the island *c.* 1425 and had long been the *de facto* governor of his *banda* there for the Prince. However, Zarco is already described as the Prince's *regedor* in the territory of Funchal in a document dated 1447.[29] It seems possible, therefore, that the donation to him, which is only known in the form of a copy made when it was confirmed by Afonso V in 1451, was then misdated and should, in fact, be attributed to the year 1440, not 1450. Zarco was a figure of considerable consequence in the story of the Henrican expansion in the Atlantic islands. He reputedly governed his part of Madeira for forty years. Of his three sons and four daughters, one daughter – Maria – married the detested Maciot de Béthencourt, the French ex-governor of Lanzarote in the Canaries. His second son, Ruy Gonçalves da Câmara, became captain of São Miguel in the Azores. Zarco himself was ennobled and granted a coat-of-arms by Afonso V in 1460. He then abandoned the name Zarco in favour of the territorial name 'Câmara de Lobos'. The grant of nobility states that he had been knighted by Prince Henry and had served both at Ceuta and Tangier.

The donations also disclose that important monopolies affecting everyday aspects of the colonists' lives were granted to the subdonatories. The latter were given the sole right to sell salt in their territory if they wished to exercise it. Only they had the right to establish mills for grinding corn for public use, though hand-mills used solely by an individual for his household's needs were permitted. Communal ovens for baking bread were also a monopoly of the sub-donatory. The owners of water-operated saw-mills already established in the mountains for cutting up timber also now had to pay regular fees to the sub-donatory for the privilege of using them.[30] The colonists thus soon found themselves experiencing, under Henry and his sub-donatories, all the rigours of seigneurial rule to escape which many, no doubt, had emigrated to the new lands.

The agricultural economy visualized in these donations continued to be one concerned principally with the growing of cereal crops – particularly wheat – with cattle-raising, and with the felling and preparation of timber. This was, no doubt, a true reflection of the situation of the Madeiran economy in the 1440s but, by the end of that period, the island's economy was on the brink of very important changes. Meanwhile, Prince Henry had extracted new privileges from the crown designed to favour the island's exports to the mainland. In 1444 he thus persuaded the regent, D. Pedro, to agree that neither the royal tenth (*dízima*) customarily payable to the crown on sea-borne imports nor the toll known as the *portagem* should be levied in Portuguese ports on goods exported by settlers living in the islands.

The economic history of Madeira was a story of rapid and successful development brought about by the pressures exerted by the *sesmaria* system but also by a willingness to experiment with new crops and new agricultural techniques. How far Henry himself was personally responsible for foreseeing the agricultural possibilities which Madeira offered is uncertain. It may well be, as contemporary sources suggest, that the decision to make Madeira a prime centre of wine and sugar production was his personally. Zurara, probably describing the island's situation in the late 1440s or early 1450s said it then had a population of some 150 *moradores*, that is, householders permanently resident on the island. The chronicler probably understood by this term only those who held grants of land; he explicitly states that the figure excludes priests and members of religious orders, merchants and traders of any kind as well as unmarried men and women, adolescents and children.[31] We must add to these figures of non-persons an unknown but growing number of criminals who had been exiled by the mainland courts to the islands. The practice, first used in Ceuta, of topping up the population of overseas possessions by commuting sentences for serious crimes to periods of exile in them, was, at Prince Henry's request, first extended to the Madeiran archipelago.[32] There was also by the 1450s a probably quite small slave population. Thanks to the abundant supplies of suitable timber available, shipbuilding had rapidly started on Madeira and in the 1440s we read of caravels belonging to Zarco and Vaz participating in the slave razzias made against the Idzagen inhabitants of the Mauritanian coast. It is likely that some at least of the captives they made ended up in Madeira performing domestic or agricultural work. Caravels from Madeira also sometimes raided the Canaries to take slaves there. It should not be deduced from the documented presence of slaves on the Atlantic islands that the system of agriculture set up by Henry and his sub-donatories in Madeira or in the Azores was, in the fifteenth century, ever one dependent on slave labour. It has authoritatively been shown that Madeiran agriculture, and particularly the sugar industry, was in fact much less dependent on the work of slaves than used to be supposed.[33]

Cadamosto, writing about his visit to Madeira in the spring of 1455, gives the earliest traveller's description of that island and Porto Santo that we have.[34] The journey from Cape St Vincent to Porto Santo with the full strength of the north-east trade wind behind his caravel took only three days to complete. Cadamosto's account of Porto Santo is more favourable than that of some later writers. He notes that cattle and wild pigs abounded there, as well as innumerable rabbits, but was more interested in the dragon trees and the way they were made to yield the 'dragon's blood' so highly prized in Europe. He thought, too, that the island produced the best honey in the world, lamenting that this was only available in small quantities. He also remarked on its rich fishing grounds, so reminding us of the great importance to the Portuguese economy of the new fisheries which had been opened up to it in this first period of expansion in the African Atlantic.

A notable feature of the Henrican period was the determination to bring into use small islands which later centuries would ignore as too desolate or waterless. Deserta, the islets off Porto Santo, and even the remote Selvagens group all have their place in fifteenth-century Portuguese documents.

Despite Henry's pretence to the Roman curia that the colonization of Madeira was a victory over Islam, he seems, in fact, to have paid rather scant attention to the religious life of the new colony. Churches, or rather chapels, were built here and there but the settlers can hardly have felt that they got their money's worth for the dues they were compelled to pay for the spiritual but also invisible overlordship of the Order of Christ. Cadamosto only alludes to the presence of some Franciscan houses and has nothing much to say about religious life on the islands. No bishop of Madeira was appointed until after the end of the fifteenth century.

Henry's prize Atlantic possession early developed an international flavour, as the Prince, anxious to secure the services of experts in marketing its products throughout Europe, did not hesitate to call on Italian merchants – specially Genoese, Florentines and Venetians – to take part in the island's trading, particularly in the nascent sugar trade. Cadamosto's long association with the Prince in fact began because Henry sent aboard the Venetian galleys bound for Flanders but detained off Cape St Vincent by contrary winds, samples of sugar, dragon's blood and other Madeiran exports. His purpose was to show the Venetians the quality of these products and to get them to make known in the markets of Europe the availability of these products.[35] Contrary to what has sometimes been claimed, Henry, neither in his Atlantic islands nor in Guinea, ever showed the slightest sign of wishing to exclude foreigners from participation in his Atlantic enterprises, still less to keep the latter secret. Secrecy was incompatible with the hunger for fame which always drove him. Bartolomeu Perestrelo, captain of Porto Santo, was, because of his long years of residence in the Peninsula, perhaps not regarded as an alien but it is known that Henry specifically ordered his sub-donatories to grant land on Madeira to Germans and probably to cultivators of other foreign nations.[36] As for Perestrelo, he may well have been one of the Prince's advisors about oceanic exploration. The anxiety which Henry showed to secure the services of the Venetian Cadamosto as well as his desire in 1455 to acquaint the merchants on the Venetian galleys with the products now on offer from Madeira tell their own story. Another example of Henry's lack of xenophobic sentiments (unless it was a question of his feelings towards Muslims or Castilians) was to be shown in connection with the colonization of the Azores.

The islands of the Azores archipelago lie in three groups spread out over a large area of the North Atlantic in the same latitude as southern Portugal. The nearest island to Lisbon – Santa Maria – is some eight hundred miles west of that port. The five islands of the middle group are situated some hundred miles further to the north-west. Some 125 miles further to the north-west still lie the rugged cliffs of the two small islands of Flores and Corvo, nearly half-way between Portugal and North America. The volcanic nature of the Azores is everywhere made apparent by the frequent sight throughout the group of volcanoes, both extinct and active, by lava flows old and new, and by the obviously volcanic origins of the soil. Compared with the obvious attractions of Madeira, the Azores must at first sight have seemed to have little to offer settlers. The islands are, however, marked by a humid and temperate climate which – despite violent winter storms – favours the growth of vegetation of all kinds wherever there is enough soil to permit it. Here, far out in the Ocean Sea, Portuguese ships had probably come some seven years before the first caravel succeeded in rounding Cape Bojador.

The circumstances and date of the rediscovery of the Azores have been the subject of much argument.[37] As already suggested, fourteenth- and early fifteenth-century charts often display lines of islands marshalled in the Atlantic, variously named and oriented in a general north–south direction, at varying distances to the west of Portugal. Medieval cartographers were certainly influenced in their hazy depiction of what some take to be the Azores by a number of supernatural legends involving Atlantic voyages like that to St Brendan's Island. What is uncertain is whether and how far these legends may have been reinforced in the fourteenth century by actual sightings of some of the more easterly islands. It is by no means impossible that Italian, Majorcan or Castilian seamen, seeking to return to Europe from the Canaries against the north-east trades, had already found that by setting a north-westerly course for a time they would eventually encounter the prevailing westerlies that they knew would carry them towards the Portuguese Atlantic coast. Though it was not usually necessary to sail as far west as the longitude of the Azores to carry out this manoeuvre, no doubt sometimes they could have found themselves within sight of some of these islands. But this is mere surmise. No narratives of Henry's time or earlier ever have anything to say about the courses taken by the caravels on their homeward journeys from Guinea or from Madeira or the Canaries, a matter which their authors clearly considered to be entirely routine. Belief in the existence of the mid-Atlantic islands, as these were depicted by fourteenth-century cartographers, was doubtless reinforced by the existence of the spurious *Book of Knowledge of all the World* whose inventive Castilian author listed and gave the names of eight of them which he claimed to have visited in his imaginary Atlantic travels aboard a Moorish ship.[38]

It is, nevertheless, to a fifteenth-century Majorcan cartographer, Gabriel de Valsequa, that we owe what seems to be the first authentic piece of information about the real Azores and about Portuguese interest in them. Valsequa drew a chart in 1439 which included the Atlantic and showed, for the first time, the Azores group running correctly from north-west to south-east, though the archipelago was still both incorrectly spaced and inaccurately drawn. Alongside the islands the cartographer inserted a legend, now difficult to decipher, which stated that they were found by a pilot in the service of the king of Portugal – that is, John I – in 1427. The pilot's name is given.[39] Valsequa's information has an authentic flavour. It seems likely, therefore, that, after Portuguese settlement of the Madeiran archipelago had started, efforts were made under Prince Henry's auspices to see whether any sign could be found of the many islands which tradition sited still further to the west.

Andrea Bianco's Atlantic chart of 1436 shows the 'Ylha de Brasil' as the most adjacent to Lisbon of the many islands he depicts in the Atlantic.[40] This fact needs to be associated with an observation recorded in Alonso de Santa María's famous memorandum to the Council of Basel in 1435 setting out the reasons why sovereignty over the whole Canarian archipelago belonged by the law of nations and other legal tests to the Castilian crown, not to the Portuguese. The bishop of Burgos there refers, as a recent event, to the finding by the Portuguese of the uninhabited island of Brazil, which he describes as lying towards the west on the line of latitude of Lisbon.[41] It thus appears that, for a time, it was presumed by some cartographers that the most easterly of the Azores – later known as Santa Maria – was the 'Insula Brasilii' of cartographical legend. The information of both cartographer and bishop was in fact already out-of-date. It is certain that by the late 1430s Portuguese navigators had discovered, reconnoitred and named the eastern and central groups of the Azores archipelagos as well.

On 2 July 1439 Prince Henry obtained permission from the crown to start planting settlers 'on the seven islands of the Azores'. The terms of the licence reveal that, already, domestic animals had been landed on some of them to ensure the supply of meat against the arrival of settlers from Portugal.[42] Tradition ascribes this first step in the colonization of the Azores to an expedition sent out by Henry in 1425 under Frei Gonçalo Velho, a commander of the Order of Christ and an important official of his personal household, to establish settlers on Santa Maria and São Miguel on his behalf. By this time, too, the archipelago had received its modern name – Ilhas dos Açores ('Islands of the Goshawks').[43] The identification of the group in terms of a bird's name is a reminder – noted in Columbus's *Journals* – of the way in which fifteenth-century Portuguese oceanic explorers used carefully to scan the skies for a sight of birds whose presence and direction of flight might reveal the existence of land beyond the horizon.

The Portuguese colonization of the Azores in the Henrican period is far less well documented than is the case with the Madeiran archipelago. D. Duarte's licence to populate, granted to Prince Henry in 1439, involved no more than a simple permission to send settlers there. The licence says nothing whatever about the juridical position of the settlers or about any rights of the Prince in the islands. Gonçalo Velho was given the title of '*Comendador das Ilhas dos Açores for the Order of Christ*' but, in practice, his connection with the islands was as Henry's nominee there. He was no doubt named as *comendador* of the islands to give some colour to the pretence that the Order of Christ was actively engaged in the work of discovery and the occupation of new lands. It has been suggested that Frei Gonçalo Velho himself never visited or resided on Santa Maria or São Miguel, but some documentary evidence dating from the 1460s seems to contradict this. Such information as is available suggests that Velho devoted his colonizing attention almost entirely to the island of Santa Maria – the nearest of the Azorean group to Portugal and one of the smallest (45 square miles).

In 1443 the Regent, at Henry's request and following the pattern used in the Madeiras, granted the settlers an exemption, for a period of five years, from the obligation to pay the traditional import taxes on goods exported from the Azores to Portugal. It would, though, be rash indeed to conclude from this concession that anything more than an occasional cargo of wheat, timber, wine and orchil ever left the islands at this stage. All the evidence suggests that Henry found few people willing to try to make a new life as colonists on what was now the most distant ocean frontier of the European world and one noted for its volcanic eruptions and frequent earthquakes. Nevertheless, at least on Santa Maria, a start was made with growing wheat and it was found that the island soil and climate were very favourable for this enterprise. Sea fishing off the islands was also good and it may have been at quite an early date that the possibilities of the archipelago as a very promising centre for whaling were recognized. Before long, sugar was to become quite an important export, though never on a scale to rival that from Madeira. Later still, the Azores would become a major supplier of woad to the dyeing industry of Europe.

Despite the nominal role of Frei Gonçalo Velho as colonizer of São Miguel for Henry, during the 1440s the regent D. Pedro used his authority to make himself the donatory of what was the largest and potentially the richest island in the whole group. A document of 1447, exempting its people from the payment of the *dízima* for all time, unambiguously refers to São Miguel as D. Pedro's property and proclaims his intention to settle it properly.[44] The regent's intervention in the Azores may have taken place because he wished to give Henry notice that, while he had been granted a monopoly of navigation and trade with Guinea in 1443, that monopoly did not extend automatically to include any islands thereafter discovered, or rediscovered, or suspected to exist anywhere in the Ocean Sea. At all events the regent's criticism of the performance of Henry and his nominee as colonizers of São Miguel could hardly have been more pointed. It may indeed have contributed to the bad blood between the two brothers which led to the Prince's failure to take any steps to protect or save Pedro when civil war between the ousted regent and the king broke out in 1449. Until the end of the regency in 1448, Prince Henry thus did not possess any general title to the lordship of the Azores. As for the donation of São Miguel to Pedro, that was, of course, annulled after the deposed regent's defeat and death in 1449. The island then reverted to Henry.

D. Pedro, in the short time he was donatory of São Miguel, seems to have set about colonizing it with a vigour which Gonçalo Velho had failed to show on Santa Maria. He certainly used his position as regent to cause the metropolitan courts to sentence criminals to perpetual or temporary transportation there; one such convict complained that Pedro's pressure on the Portuguese magistrates to sentence men to transportation to São Miguel to augment the settlers' numbers was such that he had been despatched there without even a formal trial. Another convict, in 1453, succeeded in having his sentence of transportation to the Azores for life changed to exile on the grounds, accepted by Afonso V, that the archipelago did not then offer conditions of life that made them suitable for permanent residence even for convicts.[45] Nevertheless, some progress was made with the settlement of São Miguel. In the regent's time the prospects or potential prospects for the export of wheat, wine, fish and vegetables were thought particularly promising. One of Pedro's acts as donatory there, according to the somewhat dubious evidence of Diogo Gomes, was to import trotting horses from Germany for breeding purposes. At the time of Henry's own death in 1460, Gonçalo Velho was still described by him as his captain on São Miguel.

The Prince's ceaseless concern to extend his authority and power beyond that permitted by the terms of royal donations to him is again illustrated by what happened in the Azores at the end of the regency. Immediately after this, in addition to recovering São Miguel, Henry's chancery began to issue documents and donations in terms which show that he now claimed to possess the lordship (*senhorio*) of all the islands on terms identical to those on which he undoubtedly held the lordship of the Madeiran archipelago. Indeed he went further by claiming that he now had the right to exercise 'royal authority' in the Azores. But nowhere among the surviving documents is any donation of this kind to be found. Indeed assertions in them such as that the Azores 'had never known any lordship but his' – a statement that, as far as São Miguel at least is concerned, was clearly untrue – may in fact be interpreted as evidence that, so far, the Prince had not succeeded in extracting any such donation from the crown. There are signs, too, that, as far as his pretensions in the Azores were concerned, Henry had at this time run into difficulties at court with the Braganza family which more and more began to challenge his ascendancy there.[46] It was inevitable that, envious of the success he had made of his lordship in the Madeiras, other magnates should also turn their attention to the Atlantic islands. Henry cannot have been pleased when, very soon after the westernmost group of the Azores was found (c. 1452), Afonso V promptly made a perpetual donation of the island of Corvo to his septuagenarian and illegitimate uncle, Afonso, the first duke of Braganza.[47] This looks very much like an orchestrated move to block further expansion of Henrican control in the Azores at a time when the aged duke and his sons were rapidly becoming too rich and too politically powerful at court for even a person of Henry's stature to risk challenging them too openly.

The donation of Corvo to the Braganzas was a more nearly perfect feudal donation than any of those so far examined in this chapter. The islanders were obliged to serve the king in time of war. The crown did not reserve for itself the customary right to hear appeals in capital cases. It also relinquished to D. Afonso all royal dues on Corvo, reserving only the tenth payable to the church. The donatory was not permitted to alienate the island in favour of anyone not a subject of the Portuguese crown and must see that only Portuguese currency was used there. For the rest, the duke's authority was supreme. Of course, in 1452 none of this had any immediate practical effect. Neither Corvo nor the neighbouring island of Flores had any settlers, nor did the duke of Braganza, as far as is known, try to send any there. The donation was probably significant for the time being only in terms of Portuguese court politics.

The next island to be colonized, after Santa Maria and São Miguel, was Terceira, the 'third' island – then more often known as the Ilha de Jesus Cristo. A copy exists of a donation allegedly granted by Henry on 2 March 1450 in which the Prince is said to have made sub-donatory of Terceira one Jacques de Bruges, a Fleming who had long resided in the Iberian Peninsula and was a member of Henry's household.[48] This donation, in the form in which it has survived, is a forgery. It contains legal provisions which the Prince would never have attempted to grant but which were plainly inserted to further an inheritance claim put forward some time after his death.[49] However, it is quite possible that the forged document was based on a genuine one that really had recorded the appointment in 1450 of Jacques de Bruges as captain–donatory of Terceira. There is firm evidence that, before his death *c.* 1474, the Fleming had held the *capitania* of that island for some time.[50] Jacques de Bruges is important in the history of the Portuguese maritime expansion as the harbinger of the massive influx of Flemish settlers into the central group of the Azores after Henry's death. This had the result that, for a few decades, these islands, while Portuguese in name, were in fact dominated by and ruled by Flemings. The Bohemian cosmographer and globe-maker Martin Behaim confirms that this Flemish immigration into the Azores was sponsored by Henry's sister Isabel, the duchess of Burgundy.[51]

A number of documents issued by Prince Henry's chancery during the last months of his life throw some light on the jurisdictional situation in the islands at that time. Gonçalo Velho, after some twenty years, was still nominally Henry's captain on the islands of Santa Maria and São Miguel.[52] He had apparently been getting too big for his boots, for Henry complained that he had been usurping judicial functions that were outside his competence, a complaint not without irony, coming from the Prince. He was brusquely reminded that neither he nor any other of Henry's island sub-donatories had the power to carry out sentences of death or judicial mutilation. But the same document also suggests that Henry himself may have been in conflict with the crown over his own rights in respect of appeals from the island courts. Thus Gonçalo Velho was also ordered not to transmit appeals from the island courts to anyone in Portugal other than to Henry himself. These he alone would transmit as he thought appropriate to the royal *Casa do Cível* and he would be solely responsible for communicating that tribunal's decisions to Frei Gonçalo. One rather imprecise sentence in the document hints that Henry was determined not to allow the king's judicial representatives to visit any of his islands in the Azores.[53]

In August 1460 Henry made a full donation of his lordship over the islands of Terceira and Gracioso to his heir, D. Fernando, duke of Beja. This grant was made, the document explains, because the duke wanted to be responsible for colonizing some islands in the archipelago and had asked his adoptive father to relinquish to him some of his which were as yet unpopulated so that he could carry out this desirable task.[54] The timing of this formal declaration of D. Fernando's interest in following up Henry's concern to forward the Portuguese overseas expansion is significant. The inclusion in the donation of Terceira as an allegedly unpopulated island shows, in any case, something less than a strict regard for truth, since it had probably been ruled by Jacques de Bruges for the Prince since 1450. These Henrican donations regarding the future lordship of the various Atlantic islands can be better understood if we remember that Afonso V must already have made clear the crown's intention, on Henry's death, to repossess itself of his monopoly rights in Guinea. There could be no question of D. Fernando inheriting these. The question was whether he should be allowed to succeed to the lordship of Henry's Atlantic thalassocracy. In the last months of the Prince's life the crown, it seems, was under pressure not to allow the lordship of the Azores as a whole to be inherited by Fernando. In a testamentary letter of September 1460 Henry surrendered to Afonso V himself all his temporal rights as lord of the islands of Pico, Faial, São Jorge, Flores and Corvo.[55] The significance of this donation is that, on Henry's death a month later, strictly speaking only São Miguel and Santa Maria remained in the Prince's hands and that only in his capacity as governor of the Order of Christ to which he had donated them 'many years ago'. These attempts by the crown to recover most of the Azores and by Prince Henry to keep them out of his heir's hands were, however, both in the end frustrated. Shortly after Henry's death Afonso V, ignoring the Prince's testamentary wishes, made D. Fernando donatory of all the Atlantic islands which had belonged to Prince Henry with the same rights he had enjoyed there. The royal donation included all nine islands of the Azores group without distinction.[56] It seems clear that some strenuous disputes about what was to happen to Henry's Atlantic possessions went on at the Portuguese court in the last months of his life, disputes from which, immediately after his death, D. Fernando emerged triumphant.

A third group of Atlantic islands was discovered in the last decade of Henry's life by navigators sailing to Guinea under his direction or with a licence issued by him. This was the Cape Verde archipelago, a group eventually found, after Henry's death, to comprise as many as ten main islands lying roughly in latitude 14° N, and some three hundred miles west of Cape Verde on the African mainland. Several navigators, Italian and Portuguese, contended for the honour of having been the first to discover the Cape Verde islands. Prince Henry seems to have recognized the claims of a Genoese merchant and navigator, Antonio da Noli, to have been the discoverer of the four islands of the group seen during his lifetime.[57] Unlike the other Atlantic islands discussed in this chapter, the Cape Verde islands fell within the scope of Henry's Guinea monopoly which specifically included islands as well as the mainland. No attempt to colonize the Cape Verdes was made during the Prince's lifetime. That task was left to D. Fernando, in whose time the island of Santiago rapidly became a privileged and prosperous offshore emporium and staging-post for the Upper Guinea trades in general and the slave trade in particular.

The Janus-like nature of Prince Henry is well illustrated by the events examined in this chapter. When his ambitions were thwarted, as in the case of the Canary Islands, Henry unhesitatingly donned his metaphorical armour, assumed a crusading posture and turned to war and threats of war to achieve whatever his ends happened to be at the time. When, as in the case of the other Atlantic islands, no hominoid obstacle stood in the way of his designs, he could easily present himself no less convincingly as a far-seeing seigneurial entrepreneur engaged in converting uninhabited Atlantic islands into flourishing outposts of metropolitan Portugal. Because the islands which made up Henry's Atlantic thalassocracy have so long been familiar sights on the modern world's trade routes, it is easy to forget that, in the fifteenth century, this achievement meant (as in the case of the Azores) cajoling often unwilling settlers with promises of better things to come to start life anew far across the ocean on what was then the westernmost limit of the known world.

Contemporary narratives and documents, as was the medieval custom, leave it to be supposed that Henry alone was personally responsible for all aspects of the events we have been concerned with in this chapter. This is unlikely. The Prince, as long as his crusading commitments were not at issue, seems to have been entirely ready to take expert advice where he could find it, whether it was a question of finding the most suitable vines to plant on Madeira, or realizing that the soil of some of the islands of the Azores was highly suitable for growing wheat, or securing from Italian merchants the know-how about placing sugar and other products of the Atlantic islands on the European market. Unfortunately, scarcely anything is known for certain about who these advisors were. As Zurara's remarks quoted in the epigraph at the beginning of this chapter suggest, it is probable that, for the average Portuguese of Henry's time, the economic benefits brought to the population at large as a result of the Prince's endeavours in the Atlantic islands had a far wider impact on everyday life in Portugal than those arising from the discovery of Guinea.

Three hundred miles south of Madeira, however, Henry was engaged for most of this time in far from benign activities. Thwarted in his obsessive attempts to make the Canarian archipelago his, he had not hesitated to declare open war on the Castilians settled on some of the smaller islands and to persist with his doomed military attempts to defeat on their own ground the warlike pagan inhabitants of the larger ones. Astrologers and ancestral voices made sure that, even when he seemed to be engaged in the ways of peace, he always had war in his heart.

Chapter Five

Beyond the Cape of No Return

Cabo Bojador (lat. 26° 07′ N), when seen from northward, shows as a mass of red sand with a gentle slope to the sea. Its western extremity, which is very low, forms a small bay with the adjacent cliffs; the eastern part of these cliffs, about 70 feet (21m.) high, is prominent . . . The best landing place is on a beach about 2½ cables southward of the cape.[1]

In 1434, according to Zurara's *Chronicle of Guinea*, one of Prince Henry's ships rounded the Saharan cape which the chronicler identified as the legendary Cape Bojador, a promontory traditionally accepted by cosmographers, cartographers and mariners, Arab and Christian, to mark the furthermost southerly point on the coast of West Africa as far as which it was safe to navigate.[2] The Portuguese mariners, after effecting a landing to the south of the cape, returned to Portugal and reported that, as Henry had predicted, they had found no evidence of the major navigational perils that tradition asserted would confront them there. Neither the promontory itself nor the appearance of either the sea or the land in its vicinity seemed to differ, they said, in any significant way from the features already familiar to anyone navigating along the Saharan coast to the north of the cape.

The Prince's successful prediction immediately established his reputation in Portugal as a student of cosmography, cartography and navigational techniques who had shown himself on this important occasion to know more than the professionals did. Henry set about making the most of his role as the man who had demolished the myths surrounding Cape Bojador. In Portugal, however, recognition of the importance of that achievement was by no means immediate or universal. A number of the Prince's traditionally minded compatriots in high places still thought, in 1434, that these new fangled enterprises in the African Atlantic were likely to prove an expensive waste of time. Even Zurara, after mentioning the initial unwillingness of the Portuguese to go as colonists to the Atlantic islands, admits that, in his words

> during the first years, seeing the great number of ships that the Prince [Henry] fitted out for this purpose at such expense . . . they gave themselves up to criticizing something of which they had little understanding. The longer it took for the enterprise to produce results, the more their criticisms grew. The worst of it was that not only plebeian people but also those of higher rank spoke about the issue in a contemptuous way, believing that no profit would come from so much expense and effort.[3]

He adds, with a touch of cynicism that perhaps recalls Henry's own criticism of these sceptics, that it was only when cargoes of slaves began to arrive in Portugal from Guinea that his critics changed their tune.

It should be noted that the commander of the little ship which had made the passage of Cape Bojador was not the vessel's professional captain or pilot but a squire attached to Henry's household. In accordance with medieval protocol, it was he who got all the official credit for the success, though this must largely have depended on the skill of the pilot using Henry's charts and briefing.[4] The Prince always insisted that the exploration of the coasts of Mauritania and Guinea proper was a military and crusading enterprise directed against Islam. Accordingly, in the early years of the discoveries the caravels each carried a small number of bowmen and other soldiers under the command of a squire or, occasionally, of a knight whom Henry wished to favour. They were under orders to wage war against any inhabitants they found on land in West Africa and to seize captives whenever they could. Another task of the squire commanders was to see that the professional seamen of whom we hear so little, duly carried out the Prince's sailing orders however risky they reckoned these to be. If Zurara is to be credited, Henry thought, at least in the beginning, that professional seamen were liable to be superstitious and too set in their routine ways to make good explorers.

There is no doubt that, with the passage of the promontory the Prince had identified as Cape Bojador, an effective if wholly illusory psychological barrier to the maritime exploration of the African coast by Europeans had been removed. The event represented the testing by Henry of a geographical hypothesis which he had apparently developed for himself on the basis of his own study and intuition. Looked at that way, it can properly be regarded as a genuine scientific achievement whose consequences would go on to change European man's traditional notions about the world in which he lived. All the same, there are reasons to believe that the successful passage of Cape Bojador was a much less straightforward event than Zurara would have his readers believe.

To start with, it is almost certain that the promontory rounded by the Portuguese in 1434 was not identical with the one shown on modern maps as Cape Bojador. The cape known to cartographers today by that name lies on the Saharan mainland at latitude 26° 07′ N, that is, some 130 miles south of the latitude of Grand Canary. There are reasons to conclude that, in Henry's time, European map-makers located it much further north. The authors of *Le Canarien*, for example, describe a landing made on Cape 'Bugeder' about 1401 by a party of fifteen unidentified Europeans who had simply crossed the strait between the mainland and the island of Fuerteventura. They explain on several occasions in the chronicle that this cape lies only twelve leagues from 'where we are' (i.e. on the island of Lanzarote).[5] Plainly the promontory referred to here was not the Bojador of modern charts. It was almost certainly the one later cartographers know as Cape Juby (27° 57′ N). As the epigraph at the head of this chapter explains, the Cape Bojador known to cartographers today is so modest a promontory that it is hard to believe that it really can ever have been identified by any who had seen it with the legendary cape beyond which medieval geographers, pilots and sailors alike claimed that further navigation southwards along the African coast became impossibly dangerous. Associated with these legends was one which, according to Zurara, was incorporated into some seaman's charts of the region before 1434. According to the chronicler, who is almost certainly copying Afonso Cerveira, these charts showed, in the vicinity of the cape, shallows extending a whole league out to sea, so making it impossible for ships to approach the land. The chronicler invites his readers to examine the charts of the region made on the Prince's orders after that date. These, he explains, remove this ancient error.[6] There is, though, a query involving the Bojador legends. Since the Saharan coastline was inhabited by fishermen and its immediate interior regularly visited by Arab and Beduin chiefs and traders, the Moroccans can hardly have supposed that there was any truth in these legends about what happened to the surface of the Ocean Sea beyond the cape. It seems likely that these tales had been deliberately circulated by the Muslims to deter Christian shipping from venturing into a region well served by the trans-Saharan caravan routes.

Modern scholars have proposed quite convincingly that medieval European cartographers and others had wrongly taken Cape Juby, which lies some 140 miles to the north of the Cape Bojador known to the Arabs and Berbers, to be the legendary promontory. Cape Juby, on the mainland opposite the Canary Islands, fits the bill as far as the location given in pre-Henrican narratives and charts is concerned. It is an even more low-lying promontory than the real Cape Bojador and is indeed fringed by dangerous reefs, though these do not extend far out to sea. What always made sailing vessels wary of Cape Juby was, however, the Canary Current, here funnelled between Fuerteventura and the mainland, where it sometimes flows south-west at a speed of six knots. It has, moreover, a dangerous tendency not to flow parallel to the coast but to strike obliquely against the shore. Unsurprisingly, inshore navigation in the vicinity of the cape is, even today, considered dangerous for sailing vessels, particularly those attempting to sail northwards.

Definite evidence that the real location of Cape Bojador became known to Henry during his lifetime is suggested by a portulan chart of *c.* 1460 where the famous promontory is shown more or less in its modern position. When and how did Henry first learn that a mistake had been made? It is likely that this not very welcome information was given to him in about 1445 by his Arab-speaking squire João Fernandes, one of the unsung heroes of the Henrican discoveries, who voluntarily spent seven months ashore in 1444 and 1445 living mostly among the Berbers of the Río de Oro region so that he could eventually report to the Prince on the physical and human geography of the whole territory.[7] It seems highly probable that it was he who told Henry that the cape the people of that area identified by the toponym 'Bugeder' was located considerably further south than European cartographers had supposed. Henry insisted in documents for many years that the discoveries had begun at Cape Bojador but, of course, once his caravels had reached, identified and passed the real promontory which the local people knew by that name, the error made in 1434 could hardly be concealed from map-makers and those involved in navigation on the coast concerned. It probably embarrassed the Prince less than we might expect since he could claim that he had been responsible for correcting an ancient and important cartographical error.[8] What mattered in 1434 was that the facts as they were known made it seem certain, as Zurara explains, that the legendary cape had duly been rounded and the traditional dangers associated with it shown to be merely chimerical. To Henry's contemporaries, what was important was that the Prince had been proved right when, challenging the received wisdom of scholars and seamen alike, he had declared that his men would find no Cape of No Return on the Saharan coast.[9] Given the ambiguous status of the term 'Cape Bojador' in fourteenth- and fifteenth-century documents and texts, in the rest of the present work I shall follow the usage adopted by the particular contemporary sources concerned.

Why was Henry so confident that, contrary to what both charts and mariners assured him, the supposed insuperable barriers to further navigation southwards off the mainland south of the Canaries did not exist? No contemporary source names any of the works which Henry studied after he began to ask himself what the African coast was really like south of the Canaries. Nevertheless, given the problem and what narrative information was available, it is pretty safe to assume that he owed this confidence not only to his intuition but, more significantly, to his acquaintance with a well-known Castilian account of the physical and political geography of the world, the *Libro del Conosçimiento del Mundo*. This was an anonymous and fictitious account of a fourteenth-century Castilian traveller's journeys round the known world made by prosifying in autobiographical guise a now lost world map of that time.[10] His journeys included more than one routine sea voyage made far to the south of Cape Bojador to various fictitious African countries and ports. If one believed this tale, and the evidence is that many did, then it followed that, of course, Cape Bojador presented no problems to seafarers, Christian or Moorish. Given Henry's interest in the Canary Islands, it is also likely that he had read, in the original French or in a Castilian translation, *Le Canarien*, a chronicle of the over-bold attempt that began in 1401 of two French knights, Jean de Béthencourt and Gadifer de La Salle, to conquer and colonize that island archipelago. The French chronicle also contains a lengthy eyewitness account of a reconnaissance of the islands and their inhabitants made by Gadifer de La Salle.[11] We know that Zurara had access to what he calls 'ancient writings' among which was one which contained an account of the French attempt to colonize the Canaries. Given Henry's obsession with these islands from 1424 onwards, it seems likely that this may have been a lost Castilian version of *Le Canarien*.

Neither Zurara, in his account of the 1434 voyage, nor Henry himself in documents issued by him or at his instigation, ever suggest that the region of Cape Bojador had been successfully visited by any other explorers from Europe before the Portuguese. This event is thus traditionally seen as a Portuguese 'first'. In fact, it appears from *Le Canarien* that, strictly speaking, this was not the case. Writing in 1402 from the tenuous French settlement their expedition had established on the island of Lanzarote, the chronicle's two French authors record that, two years earlier, a landing had been made on the African mainland at the cape and prisoners taken there by an expedition of unidentified Europeans starting from the island of Fuerteventura. The passage reads

> The season before we arrived in these parts [1401] a craft with a company of fifteen aboard sailed from one of these islands called Erbania [Fuerteventura] and went to Cape Bojador ['cap de Bugeder'] which is in the kingdom of Guinea twelve leagues away from where we are. There they took prisoner some of the native people and returned with them to Grand Canary where they found the rest of their companions and their ship which was waiting for them there.[12]

The very casualness of the entry in *Le Canarien* and the closeness of the date of the landing on Cape Bojador to the time when the chroniclers on the spot recorded it, combine to give a convincing impression of veracity. The 'Gadifer' version of *Le Canarien* is in any case notable for its factual accuracy.[13] The nationality of these first recorded European explorers to have set foot on this part of Guinea is not clear from the text. They may have belonged to another French ship bringing supplies in preparation for the expedition of Jean de Béthencourt and Gadifer de La Salle the following year, or they may have come from a vessel from Italy or from the Iberian Peninsula routinely engaged in raiding the islands for slaves. The important thing to be noted is that the French chroniclers evidently regarded a voyage to and a landing on the Saharan mainland near 'Cape Bojador' as a marginal operation of no great significance. The horror stories associated with the cape had evidently not come their way. Thus, if it were established beyond doubt that Prince Henry had read the French chronicle, we would need to look nowhere else for an explanation of his absolute certainty that the stories of the great dangers mariners would meet if they attempted to pass beyond the cape were all nonsense. The French chronicle was not the only source available to Henry which made this point. The fraudulent world traveller who wrote the *Libro del Conosçimiento* recorded more than one sea passage made by him far to the south of what he called the 'Cabo de Buyder'. He, too, did so without any suggestion that there was anything about the geography of the cape that made it different from other Saharan capes.[14]

In 1443, when the Prince secured from his brother the Regent D. Pedro the grant of a monopoly over navigation and trade in Guinea and the waters adjacent to it, the document unambiguously declared that the principal reason for his involvement in the voyages of discovery was cartographical: he had noted that neither the portulan (navigational) charts nor the world maps he had seen drew the coastline south of Cape Bojador on the basis of visual observations. The region was depicted in these documents merely as the individual map-maker fancied it might be. Thanks to the explorations sponsored by Henry, the grant goes on, an accurate chart of the first part of the coast beyond the cape had been made under his direction and it was now the Prince's intention to continue exploring southwards to follow up this success.[15]

Remarkably in view of later events, nothing whatever is said in the 1443 grant about crusading or Christian evangelization in the region, those twin purposes which Henry would later invariably insist in official documents were the main reasons why the Portuguese were in Guinea. For his part, Zurara (or, more probably, Afonso Cerveira), while duly giving weight to Henry's pious purposes there, adduces two more practical reasons which, the chronicler says, also led Henry to become involved in exploration. He wanted to find out how far south of the known boundaries of the Islamic states of North Africa the rule and power of Islam extended. He also wished to know if it was true, as the *Libro del Conosçimiento* claimed, that, well south of Cape Bojador, ports existed where large amounts of valuable merchandise could be cheaply bartered in exchange for goods routinely brought from North Africa by sea.[16]

If *Le Canarien* seems to prove that Henry's men were not the first Europeans to land on 'Cape Bojador', it also discloses that Henry himself was not the first European to contemplate launching a seaborne crusading front in Saharan and sub-Saharan Guinea. In their opening words the two authors of the chronicle set out the motives which had led Gadifer de La Salle and Jean de Béthencourt to undertake their expedition to the Canaries. These recall the account of Henry's motives for the exploration of Guinea attributed to him by Zurara and which the Prince himself would repeatedly refer to in various petitions to the Roman curia. The expedition of the two knights, *Le Canarien* explains, was undertaken in the spirit of the crusades of old for the purpose of conquering infidels and converting them to the Christian faith. Gadifer de La Salle accordingly proposes, it goes on, 'for the honour of God and the increase of our holy faith in the southern regions' to conquer and to convert the pagan Canarians.[17] The intentions of the two knights in 1402, or, at least, those of Gadifer de La Salle, did not however only envisage the conquest of the Canary Islands. After that had been completed, Gadifer, the chronicle explains, contemplated leading an eventual Christian conquest of mainland Guinea itself. In a passage probably taken down on Lanzarote by the compilers of the chronicle from Gadifer's own dictation, we read:

> Now it is Gadifer's purpose and intention to travel to and to reconnoitre all the coast of the mainland from Cape Cantin – which is half-way between here [Lanzarote] and Spain – to Cape Bojador, which is the point on the mainland nearest to us, and thence all the way to the Gold River (flun de l'Or), to see if he can find there, when the time is appropriate, some good port and suitable place which could be fortified and made defensible. If that proves to be possible, entry to that country [of Guinea] will be assured and it can be made to submit.[18]

Here then, more than thirty years before Henry succeeded in sending a ship round the promontory he believed to be Cape Bojador, is clear evidence of the existence of a project, however preposterous in retrospect, for the despatch of an armed European expedition, based on the Canaries, to reconnoitre the whole West African coast from that cape as far as the Río de Oro and beyond. Gadifer's notions of the physical and political geography of this part of Africa were derived, as the authors of *Le Canarien* themselves point out, from the *Libro del Conosçimiento*, a copy of which Gadifer had with him on Lanzarote.

It will be seen that the French knight visualized the reconnaissance referred to as a mere preliminary to the establishment of a Christian fort somewhere on the mainland coast from which the fabled lands of Guinea could be eventually conquered. It needs to be remembered that we do not have to do here simply with a wild-cat project dreamed up in faraway Europe. When the authors of *Le Canarien* described Gadifer's intentions to invade Guinea they were writing from an island in close proximity to the very mainland territory whose conquest he planned. The project was of course always doomed to be a non-starter. Gadifer must soon have realized that when the French force on Lanzarote mutinied against him. Béthencourt, meanwhile, had taken himself off to Castile, and, without Gadifer's knowledge, there paid homage for the Canaries to Henry III of Castile as his liege lord. Gadifer returned in disgust to France in 1406. All the same, in a strictly literal sense, it has to be conceded that Henry was not the first European we know of to contemplate combining discovery with crusading in West Africa. The odds are that it was his reading of this passage in *Le Canarien* that first made him think of combining discovery with crusading, conquest and evangelization in Guinea.

The evidence in the grant of 1443 that the Prince had studied world maps before he started to organize maritime exploration beyond Cape Bojador immediately invites the question: what did he, in consequence, suppose the interior of Saharan and sub-Saharan Africa to be like and what possibilities for Portugal did he expect the exploration of its coasts to open up? As far as the coast beyond Cape Bojador was concerned, the surviving work of the makers of portulan charts and *mappae mundi* seems at first sight to confirm the Prince's criticism that these were no help to mariners. Thus the chart of the Venetian cartographer Giovanni Pizzigano, drawn in 1424 and one of the last of the pre-Henrican charts of the region to survive, gives up any pretence, south of Cape Bojador, that it is any longer realistically depicting the coast. A straight line running for some distance south-east demonstrates that the map-makers worked without any first-hand information about the lie of the land.

As far as the interior of the African continent was concerned, however, matters were entirely different. Cartographers from quite early in the fourteenth century wrote on the face of their work brief snippets of information about the Sahara and the lands lying immediately to the south of it. This material makes it plain that the factor responsible for awakening European interest in what Africa was like south of the Muslim kingdoms of the Mediterranean basin was

Europe's hunger for gold and its desire to learn all it could about where and how it was mined and how it reached the gold merchants of the north. This interest was not surprising since it has been estimated that about two-thirds of the minimum annual intake of the metal needed by Europe in Henry's time came by camel caravan across the Sahara from the far-off and mysterious alluvial mines of Black West Africa – Guinea.[19] A number of important facts about the gold trade were recorded by the cartographers at least as early as *c.* 1320, when descriptive legends inscribed on Giovanni da Carignano's chart of Africa, made in Genoa, contrived to make known information about the trade which the cartographer said he had obtained from a Genoese merchant resident in Sidjilmassa – an important caravan 'port' on the northern (Moroccan) edge of the Sahara. Carignano was also well-informed about the organization of the trans-Saharan camel caravans. He uses, for the first time, the term 'Guinea' to describe the lands to the south of the desert, the 'Sudan' of the Arabs. His chart also shows, flowing right across the continent from east to west until it debouches into the Atlantic, the river which European and Arab geographers called the 'Western Nile' because they imagined it to be a branch of the Egyptian Nile – a belief still held by the Portuguese when the Henrican discoveries were well under way, and afterwards. Giovanni da Carignano also shows, located as far into the African interior as the longitude of Sicily, a large island that divides this river into two branches for a considerable distance. This island he calls the Insula Palola. It was from this imaginary island that Europeans – the Prince among them – believed until mid-century that the gold of West Africa came.

Information about the gold trade was steadily added to and refined by other map-makers who followed Carignano, notably those of the Majorcan school. In 1346, an intrepid Majorcan, Jacme Ferrer, had actually set out by sea to find the Río de Oro ('The Gold River'), as the 'Western Nile' was also often known in Europe.[20] Though the memory of Ferrer's journey was regularly recorded by Majorcan map-makers at least from 1375 onwards, nothing at all is known about the Majorcan's fate. His journey is first shown in illustrated form on Abraham Cresques's famous world map completed in 1375 and pre-sented by Peter IV of Aragon to Charles V of France in 1381. It has a painting of Ferrer's ship, not a caravel, off the Saharan coast in the neighbourhood of Cape Bojador. Some supporting details are given in writing. This map, in eight panels, caters, as Leo Bagrow remarked, not only for cosmographers, merchants and mariners but also for curious amateurs like royal princes, rich merchants and any who wanted to know about the world outside Europe. The sixth panel carries Cresques's depiction of Western Africa and includes a small section of the eastern Atlantic.[21] Though earlier maps had attempted to cater for the interest of Europeans in the gold trade and to identify the Saharan caravan routes, it was Cresques who authoritatively established in the consciousness of those Europeans who had access to his world maps a detailed account of the political and economic characteristics of sub-Saharan West Africa as he believed these to be. Mansa Musa, a former emperor of Mali, is depicted seated on his throne and holding out in his right hand what appears to be the legendary great nugget of gold supposedly inherited by the Mali rulers from the emperors of ancient Ghana. His right arm is stretched out towards the figure of a veiled Toureg mounted on a camel. The veiled figure is there to represent the *de facto* masters of the Sahara who controlled the camel caravans which carried the gold northwards across the great desert from the kingdoms of the sahel. A later map signed in 1413 by another Majorcan map-maker, Mecià de Viladestes, provides more information about West Africa and the Sahara. It declares that the Río de Oro is over a league wide at its mouth when it debouches into the Atlantic. Viladestes depicted a ship lying off shore there to illustrate his further claim that there was sufficient depth of water in the estuary to take the largest ships in the world. The implications for Prince Henry are obvious enough. If ordinary sailing ships could reach the Río de Oro, then this provided yet another reason for believing that the passage of Cape Bojador presented no difficulties – as the *Libro del Conosçimiento* asserted. If the depth of water at the river's mouth was as great as the map-maker said – and its estuary so wide – there was also a good chance that it would be possible for ships to sail up it as far as the fabled Insula Palola and its gold.

Other inscriptions on the Viladestes map, following statements already made on that of Abraham Cresques, describe how in the region of Cape Bojador and just to the south of it, there were beaches where amber deposited by whales was to be found. According to the cartographer, there was also much ivory in the region because of the many elephants that, he alleged, frequented it. The traditional doubts about whether this part of Africa was inhabited or not appeared by now to be definitely settled in the affirmative; Mecià de Viladestes located a number of towns in the area and described the local people as negroes who, he said, went naked. The Viladestes map also shows a second great river debouching into the Atlantic a considerable distance south of the Río de Oro. This the cartographer calls the 'Flum Engelica' or 'Angelic River' which flowed through the realms of Prester John before turning towards the Atlantic.[22] The likelihood that Prince Henry possessed or had seen a map of 'Guinea' in the Majorcan tradition but more up-to-date than that of Viladestes, is increased by a statement made in Duarte Pacheco Pereira's *Esmeraldo*. In a passage in this work written more than forty years after the Prince's death, Pereira claims that

> [Henry] sent to bring from the island of Majorca one Master Jacome, a skilled maker of mariner's charts, which were first made on that island. By many gifts and grants he secured his services in these kingdoms and from this man the predecessors of those who make such things in our day learnt how to make them.[23]

A lot of scholarly ink has been spent on Pacheco Pereira's assertion and on the possible identity of the 'Master Jerome' (Mestre Jacome) he refers to here. No other document has been found to substantiate Pereira's information. On the other hand he had no possible reason for inventing such a circumstantial story so long after Henry's death. Given the Prince's undoubted interest in cartography, it therefore seems probable that the author of the *Esmeraldo* may have seen in Portugal a map bearing the signature in Catalan of a 'Master Jacome' together with other identifying material to show that the map-maker came from Majorca and perhaps, even, that he had done so at Henry's behest. The long-accepted hypothesis that Mestre Jacome was none other than Jaffuda Cresques (known after his conversion to Christianity as Jacme Ribes), the son of the fanous Abraham Cresques, now looks improbable. The chronological information available about Jaffuda's life means that he could only have gone to Portugal in Henry's time as a very old man. There were of course other expert cartographers than the Cresques family in Majorca at this time.

Henry's practical concerns at the start of the discoveries were not just related to the search for gold and the gathering of geographical and ethnographical facts. He had now come to think of himself as a leader whose destiny was to show all Europe that crusading for the Faith against Islam could, as Gadifer de La Salle had supposed more than thirty years earlier, legitimately (and profitably) be just as well undertaken on the Atlantic coasts of Saharan and sub-Saharan Africa as in the Mediterranean world. Perhaps, if things went as planned, Henry's

Portuguese crusaders there might even one day be fighting as allies along with the fabled Christian armies of Prester John.[24] The spirit of simple nationalism that spurred on all Henry's crusading – and indeed all his other endeavours – must never be lost to sight when assessing his motives.

The notion of a link-up in Africa with the armies of Prester John was not an original idea thought up by the Prince. In his time and earlier the Roman curia had often thought of bringing the fabled might and wealth of the Prester in far-off Christian Ethiopia into an alliance with Christian Europe against Moors and Turks. Apart from the curia, Henry's brother-in-law Alfonso V of Aragon was, from 1428 onwards, involved in diplomatic relations with Zar'a Yâqob, the real-life Prester in East Africa. One of the subjects discussed was a dynastic marriage between some of the Prester's children and those of the Aragonese king. Relations between the Portuguese and Aragonese courts were always close after Duarte's marriage in 1428 to the Aragonese king's sister, Leonor. It seems probable that Henry's interest in an alliance with Prester John was kindled by his awareness of the attention both the curia and Alfonso the Magnanimous were giving to the matter. Henceforth the Prester would always figure prominently on the Prince's agendum of discovery as when, in 1441, he instructed Portuguese explorers of the coasts of Guinea to try to find news of the 'Indies' and of the priest–emperor in East Africa. Precise information about what was in Henry's mind is contained in the petition sent to Nicholas V in 1454 requesting that the pope grant him a monopoly over navigation and trade in the African Atlantic. This petition declared that the Prince expected to be able to open Atlantic navigation 'as far as the Indians who, it is said, worship the name of Christ, so that we can communicate with them and persuade them to come to the aid of the Christians against the Saracens . . .'[25]

Such references to 'the Indies' and to 'Indians' used sometimes to be taken as proof that Henry's ultimate goal was nothing less than the opening of the Atlantic sea route to Asia by finding and rounding the southern tip of Africa into the Indian Ocean. Unfortunately, this reading does not hold water. It is based on a misunderstanding of the various meanings the term 'India' had in the Prince's time as well as a failure to take into account the configuration of the western coast of Africa as this was imaginatively described in the *Libro del Conosçimiento* and depicted by some fifteenth-century map-makers. The 'India' that Henrican documents have in mind is in fact north-east Africa. Ever since the supposed location of Prester John's legendary

Christian empire had been transferred by southern European publicists from Asia to Africa early in the fourteenth century, the area of the African continent lying east of the Nile and south of Egypt had become known to cosmographers as 'India Tertia'. Thus, when Henrican documents speak of 'Indians', it is to the black Christian inhabitants of the Prester's empire in north-eastern Africa that they refer. The inhabitants of that empire were regularly referred to by Europeans in the fifteenth century as Indians.[26] According to Jourdain de Séverac's book *The Marvels of Asia* (*c.* 1320), which puts together many of the legends of Prester John, the Ethiopians were heretical Christians three times more numerous than the total population of western Christendom.

The assertion in Angelino Dulcert's world map of 1339 that the Prester ruled over no less than seventy-two vassal kings[27] makes more intelligible the readiness of medieval Europeans to credit the Prester with command of a standing army of 100,000 warriors permanently engaged in war with their Saracen neighbours. A learned cosmographer like Fra Mauro, in the world map he completed for the king of Portugal *c.* 1460, estimated the size of the army Prester John could put in the field to number one million men, many of whom, he said, went into battle naked, the rest in crocodile skins.[28] Nor was the empire just rich in manpower. 'I believe', wrote Jourdain de Séverac, 'that the ruler of this land is more powerful than any other man in the world and richer than any in gold, and in silver and in precious stones.' A more down-to-earth statement about the Prester on a map made by the brothers Pizzigano in 1367 reveals, too, how these tales must have kindled the imagination of gold-hungry Europeans. An inscription on their map declared that there was so much gold in the Prester's country that the roofs of the houses and their interiors were made of or decorated with the metal and even the weapons of the Prester's soldiers were forged from it.

The Prester John legends obviously catered for medieval belief in the marvellous, whether decked in religious or secular forms. In the later Middle Ages, however, in the face of the the Turkish onslaught on Europe, they seem to have come to have an important role in sustaining morale in hard-pressed Christian Europe with their stories of the priest–emperor's huge and always invincible Christian army waiting in the wings to join the Europeans in crushing Islam. The trouble had always been that the Prester lived so far away to the south of Mameluke Egypt that communications with him were so slow and so hazardous that organizing any joint military action against the Islamic states seemed impossible. Now Henry had appeared on the scene to explain that, thanks to his planned opening of the Atlantic route to Prester John's empire via the Sinus Aethiopicus (see below), the communication problem should soon be solved. The modern reader may find it hard to believe that an individual of Henry's intelligence – and with his marked tendency not to go along with consensus ideas if he had a hunch they were wrong – could apparently accept the Prester legends at face value. That would be to forget that he was also a deeply religious man of the later Middle Ages brought up to believe in the marvellous and in the reality of miracles as a rational part of everyday living. No doubt it would be a mistake to suppose that therefore Prince Henry was entirely credulous of the more sensational stories associated with Prester John. Some of his earlier allusions to the Prester as reported suggest that he intended one of the jobs of his explorers in the African Atlantic to be to verify empirically information about the priest–emperor which might be relevant to his own concerns. In more general terms, that, after all, is what the Henrican discoveries were about. What Henry could never do was to question that Prester John existed or that many marvellous things were to be found in his country.

How was it, the reader may well ask at this point, that Henry was so confident that contact with the Prester could be made by sea from the Atlantic? The explanation may be readily found by looking at the surviving work of two or three fourteenth- and fifteenth-century cartographers or by reading what the Libro del Conosçimiento has to say on the subject. From them Henry would have learnt that, some considerable distance to the south of 'Cape Bojador', a great eastward oriented gulf interrupted the southward continuity of the African coast, almost cutting the continent in two. Some cartographers called this waterway the Sinus Aethiopicus, a name it still retains on Fra Mauro's world map.[29] Readers of the Libro learnt that by sailing eastwards from the Atlantic for some fifteen days inside this waterway they would find themselves able to disembark within striking distance of the frontiers of the Prester's empire. This possibility was to influence all Henry's plans for exploration in the African Atlantic. If it were indeed true that in eastern Africa there were to be found great numbers of black Christians over whom the Prester ruled and who were perpetually at war with their Islamic neighbours to the north, then the whole strategic and political map of the Mediterranean world might be changed in favour of the Christians if Christian Europe's vision of a military alliance with the priest–emperor could ever be turned into a reality. Henry's belief in the existence of an Atlantic route to Ethiopia and in a possible military alliance between Portugal and the Prester's mighty Christian armies was heady stuff but, where the urge to go crusading against Islam was concerned, the Prince was not a man who ever allowed prudence to overrule his wishful thinking.

It seems very likely that the *Libro del Conosçimiento's* account of an alleged visit made by its author to the land of Prester John via the Sinus Aethiopicus was first responsible for persuading Henry that contact with the Prester from the Atlantic was possible as a more secure alternative to the lengthy and dangerous land route through Rhodes, Cyprus, Jerusalem and Egypt which the envoys of the pope, those of Mediterranean rulers like Alfonso the Magnanimous and those of the Prester himself were forced to use. The *Libro's* bogus author-as-traveller claimed that, on one of his voyages south of Cape Bojador aboard a Moorish ship, he had sailed southwards without any problems as far as the entrance to the gulf and disembarked there. Further travelling had brought him to the city of Graciona, ruled over, he said rather confusingly, by one Abdeselib, 'defender of the [Christian] church in Nubia and Ethiopia who protects Prester John and rules over very great lands and many cities belonging to Christians'.[30] Of special interest too is his brief account of the people over whom the Prester ruled. He writes, 'They are black as pitch and they burn the sign of the Cross [on to] their foreheads with fire to show that they have been baptized, but although they are black they are people of good intelligence and common sense and they possess both knowledge and understanding.'[31]

This deceptively simple observation communicated, in fact, serious theological and ethnographic things to readers in the later Middle Ages. The author of the *Libro*, undoubtedly here copying a legend written on the world map which was his base text, gives supposedly first-hand authority to some highly important observations about the Prester's subjects not only in the context of the Henrican explorations, but also in that of the European project for a grand Christian alliance with the priest–emperor. Since the Prester's subjects were Christians, it would have been no surprise to any European reader of the book to have it confirmed that, though black, they were intelligent, rational and even learned beings. How else would one expect the members of a Christian state to be? All the same we have here a first hint of the ideological contradictions destined to plague the Portuguese overseas expansion in Black Africa long after Henry's time. If black Africans after Christian baptism became culturally no different except in their skin colour from white European members of what Christian publicists called the *communitas fidelium*, how could the Portuguese both insist on baptizing pagan blacks and on enslaving them? We shall encounter the Prince's answer in later chapters. Being of a casuistical turn of mind, whenever theology seemed to be at odds with profit he was always able to dispose of such apparent contradictions without embarrassment.

Henry's hopes of finding Prester John by way of the Atlantic persisted even though the years went by without any evidence being uncovered that the Sinus Aethiopicus actually existed. All that happened was that, when after much searching no trace of that waterway was reported, Henry decided that it must have been by sailing up one of the great rivers of West Africa that access to the Prester's lands as described in the *Libro del Conosçimiento* had been attained. This revisionist view of the problem is already found in a letter written by a Genoese merchant, Antoniotto Usodimare, to his creditors in Genoa. Antoniotto made a voyage up the Gambia River under licence from Henry in 1455 and seems to have claimed in the document that, as a result, he had got to within 300 leagues (perhaps 900 miles) of the frontiers of Prester John's empire.[32] This must have been a purposeful lie designed to impress and hold off Antoniotto's restless creditors in Genoa but his choice of lie suggests that he had found in Portugal that contact with the Prester was then still very much part of Henry's agenda.

Portuguese faith in the accessibility of Prester John from Guinea was to be long-lived. John II, near the end of the fifteenth century, still directed his exploring caravel commanders, when they had got as far south as the kingdom of the Kongo in sub-equatorial Africa, to try to make contact with the Prester by sailing up the River Zaire.

What is peculiar about all this questing for the legendary Prester John via the Atlantic is that, at this very time, envoys from the real Prester John were quite frequently to be found in Europe. In 1428, as already mentioned, Alfonso V of Aragon had received a letter from the Ethiopian ruler in which the Prester proposed a dynastic alliance between their two countries. At the same time he asked that a number of artisans, subjects of the Crown of Aragon, should be sent to his country to teach his people their trades. His envoys were in Valencia in May ready to return home – 'to the said regions of the Indies' – with a favourable reply from the Aragonese king.[33] They were to be accompanied by Alfonso's own ambassador, an Arab-speaking Valencian noble called Pedro de Bonia. The ambassador was not just to engage in diplomacy at the Prester's court. He was instructed to provide

Alfonso V with a full account of the country, including details of the Prester's military power and 'the great treasure and riches he has'. The fact that D. Duarte's marriage to Leonor of Aragon took place in Coimbra in the very same year makes it unlikely that Henry and the rest of the Portuguese court did not learn of the Crown of Aragon's flirtation with the Prester. It may well have been that information which originally set off Henry's own obsessive dedication to the notion of contacting the fabled priest–emperor by way of the Atlantic and the Sinus Aethiopicus.

Representatives of Prester John made their appearance at the Council of Florence (1441–2) and in Castile.[34] Early in the 1450s Henry's long cherished hope of making contact with the Prester materialized, though not in the way he had imagined. Records show that, in 1452, a person described as 'George, ambassador of Prester John' spent some time at the Portuguese court. His maintenance while there was paid for out of the revenues of the Casa de Ceuta, no doubt because the king accepted that relations with Ethiopia were an African matter that therefore fell within Henry's bailiwick.[35] We may be sure that, before he was despatched by the Portuguese to the Burgundian court to be interviewed by Henry's sister, the Duchess Isabel, he was interviewed by the Prince and what he had to say about Prester John's country was duly noted.

The envoy cannot have given much encouragement to Henry's illusions when he was asked about the Sinus Aethiopicus or other possible ways by water from the Atlantic to the borders of the Prester's lands. Nevertheless, the Prince remained convinced that direct access to Ethiopia from the Ocean Sea must be possible. Though he was, up to a point, of an empirical turn of mind and, as we have seen, could mock the traditional beliefs of sailors when he considered these to contradict the weight of the evidence he had worked on for himself, the general set of his intellect was, in a thoroughly medieval way, to respect traditional authority. There was no question of casting the latter aside simply because empirical evidence seemed to contradict it. Medieval men like Henry looked for a way of reconciling the two. One is reminded of the fifteenth-century map-makers who, while duly recording new toponym by new toponym the Portuguese advance down the coast of Guinea, continued to set these in the broader context of all the old cartographical images of the region. Similarly, Henry was unwilling to call into question in their entirety theories or conclusions reached long ago by thinkers, scholars or even charlatans who enjoyed the status of what the Middle Ages called *auctoritates*. Given the extent to which religion coloured his view of himself and the way he interpreted things, such a respect for traditional learning and beliefs was inevitable. It might be the case that the priests, envoys and merchants who managed to make their way in safety from Ethiopia across Egypt to Europe or North Africa seemed to know nothing about the existence of the Sinus Aethiopicus or the other fabulous stories associated with Prester John but, since these things had authoritatively been believed to be true in Europe for a long time, and since Prester John was recognized by the Holy See, they could not be dismissed on the say-so of individuals who themselves might be acting under orders or out of ignorance.[36]

It is time to return to the passage of the amphibolous Cape Bojador and, in particular, to the way in which the Portuguese passage of that supposed promontory of destiny came about. The first officially documented account of the history of this event is enshrined in the 1443 letters patent by which the Regent granted Prince Henry monopoly rights over navigation and trade south of the Cape. Using information supplied by Henry, the document declares that the Prince despatched ships to the region of the Cape without success at least fifteen times before he finally obtained knowledge of the lands he was looking for.[37] Zurara states that twelve years were spent fruitlessly before this goal was achieved. Whether the chronicler was quoting Cerveira's lost text or whether this figure was his own contribution to the discussion cannot, unfortunately, be established. This story of the twelve or fifteen years of frustration endured by the Prince was no doubt intended to build up an impression of the strength of Henry's will to overcome setbacks and of the self-confidence in his own judgement that his knowledge of cosmology and cartography had given him. It has always, however, seemed implausible that, for twelve years or more, a succession of ships fitted out at Henry's expense and carrying detachments of his squires avid for glory should always have turned back from the start of the work of exploration because of the terror they felt when they approached the perilous promontory. All the more so since they can have seen nothing during their faltering approaches to it to support the dire fears mariners' traditions associated with any attempt to pass beyond the cape they believed to be Cape Bojador. It must be remembered too, when examining this question, that sailings to the Canary Islands from European ports had long been routine and, though the nearest of the islands was less than a hundred miles from Bojador, no source suggests that those making this journey to the Canaries were aware of or fearful of any specially dangerous obstacles to navigation in the vicinity of the archipelago.

The story of the rounding of the cape that Henry put about when seeking his Guinea monopoly – and that Zurara's chronicle largely supports – involved an assertion that his attempts to get his ships to round Bojador and make a landing there must have begun about 1422 and gone on continuously until 1434.[38] It may be noted that, if we credit this history of events, Henry's attempt to explore the uncharted shores of Guinea must have begun about the time when he was also preparing to send a large private army to capture the pagan-held islands of the Canarian archipelago and was engaged in the colonization of the Madeiran archipelago. There is, though, another version of how the exploration of Guinea came about. This is to be found in the Proemio with which Cadamosto introduces his *Navigazioni*. The Venetian explorer, after explaining to his Italian readers that the Prince dedicated himself to making war against the Moroccans, goes on:

> The said lord [Henry] strove by every possible means to do harm to this Kingdom of Fez many places belonging to which border on the Ocean Sea, beyond the Straits of Gibraltar. Thither every year the said prince sent his caravels, which wrought such loss to the Moors that he urged them year by year to sail still further [south] so that they finally came to a promontory called Cabo Non. This cape was called thus then and still is today. It had always been thought to be the end [of navigation] because it could not be shown that anyone who passed beyond it had ever returned; [hence] 'Capo de Non – who passes beyond it will never return'. The said caravels at last reached this cape and did not dare to go beyond it. The said lord, desiring to know more, determined that the following year, with the favour and aid of God, his caravels should pass this Cabo Non.[39]

When he wrote that passage Cadamosto had just returned to Venice after spending six years in Portugal and in Guinea where, working directly for Prince Henry, he had been deeply involved in the exploratory and commercial sides of the discoveries in the 1450s. We have therefore to take very seriously his assertion that the question of what lay beyond the traditional barrier to further navigation southwards arose only when the ships the Prince had been sending annually to raid the Atlantic coast of Morocco had extended their hostile activities as far south as the sultanate's southern borders and asked for further orders. Since Cadamosto knew the Prince personally and was an unconditional admirer of him and especially of his efforts to further exploration and trade in Guinea, his omission of any reference to the fifteen (or twelve) epic years of supposedly unsuccessful attempts to round the Cape cannot be dismissed as the remarks of an ill-informed or ill-intentioned person. Cadamosto's account of the way the discoveries began is certainly much more plausible than that given in Henrican documents and by Zurara. We know that after 1415 Henry's corsairs did regularly carry out attacks on Morocco's Atlantic coast. It obviously suited Henry, when producing reasons why he should be granted a monopoly of navigation and trade in Guinea, to claim that what had actually been no more than annual raids by his caravels on the west coast of Morocco, had all along been part of a plan to find and round the perilous cape.

A question that inevitably arises in relation to all this is: why did the Moroccans themselves not attempt to sail further south and why did they apparently do nothing to stop Portuguese attempts to do so? It is, of course, entirely likely that, long before Henry's time, they had done so and had concluded that, as far as North Africa was concerned, sending ships along the Saharan littoral could serve no profitable purpose. This was not because navigation was particularly dangerous but because the trans-Saharan caravans could do a much better job. The Arab merchants and Berber nomads who knew the region, not to mention the Idzagen fishermen who made their living from the beaches, were more than capable of making sure that their co-religionaries throughout the sultanate were perfectly familiar with the sort of information about the regions of the Sahara bordering on the Atlantic that the Henrican explorers were now setting out with difficulty to acquire. From the Moroccan point of view there was no particular reason to encourage coastal shipping in the area. The web of caravan routes that for thousands of years had maintained the trans-Saharan trade between North Africa and the famous Black Muslim empires to the south of the desert functioned regularly, reliably and efficiently in the hands of the Touregs who controlled them. As for the horror stories of Arab origin about the navigational perils and travails that awaited seamen attempting to sail beyond the ill-reputed cape, it is to be supposed that the Moroccans knew these to be unfounded but kept them in circulation to scare off any would-be European interlopers. The ploy had been highly effective until Prince Henry subverted it with much publicity in 1434.

No source suggests that at any time the Moroccans attempted to turn back the Portuguese invasion of their Saharan coastal space. This is partly explicable because Moroccan sea-power and seamanship were then at a very low ebb – so much so that much of the coastal carrying trade on the sultanate's Atlantic coast had been allowed to fall into the hands of the Genoese and other European traders and seamen. Some Moorish corsairs certainly operated in the Atlantic, but in Henry's time surviving records do not mention any attempt by them to harry the Guinea caravels as they went about their business. Moroccan weakness on the seas, as well as facilitating the Portuguese success at Ceuta, should also be recognized as an important factor in the success of the Henrican discoveries of the 1430s and 1440s.

The chronology of events after the successful passage in 1434 of the promontory Henry then believed to be Cape Bojador shows that, despite an immediate flurry of activity, exploration in the African Atlantic was not, or not yet, the main interest in the Prince's life. In the eyes of his countrymen he might have taken the first steps towards uncovering hitherto unknown secrets as predicted in his horoscope but for the moment it was the great conquests of a more traditional kind that that document had predicted which concerned him more. By 1434 he was already engaged in preparing at home the political ground which would, he hoped, lead to another Portuguese army under his command going crusading in Morocco.

In 1435 Henry followed up the previous year's achievement by sending Gil Eanes back to Africa accompanied in another ship by an officer of his household, Afonso Gonçalves Baldaia. Their instructions were to sail as far south of the cape as they could. On this second voyage the two ships reached the place later known to English-speaking cartographers as Garnet Bay (24° 55′ N) which lies on the Saharan coast some seventy miles south of the modern location of Cape Bojador. This was thus probably the first occasion on which Henry's men really succeeded in reaching a part of the coast hitherto unseen by European ships.

Zurara's *oratio directa* account of Henry's considered response to what Baldaia had to tell him on his return is worth quoting in full because it is the first occasion we have which attempts to picture the Prince listening to the reports of his explorers and evaluating the significance of what they had to say. After commenting on their discovery of the detritus of men and camels south of the Cape the previous year, Henry is made to observe since you have found traces of men and camels it seems likely that a town ('*pouoraçom*') cannot be very far away from that place, or perhaps they were the traces of people who passed by with their merchandise on their way to some seaport where there is a secure anchorage in which ships can load.[41]

The suggestion in this passage that, in the region beyond the Cape, there might be a port where cargo was routinely loaded aboard ships (presumably Moorish) for their return journey north, shows that Henry continued to be much influenced by information about the region supplied in the *Libro del Conosçimiento*.

In the following year (1436) Henry took time off from his prepara-tions to go crusading in North Africa to order a single ship to sail still further south along the Saharan coast. Henry, as was always to be the case, was not content simply to have the coast surveyed and charted, though he attached great importance to this side of an explorer's task. From the start he was eager to have any information his people could pick up about the economic, ethnographical and political situation in the interior of the regions visited by his explorers. Henry early realized that a better source for this material than anything Portuguese eyewit-nesses could supply was, provided the linguistic problems could be overcome, the local inhabitants of these regions. In consequence, during Henry's time and always after it, the sailing orders (*regimento*) – without which no vessel could depart for Guinea – included instruc-tions that, when a new country was discovered, one or two local people must be secured by force or deception and brought back to Portugal so that he or his officials could interrogate them at leisure about the land whence they had been kidnapped. It is likely that Henry followed a practice employed since the previous century by European traders and others in the Canary Islands.[42] Zurara goes so far as to claim that two horses were shipped with the 1436 expedition so that potential kidnap victims could be pursued across the desert sands more effec-tively than on foot by Portuguese squires rather unsuitably dressed in their armour.

The *mappae mundi* and charts of the region, it will be recalled, often showed the Gold River flowing into the Atlantic no great distance south of 'Cape Bojador'. The author of the *Libro del Conosçimiento*, unsur-prisingly, confirmed the cartographers' account and claimed to have seen the estuary of the river when travelling south on a Moorish galley. He gave it the inappropriate Spanish name 'Río de Oro', by which this arm of the sea has been known ever since, so perpetuating a medieval legend about the source of African gold, reminding us of Henry's debt to the *Libro del Conosçimiento*, as well as proving that, despite his later claims to have been first and foremost a crusading evangelizer, the search for ways of access to that half-magical precious metal was perhaps uppermost in the Prince's mind when he first ordered the exploration of the Saharan coast. One hundred and twenty-five miles south of Garnet Bay the explorers duly reached what they first took to be a very large river estuary and presumed it was the Gold River Henry had told them to find. In fact what they had discovered was no more than a very large bay some thirty miles deep running northwards into the interior and separated from the Atlantic by a long peninsula. Baldaia, however, returned to Portugal still convinced he had discovered the legendary Gold River.

On this occasion the first recorded skirmishing with the local inhabitants of the region took place and gave Zurara his first chance to depict as deeds well worthy to be included in the annals of chivalry the encounters between the trained and well-armed Portuguese squires and their retinues and the poorly armed and uncomprehending Idzagen fisherfolk of the Saharan littoral. The latter, considering the odds, seem to have fought the invaders with some spirit.

Incongrously, what the 1436 expedition brought back from the newly named Rio de Oro, instead of the hoped-for gold, was a full cargo of pelts and oil obtained from the seals that were found basking in enormous numbers on the sandbanks and islands in the estuary.[42] It was hardly a cargo worthy of the toponym but the Prince, as the holder of a monopoly over the manufacture and sale of soap throughout Portugal, may not have felt as let down as we might suppose.

Hoping that he might manage to find a more propitious place for taking more captives, Baldaia then sailed on some ninety miles further to a location south of Cape Barbas (lat. 22° 20′ N) which the Portuguese explorers named Pedra da Galé (modern Piedra Galha). The toponym doubtless recalls the exciting first impression which must have been made on the Portuguese when they descried ahead of them what looked like a galley proceeding off-shore under sail. Here at last seemed to be proof that, as the *Libro del Conosçimiento* asserted, Moorish galleys in search of merchandise did indeed sail these waters. For a short time it even seemed that there would be news of a sea battle against a Muslim ship in this remote place to take back to Prince Henry but this proved to be a false alarm. When the Portuguese approached it, the 'galley', sadly for some and no doubt to the relief of others, turned out to be an islet which, seen from a distance, did and does look like a ship under sail. A landing was made there and some fishermen's nets constructed from bark were picked up as trophies. There was no sight of their owners. As Zurara remarks, the Portuguese sailed for home still without having found out even if the inhabitants of this part of the Saharan coastline were Muslims or pagans.

Gonçalves Baldaia had explored more than 200 miles of coast. This was not bad going for a single season's work when we remember that a great deal of an explorer's job was cartographical and involved not only charting the coastline but also taking soundings to establish the presence of shallows, tidal sandbanks and other obstructions to navigation that needed to be shown on the first portulans of the region ever to be made. Exploratory landings had also to be made from time to time from the ship's boat. This was often no simple task because of the dangerous breakers which are characteristic of the open coasts of West Africa. The landing parties not only had to record any signs of the presence in the neighbourhood of local people. They also had the more mundane task of searching for and recording on the new maps the location of water holes and springs and places where their successors could find the large quantities of brushwood that each caravel needed when at sea to make fires for cooking.

Zurara continuously praises the heroic conduct of Henry's squires-turned-explorers. It never occurs to him to mention, as further proof of their brave endurance, what they had to put up with aboard caravels now required to remain at sea for many weeks longer than ever before. One can only imagine the gross over-crowding, the total lack of privacy, the rats and the cockroaches and other insects with which these ships were infested, the stink of the bilges, the inescapable smell of bad fish, the shortage of food, and all the other inconveniences that attended long ocean journeys aboard small vessels – conditions that would soon be exacerbated when it became the norm for the holds of the homeward-bound caravels to be filled with slaves. Zurara did not think such things worth mentioning because, of course, they were part of the expected experience of those who went to sea in ships in those days and reference to them had no place in a narrative of heroic achievement.

Baldaia, soon after his return, was rewarded, at Henry's request, with appointment to the important post of receiver of the royal taxes (*almoxarife*) in the city of Oporto.[43] It would be the Prince's habit to see that those who distinguished themselves on his voyages of exploration were rewarded by offices in the king's gift, a procedure which, as well as saving Henry the expense of having personally to reward from his own resources those who served him, also made the point that the Crown benefited at least in terms of prestige from the Henrican explorations. We hear no more of Gonçalves Baldaia as explorer. There are some indications that Henry did not seek to turn any of the squires he sent to Guinea in the early days of the discoveries into professional explorers, preferring to replace them by others after one or two voyages. It was, after all, on land that an aspirant to knighthood had, in the last resort, to prove himself worthy.[44]

Baldaia's voyage in 1436 marked the end of active exploration in the African Atlantic for five years, a period during which Henry had more conventional forms of crusading on his mind. These would end up by confronting him with a public and a personal crisis of major proportions. However, voyages to Guinea do not seem to have ceased entirely. Zurara reports that two vessels were sent to the Río de Oro in 1437 to load seal pelts and seal oil. In 1440 the Prince sent two caravels to the Atlantic Sahara. Zurara limits his comments about their voyage to the enigmatic statement that 'because they experienced adverse happenings we have nothing more to say about their journey'. It sounds as if he is here omitting information given by his source (presumably Afonso Cerveira) because he considered it unworthy of inclusion in what is essentially a chronicle of successes. Perhaps Cerveira told of the loss of the vessels or even of a mutiny by their crews. In any case, exploration in the African Atlantic now remained at a standstill. The prestige that had accrued to Henry as a successful patron and organizer of oceanic discovery was about to be gravely diminished for a time by his disastrous performance in the field as an army commander.

~ Chapter Six ~

A Just War? Prince Henry's Ambitions in the Sultanate of Morocco

Did not St Augustine, asks Aegidius Romanus, specifically state the principle that the only true respublica *is one in which* iustitia *is to be found, and how can this refer to any community other than the Christian society? Therefore, unless [infidels] and pagans have been regenerated by conversion to the faith, it is safe to assume that they are not justified in possessing anything, and may be deprived of all that they hold. There cannot be any dominion worthy of the name among infidels.*

Aegidius Romanus, *De ecclesiastica potestate*[1]

On 23 August 1437, after several years of intense political arguments and quarrelling at court and amid an appropriate blaze of religious and chivalric display, a major Portuguese expeditionary force once more set sail from Lisbon for Ceuta. This time Prince Henry was its commander. Now, however, its purpose was not just to expand Portugal's toehold in northern Morocco. The immediate plan was to capture the port city of Tangier and the ports of Ksar-es-Seghir (to the east of Tangier), and Asilah (Arzila), on the Atlantic coast. Henry, however, secretly nurtured plans that went well beyond these stated objectives.

That the expedition sailed at all was proof of the apparently irresistible political power that, when the chips were down, Henry now had at the court of Duarte I. Lengthy and well-documented arguments put forward against the project by individual members of the royal council ever since 1432 reveal both the strength of the opposition there to the project and its inability to carry the day against the Prince. The arguments were not just about strategy, economics and the political and diplomatic consequences of a new embroilment in Morocco. These records also show that there were many doubts at court as to whether Prince Henry's temperament made him a suitable person to be in command of so risky an expedition as this one would be. Yet the new king, Duarte I, ignoring all the points made by the opposition and against his own better judgement, duly sanctioned the expedition and agreed that Henry should command it.

The records disclose, too, that some of those opposed to a new invasion of Morocco did not always base their arguments on practical grounds alone. Powerful figures at court questioned the legitimacy of the proposed crusade in terms of canon law, thus, by implication, also calling in question the right of the Portuguese to be in Ceuta. Nearly a century before the Catholic Monarchs had to face questioning at home about their right to exercise *dominium* in America, the Tangier project made Duarte I aware that there was now a body of international opinion, ecclesiastical and lay, which denied the unrestricted right of the papacy to authorize, or Christian princes to undertake, wars of conquest against infidel or pagan states merely because these did not belong to the Christian community. A letter written in 1437 by one of the court lawyers to D. Gomes Ferreira, the Portuguese abbot of the Benedictine Badia in Florence who was also Duarte I's agent at the council of Basel, helps to explain the concern of the royal counsellors. Henry, it reveals, did not intend simply to conduct a summer campaign in Morocco and then return to Portugal to attend to his multifarious other concerns. The letter contains the surprising revelation that it was his intention, if all went well, to spend three or four years crusading in Morocco. It also confirms that he had concluded all the legal arrangements necessary to transfer the day-to-day control of his affairs in Portugal to an administrator during what might well be a prolonged absence in North Africa.[2] It thus seems quite possible that, already in 1437, Henry saw himself as a prospective viceroy of Morocco on behalf of the Portuguese Crown – a post he would openly seek in later years. Just when we might suppose, then, that the rounding of Cape Bojador had awakened Henry to his destiny as a pioneer of exploration in the African Atlantic, what was really at the front of his mind between 1432 and 1437 was, instead, his determination to organize a major Portuguese military crusade against Islam in Morocco. Even allowing for the Prince's immense energy and his remarkable capacity for keeping a number of different projects running concurrently, he had no choice but to put oceanic exploration on hold very soon after Cape Bojador had first been rounded by his men.

Henry had in fact been actively canvassing his plan for a new Portuguese crusade in Morocco at least since 1432, while John I, the victor of Aljubarrota and founder of the dynasty, was still alive. Now an aged and ailing patriarch of seventy-six, John was still nominally the ruler of the kingdom, though in fact it was the heir to the throne, D. Duarte, who now attended to its day-to-day affairs. Henry, as John's favourite son and the man who had persuaded his father of Portugal's crusading destiny, had hoped to secure the old man's approval for his project before death removed him from the political scene. A clutch of written opinions on policy (Port. *pareceres*) presented to Duarte by members of the royal council in 1432 reveal what the Prince was then up to. He seems to have tried to secure from his father a kind of testamentary direction to his heir to undertake an expedition against Tangier.

The *pareceres* of 1432 deserve close attention, both for the information they provide about the way the Prince's peers regarded him then, and for the detailed account they give of the sort of arguments that were used when the question of Portuguese policy in Morocco was discussed by the royal council.[3]

One of these documents was submitted by the Infante D. João (a younger brother of Henry and administrator of the military order of Santiago) who cuts a less spectacular figure in history than any of his other brothers but whose intellectual abilities may, on the evidence of this *parecer*, have been underestimated. His examination of the pros and cons of expansion in Morocco, while well written and lucidly argued, ends on a perhaps significantly indecisive note. D. João began his paper by declaring that the dictates of chivalry and those of prudence were, by definition, opposed to each other – a view that he clearly regarded as a self-evident commonplace. He then proceeded first to examine Henry's proposals from the point of view of prudence. His first observation was that such a project could only be financed by imposing the hated special war subsidy on a kingdom whose already hard-pressed commonality would thus have to bear the costs of the enterprise. This raised the question of the justness of a war against the Marinid kingdom. Princes had a general duty to avoid as far as they could placing burdens on their subjects that would cause the latter suffering; it was particularly improper for them to do so if, as in the present instance, the burden was imposed to sustain what might well be an unjust war. D. João then took up the question of the justness of a crusade against Islam in Morocco in terms which reveal, yet again, that, contrary to what one might suppose from a reading of contemporary official documents or chronicles, it was known in Portugal that some European canonists, Roman lawyers and theologians of authority now doubted the right of the pope to authorize, or princes to undertake, wars of conquest against infidel states simply because of the latter's non-Christian status. João further put forward the rigid and historically quite unrealistic view that crusading could anyway only be defended in terms of Christian law provided that the motives of the Christian crusaders could be guaranteed to be strictly religious in character and were unsullied by any thoughts of achieving private honour or profit – a notion that would have astonished the crusaders of earlier times. Not surprisingly, he concluded that it was unlikely that many of those taking part in Henry's proposed crusade would pass this test of highmindedness. In consequence, the killing of Moroccans by them would of necessity be unacceptable to God since the Christian who kills a Moor for such a purpose [i.e. for personal honour or profit] sins no less than if he had killed a Christian.[4]

After these preliminaries the prince then moved to the core of the problem when he challenged the legitimacy of the Henrican project using the arguments employed at the time by 'anti-papalist' lawyers, theologians and publicists – so-called because they, in many varying degrees, denied the temporal authority of the pope over non-Christian peoples and sometimes placed considerable limits on even his spiritual jurisdiction in their lands. What, asked the prince, was the scriptural authority for the view that Christians could justly wage war against infidels who posed no threat to their attackers and did not occupy territory that had ever belonged to the latter? On what grounds was it asserted that such a war was pleasing to God? Was it not true that holy writ proclaimed that the infidel must be converted by evangelization, not by war? Such suggestions, of course, were directly contrary to those of Prince Henry who, both then and always, passionately upheld the traditional, 'papalist' view that the pope, as God's vicar and sovereign lord of the world, could always make legitimate a war against infidels or pagans anywhere. D. João did not, however, base this section of his *parecer* solely on legal and religious arguments. In a more practical vein, he pointed to the intolerable financial burden for Portugal that the occupation of Ceuta had proved to be. The occupation of further bits of Morocco would simply redouble the burden. Duarte should also ask himself, he added finally, whether the despatch of the flower of Portuguese military strength to North Africa on a crusade might not prove too great a temptation to her enemies in the Iberian Peninsula itself. As he put it, 'it would be a bad joke if Portugal itself were lost to gain Asilah [Arzila]'.[5] The reference was, of course, to the threat from Portugal's eastern neighbour. Peace or no peace, the Portuguese were always conscious of the looming Castilian presence on their frontiers and did not believe that the Castilians had really renounced their dreams of annexing Portugal.

Having effectively stated the case against the Henrican project on grounds of prudence, common sense and legality, João, however, then proceeded to look at it, as he explained, from the point of view of those who were committed to the ideology and obligations of chivalry. There could be no denying, he admitted, that these imposed a duty on all who practised the chivalric way of life to favour a crusade against the Marinid kingdom. Men of noble status were bound to pursue the kind of honour that could only be secured by performing chivalric deeds in war. The Portuguese were not involved in hostilities with any Christian land so that option for winning chivalric honour was closed to her knights and squires. Granada was another possible target, but they could only go crusading there with the permission of the Castilian crown; though he did not actually say so, João plainly regarded this as an obligation that was unacceptable to the dignity of the Crown and knights of Portugal. Morocco was, therefore, the only territory where the Portuguese could freely and naturally pursue chivalric honour. It is plain, as indeed the other *pareceres* of 1432 show even more clearly, that Granada had once again been formally proposed by some counsellors as an alternative goal for the proposed crusade. It is not clear, though, whether the suggestion was made by those who wanted at all costs to put a stop to the Moroccan project or whether it had once again been put forward by Prince Henry himself as a fallback position if he failed to get royal consent for the latter.

Some other points made by D. João in support of the chivalric point of view read today as if they were perhaps made ironically, but this is unlikely to be the case. What was the use, asked the prince now in his chivalric mode, of conserving the monetary reserves of the kingdom in hard cash in the royal treasury where it could be spent on mere trivialities, slipping away out of sight as easily as mercury flows? The true wealth of a kingdom was measured, he wrote, not in terms of bullion in its treasury but by the extent of its territory, the size of its population and the number of goodly cities and towns in it. Once that was understood, it was plain that a war of conquest in Morocco, apart from its religious and chivalric aspects, was the only way open to the Portuguese to make their country richer. Such an essentially seigneurial, aristocratic view of economic problems no doubt mirrors the sort of views that João had heard Henry put forward when the practical utility of the Moroccan crusade was challenged. It will be noted, too, that such a theory served to supply a justification for imperialist expansion without recourse to the sort of ideas canvassed by the prince in the first part of his *parecer*.

In the last part of the document João dealt with some objections to the chivalric approach to the problem. It might be said that a people so few in number, so poor and so badly organized militarily as the Portuguese would be bound to lose if they tried to measure themselves against so numerous an enemy as the Moroccans. Even if they managed to win, where, he asked, were they going to find the colonists they would need to settle the conquered territories? It could not be supposed that the plan envisaged allowing their present Muslim inhabitants to remain there under Portuguese sovereignty. People so alien by faith, language and custom would never obey a Christian ruler. D. João himself supplied the reply to his own questions, again echoing, one suspects, Henry's assurances. History, he wrote, offered many examples of small nations conquering big ones. Moreover, as he put it (forgetting his earlier stress on the need for crusaders to be unmoved by the hope of personal gain), 'great greed breaks down strong walls'. Certainly here repeating erroneous information circulated by Prince Henry, he asserted that the Portuguese had no reason to be concerned about their lack of military equipment; the Moroccans were worse equipped. As for the difficulty about holding down conquered Islamic territory if the original Moorish inhabitants were allowed to remain, the history of the Iberian Peninsula showed that this problem had caused no difficulties during the reconquest of the Iberian Peninsula and there was therefore no reason why it should trouble the Portuguese conquerors of Morocco. The demands of chivalry, concluded D. João in a burst of patriotic euphoria, dictated that Henry's project should be approved: fortune favours the brave and none could deny that the Portuguese were among the bravest of peoples. Even if the whole enterprise failed, then the sanctity of the intentions of the crusaders would guarantee them (in death) the pleasure that surpasses all others and endures for ever – i.e. the salvation of their souls.

It might be thought that all this meant that, in the end, D. João had come down on Henry's side, but this he did not do. He brought his *parecer* to a close by pusillanimously claiming that each side of the argument was so evenly balanced that he must leave it to D. Duarte to decide between them. The usefulness of this document, though, is that it gives us in carefully reasoned form direct access to the kind of political debates that went on at the Portuguese court in connection with Henry's demand to lead a new crusade against the Moroccans. The second part presumably faithfully represents the sort of arguments in favour of that project that João had heard from the lips of his brother. Also worth noting is the prince's acceptance that the approach to the problem dictated by the ideology of chivalry, though admittedly at odds both with prudence and with the rules of common sense, nevertheless represented an intellectual position which had to be taken very seriously.

The Infante D. João was the only one of Henry's full brothers whose *parecer* of 1432 survives. That of D. Pedro has not been found though one he wrote four years later (before the expedition to Tangier actually sailed) makes it plain that he had always been entirely opposed to the whole project. If Henry himself presented a written defence of his plan to the royal council at this time, it, too, has disappeared. We do, however, have the opinions of three other members of the royal council, those of John I's even then very influential illegitimate son, Afonso, count of Barcelos – the future duke of Braganza – and of the latter's own two up-and-coming sons, the count of Ourém (also called Afonso) and Fernando, count of Arraiolos. These documents all reveal an unambiguous disapproval of the projected Moroccan crusade.

The opposition of the fifty-year-old count of Barcelos was particularly dangerous to Henry for Afonso enjoyed much prestige because John I was his natural father and because of his territorial wealth resulting from his marriage to the daughter of Nun'Alvares Pereira, the 'Holy Constable' and veteran of Aljubarrota. The old king, moreover, seems to have favoured his illegitimate son almost as much as he favoured Henry himself. Barcelos's *parecer* is dated 19 May 1432.[6] Like the Infante D. João, he began by drawing attention to the harmful economic consequences of the undertaking Henry proposed. It was not only that a special war subsidy would be required to finance it, with the damage that would cause; the arrest of shipping needed to transport and sustain an expeditionary force operating in Morocco would do grievous damage to trade, as such maritime expeditions always did. Agriculture would also be harmed because of the mobilization of agricultural labourers for military service. The consequence of all this was that, if the king accepted Henry's proposals, great popular hostility to the Crown would inevitably be aroused. The concern of these great nobles for the economic well-being of the commonality shows that they were mostly perfectly aware of the economic consequences of war, though their concern was not as altruistic as they liked to suggest since they themselves would, of course, suffer those consequences too. In any case, Barcelos went on, whether the plan was successful or not, the experience of the Portuguese occupation of Ceuta provided evidence that even victory could prove to be financially a great disaster: 'you have only to look at the damage that the occupation of Ceuta's does', he observed. How could the kingdom sustain new burdens of the same kind? He concluded that, whatever its outcome, Henry's project would put the safety and well-being of Portugal in jeopardy.

Barcelos next dealt with the assertion, presumably put forward by Henry or on his behalf, that, whatever the risks, a crusade in Morocco must of necessity both be pleasing to God and an enterprise by definition worthy of praise. He declared that neither assertion was true. It could not be pleasing to the Almighty when a sovereign, unmoved by necessity, deliberately undertook actions that were bound to bring harm to the people committed to his governorship. As for the alleged praiseworthiness of the project, to be worthy of praise a project must be potentially capable of being carried through successfully and there was no reason to suppose that that condition was met in the present instance. The count, secure in his rank, his seniority and his reputation, did not hesitate to condemn Henry's crusading intentions in uncompromising terms: 'for these reasons', he concluded, 'as far as my poor wisdom serves me, I think there is neither profit nor pleasure to be found in this expedition, nor can it be pleasing to God or to those who live in this world'. At the end of the document Barcelos, like the Infante D. João, referred to the possibility of an attack on Granada. Unlike the latter, however, he did not reject this alternative. Such an attack, he claimed, could lead to a final elimination of the Nazrid kingdom in Spain and its success was, at the same time, obviously a practical possibility. Unlike the Moroccan project, it, therefore, could be regarded as pleasing to God.

No one could learn of the contents of the *parecer* of the future duke of Braganza without seeing it as something more than an expression of opinion on a particular question of policy. It was an open political challenge to Prince Henry's overriding influence at court. It suggested that the Prince lacked both strategic and political common sense. Its unambiguous assertion that the occupation of Ceuta was a disaster was calculated to infuriate Henry.

The *parecer* of the count of Arraiolos is the earliest in the collection. It is dated 22 April 1432 and much of it deals with political questions relating to Portuguese involvement in Castilian affairs. Arraiolos, however, also took the opportunity to set out his opposition to the Moroccan project, taking much the same line as did the two documents already examined. Even if the Portuguese did manage to conquer the whole of the 'kingdom of Fez', what benefits, he asked, would that bring either to the Christian cause or to Portugal? The Portuguese certainly had neither the men nor the money to defend two kingdoms. If they contented themselves with seizing and holding some more Moroccan ports, that, too, could only be harmful; they did not have the resources to garrison any more enclaves in Morocco and the effort to do so would certainly lead to the general ruin of the country. How could anyone claim that a result of that kind would please God? The count of Arraiolos, like his father, even aimed a direct shaft at Prince Henry: 'matters that are undertaken in a spirit of vainglory', he wrote, 'necessarily end as they began [badly]'.[7] He urged that no time should be lost in acquainting the old king with the general disapproval his counsellors felt towards the Henrican project before this acquired a momentum that it would be difficult to stop. Arraiolos employed an unexpected simile to reaffirm his view that it would be intolerable to impose a special subsidy for the suggested crusade. He wrote pessimistically:

Portugal is like a man of great age whose appearance does not as yet reveal much sign of the passage of time but which suddenly decays in his final years. So it will be with this kingdom, for while it may seem now that a new demand for a subsidy can still be met without destroying it, any such demand will, in fact, reveal its collapse for all to see.

The image may well have been suggested by personal observation of what had happened to the old king during these final years. It is, in any case, a revealing one. Contrary to what is sometimes suggested today, it is plainly not true that all the great nobles, apart from Prince Henry, were heedless of the economic consequences of war or allowed their attachment to chivalric ideals overrule their judgement. The passage also makes it clear that, just two years before the successful passage of Cape Bojador, most Portuguese leaders were far from thinking of Portugal as a land in any way ready for fresh ventures or, still less, with any capacity for greatness. They thought of it rather as an exhausted and overburdened country requiring careful nursing of an unadventurous kind if it was to survive. Only the Prince and his followers refused to accept such an uninspiring vision of Portugal's future.

Rather surprisingly, the count of Arraiolos, like his father, declared himself all in favour of Portuguese participation with Castile in an attempt to conquer Granada. It is possible that this enthusiasm by both nobles for an attack on Granada was simply a device to defend themselves against a charge that they were lacking in chivalric ardour, knowing that, in reality, no Castilian government would ever give its consent to a Portuguese intervention in the Nasrid kingdom. All these 1432 *pareceres* were written as part of the internal political manoeuvring that went on as John I's death drew near. Their writers would not necessarily stand by them when the politics of the court had changed. Five years later, for example, we shall find the count of Arraiolos installed as the constable of the expeditionary force sent under Henry's command against Tangier and he was one of those who, after the Portuguese defeat, opposed the return of Ceuta to Morocco.

The last of this particular series of *pareceres* is that of the count of Ourém, written on 4 June.[8] In it the Granada project is again defended at length and with enthusiasm. War against Islam, said the count in terms that Prince Henry would have approved of, is, by definition, a pious and praiseworthy act. It is against Granada that the Portuguese can most properly undertake such a war. It may be said by some that it would be an act of folly to use Portuguese money and Portuguese soldiers to help to carry through a conquest whose necessary result would be to add to the power of a country – Castile – that had never shown itself to be a friend of Portugal. Such unworthy considerations must be put aside: the business of kings is to serve God and if that service can best be carried out by helping Castile to conquer Granada, then that is what must be done. The count was insistent, too, that the Portuguese should not ask the Castilians for any territorial or other material rewards for their participation in the conquest of the Moorish kingdom. They must take care that their crusade was not contaminated by any suggestion that considerations of profit had moved them – a concern that, again, would have astonished the Christian crusaders of earlier ages who thought that, in a crusade, piety and profit went naturally together. What the count was concerned about, though, was that the Portuguese should make sure that they secured the maximum international fame from their chivalrous offer to join Castile in an attack on Granada. The embassy to John II of Castile to make it must, he explained, be a very high-ranking one. In that way news of the Portuguese offer would secure the maximum publicity in Europe at large and that, in turn, would make it hard for the Castilian king to reject. He dutifully went on to suggest that his father and his elder brother should be charged with this diplomatic task. Also of interest to students of Henry's career is the count of Ourém's insistence that the command of any Portuguese army sent against Granada should be in the hands of Duarte himself – an insistence plainly directed at making sure that Henry did not lead it.[9]

At the end of the document Ourém turned his attention briefly to the Moroccan project as such. His comments are valuable since they probably show how the Prince had by June reacted in the face of the general opposition of the royal council to it. Henry had apparently declared that, if he was denied permission to take a royal army across the Straits, he would be willing to go to Ceuta, taking with him just his personal retainers at his own expense. Once there, he would campaign against the Moroccans to the extent that the forces he possessed permitted. This was now presented by him as an alternative to the large-scale war of conquest directed against Tangier and other places backed by the resources of the Crown.

Ourém dealt first with the more ambitious alternative. Once again, he was insistent that Henry should not be given command in Morocco. Assuming, as everyone must hope, that the Portuguese defeated the might of the Marinid state in battle, then, he said, the greatness of the fame and honour that would accrue to the victorious commander was such that the only person properly fitted to claim it was, in the inevitable absence of the aged king, the heir to the throne. As for the notion that Henry could do anything worthwhile with the support only of his own retainers operating from a base in Ceuta, the count was scornful of such a notion: though the Prince said he had enough men, the truth was that his household held only a quarter of the number he claimed and everyone knew that he, like his brothers, had great difficulty in finding the money to pay even those. The result was bound to be that, in the end, the Crown would have to bail him out with money and men. It would be more sensible, if the royal treasury was in the end going to be committed anyway, at least to make sure that the money was spent on something more effective in the way of a campaign than on the minor results that were all that could be hoped for from Henry's second option. There was, in any case, he wrote, another good reason for rejecting the latter. The count declared with some delicacy,

> Since Prince Henry is such a great-hearted man, he would not be content to remain in Ceuta without attempting great feats of arms. The outcome of these would necessarily be doubtful because he would only dispose of such small forces to undertake them that, if things went awry (which God willing they should not) you would then be obliged to go to his rescue with all the forces you could raise.[10]

The conclusion the count drew was that either Duarte must lead a royal crusade in North Africa himself or there should be no expedition of any kind there. He had, of course, already committed himself to the opinion that, in any case, the proper place for such a crusade was in the Iberian Peninsula itself.

These documents make one thing quite plain. In 1432 Prince Henry's crusading ambitions, his judgement and his soldierly competence already aroused intense distrust in some of the most influential figures among the royal counsellors, including his own brothers. Rashness seems to have been the quality that those who knew him considered to be Henry's most dangerous personal characteristic. Royal chroniclers of the time like Fernão Lopes or Zurara seek to depict the sons of John I and Philippa of Lancaster as sharing both an obedient respect for their parents and a strong and supportive affection for each other. Documents (not to mention deeds) tell a very different story. Far from Henry's projects being enthusiastically supported by all his near relatives at this time (or later), it is plain that he had to face almost unanimous opposition at court from them.

The death of John I in 1433 meant that the question of resuming the crusade against Islam had to be put aside for the time being, though it is certain that Henry did not cease to press his case with the new king. The passage of Cape Bojador in 1434 did not diminish his concern for the Moroccan plan in the slightest. The *parecer* of the count of Arraiolos already examined contains information which suggests that Henry's addiction to the pursuit of diverse and often contradictory ambitions may, at this time, also have led him to toy with yet another project that has largely escaped the notice of his biographers. There are suggestions in the document that the Prince thought seriously at this time of intervening in the endemic civil turmoil that had persisted for a decade in Castile. Much though he disliked Castilians, he seems to have considered using the political troubles there to make himself arbiter of that country's affairs.

This opportunity presented itself because D. Duarte's queen, Leonor, was, it will be recalled, the daughter of the Castilian prince, Fernando of Antequera, who had been elected to the throne of the Crown of Aragon in 1412. Leonor had four brothers. The eldest had succeeded his father on the Aragonese throne as Alfonso V. John, her second brother, had become king of Navarre. But her two youngest brothers, Enrique and Pedro, had elected to seek their careers in their father's native land – Castile – where he had retained great estates. There, these two, known as the 'Infantes de Aragón', had joined the rebel magnates opposed to the Castilian government of John II (1406–54) which was controlled for more than twenty years by the all-powerful royal favourite Don Álvaro de Luna, Constable of Castile. Portuguese involvement in these Castilian affairs began because the Infantes de Aragón insisted that their royal sister should try to persuade the Portuguese king to send military aid to them under the leadership of one of his brothers.[11] D. Duarte asked his council for its views on this awkward question in 1432. A suggestion that Henry should be sent to Castile to help the Castilian rebels had evidently then been put forward.

Arraiolos's advice was that, instead of doing any such thing, Henry should be sent with a Portuguese army to support the legal Castilian government. Such a move, said the count, would ensure that Henry thereafter secured great influence at the court of John II – by which he doubtless meant ousting that of Álvaro de Luna. From such a position he would be able to make sure that the claims of the Infantes de Aragón were favourably dealt with. He would also enjoy the support of the other rebel magnates in Castile because he would be able to see that they too were restored to their lands and influence. Arraiolos naïvely suggested that gratitude to their Portuguese protector would then guarantee that Henry enjoyed the support of the former rebels. Who knows, he asked, what rewards the Prince might not receive for his services to both sides. He might, for instance, be granted sovereignty over Granada once it had been conquered (thus becoming a king in his own right). Warming to the possibilities, the count, in his *parecer*, saw other opportunities for Henry in Castile; if he managed matters rightly, he himself might end up ruling large chunks of that country. Another result of making himself agreeable to John II could be that the latter would cede Castilian sovereignty over the Canary

Islands to him so that he could become, as he had been seeking to do for a number of years, that archipelago's legal lord. The pleas of Duarte's wife in favour of her brothers should therefore, concluded Arraiolos, be rejected and Henry sent, instead, to help the beleaguered Castilian king. As he put it to Duarte,

> it seems to me, my lord, that it would be preferable and more in your interest that control of Castile should be in the hands of your brother rather than in those of your brothers-in-law. If that were so, you would be sure that you would enjoy the great friendship and perpetual trust of a very powerful king who is also your very close relative and therefore would be anxious to handle everything in accordance with your wishes.[12]

A recent editor of the Arraiolos text has suggested that this project for establishing Prince Henry in Castile represents no more than private fantasizing by the count.[13] There is certainly more to it than that. His *parecer* makes it plain that the project had at least been mooted openly among some of the royal counsellors. Chronicle sources establish that the Prince did intervene directly in the political imbroglio in Castile at this time, though not to the extent of going there with an army.[14] Did Henry seriously contemplate removing himself to Castile, or did the count and those who thought like him see in the affair of the Infantes de Aragón a heaven-sent opportunity for ridding themselves of an overmighty political personage and rival by exporting him for good to Castile? We do not know the answer, but it would certainly be unwise to assume that Henry's ambitions elsewhere necessarily ruled out the first possibility. Though he was obsessive, he was also nothing if not an opportunist. To threaten to go abroad in search of fame and fortune (and sometimes actually to do so) was a favourite ploy of the sons of John I and Philippa of Lancaster. Henry would never find it easy to reject categorically an option that might bring him new power and reputation, especially if the chance of a major European throne of his own went along with it.[15] Nor was it so absurd to suppose that he might even become king of Castile; the troubles of the Infantes de Aragón originated, after all, because a Castilian prince with no hope of succeeding to the Castilian throne had been elected to the Crown of Aragon. It must not be forgotten, either, that Henry's obsession with the Canary Islands was so great that, even if he had no other ambitions in Castile, the thought that, by making himself agreeable to the Castilian king, he might secure the cession of the archipelago to himself as a reward was probably enough cause to make the plans sketched out in Arraiolos's *parecer* attractive to him.[16]

In July 1432, a Portuguese ambassador once more formally presented to Don Álvaro de Luna and his sovereign an offer by John I of Portugal to join Castile in a crusade against Granada. Once again the offer was rejected. The Granada option discussed in the consultative papers we have looked at was thus ruled out, though Duarte perhaps made one more approach to Castile in 1434, after his accession. Whether an offer to send Henry with a Portuguese army to aid John II against the Castilian rebels was ever made we do not know, but it seems unlikely. If it was, then Álvaro de Luna, an intelligent statesman, would certainly have turned it down. Thus, when Duarte came to the throne in 1433, it really was Morocco or nothing as far as crusading was concerned and, apart from Prince Henry and his few supporters among the counsellors, it must have looked then very much as if the noes would have it. But anyone who thought then that the Moroccan enterprise had been effectively scotched seriously underestimated the relentless determination with which Henry always pursued any objectives on which he had set his sights, even though his unwillingness to make choices between them seems at times to have irritated his contemporaries as much as it disconcerts modern students of his career.

The personality of the new king, Duarte I, is the subject of some controversy. Rui de Pina's word portrait of him placed at the beginning of his chronicle depicts him as in every respect a perfect prince. Duarte is presented as an effective figure both in war and in peace, pious, an excellent horseman and hunter, cheerful and courteous in demeanour and so on. More convincingly, Pina also depicts him as a dedicated student of learning and letters, albeit in a self-taught way, who was also an author in his own right.[17] But this eulogy is tailored to the special perspectives of the exemplary theory of history and is largely at odds with the account of Duarte's reign given in the chapters that follow. Traditionally, Duarte has been seen in fact as a weak, ailing, bookish and melancholic man, anxious to do the right thing but unable to make up his mind and easily manipulated by those, like his Aragonese wife or Prince Henry, who knew what they wanted and badgered him until he conceded it, often against his better judgement. There is a good deal of evidence to support some of this criticism, but it is not the whole story. Though doctrinal, moralistic, legal or religious works figure predominantly in the king's library, popular works of entertainment in the vernacular were not excluded. The inventory lists a number of romances of chivalry and the Archpriest of Hita's sometimes bawdy

Libro de Buen Amor.[18] The king's own *Leal conselheiro* is an essentially didactic, moralizing work in a well-known medieval tradition
and, as was customary, frequently borrows its material directly from
other authors. Though diffuse and by later standards not
well-structured, it has been correctly noted by critics that its
self-questioning is quite often associated with real insights into the
working of the human mind under stress.

A feature of Duarte's mindset was his belief in the value of written
rules for dealing with the organization of daily life or with more important problems that might crop up, like military strategy and tactics. In
view of this, it is unsurprising that he was interested in the law and in
law-making. In his short reign he managed to do some important things
in this area, such as the promulgation of the celebrated *Lei Mental*.
This law sought, by placing restrictions on the ability of holders of
what had originally been crown lands to pass these on to their heirs.
Its purpose was to check the permanent alienation of the royal patrimony by territorial donations which had been a feature of John I's
reign. Nor was Duarte ineffective in the diplomatic field. Faced by what
he regarded as a serious Castilian diplomatic attack on the prerogatives of the Portuguese crown at the Council of Basel, he caused these
to be defended energetically and with skill. Once he had decided,
despite his misgivings, to permit Henry's Moroccan project to go ahead,
he was active in promoting it, both administratively and diplomatically.
Duarte was undoubtedly a well-intentioned monarch, but the fact that
he was destined to follow and inevitably to fail to measure up to the
heroic figure of his father evidently weighed heavily on him. It seems
to have been his fear of appearing ineffectual and his ever present consciousness of the chivalric fame achieved by his Plantagenet ancestors
that made him, in the end, unable to resist Henry's demands that
Portugal should undertake a new crusade in North Africa. As events
were soon to show, this inability to counter Henry's view of Portugal's
destiny would lead to a great national disaster quickly followed by his
own premature death.

According to custom, a year's mourning followed John I's long-
expected death on 14 August 1433. John thus missed by only some
months hearing the news of the passage of Cape Bojador. When the
mourning was over the Cortes were summoned (in August 1434), as
was usual at the start of a reign. Nothing was said there about any
future military projects but the representatives of the towns (*procuradores*) took the opportunity to show their antagonism to Henry by
attacking the lucrative commercial monopolies that he had secured

from his father; they asked for at least partial annulment of the most vexatious of these – the Prince's sole right to manufacture and distribute all soap used in the kingdom, even that intended for private domestic use by individual households. The request was denied by the new king.[19]

One of Henry's earlier moves when the new reign had begun was, according to Pina's chronicle, to persuade his youngest brother, D. Fernando, to inform the king, that, unless he were granted additional territorial possessions in Portugal more consonant with his princely status than those he had, he would request permission to go abroad to serve the pope, the emperor or the kings of England or France in order to seek the honour on the battlefield that he alone of his brothers had been denied so far. Henry's advice was obviously intended as one way of putting pressure on the Portuguese king to consent to a new crusade in Morocco. Frei João Alvares's biography of Fernando confirms that the Infante made such a threat but declares that it was to England that Fernando threatened to emigrate. Henry, unsurprisingly, then quickly expressed his understanding of Fernando's situation and urged the king to remember that it had been John I's intention, once peace with Castile was assured, to keep his knights busy on conquests that would ensure that they had plenty of practice in the art of war. Let Fernando and himself, neither of whom, he said, were encumbered by wives and families, go to Africa to continue the pursuit of chivalry there as the old king had done at Ceuta some twenty years before. In that way Fernando would stop badgering him for more lands and the knights of Portugal would renew or acquire experience of war at first hand. João Alvares also states that Henry himself, no doubt with connivance at the other end, received an invitation at this time from his sister Isabel, Duchess of Burgundy since 1430. This proposed to him that he should go to Burgundy to support her husband, Philip the Good, in the civil war in France. Henry's reward for this intervention was to be nothing less than sovereignty over the Peloponnese![20] There is no independent evidence to support the assertion that Philip the Good seriously tried to tempt Henry with the offer of a Greek duchy, but equally the story is unlikely to have been invented by João Alvares given that his work was commissioned by the Prince himself. One may reasonably suspect that we have to do with a put-up job arranged between the Duchess Isabel and Henry, with Fernando's collusion, intended to help to convince Duarte that the country's most important leaders would leave Portugal to make their fortunes abroad unless the Moroccan venture was agreed to.

Rui de Pina reports that the king refused at first to consider Henry's suggestion on the grounds that the country could not afford ventures of this kind; it was quite difficult enough, he very reasonably pointed out, for the royal treasury even to find the money to hold Ceuta. To placate Fernando, however, Duarte secured for him from the pope, not without some difficulty, the administratorship of the military Order of Aviz, thus completing the crown's take-over of the most important Portuguese military orders. This move, however, proved somewhat counterproductive since it only made the young D. Fernando even more anxious to show his mettle as a crusader knight.[21]

Henry's next move, according to the chronicler, was to enlist the support of Duarte's Aragonese queen for his project. This he did by playing on her justified suspicions that the king's brother, D. Pedro, was hostile to her and probably by promising to use his influence to aid her against Pedro if the need arose. Pina's account is, however, somewhat at odds with other sources. A personal letter written by Dona Leonor shows that, at least at the end of 1436, the Portuguese queen was much worried about the wisdom of the coming expedition against Tangier and, particularly, by the possibility that her husband would find himself forced to command it.[22] What is certain is that Henry was very active at court at this time trying to win support for his project. Among his various other ploys he seems to have suggested that, if he secured permission for it to go ahead, he and Fernando would take up semi-permanent residence in the conquered regions of Morocco with himself as viceroy there – a suggestion that, one may suspect, he rightly thought would not be without its attractions to his opponents at court.

From early 1433 he had also been busy petitioning the pope to grant to him in person crusading privileges against the Moroccans. This was, no doubt, yet another way of putting pressure to commit the crown to authorize his plans. These direct approaches to the curia by Henry on a matter that clearly involved the royal prerogative and should there-fore have been made by the crown on his behalf represent a pattern of behaviour that was a feature of the Prince's dealings with the papacy throughout his life. In this, as in other matters, he frequently sought to exceed the limited powers on the international (or, for that matter, national) scene that Portuguese custom or law allowed a royal prince to exercise in his own right. Another example of this behaviour also occurred in 1433. He had already sought ecclesiastical privileges in Morocco, informing the curia that he expected soon to conquer various places in the neighbourhood of Ceuta, including the port of Ksar-es-Seghir. He sought a promise from the curia that these places, when captured, should not be annexed to the see of Ceuta as normal ecclesiastical procedures required but, instead, should be annexed to the parish church of Santa Maria de Àfrica in Ceuta which he himself had founded there. In the spring of 1434, despite the fact that nothing had yet been settled, he petitioned again for a bull granting plenary remission of sins to all who accompanied him on the expedition he declared he was about to lead in person against the Saracens.[23] It must be remembered that these petitions were sent during the period when the Council of Basel was in session; it was plainly Henry's wish to impress the international assembly of delegates there with news of his crusading zeal, and in this way also to increase the pressure on D. Duarte to authorize the expedition.

The new king had, meanwhile, become concerned to hear, perhaps from his representatives at the Council, that many scholars and publicists now questioned whether Christian princes had any intrinsic right to make war on infidels or pagans simply because they were not Christians. Since the kings of Portugal had always been careful to secure papal approval for their crusading projects, it must have worried D. Duarte to learn that many canonists and civil lawyers in Italy and elsewhere also now questioned whether the papacy had any unlimited authority to give approval to Christian princes undertaking wars of conquest against non-Christian states. By the fifteenth century it was quite widely held among scholars and publicists in Europe generally, though with a variety of nuances, that the jurisdiction of the popes only extended to spiritual matters and that they did not have unlimited temporal authority even over Christians.[24] This was disturbing news for the ruler of a kingdom which, since the twelfth century, had regarded itself as under papal protection and had always accepted, though sometimes more in name than in practice, the temporal authority of the papacy. The problem now arose not only in connection with the Prince's wish to go crusading in Morocco but also because of his expressed determination to seek papal authority to conquer the pagan-held major islands of the Canarian group.

D. Duarte was sufficiently concerned on hearing of the views of the 'anti-papalists' to ask Pope Eugenius IV to let him have an authoritative ruling on the circumstances in which a Christian prince could wage a just war on infidels or pagans. The pope, no doubt to Duarte's surprise, did not immediately assure him that both projects fell within the definition of a just war. Instead he invited two distinguished Italian lawyers, one a canonist, the other a Roman lawyer, to study the problem and each let him have their opinions in the form of what was known in the curia as a *consultum*. They did not present their conclusions until October.

While matters were thus in suspense the king asked both D. Pedro, the future Regent, and Prince Henry to present him with reasoned *pareceres* giving their opinions for or against the proposed campaign. The contents of Pedro's response are only known to us through the version given by Rui de Pina in the *Crónica de D. Duarte*. This account may have been tampered with by the chronicler using his knowledge of what eventually happened.[25] What Pedro presented was an intelligently argued opinion hostile to the project. He agreed in principle, he wrote, with the notion that it was right for the Portuguese to make war on the Moors, but only if it could be shown that such a war did not cause greater evils than any good it could achieve. It was not possible to do that in the present case. There were no funds presently available to the crown to finance such a campaign without resort to special taxation. Since the invasion of Morocco was not one forced upon the Portuguese in self-defence, it would represent an act of war voluntarily initiated by their sovereign. In such circumstances Duarte had no right to impose special financial burdens on his people without, as the text puts it, 'greatly burdening your conscience, which is something you should not do'. Pedro then went on to enumerate his other objections to the project. There was no similarity, as Henry had presumably suggested, between the situation of the Castilians and the reconquest of Granada and the plans put forward by those who wanted to see a Portuguese invasion of Morocco. In Granada each castle taken from the Moors could be effectively garrisoned by Castilian troops while the size of the territory seized with it enabled contact to be maintained with the other fortresses formerly in Moorish hands. The Portuguese plan to seize a number of widely separated Moroccan cities and towns like Tangier, Ksar-es-Seghir and Asilah would require an entirely different strategy. Since continuous contact between the garrisons of these places after their capture would obviously be impossible, the available forces would have to be permanently split between each of them. In any case, asked the prince, how was it supposed that they could be permanently garrisoned, let alone colonized, by such an underpopulated country as Portugal? And what was to be the situation in the great tracts of country between the places named? There could be no question of subduing them, still less of planting Portuguese settlers in them. These facts, Pedro considered, pointed up the cardinal weakness of the whole project. According to Pina, he summed up his opposition by observing:

Prudent kings respect the fact that any prince or lord who seeks to conquer a foreign kingdom must be quite certain that he has enough strength to dominate the countryside so that his forces may range through it at will and benefit from the prizes and booty that may be found there. If his strength is [too] small he will be unacceptably forced to rely [for defence] on stockades and artillery to protect himself from a supposedly conquered enemy, something that does not bring honour to a conqueror.[26]

Pedro's ideas on strategy, though in accord with the traditional manuals on warfare then in use, were destined soon to be proved by the Portuguese themselves to be too inelastic. The future regent evidently had at this time no sense of what naval power could achieve to overcome the problems he mentioned. The strategy condemned by him in the passage just quoted was, in fact, destined to be the strategic means by which, despite their lack of manpower, the Portuguese would be able to establish themselves as a European world power. Starting with the castle built in Prince Henry's time at Arguin in Mauritania, the Portuguese overseas expansion was based whenever possible on defended strong points set on strategically sited islands or peninsulas throughout a large part of the world. These, of course, were dependent on Portuguese naval power. It was thanks to sea power, too, that the Portuguese would be able, until the disaster of 1578, to hold securely a string of ports on the Atlantic coast of Morocco. Since it was Henry who authorized the establishment of a military post and a permanent trading factory at Arguin, he must be given the credit for inaugurating what would develop into a key feature of Portuguese imperial policy. It is improbable, though, that he thought of Arguin in such terms. No doubt for him it was simply a case of how best to exploit the commercial opportunities the Portuguese arrival on the coast of Mauritania had to offer. Where Pedro was to be proved correct was in his assertion that Henry's Moroccan project was ill-conceived because it was, in terms of Portugal's resources, hopelessly ambitious.

Pedro's *parecer* had other, more practical criticisms to make. The total lack of secrecy surrounding the proposal to invade Morocco – in contrast to the remarkable secrecy that had marked the plan to attack Ceuta in 1415 – was rightly condemned by him. He also deplored the intention to risk all on an attempt to capture so large and densely populated a city as Tangier. How, he asked, could the numerically limited Portuguese forces available be expected to encircle the place completely enough to enforce a proper siege while, at the same time, deploying adequate forces to combat the strong enemy garrison manning the city's walls and able to be switched at will by their leaders to attack the besiegers at any point they wished? Nor, of course, would they be able to devote all their attention to the siege of the city since they would also have to contend with the Moorish reinforcements that would certainly be sent to relieve it. Pina makes Pedro say with a real touch of foresight that the Portuguese besiegers might easily find themselves the besieged. He summed up his opinion, according to Pina, by advising the king that the entire project ought to be abandoned, both as too risky in itself and because, even if it succeeded in its immediate objectives, that success would, in the long run, prove disastrous.

At the beginning of this *parecer* Pedro had noted that, since a formal decision to proceed had already been taken, his views were likely to be unwelcome and would probably go unheeded. And so they were. It seems likely that, in his heart, Henry never forgave so public and so effective an attack by his elder brother on the moral propriety or the strategic viability of his pet project, especially as it was soon to be proved that D. Pedro's objections were all too well-founded.

Duarte's request had also produced, probably at Estremoz in March 1436, a written defence of the Moroccan project from its instigator.[27] This document, though of great importance to any biographer, seems, on the face of it, to do little to enhance the Prince's intellectual reputation. When compared with the *pareceres* of his brothers and nephews, it is incoherent and rambling. It makes no serious logical attempt to state the case for a Portuguese crusade in North Africa or to meet any of the arguments his peers had put forward against that project. What it does do is to convey very plainly the way in which emotion took over from reason in Henry's mind whenever the propriety of crusading against the Moroccans was up for discussion. He then did not find it in him to set about dispassionately putting the pros and cons on paper as the king required. The impatient and at times disjointed tone of his document seems to show that he much resented the demand that he should state a case in writing in favour of a project the rightness of which he considered so obvious to any knight conscious of his Christian duty that there was no possible reason to debate the matter.

The tone he adopts throughout is that of a preacher setting out to appeal to Duarte's religious feelings rather than to his reason. The document is spattered with emotive quotations and allusions taken from the Old Testament and intended to ginger up support for the

ideals of the Church Militant. The New Testament receives less attention, though it was typical of the Prince's religious attitudes that he
should cite with approval Christ's declaration that he came to bring a
sword, not peace, to the world (Matthew, 10, 34), while ignoring all
his other utterances in favour of peace.

Henry begins with a text listing his view of what the objectives of
any man's life are. There are seven of these. First of all is man's duty
to secure salvation for his soul. This is by definition the most important goal of human life. Next is the pursuit of honour for himself, his
name, his lineage and his nation. Honour, declares the Prince, is passed
on by inheritance from generation to generation and so concerns the
very essence of worldly existence. If he possesses honour, a man's name
and reputation will endure until the world's end. Not surprisingly
Henry has little time for the normal pleasures of life but, more unexpectedly, in a deeply pessimistic outpouring, he dismisses as worthless
most of the activities necessary either to make life tolerable or, indeed,
to keep it going at all.

> It is obvious that eating, drinking, sleeping, singing, [too much]
> moving about, looking, listening, the company of women, marrying,
> telling jokes, talking and all the other things one can do [for
> pleasure], bring weariness and loss of happiness until old age and
> its pains diminish [such indulgences] and death puts an end to them.[28]

We have here the Prince, with an eye on posterity, seeking to present
himself as a life-denying ascetic, a posture which must have aroused
some cynical comment among his peers coming as it did from the pen
of a most active and determined seeker after power and riches. Henry
has, however, not yet done. He goes on to make the point that those
who pursue material gain for its own sake deserve no respect and even
has the temerity to quote in this connection Christ's observation about
the rich man, the camel and the eye of a needle. A closer look at the
parecer reveals, however, that Henry does not entirely condemn the
pursuit of material gain. It all depends on the aims which motivate the
pursuit of wealth. If these are good (in a religious and moral sense),
then material profits are justifiable; if they do not measure up in this
way, then they will be tainted by evil. The document concludes by
declaring that there are really only two matters that men should
concern themselves with: serving God and seeking honour.

The second part of the document seeks to show that crusading
against the Moors provides the ideal way of accomplishing these two

tasks. Henry makes short work of any suggestion that a war against the Moroccans might be unjust. The Church, he asserts, has determined that such wars are just, and the correctness of this view is guaranteed by famous miracles and by the chroniclers and is believed in by all decent people. Naturally, no mention is made of the opinions of the many canonists and theologians who did not share the Prince's certainty. Henry characteristically contents himself with commenting impatiently that it is unnecessary to set out the many reasons that could be given to show why wars against the infidel are just and good wars: faith requires no buttressing in that way.[29] Nor is it necessary to explain why to make war against the infidel Moors in Morocco is an honourable thing. It is self-evident that to participate in such a war brings with it the greatest honour to its participants that is available to Christians in this world. Appropriate allusions to the capture of Ceuta follow. Henry reminds Duarte that their father on that occasion ordered all his sons to stop mourning for their deceased mother, Queen Philippa, because war ought not to be undertaken with sadness but approached as a happy and pleasurable affair. After a good deal more in this vein, and a warning against paying any great attention to the dangers, difficulties or expense of crusading, Henry declares, with no great justification, that he had now proved a war against the sultanate to be just, reasonable and legal and that the Portuguese should undertake it. In his only allusion to the practical aspects of the matter he added the assurance that the Moroccan state was now so politically divided, so short of arms, and its castles so weakly defended that its conquest would be easy. For good measure, he also claimed that wise men in the sultanate were destroying the morale of its people by telling them that it was their destiny to be conquered by a lord from Portugal – presumably himself. These assurances were not ones that would, when put to the test, do much for Henry's reputation as a prophet or even as a collector of military intelligence.

This document cannot be dismissed simply as a piece of rhetorical propaganda dictated solely by Henry's need to combat opposition to the projected crusade. Its assertions may lack coherence and logic, but they clearly come from the heart and faithfully reflect the passionate responses which religious zealotry, when associated with the tradition of the crusade and the ideology of chivalry awakened in the Prince. It was pointless for his peers to suppose that he could be dissuaded from his purpose by drawing attention to the enormous dangers involved in going ahead with it. It was the very enormity of those dangers which, as at Ceuta, made the whole project worthwhile. Like many another crusader, Henry believed that he stood to gain whether the crusade was won or lost. Either way he would triumph, for, even if he were killed fighting the infidel, both his eternal life and his worldly fame would be assured. One may be sure that he never gave a thought to those who might be sacrificed in his pursuit of personal glory, or to the third possibility: that of defeat but his own personal survival. The problem about Henry's *parecer* of 1436 is not its incoherence or the fanatical crusading zeal which makes him despise both the infidel enemy and the voice of what we think of as reason. The problem lies in the difficulty that we have nowadays in believing that the man who devoted his life to serving and cultivating the beliefs and emotions set out in this document could, at the same time, be the calculating, unscrupulous and sometimes conscienceless political manipulator or the cool-headed planner and organizer of oceanic discovery and colonization who also appears in the pages of this book. We may, up to a point, be able to understand what the strange ideas and concepts which sometimes motivated the medieval mind were; what eludes us is the ability, as in this case, to share the feelings and emotions that they generated in those who believed in them. It would certainly never have occurred to Henry that his *parecer* was less firmly grounded in what he thought of as authority and reason than were, in their different way, those of his brothers.

In fact, as the memorandum of D. Pedro's indicates, by March 1436 the Prince had already secured the king's provisional consent to the enterprise. It was agreed that Henry would command the expeditionary army and that he should take his youngest brother, Fernando, with him. The planned size of the army at that time was considerable. João Alvares give the figures as 4,000 mounted men and 10,000 footmen. Rui de Pina, who clearly had access to some exact figures, agrees with those given by João Alvares but breaks them down into the following categories:

mounted men-at-arms	3,500
mounted bowmen	500
unmounted bowmen	2,500
footmen	7,000
servants	500[30]

To save money, only their keep would be provided by the crown to individuals. The various captains of companies would be paid according to the number of men they managed to enlist in their service. Henry, in his exalted mood at this time, no doubt thought it entirely proper that crusaders against Islam should, if necessary, serve without being paid for their efforts. In the real military world this notion was to prove fatal to the intended strength of the Portuguese army.

There could be no question, even so, of financing an expedition of this size from existing royal revenues. Recourse to the Cortes to secure a special war subsidy was inevitable. The gist of the speech made to the Cortes of Évora in 1436 on Duarte's behalf is to be found in the arguments the king employed after the Portuguese defeat to justify his decision.[31] The voice may nominally be that of the sovereign but the arguments were certainly those of the Prince.

The last words of John I, said Duarte's spokesman, had been to urge his sons to continue the war against Morocco. Filial piety therefore required that his wishes should be respected. Such a war was necessary, anyway, if the Portuguese were not to lose the warrior reputation they had won in the late king's time. Soldiers, he said, repeating an argument used twenty years before to justify the attack on Ceuta, must have chances from time to time to practise war, otherwise they would settle down to a lazy and virtueless life. Moreover, many leaders of the kingdom had shown signs of wanting to go abroad unless they were given something worthy of them to do for Portugal, and it was plainly better that they should serve their own king than foreign ones. It was also the case that his brothers were very keen on the project and it was only proper that he should give them a chance to serve him and God in the way they wished. The war would certainly be a just one. He asserted, not very truthfully as we have seen, that a majority of his counsellors supported the plan, as did his confessors.[32] Towards the end of his speech to the Cortes, Duarte added a new and interesting point. A war in Morocco, he declared, no doubt thinking of the alliance with England, would provide him with a good excuse for not getting involved in the current wars between the Christian rulers of Europe. Later, repeating Henry's dubious strategical advice, he assured the Cortes that the moment was well suited for an invasion of the sultanate. Morocco was, he assured the *procuradores*, without a ruler and wracked by rebellions and civil discord generally. Finally he turned to the material advantages to be gained from a successful war of conquest in Morocco and put forward a claim that can scarcely have carried much conviction with most of his audience. The increase in the size of Portugal's territorial possessions would, he declared, do more than augment the honour and prestige of the crown. New revenues would become available that would largely compensate for the present burdens he was forced to impose on his people. Remembering the unfulfilled promises of this kind made when the conquest of Ceuta was undertaken, the representatives of the *conselhos* in particular must have received this one with particular scepticism.

The Cortes reluctantly conceded the subsidy asked for ($1\frac{1}{2}$ *pedidos*), and the king directed the collectors of the subsidy to begin their work at once.[33] On 8 September 1436 Eugenius IV issued the crusading bull *Rex regum* that gave the expedition the papal authority that it needed.[34] Written in the inflammatory language used by the curia on such occasions, it ordered archbishops and bishops everywhere to preach in favour of the Portuguese crusade and, taking for granted the temporal authority of the papacy over non-Christian peoples, declared that all the conquered territories would pass for ever under the sovereignty of the Portuguese crown. A feature of the bull was that it conceded to the Portuguese in Africa the right to make war not only on the Moors but also on 'other infidels' (*ad debellandos, in Africanis partibus, sarracenos et alios infideles*). This wording was no doubt seen in the curia as no more than a rhetorical flourish but, when exploration in Guinea began again in the 1440s, it would be regarded by the Prince as giving him all the papal authority he needed to make war on the coastal people of that region too.

Military preparations went ahead very slowly. It was proving difficult to raise and equip an army totalling 14,000 men. There was also once again the problem of transporting a Portuguese army of this size overseas. For a second time, a large number of foreign ships would have to be found and chartered – a time-consuming operation mostly carried out by Duarte's agents in England, Flanders and Castile.

In the early autumn the king received from Eugenius IV the conclusions of various Italian jurists about the rights of the pope to authorize and Christian princes to undertake wars of conquest against Muslims and pagans which he had requested months before. One was the work of Antonio Minucci da Pratovecchio, a professor of civil law at Bologna. He had examined the question put by the Portuguese king from the standpoint of a specialist in Roman law. His deeply researched investigation of the problem occupies more than thirty-four printed pages of *Monumenta Henricina*. The second *consultum* was provided by Antonio de Rosellis, one of the best-known jurists of his day and also a professor at Bologna. His investigation occupies twenty-two printed pages in the same work.[35] Since the two jurists had been invited to rule on general questions of canon and civil law, their work does not make any particular reference to the problems of the Portuguese king but the way the two *consulta* are placed in the Vatican registers makes it plain that the work of the two experts was the result of Duarte's request to the pope and the Council of Basel for advice.

From Henry's point of view, what they had to say was decidedly disconcerting, all the more so since the two men were not members of the 'anti-papalist' camp but were advisers to the curia. The two *consulta* reveal the surprising extent to which, within the curia itself, the traditional view of earlier canonists like the famous Henricus de Segusia (Hostiensis; d. 1271) that the spiritual and temporal powers of the papacy were unlimited had been undermined by more than a century of debate. Each *consultum*, citing an avalanche of authorities in support of their various conclusions, exposed for what they were the simplistic assertions about a just war made by the Prince. It seemed that there was no problem concerning the right of a Christian prince to expel the Moorish occupiers of lands that had belonged to his predecessors. That, however, was not the situation here. In ancient times Morocco (Tingitania) had belonged to the Visigothic rulers of Hispania, whose successors were the kings of Castile. According to the best legal authorities, said Pratovecchio, the Portuguese king, before invading this former Visigothic province would therefore have to obtain the permission of the Holy Roman Emperor. As for the right of the papacy to dispossess Muslims of their territories just because they were Muslims, the jurist, citing, among others, the authority of the *Digest* and of Innocent IV, pointed out that, in general terms, no such right existed. If infidels held their lands in accord with the law of nations (*jus gentium*), then they were entitled to do so because 'dominion, possession and jurisdiction are permitted to infidels since they have been created not only for the benefit of the faithful but for all rational creatures'.[36] As for the pope's temporal powers in general, while it was true that it could be deduced from the Scriptures that, as Christ's vicar on earth, even non-Christian peoples were under his jurisdiction, this was a *de jure* not a *de facto* jurisdiction. The only circumstance in which a pope could properly exercise any jurisdiction against non-Christians – who, by definition, were only subject to natural law – was if they offended against that law. There were however certain exceptions: it was permissible for a pope to authorize the punishment of infidel rulers if these refused to allow Christian missionaries to enter their lands to preach the gospel. It would, of course, be difficult to rely on this finding in the case of Morocco, with its bishop and its various Christian minorities. Rosellis did, however, find a possible way by which the Portuguese king might justify an invasion of the sultanate. It was the duty of the (Holy Roman) Emperor to concern himself with the recovery of the lost lands once subject to Rome. If the emperors proved negligent about performing this duty, then, according to some authorities, the pope could authorize other Christian princes to undertake the task.[37]

The *consultum* of Antonio de Rosellis was somewhat stricter in the limitations it placed on the right of Christians to interfere with infidel jurisdiction. By both natural law and divine law infidels, Antonio affirmed, had an indisputable right to rule themselves and to resist by force anyone seeking to deprive them of that right. No pope or Christian prince could make war on them unless it fell within the lawful definitions of a just war. In a declaration that attacked the very core of Prince Henry's crusading ideology, Pratovecchio added that the mere proclaiming of an intention to convert infidels to Christianity by force or simply to make them better persons did not constitute a just cause.[38] As the texts of both *consulta* constantly bracket pagans with infidels, this was potentially bad news for the Prince in regard to his ambition to conquer the pagan peoples of the Canary Islands in order, he claimed, to procure their forcible conversion.

Like his fellow jurist, Rosellis did contrive to find some reasons that might give the Portuguese the right to intervene in Morocco. He was more inclined than Pratovecchio to accept, without imposing conditions, the simple point that the lands the Portuguese wished to reconquer had once been Christian. In the second place, he helpfully gave it as his opinion that, since every Christian prince had the duty to defend his kingdoms, it would be in order for him to make a preemptive strike against an infidel country if he had genuine grounds for believing that the latter was itself planning an attack on him. It was, however, going to be difficult for the Portuguese king to make use of this argument in view of Henry's recent declaration that the sultanate was in a state of political disintegration and incapable of effectively resisting an invasion.

According to Rui de Pina, the contents of the two *consulta* gave Duarte I an unpleasant surprise when he received them.[39] As he already had his own doubts about the legality of Henry's project but had nevertheless authorized it, the discomfort they caused him was hardly to be wondered at. However, since preparations had already progressed so far that turning back was impossible, he seems simply to have archived the *consulta* and gone along with Prince Henry's traditionalist views about the justification for crusading. What the response of the Prince himself was when he heard of the contents of the two *consulta* is not recorded, but it is plain from his subsequent behaviour and utterances that he dismissed their caveats and restrictions as mere legal quibbling of the sort he despised. As for the curia, it, too, seems to have paid little attention to these documents. Successive popes would authorize each step of the coming maritime expansion of Portugal, acting, they were always careful to assert, as temporal as well as spiritual lords of the whole globe, discovered or yet to be discovered. It was, after all, unlikely that any pope would find legal grounds for questioning the actions of a ruler who wholeheartedly espoused the doctrine of the universal sovereignty of the Holy See at a time when this doctrine was under severe attack from within the Church.

Another and more practical threat to the Tangier project made its appearance on the diplomatic scene late in 1436 as a result of Henry's clumsy attempts to mislead the curia about the status of the Canary Islands. At the Council of Basel a bitter quarrel between Castile and Portugal had emerged over the sovereignty of that archipelago. Its causes and course can be followed in the private letters and secret instructions which Duarte I sent at this time to D. Gomes Ferreira, his personal representative at the Council.[40] The cause of the trouble was Castilian anger over Prince Henry's repeated attempts to usurp Castilian sovereignty over the Canaries. These led to the issue of a bull by Eugenius IV in September 1436 granting sovereignty over the islands still in pagan hands to the Portuguese Crown. The leader of the Castilian delegation to the Council, the formidably learned Alonso de Cartagena, bishop of Burgos, riposted by presenting a devastating legal memorandum of enormous length in which he showed that, from every point of view, the Castilian crown had a firm title to the archipelago – a fact, he revealed, which had at one stage been formally recognized by Prince Henry himself. The pope was forced to withdraw the offending bull, declaring that he had been misled by the Portuguese.[41]

The Castilians at the Council also turned their attention to the bull of crusade *Rex regum* authorizing the Portuguese king to undertake the Moroccan expedition. They declared on instructions from John II that Castile was the only Christian power entitled to attempt the reconquest of Morocco and threatened to force the pope to withdraw his support even for the Portuguese occupation of Ceuta, describing this as a notorious infringement of Castilian rights. The Castilian delegation also raised other matters at the Council which were calculated to punish the Portuguese for pursuing their claims in the Canaries. They now demanded that a variety of ecclesiastical jurisdictions possessed in Portugal by Castilian prelates before the Great Schism should now be restored to their original overlords. They also demanded that the military Order of Aviz and the Portuguese branch of the Order of Santiago should come once again under the rule of the Castilian masters of Calatrava and Santiago respectively, a demand that was all the more offensive since two of the king's brothers, João and Fernando, now headed these orders in Portugal. Duarte was outraged, as, no doubt, was Henry. In March 1437, the Portuguese king told D. Gomes that, if the pope granted any of these Castilian demands, war between the two countries would be inevitable and the expedition against the infidel in Morocco would have to be cancelled. He wrote to the abbot,

> finally, inform the Holy Father that, if he gives way on these matters, it will become our duty to appeal from his decision to that of God himself, pursuing our appeal sword in hand to defend these rights as the king my lord and father and our ancestors did, for we are very sure that, if such a thing came to pass, war between our two countries could not be avoided and our allies would join us in it and all this would have been brought about by the Holy Father himself.[42]

The words are those of the king but the aggressive tone towards the pope and towards Castile seem to reflect Henry's customary uncivil language towards those who opposed him rather than that of the cautious Duarte.

Even in late June 1437 this international crisis was still not officially resolved, but the Portuguese king seems to have received some assurances that the pope would not, when it came to it, do what the Castilians had requested about restoring their ancient ecclesiastical jurisdictions in Portugal. Final preparations for the invasion of Morocco continued despite the public tension with Castile. Though we have no information about the role the Prince played in these events after Eugenius IV had annulled the bull granting the Portuguese sovereignty in the Canaries, it is likely that it was he who urged his brother not to cancel or postpone the departure of the army for Morocco.

All these problems had, of course, arisen because of Henry's obsession with the Canaries and his inability to let that question rest while he got on with the Moroccan project. More important for the history of the overseas expansion of Europe in the fifteenth century were the results of the enquiry by Pratovecchio and Rosellis into the rights of Christian princes to invade and conquer lands belonging to infidel or pagan states, and into the temporal authority of the papacy outside the *communitas fidelium*. Here were set out in embryo for the Portuguese king and his counsellors to read in the 1430s the kind of arguments against the right of the papacy to become the patron of European imperialism overseas, or of Christian princes to seize infidel or pagan lands – subjects which, nearly a century later, would be publicly and hotly debated at the behest of the Catholic Monarchs by some of Spain's most distinguished theologians and scholars. Nothing of the sort happened in Portugal. For all the influence the *consulta* drawn up at Duarte's request had on the subsequent behaviour of the Portuguese king, or on Prince Henry's thinking, these documents might never have been seen by them. As for the curia, the various popes approached by Prince Henry and Duarte I in their capacity as temporal as well as spiritual lords of all the globe, naturally greatly welcomed this influential reinforcement of what had almost seemed to be a lost cause. The curia therefore asked no embarrassing questions and freely granted to the Portuguese territorial *dominium* as well as monopolies over navigation and trade in the newly discovered Atlantic world. When, on an August day in 1437, the new crusading army at last set sail for Ceuta on its way to attack Tangier, there were many who doubted if such an expedition served Portugal's best interests. It is unlikely that more than a handful of Portuguese knew that, in the rest of Europe, an ever more influential college of theologians and lawyers now held that what Prince Henry was hoping to achieve in North Africa in their name was probably contrary to civil and church law.

Chapter Seven

Débâcle at Tangier

When men are hot with drinking wine
And idly by the fire recline,
They take the Cross with eager boast
To make a great crusading host.
But with first glow of morning light
The whole Crusade dissolves in flight.

Lines by the thirteenth-century jongleur Rutebeuf[1]

Despite all the problems discussed in the previous chapter, military and naval preparations for the new crusade in Morocco had continued to go ahead slowly throughout 1437. Though the project had originally been given the go-ahead by the king in the spring of 1436, no one even then had expected the army to be ready before the summer of the following year – proof both of the size of the enterprise the Prince was relentlessly driving his sceptical countrymen into undertaking, and of the difficulty of raising and equipping an army of 14,000 men in Portugal. There was also, as we have seen, the problem of transporting it to North Africa, a problem that could only be solved, as had been the case in 1415, by the time-consuming, expensive and unreliable process of chartering a large number of foreign ships.

Meanwhile those who were to go crusading went about the business of settling their private affairs. It was usual for kings, princes, great lords and even quite ordinary knights to make their wills or bring these up-to-date before setting out on an important campaign. They are valuable documents for a biographer as they often reveal things about the testator's life not to be found elsewhere. Unfortunately, the biographer who looks for a will made by Prince Henry at this time will be disappointed. Instead of causing a normal testamentary document to be drawn up, all Henry did to cover the eventuality of his death in battle was to issue, on 7 March 1436, brief but nevertheless rather curious letters patent (*alvará*) dealing with the disposal of his possessions after his decease.[2] It also contains his statement that he has never had a son and does not expect to have one.

The document then goes on to declare that, in these circumstances, he makes the king's second son, D. Fernando (b. 1433), his son and heir and leaves to him, just as if he were Fernando's real father, all his possessions of any kind apart from the third reserved for the suffrage of his soul.[3] The haste with which this unusual arrangement was finalized strongly suggests that we have to do here with an arrangement made between king and Prince by which the two had agreed that, if Duarte allowed the expedition to Tangier to go ahead, Henry would make D. Fernando the heir to his very extensive territorial possessions including those he held on a hereditary basis (*de juro e herdade*). But a problem remains. Why, in the months between March 1436 and the expedition's departure in August of the following year, did Henry not follow the example of his younger brother and make a proper will? In fact, Henry would put off making a proper one until a few months before his death in 1460, when, it seems, the officers of the Order of Christ probably forced him to do so. Perhaps, despite his deep religious sense, he had some psychological or superstitious aversion to facing up to the possibility of his death in battle. But that hardly explains why the already ageing Prince did not choose to put his testamentary affairs in proper order during the prosperous 1440s and 1450s. Whatever the truth, his behaviour in this respect adds another measure of ambiguity to the perplexing conundrums that any search for Henry's real motivations is liable to unveil.

His youngest brother and lieutenant, D. Fernando, made in August 1437, shortly before he set out for Tangier, the sort of will one would have expected Henry himself to have made. Written in the proper legal form then appropriate for such documents, it occupies (with annotations) twenty-five pages of print in the relevant volume of *Monumenta Henricina*.[4] In the document's *exordium* Fernando goes out of his way to stress the need for men to realize that death may strike at any time and draws attention to the disastrous consequences that those who fail to make a will 'through negligence or weakness' are liable to bring about after their death. One wonders whether this was perhaps an indirect comment on Henry's refusal to take heed of this lesson. If so, it was without effect. Fernando accepts the possibility of his death during the campaign and requests that, if it occurred, he should be buried in the Franciscan convent in Ceuta until his body could be brought back to Portugal for burial in Batalha with, he requested, no more ceremony than that accorded to any ordinary knight.

Right up to the end of June, in his letters to D. Gomes in Italy, the Portuguese king had insisted that the expeditionary army would be up to the strength decided on more than a year before: 14,000 men including 4,000 mounted men-at-arms were, he claimed, getting ready to leave. The expedition would be commanded by Prince Henry. D. Fernando would be given, as second-in-command of the army, his long-demanded chance to show his mettle. The fact that he had no military experience whatever was not seen as supplying any objection to his nomination. Their cousin, Fernando, count of Arraiolos, would accompany them as constable.[5] Since Arraiolos had written so tellingly against the Moroccan project several years before, this was, on the face of it, an unexpected appointment. Perhaps, though, the king hoped the count, known as a man of strength, would restrain Henry's well-known rashness. In the light of what was to happen, the fact that Arraiolos was one of the expedition's leaders would prove of great political help to Henry.

Duarte himself had been persuaded not to take command, whether by Henry or by the queen is not certain. Though Leonor had originally supported Henry's crusade, she had, as already noted, later plainly been influenced by those at court who regarded the whole project with alarm. So, on 31 January 1437, writing to the bishop of Lérida (an old friend), she observed 'we are much concerned with this expedition that the king is mounting and about which I am very worried'.[6]

A letter sent from Lisbon by a royal official to D. Gomes in Florence on 22 May had been encouraging. The expedition, he then reported, was said to be due to sail in July. Fifty ships to transport it were already lying off Lisbon and more than a hundred in all were expected to constitute the fleet which, if all went according to plan, would sail then.

Meanwhile, said the letter-writer, there was already a continuous flow of nobles and their retinues, with horses and arms, to Ceuta. The whole expedition would sail for the latter stronghold and would set out on its conquering march to Tangier from there. The king and D. Pedro would at the same time move southwards to the Algarve so that they could more closely monitor events in Morocco and order from there any additional support that might be needed. The most striking statement in this letter, however, is that, as we have seen, the Prince now expected to be away engaged on the conquest of Morocco for three or four years.[7] Another letter from Lisbon to D. Gomes, written on 3 July, revealed that the assembly of the expeditionary army was behind schedule but it was still believed in the Portuguese capital that it would sail sometime in August. The document also reminds us of something easily forgotten by the chroniclers: the very large number of pack animals that a medieval army needed for transport purposes. In addition to 4,000 horses for the mounted troops, the letter writer explained that 5,000 mules would also be required to transport the army's equipment and supplies. This gives us some idea of the scale of the enterprise the Portuguese were engaged in. Fodder alone for so many animals, since little was available in Ceuta, would constitute a major demand on shipping capacity. The writer also reported that the Portuguese forces already in that fortress had started making large-scale raids into Moorish territory and were building roads in Moorish territory up to a distance of five leagues from the city, along which carts and wagons could move towards Tangier when the signal was given.[8] On 17 July Duarte himself wrote to the bishop of Viseu, one of his delegates to the Council of Basel, to provide him with the latest news of the expedition which was to be passed on to the Council. The king's letter describes the various religious ceremonies, sermons and processions that had taken place in Lisbon on 12 July in connection with the publication of the bull of crusade, *Rex regum*. For reasons best known to himself, Duarte had then wanted the Council informed that embarkation would take place on the Feast of St James, 25 July, though he must have known very well that this was now impossible. He still claimed in the same document that the expedition was up to strength and reported that the Portuguese in Ceuta had recently carried out a successful raid into enemy territory as far as Tetuan, thirty miles south of the enclave. They had also, said the king, defeated a much superior enemy force in a large-scale skirmish.[9] He instructed the bishop to ask for the councillors' prayers for the success of the enterprise and to point out to them that, for the past seven hundred years, no Christian army of the present size or formed of so many excellent men-at-arms had crossed into Africa.

It must have been at this time that the king handed over to Henry, Fernando and the count of Arraiolos his general written instructions for the conduct of the coming campaign. Two other documents intended by D. Duarte for the Prince's eyes alone contained detailed personal advice to his brother about tactics and also drew his particular attention to the kind of mistakes Henry, as commander-in-chief, should avoid. These documents supply a number of important insights into the fears felt by Duarte about his brother's future conduct as a commanding general. They also set out the Portuguese king's own notions of military strategy and tactics and reveal much about Duarte's own mindset.[10] A notable feature of the latter is the great admiration the king expresses for English military tactics and battle discipline and Duarte's insistence that Henry should encourage his soldiers to imitate these. The Portuguese king was well versed in the rules for war as set out in works like Vegetius's *De rei militaris* and other Latin manuals and popularized in some medieval treatises. Henry, who considered himself the most soldierly figure of all his brothers, can hardly have been grateful for these royal instructions on how to do his job. It has sometimes been supposed that Duarte's admonitions to the Prince represent a series of generalities about human behaviour which should not be regarded as directed at Henry's personality in particular. This is not a tenable position. In all three documents it is clear that the king is full of foreboding about the future of the expedition under its headstrong commander and is making a last-minute attempt to get him to behave as a prudent general should.

The general instructions issued to the three leaders were meant to be encouraging. Though the Portuguese would be much outnumbered by the enemy, wrote the king, they had God on their side and, anyway, most of their Moorish opponents were worth little. The Portuguese had better horses and better arms and were united by a great purpose. Worry about the leaders' ability to enforce proper order in the army is revealed several times in all three documents. The commanders must, said Duarte, see to it above all that their men were properly trained and tight discipline enforced as it was in English armies. He wrote:

Bear in mind, apart from other examples, the example of the English who, principally for this reason, continuously win their battles. They make use of [training] in such a way that, wherever they find themselves and even if they are few and without a captain, they rapidly take up such effective positions that their enemies are made very afraid.[11]

This son of Philippa of Lancaster never forgot the successes of the English in battle his mother had told him about.

Five pieces of advice were directed particularly to Henry himself. He must remember, his brother reminded him, to attend properly to the wider responsibilities of a commander, not just to those immediately concerning a battle. He must take care, when he had to, to administer justice to the army fairly, not allowing his judgement to be influenced by personal affection – one recalls that this propensity of Henry for letting even his seriously erring favourites off lightly is one of the very few things about him that Zurara allows himself to criticize. Another warning the document contains is against acting precipitately and without first taking good advice. At the same time Henry must not accede too readily to the promptings of those around him: 'do not just follow the inclination of your own strong and excellent will, nor should you accede to every suggestion of others', wrote the king.

The warning seems to confirm other evidence which suggests that, while Henry was accustomed to ride roughshod over any opposition to his plans, this was not incompatible with a tendency to accept over-readily advice tendered by those close to him. Perhaps Duarte's insistence that the Prince should show mercy whenever possible to women, children and prisoners and take care to prevent indiscriminate and unjustified killings of them did not only represent an expression of general Christian piety but was prompted by the Portuguese king's memories of the savage behaviour of Henry and his retainers at Ceuta in 1415.[12]

Another document containing further special advice to Henry carries the exploration of the likely errors he might commit as commander still further.[13] Let him be careful, said Duarte, to set time limits for completing any commitments he undertook; let him also avoid promising to do things that he was not in a position to perform, simply in order to please those who made requests to him; 'he who wants to please everyone ends up by displeasing everyone' remarked the king in a rather obvious aphorism which, however, points again to a somewhat unexpected feature of the Prince's heroic persona. Duarte also recommended his brother to avoid reaching decisions until he had thought quietly about the matter in question, and, as if he were a twentieth-century general, warned him against making public statements on the hoof or giving unconsidered replies to questions put to him. The document also repeats the injunction to the Prince not to treat things as already dealt with when, in fact, no action on them had yet been taken.[14] He was also warned by the king, again not without justification, to try to avoid involving himself in 'disorderly' expenses.

The general impression about Henry which all these admonitions suggest is a thoroughly contradictory one. On the one hand he is presented as rash, liable to act without thinking, bloodthirsty in war, careless about administrative details and – a serious matter in any commander-in-chief – not concerned for the proper training of the men he was to lead. On the other hand he is also depicted as inclined to be dilatory, liable to make promises he cannot keep, unable to be trusted to carry things through until they are done, too ready to listen to the advice of others, deserving of criticism for treating the misdemeanours of those he favoured more leniently than he did those of others, and finally as known to be bad at keeping control over financial disbursements which required his authority. Grounds for most of these criticisms, contradictory or not, are to be found or hinted at in other contemporary sources. Somewhat inconsistently, perhaps, Duarte ended what must have been a highly irritating series of admonitions by assuring Henry that he had the qualities of a good commander!

The last of the documents is a short treatise advising the Prince on how to make war on the Moroccans. Much of it seems in accord with the recommendations of Roman writers on military affairs.[15] Thus the king reminds Henry of the importance of scouts when an army is on the march and stresses the need to make sure that troops always move in disciplined formations. He emphasizes the necessity to see that both captains and standards are always escorted by properly armed men – a warning perhaps inspired by memories of how Henry's rashness at the capture of Ceuta had caused him to become separated from his bodyguard. Various other admonitions made good sense. It was necessary for a commander to make sure that mounted men did not get mixed up with those on foot. Casual skirmishes with the enemy should be avoided, not sought; the correct way of maintaining contact with the enemy was to manoeuvre up to his vicinity and then return to the body of the army without actually engaging him. A good lookout must be kept when the army was in camp and no one standing to on guard duty should ever be permitted to leave his post for any reason, even when it seemed quite safe to do so. The king's ideas about how to deal with a Moorish attack were also sensible. The Portuguese should let the attackers approach without responding until they came within range of the Portuguese cannon, culverins and bowmen; only when the enemy formation had been broken up by their fire should a counter-attack be launched. Here, too, Duarte repeated his warnings about the need for strict discipline and battle drill. He also drew attention to the imperative need to make sure that the army's supplies were always safe-guarded. Very characteristically, too, Duarte also recommended Henry, rather late in the day it must have seemed, to study books about war whenever he had the chance and, in particular, to 'remember to make a habit of reading the books of advice on battle tactics that D. Fernando and the count of Arraiolos carry with them'.[16] He did not expect the Prince, it would seem, to be likely to carry military manuals for the use of field commanders in his own baggage. Henry probably found Duarte's worries about the chastity of the Portuguese soldiers more to his taste. Once again the king cited English practice as the model to be followed by the Portuguese army. He wrote

> I recommend you to place a strong guard [on any camp] to safeguard the virtue of chastity for you well know how pleasing that is to the Lord, particularly in such circumstances as these. Remember [the custom] of the English who, though in times of peace they are much embroiled with women, as soon as they find themselves at war keep away from them and allow no women in camp except those whose duties there make it proper to admit them.[17]

It is unclear what the authority for Duarte's belief about English campaigning celibacy was, but the whole topic was clearly one which obsessed Philippa's sons. In addition to Henry's much publicized chastity, D. Fernando's contemporary biographer assures us that he too maintained a lifelong celibacy and would not even allow the young men of his household to have relations with women before they were twenty.[18]

The final part of the document takes a more practical turn. The royal galleys, the king noted, were all undermanned because of the shortage of sailors (and, presumably, of rowers). They must therefore be sent back to Portugal as soon as possible – certainly not later than October – because they could not safely remain in Moroccan waters during the winter. The same applied to the large number of caravels and sailing barges (*barcas de carreto*) that formed part of the fleet. Transport, trade and fishing, Duarte reminded his brother, were all gravely affected by the continued detention of these craft for military purposes. Other instructions reveal the king's distrust of the courage of the crews of the foreign merchant ships under charter. They, he assumed – no doubt rightly – would be anxious to get out of the war zone as soon as possible. Guards should be posted on these vessels during unloading in North Africa to see that they did not try to make off with some of their cargo still undischarged. Noting that most of these chartered vessels were either English or Basque and that English and Basque seamen did not get on with each other, Duarte also insisted that care should be taken to see that fighting did not break out between these two groups since such quarrels could endanger the whole fleet. No time should be lost in releasing the foreign ships once unloading was completed because the expense to the crown of chartering them and paying their crews was very great. All in all, it could hardly be said of the Portuguese king that he wrote like a ruler confident that victory for his army under Henry's command was a foregone conclusion.

A letter from the royal secretary to D. Gomes in Florence dated 12 September 1437 reported that the fleet had finally left the Tagus on 22[19] August in favourable weather conditions. The same letter reports the fleet's safe arrival at Ceuta four days later, since when no news of interest had been received from there. Another letter from Oporto to the abbot written rather later was a bit more informative about what was happening in Ceuta. A well-equipped force of nobles and their retinues, it reported, was camped outside the city walls and the new tracks westwards over the sierras towards Tangier that had been made by Henry's order were now said to be complete and guarded by men-at-arms and bowmen.

In fact, however, already all was far from well. For one thing the whole army, when a formal muster was held in Ceuta, proved to be alarmingly under strength. The king, in a letter written six months later, reported that more than a quarter of the soldiers available in Lisbon (that is, about 3,500 men) had had to be left behind there because many of the foreign ships chartered as transports had failed to show up. Rui de Pina says that 8,000 men were missing, leaving Henry with only 2,000 men-at-arms, 1,000 bowmen and 3,000 foot soldiers under his command, but he may have exaggerated the shortfall to excuse the Portuguese defeat.[20] João Álvares, who was of course present at these events with D. Fernando, says that only 7,000 men sailed from Lisbon in August but presumably to these must be added those from Oporto under the count of Arraiolos and all the others who had reinforced the regular Ceuta garrison during the preceding months. Duarte's letter about the disaster written to D. Gomes in March 1438 was precise on the reasons for the shortfall:

Of those we had decided should make up the army more, than a quarter of the cavalry, foot soldiers and archers were left behind because of the shortage of shipping. The vessels we had chartered in England and Flanders did not come on account of the war between the king of England and the duke of Burgundy and, at the same time, many ships chartered in Castile did not turn up because of other problems.[21]

Certainly the army with which Henry still proposed to conquer not only Tangier but perhaps also Ksar-es-Seghir and Asilah was now ludicrously small for the job. To increase its numbers, a proposal was made that the troops who had been left behind in Lisbon should march overland to the Algarve and thence to the Castilian port of Tarifa to make the passage of the Straits at its narrowest point. Henry, according to Pina's chronicle, opposed this plan because he believed that at least some of the missing vessels would soon turn up to transport the troops who had been left behind, and because he did not believe, no doubt rightly, that the Castilians would permit the Portuguese, crusade or no crusade, to use Castilian territory in the way suggested.

The two narrative sources for the Tangier campaign are João Alvares's biography of D. Fernando and Rui de Pina's *Crónica de D. Duarte*, the latter generally thought to be based on a version of the affair originally written by Zurara. Both narratives broadly agree in their account of events and both, of course, seek to present the ensuing disaster as favourably to Prince Henry as they can. João Àlvares's status as an eyewitness in D. Fernando's retinue has to be balanced against the fact that his biography of the martyred prince was commissioned by Henry so that, when it deals with the 1437 campaign, it is concerned with laying the groundwork for his hagiographical account of Fernando's subsequent experiences in the hands of the Moroccans.

Given the diminished size of the forces at his disposal, Henry was advised by his subordinate commanders not to attempt to march on Tangier at least until he had received new orders from the king. Henry, according to Pina, rejected this counsel out of hand, saying characteristically that, even if the army were smaller than it was, nothing would deter him from carrying on with the purpose which had brought him to Ceuta. The campaign proper began on 9 September when the Prince ordered most of his troops to begin their march to Tangier. Some 2,000 men under the command of the now ailing D. Fernando, who was unable to ride because of 'a poisoned ulcer' – more probably an attack of piles – were ordered to embark with the fleet and sail along the coast to blockade the port of Tangier pending the arrival of the main army by land. Meanwhile Henry, in Ceuta, did his best to inflame the religious and crusading zeal of the expeditionary force. The day before its departure from that city, all took communion, listened to yet another crusading sermon and received plenary absolution. When it set off on its march on Tangier, the army carried appropriate religious and patriotic impedimenta – a banner showing Christ as a crusader, an image of the Virgin, an image of John I's Holy Constable, Nun'Alvares Pereira, a banner with a representation of John I's own face on it and, for good measure, the portion of the True Cross sent by Eugenius IV specially for the occasion.[22] The evidence suggests that by this stage Henry had been very successful in communicating his own fanatical hatred of Muslims and his certainty of victory to his troops. Otherwise, it is impossible to explain how the Portuguese fought with such tenacity for as long as they did against ever mounting odds. It was more as strategist and tactician, not as a leader of soldiers in the field that Henry was about to fail miserably in the task he had demanded should be his.

His original intention had been to march directly on Tangier across the coastal sierras – hence the road-making works referred to in the contemporary documents already mentioned. The Moroccans, alerted to what was intended, were found to have moved substantial forces into this mountainous area, forcing the Portuguese instead to make a long detour to the south by Tetuan. This took five days to complete, giving ample time to the defenders of Tangier to complete their final preparations. However, not all the signs were unfavourable to the Portuguese. What seems to have been a major skirmish in the mountains west of Ceuta had gone in their favour and the Portuguese army was not seriously opposed on its march from Ceuta to Tangier. Whether this was because the Moroccans did not wish to risk an action in the field or because they hoped to destroy the whole enemy army outside Tangier is not known.

Fresh doubts must have begun to trouble some of the Portuguese leaders when the army finally camped before the city and they realized that their commander had seriously underestimated the strength and spirits of their opponents. Tangier was seen to be a larger city than they had supposed and a strongly garrisoned one. Its walls, contrary to the assurances Henry had given the king, were in good condition. Ample forces of bowmen, some of them from Granada, were to be seen manning the battlements. The Portuguese also found that the defenders had artillery at their disposal for use against the besiegers. It was evident, too, that, exactly as D. Pedro had predicted, the size of the city and the shortage of numbers on the Portuguese side meant that no close investigation of it was going to be possible. The Portuguese army, whose main camp had been set up on the ground between the walls of Tangier and Cape Espartel, would therefore have to try to take the city by assault. A further unwelcome discovery was that the governor of Tangier was none other than Henry's old enemy, Salah ben Salah, the ousted governor of Ceuta when it was captured by the Portuguese in 1415. He could be counted upon to do everything in his power to take his revenge.

Though the narrative sources are contradictory on the point, the Prince appears not to have brought with him from Ceuta artillery in sufficient quantities to allow a major attack on the city to be made before further Moroccan reinforcements arrived. According to Pina's account, six days (from 14 to 20 September) were wasted while more equipment was brought in by sea and unloaded on to the beaches. João Alvares claims that, during this waiting period, three unsuccessful assaults on the city were attempted.

What figures prominently in the narrative accounts of the siege of Tangier and in a number of documents about it is the key role of the wooden stockade or *palanque* set up by the Portuguese to protect the camp they had established to the west of the city. The fencing on its north side was erected not far from the sea but, contrary to Duarte's explicit orders, no protected corridor running from the camp to the beach to give secure access to the fleet anchored offshore had been constructed. The beaches were therefore open ground. This was perhaps Henry's greatest tactical blunder, as events soon revealed. Though it was quite normal for a besieging army to construct a stockade to protect its supplies and baggage against raiders or sallies by the besieged, the provision of a stockade into which all the besiegers could retreat for defensive purposes was out of character with Henry's preference for an entirely aggressive attitude where military operations were concerned. He may well have considered that any protected corridor from the camp to the beaches was not acceptable precisely because it could be seen by his troops as a potential safe line of retreat if things began to go badly for them.

The stockade was clearly a very substantial affair, since it accommodated within its perimeter a tented camp capable of containing the whole Portuguese army of some 7,000 men together with its horses, pack animals and such supplies as had been unloaded from the fleet or brought overland from Ceuta. I presume that the material for the stock-ade must have been prefabricated in Portugal and shipped from Ceuta in sections to Tangier. Duarte's instructions to Henry show that the stockade's role had been decided on as part of the tactical plans for the attack when these were worked out in Portugal.[23]

All the Portuguese assaults on the walls of Tangier failed for reasons that probably had nothing to do with the courage of the attackers but all to do with the lack of proper equipment for the task in hand, a defi-ciency caused by an obvious failure to secure full information about Tangier's fortifications before the campaign. Thus it was soon discov-ered that the scaling ladders brought from Ceuta were not only too few in number: no one had taken the trouble to make sure that they were long enough to reach the top of the city's walls. They turned out not to be, so more time was then wasted while ladders of the right length were procured. It was also discovered that the cannon the Portuguese had with them were only capable of firing balls whose weight was too light to do effective damage to the walls of the city. Attempts had to be made to bring heavier artillery from Ceuta. Documents explain, too, that cannon balls and gunpowder were found to be in short supply. These, again, had to be fetched from Ceuta by sea.[24] This succession of slip-ups cannot have helped the morale of the Portuguese troops or served to further their regard for their fire-eating general's abilities as a military planner.

The king, according to Pina, had issued firm orders to Henry that no more than three major assaults on the city were to be attempted, and that no more than, one week in all was to be spent on these operations. If victory had not been achieved by then, the army and fleet were to return to Ceuta and winter there until Duarte made new arrangements for another offensive in the spring.[25] The reason for imposing a tight time limit on operations in September was obvious. The capture of the city must either be achieved quickly or abandoned before the Moroccans had time to bring up the further massive rein-forcements they had started to raise when news of the enemy landing reached Fez. Also, the Portuguese had learnt from the Ceuta experi-ence in 1415 that autumn was a risky time for campaigning in the Straits of Gibraltar. The king's belief that it should be possible for the Portuguese to take a city of the strength and size of Tangier within a week was plainly quite unrealistic. Memories of the lightning victory at Ceuta, secured in very different circumstances, seem to have made it difficult for Henry or the king to understand what they were up against this time.

The Prince ignored Duarte's instructions to withdraw to Ceuta if Tangier had not fallen after a week's siege. The strategy of *reculer pour mieux sauter* was one entirely alien to Henry's temperament when he was functioning in crusading mode. The Portuguese army in fact was to remain outside the city's walls for about five weeks.

Henry's assurances in his paper to the king that political discord in Morocco guaranteed that the Moroccans would only be able to put up a weak resistance now came home to mock him. As enemy reinforcements arrived from the interior of the sultanate in large numbers – though not, of course, on the epic scale suggested by the chroniclers, or as reported by the king to the pope – the Portuguese, exactly as the future regent had predicted, gradually found their role had changed. Instead of themselves being the besiegers they became virtually besieged within their stockade by the Moroccans. After the failure of his initial assaults on the city, Henry seems to have had no plan at all beyond a grim determination to remain *in situ* until God did what was expected of him and came to the aid of the Portuguese army. One can only guess at his state of mind as it became plain that the much trumpeted crusade which he had insisted on organizing and commanding was dissolving into humiliating failure before his eyes. No reinforcements could be expected from Portugal. Retreat by land to Ceuta was not an option. The only possible escape was by a withdrawal to the beaches and from there by boat to the ships lying off shore. One thousand knights and squires, with their retinues, had, according to Pina, already taken this way out even before the whole army had been ordered to withdraw to the dubious safety provided by the stockade. Zurara, in a passage in his *Chronicle of Guinea*, notes that members of the Prince's personal household were among those who abandoned him at that time.[26]

Towards the end of September, still more enemy reinforcements arrived under the personal command of the Moroccan commander-in-chief, Abu Zakariya (the 'Lazeraque' of the Portuguese chroniclers). This would have been the moment for the remaining Portuguese to attempt a fighting withdrawal to the fleet anchored off shore, even though Henry's failure to carry out Duarte I's orders to include a section of beach within the perimeter of the stockade had made such a withdrawal difficult. As the king was to point out to the Cortes of Leiria a few months later, a protected withdrawal would have been possible if Henry had constructed the stockade in the form he had been ordered to do.[27]

A letter apparently written from the Portuguese camp on 4 October by a member of the vanguard under the count of Arraiolos survives and appears to be genuine. It suggests that, despite all these ill omens, at least the vanguard of the Portuguese army under the direct command of the count was still in good heart and able to act offensively. The anonymous letter writer describes two attacks mounted by the Moroccans in the first days of that month.[28] These, according to him, were serious clashes outside the stockade with both sides in battle order. The Portuguese considered that, particularly on 3 October, they had indubitably won a victory over forces commanded by the Moroccan general, Abu Zakariya, himself. The letter writer no doubt exaggerated these successes so as to counter the stories of disaster already circulating in Portugal. One may certainly view with some scepticism his report that the morale of the Portuguese troops received a considerable lift when a cross 'as white as crystal' appeared in the sky over Tangier, causing all those within the stockade at this time to remain on their knees in prayer until the phenomenon disappeared. It was, of course, taken to be a sign from Heaven that, despite appearances, all was not lost and the city was still destined to fall to the Christians.[29] The letter, however, unwittingly confirms the dire straits of Henry's army early in October. Its statement that 3,000 Portuguese troops took to their knees when the cross appeared in the skies implies that as many as 4,000 members of the force of 7,000 men which had originally appeared before the city some weeks before had by then disappeared. Since very few Portuguese were killed in action or taken prisoner at Tangier, it has to be inferred that, as Pina suggests, they had already slipped away to the ships or set out without orders for the shelter of Ceuta.

Despite the anonymous letter-writer's brave words, it must have been obvious to Henry and to his subordinate commanders even before the end of September that, heavenly signs or not, there was not the remotest chance of Tangier falling to the Prince and every chance that the Portuguese army might be destroyed by the Moroccans. Now it was a question of securing terms which would allow the invaders to depart with some dignity. They had only one possible card to play, and that was to offer to surrender Ceuta. According to João Alvares, envoys had already been sent to the Moroccan lines before the end of September to hint that if the Portuguese were allowed to withdraw freely and with honour to their fleet, Ceuta could be returned to Morocco. It is not known whether Prince Henry agreed or pretended to agree with this proposition from the start or whether he was forced to accept it by pressure from his commanders. Either way, now began the darkest days he was ever to experience. It was not just the humiliation he had to suffer as the commander of an army he had led to defeat. The offer to surrender Ceuta represented for him a potential moral defeat of crisis proportions. Had he not been made by John I responsible for Ceuta's defence, and was it not he who had made the occupation of that city by the Portuguese a symbol of a new age in Portugal's history? It was also the place where he had won his spurs and defined himself as a dedicated if somewhat anachronistic successor to other famous Iberian crusaders for the Faith.

Moroccan opinion about what to do was divided. Many held the view that, in revenge for the capture of Ceuta, what remained of the Portuguese army should be annihilated. But that would mean that Ceuta would continue in the hands of the Christians who had shown themselves well able to hold on to it. In the end, therefore, the Moroccans agreed to let the Portuguese depart in exchange for Ceuta's return to them. The capitulation to which Prince Henry put his hand on 17 October was unambiguous.[30] It read,

> For the sake of peace and concord I give my undertaking to you, Salah ben Salah, that I shall hand over to you the city of Ceuta, together with all captive Moors who may be held there or those who are there as hostages for other captives; also those who are held aboard the fleet or in the camp here. To guarantee that these things will be done I shall give you [as a hostage] the Prince D. Fernando, my brother.[31]

Among the humiliations the capitulation imposed on the Portuguese was one that must have been keenly felt by Henry. The authority to conduct these negotiations on the Moroccan side had been wholly vested in the commander of the Tangier garrison, his old enemy Salah ben Salah.

Shocked and humiliated as he was, Henry was enough in command of himself to make sure that no one could say that he alone was responsible for the capitulation. He insisted that it should begin with a declaration that, in addition to himself, it was drawn up with the accord and consent of his brother, the Infante D. Fernando, as well as that of the constable of the army (the count of Arraiolos) together with the marshal (Vasco Fernandes Coutinho), the bishop of Évora (as papal delegate to the crusade) and eight other named captains. The document also concluded with a statement that the Portuguese king himself had given his consent to the capitulation. This latter statement was certainly untrue. Judging by its placement at the end of the document, it was probably included as an afterthought lest Salah ben Salah should – as well he might – start asking questions about Henry's right to agree to the surrender of a possession of the Portuguese crown.

The additional terms of the capitulation were designed to add to the Prince's humiliation. Though the personal liberty of the surviving Portuguese troops was assured, 'all the animals and arms and everything else that is in the camp' were to be left behind, the Portuguese taking nothing with them except the clothing they were wearing. The only concession won by Henry was that his men should be allowed to retain their weapons until the moment of embarkation aboard the boats lying off the beaches. As a sign of his own good faith, Salah ben Salah agreed that his son would be handed over as a hostage and kept aboard one of the Portuguese ships until all the Portuguese were safely embarked. Most astonishing of all the undertakings, however, was Henry's agreement that a royal prince should be handed over to the Moroccans as a hostage until Ceuta had been surrendered to them as the capitulation stipulated.

Further undertakings followed. The Portuguese promised to surrender Ceuta exactly as it then stood; no demolitions of its fortifications were permitted. The Tangier capitulation was, however, not just concerned with military matters. The Moroccans aimed to put an end for good to Portuguese expansionist ideas in North Africa. Henry promised to use his influence with the Portuguese king to make him conclude a treaty of peace for a hundred years with 'all the Moors of the coast of Barbary' and to guarantee them freedom of trade by land and sea.

So ended, at any rate as far as combat operations were concerned, the unpopular crusade against the sultanate of Morocco which the Prince had used his political power to force the crown to agree to. He had not only planned it. He had insisted on commanding it in the belief that it would confirm his destiny as a great conqueror. Instead he had conspicuously failed both as a planner of military operations and as a commander in the field. How, too, would he be able to explain to his fellow countrymen that he had escaped from the beaches of Tangier with what remained of the Portuguese army at the price of leaving his younger brother in the hands of Salah ben Salah as a guarantor that Ceuta would be handed over? Rui de Pina claims that Henry himself had wanted to be the hostage and had intended, once in that situation, to sacrifice himself rather than to allow the surrender of the city. According to the chronicler, the royal council forbade Henry to do this.

The claim does not carry conviction. There had certainly been no time for the council to intervene at all in the negotiations leading up to the capitulation. A question that cannot be answered is whether Henry, when he agreed to the terms of this document, was at that point genuinely ready to see Ceuta returned to the Moroccans. Or did he, from the start, intend to break his undertaking? The question is of some importance since, were the latter to be the case, Henry would have to be convicted of having planned, even while the two princes were still in camp together, to betray his younger brother should needs be in order to save Ceuta. While Fernando's hagiographers and Henry himself would always assert that the Infante was a willing hostage, it is far from certain that this was so. Fernando certainly believed when the capitulation was signed that the return of Ceuta to the Moroccans was agreed policy and that his time as a hostage would be short. Salah ben Salah must have taken the same view, for he allowed Fernando to bring with him into captivity his secretary and future biographer, Frei João Alvares, as well as the head of his household, his confessor, his doctor, the keeper of his wardrobe, his head cook and his longtime confidant, João Rodrigues, probably his chamberlain. The whole party was taken to the port of Asilah, about thirty miles down the coast. While there, Fernando was allowed to send letters to Portugal as well as to receive them, and to establish personal and financial relations with the Genoese and with the Iberian merchants established in the Moroccan port. His troubles would begin later.

Henry, before departing by sea for Ceuta, made no attempt to get any message of reassurance to his brother, a fact which disturbed the latter. According to João Alvares, Henry's silence even led Fernando to fear that he must have been killed during the fighting that took place during the final stage of the Portuguese embarkations. Salah ben Salah obligingly had the corpses of the Portuguese killed at that time examined. He informed the captive prince, perhaps not without irony, that no body of any person of quality had been found among them.[32] Henry's failure to reassure Fernando was probably the first hint to reach the royal hostage that things might not be going the way he had been promised.

The evacuation probably began on the day after the capitulation. The Portuguese chroniclers make much of the fact that, confronted with the sight of the Christian troops embarking scot free, Salah ben Salah found it impossible to stop some of the Moroccans attacking them as they were boarding the boats from the beach. They do, though, admit that some of the fighting there was between the Portuguese troops themselves after discipline broke down and many struggled to get aboard ship any way they could. Henry would afterwards claim that the minor Moroccan attacks on the embarking Portuguese were so serious a breach of the capitulation that they released him from all his own undertakings. Writing to D. Gomes about the Portuguese embarkation in March 1438, the king thus declared with evident satisfaction that, because the Moroccans had not respected the capitulation, the troops had brought away with them not only all the church paraphernalia that accompanied the army but also their arms and everything else readily transportable. Only horses, tents and some cannon had, he said, been left behind.[33] Portuguese casualties, at least among the knights and squires, do seem to have been remarkably light. Taking all these reports at their face value, the king now began to suggest to the curia that the defeat at Tangier had at least some of the characteristics of a victory. Few in Portugal can have been taken in by this, least of all Duarte I himself.

The count of Arraiolos and most of the other captains of the defeated army sailed directly back to Portugal from Tangier. Henry was not among them. He should, of course, as the expedition's commander, also have returned immediately to report to the king. Unsurprisingly, he could not face the brother whose instructions he had disobeyed with such disastrous consequences, or the mockery of those councillors and others who had opposed the whole project from the start. Using the dubious excuse that he must remain in Morocco to see to the release of Fernando, Henry took to his bed on his arrival in Ceuta and remained there for some weeks, putting it about that he was worn out by his crusading exertions. The recently appointed governor of the fortress, Fernando de Noronha, was, perhaps, none too pleased to have to receive as an honoured guest a man who had just promised to see that his governorship would be speedily terminated by the surrender of the place to the Moors. Henry remained in seclusion in Ceuta for several months. No first-hand information exists to supply any insights into his state of mind after what was now referred to euphemistically in Portugal as 'the misfortune at Tangier'.[34] It is, however, plain from his behaviour that during his months in Ceuta, he went through, as well he might, a serious spiritual crisis during which he perhaps fell into one of those periods of apathy towards the affairs of the world which Zurara implies sometimes overcame this normally hyperactive and apparently self-confident man.[35] Certainly there was much to discompose a man as concerned as Henry was with his posthumous fame. However, any of his rivals at court who thought that the catastrophe

at Tangier had mortally wounded his influence at court or the bur-
geoning of his multifaceted career would learn before long how wrong
they were. It is not even certain that the length of his self-imposed
absence in Ceuta was entirely due to the traumatic experiences he had
undergone outside Tangier. Not only did his stay there enable him to
present himself as overwhelmingly concerned with his brother's rescue,
but he may well have calculated that, as long as he was absent from
the kingdom, it would be very difficult for any moves to surrender
Ceuta to be set in train. It is also likely that the length of his stay in
the city with all the first-hand memories of 1415 and 1419 it brought
back served to reinforce his determination that, come what might, it
should never be returned to the Moroccans.

Duarte I was appalled by the disaster that had overtaken Henry's
army. While Henry was supposedly prostrated with grief and guilt in
Ceuta and Fernando was under house arrest in Asilah, the Portuguese
king, when the news of the disaster first reached him, had needed the
immediate aid of his doctors and the spiritual support of holy men to
see him through the personal crisis that now afflicted him.[36] He was,
indeed, destined never to recover his health again. Duarte had every
reason to feel distraught. It was he who, ignoring the warnings of some
of his most experienced councillors and against his own better judgement, had allowed himself to be swept off his feet by the religious
zealotry, the single-minded importunities and the tempting promises of
a great victory made by his younger brother. Now he was certain to go
down in history as a king who had proved a quite unworthy son of his
hero father and of his English ancestors. Now, too, he was faced by a
dire choice: to become the sovereign who handed back Ceuta to the
Moroccans or to be the ruler who broke a contract solemnly if illegally
concluded in his name by Henry, knowing that the latter course risked
abandoning his youngest brother to a miserable fate. It must have
looked to him as if the warnings of his astrologer, Mestre Guedelha,
about the ill-omened hour he had chosen for his proclamation as king
were proving to be fully justified.

Duarte undoubtedly possessed the right, under the royal prerogative,
to surrender Ceuta if he so decided. But this was a decision he was not
willing to take on his own responsibility. It soon became plain that the
royal council was divided on the question and was unable to give him
a firm lead. As the weeks passed without anything being done, news
started to come from Ceuta that Henry, now beginning to arouse
himself, was starting to put it about, as we have seen, that, as his men
had been attacked by the Moroccans when they were embarking, the

entire capitulation agreement had thereupon become void. The fact that
they were attacked because, in contravention of the terms of the capitulation, the Portuguese were attempting to carry off not only arms but
various other forbidden impedimenta was of course not mentioned.
Henry's only practical suggestion at this time was that Salah ben Salah's
son – who seems still to have been held illegally as a hostage by the
Portuguese after their embarkation was complete – should be sent back
to his father in exchange for the release of D. Fernando. In this simple
way, said Henry, the whole unhappy problem would be solved. The
utter ingenuousness of this proposition was, however, exposed by the
arrival of letters sent by the captive Fernando from Asilah to the king.
These complained of his steadily increasing sufferings at the hands of
his captors as the weeks passed without any action being taken to hand
over Ceuta. He still nevertheless affirmed his complete confidence that
his brother would, as he had solemnly promised, see to it that the city
was returned to the Moroccans. He also informed D. Duarte of the
absolute determination of the Moroccans not to release him unless
and until that had taken place.[37] Any suggestions for some alternative
arrangement would, he declared, be rejected out of hand by them.
Henry's assertion that the Moroccans had broken the capitulation
by attacking the embarking Portuguese was, Fernando wrote, quite
untrue.

The king decided to pass the buck on to the Portuguese Cortes, which
were summoned to meet towards the end of January 1438 to advise
him. Henry refused to obey the summons to him to attend and
remained in Ceuta rebuilding his shaken confidence that his destiny
was to be a military conqueror as the stars had predicted. A failure to
respond to a royal summons to attend the Cortes was a serious matter,
all the more so since the gathering had been called specially to discuss
what to do about the situation in which the Henry had placed the
king.

Two sources contain information about what happened at the
Cortes of Leiria. One is Rui de Pina, who claims to have followed
a contemporary documentary source – probably the official record
of the proceedings there.[38] The other is an account contained in a
newsletter from Oporto dated 25 February and sent to D. Gomes in
Florence.[39]

The opening address made to the Cortes on the king's behalf did not
hesitate to tell those present that, had Henry followed the instructions
for the campaign that Duarte had given him, the disaster would
not have occurred. He also criticized the Prince for having agreed to

surrender part of the crown's dominions without even consulting him. That the king felt able to blame his most powerful subject so openly in order to clear his own name is a measure of Duarte's anger at the situation in which Henry had placed the crown.

In its reply to the king's request for advice, the Cortes proved to be as divided as the royal council. D. Pedro, to no one's surprise, voted in favour of surrendering Ceuta. He had been against its continuing occupation by the Portuguese for more than twenty years. His brother, D. João, also voted for surrender.[40] The writer of the newsletter declared that most of the prelates were also in favour of carrying out the terms of the capitulation, as were most of the representatives of the municipalities. They were doubtless delighted that an excuse had arisen for the crown to divest itself of the financially burdensome Moroccan fortress. The newsletter, however, states that Lisbon and Oporto and some of the Algarve municipalities had voted against surrender, asserting it as their view that territory that formed part of the royal patrimony should not be given away simply to secure the liberty of a single prince, however worthy. The cynically minded no doubt noted that the places taking this line were among the very few in the kingdom that derived economic benefit from the business of keeping Ceuta supplied with its many wants.

The chief spokesman for the policy of no surrender was the count of Arraiolos who had by now entirely abandoned the vigorous opposition to Henry's policy in Morocco which he had expressed in 1432, and who had also apparently contrived to forget that he was a signatory to the capitulation at Tangier. Why he had changed sides we do not know. Now, speaking as constable of the Portuguese army during the recent campaign, the count rejected the captive prince's criticism of Portuguese behaviour after the capitulation and went on to join those who asserted that a subject could not, without the express authority of his king, promise to hand over part of the royal patrimony. Arraiolos thus unwittingly admitted that the clause in the capitulation claiming that Duarte had agreed to the surrender of Ceuta was fraudulent. To explain away the fact that he himself was a signatory to the capitulation he claimed that it was legitimate, in cases of *force majeure*, for knights, in order to save their lives, to make promises to an enemy which they had no intention of keeping. While such a claim hardly accorded with the laws of chivalry, there was ample authority for it in canon law. Indeed it was precisely for that reason that hostages were routinely taken to ensure that agreements even between Christians were carried out.

Many of the magnates present at the Cortes supported Arraiolos's views. Confronted by such divided opinions, the king agonized for a time but eventually decided in favour of refusing to surrender Ceuta for the time being; a policy supported, he claimed, by the most powerful lords in the land. Instead he would try to secure Fernando's liberty by means of exchange, ransom or diplomacy. All this was, of course, decided in Henry's absence, though, as we have seen, he had let it be known that he, too, favoured jettisoning the agreement with the Moroccans of which he was the principal signatory.

It had now become essential for Duarte to discuss the position face-to-face with the Prince whose prolonged absence from the court was becoming an embarrassment. Henry, soon after the closure of the Cortes, at last agreed to leave Ceuta for the Algarve. Once there, however, he refused to travel further north than Portel (half-way between Beja and Évora) to meet the king.[41] Pina puts the meeting between the two brothers as late as June 1438 (some eight months after the withdrawal of the Portuguese from Tangier). The chronicler says that Henry eventually presented himself in Portel wearing mourning clothes. From there he asked to be excused from joining the court, giving as his reason that he felt unable to appear there again until he could do so with D. Fernando by his side. This was of course mere play-acting for public consumption. Henry, the least sentimental of men, had better reasons than pretended concern for D. Fernando for avoiding an appearance at court.

The king now decided that he would travel from Évora to Portel to meet his brother. This reversal of protocol served to show that, despite all that had happened, Henry was still the most important magnate in the kingdom and could still make D. Duarte dance to his tune when he wanted to. We know little about the meeting except that it did nothing to resolve the king's problems, for it emerged there that Henry seemed to have learnt nothing from what had happened to him a year before. He told D. Duarte that he fully approved of the decision not to surrender Ceuta and tried to convince him that the disaster had not really been so bad as people thought. It was agreed that an attempt should be made to secure D. Fernando's freedom by offering to pay a large ransom for him and to release a large number of Moorish captives held, not just in Portugal but in the neighbouring Hispanic kingdoms. Just how Duarte's fellow monarchs were to be persuaded in this way to pick up part of the tab for Henry's incompetence as the leader of a campaign they disapproved of was not gone in to. It was also planned to call on Europe's rulers generally to put diplomatic pressure on the Moroccans to release the Infante.[42] It is not to be supposed that Henry seriously expected these suggestions to be taken seriously. If we are to credit Pina, he now, however, also proposed an alternative solution to the problem of Fernando's release. This once again confirmed that, whenever the Prince switched himself into his crusading mode, common sense no longer ruled his thinking. What he suggested was more of the strategy that had just so spectacularly failed. A new crusade in Morocco, he declared, was the obvious way out should Fernando's captors refuse to ransom him. An army of 24,000 men, he estimated, ought to suffice to crush any Moroccan army that could take the field. Admittedly it might be a problem for Duarte to raise that number of troops in Portugal, but his Christian allies and neighbours would doubtless be ready to respond to his call for military support.[43] Henry, as was his wont, predicted certain victory if his project was adopted and he was in charge of carrying it out. How a new invasion of the sultanate would secure Fernando's release, he did not explain. It seems likely that he had already written off his brother and that his proposal that he should take a new army to Morocco allegedly to force the Infante's release was no more than a ruse to give him a new chance to go crusading in the sultanate. We should not be surprised that Henry emerged from his dark night of the soul with his obsession about crusading in Morocco intact. Deeply rooted in his religious instincts and in his sense of his historical destiny, it had become a core part of his personality.

An unsought martyrdom had begun to look more and more like a probable ending for D. Fernando. In May the Moroccan Regent had issued orders that the Portuguese prince should be moved from relatively comfortable confinement in Asilah to a prison in the capital city of Fez. Here, Abu Zakariya himself took charge of matters, declaring that he did so because, after more than six months since the signing of the capitulation, and despite continuous attempts at negotiation, the Portuguese had still not taken any steps to hand over Ceuta. João Álvares's record of Fernando's life as a hostage in Fez shows that the Portuguese court had not yet totally abandoned him to his fate. By a series of letters and verbal messages, they attempted to keep negotiations going and the Infante's spirits up while actually doing nothing towards implementing the principal undertaking in the capitulation. Abu Zakariya now rapidly lost patience and increasingly subjected the Portuguese prince to more and more humiliating treatment in his new prison. João Álvares, who was still there with him, describes his sufferings at very considerable length, no doubt in the process making the worst of what was undoubtedly a bad job.

This was the state of matters when, in late August 1438, the Portuguese king fell seriously ill and died at the age of forty-seven. His death was almost certainly the result of pestilence, but the temptation to assert that he died of grief and guilt proved too much for many of those around him, among them Henry's enemies. Pina sententiously concluded that his end showed what was liable to happen when a ruler ignored the advice of those most competent to give it. Henry and his apologists, once Duarte was out of the way, unscrupulously put it about that, as was technically true, the Tangier expedition had been undertaken by order of the late king and that therefore the real responsibility for the disaster was his, not theirs – an attempt to shift the blame that can have convinced few.

Duarte left a six-year-old heir, Afonso V, and, in his will, nominated his much disliked Aragonese queen to be regent of Portugal during Afonso's minority. The kingdom was at once plunged into political crisis. Very conveniently from Henry's point of view, the problems caused by the disaster at Tangier had, perforce, to be set aside. When the news of Duarte's death reached Fernando in his prison in Fez he is said, rightly, to have feared that his chances of ever securing release had now been much reduced. As for Henry, he at once saw that the regency crisis gave him his chance to rehabilitate his political fortunes. He now offered himself as peacemaker between the rival factions at court – between those who thought that Duarte's will should be respected and those who found unacceptable an arrangement that, apart from marginalizing the surviving legitimate sons of John I, would put the government of the country in the hands of an Aragonese queen with openly pro-Castilian interests. In December 1439, after various compromises suggested by Henry came to nothing and the kingdom was close to civil war, D. Pedro, as John I's eldest surviving son, was elected by the Cortes of Lisbon as sole regent for the period of Afonso's minority. Henry accepted the decision of the Cortes. He had no cause to like an elder brother who had always opposed Portugal's involvement in North Africa and was an effective critic of some of the other causes to which he had dedicated himself. A few years later he would abandon Pedro to his fate as coldly and with as much calculation as he was now abandoning Fernando. For the moment, however, he recognized that he needed to be on good terms with the man who now ruled the kingdom. There was a formal reconciliation between the two brothers, after which they established for some years an effective working relationship. It is possible that Henry's price for supporting Pedro in this crisis was a promise by the latter to give him a free hand in the African Atlantic and in the Canaries.

What of D. Fernando in his prison in Fez? Duarte's will had stipulated that, if all attempts at ransom failed, then Ceuta should be surrendered to secure his brother's freedom. By now, however, it was generally accepted that such a surrender was unacceptable. Henry now did not hesitate to resort to deceit and hypocrisy to silence his critics. He spread the word that Fernando, in order to keep Ceuta both Christian and Portuguese, had declared himself willing and ready to accept martyrdom for the Faith in Fez. Henry knew quite well that the truth was very different. A series of letters sent by the unhappy prince from his Moroccan gaol pleading that Ceuta should be surrendered to secure his release notably fail to suggest that he then had any taste for a martyr's death. One such letter survives. It was written in the summer of 1441, not to Henry but to the regent.[44] In it Fernando complains that the Genoese and Majorcan merchants located in the sultanate whose loans had been keeping him from starvation had not been paid what was owed them. He feared that unless their bills were soon paid, they might soon conclude that the Portuguese court, as he put it, 'is now very little concerned about my sufferings' and therefore would cease to finance him. Fernando's letter does indeed declare that he would prefer death 'to going on suffering the continuous tribulations and frequent new forms of misery which we are enduring here and which every hour of the day we expect to be visited on us . . .' But these were not the words of a man anxious to become a Christian martyr. The distressing picture they painted was clearly intended to arouse the regent's pity. So far from looking forward to death, Fernando's letter went on to show that, as late as 1441, he still hoped that the regent would authorize the long-delayed surrender of Ceuta and so secure his release. It is noticeable that the unfortunate royal captive's letter never once mentions Prince Henry, his one-time protector and recent companion-at-arms to whom he had been so close – an omission which suggests that he knew for sure by this time that Henry had betrayed him.

The spectacle of Henry actively promoting a policy likely to lead to the execution or death in a Moorish prison of a brother for whose presence there he was wholly responsible was, even by the accommodating standards of fifteenth-century *Realpolitik*, difficult to explain away. Zurara's brief references to the matter in the *Chronicle of Guinea* reveal his embarrassment at his inability to find anything uplifting to say about Henry and Tangier.[45]

After Fernando's miserable death in prison in Fez, Henry took steps to see that the story of his brother's supposed martyrdom was properly recorded in writing. He commissioned João Alvares – the Infante's secretary and companion in prison – to write an account of his brother's sufferings and death. This work, the *Trautado da vida e feitos do muito vertuoso Senhor Ifante D. Fernando*, became a well-known work of Christian hagiography in the early modern period. It was the source, in the seventeenth century, of one of Calderón's best-known martyr plays, *El príncipe constante*.

Seen from today's perspective, nothing connected with the Tangier disaster stands to Henry's credit. His strategy was founded on arrogance and wishful thinking buoyed up by expectation that divine intervention would make up for the deficiencies of men and material from which the Portuguese suffered. This hope, with which Christian crusaders through the ages were accustomed to dupe themselves, proved as illusory on this occasion as on many others. Exactly what motivated Henry when he signed the capitulation with Salah ben Salah cannot now be determined. The possibility certainly cannot be ruled out that he simply did so out of despair, fearing that, if he did not give the Moroccans everything they demanded, the destruction of what remained of the Portuguese army would follow and he would be blamed for permitting that. Or he may have put his name to the capitulation having already made up his mind that in no circumstances would he allow his promise to surrender Ceuta to be honoured, despite the probable consequences for his brother. The one thing that is clear is that, at this critical time in his career, Henry failed to behave like the model Christian paladin he had set himself up to be. Devoted readers of the chivalry books then popular at the Portuguese court would certainly have found Henry's actions after Tangier falling well short of knightly *courtoisie* as practised at the court of king Arthur. Nevertheless, given the religious and cultural climate in which the nobles of fifteenth-century Portugal lived, it was inevitable that many of Henry's peers, while hard put to excuse his defeat, reckoned his subsequent behaviour worthy of praise, not criticism. By remaining in close seclusion in Ceuta he had, for some, shown a proper sense of the guilt and shame the leader of the failed crusade ought to feel. Paradoxically, the disaster also weakened the opposition to Henry's expansionist policies in Morocco. Many evidently now agreed with him that to return a Christian city to the infidel in order to save the life of a single prince would be a wholly unacceptable act. Others even seem to have been persuaded that, especially on account of his rank, the unfortunate Fernando should glory in the opportunity to suffer the Christian martyrdom which his brother now planned for him. Especially after his death in 1443 and the ignominies to which his body was then subjected in Fez, the desire for revenge when the time was ripe helped to prevent any cool appraisal of Portugal's crusading stance in Morocco. Thus it was that the damage to Henry's reputation and to his political power from the Tangier disaster proved to be much less enduring than might have been expected. The constitutional crisis which arose after Duarte I's unexpected death effectively diverted attention away from that defeat and from the problem presented by Fernando's captivity. It was soon found, too, that Henry's political authority and his influence both with the queen and with his brothers was needed in the search to find a solution to the crisis. He took full advantage of the opportunity this gave him to recover lost ground. He had also seen to it that his nephew the boy king Afonso V was thoroughly indoctrinated with the belief that it was Portugal's historical mission to reconquer Visigothic Tingitana for Christianity.

Chapter Eight

Discovery Resumed: The Portuguese Sahara

There are many events in the womb of time which will be delivered.

William Shakespeare, *Othello*, Act 1 Scene 3

In 1441, with the Tangier disaster conveniently pushed into the background by the political turmoil preceding the regency of D. Pedro and D. Fernando abandoned to await death in a Moroccan prison, the Prince once again set about giving his attention to uncovering the world's secrets hitherto hidden from men, as predicted in his horoscope. The exploration of the Saharan coast and its hinterland was accordingly taken up again under his auspices at the point where it had been suspended several years before. Some of his captains were assigned to return to the Río de Oro to trade and to take prisoners who were to be brought back to Portugal for interrogation. Others were given the duty of exploring the coast beyond Punta Galha, the furthermost point reached by Henry's men in the previous decade. Journeying further south and keeping within sight of the surf that continuously broke on the desert shores, the explorers soon found Cape Blanco (20° 46′ N) and, having rounded it, reconnoitred and charted the great bay it enclosed. This they named Angra de Santa Maria.[1] Its discoverer, Diogo Afonso, erected on the cape a tall wooden cross to inform others who passed that way afterwards that he and his men were the first European discoverers of the cape. The setting up of such wooden crosses on important coastal landmarks was a practice regularly followed by the discoverers in the Henrican period and afterwards. They did not simply record the first discovery of the region concerned. The cross signalled a claim that it had been recovered for Christianity by the Prince's efforts. Zurara comments that the cross erected on Cape Blanco in 1441 was reported still to be entirely intact at the time he wrote this chapter of his chronicle.[2] In the time of John II, for durability's sake, the wooden crosses of Henry's time were superseded by the famous and much more elaborate stone crosses or *padrões* prefabricated in Lisbon.

As was the case with the first phase of the discoveries, no personal records exist to tell us what these early explorers thought of their task or how they responded to the new sights and people they encountered on the coasts of the Sahara or of Guinea proper. Their leaders had some idea of what to expect from the briefings of the Prince and the charts and other information he supplied to them. The squires of his household who, until 1448, had orders to make war on the coastal inhabitants of Mauritania and Senegal no doubt tended to see the people and their culture simply as manifestations of Islam or paganism which it was their duty as Christian crusaders to destroy or subdue. It was not a frame of mind likely to encourage curiosity. What the ordinary Portuguese sailors thought of the new world they were helping to uncover or how willingly they took part in this work we have no means of knowing. They seem to have behaved bravely enough both when armed encounters were the rule and when the perils of the seas overtook them. No doubt the lure of gold was also an important factor when it came to finding crews.

Proceeding on their way south, the explorers found that the configuration of the coast and the aspect of the sea offshore beyond Cape Blanco changed markedly. They now found themselves in a region of strong tidal streams, shoals, sand banks and offshore islands that stretched south for more than seventy miles, making inshore navigation hazardous. Some of the islands showed signs of human habitation.

Despite the navigational problems the region offered safe if shallow anchorages and easy access to the Saharan mainland. The area, now part of the Islamic Republic of Mauritania, has been known to European navigators since the fifteenth century as the Arguin Bank after the name finally given by the Portuguese to one of the principal islands lying just off the coast at the northern end of the bank – Arguin Island.[3] The first discoverers found the island to be quite densely populated by Idzagen (Sanhadja) fishermen. When they landed, they soon discovered why: a perennial spring of excellent fresh water flowed from the greenstone in the north-east corner of the island. There were also a number of other points where springs of more saline water were to be found. Such a discovery, on this thirsty Saharan coast where wells were scanty and, above all, difficult for the invaders to discover, meant that one of the gravest problems facing the Prince's caravels when they attempted to push further south was solved. It was also a great piece of good fortune for the Portuguese that water should have been found on an island, about three miles long at its greatest length, which lay nearly two miles off-shore at its nearest point to the potentially hostile mainland. It was also unique among the other islands on the Arguin Bank because, towards its northern, land side, it rose steeply to an elevation of 25 feet. From here, it commanded the strait between it and the mainland. Here, too, the Portuguese, accustomed to depend largely on a diet of fish while at sea, could replenish their supplies with the greatest ease, and dry their catches on shore in complete security. Arguin offered a relief from a fish diet as well. The spawning fish in the shallows of the Arguin Bank attracted large numbers of birds such as pelicans, flamingos and the like to Arguin and its vicinity. These supplied eggs as well as fresh meat. The presence of this wildlife was to prove important later on, when Arguin Island became one of the centres in West Africa where slaves were held for shipment to Portugal and the Portuguese had to try to feed them as cheaply as possible until the slave ships arrived. Arguin was destined to play a significant role in the early history of Portugal's maritime expansion.[4]

Soon after exploration recommenced, Henry set about obtaining legal or quasi-legal cover to justify the presence of his own ships and men in the region and to make sure that no one else ventured there without his authority. Two papal instruments were issued at his request with this in mind. The bull *Illius qui se pro divini* of Eugenius IV dated December 1442 did not, on the face of it, have anything special to do with exploration in the African Atlantic. It granted plenary indulgence to the knights and friars of the Order of Christ and to all other

Christians who, led by Henry, might go crusading against the Saracens under the banners of the Order. Significantly, however, a further clause provided that the indulgence would be valid even if the Prince did not participate personally in any such crusade.[5] Despite its general scope, the relevance of this bull to the renewal of Henrican-sponsored exploration was recognized by Zurara (or, more probably, by Afonso Cerveira). The chronicler, casting aside for once his declared reluctance to reproduce the text of archival documents in the *Chronicle of Guinea*, included a partial transcript of the bull in his account of the renewal of exploration along the Saharan coast.[6] He clearly saw the document as having served to establish the point that, as far as the curia was concerned, the operations of the Prince's men in that region represented, in a new location, a continuation of Henry's crusade against Islam. As we have seen, the notion of moving European crusading endeavours to the African Atlantic was not an entirely novel one. Crusading had already been proclaimed by the French would-be colonizers of the Canaries at the beginning of the century as the motive which impelled them into those waters.

In October 1443 Henry secured from the regent the all-important letters patent already referred to in previous chapters. This, it will be recalled, granted him a personal monopoly over all navigation south of Cape Bojador, whether for the purpose of making war or simply to trade. Any vessel not travelling beyond the Cape under the direct orders of the Prince or with a licence issued by him would from now on be confiscated with all its cargo and become Henry's property. To help to reimburse the Prince for the great expenses he had incurred and expected to incur in future on the work of exploration, the crown also surrendered to him the customary royal fifth and tenth nominally due to it on anything imported from the newly discovered regions south of Bojador. Given that the search for gold was at this time the main practical motive behind the Henrican voyages, such a casual surrender of potential future crown revenues is difficult to explain. Perhaps, as already suggested, it was part of a bargain between the regent and Henry. Or perhaps D. Pedro was one of those who doubted in 1443 whether anything worthwhile would emerge from his brother's Atlantic enterprise and therefore believed this surrender likely to prove a dead letter.

The document included some statistics supplied by Henry. Up to the date of the issue of the letters patent he claimed that he had sent ships on fifteen occasions to the Atlantic coast of Africa on voyages of exploration. On two of these occasions a total of thirty-eight captive 'Moors' had been brought to Portugal.[7] This second document effectively established that the Portuguese maritime expansion would be organized and financed as a state monopoly. The bull of 1441 formally gave papal approval to the ideological cover that would be used to justify that expansion.

No crusading or evangelistic motive was suggested in 1443 as a reason for the grant of the monopoly. The grant, instead, presents the Prince solely in his role as sponsor of cartography and instigator of exploration in the African Atlantic. It also already accepts that trade, not war, might be the main motive for some of the Henrican or Henrican-licensed voyages.[8] Some scholars have seen in these facts evidence to support the theory that the regent's interest in discovery in the African Atlantic was solely directed towards its commercial possibilities and that he had little time for his younger brother's desire to wrap the twin ideologies of crusade and chivalry round the work of the explorers. Since the document, as was customary, simply reproduces the grounds on which Henry had asked for the grant from the crown, any such reading of it seems far-fetched. The active participation of men and ships belonging to the regent alongside those of the Prince in some of the voyages of exploration carried out in the 1440s indicates, however, that there was at least a tacit understanding that the Henrican monopoly was not to be taken as excluding other members of the royal family from sending their vessels to Guinea if they wished, though, according to Zurara, they, like everyone else, had to obtain Henry's formal licence to do so. After the regent was killed in 1449, but before the Prince's own death, royal caravels belonging to Afonso V also continued from time to time to make the journey.[9] The 1443 monopoly granted to the Prince by the regent was, of course, only effective as far as the subjects and territories of the Portuguese crown were concerned. It could have no international validity unless it was underwritten by the authority of the pope.

Zurara's detailed and enthusiastic account of the various military actions carried out by the Prince's knights and squires in the 1440s against the inhabitants of the Saharan coast between the Río de Oro, Cape Blanco and the islands on the Arguin Bank has often been criticized in modern times because of the chronicler's insistence on presenting as major military and chivalric actions what were often only trivial skirmishes between trained Portuguese soldiers and groups of poor Idzagen fishermen or ill-armed nomadic Arab and Sanhadja [Zanaga] tribesmen.[10] Modern readers are likely to think it incongruous when they read in Zurara that the Portuguese knights and squires of Prince Henry's household attacked such groups in full armour shouting the battle-cry 'Portugal and St James!' for all the world as if they were about to engage the seasoned warriors of the armies of Morocco or Granada. On a number of occasions the chronicler records that individual squires who were thought to have distinguished themselves in such encounters were knighted in the field for their bravery. But, when he did this, Zurara was, in fact, doing exactly what was expected of him as official chronicler of 'the deeds of arms' that eventually brought about what he describes as 'the conquest of Guinea'. By presenting these events as the actions of tyro crusaders given by the Prince a chance to win honour by fighting against the enemies of the Faith in new lands, the chronicler, himself an ardent believer in the meaningfulness of chivalry, dutifully interpreted them as he knew the participants wished them to be recorded for posterity. What the chronicler in fact describes in these chapters of the *Chronicle of Guinea* is, of course, another of the earliest of Europe's colonial wars.[11] Zurara's critics do not always remember that, as late as our own century, European soldiers frequently behaved and were praised by contemporary historians for behaving in other peoples' lands in a way very similar to that of the Prince's young men on the Saharan coast or in Senegambia. Nor, despite the disparity in training and equipment between the Portuguese and their indigenous opponents in the 1430s and 1440s, were the odds always as unequal as might be supposed. Even the chronicler was forced to admit that the people of the desert, Arabs and Berbers alike, on occasion defended themselves with spirit and some skill.

On at least one occasion recorded by Zurara, Henry tried to send an expeditionary force of some size to the African Atlantic. In 1445 a fleet claimed by the chronicler to have numbered no less than twenty-six caravels, fourteen of them from Lagos, set out with orders to reach the land of the blacks. These figures must be treated with caution, but clearly a force of some size was involved, partly funded by the Prince and partly by private caravel owners and merchants. Even so, the financial cost to Henry's treasury of mounting a fleet of this size gives meaning to his references to the great expenses he had incurred as sponsor of oceanic exploration in the African Atlantic. As it turned out, the 1445 expedition's achievements fell well short of what was planned though quite large-scale combats were fought when landings were made from up to half-a-dozen caravels at a time on the populated islands south of Cape Blanco. One is left with the impression that, when he sent a fleet of this size into action on the Saharan coast, Henry over-reached himself because the captains of the various vessels had no experience of navigating or manoeuvring jointly on such a scale. He would never again repeat the experiment.

Even at this early stage, though, the Portuguese did not always rely on armed force. If Henry's squires were anxious to win fame by making war on the inhabitants of the Saharan coast, the merchants who partly funded these explorations were, for their part, more interested in opening ordinary trading relations with them. In consequence, we find two entirely contradictory purposes at work from the beginning of the Portuguese arrival on the Saharan coast. One group saw the region as a theatre of war against Islam. The other wanted to exploit the discoveries commercially. It would be several years before the Prince was forced to recognize that he must choose between making war on the inhabitants of Mauritania or seeking to trade with them. Serious attempts to open trading relations were evidently made at an early stage. A quittance issued to the royal *contador* in the tax-districts of Guimarães and Ponte de Lima for monies collected and disbursed by him in 1444 records a payment of 34,538 *reais brancos* which had been spent on the purchase of no less than 2,442 *varas* – about 2,847 English yards – of linen cloth packed in sacking which had been purchased and handed over 'to Gomes Pires, our captain, to be taken to the Río de Oro'. Here we have to do with a caravel belonging not to the Prince but to the Crown. The receipt for this cargo was signed by a squire of the Regent's household who, as the quittance explains, was himself to make the journey to the Río de Oro as ship's scrivener aboard the royal caravel which would carry the aforesaid cloth there.[12] It was also countersigned by Gomes Pires himself.[13] This quittance appears to be the first official document that has so far come to light which supplies detailed factual information about Portuguese exports to the newly discovered regions of West Africa. It survives since, because a royal caravel and cargo was involved, the expenditure needed to be covered by a quittance issued by the royal chancery. The journeys of Gomes Pires to the Río de Oro and further south in a caravel belonging to the Crown are described at some length in Zurara's chronicle. Pires, though one of D. Pedro's captains, played an important part in the explorations of the 1440s. In the summer of 1445 his vessel, accompanied by a caravel commanded by one of the Prince's men, Lançarote da Ilha, actually reached the mouth of the River Senegal, the river which traditionally marked the boundary between the Berber and Arab tribes of the Sahara and Black Africa proper.[14] On its 1444 voyage to the Río de Oro, Pires's caravel was apparently accompanied by two others belonging to Prince

Henry. Zurara, perhaps to play down the participation of the Regent's ships in this stage of the discoveries, implies that the expedition was under the command of another of Henry's most successful explorers, Antão Gonçalves. He confirms that its purpose was to try to establish trade with the people living in the Río de Oro region. In this respect it proved a failure.[15]

It is not difficult to imagine what may have gone wrong. The Portuguese did not yet understand the mechanics of nomadic commerce in the Sahara. Prince Henry, still perhaps crediting what the *Libro del conocimiento* had to say on the subject, evidently encouraged his explorers to believe that they would find on or near the coast permanent settlements where trade was continuously carried on and where merchants able and ready to do business with them were to be found. It took time for the Europeans to understand that the coming of caravans and merchants to these remote and peripheral regions was infrequent and seasonal, and that therefore contacts with the merchants of the Sahara must be carefully arranged in advance. It is to be supposed, too, that the people of the Río de Oro – like those of the regions further south – were not particularly interested in buying bales of linen cloth manufactured to meet the needs of the Portuguese market and which would have to be made up locally into garments. What they wanted was to be able to buy from the Portuguese the various types of garment they were accustomed to buy ready-made from the itinerant merchants of the desert, a fact that was to have immediate and unforeseen consequences for the pattern of Portuguese trade with these regions.

Despite their failure in 1444, the Portuguese continued to believe that the Río de Oro offered good prospects for developing normal trading relations. In 1445, on a journey back to Portugal from Cape Verde, Gomes Pires again went out of his way to make a call there and received a promise that, if he returned the following July, many black slaves from Guinea proper as well as gold and other articles would be available for barter. We know from other sources what these other articles were: the highly prized skins of the oryx antelope – a luxury item which, like ostrich eggs, had so far only reached Europe among the cargoes of the trans-Saharan caravans; amber – found on the Atlantic beaches; civet musk (the immensely valuable musk obtained from the anal glands of the civet cat); live civet cats; gum arabic (exuded by certain types of acacia and used in the textile industry of Europe to give a gloss to cloth); sweet resin (used in Africa and Europe as a vulnerary); turtle fat (thought to be a cure for leprosy); seal oil; dates from the Mauritanian Adrar.

Gomes Pires duly kept his new rendezvous with the people of the Río de Oro in the summer of 1446. He caused a smoke signal to be made on the top of a high dune to announce his arrival and, when some local people eventually turned up, offered to barter cloth for slaves, preferably blacks imported from the south. It was then explained to him that such affairs were the business of merchants and that these were at present in the interior and must be sent for. Though he was assured that this would be done and that the merchants would be found very willing to trade, none turned up. After three weeks – not a long time in the circumstances – Gomes Pires lost patience, perhaps because he was running short of supplies, and started slave-raiding on his own account in the region. This, of course, did nothing to advance any prospect of establishing peaceful trading relations with the Río de Oro, though the change was no doubt to the taste of Henry's young warriors who, disappointed by the small quantities of gold dust and gold ornaments that had been found in the region, turned covetous eyes on the brown-skinned and strangely garbed Sanhadja men, women and children. If captured by force as individual crusader's booty and taken to Portugal for sale as slaves, they would bring them not only honour but hard cash as well. Unsurprisingly and inevitably, the exploration of Mauritania now became inextricably associated with slave razzias and equally inevitably with attempts to find reasons for scorning the humanity of the captives destined to become slaves. Cadamosto reflects the popular attitude in Portugal towards those captured on the Saharan coast when he says of them that they were all great liars and thieves who anointed themselves with fish fat, smelt bad and had other unpleasant habits.[16]

It will be recalled that, when his ships first began to sail beyond Cape Bojador, the Prince had issued instructions to his captains that one or two members of any local populations encountered should be seized and brought to Portugal to be interrogated for information about their people and the world in which they lived. Henry's urgent wish to obtain any reliable knowledge he could about the Western Sahara and its inhabitants was impressed from the start on the leaders of all the expeditions he sent there. One of his squires, João Fernandes, stirred by a wish to serve the Prince in a way which would earn him special merit, now offered to perform a remarkable piece of information-gathering in the desert. The novelty and importance of what he did has not received in modern times the recognition it merits, perhaps because of the emphasis historians of the Portuguese discoveries have always put on seaborne exploits.

The squire concerned was serving aboard a caravel that put in to the Río de Oro in 1444. He realized while there that the most effective and quickest way of supplying the Prince with the information he sought about the interior of the Western Sahara would be for a Portuguese like himself to spend time living among the people there, so cutting out the reliance on captured native informants on whose information Henry had so far largely depended. João Fernandes was just the man for the job. He had been a prisoner of the Moors in North Africa and had first-hand experience of Islamic customs. He knew some Arabic and so could expect to be able to communicate at least with some of the people he would encounter. He himself requested he should be marooned on the shores of the Río de Oro so that he could carry out his self-appointed task over time. All he demanded was a firm promise by his companions that they would make sure that a ship came to pick him up the following year.

João Fernandes now spent seven months exploring various parts of the Western Sahara and questioning its people, often travelling in company with bands of nomadic pastoralists and once joining the wanderings of a tribal chieftain and his retinue. He was found waiting on the beach not far from Arguin Island in 1445 by a caravel despatched by the Prince to pick him up. This was some 260 miles south as the crow flies from his original landing place near the Río de Oro. Zurara, who declares that he was personally acquainted with João Fernandes, not unjustifiably devotes a good deal of rhetorical prose to praising the courage of Henry's squire, who probably was the first of those European explorers who, over the centuries, and starting from the Atlantic coast, were to traverse the Sahara half as honoured guests, half as prisoners of nomadic tribesmen.

João Fernandes reported to Henry that the first thing insisted upon by the shepherds who allowed him to join them was that he should abandon his European clothing and wear that used by them – what the Portuguese called an *alquicé* (Ar. '*el-ksa*'), the Moorish white woollen cloak with hood. Zurara does not say if he also wore the famous blue or black veil (*litham*) of the Touregs which Cadamosto says was also a normal part of Sanhadja dress. It is likely he did so since travel in the desert without it was hardly possible. Zurara, who felt obliged to defend João Fernandes's adoption of Islamic dress, perhaps thought it prudent to omit this detail. The Portuguese squire appears to have been a discerning and objective observer of Saharan life as this appeared to a fifteenth-century European. Despite his complaints about the heat and the sand and dust of the desert, he seems to have enjoyed an experience totally alien to anything he had previously known, even in Moorish captivity. He rightly noted that the Western Sahara was by no means everywhere as totally barren and uninhabited as was generally supposed. The nomads, he reported, as long as they kept moving on, knew where to find pasturage for their flocks of camels, sheep, goats and even some cattle. While camels provided the principal means of animal transport, a privileged few rode imported Barbary horses, though these were rare and much prized. The poor, he observed, simply walked the desert on foot. He was struck, too, by the fact that the camel caravans navigated by means of a compass like those seamen used. He also observed that, to detect the whereabouts of the next well, their drivers looked out for places where the desert crows could be seen wheeling in the sky. He was particularly impressed by the amount of wild life encountered in the desert. Ostriches, antelopes, gazelles, hares and partridge were frequently to be seen. Nor, he reported, was the region completely treeless. Date palms grew where there was some water and drought-resistant shrubs like acacias were to be found even where there seemed to be none. The Portuguese squire found that milk, especially camel's milk, provided the staple food of the nomads. Zurara, since he was primarily concerned to report on things the Portuguese did not know about, does not trouble to mention the importance of fresh or dried fish and other sea foods in the diet of those whose wanderings brought them near the ocean. As for gold, the hope of finding which still fired the imagination of the Portuguese at this time, João Fernandes was encouraging, claiming that the notables of the interior possessed it in abundance.[17] He also noted that wheat was a scarce but much prized article of food, a discovery that the Prince was not slow to capitalize on. Walled towns and villages in the European sense were, reported the explorer, virtually unknown in the region. The nearest such place to the coast was Wadan in the Mauritanian Adrar. Cadamosto's account of Wadan describes it as located six days' journey by camel eastward from Arguin Island. The news about the existence of Wadan brought by João Fernandes was a major event in the reconnaissance of the Western Sahara by the Prince's explorers. Wadan, whose one-time importance can still be recognized today from the extent of its ruined houses and abandoned buildings, was, in the Middle Ages, an important trading centre on the most westerly of the trans-Saharan caravan routes. It was certainly João Fernandes's reports about the existence of Wadan that determined the Prince to set up a permanent trading-post at Arguin and it was from there that his aim to outflank the north–south caravans by sea began for the first time to look plausible.

João Fernandes evidently was somewhat baffled when it came to understanding the ethnology of the region. He recognized the existence there of social divisions based on relative wealth and tribal status, and the role of nomad chiefs, at least one of whom he thought to be a person of sufficient grandeur to be considered of knightly status in European terms. His tented encampment, reported the Portuguese explorer, sheltered a retinue of some one hundred and fifty persons. He was, though, unable to discover any evidence that the various tribes and sub-tribes – Arab or Berber – whom he encountered owed allegiance to any sovereign ruler or had any sense of political statehood. In consequence, he described it as a land without authority or justice, a point also emphasized by Zurara and Cadamosto. Such a description of the political and social situation of the people of the Sahara was bound to suggest to fifteenth-century Christians that any Christian prince was free to impose his own authority there if he so chose. Despite his seven months with the peoples of the desert, the adventurous Portuguese squire, entirely excusably, failed to understand either the complex tribal and caste cultures of the Ma'qil Arabs and the Berber Sanhadjas, or to notice that Koranic law was a unifying force accepted and obeyed by all the peoples of the Sahara. The general impression to be garnered from the account of his observations as this is transmitted by Zurara is that, had the Portuguese not insisted from the start on treating the desert peoples as their natural enemies, peaceful trading could easily have been established. João Fernandes's travels in the Sahara antedated by about two years the better-known journey of the Genoese Antonio Malfante to the Saharan oasis of Tuat.[18]

Zurara, whose chronicle about the discoveries of Guinea regrettably ends with its account of the events of 1447, makes no mention of the existence by that time of any permanent trading-post on Arguin Island, though we know that one had long been established there by the time he finally revised his chronicle of the conquest of Guinea about 1468. For a while in the 1440s the Prince's hopes of setting up a permanent *resgate* on the Saharan coast still seem to have been directed towards the Río de Oro. Arguin, effectively depopulated by the recent slave razzias of the Portuguese, was at first used simply as a place where the caravels called to water ship. Yet only eight years later, according to Cadamosto, the island was the centre of an organized and regular trade dependent on its contacts with the merchants of Wadan. The Venetian's account of Arguin as it was in the mid-1450s is included in his account of his first voyage to Guinea in 1455. In it he discloses that Prince Henry had by then leased the Arguin trade as a monopoly to a consortium of merchants for a ten-year period.[19] These leaseholders had, he added, already constructed a building on the island where their factors continuously resided to trade with the Arabs who came down from the interior to the coast for that purpose. There is no reason to doubt Cadamosto's evidence. Though he does not specifically claim to have visited Arguin himself on this occasion, his narrative shows that he was very well and accurately informed about the place and about the commerce and ethnography of the Sahara in general.

The motives the Prince had for leasing the Arguin trade to a private consortium can only be guessed at. Leasing out parts or all of the Guinea trades as private monopolies to merchant adventurers was a procedure that the Crown would follow very successfully on a number of occasions after Henry's death. Its advantage was that it secured a guaranteed annual rent to the lessor and saved the latter from shouldering the expense, trouble and risks involved if he himself handled the trade directly. In this case it left Henry free to deploy his own resources in exploring and developing commercial markets beyond the River Senegal. Henry, nevertheless, did not wash his hands of Arguin. It was he who, according to Cadamosto, was responsible for building a 'castle' on the island to protect the trade.[20] No doubt the castle was garrisoned by his own people who would also have been charged with the task of keeping an eye on the doings of the lease-holders. Cadamosto does not state what the nationality of these lease-holders was. They are not referred to again for the rest of Henry's lifetime.

We should probably not think in exaggerated terms of the Henrican *castello* at Arguin mentioned by Cadamosto. It may well have started its existence as no more than a large hut defended by a wooden stockade made of timber brought from Madeira for the purpose. Given the lack of essential building materials on the Saharan littoral, it is probable that these were shipped from Portugal as was to be the case with the much more famous castle of São Jorge da Mina erected on the Mina Coast in 1482 by John II. At most in Henry's time, the *castello* can only have been a sturdy fortified tower like the so-called 'castle' that was rapidly erected by Jean de Béthencourt and Gadifer de la Salle at Rubicón, on Lanzarote, at the beginning of the century. The memoirs attributed at the end of the century to the long-retired Guinea pilot, Diogo Gomes, claim that it was in the Henrican *castrum* that the first mass ever to be celebrated in Guinea was celebrated. This text even names the priest from Lagos who was the celebrant, though Martin Behaim (Martin of Bohemia), who took down Gomes's recollections in German or in Latin, probably got the priest's name wrong. Pacheco

Pereira credits Afonso V with the construction of a proper fortress on Arguin after Henry's death and recalls the name of the soldier the king appointed as the first captain (*alcaide-mor*) of the place. This was a *fidalgo* of his household, Soeiro Mendes de Évora, to whom he granted this office in 1464, justifying his choice by explaining that Soeiro Mendes, in addition to his services in North Africa, had been responsible for overseeing the building of the castle as ordered by the king.[21] The office of *alcaide-mor* at Arguin seems also to have embraced responsibility for trade with the interior as well as the conduct of the *resgate*. In Prince Henry's lifetime and after his death the trade centred on Arguin (*os tratos de Arguim*) was always regarded as belonging to a semi-autonomous organization responsible for trade relations with the Atlantic Sahara. The place must have been serviced by the already-mentioned Imragen fishermen (Port. *schirmeiros*). These were much despised by the people of the desert and even the Portuguese commented on their extreme misery. They subsisted, it was said, on a diet of fish, turtle meat and an occasional piece of camel flesh half-cooked on a fire of dried seaweed. João Rodrigues, a Portuguese who spent several years on Arguin Island in the 1490s, told Valentim Fernandes that the Imragen stank like goats – a comment which is difficult to reconcile with his other statement that they had the unpleasant habit of anointing their bodies and hair with the grease of fish.[22] By the 1460s there already seems to have been a settlement of sorts (*cassas e villa*) outside the castle walls and under Portuguese protection. This foreshadowed what would later come to be the norm in the case of all the later castles set up by the Portuguese in Africa.

The 1464 document appointing an *alcaide-mor* at Arguin implies that the building of a fort carried with it at least a *de facto* if not a *de jure* assumption of sovereignty over the island by the Portuguese crown, a claim which is asserted pictorially on later maps of the coast of Guinea. It was customary to show on these, adjacent to the toponym 'Arguim', a large vignette of the royal standard of Portugal flying over the island.

Henry had perhaps an even more important reason than those already mentioned for farming out the Arguin trade to a consortium of merchants. It had become apparent from the earliest attempts of the Portuguese to trade with the merchants and peoples of the Western Sahara that many of the articles the latter wanted from the newcomers, particularly clothing and textiles, had to be the same as those they were accustomed to receive from North Africa by caravan. This inevitably meant that the Portuguese soon found themselves obliged to import from Morocco – or to buy there directly – Moorish clothing and other goods for barter at the Saharan *resgates*. Such a requirement would present no moral or other problems to the Genoese or other Italian merchants or to those of Castile and the Crown of Aragon who were accustomed to trade freely with the Muslim kingdoms of North Africa. The Genoese, indeed, now virtually dominated the maritime trade of Atlantic Morocco. It did, however, present difficulties for Prince Henry. Since the capture of Ceuta, Portuguese trade with North Africa had been at a standstill and it could hardly do Henry's crusader's image much good if he was suddenly to be found trying to persuade the Moroccans to allow his ships and crews to enter their ports to pick up cargo destined for barter with the Muslims at Arguin or on the Río de Oro. Moreover, since his privateers had harried Moorish shipping on the Atlantic coast of Morocco for several decades, and since he never ceased proclaiming himself the inveterate enemy of Islam, it was unlikely, anyway, that Portuguese ships would be given permission to enter Moroccan ports to trade. This problem, too, could be circumvented by leasing the trade of Arguin for the time being to a consortium of professional merchants who either had free access to these Moroccan ports or could buy from those who had. When it had become generally accepted that trading, not crusading, was what the Portuguese were really about in Arguin and further south, such camouflage would become superfluous.

All that remained of the Portuguese castle at the beginning of the twentieth century when the site was visited and examined by Gruvel and Chudeau was the smaller of two cisterns that once stored the water from Arguin's famous spring. This was built in the form of a vaulted grotto hewn out of the rock and reached down a flight of steps. In the grotto were two stone-faced circular basins, each of considerable depth, into which the water was collected as it filtered through the rock.[23] The cistern was clearly the work of skilled artisans and serves to confirm that masons and other building workers must have been shipped to Arguin Island to carry out this work – probably not until the time of Afonso V or John II.

From the Arab and Sanhadja merchants on the mainland, the lessees of Arguin and those aboard individual caravels operating off the Saharan coast bought gold dust and gold ornaments and the various luxury items listed earlier in this chapter. Though the search for gold was always a priority of the Henrican explorers, during the Prince's lifetime they were never destined to find it on offer anywhere in Guinea in the sort of really large quantities they and their master had hoped for. At Arguin the most valuable commodity available soon turned out to be not gold but slaves, particularly black slaves imported from Guinea proper by the trans-Saharan caravans. In exchange, the Portuguese bartered wheat, for which there was a ready demand in the desert where it was a luxury import. Other exports to Arguin at this time were the various types of clothing commonly worn in North Africa, woollen textiles of various sorts, linen, some silver and other unspecified articles.[24] Diogo Gomes offers an account of the way the Arguin trade started which diverges from the account given by Zurara. According to Gomes, the trade only began in earnest when the Prince sent an *urca* (in English terms, a square-sailed cog) there with an experimental cargo of wheat, Arab clothing and other merchandise.[25] This initiative, he says, was successful and trade continued at Arguin ever afterwards.[26] The account attributed to Gomes by Martin Behaim has perhaps, as often, got the details of what happened wrong. However, the old sea captain's supposed reference to the sending of a square-rigged ship to this coast by Henry is intriguing because it calls in to question the assertion, always sedulously put about by the Portuguese in the time of the Prince and Afonso V, that only caravels, with their special navigational qualities, were capable of making the return journey to and from Guinea.

Cadamosto's account of Arguin in his *Navigazioni* is associated there with his important descriptions of the Saharan caravan trade and the empire of Mali and with his extremely well-informed account of the famous silent trade in alluvial gold by means of which the gold merchants of the Sudan obtained the precious metal mined in Bambuk and Bure from the elusive black miners who extracted it there. Cadamosto did not obtain all this information in 1455. He himself remarks that he had secured much of it by interrogating Sanhadja and other slaves in Portugal.[27] The description of the island's trade and the reference to its *castello* were certainly noted down by him or for him before Prince Henry's death in 1460.[28]

Arguin was thus the site of the very first of those overseas fortified trading factories (*feitorias*) through which the Portuguese were later to conduct their commerce in the African Atlantic, in the Indian Ocean and in Brazil.[29] Unlike the *fonduqs* maintained by the Italians and other European merchants in Muslim North Africa, the Portuguese *feitorias* world-wide were, after the Prince's death, usually under the control, direct or indirect, of the crown. The king appointed the *feitor*, gave him his instructions and received from him his detailed accounts for scrutiny and quittance together with the profits from the factory, if any.

If Cadamosto's information is correct, the first foundation overseas of what was to be a characteristic institution of the Portuguese empire must be attributed to Henry and not, as is sometimes the case, to Afonso V and his advisers.

Cadamosto is also our only reliable source of information about the trade of Arguin as it existed in the Prince's time, though he only provides quantitative information in relation to the trade in slaves. The most authoritative text of his work states that during the time he served Henry in the 1450s, the place exported to Portugal eight hundred to one thousand slaves annually.[30] This included not only Sanhadjas and other natives of the desert, but also a considerable number of blacks bought from the merchants of Wadan. Cadamosto's figures have been criticized as too high when compared with those shown in end-of-the-century quittances. It is, however, quite likely that the establishment of the Arguin factory brought about a boom in the slave-trade there in the 1450s which was not maintained later when the Portuguese were able to obtain slaves freely in Senegal and further south.

The Venetian explorer does not, unfortunately, give any figure for the value of the gold dust obtained annually at Arguin in the 1450s, though he duly notes that it reached there from Wadan, where the merchants of that desert entrepôt obtained it from the northbound caravans from the Sudan.[31] He clearly perceived that the gold trade of Arguin represented a challenge not only to the trans-Saharan caravan trade itself but also to the long-established operations of Italian and other European buyers of Sudanese gold at Asilah, Safi, Massa and other ports on the Atlantic coast of Morocco.

Regular documentary evidence for the history of the Arguin trades only becomes available for the period well after Henry's death and is therefore largely outside the scope of this book. However, some of it is probably applicable to what went on in the Prince's time too. The content of the notes made by Valentim Fernandes early in the sixteenth century from an oral account of the affairs of Arguin given him by João Rodrigues present a case in point even though the notes refer specifically to the last two years of John II's reign (1493–5). The main items sought by the Portuguese at Arguin when João Rodrigues was there continued to be black as well as Sanhadja slaves and gold. To these he adds oryx skins, gum arabic, civet cats, ostrich eggs and, rather surprisingly, camels, cattle and goats. The musk obtained from the civet cat was always one of the most prized items sought by the Portuguese at Arguin. They bought both the musk itself and, when they could obtain one, an actual cat. Two such animals were shown by Afonso V in 1466 to the German traveller Gabriel Tetzel, who tested the odour, which, he says, he found exquisite. In addition to its value to perfumers, Tetzel reveals that the Portuguese king regarded civet musk as a valuable specific against the plague.[32] The camels were probably exported in João Rodrigues's day to the Cape Verde Islands along with the cattle and goats, apart from those whose meat was used locally to supply the garrison and visiting caravel crews.

Administratively, from Henry's time onward, the Arguin trades, as already mentioned, always constituted in Portugal a separate agency and were not subsumed into the Guinea trades generally. The agency was located in Lagos until Henry's death, when Afonso V removed it to Lisbon, alleging that he did so because of corruption practised by Henry's officials in the Algarve port.

It seemed, up to 1447, that the exploration of the Saharan coast and beyond and the opening of trade in its wake had settled into a firm pattern. After reaching a hitherto unexplored part of the coast, the Prince's men would land in force to intimidate the local inhabitants and to take one or two prisoners so that these could be taken to Portugal to be quizzed for information by the Prince personally, or by one of his advisers. If the local people seemed willing to trade, then no further military action might be taken but usually the Portuguese, treating them as their natural enemies, launched the armed assaults so enthusiastically chronicled by Zurara. Suddenly, in 1448, Henry completely changed this strategy. He issued orders that no further military actions were to be initiated in any part of Guinea. In future, peaceful trading was to be the order of the day. Arms might only be used in self-defence if his men were attacked. Zurara comments on the new arrangements with a note of regret in the penultimate chapter of his *Chronicle of Guinea*:

> It seems to us appropriate that we should ... bring this volume that we have already written to an end here, [but] with the intention of writing another work which will be continued until the end of the feats of the Prince even though the affairs which followed were not handled with as much effort and courage as the earlier ones for, from this year [1448] onwards, what was done in this region [Guinea] was dealt with more by means of exchanges of merchandise and by pacts than by displays of bravery or the travail of arms.[33]

What had brought about a change at first sight so much at odds with the Prince's determination to make sure that exploration in the African

Atlantic carried with it a crusading image? One thing that contributed to the change was, no doubt, what João Fernandes had told him about the Western Sahara. The squire's report must finally have convinced Henry that the supposed travels of the author of the *Libro del conocimiento* in this region were entirely fictitious. There had been no sign of the easy access to gold that the latter promised, nor of the towns, ports, merchants or Moorish shipping which he said he had seen with his own eyes on the coast. Instead of gold, the Portuguese, however, had found that slaves represented a valuable and relatively easily available commodity in the region. They had also discovered that slave-taking did not necessarily require the use of military force; slaves could quite easily be obtained in the Sahara by barter just like any other commodity traded there. But there was another and more powerful reason that led the Prince to call a halt to any more routine acts of military aggression either in the regions so far discovered or in those yet to be explored. Between 1444 and 1447 Henry's caravels had reached the mouth of the River Senegal and then managed to sail for a considerable distance along the coast of Black Africa beyond Cape Verde, perhaps as far as the River Gambia, certainly as far as the River Salum.[34] However, what should have been celebrated as a triumph of exploration by the Prince and his men – involving as it did the uncovering by them of a world never before seen by Europeans – was overshadowed by the disagreeable experiences they had undergone at the hands of the coastal people of what is now Senegal. These forcibly made the point that to make war on the peoples living on or near the sparsely populated Saharan coast was one thing but that making war on the inhabitants of the coasts of Black Africa was quite another. The latter had turned out to be able at short notice to put in the field large numbers of warriors who were usually not in the least intimidated by the small forces the Portuguese could put ashore, or by the fire from the bombards and culverins with which the caravels were equipped.[35] The Portuguese, on the other hand, were much frightened by the effectiveness of the poisoned arrows and lances fired or hurled at them by the massed African warriors. A wound from one of these, as Zurara explains, usually meant certain death. Sometimes during these actions the Portuguese had to retreat so fast that they were unable to recover the bodies of their dead comrades. Nor did the Africans always wait to be attacked. They were liable, using dugout canoes, to launch themselves against caravels lying at anchor. In these various encounters some knights and squires and a considerable number of soldiers and sailors were killed. Among them were Nuño Tristão, an intimate of Prince

Henry and prominent among the explorers of the Saharan coast, and a Danish knight, Abelhardt. Abelhardt had been charged by the Prince, in what seems to have been a case of Henry placing chivalric *courtoisie* above common sense, with the task of negotiating a pact with the Wolof ruler of that part of the coast. Afonso Cerveira was presumably the source from which Zurara took his account of the Portuguese defeats, but it is to the chronicler's credit that he did not attempt to minimize these. Nor, unlike Henry when he found himself in a similar situation in the Canaries, did Zurara seek to attribute the successes of the black tribesmen against the Portuguese to the uncivilized way indigenous people made war. He accepted the military ability of the Africans, saying of the complacent assertion made by one Portuguese commander that it would be easy to capture some of these blacks, 'They were not as easy to capture as he thought for, believe me, they are very strong and skilful in defending themselves as you will see in the chapters which follow where we shall speak about the way they made war.'

Later he had to report that, in 1447, the fighting men from a fleet of caravels from Lagos had come off second best in an engagement with the local warriors that had taken place well south of Cape Verde. As a result of this defeat the Portuguese captains abandoned any further exploration and returned home, giving as an unconvincing excuse for this behaviour that their vessels were overcrowded because they had had to take on board all the men from one which had been wrecked. The feebleness of the excuse was noted by Zurara, who commented,

> Although this is what they said, I am more inclined to believe that the main cause of their sailing away was their fear of their enemies whose awesome way of fighting gave any sensible man good grounds for alarm. One could not have called it true courage if, in the absence of any greater need than the one they then had, they had determined [to stay] to fight people who they knew could do them great damage.[36]

Such words come unexpectedly from the pen of Zurara, who spent much of his life as a chronicler praising the chivalric derring-do of those who conducted themselves in precisely the way he condemns here. With his change of attitude, the chronicler is clearly preparing the way for his forthcoming need to justify the Prince's decision to abandon the attempt to achieve his purposes in Guinea by force of arms. Henry, despite his obsession with the idea of himself as a predestined crusader, was, except perhaps where North Africa was concerned, disconcertingly capable of rearranging his policies to meet new situations when circumstances showed that the existing ones could not work. When it had become plain that he had to choose between abandoning the use of arms in Black Africa or abandoning any idea of exploring and trading there, he did not hesitate. Never averse to the use of casuistry when he found himself caught between the claims of ideology and the practical requirements of the moment, he simply explained that the switch to peaceful trading meant continuing the war against Islam by other means.

This readiness to rearrange policies was not, of course, limited to the affairs of Guinea. Zurara, in the middle of his account of various Henrican expeditions there and to the Atlantic Sahara, suddenly inserts into his narrative an account of a carefully prepared attempt by Henry to open trading relations with the Moroccan port of Massa, located near the southernmost coastal border of the sultanate. In the fifteenth century, despite the fact that its anchorage was not particularly safe, Massa was an important maritime outlet for the wheat and other agricultural produce of the rich plains of the Sous. It was also one of the ocean terminals for the trans-Saharan caravan trade. Its maritime commerce was mainly in the hands of the Genoese and other Italians, though Castilian shipping was also often seen there.

The Prince, according to Zurara, feared that it would prove impossible ever to open up peaceful trade with the Río de Oro. He therefore decided to explore the possibility of establishing normal trading relations with Massa. Zurara's account of the attempt is not very informative about what no doubt seemed to him a regrettable example of economic advantage triumphing over chivalric ideals. The truth was that Henry wished to find fresh sources from which he could obtain slaves brought to Morocco from Black Africa by caravan, and had had pointed out to him that, if he could put his crusader's prejudices on hold, this could be done more inexpensively through the ordinary processes of trade in Massa, Safi and other Moroccan Atlantic ports than by expensive journeys to Guinea. The Atlantic wind systems off this region of the Atlantic coast permitted at most seasons of the year both a quick passage to these ports from Europe and a return that could be calculated in days, not weeks. This contrasted with the situation further south where, from Mauritania onwards, the north-east trade winds blew relentlessly throughout the year, causing the homeward journey at times to take six weeks or more.

The Portuguese chronicler characteristically assures his readers that the Prince was not particularly concerned with any material profit he might make from slaves he bought at Massa. He thought of them, Zurara assures his readers, primarily as potential converts to Christianity.[37] It was an interpretation of Henry's motives for engaging in the slave trade in general which the Prince would stick to all his life.

There was absolutely nothing unusual about Europeans sending vessels to Massa to buy slaves, gold and other products arriving there by caravan from Black Africa. In addition to wheat, Massa was also a main outlet for other agricultural crops produced in the fertile Sous itself – barley, skins, honey and wax among them – as well as horses. Christian merchants regularly traded there, but the Portuguese were not among them. Portugal's implacable hostility to the sultanate under the Prince's direction and the years of attacks on shipping off its Atlantic coast by his caravels had made sure of that. Yet here he now was in 1447, seeking to place himself and his caravels among the other Christian traders who routinely used the port.

Zurara may be right when he suggests that one factor in this decision was gloom felt by the Prince about the prospects of developing a worthwhile trade with the peoples of the Atlantic Sahara. If so, as the chronicler's own narrative shows, this was only a transient mood. It was not only because he could buy slaves there that Henry wanted to secure trading rights in Massa. There was also the fact that the peoples of all the regions so far discovered by the Portuguese navigators insisted, as we have seen, that what they wanted were the kind of materials and other goods manufactured in North Africa that they were accustomed to secure from the southbound caravans. However much it might go against Henry's crusading grain, there was no gainsaying the fact that it would make good economic sense for his caravels to pick up such goods themselves in Morocco on their way south rather than have to purchase them in the Peninsula from Italian, Castilian or Catalan merchants. Since Henry had hit on the idea of announcing to the world that his principal aim in seizing or buying slaves was to give them the opportunity of converting to Christianity, the fact that he was now proposing to buy them from Muslim merchants in Morocco could, with some suspension of disbelief, be presented to the Christian world as a benevolent act of Christian charity.

Larger ambitions may, however, have influenced the Prince at this time. The extension of Portuguese power in Morocco was an aim never far from Henry's mind. The political disintegration of the Marinid state and the consequent virtual collapse of the central government's authority in the more southerly Atlantic regions of the sultanate may already have caused him to wonder if it might not be possible to detach some of the ports there from the rule of Fez altogether and turn them at least into Portuguese protectorates, as indeed would start to happen later in the century.

Henry's attempt to establish contact with Massa was carefully planned. He realized that, since the Portuguese had, by their own acts since 1415, virtually excluded themselves from participation in the Moroccan trade, it would not be possible to send a Portuguese ship there under his auspices expecting the authorities to give it a friendly reception. Exceptional incentives would have to be provided to persuade them to do so. There is reason to suppose, reading between the lines of Zurara's text, that João Fernandes, the explorer of the Río de Oro, may have been responsible for persuading the Prince to try his luck at Massa. The ruse used in 1447 to get a Portuguese ship into the Moroccan port was an astute one. A Castilian merchant was found who had come into possession of twenty-six Moorish captives, natives of Massa and doubtless part of the booty of some Castilian privateering operation. Their ransom in exchange for a larger number of black slaves had already been arranged. The Castilian merchant, for a suitable reward, was persuaded to agree to return the prospectively ransomed Moors to Massa aboard an armed Portuguese caravel belonging to one of Henry's squires. It was thought to be unlikely that the town's officials would refuse to allow a number of their fellow citizens to be rescued from Christian captivity simply because they had arrived home on a Portuguese ship.[38]

Zurara's account reveals that, though the Portuguese vessel with its Moorish prisoners aboard seems to have been permitted to anchor off Massa, no one was allowed to land while lengthy and at first inconclusive discussions took place with the local officials. The project was saved by the active intervention of the indispensable João Fernandes who managed to get their permission to go ashore. No doubt because of his knowledge of Arabic and his familiarity with the Moorish scene, he succeeded in reaching a partial agreement that eighteen of the imprisoned Moors should be exchanged for fifty-one black slaves. This was done. Fernandes was still ashore seeking to complete the exchange when, according to Zurara, a southerly storm forced the Portuguese ship to put to sea. It then sailed for Portugal without returning to Massa.[39] Unfortunately, Zurara has nothing further to say about any long-term results of this Henrican voyage of reconnaissance to the Moroccan port, but it seems from such evidence as is available that Portuguese shipping now at least ceased to be rigorously excluded from any of the sultanate's southern harbours. Zurara, as we have seen, supplies an economic motive for the Prince's decision to try to secure access to southern Moroccan ports for his ships. The chronicler plainly did not feel that Henry's attempt to establish trading relations with Massa was in any way at odds with the Prince's crusader's stance which he so zealously promoted. Presumably neither the Prince nor his supporters at the Portuguese court did so either, for, in fact, Henry had, or believed he had, papal cover for his attempt to establish direct trading relations with Massa. While the Portuguese were still celebrating the capture of Ceuta in 1415, his father, at his request, had secured from Martin V permission to trade freely with the Moroccans except in arms, iron and other prohibited goods.[40] At the time it was claimed that this concession would give the Portuguese a chance to convert the Moroccans by love as well as by fear. It was never revoked by the curia. No doubt, therefore, Henry reckoned that his attempt to secure access to Massa for his ships could be justified on the same grounds. He could hardly claim, as he had done in the Portuguese Sahara, that sending his ships to trade in the ports of southern Morocco along with those of other Christian states was an effective act of war against Islam.

That something more was involved, however, than an attempt to open Massa to Portuguese shipping soon became clear. In February 1449 the Prince secured from the new government of Afonso V yet another monopoly in the African Atlantic.[41] This grant may well have been a quid pro quo demanded by Henry as a reward for his failure to rally to the cause of his brother the ex-regent in the civil war which had just ended with the latter's death in battle. In 1443, as we have seen, D. Pedro had granted him exclusive control of all commerce and navigation from Cape Bojador southwards. It would therefore have been logical to extend the monopoly to the north as far as Cape Noun and the southern frontier of the sultanate. But the new monopoly went far beyond this. The 1449 grant declares that, in accordance with Henry's request, his monopoly now embraces the entire coast northwards from Cape Bojador as far as Cape Cantin (Cape Beddouza), a promontory just north of what was then a major Moroccan port, Safi. It thus included more than 200 miles of coast that formed part of the sultanate and included a number of other ports also regularly visited by international shipping. As in the case of the 1443 grant, no mention was made of any evangelizing intentions. The document justified the new grant solely in commercial terms and in so doing disclosed that the crown was well aware that, behind the ambiguous geographical statements made at Henry's request, what was really involved was the opening of the Moroccan ports to Henry's ships. Portuguese commerce there, the document explained, had been at a standstill for thirty years [i.e. since the capture of Ceuta] and the Prince had undertaken to reestablish it. To quote the relevant passage,

> since the greater part of that land [between Cape Bojador and Cape Cantin] is uninhabited and for a very long time there has been no trading of merchandise between our kingdoms and it, he [the Prince] has asked us to grant to him the dues that belong to us on all merchandise and everything else that it may be traded from Cape Cantin as far as Cape Bojador because it is his intention to serve God and ourselves by working to bring it about that merchandise from the said lands reaches our kingdom.[42]

The passage offers a good example of the Prince's willingness to be economical with the truth when it suited him. No one reading it without knowledge of the geography of north-west Africa would realize that Henry was being granted exclusive rights to control trade with some of the major trading ports on the west coast of the sultanate, or that the crown had once again ceded to him most of the imposts due to it on the highly valuable merchandise Henry planned to bring to Portugal from those ports.[43] But there was more to this document than a plan to open the latter to Portuguese shipping. A clause in the grant explained that Portuguese ships of war could seize *any* vessels that were found to be trading in the region concerned 'without a licence issued by my said uncle, whether they be from our kingdom or from abroad'. Henry thus now sought, through a licensing system managed by him, to control not only Portuguese trade with Morocco south of Cape Cantin but that of all other countries too. One possible interpretation of the document is that, having failed in 1437 in his bid to expand the Portuguese hold on the sultanate by military means, the Prince had now hit on the idea of using a combination of economic controls and naval force to establish his political and commercial domination over the sultanate's southern Atlantic coastline. If so, the ploy seems to have worked, at least in part. Events suggest that, when information about the new grant reached the authorities in Safi, Massa and the other ports concerned, and when the Genoese, Castilians and other merchants heard of the Portuguese threat to their trade, these parties agreed that the time had come to lift the long-standing embargo on Portuguese shipping. It must be admitted, however, that there is no evidence that the Prince, in practice, attempted to control foreign shipping in the region.

Though the documentation is scanty, by 1452 Safi seems to have been a regular port of call for Portuguese caravels. In accordance with the terms of the 1449 grant, licences to travel there were now issued by the Prince's chancery. However, a royal document of that year provides clear evidence that a Portuguese caravel called at Safi at that time to acquire black slaves from a Genoese merchant who acted as the Prince's agent there.[44] All the same, the Moroccans remained suspicious about Henry's real intentions on this part of the coast. About 1456 a Jew living in Lagos, obviously himself a merchant, was found guilty in Portugal of the charge of sending a letter to the *cadi* of Safi warning him that a forthcoming call there by a Portuguese caravel from Lagos was not mainly for commercial purposes. Its real task, said the alleged letter, was to report on the defences of the place and suggest how it might most easily be captured by the Portuguese.[45] The royal document's denunciation of this act of treason does not make it clear whether the culprit was simply guilty of spreading damaging falsehoods, or whether he really had betrayed a forthcoming Portuguese spying expedition engineered by the Prince. Since a Jew was involved, one cannot rule out, either, the possibility that the alleged traitor was the innocent victim of a ruse designed to alarm the authorities in Safi about what might happen if they did not show themselves sufficiently co-operative with Henry. Whatever the truth, the affair suggests that the possibility of a Portuguese (i.e. Henrican) attempt to seize Safi was then in the air.

Portuguese chancery records reveal, too, that, about the same time, grave charges were brought against some Lagos mariners by a former member of their ship's crew. He claimed that they had attempted to smuggle forbidden exports, including arms, to Safi in a Guinea-bound caravel duly licensed by the Prince. The matter was particularly serious since the captain of the caravel concerned, Leonel Gil, was not only a member of the Prince's personal household but also the son of Gil Eanes, the hero who had rounded Cape Bojador and who, in 1449, had been taken under the King's special protection at Henry's request.[46] The accusation was that, after loading in Lagos its normal cargo for Guinea, the caravel commanded by this squire had gone to the Guadiana estuary in the eastern Algarve, allegedly for the purpose of taking on cloth to be exchanged at Safi for locally made Moorish *alquicés* for sale in Guinea. The real purpose of the call in the estuary, it was charged, was to smuggle on board there by night, prepacked so that they could not be identified, arms and other goods whose export to infidel lands was prohibited. These included, it was alleged, vegetable poison used by bowmen in Europe on their arrow heads. The sale of this material to infidels, if proven, would be seen as a particularly heinous offence.[47] Unfortunately, no further information about this case is available. It must have caused a scandal at the time because of Leonel Gil's alleged involvement and his closeness to the Prince as well as to the royal household. While we cannot be absolutely sure that the allegation was true, the convincing eyewitness detail provided by the accuser about the nature of the illegal cargo and the circumstances of its loading suggests that may well have been. Quite apart from the particular facts of this case, the information supplied in it serves to remind us of the tainted realities of everyday fifteenth-century commercial life that, even in the Prince's immediate circle, lay behind the rather smug heroics of Zurara's chronicle. Thus Leonel Gil had got his post as a tax collector in Lagos because the previous incumbent, a squire attached to the royal household, had murdered one of Henry's squires. Gil himself was plainly a man of violence. As late as the 1470s, though by then a knight in the king's service, he was exiled to Ceuta for having hit a nobleman's servant on the head with a stone. The affair also, of course, gives us a glimpse of the new opportunities for illegal self-enrichment that the discoveries had opened up for all levels of society.

In the light of the evidence examined above, it is probable that Prince Henry's surprising despatch of a caravel to Massa in search of slaves in 1447, though presented by Zurara as if it were an isolated episode, did mark the opening of an entirely new development in the complicated early history of the Portuguese expansion in West Africa. Its practical effect was to pit, in Henry's own person, the crusader against Islam in northern Morocco against the entrepreneur determined to open the ports of southern Morocco to his ships so that these could carry to Guinea the goods that the people there wanted. The new policy would lead eventually, after the Prince's death, first to the establishment of Portuguese protectorates over Azemmour, Safi and Massa and then to Portuguese military occupation of these and other Moroccan Atlantic ports.

The grant to the Prince in 1449 of the monopoly over navigation between Capes Cantin and Bojador had other implications too. It represented, of course, a new challenge to Castile engineered by the Prince. Neither the Portuguese occupation of Ceuta nor Portugal's ambitions in the north-west of the sultanate had moved the government of

John II of Castile, continuously enmeshed in political troubles at home, to do more than grumble. But the 1449 monopoly granted by Afonso V was a different matter. It represented a direct threat to the overseas trade of the Andalusian merchants with Atlantic Morocco. It also involved the status of the continental hinterland of the Canary Islands, an archipelago which John II's advisers were determined to keep the Prince out of even at the cost of war (see Chapter Eleven). Henry, as always, was unmoved by Castilian opposition to his plans. Early in 1446 he had secured letters patent from the regent, D. Pedro, forbidding any Portuguese to go to the Canaries unless he had a licence from him to do so.[48] Henry gave a number of reasons for his request. His ships on their way to or from Guinea, he said, were sometimes interfered with in the islands to his great loss. He claimed that no Portuguese ships had been in the habit of going to the Canaries until he had opened that route for them. Even now, he claimed, few took advantage of this new opportunity unless it was as part of one of his squadrons operating in the region. It was therefore proper, bearing in mind the great expenses he had been put to in order to open the islands to Portuguese shipping, that he should be granted the right to control who went there and to receive the royal fifth on the cargo they brought back. Like so many Henrican documents of its kind, the terminology of the grant is deliberately ambiguous. It speaks as if the trouble Henry's ships ran into in the Canaries was caused by Portuguese there, when, of course, those responsible were usually Castilians.

Less than five months after the grant of the new continental monopoly to the Prince came the Castilian riposte. Early in July 1449 the Castilian king granted to the duke of Medina Sidonia and lord of Sanlúcar de Barrameda – Juan de Guzmán – a rival monopoly over navigation and trade, with territorial and juridical *dominium*, in what the Castilian document describes as 'the newly discovered lands and seas between Cape Bojador and Cape Rhir (Cape Aguer)'.[49] The Castilian king gave as his reason for making the grant the service the duke had already done him concerning the conquest of these African territories and the further work to this end which he would undertake. The *Crónica de D. Juan II* supplies some background to the document. It explains that Juan de Guzmán had been sent, probably shortly before 1453, as ambassador to Afonso V. His task was to inform the Portuguese king that careful investigations had confirmed that the Portuguese had no rights to 'the conquest of Barbary or Guinea'. These, said the Castilian king, belonged to the Castilian crown and if Afonso did not abandon his intrusions there he could expect war. According to the chronicle, the Portuguese king was very angry when he received these threats from the ambassador but hid his anger and proposed further enquiries which, he was sure, would reveal that Portugal's rights of conquest in the two regions were legally sound.[50] No mention is made of Prince Henry in these exchanges. The Castilians probably did not wish to be fobbed off, as they had been in the Canaries, by Portuguese claims that questions relating to the African Atlantic should be taken up with the Prince to whom the Portuguese king had delegated responsibility for the region.

The donation to Juan de Guzmán specifically stated that the rich fisheries of the Mar Pequeño (the region between the islands of Lanzarote and Fuerteventura and the mainland, sometimes called the Mar Menor), were included in the grant. It will be noted that the northernmost point referred to in the latter, Cape Rhir, fell well short of the northernmost reach of the new monopoly the Portuguese regent had just granted to the Prince. It did, though, since Massa was south of Cape Rhir, intrude on some of the territory of the sultanate. This probably reflected nothing more than the Castilian court's ignorance of Atlantic political geography, since it is inconceivable that the Andalusian merchants or the Andalusian duke himself would have intended to imperil commercial relations with Morocco by making a pointless claim to territory within the sultanate's borders. The reference to the fisheries of the Mar Pequeño is important. It not only implies that Portuguese fishermen had been fishing in that Canarian region. It also reminds us yet again of the importance to the Portuguese of the rich fisheries which, all the way to Senegal, the discoveries were opening up.

With this grant of a monopoly to one of the kingdom's great Andalusian magnates, the Castilian crown served formal notice on Henry that it did not accept the validity of any claims by him to exercise any control over navigation and trade north of Cape Bojador. However, though deliberately setting up Medina Sidonia as a kind of minimalist Prince Henry, the Castilian government did not, itself, propose to give him any naval or military help in his projected struggle with Henry. Just as the Castilians had left it to territorial lords, merchants and sailors from Andalusia to resist Henrican aggression in the Canaries, so they would leave it to the duke, using his own resources, to make good his new mainland Atlantic monopoly if he could.

Afonso V had every reason to temporize when he learnt from Juan de Guzmán before the summer of 1453 about Castile's claim to the 'conquest' of Guinea. The Castilian king – who, the previous year, had made Europe's great lords tremble by executing his lifelong favourite and the effective governor of his kingdom, Don Álvaro de Luna – was known to be ill. He died on 20 July 1454. Prince Henry could safely assume that the political turmoil in Castile that would follow the accession of Henry IV would guarantee that Castilian claims in the African Atlantic would not be seriously pursued in the near future. They were, though, not forgotten. In 1475, fourteen years after the Prince's death, the Catholic Monarchs, during their war with Portugal, brought John II's claim to Guinea out of hibernation and, reasserting it, used it for the duration of that war as their justification for breaking the Portuguese Guinea monopoly in a spectacular way.[51]

Other correspondence addressed by the Castilian king to Afonso V at this time records the savagery with which Prince Henry's caravel captains dealt with alien interlopers against his monopoly. In a letter written in 1454, the Castilian king protested to the Portuguese king in the strongest terms about the brutal treatment the men aboard one of several Andalusian caravels returning from a voyage to Guinea unlicensed by Henry had received from those aboard a Portuguese ship of war. One of the charges made by the Castilian king in his letter was that 'by your command a Genoese merchant resident in Seville who was aboard the said caravel had his hands cut off. . . .'[52]

Zurara's narrative of the discovery and 'conquest' of Guinea ends, as we have seen, in 1448. Apart from the necessarily unreliable memoirs of Diogo Gomes, the next and only important contemporary narrative source for the Henrican discoveries during the 1450s is the *Navigazioni* of Cadamosto, a work which also has much to say about the way the Prince had by then organized both exploration and trade in Guinea. This is therefore an appropriate point to examine the special characteristics and qualities of the caravel, a type of ship without which Prince Henry's decisive role in the annals of the maritime expansion of Europe would hardly have proved possible.

1. Portulan (navigational) map (*c.* 1490) by Pedro Reinel depicting the eastern Atlantic and the West African coast as far as the Gulf of Guinea. It is believed to be the oldest surviving map by a Portuguese cartographer. The coast from the Gulf of Guinea southwards appears to have been added after the original map was drawn.

2–3. The four western panels of the *Catalan Atlas of Abraham Cresques* (*c.* 1380). Starting in the south-west with Cape Bojador, Cresques depicts the traditional political geography of the Sahara/Sahel as far as the Red Sea.

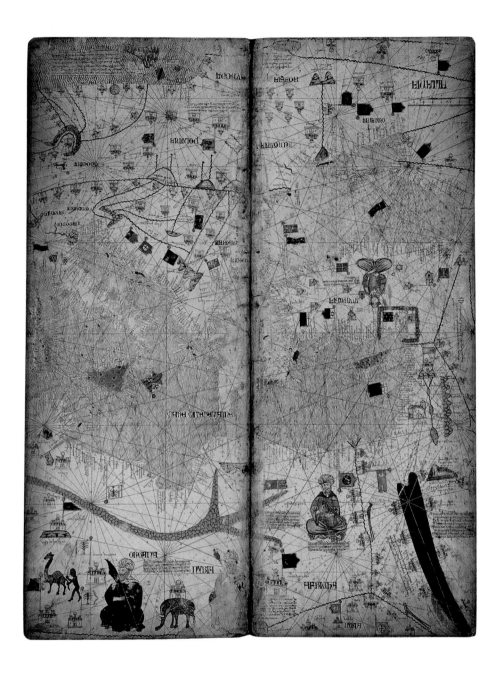

4. (next two pages) *World Map of Mecià de Viladestes* (*c.* 1410) showing more information about the Saharan coastline than that given by Abraham Cresques.

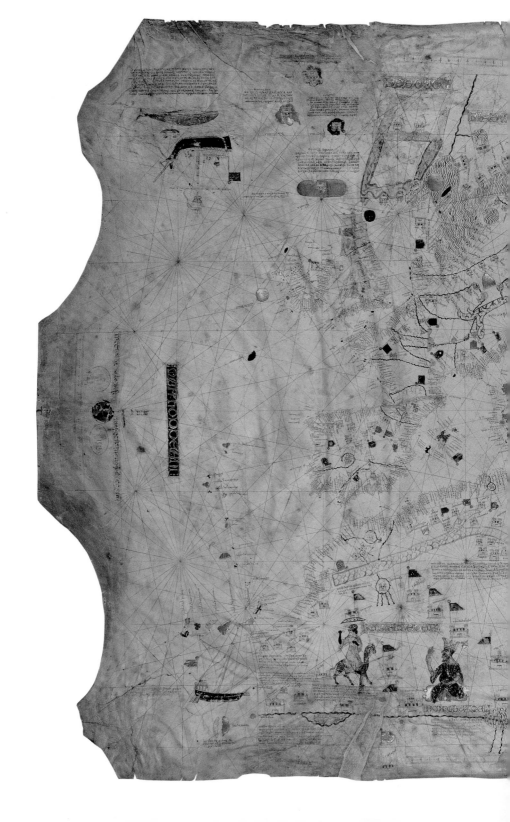

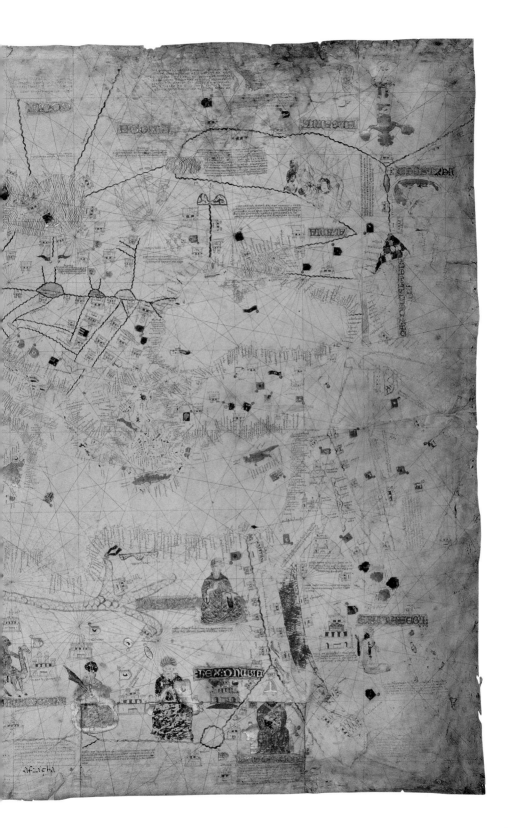

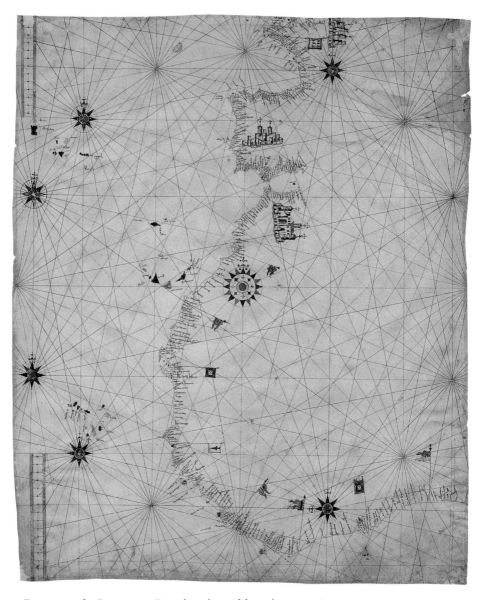

5. Fragment of a Portuguese Portulan chart (fifteenth century).

6. *Catalan World Map* (fifteenth century) shows the Sinus Aethiopicus, the great east–west gulf which was believed in Henry's time to allow direct navigation from the Atlantic to the borders of Prester John's empire in East Africa.

7. The first of Grazioso Benincasa's portulan charts (1462) of the coast of West Africa and the Atlantic Islands, mapping from northern Portugal to Cabo Blanco and Arguin.

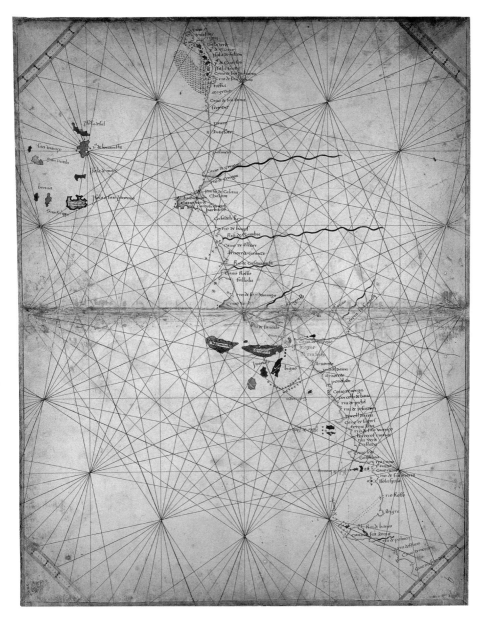

8. The second of Grazioso Benincasa's portulan charts (1468) of the coast of West Africa and the Atlantic Islands, mapping from Arguin to Cape Mesurado (60 19' N) near the most southerly point on the coast reached by explorers in Henry's time. It is believed that Benincasa used information supplied to him by Cadamosto when that explorer returned from Portugal to Venice *c.* 1462.

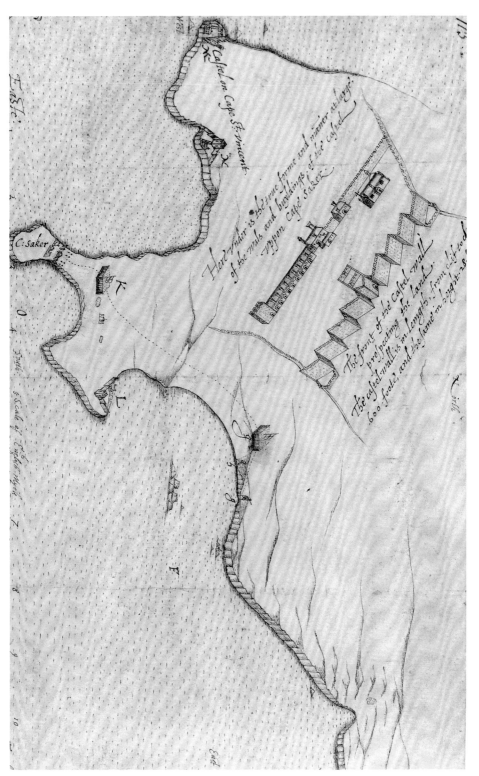

East:

The Castel on Cape St. Vincent.

C: saker

K

L

Here vnder is the same forme and maner at large
of the wals and buyldings of the castel
vppon Cape Saker.

The front of the castel wall
prospecting the land
The castel wall is in length from Cliffod
600 foote, and the same in bright.

miles

O   4   miles   The Scale of English myles.   7   8   9   10

9.

10. Late-Gothic tomb of Prince Henry in the Founder's Chapel of the monastery of Santa Maria da Vitória at Batalha. The tomb was made for him in his lifetime. Note the coat-of-arms of the Order of the Garter placed centrally on the front of the tomb between those of the Order of Christ and Henry's own princely arms. At the end of the carved inscription along the top of the sarcophogus space has been left to enable eventual insertion of the day, month and year of Henry's death. This was never done.

9. English plan of Cape Sagres and its fortifications made in the 1580s in connection with the attacks on the Algarve coast then undertaken by Drake and Essex. The sketch gives a good idea of why the shelter of the Sagres promontories was so important for sailing ships waiting for favourable winds to round Cape St Vincent into the Atlantic.

11. (next two pages) The Lisbon waterfront in the sixteenth century. Note the large number of caravels recognizable by their lateen rigging. Plate from the *Civitates orbis terrarum*, vol. 1, Braun and Hogenburg, 1572.

LISBO

CASCALE Lusitana opp.

11.

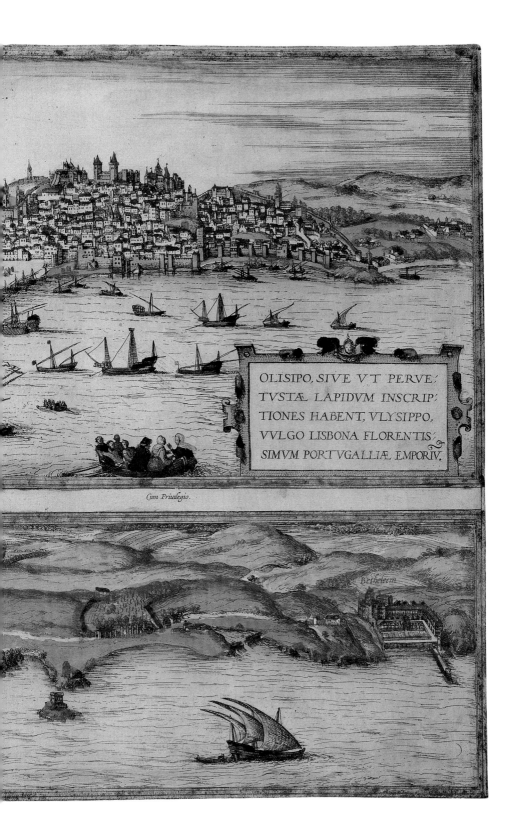

OLISIPO, SIVE VT PERVE:
TVSTÆ LAPIDVM INSCRIP:
TIONES HABENT, VLYSIPPO,
VVLGO LISBONA FLORENTIS:
SIMVM PORTVGALLIÆ EMPORIV.

Cum Priuilegio.

Betheleem

12. Portuguese Ceuta in the sixteenth century. Plate from the *Civitates orbis terrarum*, vol. 1, Braun and Hogenburg, 1572.

14. View of Lisbon waterfront in the sixteenth century from the *Crónica de D. Afonso Henriques*.

TINGIS, LVSITANIS, TANGIARA.

13. Tangier in the sixteenth century. Plate from the *Civitates orbis terrarum*, vol. 1, Braun and Hogenburg, 1572.

15. Portrait of John I (second half of the sixteenth century).

16. Philippa of Lancaster, detail from an illuminated genealogy of the Portuguese royal family.

17. The Marriage of John I of Portugal and Philippa of Lancaster in Oporto in February 1397 (a late fifteenth-century illumination).

18. Portrait located in a position of importance among the crowded figures shown in the *Polyptych of S. Vicente de Fora*, attributed to the painter Nuno Gonçalves (*c.* 1470–80) and, since the end of the nineteenth century, traditionally believed to be Prince Henry. In modern times the correctness of this assumption has been challenged on a number of grounds by some art historians.

19. Supposed portrait of Prince Henry now attached as a frontispiece to the late fifteenth-
or early sixteenth-century Paris manuscript of Zurara's *Crónica dos feitos da Guiné* to
which it did not orginally belong. It is of a later date than the Zurara manuscript itself. The
illuminator of the margins clearly accepted it as a portrait of Henry, but there are features
of his work which raise some doubt as to whether this was originally the case. The Paris
portrait appears to be a mirror image of illustration 18 so that their authenticity stands or
falls together.

20. The outer border in particular gives some idea of how the Portuguese perhaps imagined Guinea in the early sixteenth century. *The Rest on the Flight to Egypt* from the *Livros de Horas de D. Manuel I*, 1517–38.

21. Sixteenth-century Afro-Portuguese carved ivory salt cellar depicting two Portuguese knights, one visible and identifable by his long nose and carefully trimmed beard. It was long believed that artefacts like this were carved in the region of Benin (Nigeria), but it is now thought possible that they were made by the ivory carvers of Sierra Leone or even, since a considerable number survive, commisioned from African craftsmen in Portugal by wealthy purchasers.

22. The tomb in the Fitzalan Chapel in Arundel Castle of D. Beatriz, countess of Arundel – Henry's half sister and the natural daughter of John I of Portugal – and her first husband, Thomas Fitzalan. The dynastic marriage was arranged by Queen Philippa and her brother, Henry IV.

23. Detail of D. Beatriz from the tomb in the Fitzalan Chapel in Arundel Castle.

24. The original (bearing Henry's personal autograph – 'J. d. a.') of a quittance granted by him to Heitor de Sousa, his treasurer, in respect of itemized goods passing through his hands when, on the Prince's orders, he went to Guinea to visit the *resgates* there.

25–8. Prince Henry's squires and sailors can hardly have failed to be impressed when they first saw Madeira rising steeply from the sea on all sides in sequences of high mountains separated by steep ravines and observed that the whole large and apparently uninhabited island was covered with virgin forest down to the seashore.

26. Madeira.

27. Madeira.

29. View of La Gomera, the most mountainous and impenetrable of the Canary Islands. In the 1440s Henry, by arrangement with some of the local pagan clan chiefs, maintained an isolated garrison on part of the island's coast.

28. Madeira.

30. Aerial view of Cape Sagres (Algarve).

31. A view of Cape Sagres a short distance to the east of Cape St Vincent.

32. Chapel of Our Lady of Guadalupe (?thirteenth century) not far from Henry's lost palace at Raposeira (Algarve). According to tradition he was accustomed to pray here.

33. Fifteenth-century chapel on Cape Sagres.

Chapter Nine

The Caravels of Christ

The caravels of Portugal being the best ships that travel the seas under sail, he [Prince Henry] reckoned that, provided they were furnished with everything necessary, they could sail anywhere.

Cadamosto[1]

In the history of maritime discovery the name of Prince Henry is indissolubly associated with the name of the type of ship which made the Henrican discoveries possible – the caravel.[2] Henry himself had only a limited personal experience of shipboard journeys and may never have travelled in a caravel but he certainly learnt early on – perhaps as a result of his connection with the Casa de Ceuta, perhaps as the owner of ships operating as corsairs – to appreciate the sailing and other characteristics of the caravel which, as Cadamosto commented, made it the ideal craft for exploring the unknown and difficult waters of the West African coast. The Venetian explorer attributes to the Prince personally the realization that the caravel's special qualities made it uniquely suitable for this kind work of work. There is no reason to doubt his statement. All the evidence suggests that, had it not been for the availability in Portugal of this type of ship, any programmed close exploration of the coasts of Guinea would not have been possible in Henry's time. It should be noted, though, that the first successful passage of 'Cape Bojador' was, surprisingly, made by a single-masted, square-rigged *barcha* (barge) equipped with oars. One wonders whether, when deciding to send a vessel of this type to attempt the passage of the cape, Henry may not have been influenced by the vignettes of Jacme Ferrer's attempted voyage of discovery to the Río de Oro in 1346 aboard an *uxer*. Vignettes of this craft, which was very similar to a Portuguese *barcha*, appeared on Majorcan world maps of the late fourteenth and early fifteenth century and showed the vessel sailing to the south of the cape. If Henry believed at this initial stage of the discoveries that the vignettes recorded a historical truth, as seems highly probable, the reason for assigning a *barcha* rather than a caravel to make the first passage of Cape Bojador becomes more explicable. At all events it did not take the Prince long to realize that the exploration of the coast of West Africa was a task for which caravels were particularly well suited.

The special qualities of the caravel were long admired by foreign sailors as well as by the Portuguese themselves. Cadamosto spoke after much experience of sailing them to and in Guinea. His views were echoed for a long time by foreign writers on nautical matters. As late as 1604 Bartolommeo Crescentio, in his *Nautica Mediterranea*, could still single out caravels as vessels so agile and easy to handle that, he said, they manoeuvred like ships propelled by oars.

It was the sight of Portuguese caravels off their shores which provided the first visual contact with Europeans and with the maritime technology of late-medieval Europe for the peoples living near the beaches of the coastal Sahara and the shores and rivers of Black Africa. Henry was always careful to ensure that these first contacts also proclaimed visually the main purpose which, he claimed, had brought the Portuguese to the shores of lands on whose seas only canoes and rafts had previously been seen. The square cross of the Order of Christ, routinely painted on the sails of the caravels, emblematized, for Christians, the evangelizing and crusading intention behind the Portuguese enterprise in Guinea. It is likely that the Africans, however, when they first saw the caravels, found more immediately meaningful to them the sight of the traditional eye then always painted on each side of a caravel's prow in accordance with a custom of Portuguese fishermen and seamen that rested on a folkloric basis probably much older than Christianity.[3] It is reported that the Africans believed that it was through these eyes that the caravels were able to find their way across the hitherto uncharted deep.

The main explanation for the success of the caravel as a tool of discovery lay in its rig. Its large triangular sails were not – as was the case with square-rigged ships – attached to cross-spars fixed to the mast. Instead they were suspended from an immensely long yard raked obliquely to the mast and attached to it only by a rope collar, or parrel.[4] The mast itself was always inclined at a forward angle to the hull. Small caravels might only have one or two masts but three-masted caravels soon also came into use. The average capacity of the caravels used by Prince Henry's men was between forty and fifty tons, but some were smaller and a few others considerably larger. Apart from its sails, the caravel in Henry's time had other characteristics that made it immediately recognizable. Chief among these was the absence of any sort of forecastle or raised deck ahead of the mainmast. This feature was due to the need to keep the area ahead of the mainmast unobstructed, to permit the free working of the main lateen sail, whose lower edge reached down almost to deck level. The spar from which the sail was suspended could thus be swung round in front of the mainmast without encumbrance when tacking or going about. There was a small poop deck or sterncastle. The small fishing caravels often used for exploration in Henry's time may sometimes have had only one mast but two were probably more usual and the larger decked caravels must often already have had three. These subsidiary masts were, until the coming of the *caravela redonda* later in the fifteenth century, sited astern of the mainmast. Caravels carried oars as part of their normal equipment but these were only used when manoeuvring in port, or to cope with problems encountered in shallow water or when navigating in rivers, or, perhaps, when going about.

The exceptional response of the great lateen sail even to light breezes, the rapidity with which caravels manned by skilled seamen could go about and their ability to sail close to the wind made it easier for them to evade the attacks of corsairs and other hostile craft.[5] These characteristics, as well as a caravel's shallow draught, had obvious advantages as far as navigation and trade off the coasts of Guinea were concerned – for example, when navigating amid the notorious shallows of the Gulf of Arguin or far up the remoter reaches of the great rivers of West Africa. But most important of all was a caravel's ability to sail far closer to the wind than square-rigged ships. It has been plausibly maintained that, thanks to its lateen sails, a caravel sailing close-hauled could hold a course at only 30° off the wind.[6] When homeward bound from the Saharan coasts or from Guinea proper, caravels could, if need be, make their way directly home against the north-east trades which blow almost continuously, but with varying force according to the season, down to the latitude of Cape Verde and beyond. Probably at quite an early stage it was discovered, however, that it was often less chancy not to attempt to beat north against the trades but to take a north-west course to the latitude of the Azores and Lisbon where the Atlantic westerlies enabled the caravels to run before the wind directly to Portugal. A vessel taking this 'Guinea track' might take several weeks to sail from the region of Cape Verde to Portugal but the passage was predictable, unlike attempts to sail directly into the north-east trades.

On a southerly course outward bound from Portugal, and with the wind and current favourable, an average speed of six knots was easily attainable. Cadamosto states that it took his caravel only three days in 1455 to cover the 580 miles from Cape St Vincent to Porto Santo. His text also makes it clear that the Guinea caravels in his time still sailed from Portugal in February, March or April, returning three or four months later, though this custom would soon change.

The Portuguese in the Prince's day distinguished two types of caravel.[7] One was that called by Zurara a *caravela de pescar*, that is, as its name implies, a caravel modelled on those built primarily for deep-sea fishing, upon which this all-important industry of Portugal depended. They were either undecked or half-decked. Though they were very seaworthy and could make fast journeys to the Mauritanian coast and beyond, their smallness and lack of decking meant that, though useful for making the first probings in newly discovered bays, estuaries and rivers, and for taking soundings ahead of the larger caravels, their cargo capacity was very limited. Since, at the beginning, the Prince hoped that the explorers would return with quantities of gold dust and articles made from that metal, lack of cargo space posed no great problems. However, when it was found that the main cargo brought home from Guinea was destined to be slaves, and that vessels outward bound for Senegal needed to carry horses for barter there, fully decked vessels became essential. The role of the fishing caravels was largely reduced to reconnaissance duties.

The other type of caravel was that described by Zurara as a *caravela tilhada*, a fully decked vessel able to carry general cargo in its covered hold. Here numbers of slaves could be securely stowed and a few horses carried. The average length of a *caravela tilhada* in Henry's time was between forty and sixty feet. More is known about their tonnage. Thus the brand-new caravel which took Cadamosto to Senegambia in 1455 was a vessel of some fifty-four tons capacity.[8] During the Portuguese–Castilian war in the 1470s the Castilian caravels used by the Catholic Monarchs to break the Portuguese monopoly over trade with Guinea seem to have been vessels averaging some forty-five tons.[9] Even as late as 1552 a census of Portuguese caravels made then shows that the average tonnage of the traditional type (as opposed to the larger *caravela redonda*) was still only between forty and fifty tons.[10] It seems likely that the dimensions of a purely lateen rigged caravel could not, for technical reasons, be increased much beyond sixty tons.

Caravels were carvel-built, that is, the hull was smooth and not constructed of overlapping boards as was still the case with the clinker-built cog.[11] Recent investigations seem to confirm that a favourite material of the caravel builders was the wood of the cork tree. This was water-resistant and easily worked. For the rudder and ribs, the more robust wood of the holm oak was preferred. If the more easily handled pine wood was used when building a caravel, the shipwrights preferred what they called *pinho manso* to *pinho bravo* because the latter rotted more easily.[12]

The proportions of a caravel's hull differed notably from that of the ordinary merchant cog. For the latter, the normal rule was that length was only three times the beam so that cogs were decidedly tubby vessels. Caravels were considerably slimmer, a feature which, of course, also contributed to their superior speed. The caravel, however, was not without its disadvantages. Because of the clearance needed to work a caravel's lateen sails, its bow lay low in the water. This meant that the vessel was not at its best when running directly before the wind since the lateen sails, which could not be reefed, then had a tendency to bury the vessel's bows. Equally, a caravel could also be a difficult performer in a following sea. This was why, towards the end of the century, a new type of caravel, the *caravela redonda*, partly equipped with traditional square sails, came into use for deep-sea Atlantic voyages which involved prolonged running before the wind. Another disadvantage of the caravel arising from its low freeboard was that it was much more easily boarded than was a lofty cog if a hostile ship or some African war canoes managed to come alongside. Another problem the caravel presented was that, despite its small size and limited cargo-carrying capacity, it required a larger crew to handle its lateen sails than did a square-rigged ship of much greater capacity. A crew of about twenty was the norm. This made it a relatively expensive vessel to operate. When, as was often the case, the vessel carried a couple of bowmen and a handful of soldiers, these vessels were decidedly crowded, even when there were no slaves held below deck. The seamen and soldiers were, of course, expected to sleep, eat and live on deck. The pilot needed the limited shelter of the sterncastle to read his navigational tools, study or amend his charts and set courses. The ship's scrivener no doubt also needed to be under cover when keeping his records. It is to be presumed, too, that the *capitão* and any persons of rank carried also dossed down in this limited space. Narratives and documents of the Henrican period make no reference to the hardships endured by those who sailed aboard a caravel on sea voyages that lasted several months.

The ship-owners of Andalusia also used caravels extensively. They considered the caravel to be a vessel whose Peninsular origins were Portuguese. This belief is confirmed by a late fifteenth-century document which makes a clear distinction between 'small, lateen-rigged caravels like those of Portugal' and caravels 'according to the style of Andalusia'.[13] The latter by then routinely had a square-rigged main-mast and a foremast in the prow also intended to carry a square sail, the mizzen mast only still being lateen-rigged. There were other differences. These Castilian vessels now developed a substantial forecastle as well as a stern castle since, once the mainmast was no longer lateen-rigged, it was no longer necessary to keep the fore deck of the caravel clear.

There is some uncertainty about the chain of command aboard the Guinea caravels in Henry's time. Zurara clearly attributes final authority to the vessel's captain (*capitão*). If the voyage had any other than a strictly routine commercial purpose, the *capitão* was often a squire (or sometimes a knight) of Henry's household. The captain was ultimately responsible for seeing that the written sailing orders (*regimento*) issued by the Prince to his own men and to those who sailed under licence from him were duly followed. The *regimentos* contained detailed orders for the voyage, specifying what region of Guinea the vessel was to visit and what trading activities it was permitted to carry out there.[14] It was by means of these *regimentos* and licences that Henry retained close control over the working of his Guinea monopoly. The *capitão* was, of course, also responsible for organizing any military operations that had to be undertaken.

The *piloto*, was, as his name implies, a professional sailor who was responsible for a vessel's navigation. It is to be supposed that, particularly in the early days when Henry's squires were eager to win military glory for themselves in Guinea, there must have been many occasions when captain and pilot tended to be at odds. Cadamosto's *Navigazioni* makes it clear that, on private trading voyages sponsored by a merchant or a group of merchants holding Henry's licence, these merchants or their factors normally travelled aboard the caravel to Guinea to carry out their trading on the spot. They could insist that the ship call at a *resgate* named in the licence even if the pilot thought this imprudent.

Another extremely important personage on the Guinea-bound caravels was the ship's scrivener (*escrivão*). Even on privately sponsored voyages it appears that he was always appointed by and represented the interests of the Prince. It was his business to keep all the accounts concerned with the voyage and to see that the terms of the Prince's *regimento* were strictly respected by captain and pilot. It was also his obligation to keep details of all commercial transactions made during the voyage so as to make sure that Henry received the royal fifth and the other dues to which he and the Order of Christ were entitled on goods imported from Guinea. He was also the first line of defence against the smuggling thence by officers, merchants and crew of gold ornaments, gold dust and other small but valuable items. The second line was the strict ship search always carried out by customs officers when a Guinea caravel reached Lagos or another Portuguese port. Judging by Cadamosto's account of the voyage of Pedro de Sintra surreptitiously given him by that explorer's *escrivão*, it may also have been the scrivener's business to keep his own detailed log of the voyage. The information in it was no doubt intended for Henry's eye so that he could collate it with all the other information about Guinea with which the returning caravels continuously supplied him. The scrivener's job was a difficult one. As Henry's personal watchdog he can hardly have been a popular figure with the other crew members, whatever their status. On that account, the post was often given to a young member of Henry's personal household whom he could trust to look after his interests.

Documents show that the caravels carried as crew members a number of apprentice seamen (*grumetes*). These were lads in their late teens. There were often more of them than ordinary seamen in a caravel's crew. One or two ship's boys (*pagens*) were also carried. They acted as servants or general dogsbodies. Henry seems to have wanted the crews of the Guinea caravels to contain a high proportion of young men. A cynical view might be that young seamen came cheaper. However, judging by the comments attributed to him by Zurara, after the early failures to round Cape Bojador he distrusted the conservative outlook and the superstitions he had learnt to associate with older mariners.

Another important if despised figure regularly carried by the Guinea caravels was the African slave–interpreter who might be a man or a woman and whose essential but unenviable role in the slave trade is discussed elsewhere in this book. Though, as a confidence-building exercise, it might in theory have been advantageous from the 1440s to have employed some black Africans as crew members aboard the Guinea-bound caravels sailing to the established *resgates* in Senegal, it seems certain that this never happened in Henry's time, though it did much later on. No doubt the racially prejudiced Portuguese crews of that era would have objected to working alongside black slaves or those whom they thought of as slaves. More importantly, various papal bulls specifically forbade any Portuguese attempt to teach Africans about navigation. To do so, the curia feared, might be to undermine the position of the Europeans.[15]

The cost of provisioning the Henrican caravels for their long journeys carrying crews of twenty men or more was not negligible. Large quantities of biscuit as well as dried or salted beef, wine, oil and vinegar were taken on board in Portugal. The caravels on their outward voyage to Guinea also took on additional supplies of water, firewood and meat in Madeira or Porto Santo or in those islands in the Canaries where the Prince maintained a toehold. We know from Zurara that, at Arguin, the Portuguese crews were accustomed to stock up with turtle-meat and edible sea birds. In Senegambia native rice, honey and goats' milk butter was obtained. But it was, in the fifteenth century, not as easy to secure provisions ashore in West Africa as today's visitor there might suppose. Protein seems, in fact, to have been rather scarce. Many of the food-producing trees and plants which we now associate in abundance with the region were carried there by the Portuguese after the discovery of India and Brazil. What the Prince's seamen could usually rely on were ample supplies of fish, either freshly caught at sea or dried for later consumption. Since their outward course took them through what are still some of the richest fishing grouds in the world and the Portuguese were expert deep-sea fishermen, they must usually have been able to count on this staple food.

Water was always a problem for the caravels, particularly when they were taking the 'Guinea Track' home, or charting the Saharan coast.

Less obvious but almost as important was the need to secure sufficient quantities of firewood for cooking. Locating and charting the whereabouts of springs accessible near the shore and of areas where brushwood was to be found constituted, until they had left the Sahara behind, a main concern of Henry's explorers. It was, of course, not the custom of the Portuguese pilots to sail by night in West African waters. When they could find one, they always sought to anchor for security's sake in a secluded bay where no native huts were to be seen or, better still, near an uninhabited offshore island where they could take on water and firewood, stretch their legs and effect any emergency repairs needed with little risk of an attack by enemy canoes.

The Henrican caravels were normally, or frequently, equipped with cannon. Zurara, in his account of the great expedition to the Arguin Bank in 1445, refers to the presence aboard them then of bombards and culverins, the latter at that time an early form of handgun.[16] Given the dimensions and build of a caravel, the ship-borne bombards must have been smaller than the large bombards of the same name by then commonly used by armies on land. Cadamosto, in his account of his voyage to Senegal in 1455, mentions how he caused one of his caravel's bombards to fire a shot to impress some Wolofs visiting him on board it. Later, when he and his accompanying caravels were attacked in the Gambia River on the same journey, the Venetian navigator describes how the Portuguese ships first fired a simultaneous broadside of stone cannonballs from four bombards and subsequently continued to employ these weapons in the hope of driving off the canoes of the attackers. He himself admits, however, that the Africans soon got over any consternation this first encounter with Portuguese artillery caused them.[17] It is known that Castilian caravels operating in the Canary Islands in 1451 were also armed with bombards. These ship-borne cannon do not seem at first to have been very effective. John II of Portugal, according to his biographer, Garcia de Resende, carried out experiments towards the end of the fifteenth century in the hope of improving the firepower and aim of the guns carried by the caravels of that time. One result of these experiments was that he ordered them to be equipped with larger bombards which were capable of firing their stone balls in a lower trajectory over the water. This, it was claimed, would make it easier to hit chosen targets.[18] Bombards did not come cheap since they usually had to be imported from Flanders and Germany, so adding further to the cost of fitting out a caravel destined for Guinea. The inventory of Henry's possessions in the Lagos dockyard and elsewhere in the city in 1460 lists an unspecified number of '*troons e canoõs*', specifying that they were made of iron.[19]

Though the navigational tools at the disposal of pilots when the Henrican voyages began were unsophisticated, surprisingly fast passages south are recorded. With a favourable wind and current, a caravel could easily average six knots an hour. Cadamosto, as we have seen, states that, sailing under such circumstances, it took his caravel only some three days after leaving Cape St Vincent to make Porto Santo, near Madeira. It is not known exactly when the Portuguese pilots discovered that, by setting a course north-north-west from the region of Cape Verde, the caravels, thanks to their lateen rig, could make the otherwise difficult return journey home against trade wind and current a routine matter. This was done by keeping the direction of the prevailing north-east trades at an offing of about 30 degrees to the east. When they reached the latitudes of the Azores they were able to pick up the Atlantic westerlies to carry them straight to Portugal. This course thus took the form of an arc that later became known to navigators as the 'Guinea Track' ('*Volta da Guiné*').[20] Though taking the Guinea Track could mean that the return journey might last as long as two months, it was free of the difficulties and uncertainties that attached to the task of beating a course directly north from the latitude of Cape Verde in the face of the prevailing wind and strong currents near the African coast, though this was probably more often done than is usually supposed. Neither Zurara nor Cadamosto unfortunately have much to say about the return journeys of the caravels from Guinea in Henry's time. They plainly regarded the homeward voyages, whichever of the two routes was taken, as a matter of navigational routine and of no special interest. A passage in Zurara does refer to an occasion in 1446 when most of a caravel's complement had been killed in an action in the estuary of the River Geba. The ship's scrivener, who knew nothing about navigation, is said to have managed, with a mere handful of survivors, to sail the caravel successfully back to Portugal. The voyage, according to the chronicler, took two months, during which time no land was seen.[21] This makes it likely that the scrivener took the Guinea Track or at least a modified form of it. The narrative attributed to Diogo Gomes refers to an occasion in the middle of the century when contrary winds encountered off Madeira on his return journey from Guinea forced him to return home via the Azores. The implication is that he was in the process of sailing directly home to Portugal via the Canary Islands and Madeira when he altered course. The same document confirms that a caravel piloted by the Italian Antonio da Noli, which was travelling in convoy with the Portuguese captain, managed to make a speedier return to Portugal than the latter by setting 'a more direct course to the north'.[22] It would plainly be unwise to presume that, in the last two decades of Henry's life, the caravels, specially when their business was to the north of Cape Verde, routinely took the Guinea Track. It was obviously possible for them, by tacking and taking advantage of such offshore winds as offered themselves, to make their way back to Portugal by sailing against the north-east trades at no great distance from the continent. Later, when exploration had opened up navigation much further south than in Henry's day, it obviously made sense for ships normally to use the Guinea Track.

In the 1440s and 1450s the normal season for the departure of the caravels from Portugal was the early spring. Cadamosto, for example, set sail from Lagos in March for his first voyage to Guinea. The caravels in Henry's time reckoned to return home before the autumn storms on the West African coast. This pattern would be drastically changed later on in the century when navigation to the Malagueta and Mina coasts, or further south still, had to be undertaken. It was then soon discovered that more favourable wind and weather conditions for journeys to those regions of Guinea were encountered if the caravels sailed from Portugal in September, October or November when the north-east trades blew as far south as latitude 5° N. When, for example, Eustache de la Fosse sailed from Cadiz on his illegal voyage to the Malagueta and Mina coasts in 1479, the month selected for departure from Seville was early October.

The outward journey presented few problems once the northeast trades had been picked up. Münzer agreed with Diogo Gomes's comment that from Lisbon to Cape Verde – some 1,750 nautical miles on a direct course – could, in normal conditions, take no longer than twelve days.[23]

Cadamosto's *Navigazioni* gives important additional information about the courses followed by his caravels when sailing to Guinea or exploring new regions there. From the Canaries he would sail due south out of sight of land for some distance before altering course to the east to make for Cape Blanco. From there, unless a caravel's first destination was Arguin Island, he would sail south again, keeping well west of the dangerous Arguin Bank, before picking up the African coast again north of Cape Verde. South of that cape, Cadamosto's caravels navigated always keeping within sight of the shore, so that they could pick up the succession of landmarks and bearings shown on the charts made by the first explorers. When they reached uncharted waters, their first task was to make new charts that recorded – for the eyes of the Prince and future navigators in that region – this kind of information, as well as the results of soundings taken by the lead.

Little is known about the capital cost of building and equipping a caravel at this time, or about the running costs involved in sending one to explore, or to trade in Guinea. Hieronymus Münzer, writing in the 1490s, commented on the short life caravels operating in tropical waters had because of the ravages of the worms which attacked their hulls. According to him, their timbers were liable to give way altogether after only three or four round voyages.[24] Outsize barnacles were another trouble, slowing up a ship and making necessary frequent careening.[25] The hulls of the Henrican caravels of forty and fifty years earlier were certainly not immune from these hazards.

Though this chapter is about ships, not trade, the role of the Guinea caravels as equine transports merits attention here. The export of horses to the Senegal *resgates* was the mainstay of Portuguese exports to the Senegalese kingdoms in Henry's time. There they were exchanged for slaves. Diogo Gomes claims that, in about 1462, he took ten horses to Senegal aboard a caravel commanded by him and that the outward journey lasted twelve days.[26] As we have seen, this was not an unusual time for such a passage when the weather was favourable. During the European Middle Ages generally, the movement of horses by sea for military or other purposes was, of course, a commonplace procedure. If any distance was involved, ships equipped with a stern door through which the animals were loaded and unloaded were often used. There is, however, no indication that, in the Prince's time, caravels were ever modified in this way. Their lines hardly permitted such a thing. It remains, though, something of a mystery how the Portuguese managed with apparent success routinely to transport horses to Senegal in the holds of vessels no bigger than caravels.

How did the Henrican caravels engaged on exploration navigate? The myth about Henry's supposed school of navigation on Cape Sagres is now entirely discredited, though, given the indestructible nature of historical legends, it will no doubt live on to provide romantic entertainment for tourists. It seems certain that, at least until mid-century and perhaps later, Henry's pilots relied on the traditional techniques of oceanic navigation based mainly on the compass, the mariner's chart (when this was available), the lead (to take soundings) and on estimated latitudes. The latter were obtained by noting with the eye the height of the Pole Star above the horizon. Dead reckoning, dependent on a seaman's intuition but helped by half-hourly checks made with the help of a sandglass and recorded on a traverse board, may also already have been used aboard the caravels. Such methods were necessarily rough-and-ready, though the skill of medieval pilots relying on instincts developed by a long tradition probably made them much more reliable than we might imagine. Once a region of Guinea had been explored and charted, families of so-called rhumb lines radiating out from a number of central points on the chart told pilots what compass courses they needed to set, whether they were in port or at sea, to reach the latitude of the required destination. The next stage was to make available on board ship an instrument capable of estimating more accurately than a seaman's eye could the height of the Pole Star above the horizon. Later on in the century this measurement would be correlated with a table of latitudes worked out by shore-based astronomers. There is some evidence that this more sophisticated system, which involved the use of a seaman's quadrant, was being experimented with on Portuguese ships in the early 1450s;[27] the narrative of the Infanta Leonor's ocean journey from Lisbon to Leghorn in 1451–2 to become German empress notes that the Portuguese fleet, in addition to skilled pilots, carried, for greater security, 'master astrologers' well-experienced in reading their way by the stars and the Pole'.[28] This statement suggests that the Portuguese pilots of that time were not yet familiar with navigation by astronomical instruments and that the despatch of professional astronomers-cum-astrologers aboard the fleet was an exceptional measure taken because of the importance of the Infanta's journey. Certainly the observant Cadamosto's account of his two voyages to West Africa in 1455 and 1456 gives little support to the view that these new methods of navigation were by then routinely used by the Portuguese explorers. In a note on the height of the Pole Star and the appearance of the Southern Cross – the latter first sighted by Cadamosto's caravels off the Gambia – the Venetian navigator clearly implies that the only instrument available for fixing the new constellation's position was still the caravel's compass and the human eye.[29]

Against this evidence, two pieces of information have sometimes been cited to suggest that the pilots of the Guinea caravels in the Prince's time *did* know how to employ the new tools used for astronomical navigation. Diogo Gomes claims to have used a quadrant in West African waters c. 1460. He may well, however, have anticipated chronologically the later use of this instrument by himself and others. The quadrant was certainly employed by Portuguese pilots before Gomes retired from the sea later in the century. On the whole it seems likely, however, that the Henrican explorations in Guinea, certainly until towards the end of the Prince's life, were carried out using only the limited navigational aids that had traditionally served pilots well in the Mediterranean and on the route from there to Northern Europe, a fact which makes the achievements of Henry's navigators especially noteworthy. Far from teaching practical navigation to his pilots as the myth has it, it is much more probable that at first it was they who taught the Prince about their craft, so enabling him to relate his book knowledge of astrology, astronomy and cartography to the needs of practical navigation, even though he had little direct experience of the latter. He sometimes personally briefed his pilots about what they might expect to find when they reached any hitherto unvisited destination in Guinea, using for this purpose the background information he had accumulated both from his reading of books and maps and from the reports of previous explorers. Since he was keenly interested in new developments, where matters of concern to him were involved, it may be supposed that he took whatever opportunities came his way, such as the presence of the storm-bound Venetian galleys off Cape Sagres in 1454, to find out what the latest navigational devices used by foreign seamen were and how they worked. How successful he was in persuading his pilots to adopt new tools and new practices is perhaps another question.

All the new information and guidance Henry could offer his pilots and captains would have gone for nothing if their hearts were not in the enterprises he asked them to undertake. Here his moral authority was the decisive influence. Everyone knew that, in the face of intense scepticism from his peers, from experienced pilots and from cosmographers, he had been proved right when he said that the fears seamen associated with the name of Cape Bojador were mere superstitions. His own unshakeable self-confidence that it was his destiny to succeed as a sponsor of oceanic exploration communicated itself to mariners and sea-going knights and squires alike, even before the caravels started to trade profitably in Guinea. All these people trusted Henry because they believed, probably not always correctly, that he knew what he was about. It was also a touch of genius on his part to exploit the religious and chivalric sentiments of the squires of his over-large household by offering them the chance to win in great waters, as crusaders for the Faith on remote African shores, the fame and glory they sought.

Chapter Ten

Prince Henry and the Atlantic Slave Trade[1]

I have determined . . . that on all things which are traded or
secured . . . in the said land of Guinea from Cape Noun onwards,
whether they be male or female slaves, gold, products of the
fisheries or any other objects and merchandise whatsoever, there
shall be . . . paid to the said Order of Christ the vintena . . .

> Prince Henry in a donation to the Order of Christ dated 26
> December 1457[2]

The beginnings of serious Portuguese involvement in the maritime slave trade, and evidence of the enthusiastic welcome this innovation received from the Portuguese population at large, can be precisely dated and reported on, thanks to the special attention given to the trade by Zurara in the *Chronicle of Guinea*. The first Portuguese expedition beyond Cape Bojador to be overtly concerned with nothing except slave-raiding on a substantial scale was organized in 1444. The organizer was one of Henry's henchmen, Lançarote da Ilha, the royal tax-collector in Lagos. He mounted an expedition of six Lagos caravels for the express purpose of taking slaves on the islands on the Arguin Bank. The costs of fitting out and supplying the expedition were not borne by the Prince on this occasion but by Lançarote and a consortium of Lagos merchant-adventurers. They had, of course, to obtain Henry's licence for the project and to agree to surrender to him, as was now routine in such cases, the royal fifth (*quinto*) of whatever number of slaves they might bring back, the slaves being seen as war booty. The expedition was organized as a naval and military operation. To the normal crew of each caravel were added one or two bowmen and a small number of other fighting men in each case under the command of one of Henry's squires. Zurara's factual source for what followed was, as usual, the lost narrative of Afonso Cerveira. The chronicler, however, added various rhetorical comments and embellishments of his own to Cerveira's work, together, perhaps, with the occasional personal memory of slave auctions at which he had been present.[3]

During the first part of June 1444 the inhabitants of the islands on the Bank, mostly but not solely poor Idzagen (Sanhadja) fishermen whom the Portuguese called *schimeiros*, were attacked without mercy by the European invaders of their space from Cape Blanco southwards as far as Cape Timiris, those of whatever sex or age who resisted often being killed to intimidate the others into surrender. The captured men, women and children were carried off to the caravels in the ships' boats or on the crude rafts (Port. *almadias*) used by the fishermen. Eventually some two hundred and forty captives in all were crammed aboard the six caravels where they were kept bound and perhaps, as was certainly usual later, fettered. Some were kept in the hold, others left on deck exposed to the worst the weather could do during the long journey back to Portugal. It must be remembered that most caravels at this time only had a capacity of perhaps from forty to fifty or sixty tons burden and that each, on account of the presence of the soldiers as well as the crew, already carried some twenty or more Portuguese. The overcrowding must have been acute, the captives terrified and the filth and stench in the holds overwhelming, even for the noses of a medieval crew. According to the dates given by Zurara, it took from mid-June to about 6 August 1444 for the six caravels to reach Lagos from Cape Blanco with their human cargo.[4]

The return of the caravels to Lagos in mid-summer, and the events which followed their return, are recounted at length in a famous, often quoted and usually misinterpreted passage in the *Chronicle of Guinea*. The factual information in the passage was presumably taken from Cerveira's narrative, but Zurara also used the occasion to give full rein to his penchant for rhetorical writing.[5] News of the expedition's success had reached the Algarve port in advance of its return. In consequence, a crowd of spectators was already assembled on the waterfront to witness what they had been told would be a novel event in the maritime history of the port. The whole event was dominated by the presence on horseback of the Prince himself. It was not, of course, the first occasion on which Portuguese ships had unloaded slaves in Lagos. Captured aboriginal inhabitants seized in the Canary Islands by private merchants had been disembarked there from time to time ever since the fourteenth century. The occasional privateer belonging to the Prince or to someone else also occasionally put in to land captive North African or Granadine Moors seized at sea by Portuguese corsairs or taken in a land raid on those coasts. A small number of Berber captives from the Sahara had already been brought back to the Algarve port by early Henrican voyages. But now something different was afoot. The occasion was intended to celebrate the fact that Portugal had now joined the Genoese, the Catalans and Valencians as a serious slave-trading nation. For this reason and for political and publicity purposes of his own, Henry had decided to make a major public spectacle of the disembarkation and disposal of the large number of captive men, women and children taken by force of arms in a distant land never seen by Europeans until about ten years before. The Lagos crowds would see for themselves that, contrary to what his many critics had been suggesting, the exploration of Guinea was not the risky and useless waste of effort and money they complained about. Although no large quantities of gold had been found so far, the Portuguese discoverers had secured direct access to what was soon realized to be an unlimited number of potential slaves from West Africa who, until now, had only reached Europe thanks to the Islamic monopoly exercised through the trans-Saharan caravans.

Lançarote, according to Zurara's account, reported to the Prince that the long sea journey under bad conditions, as well as the grief and fear of the captives, meant that they were in a lamentable condition, a report one can well believe. Nevertheless, they were kept aboard overnight while the port officials carried out their bureaucratic duties of head-counting, assessing the value of the human cargo and establishing the amounts that must be handed over to the Prince as a first priority in the form of the *quinto* as well as the twentieth (*vintena*) due to the Order of Christ, and other imposts. Any vessel returning from Guinea had also to be closely rummaged for contraband, particularly in the form of gold dust or gold jewellery.

Disembarkation took place early in the morning after the caravels' arrival. The captives were marched to a convenient open space just outside one of the town gates where the townspeople and peasants from the surrounding countryside had already gathered in force to witness the unusual sight. Before those responsible got down to the business of auctioning the slaves, they, on Henry's instructions, presented one captive to the principal church in Lagos and another to the Franciscan convent on Cape St Vincent. This was intended both as a thanks-offering to God for the success of the venture and to give force to the claim that it was concern for the salvation of the souls of these captives and nothing else that had caused the Prince to arrange for them to be brought to Portugal. When Las Casas came to comment on Henry's donation a century later, he denounced it as a wicked attempt to suggest that God himself approved of the seizure of slaves by force.[6]

The *Chronicle of Guinea's* description of the spectacle that then ensued makes it clear that Zurara was not so habituated to the insti-tution of slavery that he was incapable of recognizing and recording the human tragedy involved in what happened next, though he did not interpret the tragedy in the terms that modern writers suppose he did. The captives were divided into five groups whose market value was reckoned to be roughly equal.[7] Henry, mounted on a horse, supervised the proceedings, taking for himself as the royal fifth some forty-six of the best slaves. These already had been specially set aside for him. Zurara paints the harrowing scenes witnessed by the onlookers as the division was carried out:

> These people, assembled together on that open place, were an aston-ishing sight to behold. Among them were some who were quite white-skinned, handsome and of good appearance; others [Berbers or 'tawny Moors'] were less white, seeming more like brown men; others still were as black as Ethiopians, so deformed of face and body that, to those who stared at them, it almost seemed that they were looking at spirits from the lowest hemisphere. But what heart, however hardened it might be, could not be pierced by a feeling of pity at the sight of that company? Some held their heads low, their faces bathed in tears as they looked at each other; some groaned very piteously, looking towards the heavens fixedly and crying out aloud, as if they were calling on the father of the universe to help them; others struck their faces with their hands and threw themselves full length on the ground; yet others lamented in the form of a chant, according to the custom of their native land, and though

the words of the language in which they sang could not be understood by our people, the chant revealed clearly enough the degree of
their grief. To increase their anguish still more, those who had charge
of the division then arrived and began to separate them one from
another so that they formed five equal lots. This made it
necessary to separate sons from their fathers and wives from their
husbands and brother from brother. No account was taken of
friendship or relationship, but each one ending up where chance
placed him. . . . Who could carry out such a division without great
difficulty for as soon as the children who had been assigned to one
group saw their parents in another they jumped up and ran towards
them; mothers clasped their other children in their arms and lay face
downwards on the ground, accepting wounds with contempt for the
suffering of their flesh rather than let their children be torn from
them?[8]

It was the kind of scene which, from the dawn of civilization, most
people the world over had always been taught to regard as a normal
feature of economic and social life. The description of such scenes by
the historians of antiquity was usually concerned with the plight of
the civilian victims of defeat in war. What is unusual about Zurara's
description is that it describes in much detail an actual auction of
African slaves in Lagos and does so in terms which not only show an
ability to understand the human misery involved but set out to draw
the reader's attention to it. The facts of the auction were no doubt taken
from Cerveira's narrative, but Zurara's gloss on the original material
is obvious as when, in an introductory and highly rhetorical passage,
Zurara unexpectedly explains that, since the captives were human
beings and the children of Adam just as he was, it was natural that
their sufferings should move him to tears when he came to write about
this event. His acceptance of the humanity of the slaves-to-be evidently
embraces the black Africans despite the fact that he regarded their facial
features as 'deformed'. This, he says, caused those who stared at them
to imagine they looked as visitors from Hell might look.

The Portuguese chronicler deserves full credit for letting readers in
later centuries share his experience of what a fifteenth-century slave
auction was really like. It would, however, certainly be a mistake to
suppose that Zurara, in this passage, had any intention of suggesting
to his own contemporaries that there was anything wrong about the
slave trade or those who participated in it. The auction was, he explains

admiringly, supervised in person by his hero, Henry, and he repeatedly emphasizes, as Henry himself did, that the only purpose of the trade in slaves which the Prince was responsible for bringing to Portugal was to make Christians of infidels and pagans; any 'inconveniences' the converted slave might have to endure in this life being as nothing when compared with the certainty of eternal salvation that conversion brings with it. The chronicler also draws another lesson characteristic of the spirit of the later Middle Ages from the pitiful spectacle he has described when he comments

> Oh! All-powerful Fortune, whose wheel moves forwards and back-wards arranging the affairs of the world according to your whims, at least place before the eyes of these miserable people some aware-ness of the wonderful new things that await them [at life's end] so that they may receive some consolation in the middle of their present great distress.[9]

Zurara devotes almost the the whole of his next chapter to explain-ing how well-treated slaves are in Portugal and how easy their social relations with their masters and other Portuguese are. The chronicler wisely elected only to discuss the treatment of domestic slaves. While his contemporaries no doubt realized that his target was the laudable one of giving posterity a good impression of the Portuguese as slave-owners, some even so may have felt a certain discomfort about the excessive zeal with which the chronicler here gilded the lily. Zurara seems, in fact, to have got himself thoroughly muddled about the whole question of slavery. Despite his sympathetic account of the sufferings of these captives, he finally explains their plight as a visual illustration of the correctness of traditional Christian theology's view of the pagan state. Without access to Faith, these people, he now explains, previ-ously lived like beasts, incapable of reason and in consequence knowing nothing of the existence of bread, wine, clothing or what it was to live in (proper) houses. Worst of all, their ignorance was so great that it prevented them having the least understanding of good (and evil).[10] The reader will note Zurara's eurocentric view, characteristic of his times, that the domestic habits and arrangements of men of reason had to be, by definition, the same as those of European Christians. It was a belief that was destined to cause the Portuguese serious problems in terms of race relations with native peoples, particularly during later stages of the overseas expansion.

We may be sure that Zurara's final judgement on these matters was entirely shared by the Prince, who expressed himself in identical terms when describing to the pope his view of what the pagan Canarians must be like. It is unlikely, too, that the spectacle of the slave auction in Lagos aroused any feelings of pity in the Prince, who was the epitome of a muscular Christian and not much given to compassion – even for those who were on the right side of God – though he could simulate it when it was expected of him. Convinced of his evangelizing mission, he seems to have watched with untroubled satisfaction a happening which he had persuaded himself would be eminently pleasing to God as well as profitable to him. Zurara, anxious to make sure that future readers of his chronicle could not fall into the error of thinking that Henry was involved in the slave trade for the money, proceeded to give his readers a final assurance that it was not the fact that forty-six valuable slaves had just become the Prince's property which pleased him, but the thought of all the souls who, thanks to the action of Lançarote and his companions, had been saved from eternal perdition. The chronicler's repeated assurances on this point suggest that perhaps even in his own time there were those who found them hard to swallow.

After Henry had taken his share of the booty, the remaining slaves were handed over in lots on a pro rata basis to the various individuals who had financed or participated in the expedition. Some, according to the chronicler, were retained by their new owners and dispersed to work on the latter's own properties. Others were sold by auction or by private treaty. To put the seal of the Prince's approval on the whole thing, Lançarote himself was knighted on the spot.

In 1445, no doubt on instructions from Henry, the people of Lisbon were also given the opportunity to watch the unloading and disposal of another large cargo of slaves captured or obtained by barter on the Arguin Bank and in the region of Cape Blanco. The event seems to have caused even more excitement in the capital than in Lagos. Zurara writes:

How could anyone not take pleasure on observing the multitude of people who rushed to see the caravels? As soon as these had lowered their sails, the officers who collect the imposts due to the king were rowed out in boats from the waterfront to verify where these ships came from and what they carried. When they returned, the news [that they carried a cargo of slaves] spread in a very short time and so many people went aboard the caravels that these were in danger of sinking. The crowds were no less the following day when the captives were brought ashore from the ships to be marched to the Prince's palace, which was a considerable distance from the waterfront. From all over the city people rushed to [line] the streets through which they would have to be taken. The author of this history comments that those many who, at the beginning, as he said earlier, were opposed to this affair [the Henrican explorations] now had every reason to reproach themselves. Now there was no one around willing to admit to ever having been one of the critics. When they watched the prisoners bound with rope being marched through the streets, the tumult of the people was so great as they praised aloud the great virtues of the Prince that if anyone had dared to voice a contrary opinion to theirs he would very quickly have been obliged to withdraw it. . . . The Prince himself was away in Viseu from where he gave orders for the disposal of his fifth of the captives. As for the rest of them, the captains [of the caravels] arranged for them to be auctioned in the city as a result of which each one secured great profits.[11]

The Prince, as the *Chronicle of Guinea* and many documents initiated by him make clear, thought of his role in turning Portugal into a major slave-trading country as an evangelizing achievement of which he could be proud, and one which would make a major contribution to his posthumous fame in history as a tireless battler to bring the Christian message to infidels and pagans. In the context of the role of slavery in the world in which he lived, both these claims, with the aid of a little casuistry, could be made to seem compatible. Christianity had lived comfortably with slavery for centuries and would continue to do so for several more. He could never have imagined that time would turn his association with the slave trade into a bad memory which, as Samuel Johnson was to say, made it difficult to decide, taking everything into account, whether he had been a force for good or for evil in world history. Bartolomé de Las Casas, writing in the first half of the sixteenth century, had had no such doubts. He unreservedly described Henry and the Portuguese as violent evil-doers who, while professing to spread the Faith, had in fact broken in Guinea most of the Church's laws and teachings.[12] But his was a lone voice. Not until 1555 would anyone ever be heard in Portugal criticizing the country's involvement in the slave trade.

The Prince was not, of course, strictly speaking, the initiator and first patron of the Atlantic slave trade, though he is sometimes presented as if he were. Before his time, Genoese, Catalan, Castilian and other Christian merchants and seamen, as we have seen, had been in the habit of buying in the Atlantic ports of Morocco black slaves imported from the Sudan by the trans-Saharan caravans. From there, they had been shipped to Europe long before the Prince's caravels first started to bring them from the new Saharan *resgates*. Ever since the fourteenth century, the aboriginal inhabitants of the Canary Islands had been the constant victims of organized seaborne slave razzias frequently carried out at the behest of merchants from the Iberian Peninsula and Italy. Before the Prince's time, however, slaves, and particularly slaves from Black Africa, had rarely been seen in Portugal, hence the special attention their arrival there in large numbers attracted in 1445. What is unique about the events of that year is that the Prince was the first European to use the Atlantic for long-distance seaborne transport to Europe of Africans of diverse racial origins captured or bought by barter in the newly discovered lands beyond Cape Bojador. Nor was the Portuguese trade in slaves established under the Prince's auspices simply a venture that concerned only him and the knights and squires, merchants and sailors who, one way or another, took part directly in it. As a result of this particular Henrican initiative, Portugal became, during the Prince's lifetime, an important and ever-growing market which supplied Castile (especially Seville) and the Crown of Aragon (especially Valencia) with slaves from Black Africa. Portugal itself, thanks to this same initiative, also began to turn into a slave-owning society with all the social consequences that that would have.

How much the Prince knew about the Mediterranean slave trade and consciously borrowed its practices cannot be established, though, as he showed in connection with Madeiran sugar and viniculture, and in his choice of foreign advisers, he certainly knew about other characteristics of trade in that sea. His practical experience of the slave trade doubtless also owed much to what he had heard about slave razzias in the Canaries. Some of the ways he organized the Guinea trade seem to have been directly borrowed from procedures routinely used by slave-takers there. Nevertheless, properly to understand and assess the historical context in which Henry's appearance as a patron of the trade took place, it is necessary to take into account the extent to which the trade was carried on in the Mediterranean before – and long after – he gave it a proper Atlantic dimension.

Slave trading in the Mediterranean in the later Middle Ages had become something of a speciality of the Genoese. With scant regard for any legal or ethical prohibitions, they had long before set about enslaving members of the Orthodox Christian Church as well as those from the pagan peoples of south-eastern Europe. At their outposts on the

Black Sea, especially at Caffa (in the Crimea) and Tana (on the Sea of Azov), they bought up Tartars, Circassians, Russians and the other inhabitants of the Black Sea hinterland and the Balkans who had been captured in war or seized in razzias. These captives were then transported in Genoese ships through the Dardanelles for disposal by auction or private treaty, sometimes at Pera (near Constantinople), but most commonly at the Genoese slave-market on the island of Chios. From here, a number intended to serve as domestic servants were exported directly to Genoa itself. Others were transported to slave marts in the western Mediterranean, among them those on Majorca and Ibiza. The numbers of slaves the Genoese handled were considerable. A Genoese ordinance of 1441 forbade Genoese three-decked ships to carry more than sixty slaves at a time if they were also carrying other merchandise. This restriction on numbers significantly did not apply to vessels which specialized in the slave trade and carried no other cargo. Records show that ships on the run from the Black Sea to Chios sometimes, in fact, carried more than 100 slaves per voyage.[13] It was certainly not the Portuguese who first created the baleful image of the overcrowded slaver in the maritime history of the later Middle Ages.

By the fifteenth century, most of the white slaves sold by the Genoese at Chios were disposed of to Muslim purchasers in Turkey, Syria, Egypt and North Africa in a sort of trans-Saharan caravan trade in reverse. Even the fall of Constantinople in 1453 did not put an end to the Genoese slave trade centred on the Black Sea, though the slaves bought at Caffa and Tama were, by now, at least partly Islamicized and subject to Turkish suzereinty. By 1460 most of the slaves being handled by the Genoese merchants on Chios were prisoners taken by the Turks in the Balkans – Greeks, Bulgars, Bosnians, Serbs. As has been said, the Genoese had no compunction either about enslaving Greek Orthodox Christians who came into their hands in this way, or about selling them indiscriminately either to Muslim buyers or to Western Christian ones. All were regarded simply as commodities. Though the Genoese slave traders were most active in the eastern Mediterranean, this was certainly not the only area of their activities. As keen buyers of black slaves from the Sudan, they were also to be found at the various points in Muslim North Africa where the trans-Saharan slave-caravans debouched and where Genoese *fonduks* existed. These black slaves were then sold in North Africa itself, in Sicily, in the Iberian Peninsula and elsewhere. The appearance on the Iberian scene in the 1440s of the Portuguese caravels from Guinea with their human cargo seemed to challenge this virtual Genoese monopoly of the export trade in black slaves reaching North Africa from time immemorial by the caravans from the Sudan.

One notable difference between the Genoese and the Portuguese approach to the trade was the failure of the Italians to show any interest either in converting slaves to Christianity or in respecting the restrictions imposed by canon law and papal edict on the sale to Muslims of infidel or pagan slaves, let alone Christian ones. Prince Henry's claim that the sole purpose of his investment in the slave trade was to give the captives from Africa an opportunity to become Christians sounds like obvious hypocrisy today but, judging by what Zurara and some of his contemporaries have to say on the matter, did not seem so to them. The Prince never wavered from his assertion that the Portuguese were in Guinea as crusaders for the Faith and, as everyone knew, crusaders had the right, as a reward for doing God's work and to help to make its continuance possible, to take whatever booty of war they could. This, of course, included prisoners who, unless they could put up ransom money, were deemed to have become slaves. Nor, as long as it could be claimed that the slaves had been taken in a just war in Guinea against infidels and pagans, had the Church any objection to their enslavement. In the Iberian Peninsula the acceptance of slavery by the civil authority was fully enshrined in legal form in the *Siete Partidas* of Alfonso X of Castile, a code whose validity was recognized in Portugal as well as in Castile.[14] This work's sections on slaves and slavery, derived from Roman law, are to be found in *Partidas*, III, IV and V. The work is uncompromising on the social status of a slave. When defining the duties of a freedman towards his former master, it comments 'just as servitude is the most ignoble thing in this world that is not a sin, and the most despised, so to be free is the thing most dear to man and the most prized'.[15] The king also made short work of the problem presented by the Christian belief that all members of the human race are descended from Adam – a problem that, as we have just seen, troubled Zurara when he came to write about slavery and Prince Henry. The Castilian code simply explained that, though in natural law there may be no distinction between a free man and a slave, for the practical working of society natural law in this case had been superseded by man-made law which treats freemen and slaves differently.[16] How differently is made clear when the subject of witnesses in legal trials is being discussed in the *Partidas*. In general, the manual explains, slaves were not permitted to give evidence against anyone. An exception was made in cases of treason and certain types of murder, but with the discouraging proviso that a slave giving hostile evidence on such occasions should be tortured while doing so to make sure that he was telling the truth. The *Partida* concerned explains why such a measure is necessary:

> . . . slaves behave like desperate men because of the state of servitude in which they find themselves. Therefore everyone should expect that they will readily tell lies and conceal the truth unless force is applied to them.[17]

Three causes were accepted in the *Partidas* as justifying enslavement: (1) if a person being an enemy of the Faith had been captured in war; (2) if the person concerned was the child of a slave woman; (3) if a free man or woman voluntarily let themselves be sold into slavery. For practical purposes, the third of these can be discounted here. It was, of course, understood by the Alfonsine compilers that by 'war' they meant here a war that was 'just' simply because it was waged against infidels or pagans. The *Partidas* also contain quite elaborate rules governing the sale and purchase of slaves.[18] For the rest the code mostly follows Roman tradition. A master can do with his slave whatever he pleases except that he may not kill him or mutilate him physically. Even this restraint was relaxed if he had found a slave in bed with his wife or daughter. Any sort of profit made or earned by a slave belonged to his master – a reference to the common practice of hiring out slaves to work for others. One legal provision referred to a peculiarly Iberian problem: it was a capital offence for a Jew or Moor to own a Christian slave, though it was legal for either to own unbaptized slaves. The humiliating life-long obligations of a freedman towards his former master according to the Alfonsine code are such as to explain why, in Portugal, the distinction between the two states was, in practice, barely visible.[19]

Henry, however, had much more powerful authority than tradition or the *Siete Partidas* to justify his engagement in the slave trade. Various earlier papal bulls could be interpreted as giving him the right to take slaves in Guinea but it was Eugenius IV, in January 1455, who, basing his action on the traditional doctrine that the supreme pontiff was the terrestrial as well as the spiritual ruler of all the world, had spelt out in detail the nature of this right. The bull authorized Henry to proceed to the conquest and conversion of all Black Africa, explored and still to be explored; to enslave its people; and, more significantly, to deny their liberty to such slaves even after they became converts to Christianity.[20]

Though Henry, despite Zurara's disclaimers, was no doubt in practice just as keen as any Genoese slave trader on the profits to be made from 'black gold', it would have been impossible for a prince of his standing, and with his highly publicized dedication to religious values, to have become involved in the slave trade in a major way without the ideological support and the authority of the Roman curia. It is, though, unlikely, for the reasons already stated, that he, a thoroughly traditional late-medieval Christian of his time, saw any contradiction between enslaving Africans and converting them at the same time. Far from opening himself to the charge of hypocrisy, the pious Henry could fairly claim that, as he saw it, he was the first secular Christian leader of his time ever to concern himself about the souls rather than simply the bodies of slaves from across the waters.

After Henry's death much less would be heard of these evangelizing claims, and with good reason. By the middle 1470s Afonso V permitted slaves to be bought on the Nigerian coast, transported to the Mina Coast and there immediately sold to the merchants of Mina for gold without the slightest attempt having been made to turn them into Christians. The practice was in clear contravention of canon law. Nevertheless, when required to justify their reasons for building their spreading empire, the Portuguese always explained that what drove them above all was their pious desire to bring Christian salvation to Muslims and pagans alike the world over. It was doubtless an explanation of the matter which Zurara would have heard often from Henry's own lips and which he made his own.

By no means all the slaves imported into Portugal in Henry's time – or later – remained there. There was a strong demand, specially from Castile, for black slaves. This came particularly from the Andalusian ports, especially Seville and Cadiz. Until then, the Canaries had probably been the main supplier of non-Muslim slaves to Castile. Now black slaves imported from Guinea by the Portuguese were much sought after. Spanish end-of-the-century literary sources show that the large black community in Seville rather unexpectedly spoke the Afro-Portuguese pidgin they had picked up while in Portuguese hands.

As far as the Peninsula was concerned, Portugal was a tardy participant in the slave trade. During the fourteenth and early fifteenth centuries the eastern lands of the Crown of Aragon – Catalonia, Valencia and the Balearic Islands – were the only regions of the Iberian Peninsula where an organized seaborne slave trade was carried on and where chattel slavery was fully institutionalized. They are also the only regions for which reasonably adequate documentation about Iberian slavery at that time exists.[21] In the Crown of Aragon the employment of slaves for agricultural work and for urban heavy labour – as well as for domestic and personal service – was traditional. Until the end of the thirteenth century such needs had been largely met by enslaving Moorish prisoners-of-war and by razzias made into Moorish territory in the Iberian Peninsula itself. These sources of supply markedly diminished when, about 1265, the Crown of Aragon ceased to have any common frontier with the Granadine Moors. At the same time, as a consequence of the Black Death and other factors, the demand for slave labour steadily continued to increase. Under these conditions the Catalans, following the example of the Genoese, also turned to the eastern Mediterranean and began to import numbers of Tartar slaves, as well as Greeks, Bulgars, Bosnians and Russians. The main market through which they bought these white slaves seems to have been Majorca, but the mechanics of this Peninsular trade with the East are still obscure.

The importation of Christian, though schismatic, slaves into the Crown of Aragon at first troubled the conscience of the Aragonese rulers. John I went so far, in 1388, as to obtain from the Avignon pope a bull ordering him to release all such slaves in his dominions if they had been acquired directly or indirectly from the Turks.[22] The bull proved unenforceable because of the fierce resistance of all John's subjects who traditionally depended on slave labour.

The eastern Mediterranean was, however, unable, through the normal channels of the trade, to satisfy all the needs of the Crown of Aragon. To help to fill the gap, Catalan and Valencian privateers took to raiding the coasts of North Africa and Granada and to preying on Moorish shipping even more vigorously than they had always done. The activities of these corsairs were well-established long before the Portuguese began, in the time of John I, to do the same thing in a major way. Catalan corsairs ranged as far afield as Asia Minor, where they boldly conducted razzias against the Turkish population in their search for slaves.[23] The importance of the slave trade to the Crown of Aragon, and the material rewards it brought, can be judged from the fact that the operations of the corsairs against the Moors at sea and on land went unchecked by the rulers of that crown, even though these operations imperilled the extremely important legitimate sea-borne trade with the Muslim world in North Africa carried on out of Barcelona, Valencia and the Balearic Islands. Additional evidence of the importance of slave labour for the Catalan economy in the early fifteenth century is the fact that the *Generalitat* of Catalonia at that time sponsored a scheme for insuring owners of slaves against losses caused to them by the flight abroad of their slaves. The records compiled in connection with this scheme disclose that, about the end of 1431, some 1,700 slaves were registered under it – three-quarters of them in the city of Barcelona and its municipal district. Since slaves under the age of fourteen were not insurable and those who were valued by their owners at less than 25 *libras* (Barc.) were exempt, this figure necessarily underestimates considerably the total number of individual slaves then living in the Catalan capital.

Another region that imported slaves in the fifteenth century was the kingdom of Valencia.[24] Valencian records show that black slaves were quite commonly to be found there early in the century and that, in the 1420s and 1430s, they already sold for a higher price than those whom the registers describe as 'white or brown Moors' (*moros blancos o llors*), that is, Arabs or Berbers.[25] An indication of the rarity value which black slaves still retained at this time is given by an Aragonese document of 1400 in which Martin I refers to his intention to make a present of two negro slaves 'together with other things' to the duke of Burgundy.[26] The Portuguese, when they reckoned that black slaves were more valuable than Africans of lighter pigmentation, simply followed a feature of the slave market in the rest of Europe. The reasons for this preference were varied. As domestic servants, blacks in those early days were seen in Europe as exotic household luxuries for the rich, though the sheer numbers imported into Portugal were soon to make them available there even to quite modest urban householders. More significantly, blacks were generally believed to make better slaves because they were said to be more capable of sustained hard physical labour than whites. From the owner's point of view, black slaves had another advantage. Their colour made them conspicuous in a predominantly white society. In consequence they were also less likely to attempt to escape, or to succeed if they tried. Zurara characteristically gives another reason why black slaves were preferred; they were, or seemed to be, much easier to convert than either Orthodox Christians from the East or Africans from the Islamicized lands north of the River Senegal.

Aragonese records also merit attention because of what they disclose about the legal and social situation of slaves in the east of the Iberian Peninsula at a time when Portuguese information about those matters is scanty. In Catalonia and Valencia (and perhaps in the Balearics too) the traditional legal proviso that no individual could be legitimately assigned to the status of slave unless it could be established that he or she had been captured as booty in a just war was, at least in theory, taken seriously. Documents had to be presented to the royal officials guaranteeing that the man, woman or child concerned had been taken prisoner *'de bona guerra'*, i.e. in the course of military operations against infidels or pagans. In the Crown of Aragon the declaration to this effect had, rather oddly, to be made by the captive himself.[27] Given the realities of the captive's position, not to mention the language problems and other pressures with which he or she had to contend, it is unlikely that refusals to make the required affirmation were frequent.

There seems to be no evidence that such individual affirmations of status were required in Portugal in the Prince's time. No doubt the point was covered by the fact that, even when peaceful trading for slaves in Guinea had become the rule, Henry's claim that such trading was an integral and continuing part of his personal war against Islam was held by him to provide the necessary guarantee that every slave had been a legitimate prisoner of war.

Of equally dubious practical force were the rules in Catalonia relating to the baptism of slaves. There was a theoretical requirement there that masters should do their best to see that all immigrant slaves were baptized as soon as possible; if a slave had not been baptized before he or she was sold for the first time, the original or the new owner was required by law to arrange baptism without delay and to give the convert a Christian name. As in Portugal, baptism did not secure liberty, but in Catalonia it did give the slave some extra rights. One who had been baptized with his owner's consent was not supposed to be resold without his own personal agreement. But this right was somewhat diminished by a proviso that, if baptism had taken place *without* the owner's consent, the slave concerned could not benefit in the way described. He or she could then be sold to another Christian master without their agreement.[28] Thus, in order to maintain the slave owner's unrestricted right to dispose of a slave as he wished, all that was needed was a declaration by the owner that baptism had taken place without his consent, a ruse that no doubt was frequently employed. As had always been the case, and as would continue to be the case in the centuries which followed, whether in Portugal or elsewhere, the few laws intended to protect the civil rights of slaves were ignored or circumvented because neither slave owners nor the state had any material motive for respecting them. As the *Siete Partidas* had noted, slaves might be human beings like everyone else, but the law had intervened to make sure that, for practical purposes, they were assigned to a lower category of being than that of their masters.

In Portugal, at least in the Prince's time, genuine efforts were obviously made by him to secure the baptism of African slaves. His motives were not necessarily entirely altruistic. Conversion at least partly broke the link with a slave's past and with his or her native culture. Henry also of course needed multiple conversions in Portugal to justify his frequent assurances to the curia that, under his auspices, encouraging numbers of Africans were receiving Christian baptism. He did not explain to the curia that these proselytizing successes were achieved only among slaves after they had been brought to Portugal. It was, though, by no means unheard of for black slaves to refuse baptism. Those that refused can be identified in the records because they retained their African names.

Slaves in the Crown of Aragon could be sold either at a public auction or by private treaty. At auction, sellers were required to describe them in detail like any other chattel and to draw a possible buyer's attention to any blemishes or physical defects. This was also the practice in Portugal. Foreign travellers there later in the century noted that slaves put up for sale were inspected in the nude by potential buyers and made by them to demonstrate their physical fitness by performing exercises.[29]

Though slaves were not regarded as totally without a juridical persona, even if they remained unconverted, their rights, based on Roman law, were, as we have already seen, very few. Slaves could be disposed of in their owners' wills just like any other chattel. Everywhere the child of a slave woman normally retained the juridical status of its mother. Monetary or other redress for offences committed against a slave was receivable by his master, since such offences were treated as damage to the latter's property. Slaves could take no legal initiatives on their own behalf nor, as already noted, could they normally give evidence in a civil or criminal case, since their legal status was held to be similar to that of children, women, madmen or those who were blind, deaf or dumb.[30] Though his owner was forbidden to inflict physical mutilation on him, the slave was subject to severe punishment by the officers of the law for a great variety of offences. Attempted flight was particularly *mal vu* and could lead to a public flogging and, sometimes, also to the loss of a member which did not impair the escapee's capacity for work, such as an ear. In theory at least, a slave could never carry a knife, drink in a tavern or public place, sell anything, be given lodging by anyone except his owner, or be in the streets after dark unless he carried a light.[31] Most of the restrictive and punitive laws in force in the Crown of Aragon are eventually to be found replicated in Portugal as the numbers of slaves there grew. There is, though, some evidence that, during Henry's lifetime, the Portuguese were more tolerant and less frightened of this new racial element in their social midst than they later became. At best, the Portuguese regarded their domestic slaves as if they were grown-up or mentally retarded children who could not speak Portuguese correctly and always needed watching. The worst treated, as elsewhere in the Peninsula, were those who, in urban centres, were hired out by their masters to perform heavy duties like stevedoring on the dockside, or despised ones like street cleansing or sanitary clearance.

The real public career of the Prince as a hero of discovery may be said to have begun when he was acclaimed by the citizens of Lagos and Lisbon as they watched the columns of pinioned and terrified brown-skinned and black-skinned captives from the far-off Saharan coast marched through their streets in 1444 on their way to be offered membership of the *communitas fidelium*. Not for a moment did Zurara let his readers ask themselves if the material profits from the slave trade did not, perhaps, have something to do with Henry's satisfaction. As he puts it in a rhetorical address to his hero:

The only thing that concerned your generous heart was not the thought of the small material gain [that accrued to you], and which I can justly call 'small' when I compare it to that greatness of intellect without which you would not have had the knowledge nor the ability either to start or to finish any part of your noble deeds. Instead of that, you were moved only by your pious intention to seek salvation for those lost souls. . . . That is why, when you saw the captives displayed before you, so great was the pleasure the sight of them gave you that you reckoned as nothing the expenses you had had to lay out [on this enterprise]. But a greater happiness still was the one that was reserved for them, for, though their bodies might be in a state of servitude, that was a small matter when compared with the fact that their souls would [now] enjoy true freedom for all eternity.[32]

Zurara's commitment to this line of approach to the Henrican beginnings of the Atlantic slave trade necessarily ruled out any objective assessment of the actual situation of African slaves in Portugal in the chronicler's time. Confining himself exclusively to discussing the fate of those who became domestic slaves, he paints a picture of happy relationships between the latter and their masters which, if taken at its face value, would prove that slavery in Portugal was a positively enviable state to be in, and one far removed from that which prevailed, for example, in the lands of the Crown of Aragon. Readers of Dr Saunders's study of the social history of black slaves in Portugal from 1441 will know that, in fact, their situation was much the same, or very soon became much the same. Zurara, however, claimed that masters and mistresses treated their slaves exactly the same as they treated their free-born Portuguese servants. Sometimes, he says, they even treated them better, as, for example, by having them instructed in the mechanical arts. Warming to his theme, the chronicler asserts that male slaves who were considered capable of managing their own affairs were often freed by their masters and married off by them to Portuguese women. Sometimes, just as if the relationship was a parent–son, not a master–slave one, the newly weds were then presented with some of the master's household goods to help them in their new state. Nor was it males only who enjoyed happy domestic relationships with their owners. Widows who bought black female slaves often treated them, the chronicler declares, like their own daughters. He has praise, too, for the slaves themselves: those from Saharan and Black Africa proved themselves, after conversion, to be loyal and obedient servants, devoid of all evil intent. Unlike captive Muslims, they never sought to escape and, once they had been exposed to the goodly and godly life that was theirs in Portugal, they soon forgot all about their native lands. A final and rather unexpected advantage black slaves had over those from other regions was that, according to the chronicler, they were less inclined to lasciviousness.

No doubt Zurara knew of individual examples that could be used to support this rosy picture of domestic slavery in Portugal, but there are no grounds for supposing that even domestic slaves (who frequently appear as comical figures in later Portuguese literature) normally enjoyed such kindly treatment as he would have us believe. The chronicler prudently avoids mentioning those who were hired out by their owners to perform despised menial tasks in the cities or to work as unpaid agricultural labourers. Naturally no reference is made, either, to those who were exported to Andalusia, particularly to Seville where, by the 1470s, such a large number of Portuguese-speaking black slaves existed that the Catholic Monarchs considered them to form a separate community deserving of their own legal representative.[33]

There are few sources which enable calculations to be made of the number of slaves from Guinea who were transported to Portugal in the Prince's lifetime. As has already been noted, in the 1443 grant to Henry of a monopoly over navigation and trade south of Cape Bojador the regent D. Pedro referred only to two voyages which, up to that date, he said, had brought back thirty-eight 'Moorish' prisoners from beyond Cape Bojador. When the grant was confirmed five years later by Afonso V – that is, after the massive slave raids described earlier in the present chapter – this figure was altered to read that more than a thousand bodies of captured 'infidels' had been brought to Portugal from Guinea. This gives an average of some two hundred a year.[34] The latter figure, supplied to the regent by Henry himself, fits in quite well with the *Chronicle of Guinea's* estimate of 927 up to the end of 1447. For the years 1448–55 no figures at all are available, though it is plain from Cadamosto's narrative of his 1455 voyage that, during those years, the Wolof rulers of Senegal had co-operated with the Portuguese in establishing a regular barter trade in black slaves at the *resgates* in their territory.[35] Cadamosto, in his account of the same voyage, declares that 800–1000 slaves reached Portugal annually from the Arguin factory alone during the 1450s. These figures have been attacked as obviously exaggerated because they presuppose at least twenty separate caravel sailings to Arguin per year. It is not, in fact, impossible that this figure was achieved. Magalhães Godinho, in his calculations about the extent of the slave trade in Henry's time, concludes that, for the 1450s, probably between 1,000 and 2,000 slaves reached Portugal annually.[36] Given that all the figures available need to be treated with considerable caution, this one is probably as near the truth as we are now likely to get. Taking it as a basis, it can very tentatively be concluded that, for the whole of the Henrican period, some 15,000 to 20,000 slaves were imported into Portugal on the Prince's behalf or under licence from him. As already explained, not all of these human imports remained there. A number were always re-exported to Castile; it was not unknown for some to be shipped directly there from Guinea. Others were taken to Madeira where others – not as many as once thought – were used in agriculture or as domestic servants. The participation of caravels from Madeira and Porto Santo is a feature of the slave razzias of the 1440s on the African mainland, but it is not clear how far their owners were simply cashing in on a new and profitable source of income by taking and transporting captives from

Guinea to metropolitan Portugal, or how far they were looking for extra labour for the rapidly growing agricultural needs of Madeira itself.

It has been estimated by some scholars that the number of slaves successfully brought north from the Sudan by the trans-Saharan caravans in the fifteenth century was perhaps no more than about 4,300 annually. If that figure is accepted, then it is clear that already in the Prince's day the Portuguese had the potential one day, if shipping was available, to rival the numbers transported by the slave caravans.[37] Despite this, there seems to be no evidence that, in practice, the entry of the Portuguese into the African slave trade at this time had any adverse economic effects on the traditional transport of slaves by the Saharan caravans. To the numbers of slaves actually landed in Portugal we must, of course, add the steadily growing quotient of those born into slavery there by their slave mothers. Their numbers are unknown.

What is certain is that this new ethnic minority was, by the 1450s, already large enough to have a visible impact in a city like Lisbon. The Portuguese used the presence of this minority for political purposes, parading it in front of important foreign dignitaries to impress on them that the power of Portugal's rulers now extended into the far-off lands of the African Atlantic. In 1451, in connection with the forth-coming marriage between Holy Roman Emperor Frederick III and Henry's niece Leonor, an imperial diplomatic mission went to Lisbon to represent Frederick at the *sponsalia* ceremonies. One of the imperial chaplains accompanying the mission, Nicholas Lanckman von Valckenstein, wrote in his diary a lengthy account of the endless succession of elaborate public ceremonies, parades and other spectacles which the spendthrift Portuguese king arranged to mark the occasion.[38] Lanckman noted particularly the participation in these performances of blacks, Sanhadjas – whom he calls 'Moors', following Portuguese usage – and Canary Islanders. On one occasion, accompanied by a model of a dragon (perhaps to symbolize paganism conquered), the Africans performed native dances while paying homage to Leonor. They were followed by Canarians whom Lanckman, calling on a familiar medieval belief, described as wild men of the woods who had come from remote islands where men and women lived nude.[39] Despite their supposed uncouth nature, the Canarians carried a placard explaining, presumably in Portuguese and with some considerable disregard for the fact, that, on the orders of their chiefs, they had come from their islands which had been recently annexed by the king of

Portugal to attend the present nuptials. Those from Grand Canary performed a special dance peculiar to that island which aroused the special admiration of the German chaplain. This was presumably the famous jumping dance known as the *canario* which became so popular in sixteenth-century Castile. On another occasion, this time in the company of the simulacrum of an elephant, there was more singing, dancing and shouting of 'viva' in honour of the new empress performed by mem-bers from the various ethnic minorities resident in Lisbon. Portuguese Jews and Mouriscos took part along with blacks and Canarians on this occasion, the former two groups one may suppose not very willingly equated with the latter two.[40] Lanckman does not mention the civil status of these groups, but there can be no doubt that the blacks and Canarians must have been members of Lisbon's slave community.

The first information about the value of an African slave in Portugal in Henry's time is contained in a passing note included in Zurara's narrative. This states that a single black slave worth five gold *dobras* in Portugal had been bought in the Río de Oro in 1445 in exchange for a few trinkets.[41] If taken literally, this would value the slave concerned at only some 600 *reais brancos* in Portuguese currency. It is almost certainly much too low a figure.[42] All the narrative sources dwell on the great profits which were made from buying slaves and other 'commodities' in exchange for the trading goods the Africans wanted at the *resgates*. It has been plausibly argued that the average value of the best slaves brought to Lagos in 1444 by Lançarote da Ilhas's great slave-hunting expedition was perhaps as high as 4,000 *reais brancos* (equal to 33 gold *dobras* at the official exchange rate).[43] Saunders concludes that the price of a grade A slave from about 1457 onwards for fifty years was between twelve and thirteen gold *cruzados* (3,000–3,290 *reais*).[44]

The Prince was, of course, himself a principal proprietor and seller of slaves, so it not inappropriate that the best factual information about their market value at the end of the Henrican period should come from documents drawn up between 1460 and 1464 in connection with the execution of his will. Eight slaves were inventoried after his death as part of the household chattels associated with his residences in the Lagos region. Though an owner of slaves quite frequently made provision for some or all his domestic slaves to be freed on his death as an act of Christian piety, Henry, surprisingly, did not do so. Eight were accordingly disposed of by his executors to other owners. This is not necessarily a new example of Henry's hardness of heart. He was aware that he did not even have the funds to meet the unpaid wages of his household retainers and his officials in Lagos and perhaps reckoned that his duty to them was greater than it was to his slaves. There was also a need to make some gesture towards those to whom he was notoriously in debt. The names of the slaves and the price for which each was disposed of are of interest. They are shown in the following table:

	Name	Price in *reais* *brancos*	Equivalent in *cruzados* @ 253 *reais*
1	João Prestes	3,500	11.86
2	Inês	7,000	27.67
3	Fernando, Henrique & Martinho (sold as one lot)	30,000	118.58
4	Isabel	11,500	45.46
5	Pedro and Tavares (one lot)	13,800 (60 *dobras de banda*)	54.54 *cruzados*
	Total	65,300	250.20[45]

It will be seen that these figures are, for the most part, higher than the average suggested for individual slaves by Saunders, but special factors may have been at work on this occasion. With the exception of João Prestes, who was perhaps old or sick, or both, one may be sure, as Zurara once noted, that Henry's slaves were, using the standards of the time, of the highest quality. The fact that they had once belonged to the Prince may well have given them a special cachet which caused them to fetch considerably more than the prevailing market rates. One can only conjecture, though, at the reasons which made a knight of Évora, João Teixeira, willing to pay over forty-five *cruzados* for a slave called Isabel. I note that João Teixeira had recently sold a horse to the Prince for about half this amount (nearly twenty-four *cruzados*) for which – a frequent result of doing business with the Prince – he had never been paid. The high price of the horse perhaps indicates that it was a specially trained beast suitable for an aged prince to ride, for it was was valued at twice the amount the cheapest slave on the above table was worth.

Such a comparison between the value of slaves and that of horses is not inappropriate here for, in the Henrican period of the discoveries, the export of horses to Senegal was, from the beginning, always a major feature of trade at the *resgates* there. There was a strong demand for these animals in Wolof country where they were both used in war and prized as prestigious possessions by rulers and nobles. Horses were, however, unable to breed in Senegambia, possibly because the Arab merchants in North Africa, to protect their trade, were careful not to send any mares south with the caravans. In any case, on account of the climate and disease horses usually did not live long in this tropical region, so a constant demand for new imports was assured.[46] In the early days of exploration of the Saharan coast, the Portuguese caravels sometimes carried one or two horses intended to facilitate movement over the desert sands. Thus the discoverers of the Río de Oro in 1435 had carried with them two animals which were used for reconnaissance purposes when they landed there.[47] Cadamosto carried an undisclosed number of horses for sale on his exploratory expedition in 1455. For these, with their harnesses and accoutrements and some silk and other trade goods, he says he paid some 300 ducats (*cruzados*) in Portugal. He adds that he sold all his horses to the Wolof ruler of Cayor, the Bor Damel, for 100 slaves.[48] Diogo Gomes reports that, about 1460, he sailed a caravel belonging to the king and carrying ten horses to a *resgate* in the neighbouring land of the ruler of Sine, where he found two other Portuguese caravels also trading in these animals. According to Gomes, the normal going rate there had always been seven black slaves for one horse but over-supply had enabled the local king to lower the rate to six for one. Gomes claims, without explaining how, that he managed to restore the barter rate to seven for one while himself securing fourteen or fifteen slaves for each of his horses on this occasion, perhaps because he contrived to present himself to the Bor Sine as an emissary of Afonso V.[49] It will be seen that, in the 1450s and 1460s, the export of horses to tsetse-free regions of West Africa by the Portuguese was highly developed and probably mainly responsible – far more than the export of cloth, clothing, metal and luxury articles at that time – for the successful opening of the maritime slave trade by the Prince. It also represented another way in which the Portuguese could claim to be trespassing on a trade hitherto entirely dependent on the southbound Saharan caravans.[50] There is good reason to believe that it was the highly profitable slave trade associated with the sale of horses in Senegambia which first drew independent merchants in considerable numbers to seek Henry's licence to trade in Guinea.

The consequences of Henry's pioneering involvement in the Atlantic slave trade are not difficult to enumerate. Thanks to his efforts, Portugal became during his lifetime a state where the import of slaves from Black Africa became, and would long remain, a staple of the Portuguese economy. The presence and ownership of black slaves soon became a distinctive feature of Portuguese society and one which Portugal's rulers showed off with pride to foreign visitors. In setting all this in train, Henry had shown Europe that there now existed a radical new alternative to the traditional pattern of the African slave trade as the countries of Christian Europe had hitherto known it. Instead of having to depend for supplies of black slaves on the trans-Saharan caravan routes controlled by Islam, the Portuguese had established direct access by sea to the regions of Guinea where such slaves were available by barter in potentially whatever numbers their ships and their new slave markets at home were able to handle. More sinisterly for future history, Henry had shown the European world that it was possible to transport slaves from Black Africa to Europe on sea journeys which might last as long as six weeks without incurring losses of life which Henry and the merchants operating under licence from him would have found unacceptable.

~ Chapter Eleven ~

A Henrican Obsession: The Canary Islands[1]

The name 'Islands of the Blessed' shows by this title that almost all goodly things are to be found on them to make men happy such is the blessed richness of the fruits of the earth there. They are located in the Ocean Sea to the left of Morocco out towards the setting sun, each island separated one from another by its waters.

Alonso de Cartagena quoting St Isidore[2]

They [the Canaries] are inhabited by untamed, wild, hardly human men who are not united by any religion or restrained by any kind of law and who, unconcerned with civil intercourse, pass their lives like animals in a state of paganism.

Duarte I in a papal petition of 1436 describing to the pope, on Prince Henry's behalf, the supposed barbarism of the inhabitants of the Canary Islands.[3]

Towards the beginning of the *Chronicle of Guinea*, there is a chapter summarizing chronologically all the major achievements of Prince Henry. After describing Henry's part in the relief of the siege of Ceuta in 1419, the chronicler then inserts the following laconic sentence into his narrative: 'He also sent a very large expedition against the Canary Islands for the purpose of showing [the people] there the road to our Holy Faith.'[4] Without further explanation, the chronicler then proceeds with other matters. Zurara evidently could not quite bring himself to omit any reference at all in his heroic history of the Prince to what had clearly been the total failure of a major military effort undertaken in the archipelago under Henry's direction in 1424. Equally, he could not bring himself to admit outright that his hero had masterminded what seems to have a humiliating affair. Defeat by the Moors was something which happened from time to time and which Iberian Christians had long learnt to accept as an example of the mysterious ways of God. To admit openly in what was essentially a panegyrical history of the Prince that the expedition to the Canaries had resulted in his would-be crusaders being driven off by pagan islanders armed only with Stone Age weapons was to risk the ridicule of posterity, and Zurara well knew that ridicule was a form of humour that had no place in the account of the Prince he had undertaken to write. The chronicler got out of his difficulty, as we have just seen, by presenting the affair in a single sentence as another episode in the story of the Prince's dedication to the use of the sword as a tool employed to spread the Christian faith.

Inevitably, perhaps, the *Chronicle of Guinea* presents the Prince's activities in the Canaries as a minor side-show to the main business of exploring the coast of Guinea. Apart from an account of his temporary seizure of the island of Lanzarote, it hardly mentions the various later expeditions which Henry sent, usually without success, against individual islands of the archipelago. Thanks to his aversion to ocean travel, Henry, of course, never cast eyes on any of these semi-tropical islands towards whose conquest he devoted so much fruitless effort. Their and his history might have been different had he seen them for himself. Despite the way Zurara presents the topic, it is, though, clear enough that Henry was far from regarding his attempts to establish himself in the Canaries as a side-show.

Already from the middle of the fourteenth century onwards, the ancient Latin name for the islands used by St Isidore – *Insulae fortunatae* – had acquired a cruelly ironic meaning thanks to the constant depredations of slave raiders from the Iberian kingdoms and from Italy. In the fifteenth century, due in no small measure to the obsession of the Prince with the archipelago, it would also become a theatre of war, bloodshed and treachery as Castilians and Portuguese fought there against the indigenous Canarian peoples and against each other in what can be seen as one of Europe's first genuinely colonial wars.[5]

What created Henry's obsession with the Canaries from the 1420s onwards, at a time when, in addition to all his administrative commitments in Portugal, he was heavily involved in colonizing Madeira and Porto Santo and setting up governments there as a donatory-in-chief of the Portuguese crown? The explanation he gave for public consumption was very simple. He had learnt that the major islands were still in the hands of their aboriginal inhabitants. As a Christian paladin, it was therefore his obvious duty to bring them under Christian government and to see to the conversion of their peoples to the Christian faith. He repeatedly assured the curia that his sole purpose in seeking to establish himself in the archipelago was as a militant evangelist. We should not be too ready to dismiss these assurances out-of-hand as mere flummery. Everything we know about Henry shows that they provided him with the only ideological spur to military action that he could recognize as respectable. But evangelism was plainly not the only reason for the amount of energy he put into his attempt to make the islands his. For many scholars, the practical reason for his attempt in 1424 to establish himself in the Canaries has seemed conveniently obvious: he wished to secure control of the archipelago to protect the sea route to Guinea when this was opened. Though the rediscovery and settlement of the Madeiran archipelago guaranteed that his ships would be able to put in there for supplies and repairs while seeking to make the passage of Cape Bojador, Henry must have feared, according to this view, that the whole Guinea enterprise could be at risk if the Canaries, some two hundred and fifty miles further south, were to be in hostile or potentially hostile (i.e. Castilian) hands.[6] Henry's ill-fated campaign of 1424 is thus held to prove that, ten years before the rounding of Cape Bojador, he must have already been planning for that event. No doubt, after the passage of the cape, the potential threat Castilian occupation of the Canaries represented to Portuguese shipping on its way to Guinea entered the Prince's calculations. It seems, however, to have been at first a minor consideration. In none of the crown's communications with the papacy in the 1430s or 1440s is any suggestion made that Henry's interest in the Canaries was prompted by any strategic aim. It is plain, too, that the hope of instant economic advantage cannot have been present in his mind. As in Madeira and Porto Santo, orchil and dragon's blood was available in the archipelago and had long been sought as a secondary prize by European slave raiders. The taking of Canarian slaves on a far larger scale than hitherto attempted by European raiders may well have been in his thoughts. As we have noted in earlier chapters, in Henry's vocabulary 'conversion' and 'slavery' were closely associated words. Be that as it may, for four decades Henry now attempted, by war or intrigue, to conquer and rule all seven main islands of the archipelago with a total land area of 2,800 square miles (7,200 square km), some of them still quite densely populated by their aboriginal inhabitants. It was, of course, an ambition far beyond any resources he could command. To appreciate the unreality of these territorial ambitions, we only need remember that, towards the end of the century, it would take the well-equipped royal armies sent to the Canaries by the Catholic Monarchs much time and much hard fighting before Alonso de Lugo, the first *conquistador* and governor of Tenerife and La Palma, and Pedro de Vera, the conqueror of Gran Canaria, were able to pacify the islands for the Castilian crown.[7]

We can learn from other sources than Zurara a little more about the first of Henry's several military débacles in the Canaries. Fernando de Castro's expedition is referred to in Alonso de Cartagena's famous juridical defence of Castilian sovereignty over the Canaries sent by him to the Roman curia in 1436 or 1437. Cartagena, then bishop of Burgos, recalls in this document that, in 1425, the Portuguese under 'a certain Fernando de Castro' as he contemptuously puts it, had attacked and attempted to conquer the island of Grand Canary. He notes that they had failed in their attempt and had had to return home, leaving the island, in the bishop's words, 'in its state of freedom or, more exactly, savagery, as before'.[8] Fernando de Castro, as Alonso de Cartagena very well knew, was the governor and chief personage of the Prince's household but, perhaps for diplomatic reasons, he avoided involving Henry by name as the person responsible for this first major Portuguese act of aggression against the Canarians. More information about Fernando de Castro's expedition is supplied by the sixteenth-century chronicler João de Barros, who, having been able to examine contemporary documents, says that the Portuguese general attacked Grand Canary with no less than 2,500 infantrymen and 120 horsemen under his command. The logistical problems involved in the despatch to the Atlantic archipelago by ship from Portugal of an expedition this size, with its horses and all its weapons and stores, must have been very considerable and they were evidently not properly overcome. Nor had Henry realized, though he should have done from the various first-hand accounts of the archipelago and its peoples available to him, that the kind of war that faced his men on Grand Canary was bound to be quite unlike any kind of war Portuguese soldiers had previously experienced. Barros notes that the royal account books for the period showed that the crown made a contribution of no less than 39,000 gold *dobras* towards the cost of transporting the expedition to its destination.[9] The total costs incurred must have far exceeded this amount. Those had to be met by the Prince from whatever funds were then available to him. No doubt the Order of Christ, with or without formal approval, was among the obligatory contributors.

Like the other subsequent Henrican expeditions against the Canaries, even those directed against the Castilian-occupied islands, that of 1424 was officially regarded as Henry's private affair. He might secure diplomatic and some financial support from the crown but, in an effort to minimize trouble with Castile, John I and his successors never publicly acknowledged that the Portuguese crown actively sponsored the Prince's efforts to conquer the Canaries by force of arms. Nor, for his own reasons, did the Prince probably wish it to be otherwise. He knew that, in the middle of the fourteenth century, the curia had declared the archipelago to be a papal principality, though the declaration had not then produced any practical results.[10] He also knew that, when Jean de Béthencourt had paid homage to Henry III of Castile for the lordship of all the islands in 1403, he had then been officially proclaimed 'king of the Canaries' in the streets of Seville by that city's town crier.[11] Long after Béthencourt's time, his successors as lords of the archipelago were rebuked for trying to use the royal title. For a man who seems not so secretly to have nourished frustrated regal ambitions, these three facts may well have given Henry a special incentive for wishing to conquer the archipelago without the participation of the Portuguese crown. At all events, his assault on Grand Canary in 1424 opened up a Pandora's box from which emerged a concatenation of troubles for him personally, for relations between Portugal and Castile, and for relations between the two Iberian kingdoms and the Roman curia. As already suggested, thanks to Henry's obsession, the Canaries would also give the Portuguese their first experience of a real colonial war. His attempt to persuade the curia that his lack of military success against the native Canarians was attributable to the very savagery of their pagan state must have sounded hollow even to the Vatican officials whose lack of interest in what was going on in the African Atlantic was all too evident.

By 1446, when Henry sought and obtained from his brother the regent D. Pedro control over all sailings by Portuguese ships to the islands, he did specifically refer to hostile interference there with the free passage of his ships on their way to Guinea.[12] There is, though, a contradiction at the heart of the document which suggests that this claim may well have been made simply to supply the regent with an apparently respectable reason for granting yet another monopoly to his brother. The only shipping brought under Henry's control by the grant was Portuguese shipping. It is highly unlikely that the difficulties allegedly experienced in the Canaries by Henry's caravels on their way to Guinea were caused by any Portuguese there. The native Canarians, well known in the later Middle Ages as a people or peoples totally ignorant of navigation and of the simplest forms of boat-building, were, of course, in no position to represent a threat to Portuguese shipping passing through or near the archipelago. No source suggests that corsairs operated in the Canaries at this time, though they would do much later on in the century. The problem envisaged by the Prince, if it existed at all, must have been caused by the Castilians who were, by definition, outside the scope of the new powers now given to the Prince.

Whether it was a put-up job or not, the new monopoly represented a new accretion of power and wealth to Henry. The crown yet again surrendered the royal fifth to him, this time on all imports from the archipelago. Canarian slaves – described in the grant in accordance with a frequent Portuguese usage when referring to pagans anywhere in western Africa, as 'Moors and Mooresses' – were specifically mentioned as one of the taxable commodities obtainable in the Canaries.

The self-conscious reticence of Zurara about the major military and political setback suffered by the Prince in Grand Canary in the mid 1420s reflects his view that it was an event which there was no need to trouble posterity about over much. It may be inferred, however, that the news of it can have done nothing to silence the many voices in Portugal at that time which, as even Henry's chronicler admits, considered his activities in the African Atlantic generally were a waste of effort and money. Nevertheless his special interest in the Canaries was recognized at the Portuguese court before the passage of Cape Bojador. The count of Arraiolos, writing in 1432 about the Prince's ambitions to become the first Christian ruler of Granada and the alternative possibility that he might take advantage of the Castilian civil wars to get himself made ruler of a large part of the central kingdom, commented that, if the latter came to pass, the Canaries, too, would automatically be his.[13]

For the moment, though, another major attack on Grand Canary or one of the other islands was out of the question. Indignant representations from Castile that the Prince had attacked territory that was part of the patrimony of the Castilian crown prevented for the moment another armed intervention there. It is a measure of the strength of Henry's obsession with the Canaries that he now changed tack by trying to do a deal directly with John II of Castile. Suppressing for the moment both his pride and his well-known disdain for all things Castilian, he simply requested the Castilian king to cede to him the right to conquer the pagan-held islands, apparently suggesting that, if the king granted his request, he would be willing to accept a formula by which he acknowledged the ultimate sovereignty of Castile over them. This was a serious error on Henry's part. It is referred to with relish by Alonso de Cartagena in his lengthy legal defence of Castilian sovereignty over the whole archipelago and his rebuttal of Portuguese claims there. In this document the bishop makes effective use of the incontrovertible fact that Henry's request to John II represented an explicit recognition of the Castilian crown's exclusive rights in the archipelago. According to Cartagena's treatise, the Castilian king had politely explained to the Prince that what he proposed was impossible since the Castilian crown was legally forbidden to alienate any part of the royal patrimony in the way suggested by him.[14] It was not the only occasion on which, after the defeat of an attempt to establish himself in the islands by force, Henry would swallow his pride and unabashedly invite John II to give him by royal decree what he had just tried to seize from Castile by war. These approaches are referred to by the Castilian king in a letter to Afonso V of Portugal written in 1452 to protest against yet another of the Prince's armed attacks, this time on Castilian settlers in the islands and on Castilian shipping there.[15] It was never denied by the Prince that he had made direct approaches to John II about the future of the Canaries. It should not be assumed, however, that Henry expected them to be taken seriously. They were perhaps made for propaganda purposes so that he could say that he had tried without success to settle peacefully the Canaries problem he had created.

In the 1430s, despite the excitement caused by the passage of Cape Bojador by Henry's ships and by his intense political campaign to get Duarte I to agree to an attack on Tangier, there was no let-up in his determination to get control of the Canarian islands still in pagan hands. With the new king's permission, probably in 1434, the very year the famous cape was rounded, he sent another squadron to attack them. The identity of the particular island which bore the main brunt of the Portuguese attack on this occasion is not definitely known, but it was probably Tenerife. Details of what happened are contained in a long and revealing Portuguese petition sent to the pope on Henry's behalf in August 1436.[16] It begins by describing the aboriginal inhabitants of the Canaries in general as untamed savages living in a state of paganism without religion, law or civility 'as if they were beasts'. The document also attributes to the Canarians other alleged characteristics of the pagan state. Apart from noting, correctly, that they know nothing about navigation, it also observes that they are without letters, have no acquaintance with metals or coinage, do not live in proper (i.e. European-style) houses, go nude except for covering their private parts with a garment made of palm leaves or goat skins, do not wear shoes and, finally, are unacceptably athletic.[17] Henry, of course, knew very well that this description of the Canarians owed more to traditional Christian theorizing about the pagan state than to the empirically observed information about the far-from-savage Stone Age cultures of the archipelago's native peoples that had been available in writing since the middle of the previous century. Since it was, however, a question of securing papal permission for Henry to conquer and convert the islands to Christianity, it was necessary to present their inhabitants to the curia in terms which would convince it of their unmitigated pagan bestiality. The document goes on to remind the pope of the Prince's vocation, inherited from his illustrious father, to spread the Christian faith. Only after these defensive preliminaries have been gone through does it proceed to describe what had actually happened to the Prince's 1434 expedition. The alleged good news came first. Four hundred Christian converts, Henry claimed, had been made as a result of the attack of his men on the island. In Henry-speak, the terms 'convert' and 'slave' were, as we have seen, used as synonyms when communications with the Holy See were involved. Henry presumably by now had come to understand that he needed to win friends among the Canarians themselves if his struggle with Castile for control of the islands was to have any hope of success. It is, though, wholly improbable that 400 islanders were individually baptized under the eye of the Portuguese soldiery. Henry may simply have passed on to the pope grossly exaggerated claims that had been made to him by the commander of the expedition in order to sweeten the bad news of another failure. In Guinea, later, the Portuguese would resort to mass baptisms on the beaches to satisfy the requirements of canon and civil law when black slaves were about to be shipped from Guinea, but there is no firm evidence that this was done in Henry's time.

After reporting this missionary success in 1434, the document then gets round to admitting that the expedition had, unsurprisingly, failed to conquer the island concerned. To explain this new military failure to the pope, Henry hit on the none-too-subtle notion of blaming it on the pagan barbarity of its defenders. The island warriors, instead of confronting the invaders face-to-face in the manner of civilized soldiers, had, he said, like the savages they were, retired to inaccessible caves and crags where they defended themselves with a ferocity that clearly proclaimed their inhuman state.[18] On account of their unbecoming

resistance, the expedition had unfortunately run short of food and supplies so that it became necessary (as in 1424) for its commander to
decide to abandon the attack and return to Portugal. Henry promised
Eugenius IV that the offensive would be resumed when a favourable
opportunity occurred. He also took the opportunity to report an unfortunate happening which had overtaken the expedition and which
needed the pope's attention. When the unsuccessful Portuguese soldiers
had attempted to start their journey home, some of them had been
prevented from sailing by contrary winds. Driven by hunger, they had
been 'forced' to invade two islands settled by Christians – probably
Lanzarote and Fuerteventura.[19] Henry insisted, improbably, that they
had done nothing more than capture and eat some wild goats which
they found in abundance. The whole point of this approach to the curia
was now revealed. At the end of 1434 the bishop of the see of Rubicón,
in association with the Franciscan missionaries based at that order's
Seville house, had secured a far-reaching bull from Eugenius which
prohibited the enslavement of any Canarians anywhere in the archipelago. It also decreed the immediate release of any of them taken on
previous occasions and ordered the excommunication of 'certain
Christians' (i.e. Portuguese) who had attacked Lanzarote and other
islands, carrying off large numbers of natives, among them Christian
converts and others ripe for conversion. Given the circumstances, it was
plain that the bull was inspired by the behaviour of the members of
the 1434 Portuguese expedition sent to the Canaries by the Prince.
Henry's present petition, while not seeking to deny what had happened,
requested that the order of excommunication be modified so that it
only applied to the two islands where Christian settlers lived, leaving
him free to carry on the task – which, he said, he had been the first to
undertake – of subjugating the other islands by force, bringing their
inhabitants into the Christian Church and annexing islands and people
to the Portuguese crown. Henry's claim that he had been the first to
attempt the conversion of the larger islands was, of course, not true.
As we have frequently seen, Henry's deep devotion to religion never
made him feel obliged to be wholly truthful in his approaches to successive popes.

The petition concluded with a request that Eugenius IV, as God's
representative with unlimited temporal and spiritual authority over the
whole world, would grant him the right of conquest and sovereignty
over all the islands other than those already converted and settled.[20]
This is the first of a number of Portuguese documents relating to the
Portuguese maritime expansion in Henry's time in which the Por-

tuguese king, speaking on Henry's behalf as well as his own, unequivo-
cally recognizes the pope as supreme temporal as well as spiritual lord
of all the world with total authority to dispose of the lives and lands
of infidels and pagans as he chooses. Bearing in mind that this doctrine
had long been under attack from within as well as outside the Church,
the welcome assurance that Portugal fully supported the traditional
'papalist' view of the unlimited extent of the pope's temporal
authority was calculated to find favour with Eugenius IV and his successors, making them very ready, if they could, to do what the Prince
wanted. In September 1436 the pope duly issued a bull granting Duarte
I all that was requested in the petition, including the grant to the Portuguese of sole rights to conquer and rule any of the Canaries not
already inhabited by Christians.[21]

The curia, as has already been noted, had a policy of acceding more
or less automatically, without bothering to investigate them seriously,
to requests concerning North Africa or the African Atlantic that
sounded reasonable. It had more important matters to deal with as the
Turks approached Europe than what went on at the edge of the western
world. It was soon to learn that this casual approach could have embarrassing consequences. The storm of indignation Henry's aggressive
actions in the Canaries in the 1430s caused in Andalusia now forced
the effective governor of Castile, Don Álvaro de Luna, hard-pressed as
he was by internal political problems, to make a show of defending
Castilian sovereignty in the islands. He did so by having the matter put
on the agenda of the council of Basel and by requesting Alonso de
Cartagena to write the imposing juridical case for rejecting the claims
put forward by Henry to which reference has already been made. In
the autumn of 1436, too, the Portuguese king received from the pope
copies of the somewhat discouraging *consulta* of Antonio Minucci da
Pratovecchio and Antonio de Rosellis (see Chapter VI above) concerning the right of the pope to authorize, or Christian princes to carry out,
armed attacks on infidel or pagan rulers or peoples. The conclusions
of the two jurists on these matters cast some doubt, *inter alia*, on the
legitimacy of Henry's armed attacks on the free islands of the Canarian
group, since by no stretch of the imagination could their land-bound
inhabitants be said to constitute a threat to the Christian world, even
though it was true that their reception of Franciscan missionaries was
not always effusive. Duarte I, no doubt under pressure from the Prince
and aware that the pope himself was disinclined to heed the caveats of
the two lawyers, decided to pay no attention to their opinions.
Eugenius, though, could not ignore Cartagena's highly effective defence

of the prior rights of Castile in the Canaries presented to him by Alonso de Cartagena and also circulated among the counsellors then assembled in Bologna.[22] When the Castilian ambassadors there demanded that the pope withdraw the bull he had just made in favour of Portuguese claims to the archipelago, the pontiff had no choice but to accede. On 6 November, only three months after the first appearance of the offending document, he issued a new bull nullifying it.[23] In the new document he declared in unequivocal terms that he had been misled by the incorrect assertion made in the Portuguese petition to him that no one else had ever displayed any interest in the pagan-held islands of the archipelago. He had, he explained, now learnt that the Castilian crown had long claimed that the conquest of all the islands belonged to it by the law of nations. In consequence, to avoid scandal, the bull in favour of the Portuguese only remained valid in so far as it did not clash with the claims of anyone else. Since it had already been established that such a clash did exist, the practical effect of the bull was to render the grant to Portugal altogether null and void. On the same day Eugenius wrote a conciliatory private letter to the Portuguese king. News of the grant to the Portuguese had, he observed, produced a violent reaction from the Castilian court. In consequence, the curia, both in writing and from the mouths of the Castilian ambassadors present in Bologna, had received frequent and insistent demands that the instrument in question be revoked. In fact the Portuguese action had also goaded the Castilians into making a potentially much more dangerous assertion. The pope revealed for the first time the troubling news that the Castilian envoys at Bologna had not only publicly claimed that the Castilian crown had sole legal title to the Canary Islands, conquered or unconquered; they had also declared that the conquest of 'the lands of Africa' (*terre Africe*) was also reserved to it.[24] The pope recommended the Portuguese king to study carefully the documents he was sending him and to refrain from doing anything that might cause trouble with Castile. It was a friendly gesture by Eugenius IV, who had perhaps heard of Henry's interest in opening up a sea route to Guinea. It would not be the last occasion on which a Castilian government, when it was having trouble with the Prince, would fire this particular warning shot across Henry's bows. The pope was well disposed towards Portugal and her rulers but, when he was faced with a direct conflict of interest between the two Peninsular kingdoms, as in this case, he had no choice but to bow to the demands of the politically and ecclesiastically more powerful one.

The Castilians were not satisfied with the somewhat muffled terms of Eugenius IV's original derogation of the bull favouring Henry's ambitions in the Canaries. On 30 April 1437 the pope was obliged to issue a new document unambiguously declaring that he had not intended in any way to question Castile's rights of conquest in Africa (including, of course, the archipelago). In so far as the offending bull could be so interpreted, it was absolutely null and void and the question of who had the right to conquer the Canaries must be approached as if such a bull had never existed.[25] It will be noted that the curia's proclamation that Castile was the only Peninsular power enjoying rights of conquest anywhere in Africa took place at a time when, equipped with a bull of crusade supplied by Eugenius himself, a Portuguese army under Henry's command was preparing to attack Tangier and other Moroccan ports. Consistency was never a feature of the curia's handling of Peninsular affairs at this time – or later.

The disaster of Tangier and the political in-fighting concerning the regency which followed Duarte I's death in 1438 meant that, until the next decade, the Prince, as far as is known, made no new attempts to mount military offensives against the Canaries. He had, however, no intention of accepting the pope's advice to leave the islands alone. Zurara's chronicle makes it plain that, in the 1440s, his caravels, homeward-bound from Guinea, were in the habit of raiding the pagan-held islands when they had failed to obtain their quota of Sanhadja or black slaves on the African mainland.[26]

Despite all his posturing as a would-be crusader in the Canaries and his insistence on the savagery and bestiality of the Canarians in documents addressed to the curia, Henry appears, some time before 1445, to have tried to see what could be done by direct negotiation with Canarian chiefs. His men had by then managed to make friendly contact with the headmen of one or two of the four rival clans who inhabited the canyons and mountain forests of the island of La Gomera, securing some sort of permanent foothold there in circumstances which are obscure.[27] The island was, of course, claimed by Guillén de Las Casas's successor – Fernán Peraza – as part of the Canarian lordship he had inherited. Peraza, for his part, put a small garrison ashore on another part of the island and encouraged the pro-Castilian clan chiefs to make war on those who supported Henry.[28] The dramatic physical characteristics of the island meant, however, that it was possible for two hostile groups of native Gomerans, each with its particular European backers, to live in different regions of it in relative peace.[29] The parallel with what was to become in later ages a feature of European colonialism in the Caribbean needs no embellishment. Henry had clearly been given good advice by a source familiar with the island when, ignoring entirely the papal bulls ordering him not to interfere in the Canaries, he established what was intended to be a permanent Portuguese presence on La Gomera. The Portuguese seem to have remained there for a number of years but had probably withdrawn before 1455. When Cadamosto put in to the island on his outward journey to Guinea in that year, he noted the presence of Christian settlers there but described it as part of the Canarian lordship (señorío) of Diego García de Herrera.[30] It seems unlikely that, if any of the island was then still under his patron's protection, the Venetian explorer would have failed to mention the fact.

One reason the Portuguese cultivated the goodwill of the Gomerans was that they had found that the latter were willing to help them carry out slave razzias against the inhabitants of other pagan-held islands. The Chronicle of Guinea describes their participation in one such raid against their fellow-Canarians on the island of La Palma – a task in which, because of the extraordinary dexterity as mountaineers of all the peoples of the western islands of the archipelago, their help must have been invaluable.[31] To modern readers, the willing participation of the Gomerans in such actions is liable to appear like betrayal of their own people, but that would be to misunderstand the ethnological situation in the archipelago before the coming of the Europeans. The latter were astonished to find that the people of the islands, after many centuries without any contact with each other, had evolved separate cultures and languages and had lost any sense of common purpose. They seem not even to have thought of themselves as belonging to the same race.

Henry took good care to see that his relations with the Gomerans, whether Christian or pagan, remained peaceful. In 1445 or 1446 an over-zealous or over-greedy vassal of his treacherously seized and carried off to Portugal as slaves a number of the islanders, despite the fact that they were protected by the Prince's general safe conduct. Zurara's chronicle describes Henry's anger when he heard of this event. He did not content himself with directing it against the offending captain but apparently sent for and personally apologized to the twenty or so Gomerans concerned. He then kitted them out with good Portuguese clothing and sent them back to their island – a move which, the chronicler comments, did the Prince's reputation among his supporters there much good. Henry went further. Several Gomeran chiefs, presumably baptized ones, were, at different times, invited to visit him in Portugal and, according to Zurara, treated by him as honoured guests. The chronicler recalls that he himself happened to be in the Algarve in Henry's company when a Gomeran chief and his retinue were received in one of the Prince's palaces there. In consequence, he writes, he himself can personally vouch for the fact that Henry saw to it that their reception was beyond reproach.[32] These episodes (no doubt there were many similar ones) are of interest in a number of ways. They show once more how, when he calculated it was in his interest to do so, the Prince was perfectly capable of dismounting from his fire-eating crusader's horse in order to charm and honour visiting Stone Age warrior chiefs from the Canaries so that, once they had returned home, they would pass on favourable impressions of him and his intentions to their kinsfolk. Visits of this kind also, of course, served to enhance Henry's fame at home. The sight of these probably fair-haired and cer-tainly unusually clothed strangers from a distant Atlantic island being received by him, not as slaves but as honoured visitors, served to remind them that, thanks to Henry, Portugal was now closely linked to new worlds quite unknown to the generation before him. An aura of novelty and exoticism was now firmly associated with one who once had seemed cut out to be the quintessential Portuguese exemplar of a late-medieval warrior prince in the Iberian tradition. Nevertheless one cannot but wonder what Henry and his courtiers really thought about his visitors from La Gomera. Towards the end of his chronicle Zurara, forgetting the favourable things he had said earlier about them, includes in it an account of the island evidently taken from a written report he had come across. This treats the Gomerans particularly harshly, criticizing their filthy eating habits, their fondness for walking about quite nude and their contentment with a life entirely passed in singing, dancing and fornicating.[33] Perhaps at this stage in his chronicle Zurara became particularly severe on the Gomerans because he knew by then that, despite all the Prince's efforts to please them, their pro-Portuguese chiefs had eventually all gone over to the Castilians and accepted García de Herrera as their lord.

Henry, however, by no means confined his activities in the Canaries in the 1440s to La Gomera. We have already seen that when, about 1445, the then nominal Castilian lord of the islands disposed of his lordship to his son-in-law, one Fernán Peraza, Henry saw a new oppor-tunity to interfere in the affairs of the archipelago. Early in 1446 he secured a second navigational and trading monopoly in the African Atlantic, this time putting under his control all Portuguese sailings to the Canaries.[34] To justify the new monopoly, the regent, no doubt at the Prince's suggestion, declared, quite incorrectly, that the islands had never been visited by Portuguese shipping until the beginning of the discoveries under Henry's auspices. He went on to assert that, even now, most Portuguese vessels only went there if sent by him. The first assertion was, of course, patently untrue. Henry's advisers had forgotten that a key point in all the arguments with Castile in defence of Portuguese claims to the archipelago had been that Portuguese ships had first journeyed there in the 1340s. The document also contains a gratuitous puff for the Prince in the form of a declaration by his brother the regent on the young king's behalf that all Henry has done and is doing 'is for our service and for the honour of our kingdoms' – words that hardly support the view of some scholars that the regent himself was the real force behind the first stage of the Portuguese maritime expansion.

Henry seems by this time to have recognized, as was certainly the case, that he did not himself have access to the military, naval or financial resources needed for an attempt to conquer any of the main pagan-held islands. He also knew that he could not expect the regent's government to give him more than perhaps some diplomatic and moral support if he attempted any new attack on them. Thwarted in this respect, he now decided to go for the risky ploy of trying to oust the Castilians from the smaller and much more accessible islands originally settled by Frenchmen and Andalusians early in the century. The conversion of pagan Canarians was no longer to be the reason for Henry's attempts to establish his rule in the archipelago. Now he proposed, instead, to try to seize by force the islands occupied by Christian settlers and Christianized Canarians which had been part of the patrimony of the Castilian crown since early in the century. Nothing can better illustrate the extent of the Prince's purblind obsession with securing territory for himself in the Canaries, or his belief by now that he could personally more or less make policy as he pleased in the African Atlantic. To get what he wanted there, he was now ready, so it seemed, to risk plunging Portugal into yet another war with her old enemy, Castile.

His first step was to try to get control of the island of Lanzarote, conquered by Gadifer de La Salle and Jean de Béthencourt in 1402. It was still governed in the early 1440s on behalf of its frequently changing Castilian feudatories by Jean de Béthencourt's self-proclaimed 'nephew', the much hated Maciot de Béthencourt. Henry now invited Maciot to sell him all his rights on the island and to vacate the governorship in his favour. Maciot, as a vassal of the Castilian king, had, of course, no authority to do any such thing but a clause inserted in the terms of the sale nominally preserved, it was claimed, the sovereign rights of the Castilian crown in the island.[35] This pretence made no practical difference to Henry. He simply ignored the now internationally accepted sovereignty of the Castilian crown over all the islands of the archipelago, gambling that John II's government was too beset by internal problems for it to take any military action against him.

Maciot readily agreed to the Prince's suggestion. He was probably glad to do be rid of Lanzarote where his unwilling seigneurial subjects had earlier staged a revolt against his administration and even expelled him for a time.[36] Moreover, the current Castilian titular lord of the whole archipelago, Peraza, had made clear his determination to put an end to the anomalous situation on the island as soon as he could by ridding it of Maciot's presence. Peraza was in a position to raise enough force to achieve this goal whenever he wished, but he waited too long. An agreement dated 9 March 1448 sets out the price Henry had to pay for Lanzarote.[37] Maciot was guaranteed an annual pension of 20,000 *reais brancos* for himself and his descendants in perpetuity, the sum concerned to be a charge on the revenues of Madeira. He and his family were also promised sanctuary on that island under the Prince's protection. The document contained an odd provision. This was that Henry and his heirs must continue to pay the pension to Maciot even if Henry lost the island to Castile or France. Perhaps one may detect in this an indication that Maciot suspected, rightly as it turned out, that the Prince might not get away for long with his seizure of the island. The unpopular Norman knight was duly conveyed to Madeira with his family and belongings aboard two Portuguese caravels. He apparently flourished there until his death.[38] His departure from Lanzarote marked the final cutting of links with the original French attempt to colonize Lanzarote and Fuerteventura begun nearly fifty years before.

With Maciot's departure, a military force sent by the Prince now landed on the island and took possession of it without meeting any serious opposition. The new Portuguese 'captain' of Lanzarote appointed by Henry was Antão Gonçalves, who had won fame as an explorer of the Saharan coast and as a successful slave-taker there.[39] Gonçalves's right-hand man was another of the Prince's squires, also a veteran of the discoveries, Álvaro de Ornelas. The new governor appointed other Portuguese to the handful of administrative posts needed to run the affairs of the island. According to one account, the Castilian settlers were told that, in future, prices were only to be quoted in Portuguese currency and Portuguese, not Castilian, law would be enforced. So much for Henry's promise to maintain the sovereignty of the Castilian crown after the sale of Lanzarote to him. The Prince clearly planned to administer his new island acquisition in much the same way as he had organized the governments of the Madeiran archipelago and the Azores. But there was, of course, a great difference between the situation which the Prince and his appointees faced on Lanzarote and that involved in governing the other Atlantic islands. Lanzarote was no newly discovered, uninhabited island but a territory where French and Castilian colonists and the surviving aboriginal islanders had long been settled under the rule of a vassal of the Castilian crown. The settlers, highly critical though they might be of the oppressions practised by Maciot, do not seem to have welcomed the arrival of a Portuguese administration in his stead. Though greatly reduced in numbers, some of the aboriginal inhabitants of the island who had managed to survive four decades of Christian misrule still lived on the island. What they thought of the Portuguese occupation is not recorded. Zurara, inevitably, asserts that Antão Gonçalves proved himself a benign governor of Lanzarote, a claim which is somewhat difficult to reconcile with the fact that, two years after the Prince put him there, the settlers drove him and his garrison out for good.[40]

A first-class diplomatic row between Portugal and Castile naturally followed Henry's seizure of this Castilian island. Two letters sent to Afonso V by John II recount in great detail the charges the Castilian king now brought against the Prince for his recent acts of war against Lanzarote as well as against the other islands, occupied or free, of the archipelago. Many of the charges made in this correspondence would be confirmed in 1478 in the evidence then given by surviving eyewitnesses of these events to the commission of enquiry into the rightful possessor of the lordship of Lanzarote then set up by the Catholic Monarchs.[41] A Castilian envoy, Juan Iníguez de Atabe, John II's secretary in charge of legal affairs (*escribano de cámara*), was sent to Portugal to protest against Henry's occupation of that island and against his subsequent violent actions in the archipelago generally. The envoy was instructed to point out that Henry's behaviour constituted a clear breach of the terms of the treaties of peace between the two countries. He was also to complain that it was at variance with an earlier promise made by the Portuguese king that he would not permit the Prince to continue his attacks on the islands. Atabe reported that he had found the Portuguese court in unrepentant and even aggressive mood. Afonso V had replied to the Castilian protests by challenging the authority and rights of Fernán Peraza in the islands generally. He added insult to injury by demanding that Peraza should appear personally before him in Portugal to justify, if he could, the legitimacy of his claims. This singularly offensive demand was naturally rejected by the Castilian ambassador. In his account of this visit to the Portuguese court, given years later to the commission of enquiry, Atabe recalled that he had also had some difficult personal exchanges there with Prince Henry.

John II's letter of 1452 states that, after Henry's occupation of Lanzarote (and the subsequent expulsion of the Portuguese by the settlers), Henry, in 1450 and 1451, had organized unsuccessful attacks on Grand Canary and tried to occupy the whole of La Gomera. In 1450 a fleet of no less than eight caravels had taken part in these operations, setting fire to property, murdering a number of islanders and robbing not only them but also some Andalusian merchants who were in the archipelago on business. The Castilian king's letter of protest also contains the information that, in 1451, he had sent Iníguez de Atabe, accompanied by the bishop of Rubicón, Juan Cid, to Lanzarote with twenty-five men-at-arms in two Castilian caravels to help the settlers defend themselves against any Portuguese attempt to reoccupy the island. Atabe's mission was to sequester Lanzarote on behalf of the crown until the question of whether it was crown land or seigneurial land was settled. Before Atabe got there, protested the Castilian king, Henry had sent troops in a large fleet to retake the place. Though the Portuguese made a landing and attacked the local people, they were unable to reoccupy the island. Meanwhile, John's letter went on, the two Castilian caravels conveying Atabe and the bishop were attacked and captured at sea by an armed vessel belonging to the Prince which had fired bombards and culverins against their ship. The Portuguese, the king continued, had seized all the gold, jewels, money and victuals carried by the Castilian ships as well as some cannon intended to help the defence of Lanzarote. One of the Portuguese commanders even wanted to throw the Castilian royal secretary into the sea along with the crew of the vessel on which he was travelling. Fortunately for them, the Portuguese commander's wishes were restrained by his own officers.[42] Eventually Atabe, as he recalled, reached Lanzarote empty-handed and wearing only a cloak.[43]

In the next year (1451) Henry made another attempt to reconquer Lanzarote. Atabe, despite his misfortunes on the way there, had evidently organized the island's defence effectively. Five armed Portuguese caravels carrying, it was said, three hundred men-at-arms sent by the Prince failed again to retake the island. The Portuguese squadron, out for revenge, then proceeded to sack the other Castilian-held islands and to attack any Castilian shipping they came across in the archipelago. The Christian island of Fuerteventura, said the Castilian king, had been worst hit in these terror attacks. He also declared that he had been advised that Henry was now attempting to impose a general blockade of the Canaries. To this end, John's letter stated, the Prince had instructed his caravels

> to attack and sack any ships from our said kingdoms voyaging to our said islands and to make prisoner all persons found aboard them and take them to any Moorish territory to be sold there so that no one would dare either to travel to the islands or to send supplies there, by which means the said Prince would be able more quickly to seize control of them. All these things the Portuguese have done, alleging that they have made their captures in accordance with the rules governing [the waging of] a just war.[44]

Henry was always adept at finding casuistical reasons to justify dubious courses of action. Nevertheless, one wonders what he said to his peers at the Portuguese court to explain how he, who repeatedly claimed that his life was dedicated to combating the infidel, came to be routinely engaged in waging a private but savage war on Castilian settlers in the Canary Islands. If the Castilian king's second letter is to be believed, however, this did not prevent him, when all his attempts to retake Lanzarote by force had failed, from once again approaching the Castilian king with a new request that John should recognize him as the lord of that island because, he now declared, he had bought it legally from Maciot de Béthencourt.[45]

Henry had gone a step too far when he assumed that there was no limit to the provocations from him the Castilian government, however much it might bluster, would in the end let pass. It was true that Don Álvaro de Luna had at this time the best of political reasons for maintaining friendly relations with Portugal. But his government could not risk alienating the nobles and merchants of Andalusia by supinely standing by while their traditional interests in the Canaries were under attack by the Portuguese prince. In the early summer of 1452 Iníguez de Atabe was again sent to Lisbon as the king's envoy with instructions to give a first-hand account to the Portuguese court of what it described as Henry's contemptuous disregard for the peace treaties between the two countries. As the Castilian king then put it, Henry's behaviour had involved 'a most serious and atrocious injury to us and to the royal crown of our kingdoms'. He complained particularly about the fact that, as already noted, despite the king's formal promise before 1450 that neither Henry nor any other Portuguese subject would in future be allowed to attack the Canaries, the Prince's caravels had nevertheless assaulted Fuerteventura, Lanzarote and La Gomera in that same year, killing people, sacking storehouses and destroying cattle and crops. The following year had seen the attack on the Castilian crown commissioner on the high seas already described and, later, a new assault on Lanzarote carried out by caravels from Lagos and Madeira. According to the witnesses who testified before the 1478 commission, various other Henrican attacks on different islands in the archipelago also took place during these years.

Afonso V and his advisers, confronted by these demands from a Castilian government forced at last, so it seemed, to make a stand, tried to temporize. The fact was that the Prince, thanks particularly to the success of the discoveries, was then at the summit of his political power. In consequence, he was not someone to whom the king or the royal council could give orders relating to affairs in the African Atlantic unless they knew that Henry was ready to assent to them. Afonso accordingly informed Atabe that he could not respond to the Castilian demands until he had held consultations with Henry whose personal affair, he explained, the Canaries problem was. Since Henry, it seems, had probably decamped to the Algarve to avoid meeting the Castilian ambassador, this ensured that a Portuguese reply would not soon be forthcoming. After a long period of fruitless waiting about at the Portuguese court, Atabe and his colleague eventually insisted on a formal reading of John II's demands for redress before the Portuguese king at a public ceremony at court – a step which was often a sign that the countries involved were near a declaration of war. International diplomatic custom meant that Afonso V could not refuse to allow the reading to take place. However, no doubt advised by Henry, he set about trying to minimize its significance by refusing to permit the presence of a Castilian scribe formally to record the proceedings in writing as would have been normal on such a serious occasion. The Portuguese courtiers present, Atabe reported home to Castile, did their best to undermine the dignity of the occasion, too. The reading of the document was interrupted by offensive remarks about the Castilians uttered by the Portuguese king's brother, D. Fernando, Henry's nephew and adopted son and heir.[46] The ambassadors formally warned Afonso V of the consequences which the Portuguese now risked on account of Henry's repeated infractions of the peace.

None of this had any apparent effect. Despite their warnings, the

Castilian envoys had to return home having only secured from Afonso V an offensive declaration that the Portuguese would hold their own enquiry into the validity of Castilian claims to the Canaries. The contemptuous arrogance of this announcement surely reflects, once again, the hand of the Prince, whose dislike of Castilians was so often on display during his lifetime, though these attitudes do not seem to have stopped him once thinking about accepting the throne of Castile if it were offered to him.

In the middle of this impasse Fernán Peraza, the undoubted legal lord of the Canaries, died (in 1452); the lordship (*señorío inferior*) of the islands then passed to his daughter, Inés Peraza, and her husband, Diego García de Herrera.[47] Afonso V, under new pressure from Henry, promptly sent an envoy to Castile demanding that John II order Herrera and his wife to sell the islands to the Prince.[48] The Portuguese king also insisted again on Henry's behalf that the latter's claim to Lanzarote was quite legal, since the island had been voluntarily ceded to him by Maciot de Béthencourt.

When John II sent yet another protest to Portugal in April 1454, he listed a new series of Portuguese aggressions in the islands which he characterized as deliberate acts of war against the Castilians. His letter also contained a phrase which more openly than ever before served notice on Henry that, if he persisted in his campaign to wrest the Canaries from Castile, the Castilians, for their part, might challenge the Prince's monopoly over trade and navigation south of Cape Bojador. Among the king's complaints against Henry was one relating to an attack made by an armed Portuguese balenger on a Castilian ship in Castilian territorial waters off Cadiz. Referring to this act of piracy, he described the vessel attacked as 'a certain caravel belonging to certain of our subjects, natives of our kingdoms, resident in our cities of Seville and Cadiz, who were travelling, with their merchandise, from the land they call Guinea, *whose conquest is reserved to us*' [my italics].[49] To make the offence worse, the letter went on, the Portuguese captain, acting on Afonso's (or, in reality, Henry's) orders, had cut off the hands of a Genoese merchant resident in Seville who had been a passenger on the captured vessel. This seems to have been a punishment already meted out, wherever they were found, to those who, as the Prince saw it, were unlicensed foreign interlopers engaged in breaking his Guinea monopoly. No doubt he regarded Genoese merchants, with their special commercial expertise in the African trades, as particularly dangerous when they put their knowledge at the disposal of Castilian merchants instead of serving him. It was, however, one thing to attack such interlopers when they were caught operating inside the geographical limits of the monopoly but quite another to seize their vessels and kill their passengers after these had successfully returned to Castilian home waters. On the face of it, Castilian relations with Portugal had now finally moved near to breaking point.

Suddenly, however, what seemed to be a dangerous crisis went completely off the boil. The reason is not far to seek. Even while these apparently angry exchanges about the Canaries between Afonso V and John II had been going on, behind the scenes negotiations for a dynastic marriage between the two kingdoms were approaching completion. The principals concerned were the heir of John II, the sixteen-year-old and already divorced Henry, prince of Asturias, and Afonso V's pretty sister, the fifteen-year-old Infanta Dona Joana of Portugal. Joana was already noted for her sportive personality which, it was presumably hoped, might stir into action the rumoured unresponsiveness to female charms of her husband-to-be. The terms of the marriage contract were agreed at Medina del Campo in December 1453, though the marriage did not take place until May 1455, after Henry IV's accession to the Castilian throne. These happenings complicate the way we should interpret John II's indignant letter of April 1454 about the Portuguese prince's behaviour in the Canaries. Was it largely no more than make-believe, written to placate the Andalusians by sending to Afonso V a communication that both writer and recipient already knew was about to be overtaken by events? Or was the Castilian king persuaded to write it by a faction at court that opposed the Portuguese marriage and, perhaps, did not forgive Prince Henry his frequent displays of hostility to Castile? One thing was sure: the Prince's brinkmanship in the Canaries had paid off. There could be no question on the Castilian side of imperilling the marriage alliance for the sake of a few Castilian settlers on some Atlantic islands, still less of mounting a naval challenge to the Henrican Guinea monopoly. That would not happen until the start of a new war between the two old enemies twenty years further on.

As for Henry, he did not, in the light of the new dynastic alliance, now consider abandoning his claim to the Canaries but he does seem to have decided on another change of tactics to fit in with the spirit of the marriage. He was enough of a realist to sense that it was a good time to try yet again to secure from Castile by diplomacy what he had notoriously failed to win by force. The terms agreed between Castile and Portugal on the Canaries question in 1454 and 1455 are not known and very likely were never more than verbal undertakings. It seems, however, that Henry agreed to withdraw his men from the part of La Gomera where they had succeeded in establishing themselves, and to cease armed attacks anywhere else in the archipelago. When Cadamosto wrote his account of his passing visit to the Canaries under the Prince's auspices in 1455, he spoke of Diego García de Herrera as then undisputed territorial lord of the islands of Lanzarote, Fuerteventura, La Gomera and Hierro. He made no mention of any Portuguese claims to or presence on any of them. The Venetian explorer's silence suggests that, as part of the dynastic marriage negotiations, the Prince had agreed to leave the islands alone in exchange for a promise by García de Herrera that Portuguese ships on their way to or from Guinea would in future freely receive whatever supplies they needed in the four Christianized islands where the latter's rule was effective. Henry's final will of 1460, while going into great detail about the disposal after his death of his other Atlantic islands, makes no mention whatever of the Canaries.

In fact, though, the evidence suggests that, even after 1455, the Prince had probably not abandoned his obsession with the archipelago. Among the chief Portuguese nobles who escorted the Portuguese king's sister to Castile for her wedding there in 1455 were two important nobles, Martinho de Ataíde, count of Atougia, and Pedro de Meneses, count of Vila Real, who was about to become governor of Ceuta.[50] In a letter written in 1468, Henry IV complained that these two Portuguese envoys on that occasion, along with members of their retinues, had continuously badgered him to grant sovereignty over Grand Canary, Tenerife and La Palma to Portugal. The Castilian king claimed he had eventually agreed to do what they asked simply to put an end to their importuning, and because he then had more important and troublesome things on his mind than the international status of the Canaries.[51] Since neither of Dona Joana's escorts had shown any previous interest in the archipelago, or in the African Atlantic generally, it is a distinct possibility that the Prince was behind the importuning about which Henry IV complained. If so, Martinho de Ataíde must have been somewhat embarrassed when the Castilian king, with characteristic insouciance and with a total disregard for the rights of the Castilian ruling family in the islands, granted the right of conquest and the lordship of the three pagan-held islands not to Henry, nor even to the Portuguese crown, but to Ataíde himself personally. What Henry thought about this offhand behaviour is not documented, but since it made him look rather foolish, he cannot have been pleased. Ataíde seems to have done nothing with his unexpected and unmanageable gift. He eventually sold it, probably after the Prince's death, to Pedro de Meneses, by now governor of Ceuta. The latter, in case the erratic Castilian king had second thoughts, lost no time in registering his acquisition with the curia by asking in his turn for papal authority to conquer his newly acquired property and to convert its pagan inhabitants to Christianity.[52] But, in the end, nothing came of this either. Pedro de Meneses in his turn sold his rights to Henry's heir, the Infante D. Fernando. The latter seems to have sent an unsuccessful expedition to the archipelago in an attempt to secure his newly acquired claims there but his heart was not in it. Unlike his adoptive father, he did not allow the Canaries to distract him from the business of developing the Portuguese Atlantic islands – these now included the Cape Verdes – which had come to him on Henry's death. That, however, was still not the end of the matter since, as we have seen, in 1468 Henry IV formally revoked the donation of the Canaries he had made in 1455 to Martinho de Ataíde with as little ceremony as he had originally made it, merely saying that he had granted it under a misapprehension. He then confirmed that the sole rights of seigneurial lordship (*señorío inferior*) belonged by the due process of inheritance to his Castilian vassal, the sorely tried García de Herrera.[53] That was not the end of Portuguese fifteenth-century attempts to use naval and military force against Castile in the Canaries but further attempts took place in the context of the open hostilities between the two countries that followed Afonso V's attempt to seize the Castilian throne from Isabel the Catholic in 1478. They are therefore outside the scope of the present book.[54]

Henry's habit of pursuing with obsessive determination any cause to which he had publicly committed himself was, of course, responsible for the success which would find him a special place in the history of oceanic exploration. His obsessiveness also involved him in some notable failures of which the débâcle before Tangier is the best known. Less well-known are the details of his thirty-year-long attempt to make himself conqueror and ruler of the Canarian archipelago.

As is commonly the case with obsessives, Henry did not interpret the defeat of his army on Grand Canary in 1424, or any of the later defeats his men suffered in the archipelago, as supplying any reason for him to ask himself if the way he was going about things there was either politically wise or militarily appropriate. His instinctive response to defeat of any kind was immediately to set about organizing a repeat performance of the unsuccessful endeavour, a procedure he followed with determination in the archipelago. There were, of course, limits to his inflexibility. As long as he was satisfied that he was not being prompted to call his ideological mindset in question, he could decide to – or be persuaded to – change course when it was obviously necessary to do so if a project was to survive. On such occasions, as we have seen, Henry would sometimes resort to casuistry to persuade others that, though things might look different, in fact there had been no abandonment of his previous position. Just as, in Guinea in the late 1440s, he abandoned war and intimidation as appropriate instruments for the Portuguese explorers to use in the lands they had recently reached, so in the Canaries he came to recognize that, if he was to have any hope of establishing himself in any of the pagan-held islands, he needed, however much it went against the grain, to seek allies among some of the clan chiefs. The story of Henry's endeavours in the Canaries also repeatedly confirms what we have seen in other contexts: that, for all his piety and public displays of devotion to religion and the institutions of the Church, he was not above deliberately misleading successive popes when that served his purposes. Thus, in order to supply Eugenius IV with the sort of reasons he needed if the curia were to be persuaded to grant him the right to conquer the islands which were still in aboriginal hands, he assured Eugenius that the native Canarians in every way demonstrated the accuracy of the definitions of paganism traditionally accepted by the Fathers of the Church and by later publicists. Though he must have known perfectly well the favourable accounts of Canarian culture reported on by European observers in the Canaries since the middle of the fourteenth century, which reported that the Canarians were members of a quite complex and in many ways surprisingly advanced Stone Age culture, he did not hesitate to assure the pope that they existed on a level indistinguishable from that of wild beasts.

What the most powerful of the various motives which fuelled Henry's obsession with the Canaries was must remain a matter for conjecture. As we have seen, it is quite unlikely that, in 1424, he was already concerned with protecting a sea route to Guinea that probably then did not yet exist even in his imagination. Even had it done so, and even though he was notoriously bad at weighing up objectively the military or strategic odds against him, it is impossible to believe that, simply to provide protection for his ships when the time came, he set about the Herculean task of trying to conquer and subdue, with the limited forces available to him, the largest, most densely inhabited and least accessible islands in the group. It is certain that his obsession embraced a number of more complicated aims and motives. The desire to appear before posterity as a prince responsible for conquering and converting these quite large pagan societies existing on the fringes of the then known world was certainly one – especially if he was spurred on by the belief, revealed in his horoscope, that it was his destiny to achieve notable conquests. This pious purpose may have seemed all the more opportune to Henry on a worldly level because he did not consider the conversion of the native Canarians to Christianity incompatible with their continuing relegation to the status of slave. There is much evidence, too, that the fact that Castile claimed sovereignty over the Canaries awakened all his ingrained dislike of and contempt for every Castilian. In order to drive these interlopers out of what he early came to see as his private sphere of influence in the African Atlantic, he determinedly waged for years what amounted to an undeclared proxy war against Castile throughout the archipelago on the risky assumption, which, however, proved correct, that the central kingdom's political weakness would see to it that, however much he rode roughshod over Castilian rights, a local war there did not turn into an all-out war between the two kingdoms. Given the Prince's frustrated hopes of achieving regal status outside Portugal but within the Peninsula itself, we cannot exclude the possibility, either, that his awareness that the islands had once been proclaimed a papal principality and that Jean de Béthencourt had had himself proclaimed their king in the streets of Seville may have seemed of interest to one whose frustrated regal ambitions had been noted at the Portuguese court. Whether the accounts he had of the physical characteristics of the larger islands of the archipelago awakened in him any vision of their potential agricultural future – comparable to that developing under his aegis in Madeira – we cannot know. Given the straitened, frontier-style level of life that was apparently the lot of the Castilian settlers on Lanzarote and Fuerteventura in his day, this was perhaps unlikely. It may well have been, of course, that what caused Henry's obsession with the Canaries was simply the appetite to acquire ever more land which always characterized the psyche of medieval magnates generally, and none more so than that of the sons of John I and queen Philippa when they complained that Portugal was too small to supply them with territorial possessions conmensurate with their princely status.

The most obvious negative consequence of Henry's obsession with the Canaries was that for several decades he caused men, ships, armaments and a great deal of money to be wasted on a particularly nasty, entirely unnecessary and in the end largely unsuccessful private colonial war. If there was one thing the long story of the Prince's preoccupation with the Canaries did not do for him, it was to bring him any of the honour or fame he had hoped to find there. Nor, it must be added, did it do anything for his reputation as an organizer of military operations. Judging by his complaints to the curia, he was never able to understand that rigid adherence to the methods of warfare as practised by late-medieval European and Moorish armies would not do when used against an enemy fighting to preserve his home and freedom who was unfazed by the military technology of the invaders, and whose notions of how to wage a defensive war against them belonged to what would one day be known as the guerrilla tradition.

The treaty of Alcáçovas in 1479 put an end for good to Portuguese political claims in the Canary Islands. It was followed up by the hard-fought but in the end successful military campaigns ordered by the Catholic Monarchs to complete the conquest of the whole archipelago. Ironically, so far from these events leading to the exclusion of the Portuguese from the islands Henry had so much coveted, the reverse happened. The Castilian *conquistadores* brought in large numbers of Portuguese settlers and colonizers, often from Madeira, to open up and work the land, and later to establish the Canarian sugar industry.[55] As far as Portuguese shipping on its way to Guinea or further afield was concerned, after 1479 Castilian control of the Canaries rarely caused any problems.

~ Chapter Twelve ~

Cadamosto: A New World Observed

In this account of my journey, having seen . . . many new sights worthy of notice, and so that those who come after me will be able to understand what went through my mind as I sought out strange things in divers new places, I have decided to make a record of what I saw, for truly, when compared with the sights I have seen and ingested there [in Guinea], the way we live and the places where we live and our customs can be said to belong to a different world . . .

Cadamosto[1]

The way Cadamosto or, to give him his Italian name, Alvise da Cà da Mosto, came to be involved in the affairs of Guinea was, as he tells it in his *Navigazioni*, entirely fortuitous. In August 1454 he was aboard one of the three Flanders galleys on their routine voyage from Venice to the North. Because of unfavourable weather in the Atlantic beyond Cape St Vincent, the galleys took shelter in one of the bays sheltered by Cape Sagres from the westerlies. There was nothing unusual about this. As far back as 1443 Henry had obtained from the crown the right to build a 'town' near or on the cape. One of its functions, he claimed, would be to attend to the material and spiritual needs of the ships of various nations which found themselves obliged to anchor there while awaiting a suitable wind or favourable weather to round Cape St Vincent.[2] It is on record that the Signoria had long thought it worthwhile to maintain some Venetian ships' carpenters and other specialists permanently in the nearby inland village of Raposeira to service the galleys when they were held up on their way north.[3] Cadamosto himself belonged to an important Venetian merchant family whose fortunes had suffered because of the incurable litigiousness of his father. In 1454 he was only aged twenty-two but was on his second voyage with the Flanders-bound galleys. Despite his youth he had already had experience of sailing with the galleys of Venice on journeys to the eastern Mediterranean and North Africa.

Cadamosto's book goes on to explain that, while the galleys were weather bound off Sagres, Prince Henry, then resident in Raposeira, sent one of his secretaries, Antão Gonçalves, to call on the commander of the galleys. Gonçalves is presumably to be identified with the successful explorer of the coast of Guinea and the expelled Henrican governor of Lanzarote of that name. He came aboard accompanied by a Venetian, Patrizio di Conti, described by Cadamosto as a 'consul' of Venice in Portugal. Cadamosto, surprised to find a Venetian consul in such a remote place, seems at first to have doubted Conti's credentials until the latter produced his official letter of appointment bearing the Signoria's seal. One source significantly describes Conti as 'a man celebrated for the worth of his geographical learning'.[4] If this is correct, he may have been stationed in Lagos or at Raposeira as much to advise Henry on matters geographical as to look after Venetian interests in the Algarve. Maybe, indeed, the Signoria had appointed him as consul so that he could report to it on what the Prince was up to.

Henry's overt object in making contact with the galleys on this occasion was to show the Venetian merchants aboard them samples of the sugar now being produced abundantly in Madeira along with dragon's blood and other commodities from his Atlantic islands. He hoped thus to secure their interest in the products of the islands. Perhaps he also wanted to ensure that the Genoese had some competition from Venice as regards the purchase and marketing in Europe of the growing export production of sugar from Madeira. Gonçalves and Conti, in the course of explaining to the Venetians aboard the galleys these economic possibilities, also described how Henry's explorers had opened up trade with the Atlantic mainland of West Africa and particularly with Black Africa. They told of the great profits that could be made there by European merchants sailing under licence from the Prince. According to the two men, gains of the order of six or ten times the original outlay on trading goods were easily obtainable. The young Cadamosto, attracted by such a prospect and fascinated by what the two visitors had to say about Guinea, was more interested in this information than he was in the economic possibilities offered by trade with Henry's Atlantic islands. It seems in fact possible that the latter had instructed his two messengers to try, by talking about the profits to be gained in Guinea, to persuade one or more of the Venetian merchants aboard the galleys to join his service. Cadamosto enquired of Gonçalves and Conti if the Prince allowed alien merchants to sail independently to the newly discovered lands. It was explained to him that the answer was in the affirmative and that there were two alternative ways in which this could be done under licence. If a merchant or a ship's captain elected to fit out or charter a caravel for the journey at his own expense, and himself to supply its cargo of merchandise for barter in Guinea, he was permitted to retain three-quarters of any profit made, one quarter being payable to the Prince. If Henry himself fitted out a caravel on a merchant's behalf, leaving the latter only to supply the cargo, then his share of the profits made would rise to one-half.[5] Cadamosto was also assured that Henry would particularly welcome the participation of Venetians in the new Guinea trade because he counted on finding spices and other articles of commerce that they were especially experienced in handling.

After the licensing arrangements had been explained to him, Cadamosto was invited to Raposeira to meet the Prince personally and to confirm from him that things were as he had been told. He says that he was well received by Henry who urged him to leave the galleys forthwith and join the Portuguese in the work of discovery and trade in Guinea. The young Venetian, being, as he wrote, well fitted by his youth to cope with hardships, and anxious to see lands and sights never before seen by any of his fellow-countrymen, made a quick decision to accept Henry's invitation and become a merchant–explorer under the latter's auspices. He returned aboard his galley to collect his belongings and to buy merchandise that he thought might be useful for his new enterprise before finally parting company with his compatriots. So began an association that would last until 1460. After the Prince's death Cadamosto only remained in Portugal for two or three years. About 1464 he returned to Venice, perhaps because, with the disappearance of his patron and the reversion of responsibility for the affairs of Guinea to the crown, he felt there was no longer any place for him in Portugal.

There is much of interest to the student of the Prince's life in these opening passages of the *Navigazioni* such as the information that, when Cadamosto met him in 1454, Henry was still living on his estate at Raposeira. Many scholars have believed that, by this time, whenever he was living in the Algarve – which he did even in these years less unbrokenly than is often supposed – the Prince had taken up residence in his elusive 'town' near the modern Sagres, or on the cape itself. Given the importance to Cadamosto of his meeting with Henry and his subsequent familiarity with this region of the Algarve, it seems unlikely that, when he wrote the passage concerned, Cadamosto misremembered the location of his first meeting with his princely patron. Also of interest is the information that there was in Henry's entourage in the Algarve an official of the Signoria. As his welcome to Cadamosto himself confirms, Henry evidently had no thought of keeping foreign merchants away from Guinea or from his Atlantic islands – as long as they were not Castilians. On the contrary, he was anxious to make use of their special commercial and marketing expertise and, judging by Patrizio de Conti's presence on the scene, was also ready to discuss with foreigners geographical matters related to the discoveries.

In his *Proemio* the young Venetian duly pays brief tributes to Henry's piety, to his dedication to crusading against the Moroccans, to his heroism on the battlefield and even to his chastity. In the actual text of the *Navigazioni*, however, the Prince appears not at all in his crusader's rig but as a practical and successful organizer of discovery and trade who directly concerned himself in planning and detailed control of operations in Guinea. Cadamosto had, of course, no reason to include in an account intended for Venetian readers of three voyages of exploration to what he regarded as a new world, anything about the other concerns of the Prince or about Portugal and its political affairs. Nevertheless, since he plainly came to know Henry well, his account of the latter as a hands-on controller of operations must be given proper recognition, difficult though it may be to reconcile that view of him with the hero figure other contemporary sources depict.

Cadamosto, since he obviously had no ship of his own, had arranged with the Prince to use the second of the two methods described above to fix up his first voyage as an explorer. Henry fitted out a new caravel of perhaps some forty-three tons capacity (ninety *botte*) for the journey to Guinea of his new protegé.[6] Cadamosto sailed from Lagos on his first voyage on 22 March 1455. He had thus had seven months in which to find out all about the discoveries and the Guinea trade and to learn some Portuguese. The ship's master, Vicente Dias, had commanded a caravel in the major military expedition of 1445 to the Gulf of Arguin.

With the north-east trades behind them, Cadamosto notes that they covered the 600 miles to the island of Porto Santo in three days.

Before proceeding further it will be appropriate to draw attention to features of the *Navigazioni* that relate to its value both as a historical record and as a classic piece of travel literature. Portuguese students of the discoveries have often found it difficult to give Cadamosto his due, perhaps because of a certain unconscious resentment that the major contemporary piece of writing about the final phase of the Henrican discoveries that has survived should be the work of a foreigner. Attacks on Cadamosto's reliability have centred on his assertion that he, with another Italian, Antoniotto Usodimare, was the first to discover and partly to reconnoitre the Cape Verde Islands. The case in defence of Cadamosto's claim has been effectively made by the editor of the best critical edition of the *Navigazioni*.[7]

Though Cadamosto speaks as if he wrote his account of his own two voyages to Guinea from memory, this certainly was not, for the most part, the case. Even allowing for the remarkable ability to recall events which people of his time, trained in the discipline of mnemonics, enjoyed, it is obvious that the self-assured, highly detailed and usually accurate descriptions of happenings experienced and observations made nearly ten years previously that are recorded in the *Navigazioni* cannot have been dependent on memory alone. To appreciate this, one has only to dwell on the confidence with which Cadamosto writes not only about matters related to navigation and oceanic exploration but also *in extenso* about the ethnographical characteristics of the native societies he encountered and about the fauna and flora to be found there. As an amateur ethnographer and naturalist in Senegambia, his work as an observer has stood the test of time.[8] He must have based much of the *Navigazioni* on the re-examination of charts (some of them made by him), on what was recorded in ships' logs, on notes taken on various occasions, and on other records he had made in 1455 and 1456 or later and carried with him from Portugal to Venice when he returned there in 1463. As one of his editors has pointed out, his incorporation of such contemporary recorded material into his narrative sometimes caused him to write as if the Prince were still alive.[9]

The text of the *Navigazioni* does in fact give us a direct clue as to the kind of written material Cadamosto used. For his account of the 1462 voyage of Pero de Cintra to the coast of modern Liberia, he explains that he used the log and the verbal commentary on it brought to him in his house in Lagos by Pero's Portuguese scrivener, a friend who had previously been to Guinea with him on an earlier occasion.[10] Even when he is writing about his own two voyages as an explorer, Cadamosto very frequently acknowledges, if he is presenting information secured at second-hand, that this is the case. He often specifies what his particular source was. This could be other Europeans (Portuguese or foreign), or slave–interpreters whom he has interrogated. He frequently also indicates whether such information was obtained by him in Guinea or in Portugal. His famous account of the way the Islamic rulers of the Sahel carried on the 'silent trade' in which salt was bartered for gold with the purposefully invisible miners of the West African gold fields is an example of his skill in securing from others and then putting into his own words accurate information about the origins of the gold trade of West Africa that Europeans before his time had sought in vain to acquire.[11] Two other points need to be made about the *Navigazioni*. One is that it is primarily concerned with giving accounts of the two voyages of exploration its author made in 1455 and 1456. It seems certain, however, that he subsequently made other voyages to Guinea which were to established *resgates* in Senegambia and perhaps to the new factory at Arguin as well. The second point to be emphasized is that all the new information about Guinea contained in Cadamosto's book was, of course, made known at the time to his patron the Prince and to those who worked for him. His purpose in writing the *Navigazioni* was to make a wider world aware of the nature of the discoveries in the African Atlantic that Henry had directed, not to disclose secrets the Prince had previously kept to himself. Cadamosto, though he wrote in Italian, is thus a true chronicler of Portuguese exploration in Guinea and of the commercial exploitation of the region in the last decade of the Prince's life.

After the Venetian explorer had spent two days on Porto Santo, his caravel departed for Madeira and later put in, apparently without experiencing any problems with the Castilians there, at the Canary islands of La Gomera, Hierro and La Palma. Though his account of these places is, as we have seen in the preceding chapter, important for the history of the Atlantic islands in the Prince's time, it does not concern us here. His descriptions of Arguin and of Mauritania in general have also already been considered. Though he seems to have sailed along the Arguin Bank in 1455 and has much to say about Arguin and its fortified trading post and about the affairs of the western Sahara, it is by no means certain that his caravel actually called in at Arguin on this voyage. It seems more probable that he set a course directly from Cape Blanco for the mouth of the River Senegal and Black Africa.

Now began the serious business of mapping the coast and, when possible, landing to make contact with the local people. Navigation henceforth was, of necessity, as Cadamosto explains, a slow business, involving not only close visual scrutiny of the coastline, but also, in these uncharted seas, much use of lead and line. The caravels engaged on this work never attempted to navigate at night but always, if they could find one, sought some secure bay, river estuary or offshore island where they could anchor safely until dawn. A careful watch had to be kept at night, not only for unfavourable changes in wind and weather but also against possible attack by hostile canoes; one thing the Portuguese had very soon learnt, to their no small surprise, was that, in Black Africa, the local people were far from being intimidated by the arrival off the coast of the caravels with their strangely complexioned and garbed crews. Even when they fired their cannon, this had only a momentary effect. At dawn, sail was set again with one man aloft on the foremast and two stationed in the bows. Their main duty was to watch for any telltale breakers ahead that would reveal the presence of shoals.[12]

It is made plain in the *Navigazioni* that, before Cadamosto's own arrival off the Senegal in 1455, the Portuguese had, since 1448, succeeded in establishing peaceful and regular trading relations with the two northernmost Wolof kingdoms of Senegal (Walo and Kayor), and had already sailed some distance up the great river which would give its name to the lands on its lower reaches. According to Cadamosto, the Senegal was discovered and entered, about 1448, by three caravels belonging to Henry, after which Portuguese vessels called there every year to trade.[13] A Portuguese document of John II's time is more precise. It states that the first organized trading in the region was carried out by a certain Lourenço Dias, of Lagos, one of Prince Henry's squires.[14] The traders even then were not only Portuguese nationals: the Venetian explorer explains that, when getting himself briefed in Portugal for his own journey to the region in 1455, he consulted a Genoese merchant who had been in Senegal the previous year and who assured him that the local king was a person who could be trusted and who paid properly for the merchandise he bought from the Europeans.[15] Cadamosto also alludes to consultations he had with various Portuguese who had had dealings with the same Senegalese king. There is thus clear evidence that regular trading with the Wolofs of Walo and Kayor, north of Cape Verde, existed on a regular basis at least from the beginning of the 1450s. It is also worth noting how early the Genoese appeared as participants in this trade in the wake of the Portuguese discoverers. The merchant mentioned by Cadamosto may well have come from the important Genoese merchant community, dominated by the Lomellini family, which had long been established in Lisbon. What remains unknown to students of the discoveries is to what extent money provided by Genoese and other Italian merchant houses settled in Portugal helped to finance the Henrican voyages to Guinea.

The anonymous Genoese consulted by Cadamosto was not the only Genoese resident in Portugal who went to Senegal during these years.[16] The *Navigazioni*, in its account of Cadamosto's first voyage, reports that, off Cape Verde, he encountered two Portuguese caravels also sailing south in company together. Aboard one of them was a Genoese merchant at that time resident in Portugal, one Antoniotto Usodimare.[17] Like Cadamosto, Antoniotto seems to have been operating under a licence from the Prince which encouraged him, too, to try his hand at exploration as well as at trading.[18]

Cadamosto supplies a fair amount of information that enables us to build up some picture of the rapid growth of Portugal's trading relations with Senegal between 1448 and 1455. The trade centred on an unidentified Atlantic anchorage between the mouth of the Senegal River and Cape Verde known to the Portuguese as 'As Palmas de Budomel' or just plain 'Budomel'. The toponym tells its own story. As Cadamosto himself points out, it is simply a Portuguese transliteration of the title of the ruler (*Damel*) in whose territory the anchorage lay, preceded by the Wolof *bur*, 'chief'. This was the traditional title by which the ruler of the Wolof state of Kayor was always known.

The frontiers of the six states forming the Wolof confederation were always unstable but Kayor, in early Portuguese times, probably extended along the Atlantic coast from a point somewhat to the south of the estuary of the River Senegal further southwards to the neighbourhood of Cape Verde. The Damel of Kayor's lands did not actually extend north as far as the river's south bank. This, as well as some Wolof territory to the north of the river, belonged to the ruler of the small state of Walo. Immediately to the south of Kayor, in the neighbourhood of Cape Verde, was – at least in later times – the somewhat exiguous territory of Baol, whose ruler was called the Teny. To the east, some fifty to seventy-five miles inland from the coast of Kayor, was the inland state of Jolof whose ruler, the *Burba Jolof*, was titular overlord of the whole Wolof confederation.[19] The name the Portuguese gave to their anchorage indicates, therefore, that this was in the territory of the Damel of Kayor. According to Cadamosto, the Damel's capital was then about twenty miles from the anchorage.[20] The Venetian traveller also says that, in 1455, the ruler of Kayor, whom he visited in his capital, was a young man of twenty-two whom he calls 'Zucholin'.

It is more difficult to identify wth certainty the exact site of the anchorage. Cadamosto locates it as lying sixty-four miles south of the mouth of the Senegal and thirty-two miles north of Cape Verde. The sandy, exposed coastline north of Cape Verde has undergone, since the fifteenth-century, marked changes which have obliterated the outlets to the sea of a number of small rivers. These formerly made breaks in the heavy surf, allowing ships' boats access to the land. Modern investigations into the site of the *resgate* of Budomel, however, place it on the coast near the present village of Mboro, at a place where old maps show that a stream used to enter the sea.[21] Trading procedures here were that, after anchoring, the caravel captain sent a message inland to the Damel's capital by the Wolof interpreter carried on his caravel announcing his arrival and offering to trade. When Cadamosto did this in 1455 his message unexpectedly produced the Damel in person. The Wolof ruler arrived at the anchorage with an escort of fifteen horsemen and 150 warriors on foot. After personal contact had been made, the Damel authorized Cadamosto to disembark and invited him to visit his capital to complete trading arrangements. As a sign of goodwill he also presented his visitor with a beautiful Wolof girl of twelve or thirteen who, as Cadamosto puts it, was intended to serve him in his cabin and, we are left to infer, did so. As would frequently be the experience of the Portuguese in Guinea, trade on the African side was entirely in the hands of the local ruler.

The main trade carried on by the Portuguese in Kayor was, as explained in an earlier chapter, bartering horses for slaves. This seems always to have been the basis of trade at the *resgate* at Budomel. Horses were highly esteemed by the Wolof chiefs and nobles, less for warlike purposes than as a prestige possession. Cadamosto comments that, because of the climate and lack of proper food, the animals did not live long even in the northern (tsetse-free) regions of Senegal so there was always a ready market for them.[22] Before the coming of the Portuguese, the Wolofs had always bought from Arab and Sanhadja merchants Barbary horses which had survived the journey across the Sahara. Cadamosto emphasizes that the animals he carried aboard his caravel were from the Iberian Peninsula and had not been purchased in

Morocco. The horse trade was certainly a profitable one since, according to Cadamosto, in his time the Wolofs would offer from nine to fourteen slaves for a single animal.[23] At the beginning of the sixteenth century, when their slave-trade with Senegal was in decline, Portuguese writers complained that they could only now secure five slaves, at best, for one animal, and looked back to more prosperous days when, in a good year, four hundred slaves, mostly bartered for horses, were regularly shipped from Senegal.[24] The sale of the seven horses together with the wool and other articles of trade Cadamosto had brought with him in 1455 secured him what he regarded as a satisfactory number of slaves.[25] The establishment of the trade in horses at Budomel thus offers a clear example of the way, as already at Arguin, the appearance of the Portuguese on the Atlantic coast, by pitting caravels against caravans, represented, as Henry had promised, a deliberate attack on ancient patterns of economic intercourse between Black Africa and the Muslim world. It would be unwise, though, to exaggerate the negative effect – if any – that this attack had on the western trans-Saharan caravan trade in the Prince's time.

Cadamosto brought from Portugal some other articles which were known to be in demand in Senegal – he mentions particularly woollen cloth, saddles and Moorish silks. There was also a market in the partly Islamicized Wolof lands for *haiks* and *bedels*. These everyday articles of Moorish clothing, previously brought by caravan from Morocco, also began to be exported to Budomel by the Portuguese. There was no demand for food, which the Wolofs had in abundance, nor for cotton, since cotton was a local product. Despite the nominal adherence of the ruling class to the tenets of Islam, the Wolofs were particularly fond of the local palm-wine, a taste their leaders soon began willingly to supplement with wine imported from Portugal as a luxury article. Though Cadamosto had learnt the secrets of the way the West African gold trade was conducted, he was rightly not encouraging about the possibilities of obtaining significant quantities of gold dust in Senegal, reporting that he had seen very little gold of any kind in the local markets there.

It can be inferred from the *Navigazioni* that, in 1455, there were as yet no further established Portuguese trading posts anywhere south of Budomel, though this would soon change. There is, however, evidence in the Venetian's text that some of Henry's men may already have sailed a considerable distance up the Senegal by the time of his first voyage, though the categorical statement to this effect which appears in one of the manuscript copies of his book, and in both sixteenth-century printed versions, is not found in the oldest manuscript.[26] Though Cadamosto himself did not attempt to navigate upriver in 1455, he described in detail how to navigate in the estuary of the Senegal and was well-informed about conditions upstream. He also reported that tidal influence continued to be felt more than fifty miles from the sea.[27] As it in fact extends a great deal further than this, it may perhaps be inferred that, by 1455, other Portuguese explorers had already sailed up the river to a point near the modern Rosso, a hypothesis supported by the fact that Cadamosto was also aware that from this point eastwards lay the country of Takrur inhabited by the Tukulor, or Futa Toro Fulbe people.[28]

It was quite natural that the Portuguese should have found the Wolofs ready to open trading relations with them. They were long accustomed to doing business with Arab and Sanhadja traders. Their nominal status as Muslims, and the frequent presence in their country of marabouts and holy men from North Africa must have served to give their rulers at least some ideas about the Mediterranean world far away to the north beyond the desert. The Portuguese, on the whole, seemed to have liked the Wolofs, whom they thought to be remarkable horsemen and good warriors. Cadamosto's detailed account of them and their country is rightly famous for its objectivity. The Venetian explorer's all-embracing curiosity about this new world, and his ability to record what he had seen and heard there in detailed but always businesslike prose, is seen at its most fruitful in his description of the Wolofs and their society. Though he was critical of some aspects of their character as well as their customs and habits and, as a European, inevitably did not always find the right explanations for the latter, he never treated the Wolofs with the kind of barely concealed disdain if not active dislike with which the Portuguese of Henry's time were likely to refer to Muslims and pagans alike. Thus, while noting that the Wolofs were awkward when responding to things of which they had no previous experience, he commented that, when dealing with anything with which they were familiar, they handled it with as much skill as any European might.[29] Though he reckoned them to be inclined to deceit, he noted with approval that they were of kindly disposition. What did much surprise him was to find Wolof men performing a number of tasks which in Europe were regarded as the duties of women. It was the close relationship he had established with the Bor-Damel which gave him the opportunity to write at length and sympathetically about the latter's way of life and the customs of his court. Cadamosto's descriptions of the novel flora and fauna of

Senegambia as they were in the middle of the fifteenth century (e.g. his descriptions of elephants or hippopotamuses and their habits), are notable for the accuracy and completeness with which eyewitness observation of these and other animals and birds of the region had equipped him. Religion rarely enters his narrative, but he does refer to arguments he had with the Bor-Damel about the relative merits of Christianity and Islam, arguments in which, he says, the Wolof ruler took a decidedly open-minded stance. On the basis of these discussions, he concluded that the Bor's powers of reasoning and understanding were no different from those any European man might display.[30] In light of the fierce arguments about the legitimacy of non-Christian kings that went on in the later Middle Ages, Cadamosto's judgement that the Bor-Damel had every right to be regarded as a true king in Christian terms are significant. The Venetian explorer concluded from his contacts with the Wolof ruler and his observation of court ceremonial that, as he puts it in a remarkably unprejudiced way,

> it cannot be doubted that rulers like him are not there because they are rich in treasure or money since they possess neither, nor do they have any income to spend. Nevertheless, in terms of the ceremonial which surrounds them and the size of their retinues, they may truly be regarded as lords and rulers (*signori*) like any lords anywhere else. To speak the truth, they are more revered and feared by their subjects and better accompanied by more people than are our lords here [in Italy] by theirs.[31]

The Venetian probably knew little about the arguments of theologians and canon lawyers concerning the legitimacy and rights, if any, of non-Christian rulers, but he did recognize, when he encountered one, a person whose authority and demeanour measured up to those he associated with kingship, even if that person was black and quite without the conspicuous display of wealth that, in European eyes, necessarily went with a throne. On the question of the Wolofs' religion Cadamosto noted that, on the whole, they were very lukewarm Muslims. He claimed, somewhat over-hopefully, that contact with Christians was weakening their belief in Islam still further. As he put it, with unusual smugness, the Wolofs admired Christian habits and were much impressed by the wealth and intellectual gifts of the Christians. This, perhaps, was a rare occasion when Cadamosto gilded the lily somewhat. There is no convincing evidence that Henry ever took any serious steps to follow up the commercial penetration of the Wolof states by the dispatch there of missionaries.

Cadamosto's friendly personal relationship with the Bor-Damel and the detailed account of the latter's kingdom which he brought back to Portugal clearly had much to do with the making of the lasting close association between the Portuguese and the Wolofs which, in John II's time, would lead to the much-trumpeted conversion, in Portugal, of a Wolof king, and an unsuccessful attempt to establish a Portuguese castle and garrison at the mouth of the River Senegal. The relationship is still reflected today by the considerable number of Portuguese words which passed into the Wolof language.[32]

For the Wolof rulers, these contacts with the Portuguese in the Prince's time were by no means without political as well as economic consequences. As already noted, the Bor-Damel and the other coastal rulers of the Wolof federation were nominally at least under the suzerainty of the Burba Jolof, who ruled over the inland state named after him. The new relationship of the coastal rulers with the Portuguese enabled them to increase their independence of the Burba Jolof whose landlocked kingdom remained oriented towards the Sahel and the trans-Saharan caravans.

Seen with hindsight, there was, of course, a notable downside to the relationship between the Portuguese and the coastal kingdoms of Senegal. For decades, the most sought-after black slaves in the Peninsula were Wolofs.[33] Cadamosto's relatively sympathetic appraisal of the Wolofs and their culture did not lead him to feel any discomfort about buying Wolof slaves. As far as we can tell, his attitude to the slave trade was no different from that of everyone else engaged in it anywhere. Just as Christian baptism changed a man, woman or child into a different and better sort of person, so, in a reverse way, when any man, woman or child had the misfortune to descend into the legal or customary category of slave, they were thereby turned into an inferior kind of human being. Once the slaves had been loaded aboard the caravels, Cadamosto has no more to say about them than he has about any other goods carried in their holds. Nevertheless, when he set about exploring the coasts and rivers south of Cape Verde after loading slaves in Senegal, the local people can hardly have failed to be aware of the presence of these captives aboard the Portuguese vessels. The fear and hatred that Cadamosto himself admits the inhabitants of the lower reaches of the River Gambia displayed towards him and his companions in 1455 was certainly fuelled by their fear of enslavement and by their belief that the otherwise inexplicable eagerness of the Portuguese to purchase black slaves was due to their fondness for eating the flesh of black people.[34]

After his stay in the Bor-Damel's country, Cadamosto resumed his journey south, his aim being to reach the kingdom of the Gambia where, the Prince had told him, black informants already brought to Portugal had declared that much gold was to be found. It was in June 1455, when his vessel was approaching Cape Verde, the western extremity of Africa (14° 45' N), that Cadamosto encountered the caravel of Antoniotto Usodimare sailing in company with another one manned by the Prince's men. Enquiry revealed that Antoniotto, too, had a licence from Henry to explore and trade beyond Cape Verde. The two Italians resolved to join forces and to try together to reach and explore the River Gambia whose estuary had been sighted and named by Dinis Dias in 1444 but which had not yet been reconnoitred. At Cape Verde no attempt was made to land on the mainland fringing the modern Baie de Gorée – later known to the Portuguese as Angra de Bezeguiche – where Dakar now stands.[35] The crews limited themselves to disembarking briefly on Ilha da Palma – later known as Gorée Island, a place destined to play an infamous part in the history of the Atlantic slave trade. Here they took on fresh water and, as was the custom of the caravels, set about fishing to ensure they had sufficient supplies in dried form of this staple diet for their onward journey. The latter was not particularly rapid. Cadamosto notes that, in accordance with Portuguese practice when exploring an unknown coast, his caravels always anchored at nightfall in deep water a considerable distance from the shore, choosing a spot where there was no sign of habitation ashore in order to avoid a night attack by hostile canoes.[36] By day the need to map the coast as the Prince required, as well as the demands of navigational caution in an uncharted sea must also have slowed up the caravels' progress. One man was regularly stationed as a lookout aloft on the mainmast and another in the bows to give warning of reefs or shoals ahead.[37]

Cadamosto was always enthusiastically responsive to the novel sights that nature in the tropics had to offer him and often records in the *Navigazioni* the impressions they made on him. The everyday European vocabulary being then without any specialized terms for expressing the feelings aroused by tropical exotica, he had to extend the significance of an adjective like 'beautiful' to refer to anything in nature that struck him as new and unusual. Thus he frequently remarks on the beautiful appearance of the trees of Senegambia when he wishes to refer to the impression made on him by the sight of the lofty trees growing on the shores of Gorée Bay, the like of which he had never seen before. The height or girth which some tropical trees attain never failed to make him marvel at what he can only call their 'beauty'. He even describes as 'beautiful' the spectacle of mangroves growing in sea water near the shoreline. Here the adjective is probably used to convey strangeness rather than aesthetic pleasure in a modern sense. Cadamosto was also fascinated, more expectedly, by the birds of West Africa whose individual characteristics he was good at describing accurately. Perhaps this interest was not wholly ornithological. The export to Portugal of West African birds, particularly parrots, which were than sold throughout Europe was, from the beginning, an important secondary staple of the Guinea trade.

Cadamosto correctly noted that, in his time, Wolof-ruled territory came to an end not far south of Gorée Bay. From this point the land was mainly inhabited by the Serer and Sine peoples who, he observed, refused to recognize the authority of any overlord. He did not like the Serers, whom he regarded as cruel as well as idolatrous and all the more dangerous because they were well protected by the tropical forest in which they lived and the streams and lakes which were also characteristic of the region. It is clear from the Venetian's narrative that the Portuguese in his time had a healthy respect for the fighting qualities and weapons of the Serer and Sine people and approached them with great care. They had every reason to do so. Off the estuary of the Salum, one of the Portuguese slave–interpreters carried by each caravel was sent ashore alone with orders to discover from the people there the name of their ruler, the lie of their land, and what the prospects were for trading in gold or other articles. The tribesmen drawn up on the beach lost no time in killing the interpreter and in making it clear that they would resist any attempt by the Portuguese to effect a landing. Cadamosto and Usodimare prudently made no such attempt. Despite this experience, soon afterwards better relations must have been established with the people of the region since Porto de Ale (the modern Portudal) became an important port of call where the caravels routinely secured water, fresh meat, millet, vegetables and firewood.

Sailing south-south-east off a generally low-lying and thickly wooded coast, Cadamosto and Usodimare contented themselves with charting the various estuaries and pseudo-estuaries that characterize this part of the Senegambian coast and recording its features as seen from the sea. Eventually they came upon a twenty-mile-wide break in the coastline where the sea exhibited evidence of the presence of fresh water. They rightly surmised that this was the mouth of the River Gambia, the destination which Henry had set them.[38] They had now come to the lands ruled by Mandinka chieftains still owing an allegiance – more hypothetical than real – to the far-off emperors of Mali.[39]

The caravels of Cadamosto and Usodimare set out to sail up the Gambia without wasting much time at its mouth. The smallest of the caravels led the way because it drew the least water. From the start they met with unremitting hostility from the Mandinka inhabitants of either bank. All attempts to persuade them that the white men came in peace, seeking only to trade, failed and, after the three vessels had sailed upstream for about four miles, they were attacked by a force Cadamosto, perhaps exaggerating, put at about a hundred and fifty warriors in some seventeen war canoes. The Mandinkas displayed not only tactical sense in their attacks but also failed to show any sign that they were intimidated by the white invaders of their space or by the alien spectacle their ships presented. Cadamosto describes the scene with his customary eye for detail and his absence of racialist sentiments:

> They seemed to us to be men who were most handsome of body, very black, and all wearing white cotton shirts. On their heads they had a kind of small white cap like those Germans wear, except that these had on either side protuberances in the shape of wings and in the middle of each cap was a feather, perhaps a sign that they were warriors. A black stood in the prow of each canoe bearing on his arm a round shield, apparently of leather.[40]

The caravels, under heavy attack by arrows fired at them from the canoes, discharged their bombards against the attackers in line with the Prince's authority that they might use arms in self-defence. Cadamosto records that the cannon fire at first caused dismay among the warriors in the canoes but that, after a while, they once again resumed their attack on the caravels. The Portuguese bowmen then opened fire against them, causing many casualties but still not deterring them from moving against the smallest caravel. This was only saved from capture when the other two vessels succeeded in towing it out of range of the arrows from the canoes.

After the action had been broken off, gesticulations and shouting by the slave–interpreters aboard the caravels persuaded one canoe to come within hailing distance. According to Cadamosto the interpreters explained to the warriors that the Portuguese had come in peace as they had done in Senegal and only wished to trade and to present to their ruler gifts from their own king. The reply as the interpreters conveyed it was disconcerting. To quote the text of the *Navigazioni* again:

> They replied that they had already had news of us and of our deal-ings with the blacks of Senegal, who must [themselves] be bad men if they sought our friendship, for it was their firm belief that we Christians ate human flesh, and that we only sought to buy black people in order to eat them. For that reason nothing in the world would make them wish to be friends with us. On the contrary they hoped to kill us all and then to present everything we had to their lord, who resided three days distant. . . .[41]

Direct information like this about the thoughts the people of Guinea had about the European seaborne invaders during the Henrican period is perforce extremely rare. When it is offered, as occasionally by Zurara and sometimes by Cadamosto, it usually reads suspiciously like thoughts the European writer has decided it would be appropriate to attribute to the Africans. On this occasion Cadamosto undoubtedly faithfully reports what the interpreters told him. He did not, of course, see the rich irony involved in the fear of the Mandinka that the motive of the Europeans in coming to West Africa in their ships was motivated by their anthropophagous taste for black flesh.

Following on the action between the three Portuguese caravels and the Mandinka warriors in their war canoes, Cadamosto, Antoniotto and the Portuguese officers accompanying them discussed future action. One view was that the expedition should try to make its way much further upriver in the hope of coming across less hostile people. Their crews were, however, firmly against any such project and insisted that the time had come to return home. It was then July and they had already been away since March. Beyond noting that the first stage of the long homeward voyage involved setting a course for Cape Verde, Cadamosto says nothing about the subsequent courses set for the return journey, nor the time this took. What the Venetian did remember when he came to write up the *Navigazioni* was that, off the mouth of the Gambia where the Pole Star was very low on the northern horizon, he had had his first sight of the Southern Cross. Recognizing the import-ance of this event, he inserted in his text a sketch he had then made of the latter constellation.[42] He also wrote, in this case not entirely accu-rately, that, from timings made on the spot on July 1, it was found that a midsummer day there lasted only about two hours more than the night.[43] The care with which Cadamosto – and, later, Pedro de Sintra – record the diminishing height of the Pole Star above the horizon as they sailed southwards reminds us again that this distance, measured by eye or just possibly by a seaman's quadrant, was the only means seamen of the Henrican period had of estimating latitude or the linear distance they had sailed from their port of departure.[44]

After the expedition had returned to Portugal, Antoniotto Usodimare wrote a long letter to his creditors in Genoa. It is dated 12 December 1455.[45] Since this document purported to give some account of the Genoese merchant's experiences in Guinea at a time when we know from the *Navigazioni* that he was in Cadamosto's company, one might expect it to complement the version of events given in the *Navigazioni*. In fact it does no such thing. Antoniotto, anxious to present himself to his creditors as a lone explorer, nowhere mentions his association with Cadamosto. What he told his creditors, enclosed in a thin tissue of genuine personal experience, was mostly a farrago of half-truths and unskilful lies designed to make his creditors believe that, travelling on his own, he had explored the River Gambia far further into the interior in 1455 than either he or Cadamosto had actually done. To add colour to his claim, he asserted that he had been within measurable distance of the fabled empire of Prester John and within a mere few days' journey of a place where the army of the emperor of Mali was encamped. He even, for good measure, claimed to have come across in the jungle a descendant of the brothers Vivaldi who, in 1291, had set out from Genoa to try to reach 'the East Indies' by circumnavigating Africa via the Atlantic. Unsurprisingly they had never been heard of again, but their possible fate was evidently still a topic of discussion in Genoa. Antoniotto also described in some detail his alleged involvement in diplomatic negotiations between Afonso V and a ruler he first calls 'a certain black noble lord' but who, a few lines later, is improbably transmogrified into 'the king of Gambia'. According to him, he had brought the latter's 'secretary' to Portugal to negotiate a peace between his master and the Portuguese king and had been made responsible by Afonso for arranging the secretary's return journey. It is just possible that there was some slender basis of truth behind this tale. It will be remembered that, in accordance with Prince Henry's standing orders to his explorers, one or two inhabitants of newly discovered lands must always be kidnapped and brought back to Portugal to be interrogated about his or her country. Perhaps it was this routine procedure that the untruthful Genoese blew up into a diplomatic initiative by an African king.

At the end of the letter Antoniotto told his creditors that he would shortly be returning to the Gambia on a journey the proceeds of which, he said, would certainly enable him to settle his debts to them. He did not mention that this voyage, too, would be in Cadamosto's company. Since he returned to Genoa shortly after his second voyage and was given an important post in Caffa, the Genoese outpost on the Black Sea, it appears likely that his optimism about the improvement in his finances as a result of this voyage proved justified.

Cadamosto's new expedition probably sailed from Lagos in March 1456.[46] It consisted of a caravel hired by him, another hired out to Antoniotto and, as before, a third belonging to the Prince himself. The latter's function was no doubt partly to keep an eye on the activities of the two Italian merchants in Guinea but also to make sure that their work of exploration was independently recorded by his own men; all concerned knew that this work was dangerous and that individual ships and records might well be lost so that such duplication was highly advisable. The licences Henry had granted to the three vessels seem to have specified that they should make straight for the River Gambia without stopping *en route* and should, this time, make a determined effort to navigate as far upstream as they could towards the point on the river where gold in considerable quantities was rumoured to be available.

The journey as far as Cape Blanco, aided by the Canary Current, was rapid and without incident. On this occasion no call was made either in Madeira or in the Canaries. Near the cape, however, a storm forced the caravels to sail westwards away from the African coast for two days. According to Cadamosto's detailed descriptive account, this mishap resulted in the sighting and examination of a group of hitherto unknown islands, the easternmost of which lay some 300 miles out in the Atlantic from Cape Verde (see Chapter Four). Later explorers would discover the whole group to consist of fourteen uninhabited islands and islets. Cadamosto (no doubt in concert with Antoniotto) did a rapid reconnaissance of the islands that were nearest at hand. They looked particularly at what was to turn out to be the largest and highest of the whole group – the island of Santiago. Cadamosto claims in the *Navigazioni* that it was so named because the caravels had anchored off it on the feast of St Philip and St James in 1456. This is one of the occasions when his memory, or the carelessness of a copyist, probably played him false, since the feast referred to falls on 1 May.[47] Having satisfied himself that the archipelago appeared to be uninhabited and that the islands seemed to offer few immediate attractions to settlers or traders, the Venetian explorer decided that the caravels should not waste any further time on exploring them but should, in accordance with the Prince's explicit orders, make for the mouth of the River Gambia.

This time the three Portuguese ships entered the wide estuary of the river and proceeded upstream without meeting any hostile action, though they were followed at a cautious distance by a number of native canoes. Soon they had their first practical reminder that they had other enemies besides human ones to contend with in these tropical regions. A sailor whom Cadamosto calls Andrea died of fever and was buried on an islet in the river which the Portuguese named in his memory on their charts as 'Ilha de São Andrés' – the James Island of modern maps.[48] The sailor's death from fever was apparently the first suffered by the expedition and plainly made a lasting impression on Cadamosto. More cases of fever (probably malaria) were soon to follow.

The journey up the Gambia, made possible only by constant soundings, continued without mishap. The individual Portuguese pilots and seamen of the Prince's time are often rightly praised for the unruffled and professional way in which they went about the business of navigating in the unknown tropical waters of the Atlantic off the coast of Guinea proper. They do not, perhaps, get sufficient credit from historians of the discoveries for the courage and skill with which they also mastered the very different problems involved in sailing their caravels many miles up the great rivers of West Africa which had previously been the preserve of native canoes. The new hazards such riverine navigation presented were many. There were not only the obvious ones such as hidden shoals and sandbanks leading to sudden changes in the depth of water which could result in the grounding of a caravel, or the need to keep an ever-watchful eye open for uprooted trees and other obstacles carried down river by the current. The Portuguese pilots also had to learn to allow for tidal influence which at some seasons might be felt a hundred or even two hundred miles upstream. Present always by day and by night, too, was the need to keep constant watch in case of a surprise attack by war canoes emerging from the many creeks which flowed into the main river.

On his second voyage Cadamosto had been supplied with at least one native interpreter capable of speaking in his own language to the local Mandinka people. This time, through him, amicable contacts were soon established. Cadamosto explains that the Portuguese learnt in this way that the principal lord of the river people with whom they were now in contact resided nine or ten days' journey inland and that he himself had as his suzerain the Mali emperor. While all this was nominally true, in practice it is known that by the fifteenth century the Mali emperor's influence along the lower Gambia was slight and that the various Mandinka chieftainships established on both banks of the river were virtually independent lordships able to decide for themselves how to respond to the situation created by the appearance of the Portuguese in their midst.

The man through whom the interpreters had learnt these things voluntarily came aboard Cadamosto's caravel and offered to conduct the Portuguese upriver to the seat of residence of the local chieftain, whom the Venetian calls 'Batimansa' ('the king of Bati'). According to his account, Batimansa's capital was located near a riverine port some sixty miles from the river's mouth, possibly therefore where Bintang Bolong (Bintang Creek) joins the Gambia, which is still something like a mile wide.

The meeting with the Batimansa was highly successful. He did not appear to share the fear that the Portuguese were cannibals that had caused trouble lower down the river the previous year. He made no difficulty about authorizing his people to start trading with them, doubtless realizing that he would gain political clout as well as commercial benefits from such a relationship. Cadamosto, with his penchant for detailed description, depicts the scene which followed as large numbers of men and women arrived in canoes and boarded the caravels to barter what they had to offer. As on other occasions, the Venetian marvelled at the willingness of the Africans to accept cheap trade goods and trinkets which in Europe cost very little in exchange for commodities worth a great deal there. His description of the working *resgate* on the banks of the River Gambia is the earliest narrative account we have of a spectacle that was destined to be repeated in western Africa many thousands of times during the centuries that followed.

Cadamosto's narrative unsurprisingly reveals that slaves were the most valuable commodity available in quantity in Batimansa's country. There was one disppointment. Despite what the Portuguese had been told in Senegal, very little gold was on offer in Batimansa's lands. Cadamosto, always anxious to seek for causes and explanations, suggested that the reason for this disparity was that the poverty of the Africans led them to regard as an important amount of the precious metal a quantity that, to Europeans, seemed very little. It is more likely that the misinformation was in fact due to the Wolofs' desire to please by supplying their visitors with the kind of answers they plainly hoped to receive. If Diogo Gomes's reminiscences are to be credited, it was not long after the second voyage of Cadamosto and Usodimare that the Portuguese did find promising quantities of gold dust available for barter on the Gambia. This happened when, much further upstream, they reached the flourishing markets of Cantor.[49]

Cadamosto mentions that among the articles he bought from the Batimansa's people was the musk extracted from the civet cat in much demand by the perfumers of Europe. He also records that some live civet cats were bought too. These were specially prized since, if they survived the voyage back to Portugal, they could be repeatedly made to yield up their precious musk from their anal glands. The hope of securing malagueta pepper to which Antoniotto had referred in his letter to his creditors was probably frustrated. Though Cadamosto does not mention it, it grew much further upriver. The Venetian explorer does make much of the fact that the Portuguese sailors bought apes and baboons from the Mandinkas for next to nothing. Though it is unlikely that many of these survived to reach Portugal, those that did would be certain to fetch a good price there.

Cadamosto devotes much time to describing the way of life of the Mandinkas and the flora and fauna of the Gambia as he knew it. He was particularly fascinated by elephants. His account of them includes a description of a native elephant hunt. He also recounts that on another occasion a Gambia chief presented him with a small dead elephant so that he could taste its flesh. This seems to have taken place on a subsequent (post-1456) journey to the Gambia which is not otherwise recorded in the *Navigazioni*.[50] Cadamosto's account of the affair is worth quoting at length as an example of his determination to find out and verify everything he could about the way things were in the *novo mondo* in which he found himself. The passage is also significant for his insistence that it was only thanks to the labours of Prince Henry that these novel experiences had been made possible. He wrote

This elephant was offered [first] to me by the lord of the place, that is to say I was allowed to cut off whatever portion of it I wished. The rest was given to the hunters for them to eat. Realizing from this that blacks were accustomed to eat elephant flesh I had them cut off a . . . piece which, after it had been boiled and then roasted, I then ate on board our ship because of my wish to try out [new] things and to be able to say that I had eaten meat which had never before been eaten by anyone else from my country. To tell the truth, ele-

phant meat is not very good. It seemed to me tough and unappetiz-
ing and with little taste. I also brought back to the ship one of the
elephant's feet and part of its trunk along with many hairs from
its body. These were black and a palm and a half or more in length,
and very thick. These things along with some of its flesh I later
presented in Portugal to my lord the Prince D. Henrique who
received them as an important gift because they were the first things
he had seen from that country, and also because he was very desirous
of possessing unusual objects from far-off places that were presented
to him and which came from lands discovered as a result of his
labours . . .[51]

Cadamosto also presented parts from other elephants to the Prince,
among them a tusk twelve palms in length. Henry, he reported, subsequently presented this particular offering, together with an elephant's
foot, to his sister, the Duchess of Burgundy. The author of the *Navigazioni* concludes his account of the sights he had seen on his visits to
the Gambia with a convincing description of the appearance and habits
of the hippopotamus.

Exactly how long the Portuguese caravels remained in the Batimansa's waters is uncertain but the events described by Cadamosto
clearly suppose a stay of a number of days.[52] This was cut short when
some of those aboard them fell sick with what the Venetian calls a high
and continuous fever. In consequence, he ordered the caravels down
river with all possible speed. Once they reached the open sea, the sick-
ness, whatever it was, seems quickly to have abated for, instead of
sailing homewards, it was decided that the little squadron could continue exploring the coast further southwards. After two days' cautious
sailing and when they were some sixty miles beyond the estuary of the
Gambia, the caravels found themselves off the estuary of another great
river at 12° 35′ N. This they called the 'Rio Casamansa', following their
habit of using the name of the local ruler (*mansa*) as a toponym. The
name remains in use today.

A landing party sent ashore here discovered that the region's ruler
was away fighting a rival. Since Cadamosto had by now learnt that in
Black Africa proper trading was only possible with the local ruler's
consent and under his control, he resolved to continue his southward
exploration of a coast notable for the number of major rivers and
streams which discharge there into the Atlantic. The saints' names the
explorers gave to two of these ('Rio de Santa Ana' and 'Rio de São

Domingos') indicate that they explored this coast – now part of the Republic of Guinea-Bissau – between late July and early August 1456. Finally they came to an estuary so wide that they at first took it to be a very large bay. On further investigation, however, it turned out to be the mouth of yet another river. This was the waterway nowadays known as the Rio Geba. Cadamosto and his Portuguese pilots settled somewhat unimaginatively for the name 'Rio Grande', an adjective inspired more by the width of its estuary than by that of the river proper. The next morning, while they were still at anchor, they were disconcerted to see approaching their vessels two canoes larger than any they had yet seen anywhere in Guinea. Cadamosto recalls one as being as long as a caravel and propelled by some thirty men. The Portuguese stood to arms but the Africans, probably Cocolis or Nalus, indicated by signs that their intentions were peaceful. Communication other than by signs proved impossible when it turned out that none of the native interpreters carried by the caravels could understand a word of the language spoken by these visitors from the mainland, a situation which led Cadamosto to explain just how much the whole work of exploration in Guinea and the development of Portuguese relations with its peoples depended on the skill of these interpreters.[53] He commented,

> When we saw that we were now in a new country and that we could not make ourselves understood, we concluded that it would be a waste of time to proceed further. We reckoned that, if we did so, we would go on being confronted by yet other languages, and, since we would not understand them, nothing new would be achieved. Therefore we determined to turn back.[54]

Faced by the sheer number of different languages spoken by the tribes they encountered and were to encounter in Guinea, the dependence of the Portuguese on the slave–interpreter system was almost total. When, as here, it did not work, they were impotent to carry out the kind of information–gathering the Prince required of them. Cadamosto accordingly gave the order to set a course for Portugal stopping only to carry out a hasty reconnaissance of the Bissagos Islands, which lie some thirty miles off the mouth of the Geba. He called the islands beautiful because of the size and greenness of the trees which covered them.

Regrettably, because the *Navigazioni* is a story of exploration, its author again offers no information about the homeward journey or about the course followed by the three caravels. In particular, we do not know from him whether the little squadron already used the *volta da Guiné*, or whether it made the difficult direct journey north from Cape Verde tacking against the prevailing wind. Cadamosto's return to Portugal marks the end of his remarkable autobiographical account of his explorations in Guinea, though not quite the end of the *Navigazioni*.

~ Chapter Thirteen ~

Once More Unto the Breach: Alcácer-Ceguer

. . . when the blast of war blows in our ears.
Then imitate the action of the tiger.
Stiffen the sinews, summon up the blood,
Disguise fair nature with hard-favour'd rage;
Then lend the eye a terrible aspect

Shakespeare, *King Henry V*, Act 3 Scene 1

On his return to Lagos at the end of his second voyage, Cadamosto would have found that Henry was away in Lisbon and now had more immediately important things on his mind than the Guinea enterprise. The Venetian explorer's account of his most recent explorations therefore probably made less of an impact in 1456 than he had expected. What had happened was that the ageing Prince had heard and had responded once more to what, for him, had always been a summons which took priority over all others: he was preparing once again to take up the crusader's sword. From October 1456 and for some months afterwards, he seems to have been in the Portuguese capital where Afonso V was engaged in military preparations in response to a demand from Calixtus III that Portugal should join the grand alliance the curia was trying to organize against the onrush west of the Turks who had taken Constantinople in 1453.[1] Commercial voyages to Guinea did not of course now cease simply because the Prince was not in the Algarve but exploration further south of the point on the coast of Guinea reached by Cadamosto seems to have been suspended, not to be resumed again until shortly after Henry's death. It was now largely left to the merchants and caravel captains, under the supervision of Henry's officials in Lagos, to exploit as best they could the opportunities for trade in Mauritania and Senegambia which the discoveries had made possible.

Henry did not, of course, turn his back on the affairs of Guinea altogether from 1456 onwards. He was too much involved in them to do that, even if he had wished to. So it was that an administrative event which took place the year after Cadamosto's return from his second voyage deserves special attention. In December 1457 the Prince, in his capacity as administrator of the Order of Christ, decreed in a long document dated from 'my town' (i.e. the elusive Vila do Infante near Sagres), that the Order should in future receive the *vintena* (a tax nominally equal to one-twentieth) which was henceforth to be levied on all articles of value brought from Guinea.[2] The document gave examples of what Henry considered the most important of such articles to be – 'men or women slaves, gold and fish' – as well as any other merchandise whatsoever. In it Henry asserts that the uniform imposition of the *vintena* was intended to substitute a single rate of import duty payable to the Order of Christ for the varying rates and consequential disagreements which had until then existed. He also declared that the change had been agreed upon at a meeting of a chapter of the Order. It is not known whether Henry, at the end of 1457, had travelled specially to Tomar for such a meeting or whether it was held for his convenience in Lisbon or the Algarve.

Much of the 1457 document is concerned with giving yet another official account of the discoveries. In this Henry again states unambiguously that he had used the revenues of the Order of Christ to meet part of the great cost of the explorations he had sponsored.[3] There was now no suggestion that Cape Bojador had been the starting-point for the discoveries. The document contented itself with the revised claim that these had begun at Cape Noun, some two hundred miles further north, and that the most southerly point beyond that cape so far reached by the explorers was at least 300 leagues (perhaps 1,100 English miles) further on – an assertion which places the limit of the discoveries in 1457 in the neighbourhood of Cape Roxo (12° 20′ N). This fits well enough with what Cadamosto says about the final point he reached on his second voyage.

The document is also notable because it describes Afonso V as the first 'Lord of Guinea'.[4] Afonso's right to use this title was clearly established by the grant of sovereignty over Guinea contained in the bull *Romanus pontifex* of 1455. In fact he never seems to have used it, even after Henry's death. Henry's insistence on the point in the 1457 document perhaps arose less from a desire to encourage the king to start naming his new lordship than from a wish to use the occasion to remind both him and posterity that it was thanks to his efforts that the lordship of Guinea would, at any rate after his death, be part of the patrimony of the Portuguese crown. There are other possible explanations. It may have been a move by Henry, whose political star was now somewhat on the wane, to reassure his critics at court that, though he himslf was also theoretically entitled under the terms of *Romanus pontifex* to call himself 'Lord of Guinea' for his lifetime, he had never claimed a label which propriety demanded should belong to the crown. Afonso's refusal to use the title after the Prince's death is not easily explained. Perhaps it reflects the fact that this inveterate royal pursuer of honour on crusading battlefields regarded Guinea – despite his uncle's casuistic claims that he was indirectly engaged in a war of crusade and conquest there too – as a place where the Portuguese went to trade, not to take religious and political control. It would not be until after Afonso's death that John II, on his accession to the throne in 1481, would lose no time in including the lordship of Guinea among his royal titles and in taking both military and political steps to establish his suzerainty there.

It must not be assumed that the Henrican order of 1457 was dictated by any intention on Henry's part to repay to the Order of Christ any of the large sums he had, by his own confession, appropriated to finance the discoveries. Since the pope, in 1454, had conceded to the Order sole 'spiritual' jurisdiction over the newly discovered territories in the African Atlantic, it had had the right to receive the customary levies which went with such jurisdiction. The reality of the matter was that the proceeds of the new *vintena* would be in practice entirely at the Prince's disposal. It is not therefore unfair to see the decree of 1457 as a device of Henry to impose, for his own purposes, an additional tax on imports from Guinea over and above the royal *quinto* which the crown had ceded to him for his lifetime. Certainly there is no reliable evidence that the Order's funds were ever used in the Prince's time to carry out any missionary or other 'spiritual' work on the main-land of Saharan or Black Africa apart, perhaps, from a chaplain to serve the needs of the Portuguese factory at Arguin.

But, as already indicated, Henry had other and for the time being more important matters than Guinea to concern him from 1456 onwards. The zealotry of his protegé, the young and headstrong would-be hero king Afonso V, forced the whole Portuguese court, willingly or not, to give itself up to the heady business of planning a leading role for Por-tugal in the international papal crusade against the Turks in the eastern Mediterranean. Henry himself received a flattering personal letter from the pope expressing his admiration of the Prince's past achievements as a fighter for the Faith and urging him to join in this chance to renew his dedication to the task of making war against the forces of Islam.[5] The strategy of the crusaders, Calixtus explained, would be to go for the bull's-eye by attacking mainland Turkey itself, so, he hoped, forcing the Ottoman armies threatening eastern Europe to withdraw. The pope even suggested, with a failure to grasp strategic realities which exceeded even Henry's shortcomings in that sphere, that success in Turkey's heartland could be expected to lead to the total extermin-ation of the Turks as a people. Henry, as the Portuguese prince who, for forty years, had never ceased to proclaim Portugal's crusading destiny, plainly had left himself with no choice but to express, at least in public, his enthusiasm for the reckless plans of the pontiff and his own royal nephew. His enthusiasm for a new crusade against Islam was no doubt genuine but, in the light of subsequent events and his life-long obsession with North Africa, one may surmise that he had very serious doubts about the wisdom of taking on the Turks instead of returning again to Portugal's now traditional crusading ground in Morocco which he had done so much to create.

Since the summer of 1456, egged on by Calixtus, a number of Italian states as well as the Crown of Aragon and Portugal had com-mitted themselves to take part in 1457 in the papal crusade. The Turkish armies, after capturing Constantinople, were, as the pope had explained in his letter to Henry, now threatening Hungary and the rest of the other Christian states of eastern Europe.[6] The 25-year-old Afonso V, apparently ruled by his conviction that it was his destiny to outdo even the fame of his famous grandfather and his nearly as famous uncle as a warrior against the infidel, threw himself with enthusiasm into the papal project. He not only assured the pope that he and his kingdom were enthusiastic supporters of the crusade against the Turks but before long was presenting himself as its appropriate commmander-in-chief. His grounds for claiming the post were that, as he promised Calixtus, a Portuguese fleet and a Portuguese army of no less than twelve thousand men would be taking part in the campaign.[7]

By the spring of 1457 Afonso's ambitions had soared still further. The pope had by now been promised that the goal of the Portuguese crusaders, led by their king in person, was nothing less than the reconquest of Constantinople itself.[8] Afonso, as would be his wont all through his reign, paid scant attention either to the logistics of the enterprise to which he had so lightly committed himself, or to the ability of his kingdom to finance the very large shortfall that would remain after the Church's contribution to the crusade had been taken into account. Nor, driven by the mixture of religious zealotry, chivalric posturing and a burning desire to acquire instant fame with which the Portuguese king approached the business of kingship, did he show any signs of grasping, or wanting to grasp, the political problems involved in getting the grand alliance planned by the pope off the ground.[9] He soon began to learn what these were when the envoy he had sent to Italy to make final arrangements with the king of Naples and other Italian rulers reported that there seemed no likelihood whatever that they intended to turn their promises into military, naval or monetary realities. The Aragonese king, for his part, assured him that the resources of the Crown of Aragon's Mediterranean empire would be at the disposal of the fleet carrying the Portuguese expeditionary force – providing the Portuguese crusaders were prepared to pay his officials on the spot for whatever they required. As for the Crown of Aragon's direct participation in the crusade, the Aragonese king explained that this would not be possible until he had settled his current disputes with Genoa. In September 1456 the Portuguese king received a letter from the Duke of Milan, Francesco Sforza, which should finally have warned him that he could expect nothing but fine words from the city states of Northern Italy. The Duke, tongue in cheek, cynically expressed his admiration for the sublimity of spirit which led the Portuguese king, when barely out of his adolescence, to want to attack the infidel in a region so far away from the traditional Portuguese crusading arena in North Africa, and despite the fact that his plans might put Ceuta in danger.[10] Afonso's alarmed counsellors could not have put it better. Nothing loath, the Portuguese king characteristically announced that he would go it alone against the Turks. He was only persuaded with difficulty to accept the arguments of those around him that he would serve Portugal's highest interests even better by leading his crusading army against Morocco.

It seems very likely that Prince Henry played an important part in convincing Afonso that his preordained role was to pursue what the Prince regarded as Portugal's manifest crusading destiny in the Marinid kingdom. It was now 1458 and the crusade against the Turks was plainly not going to happen. Afonso then announced (no doubt as a face-saving device) that, to protect Ceuta from a rumoured Moroccan attack, he would, instead, lead the waiting Portuguese army in a new attempt to capture Tangier. Besides protecting Ceuta, the capture of Tangier would avenge memories of Henry's disastrous defeat there in 1437.

One might have expected the Prince to have welcomed this project, since he had often in the past proclaimed his desire to lead a new assault on the city which had been the scene of the greatest loss of reputation he had ever suffered in his life. Age, however, seems to have taught him some measure of prudence in matters military for it was agreed by him and the king's other counsellors, some of them reluctantly, that an attack should be mounted, not against Tangier but against the minor but well fortified port of Alcácer-Ceguer, midway between Tangier and Ceuta. Rumours, which may have been deliberately spread to justify the operation, conveniently confirmed that the sultan of Morocco was indeed planning an assault on Ceuta. A timely request from the governor of that fortress for succour also helped.

A fleet numbering some ninety ships, large and small, finally set sail from Setúbal on 30 September 1458.[11] On 3 October it reached Sagres, where the 64-year-old Prince Henry, ready for what could well be his last military campaign, was waiting to embark with his retainers. After hanging about off Lagos for several days the fleet, now somewhat improbably claimed by the chroniclers to have grown to number two hundred and twenty vessels all told, set sail for the African coast.[12] Whether by accident or design, it found itself off Tangier. The sight of the Moroccan city was enough to cause the mercurial Portuguese king to change his mind yet again. He promptly announced that he proposed after all to switch to his original plan of attacking Tangier.[13] Henry is depicted by Damião de Góis as having deployed at this point all the authority his age and his experience of war in Morocco gave him to reason with his nephew, urging him to abandon any such notion and to stick to the original plan. His arguments, if Góis has not invented them, included a lesson in the psychology of war. Henry explained to the overstrung Afonso that the Portuguese soldiers had been informed that their objective was to mount an attack on Alcácer-Ceguer. Suddenly to change this plan, as the king now proposed, would, Henry said, involve asking them to take part in a military venture for which they were neither psychologically prepared nor militarily equipped against a major and strongly fortified city which, moreover, they all knew had not long ago been the scene of a great military disaster for Portugal. The morale of the Portuguese troops, he claimed, would therefore be badly affected if this last-minute change of plan were to be adopted.[14] The last thing the Prince wanted, we may suppose, was to be involved, at the end of his life, in a repeat performance of what had happened in 1437. Confronted with such pressure, the Portuguese king unwillingly gave in and the fleet moved a few miles east in readiness for an assault on Alcácer.[15] By now the Moroccan fortresses in the danger area were, of course, on full alert. Unlike the secrecy and deceptions with which his grandfather had prepared the attack on Ceuta, Afonso V, following crusading tradition, wished all Europe to know what he was about.

Alcácer-Ceguer (in Arabic Ksar-es-Seghir, 'small castle') had originally been established to serve as a port for traffic between Morocco and the Nasrid kingdom of Granada. After the sultanate lost Ceuta to the Portuguese, it became especially important for this purpose, and also as a place of shelter for Moroccan corsairs now deprived of their base in that port. Alcácer-Ceguer, as its name suggested, was no Ceuta or Tangier. Its castle and walls were however in good order, its outer defences were in place against a seaborne landing and it was fully garrisoned.[16] Despite this, the Moroccans must have been surprised, given the size of the Portuguese army, when its goal turned out to be this minor port. In the circumstances the outcome could hardly be in doubt. Nevertheless, despite the presence of the king, sword in hand, along with the rest of the attackers, the resistance of the garrison of Alcácer kept the Portuguese at bay for some two days. Rui de Pina, whose account of the whole affair may be based on the lost chapters of Zurara's Crónica de Dom Duarte de Meneses, attributes to the tactics employed by the Prince much of the eventual success of the Portuguese in overcoming the defenders.[17] According to him, when Henry saw that head-on attacks on the walls of the town by conventional methods had not produced any success and that the fighting was continuing long after nightfall on the second day, he caused a large bombard to be brought up.[18] Its function was to breach the fortress's walls by cannon fire and so save the inevitable heavy loss of life the Portuguese would suffer if they were now to rely on an all-out assault using scaling ladders. Portuguese records show that, by now, numbers of bombards as well as smaller types of cannon and firearms were routinely in use by Portuguese armies operating in Morocco. Henry's move seems quickly to have produced results. The stone cannonballs from the heavy bombard duly breached the wall. Once this had happened the garrison offered to surrender both castle and town to Afonso on condition that it and all the inhabitants of the town were assured of free passage out of the place, together with their possessions. According to the same chronicler the capitulation was also organized by the Prince who seems, even when Moroccans were the enemy, to have learnt over the years to accept that the surest way to keep a garrison fighting against the odds was to let its members believe that they would be massacred if they surrendered. The terms of the surrender were honoured by Afonso V. The garrison and civilian population had left the castle and town by the morning of 24 October. The Portuguese king and the other leaders of the victorious army then entered the town in procession and proceeded to the main mosque which was promptly renamed Santa Maria da Misericórdia.[19]

The chroniclers do their best to present the capture of Alcácer-Ceguer as a notable as well as hard-fought victory for Portuguese arms. However, those who actually took part in it, including Prince Henry, cannot have failed to feel that, as an achievement, it was a somewhat low-key ending to an enterprise which, when it started two years earlier, had had the recovery of Constantinople from the Turks in its sights. This was recognized even by the Portuguese king when, after leaving Alcácer, he paid what surprisingly seems to have been his first ever visit to Ceuta. Pina writes,

> when the king contemplated the magnificence of Ceuta, its size and the strength of its location, and remembered that his grandfather had conquered it with a force similar [in size] to his own, and then thought of Alcácer and the meaning of its name, he became down-hearted and saddened because he felt that, when the two places were compared, it would be seen that such a minor achievement as his was did not measure up to the greatness and high purposes which, he believed, it lay in his heart to accomplish. So it came about that he longed to undertake some greater enterprise.[20]

Afonso did, indeed, as soon as he could, set about satisfying these long-ings. Meanwhile he made the best of things. Imitating the action of his grandfather after the capture of Ceuta, he added the title 'Senhor de Alcácer' to his royal titles and appointed Duarte de Meneses, natural son of the first governor of Ceuta, as captain and governor of this new outpost in North Africa.

Though the ageing Prince had distinguished himself in the field, he cannot have been too happy, either, about the way things had gone for him. If it was he who had insisted that Alcácer-Ceguer should be the scene of operations in 1458, he must have realized, when he saw the place close-up for the first time, that strategically it could hardly have been a worse long-term choice as a second Portuguese fortress in North Africa. On its land side the bay on whose shores the castle and township were located is quite closely hemmed in by a semicircle of hills and mountains. Since there would never be enough troops to occupy and hold these heights permanently, the Portuguese occupiers of Alcácer would be under continuous scrutiny by the Moroccans during the hours of daylight. From the surrounding heights, too, as events were soon to show, the enclave was within range of the large bombards now increasingly used tactically by both sides. Given Alcácer-Ceguer's unpromising strategic situation, it was apparent that another Portuguese military force would now have to be locked up on the north coast of Morocco and would require to be supplied and victualled by sea from metropolitan Portugal, either directly or from Ceuta.

There were other aspects of the affair which cannot have pleased Henry. Afonso V had appointed his brother, D. Fernando, the Prince's own adopted son and heir, to be second-in-command of the expedition. This made Fernando, according to Rui de Pina, the most important person in the Portuguese force after the king. Fernando, by all accounts, conducted himself well in the battle. However Henry, accustomed since 1415 to think of himself as, after the king, the natural commander of any Portuguese military operations in Morocco, cannot, either, have been happy to find himself playing second fiddle to his own adopted son in the battle for Alcácer-Ceguer. Whether this arrangement had anything to do with justified fears about the quality of Henry's generalship, or to anxiety lest his age might now make him a less doughty knight on the battlefield than he used to be, is not known. What is known is that Fernando, despite his good performance as second-in-command in the attack on Alcácer, had already made it plain that he was not altogether sound on the subject of Portugal's Moroccan destiny. Worse still, in 1460, a few months before Henry's death, he openly joined those of the king's chief counsellors who presented written opinions to Afonso V strongly opposing the king's plans to lead a new expedition against the Moroccans. Fernando's *parecer* made the case against this project at length and in no uncertain terms, employing strategic, historical, political, financial and moral arguments to support his case.[21] If Henry, before his death, got to hear of Fernando's doubts about the correctness of the Moroccan policy to which his god-father had devoted so much of his political life, that may explain why, perhaps angered by what he surely would have regarded as a betrayal by his heir, he, in the last weeks of his life, unexpectedly made a new will in which he sought to reduce considerably the inheritance which Fernando had long expected from him.

Before leaving Alcácer, Henry did however make sure that the king granted to the Order of Christ sole ecclesiastical jurisdiction in the captured town. It was declared to be part of the parish of Santa Maria de África, the Order's church in Ceuta. If anyone noticed that few of the Order's knights had taken part in this crusade against the infidel, they doubtless kept their thoughts to themselves.[22] Henry characteristically also took advantage of the royal euphoria in 1458 – perhaps more assumed than genuinely felt – to secure pardons for members of his extended household under sentence for various crimes but who had nevertheless served in the victorious army. When the crimes and misdemeanours of his retainers were concerned, Henry could always be relied on to use his influence with the king to secure a pardon or at least a reduction of the sentence. One of the few criticisms that Zurara ventures to make of his hero is that he was not always even-handed, as between members of his household and others.[23] Henry also used the occasion as new grounds for getting the king to make appointments of his people to yet more offices in the crown's gift.

Afonso, as has been noted, moved with his chancery to Ceuta a few days after the victory. It is not certain whether Henry accompanied him, either on this visit to the Moroccan fortress, or on the king's return voyage to Portugal towards the end of November 1458. At all events, Henry now seems to have remained mostly in the Algarve until his death there two years later.

From a strictly strategic point of view there were some positive consequences arising from the capture of Alcácer-Ceguer. The movement of men, food and other supplies from Morocco to Granada was made more difficult, though this was of benefit to Castile rather than to the Portuguese. The presence of another Portuguese garrison a few miles away must have somewhat relieved the sense of isolation in a wholly hostile land that had prevailed in Ceuta since 1415. As the violence of the Moroccan reaction to the loss of the port showed, the Portuguese victory was seen even in the politically unstable sultanate as a serious blow to the prestige of the sultan and his counsellors as defenders of the Faith as well as to the honour of its generals and fighting men. This became all the more so after Moorish troops many times the size of the Portuguese garrison – and fighting with every tactical advantage – twice failed to retake Alcácer. The occupation of this small Moroccan port had served notice, too, that Afonso V, if not most of his counsellors, considered that Portugal was, despite the disaster of Tangier twenty years before, still committed to a policy of military expansion in Morocco, a policy continuously promoted by the Prince since before 1415. Modern students may find it inexplicable that the Portuguese court should have deliberately elected to exacerbate its always hostile relationship with the sultanate at a time when Portuguese trade with Guinea was steadily becoming more and more dependent on textiles, wheat and horses that could most easily and cheaply be secured by the Portuguese in the ports of Atlantic Morocco, and when ready access to Moroccan wheat by the ordinary processes of trade could have easily solved the chronic shortages of that cereal in metropolitan Portugal. It is, however, unlikely that these considerations counted for much either with Afonso V or with his ageing uncle. It was enough for them that the Portuguese had, by the attack on Alcácer, demonstrated that they were still dedicated to a policy of crusade and conquest in Morocco. It is, however, difficult not to wonder if, with all his other, more unconventional achievements before him, Henry must not sometimes have asked himself whether posterity might not admire him for these as much as it did his fame as a crusader. If he did have such thoughts, he kept them strictly to himself. The fact was that Henry himself had always done his best to see to it that his public persona, not only in life but also posthumously, was and would be first and always that of a soldier of the Church Militant. It was an image from which he could not now have disengaged himself, even had he wanted to, and there is no evidence that he ever had any such wish.

~ Chapter Fourteen ~

From Senegambia to the Lion Mountain: The Henrican Discoveries Concluded

The benefits conferred on Portugal by the virtuous Prince Henry are such that its kings and people are greatly indebted to him, for a great part of the Portuguese people now earn their livelihood in the lands which he discovered, and the kings of Portugal derive great profit from this commerce; for, when the trade of this country was well ordered, from the Senegal River on the border of the kingdom of the Wolofs – where the first blacks are ... to Sierra Leone inclusive, it yielded yearly 3,600 slaves and more, many tusks of ivory, gold, fine cotton cloths and many other things.[1]

For information about the course of events in Guinea between Cadamosto's second voyage of exploration in 1455 and Henry's death in 1460, we are largely dependent on the oral reminiscences attributed to the Portuguese sea captain, Diogo Gomes. Because of the way in which these have come down to us, a difficult problem of credibility attaches to them. They were apparently dictated by Gomes near the end of the century when he was an old man. They appear in the form of a narrative in dog-Latin, under the title *De prima inventione Guinee*, in the manuscript collection of miscellaneous material about the Portuguese expansion collected in Portugal early in the sixteenth century by the well-known Moravian printer and translator, Valentinus Moravus – better known in Portugal as Valentim Fernandes.[2] A note at the beginning of *De prima inventione* explains that Diogo Gomes's memories of his voyages to Guinea had been written down in Lisbon by Martin of Bohemia. Martin of Bohemia, otherwise Martin Behaim, is well-known to historians of the discoveries for the famous globe of the then known world he made about 1492. At this time the aged Diogo Gomes held the post of royal tax-collector in Sintra, near the Portuguese capital. The *De prima inventione* contains an allusion to the death of the Genoese explorer and colonizer of the Cape Verde Islands, Antonio da Noli. This occurred in 1499. It is known that Diogo Gomes himself was dead by the end of 1502. It is, therefore, likely that he dictated his reminiscences to Martin Behaim at the very end of the fifteenth century, several decades after Henry's death. He neverthless looked back to the Prince as the much-admired patron of his professional career as a sailor.

Apart from Diogo Gomes's age, there are other aspects of the *De prima inventione* which make it necessary for students of the Henrican discoveries to approach it with caution. There is the question whether Martin Behaim's Portuguese was entirely up to the task of understanding what the old man had to say, so that an interpreter may have been involved at that stage. The translation into Latin has been supposed to be the work of Martin Behaim or Valentim Fernandes but, in view of the barbarous Latin used in it, this seems improbable unless we have to do with an instantaneous draft version made as Diogo Gomes told his story. The version of the early history of the Henrican discoveries in the African Atlantic given in the work certainly contains, among other defects, serious chronological errors. These could be overlooked if the chronology and sequence of the voyages beyond Cape Verde in which Diogo Gomes himself took part could be relied on. Unfortunately his narrative, in the state in which it has come down to us, is often incoherent and contradictory. It seems at times to have been massaged either by Martin Behaim himself or, more probably, Valentim Fernandes who, seeking to polish up or elaborate on the information supplied by Gomes, perhaps drew for this purpose on his own undoubted first-hand knowledge of the writings of Zurara and Cadamosto. One critic has been led to suggest, not without citing some suggestive evidence, that the whole narrative may be a forgery compiled by Valentim Fernandes by putting together extracts from the two writers mentioned.[3] This, however, seems unlikely since there is no apparent reason why a person of Valentim Fernandes's scholarly stature should have set about creating a forged narrative of this kind. The reliability of the *De prima inventione* was vouched for not only by Fernandes himself and, presumably, by Behaim: it was accepted as genuine by another contemporary German visitor to Portugal in the 1490s, Dr Hieronymus Münzer, who was in close contact with his two fellow-countrymen during his visit to Portugal and who discussed Portugal's new African empire with John II himself.[4]

Nevertheless, despite its obvious shortcomings, the contents of the *De prima inventione* cannot be ignored. Diogo Gomes clearly had been on several voyages to Guinea and spoke from personal experience gained during them. His account of his journeying far up the Gambia river beyond the point reached by Cadamosto in 1456, and of his visits to the Salum estuary, bear the stamp of truth. The fact, too, that Fernandes and Behaim evidently sought him out suggests that he already enjoyed some reputation in Lisbon as a teller of stories about his now far-off experiences in the African Atlantic in the Prince's time.

Gomes states that, perhaps in the same year as Cadamosto's second voyage in 1456, or more probably soon afterwards, he set out from Portugal with three caravels under orders from the Prince to try to sail further up the Gambia than Cadamosto and Antoniotto had done. The squadron, he claims, also carried instructions to sail as far as possible to the south along the West African coast.[5] The Gomes narrative makes no mention of the voyages of either Cadamosto or Antoniotto, prob-ably because the old sea captain wished to give the impression that the credit for the exploration of the lands south of modern Senegal in those far-off days had been his alone. An intriguing claim attributed to him is that, on this voyage to the Gambia, he carried with him an 'Indian' (i.e. Ethiopian) interpreter so that he would be able to communicate with the local people should the caravels reach 'India'; as we have seen in an earlier chapter, 'India' as used in Henrican documents is a reference to Prester John's country in north-east Africa. The statement, assuming it to be genuine, would thus seem to be further proof that the Portuguese navigators still expected, in the last years of the Prince's life, to find the entrance to the great eastern-pointing gulf which would carry them to the borders of Ethiopia.

The expedition sailed beyond the Rio Cacheu to the estuary of a river called by Diogo Gomes the 'Fancaso'; this was perhaps the modern Canal do Geba, in what is today Guinea-Bissau. Here the sailors, according to Gomes, were much alarmed by the same violent tidal cur-rents characteristic of the sea in this region and also described by Cadamosto. They insisted that the squadron should turn back. This it did after the Portuguese had conducted some trade with the local people who, despite the tidal rips, came out to the caravels in their canoes and offered cottons, ivory, and, according to Diogo Gomes, a small quantity of malagueta pepper, partly in the form of grains and partly still in the pod.[6] This is the first reference to malagueta pepper actually having been obtained by the Portuguese in Guinea, though, as we have seen, Antoniotto Usodimare had referred to his hopes of securing some in his letter of December 1454.

The account in the Diogo Gomes narrative of the expedition's itinerary when it turned north again is, as often, confusing. It supposes that the three caravels returned to the neighbourhood of Cape Naze (Cabo dos Mastos), near Cape Verde, but next has them sailing far up the the River Gambia. On the way Gomes claims that he succeeded, some distance upstream, in establishing relations with a nephew of a local chief and in securing from him no less than 180 'weights' of gold by bartering cloth, beads and other articles.[7] Next, leaving the other two caravels at two different points lower down the river, Gomes claims that he then ascended it, guided by a Mandinka pilot, all the way to Cantor (Kuntaur), far higher up the river than Cadamosto and Antoniotto had reached. He describes Cantor as a large town and himself as its first European visitor.[8] Modern Kuntaur is a large town on the north bank of the river. The most reliable early descriptions of Cantor, however, indicate that it was the name given to an extensive kingdom on the *south* bank of the Gambia still well to the west of the Barrakunda Rapids. These lie some 280 miles upstream from the river's mouth. According to later Portuguese sources, the importance of the market located in the town of Cantor caused the river often to be known to Europeans as the 'Rio de Cantor'.[9] The Portuguese captain claims that the arrival of his caravel at this place caused traders to come in from the whole district in the hope of bartering with the Europeans.

It seems likely that Diogo Gomes really was the first captain to sail up the Gambia to Cantor and that the date was 1457. Whether all the information the *De prima inventione* provides about this journey – particularly that describing the political geography of the Upper Gambia – was obtained at first hand must remain open to question. It is to be noted that some of it is decidedly confused and that what the narrative has to say about the empire of Mali, allegedly obtained at Cantor, in fact sometimes employs Wolof instead of Mandinka terminology, suggesting that at lest some of it came from Wolof or Serer informants.[10]

Nevertheless, it is certain that, perhaps not long after Cadamosto had sailed some distance up the Gambia on his second voyage,

Portuguese caravels did begin regularly to go all the way upstream as far as the region they knew as Cantor and its river port to which they gave the same name. Cantor was, in African terms, no great distance from the gold mines of Bambuk and was a flourishing centre of trade on the Upper Gambia. Gold from Cantor, though never in very large quantities, appears regularly in Portuguese documents relating to bullion imports from Guinea when these become available half a century or so later. If we make the reasonable presumption that the narrative attributed to Gomes is at this point genuinely autobiographical, the Portuguese navigator thus deserves special recognition as the first explorer to bring back in significant quantities from Guinea in the Prince's time the gold which had been the original prime motive behind the Henrican explorations.

Diogo Gomes states that his crew was soon prostrated by the heat on the Upper Gambia and that his caravel, in consequence, was forced to weigh anchor and sail down river. He was rejoined on this journey by the two caravels which had been left in its lower reaches. The crews of both were found to have been severely reduced by deaths due to fever. Further down river still, Gomes claims that he made peace with the Batimansa (see Chapter Twelve, p. 311) and secured from him a promise that he would never again make war on the Portuguese. Since Cadamosto, too, had established friendly relations with the same ruler, it seems likely that Gomes's account muddles the names of the various chieftains whose lands bordered the river.

Gomes is on firmer ground when he reports that the hostile reception accorded to the first Portuguese explorers to reach the Gambia had been due to the attitude of the ruler of the Barra country, who controlled the northern shores of the estuary as far as the territory of the Bur-ba-Sine and was known as the Niumi-Mansa.[11] Gomes asserts that he was instrumental in establishing friendly relations with this chief, too, though he strains credulity when he asserts that his spirited verbal defence of the Christian religion (delivered, presumably, through an interpreter) led the Niumi-Mansa to expel the Muslim marabouts from his land and to request Christian baptism from Gomes himself during a ceremony in which the chief wished, says the narrative, to be renamed 'Henry'. No more convincing is the text's assertion that the Niumi-Mansa asked the Portuguese captain to send him a Christian priest as well as some sheep, geese and pigs. He also requested that two Portuguese builders should accompany them to show his people how to construct proper houses. The whole story, while it cannot be dismissed out-of-hand, is suspiciously close to the terms of the famous request made by the Mani-Kongo to Diogo Cão when that explorer discovered the kingdom of the Kongo in the 1480s. The narrative also claims that, after the conquest of Alcácer-Ceguer in Morocco in 1458, when the Prince had time to turn his attention again to the affairs of Guinea, he honoured the promises made to the Niumi-Mansa on his behalf by Diogo Gomes, at least to the extent of sending a Christian missionary to that chief's court. Gomes's claim that the Niumi-Mansa sent the Muslim marabouts in his kingdom packing after hearing Gomes's arguments in favour of Christianity does not convince.[12]

Diogo Gomes also goes into some detail about a later voyage to Guinea made by him on the orders of Afonso V shortly after Prince Henry's death. He gives the commercial object of the voyage as that of transporting ten horses to be bartered in the land of the Bur-ba-Sine for slaves. According to the narrator, he had also been ordered by the king to intercept vessels illegally smuggling arms to Guinea and had been given general authority to monitor all vessels found sailing off the coast of Senegambia. On arriving off the Salum estuary, Gomes says he found two caravels already there. These had also transported cargoes of horses to Guinea. One of them was commanded by a Genoese already mentioned in these pages, Antonio da Noli, the future governor of the Cape Verde island of Santiago. Also present at the *resgate* was the 'king of the Wolofs' who, according to the Gomes narrative, had been driven out of his kingdom by the Brak of Walo.[13]

Gomes claims that he found that the trade in horses in the territory of the Bur-ba-Sine was being seriously damaged because the merchants aboard the other two caravels he met there had acquiesced in an unwarranted reduction in the barter rate for horses at that *resgate*: instead of the customary seven blacks for one horse, a change to a rate of six for one had been accepted by them. According to Gomes, he therefore used the authority given him by Afonso V to compel Noli and the Portuguese captain to sell their horses to him personally at the old rate. He then claims that he himself disposed of the animals to the Serers at the rate of one horse for fourteen or fifteen slaves! This tale, while it accords with the boastfulness which is a feature of the narrative attributed to the old sea captain, must also be treated with extreme reservations. It is hard to see what pressures Gomes could apply to make the Bur-ba-Sine double the number of slaves he was prepared to exchange for a single horse. The decline in the barter value of horses was plainly brought about by the steady rise in the number of these animals shipped by the Portuguese to Senegambia and, perhaps, by a corresponding reduction in the price of those traditionally brought there by camel caravan across the Sahara. Later information shows that the attempts of the Prince, and later of the crown, to dictate barter prices in Guinea from Portugal without regard for the laws of supply and demand inevitably proved ineffective.[14]

Diogo Gomes also asserts that he was responsible for detaining an unlicensed caravel – almost certainly a Castilian one – returning from the Gambia laden with merchandise, including gold.[15] The vessel was intercepted by him off Cape Verde and sent under escort to Portugal so that appropriate action could be taken against the interloper by the Portuguese king. Gomes reports, without explaining why, that the intruder was eventually executed in Oporto. This is possible, but once again the narrative strains credulity when it asserts that the executed man's body, together with the goods he had obtained in Africa, gold included, were thrown on to a fire after the execution. It seems highly unlikely that, even for punitive purposes, the interloper's bullion was or could be disposed of in such an operation. There is no doubt, however, that from the Prince's time onwards, as we have already seen, savage penalties were inflicted at his behest on any unlicensed foreign merchants and sailors who tried to break his Guinea monopoly.

Very different in quality from the conjectural narrative attributed to Diogo Gomes is the account of a voyage of exploration to Sierra Leone and beyond made in 1461 or 1462 by a Portuguese navigator, Pedro de Sintra. This, written up by Cadamosto from first-hand oral and documentary material he had been allowed to see, is contained in the third part of the Venetian explorer's *Navigazioni*. Though this journey did not take place until after the Prince's death and was therefore nominally made on the orders of Afonso V, Cadamosto correctly regarded it as marking the end of the work of exploring the waters of Guinea for which the Prince had been responsible. It has been suggested on the basis of a remark made decades later by Pacheco Pereira that *two* voyages were made by Pedro de Sintra at this time, one before and one after the Prince's death. There is, however, no reason to doubt Cadamosto's word that the account he gives refers to a single voyage made in 1461 or 1462. He does note that, after his own second voyage in 1456, there had been other voyages before his departure from Portugal but makes it clear that, as far as exploring was concerned, he considered the expedition of Pedro de Sintra to be the most important of these. After it, he reports, no further voyages of discovery had gone to Guinea up to the time he left Portugal early in 1463.[16] In fact no record exists of any other attempts to explore the coast of Guinea beyond the 'Lion Mountain' until the end of that decade when, in 1469, the Portuguese king was persuaded to farm out the task of starting up the discoveries again to a rich Lisbon merchant, Fernão Gomes. This was to prove a turning-point in the history of the Europeans in West Africa as, under the energetic régime of this Gomes, exploration progressed at a speed never matched in Prince Henry's time. Some fifteen years after his death, Fernão Gomes's explorers reached what is now Ghana (known to the Portuguese as the Mina Coast and to the British as the Gold Coast). There they were at last in a region where the large quantities of gold that had always eluded Henry were available for trading.

Pedro de Sintra has sometimes but perhaps wrongly been identified with a knight of the Prince's household of that name. Cadamosto describes him as a squire in the king's service as does a royal document of 1464.[17] Sometime before that date, but almost certainly after Henry's death, he had been appointed receiver of the dues owed to the crown on goods arriving in the Algarve from Guinea. In the same year Afonso V made him a maintenance grant of 4,000 *reais brancos* a year for his many services to the crown. Pedro de Sintra was evidently an important figure in the rather shadowy history of the Portuguese in Guinea in the first decade after the Prince's death. He continued to play an important role in its affairs until his own possible death there in the 1480s.[18] Pacheco Pereira mentions a toponym in what is now Nigeria he calls 'Rio de Pero de Sintra' located some distance to the east of the estuary of the New Calabar and Bonny Rivers. By the mid-1470s Portuguese caravels regularly frequented the slave markets on the Nigerian coast, so a tenable hypothesis is that the toponym was intended to commemorate the demise of the navigator at that spot.

Setting sail from Lagos with two caravels, Pedro de Sintra took up the work of exploration from the point where Cadamosto had abandoned it in 1456. After reaching the Bissagos Islands (11° 50′ N) off the Geba estuary (in modern Guinea-Bissau), he managed to sail some 500 miles further south-east along the coast almost as far as the Junk River (6° 10′ N), in modern Liberia. Cadamosto's account of this journey was not obtained directly from Pedro de Sintra himself. He explains that he used information supplied to him by a young Portuguese friend who had served under him as ship's scrivener on one of his own voyages and had just returned from performing the same function under Pedro de Sintra's command. According to Cadamosto, this friend, whom he does not name, visited him at his house in Lagos immediately after the expedition's return and gave him a detailed account of Sintra's discoveries. The Venetian explorer specially praised the orderly sequence in which the young Portuguese scrivener told the story of the voyage. He was no less impressed by his ability to name the countries the two vessels had visited and to recall the toponyms the explorers had given to the features they were the first Europeans to see. He also passed on to Cadamosto the rather scanty information Pedro de Sintra and those with him had been able to secure about the lands and people with whom the two caravels had managed to make shore contact. It looks very much as if Cadamosto had been able – probably in contravention of the rules – to copy the chart made during Sintra's voyage, using this to check his notes of what his informant had had to say about his voyage. However, the main thrust of this narrative is to supply information of concern to future navigators. Only occasionally does it have anything much to say about the African peoples with whom the explorers had managed to have dealings. It is especially interesting for its account of the way navigators of the Henrican period went about the task of exploring Guinea.

The scrivener's report begins by recording a new attempt to reconnoitre the Bissagos Islands – already visited by Cadamosto in 1456. These lie off the estuary of the Geba. As noted in an earlier chapter, the Portuguese and their Italian colleagues were always careful to investigate any islands they came across. Islands, especially if they were thickly wooded, promising access to fresh water and firewood. If they were uninhabited, they also might well offer safer and healthier anchorages than did the mainland. A landing was made on one of the Bissagos Islands. This was found to be inhabited. Cadamosto's informant described how, on a visit to a village on it the Portuguese explorers had seen wooden carvings of 'idols' which were worshipped by the local people. These may well have been the same kind of anthropomorphic carvings in an original style peculiar to the archipelago which have attracted the attention of modern students of African art. Cadamosto, as was his wont, lets the report of the existence of these emblems of a pagan culture pass through his fingers without thinking it necessary to add any reproving personal gloss. The African slave–interpreters carried aboard the two caravels proved no more successful in establishing communication with the inhabitants of the Bissagos Islands than those carried by Cadamosto had been in 1456.

Some forty to fifty miles further south, the expedition came on yet another of the wide river estuaries which characterize this part of the African coastline. This one was probably either the modern Río Cacine or the Rio Grande de Buba. Pedro de Sintra called it the 'Rio de Besgue' which, Cadamosto's informant told him, was the name of the local ruler.[19]

Continuing south-east for some 140 miles along the low and swampy coast of what is now the Republic of Guinea as far as latitude 10° 12′ N, the explorers unexpectedly came upon an elevated promontory to which they gave the name Cape Verga. Inland from the Cape they saw mountains covered with forest trees whose girth, height, greenness and beauty drew an appreciative comment from Pedro de Sintra's scrivener just as similar sights had done in the case of Cadamosto himself.

Sixty miles as the crow flies beyond Cape Verga, another long narrow promontory was sighted which in fact was the western end of the cape on which the city of Conakry now stands. Pedro de Sintra named the promontory Cabo de Sagres (9° 30′ N) in honour of the Prince and 'the fort' (sic) he had built on the now famous cape east of Cape St Vincent in the Algarve. The Portuguese explorer might now be working for Afonso V but he plainly still thought of Henry as his real patron.[20] The narrative is confused at this juncture, perhaps because Cadamosto muddled up what his young informant told him. Thus the Venetian's narrative states that Cabo de Sagres was the highest cape the Portuguese had ever encountered on this voyage. In fact the Île Tombo of today, though rocky low cliffs enclose most of it, is not particularly high. Cadamosto's informant is also reported as declaring that a tall mountain with a conical peak 'like the edge of a diamond' rose from the middle of the promontory.[21] The reference can only be to Mount Kakoulima (3,297′), the highest mountain visible in this locality but which rises some distance inland. Mention of offshore uninhabited islands here, however, makes the identification of Cabo de Sagres with the western end of the Île Tombo certain. The offshore islands are the present-day Îles de Los (Port. Ilhas dos Ídolos) which are a feature of this locality. The Portuguese name refers back to the large number of carved figures which the explorers found on the islands. Pacheco Pereira asserts that, when the people from the mainland went to the islands to plant rice, they took with them these figures to worship, leaving them behind when they left. Though Cadamosto's text does not say so, the appropriateness of the toponym Cabo de Sagres was probably clinched by the fact that, as is the case with its Algarve homonym, bays on both the north side and also on the south side of Île Tombo offer good shelter for shipping.

At this point in the narrative, the Sintra text includes its most detailed account of the ethnography of this region. Though no attempt is made to identify the tribal status of the people encountered there, they were probably Buloms. They, the document explains, are brown rather than black in appearance. They worship wooden statues of human appearance to which they make offerings before eating or drinking. They bear on their faces and bodies marks made as if with hot irons and are naked except for loin cloths made of bark. The Portuguese were much struck by the habit common to both sexes of wearing a number of gold rings hanging from their pierced ears and nostrils. Even more remarkable to them was the fact that the wives of the local king and of the chiefs and men of high standing in the group had the lips of their sexual organs pierced as well as their ears, and wore gold rings hanging from them. The Portuguese were also once again impressed by the size of the canoes in use in Guinea. In the Cabo de Sagres region, craft carrying thirty or forty men were seen paddled by rowers who did so standing. Cadamosto's informant thought these people to be without weapons because, he said, iron was unknown in their country. This was clearly a mistake since iron was available from indigenous sources in this part of Guinea. Presumably what he told Cadamosto was that the inhabitants of the Cape Sagres region did not at that time have iron weapons. Later Portuguese writers refer positively to the highly toxic poison with which the warriors there tipped the arrows and assegais they used. The text describes the whole area as well provided with rice, millet, vegetables such as beans, and some beef and goat meat.[22]

Continuing their course south-east, Pedro de Sintra and his men found themselves off the coast of what is now the modern Republic of Sierra Leone (Port. *Serra Lyoa*), a region remarkable for the forested mountain ranges of the Sierra Leone peninsula and the rocky promontory (8° 30' N) which nowadays bears the same name. Pedro de Sintra named it Cabo Ledo (Cape Cheerful), it is said because of the encouraging impression made on him and his crews by the lofty sierras and their pleasing hinterland.[23] Pursuing their journey coastwise parallel to the Sierra Leone range, the explorers duly recorded the group of islands some distance out to sea known today as the Banana Islands. Sintra's caravels then continued south off the flat shores of modern Yawri Bay until they came across a region of red sandstone. Because of the way the sandstone discoloured the waters of a river which entered the sea there this they named the Rio Roxo (Red River). This was probably the Kagboro River shown on modern charts. The cape just to the south, known to cartographers today as Shenge Point (7° 55' N), was marked on Portuguese charts as Cabo Roxo. The explorers disembarked here on a lofty, wooded uninhabited island which they also called Ilha Roxa (today's Plantain Island). Portuguese coastal toponyms in Guinea often appear unimaginative and repetitious to modern students, but it must be remembered that the explorers were mainly concerned with making sure that the labels they invented, when placed on the charts recording their discoveries, would serve to make the geographical features to which they referred easily recognizable by future pilots. However that was not the whole story. As has been noted in an earlier chapter, the act of providing the geographical features of the coast of Guinea with a string of Portuguese names can be seen symbolically as the first step in bringing the region into the embrace of Portuguese imperialism. It also may be interpreted as evidence of the inability of the interpreters carried by Sintra's caravels to establish, south of Senegambia, oral contact with the inhabitants of the region. Further north, as we have seen, linguistic interchanges had sometimes allowed the explorers to incorporate the names or titles of local rulers into the place names created by the Portuguese. Such connections were now rare.

An essential part of a fifteenth-century explorer's task was to supply fixes on the Pole Star from hitherto unvisited locations for the benefit of future navigators. Such ocular fixes, still probably made without instruments other than a compass, continued to supply the most used method of estimating latitudes. Reflecting this concern, Pedro de Sintra's scrivener told Cadamosto that, as seen from Ilha Roxa (Plantain Island – latitude 7° 55′ N), the Pole Star was only 'a man's height' above the horizon.

Sintra's caravels were now south of the modern port of Freetown, in Sierra Leone. Beyond Shenge Point, the Sintra text records the discovery of a very wide opening in the coast towards the east. At its head debouched a large river the Portuguese named Rio de Santa Maria because it was found by them on the feast day of Our Lady of the Snow (5 August). The reference is to the Sherbro 'River' of later times, really a large sound (or 'gulf' as Cadamosto terms it) twenty miles wide that extends to the east and then to the south. On its southern side the explorers came on 'a great cape' which they named after St Ann, whose festival (26 July) it was. There was either some confusion about these two dates or the naming of the features concerned was not carried out in strict chrolological order. The map they made of this part of the coast of Sierre Leone must also have been faulty, or was misinterpreted by Cadamosto, since the Cape St Ann (7° 34′ N) of today is in fact a low, sandy point. Some scholars have reckoned that the modern Cape St Ann therefore cannot have been the promontory referred to. This is improbable since the text correctly draws particular attention to the notorious Shoals of St Ann which extend for many miles to the north of the cape and to the violence of the tides and currents which sweep over them.[24] The whole passage is an impressive example of the thoroughness with which Portuguese explorers like Sintra and Italians like Cadamosto, working under the routine instructions laid down by the Prince, went about the task of mapping the coast of Guinea.

No landings seem to have been made in this region. Seventy miles beyond Cape St Ann, sailing south-east in shallow water, the next river encountered was named the 'Rio das Palmas' because of the many (oil) palms seen growing in the vicinity of its mouth. This was probably the Sulima River of later map-makers. The Portuguese reckoned that it was too dangerous for any attempt to enter it to be made, an assessment with which the *Africa Pilot* concurs. Soon afterwards, the caravels would cross the modern boundary between the states of Sierra Leone and Liberia but in mid-fifteenth-century terms they were still off the land dominated by the Lion Mountain. The next river they encountered, some seventy miles further on, was named the 'Rio dos Fumos' ('Smoky River') because, as the text explains, when they discovered it they also saw smoke rising on shore from fires the local people had made along the whole stretch of coast.[25] Given the fact that it was now the height of the rainy season, it is unlikely that the smoke was caused by the normal processes of African agriculture. It may well have been intended as an alarm signal to warn the people of the region of the threat represented by the presence of the two caravels in these waters. The Portuguese explorers were unable to effect a landing, no doubt because of the combination of shallows and heavy surf which are a feature of this coast. The 'Rio dos Fumos' may well have been the Mano River which, today, marks the border between Sierra Leone and Liberia.

Pedro de Sintra and his men were now approaching the end of their remarkable voyage. Twenty miles beyond the Rio dos Fumos they came upon a bay ending in a cape which formed the western extremity of a range of hills. To this, with some inevitability, they gave the name 'Cabo do Monte' – the Cape Mount of modern charts. Sixty miles further on, they sighted another small but steep-sided cape described in the Portuguese text as dominated by a hill. To this they gave the name Cabo Mesurado (6° 19′ N).[26] The name survives today and marks the southernmost point of the bay in which is located the Liberian capital, Monrovia. Here too, as the caravels lay anchored off shore for the night as was their custom, they noted many signal fires burning among the trees and in open ground. The text attributes this phenomenon to the surprise of the local people at their first sight of Portuguese caravels standing off shore. Early narratives of the exploration of Guinea like to stress the astonishment the Portuguese vessels caused to the local people when they appeared. They certainly excited much curiosity. It is, however, highly unlikely that news of the presence of the Portuguese vessels off these coasts was not already known to the native people who had their own ways of passing news and warnings to each other over considerable distances. In addition to acting as a warning to their own people it may have been hoped that the fires would dissuade the Portuguese from attempting a landing. If so, the warning appears to have been heeded.

Sixteen miles further down the coast by Cadamosto's reckoning, Sintra and his men came upon what is described in the text as a great forest whose trees grew right down to the water's edge. They named the place 'Arvoredo de Santa Maria' (St Mary's Grove), probably because they sighted it on the Feast of the Assumption (15 August). Here contact *was* made with the local people, a few of whom ventured out to the anchored caravels in their small canoes. Three were actually persuaded to board one of the ships. All carried pointed wooden darts. Some had metal knives. Two were equipped with leather shields and bows. Some wore necklaces of teeth, which the explorers believed to be human. The slaves aboard each caravel were ordered to try to have speech with the visitors but the attempt proved totally abortive. In consequence, as Cadamosto himself had done in a similar situation, Pedro de Sintra decided that, since they could not secure any information about the country except what they could see for themselves, it was an appropriate time to call a halt to further exploration and to start the long voyage back to Portugal. He could not of course know that he had reached the beginnings of what would later be known as the Costa de Malagueta or Grain Coast where, less than a decade later, the Portuguese would start to obtain large quantities of malagueta pepper, or grains of paradise.

Before they set sail for home, Pedro de Sintra ordered one of the blacks who had boarded the caravels to be kidnapped and taken to Portugal. Cadamosto confirms that this was done in accordance with Afonso V's orders that, if the explorers reached a land where the native interpreters were unable to communicate with the local people, they should try to bring back to him, by force or by persuasion, 'one of the blacks of that land so that he could give an account of his country, either through the many black interpreters to be found in Portugal, or because, with time, he himself became able to make himself understood [in Portuguese]'.[27] Though now done in the king's name, this was, as we have seen, a continuation of standard procedure in Prince Henry's time when the explorers found themselves linguistically impotent despite the efforts of the interpreters they carried. Cadamosto adds a revealing comment based on his own information about what happened to the kidnapped African on this occasion. He explains that, after many unsuccessful attempts in Portugal, a female slave belonging to a Lisbon citizen was found who could communicate with the man concerned, not in the native language of either of them but in another language which both knew. Perhaps some indication of the way Cadamosto found himself isolated in Lagos after Henry's death and the removal of the control of Guinean affairs to Lisbon, is his dry comment that he was not informed about what kind of information the man, through the woman slave–interpreter, had given the king about his homeland except that there were unicorns there.

This African informant was luckier than those kidnapped for similar reasons in the Prince's time. The king did not enslave him but, over a period of some months, caused him to be shown many features of Portugal and then sent him back to his homeland with gifts aboard another caravel which, before February 1463, retraced the route taken by Pedro de Sintra. No doubt it was hoped that in his role of interpreter he would reassure his people that the Portuguese had come to their country in peace and wanted only to trade. Cadamosto is emphatic that, up to the time he left Portugal on the date mentioned, no other vessel had gone further south than Pedro de Sintra had.

The discoveries of Cadamosto and Pedro de Sintra and the toponyms associated with them (about forty new names) are all shown on a portulan atlas drawn in Venice in 1468 by the chart-maker Grazioso Benincasa.[28] These place names, all in Portuguese, clearly represent the latest information then available in Italy about the results of the explorations of Cadamosto and Pedro de Sintra and may well have been given to Benincasa in Venice by Cadamosto himself. The atlas terminates slightly beyond Cape Mesurado. A number of the Portuguese toponyms shown on it are not mentioned in Cadamosto's account of his own voyages. It has been suggested that these may be relics of earlier Portuguese exploration. It is far more likely that they appeared on Cadamosto's charts and in the logs he kept but that he did not include references to them in the *Navigazioni* so as not to overload his text with too much minor cartographical detail.

So ended the Henrican voyages of discovery. In the twenty-seven years or so that had passed since the rounding of the elusive Cape

Bojador, the caravels had explored, as the crow flies, some 2,000 miles, but the actual sailing distances covered coastwise and up rivers like the Senegal and the Gambia was, of course, more of the order of 2,500 miles. At first sight this does not seem a particularly impressive achievement, especially when we remember that one-third of this distance had been covered by Pedro de Sintra in a single voyage, or compare it with the distances routinely covered after 1469 by individual explorers working for the farmer of the Guinea trades, Fernão Gomes. Such comparisons are, of course, invidious. Fernão Gomes's captains had at their disposal all the accumulated knowledge gained by Henry's captains and pilots about the navigational and other special problems associated with long-distance sailing on the coast of West Africa. They also had access to all the cartographical and other eyewitness information about the region which the Prince had painstakingly collected over twenty-seven years from both navigators and African informants.

One must not, of course, suppose that the voyages described in the narrative sources that survive, or which are known about because they are referred to in chancery documents, were the only ones that took place in the years with which we have been concerned. Cadamosto makes it plain that, before he came on the scene, purely commercial voyages from Portugal to Senegal were already routinely made. There was, of course, no clear distinction made in Prince Henry's time (or later) between such voyages and those which involved exploration. The discoverers of the Prince's day knew that, as well as exploring, they were expected to trade whenever an opportunity occurred.

The Henrican voyages dedicated to exploration were sporadic, depending on what other distractions demanded the Prince's attention, on his ability to raise the necessary finance and to find navigators whom he considered likely to measure up to the tasks he set them. Given the aggressive nationalism he displayed in his dealings with Castile, it is perhaps surprising that he made no attempt to exclude foreign navigators or merchants from Guinea or from his Atlantic Islands – as long as they were not Castilians. On the contrary, he went out of his way, as in the case of Cadamosto, personally to recruit them. Genoese merchants found no problems about securing licences from him to admit them to the area of his monopolies. He showed no inhibitions about sending to Italian cartographers the latest information about the exploration of Guinea and, by the 1450s, seems to have had one or two Italian advisers with him in the Algarve. It is much to Henry's credit that he recognized early on that he needed access to Italian commercial know-how if the new materials arriving from Guinea and the

Islands were to be properly marketed in Europe. As has already been mentioned, it is likely, too – though as yet unproven – that some of the money for the Henrican and later discoveries was furnished by the Italian merchant houses established in Lisbon. This, if correct, would help to explain why the Prince, while fiercely defending his Atlantic monopolies, did not try to deny access to them to properly accredited foreigners.

There are in the various narrative accounts of the voyages to Guinea made in Henry's time silences which the modern reader wishes were not there. Thus, not much is said in them about the many new navigational perils and problems that the Portuguese mariners undoubtedly encountered and learnt to handle. The authors of these narratives evidently took it for granted that everyone knew that the sea was a routinely dangerous place, particularly when uncharted waters were involved, and did not think that such matters merited special mention. The relative lack of attention given in these narratives to the threat to life posed by tropical diseases is also surprising. It must be remembered, however, that the risk of contracting mosquito-borne fevers while a caravel was anchored some distance offshore was slight. The danger came when the vessel sailed far up great rivers like the Senegal or the Gambia; significantly, these are the circumstances in which the narratives do report casualties due to fever. As rapid a return as possible to the open sea seems to have put a stop to such outbreaks. It was only later on in the century, when Portuguese garrisons were permanently stationed ashore in Guinea in fortresses like those of São Jorge da Mina or Axim, and when missionaries and traders took up residence in the Kongo, that it become recognized in Portugal that, for Europeans, tropical West Africa was a place of death. As João de Barros was to write, after listing the benefits Portugal received from and gave to Guinea in his time,

> Nevertheless it seems that – on account of our sins or as a result of some judgement of God hidden from us – at the entrance to this great land of Ethiopia [Guinea] where our ships go, he placed a menacing angel with a sword of fire in the form of mortal fevers which prevent us penetrating into the interior to find the springs which water this earthly garden and from which flow down into the sea, in so many of the regions we have conquered there, rivers of gold.[29]

There is no evidence that in Henry's time the health hazards which awaited the Europeans in West Africa had yet become recognized as the fearsome menace to which Barros refers. That would not happen until the 1480s, when Portuguese garrisons began to be established on the mainland of tropical Guinea and the islands in the Gulf of Guinea were colonized by Europeans.

~ Chapter Fifteen ~

The Necessary End

. . . death, a necessary end,
Will come when it will come.

Shakespeare, *Julius Caesar*, Act 2 Scene 2

The necessary end came for Prince Henry on 13 November 1460 when he was in his sixty-seventh year.[1] It seems certain that, at the time of his death, he was in residence in the Vila do Infante, the embryonic town on or by the sea-girt promontory of Cape Sagres that, as we have seen, he had founded in 1445 and characteristically named after himself. No account of his final illness and death exists. It may be noted, however, that some of the documents issued by him in the weeks before his death contain amendments inserted by him in his own hand. Neither these nor his characteristic signature – 'J.d.a' ('Jfante dom anrique') – give any grounds for supposing that, up to a short time before his demise, Henry was seriously failing physically or mentally.

It was not until the autumn that he got down to – or was persuaded by those concerned for the future of the institutions, enterprises and the Atlantic colonies of which he was master, to get down to – the task of arranging his affairs in testamentary order to meet the eventuality of his approaching death.[2] His final will was only witnessed, signed and sealed seventeen days before this occurred. Associated with it are fifteen individual testamentary instruments. In addition, there is also a so-called *Escrito das Capelanias* (register of chaplaincies) in which, among other good works of his, he listed all the churches and chapels he had caused to be erected outside metropolitan Portugal. These documents also contain liturgical instructions about the masses for his soul which were to be said for ever in all these places on Saturday of every week of the year. He admonishes all future officers of the Order of Christ to see that his instructions were regularly carried out for ever, not only in the churches and chapels named in the document but in any new foundations established anywhere in whatever regions of Guinea might be discovered after his death. There are no other instructions concerning Guinea in these documents, nor were any called for since his monopoly there automatically reverted to the crown on his demise.

Suggestions have been made that Henry's attitude to religion reflected the pietistic trends that were around in his day. There is nothing in these documents to support such a notion. They show his interest in liturgical correctness and his concern to ensure that religion played a full part in seeing to it that his name and deeds were never forgotten. As far as religious practice was concerned, Henry's general position seems to have been conventional enough for his times and royal rank. What was unconventional about it was his dedication to a militant activism that he persuaded himself represented a return to the now dated aims and values of the Iberian *Reconquista*. These, however, in their turn, had been reinvigorated in his case by exposure to the cult of chivalry as practised by his English forebears, heroic stories about which he and his brothers had heard, one presumes, from the lips of his mother.

To the clutch of papers dictated in his last weeks of life by the Prince, we need to add two inventories made on behalf of his executor, the king. These itemize his movable and other possessions in the Algarve and deal with their disposal. No similar inventories exist for the contents of his palaces in Lisbon or his residences in Viseu and in other regions of the kingdom. A few related documents give information about how some of his possessions were disposed of, or refer to his outstanding debts. From these sources we can secure some much-needed data about his personal household in the Algarve and the way he lived there. They also supply some account of the Lagos dockyard which, under his control, had served as the main home base for all departures for Guinea as well as for sailings to his Atlantic islands.

There was, of course, nothing unusual about the fact that the Prince made a will shortly before his death. As has been remarked on earlier, what was decidedly unusual for a person of his standing is that this seems to have been the first time in his life that he had ever made a proper will. There is no evidence that, despite his age, he had taken this routine precaution before any of the campaigns in North Africa, including the recent attack on Alcácer-Ceguer. One may contrast this omission with the testamentary care taken by his brother, the ill-fated D. Fernando, just before the attack on Tangier in 1437. The text of Fernando's will, made strictly in accordance with prescribed legal forms, takes up (with annotations) twenty-five pages of print in the relevant volume of *Monumenta Henricina* and so gives valuable insights into the domestic side of Fernando's life.[3] Almost as if Fernando was aware of and condemned his elder brother's failure to follow his example, this document contains a longer than usual exordium which stresses both the need for men to recognize that death might strike them at any time and the disastrous consequences that failure to make a will, in Fernando's words 'out of negligence or weakness', could lead to after their death. Was it the case that Henry, despite his deep commitment to Christian beliefs, could not bring himself fully to contemplate the inevitability of his own disappearance from the world scene? Or did he simply think it useful as an experienced politician to keep his options open until the last minute? One can only surmise.

Be that as it may, the Prince did not follow his brother's example until it was past the eleventh hour. The only testamentary disposition he is known to have made before 1460 consists of a brief and hastily written document he had issued in letters patent (*alvará*) form in March 1436. This does not conform to any of the legal rules or customs of the time regarding the making of a will. He nevertheless persuaded Duarte I to ratify it and, for twenty-four years, it represented the only posthumous arrangement for his affairs he is known to have made.

For all its brevity, the 1436 document is a crucial one for students of the Prince's biography. In its opening paragraph he comments that all men desire to enjoy a lengthy life – a desire which divine ordinance does not permit. To combat the inescapable certainty of death and 'so that their names may remain [known] on earth', men therefore wish to have children. He then goes on to declare, without further explanation, that, since he has no son of his own and does not expect to have one, he adopts as his heir and adopted son his child nephew, D. Fernando (b. 1433), brother of the future Afonso V.[4] To this then two-year-old boy, he bequeathed his possessions and property, though reserving no less than one-third of the income derived from them to pay for masses and prayers for his soul. The *alvará* also requested the king to issue a dispensation allowing the inclusion in Fernando's inheritance of any lands Henry held from the crown, lands which, according to Portuguese law, could only pass to a legitimate child born to the testator. Another feature of the earlier document is Henry's characteristic attempt in it to ensure that these territories he held from the crown on a life tenancy could be inherited by D. Fernando as if they represented property held by his godfather in perpetuity (*de juro e herdade*).[5] As we have repeatedly seen, the Prince, always conscious of his mother's injunction to him to make it his business to protect the rights of the great nobles, dedicated himself to the cause of permanently alienating crown lands in this way. The *alvará* was reconfirmed in its original form in 1451 by Afonso V after he had assumed the governance of the realm. This was done somewhat surprisingly not at Henry's request but at that of the beneficiary himself, D. Fernando.[6] Did D. Fernando already have reason to believe that his godfather might be contemplating reducing the inheritance promised him since 1436?

There are grounds for supposing that the 1460 will and related documents were perhaps drawn up as a result of particular pressure from the chief officials of the Order of Christ seeking to persuade him that the time had come, in the interests of the Order, for him to make proper arrangements for his necessary end in respect of his role as administrator of the Order. It is unlikely to be a coincidence that many of the testamentary letters are concerned with confirming in perpetuity Henry's donations of overseas privileges to the Order and were expressly dictated by him for deposit in the archives of its mother house in Tomar.[7] The *Escrito das Capelanias*, dated 13 October 1460, reveals that, by then, Frei Fernando, the vicar-general of the Order, had turned up in Vila do Infante to witness this document. The Order also seems at this time to have supplied him with a new confessor to see him through the last weeks of his life.[8]

In both the 1460 will itself, and in the testamentary letters, Henry refers to himself with that air of slightly aggressive hauteur which he customarily adopts in formal documents as if to remind those for whom they were intended that, though the form may be commonplace, the issuer certainly is not. The opening passage of the will supplies a piece of biographical information not generally known. The Prince refers there to his devotion to St Louis 'to whom from the time of my birth I was dedicated'. The allusion is to the French crusader king, St Louis (d. 1270). This information further supports the view that Henry was, from childhood, encouraged by his horoscope and by his parents' interpretation of it to believe that it was his destiny to be a Christian crusader. The choice of a French royal saint perhaps reveals the hand of Queen Philippa in the matter.

The main surprise about the 1460 will, however, is that, in it, Henry attempted drastically to reduce the number of territories included in 1436 in the blanket donation to his adopted son. Then the latter had been his universal heir. The new document now names Afonso V himself as the inheritor of everything now not specifically left to Fernando. It also appoints the Portuguese king as the Prince's sole executor.[9] Under the new dispensation Fernando, by now duke of Beja, was only to inherit the lordship of two islands in the Azores group (Terceira and Graciosa), the lordship of all the others reverting to the crown. Moreover, though Henry authorized the king to grant to Fernando any other of his possessions Afonso thought fit, he specifically decreed that the by now economically flourishing island of Madeira was to be excluded from the territories willed to Fernando. A similar exclusion was applied to the port of Lagos – at that time, as we have seen, still the main base for all voyages of exploration and trade with Guinea.

The exclusion of Lagos from Fernando's inheritance makes it look as if the Prince perhaps intended to ensure that his heir did not indirectly get his hands on the Guinea trade through possession of the Algarve port and its castle. The exclusion of Madeira was a more serious matter for Fernando since, if it became effective, it would deprive him of the very considerable wealth that, as Cadamosto noted during his visit there in 1455, the economic development of the archipelago was already bringing in 1455 to its territorial lord.

It certainly cannot be assumed that the Prince made these changes out of any concern for the conservation or restoration of the crown's patrimony. As we have seen, he was, throughout his life, a leading despoiler of that patrimony, relentlessly using his political power to have transferred to himself crown lands and the crown's traditional commercial monopolies. He had also repeatedly sought to extend his seigneurial jurisdiction to include powers traditionally reserved to the sovereign. Docunent after document in the fifteen volumes of *Monumenta Henricina* shows him successfully petitioning the reigning king, too, for permission to appoint his own people to dozens of crown offices, major and minor, spread across the entire kingdom. The appointees thus became technically members of his princely household. He, indeed, alludes to all this accumulation of powers into his hands with some complacency in the 1460 will when he remarks, 'I, thanks be to God, have many servants whom I have contented by means of commanderies [in the Order of Christ], church livings, marriages, annuities and offices. Others have lived as part of my household, and some did not deserve what I have given them.'[10]

The incorporation into the will of this last and unexpected passage was thought by Dias Dinis to reveal Henry's continuing bitterness against those who had deserted him in 1437 at the time of the Tangier disaster. It reads, however, more like an angry comment inspired by much more recent behaviour by members of his household. Perhaps some of the latter, aware that the Prince was nearing his end, had, as often happened and happens in such cases, already started to desert the sinking Henrican ship.

We do not know for sure what lay behind his attempt in 1460 partially to disinherit his adopted son. Afonso V was then in serious political and financial trouble because of his spendthrift ways and his readiness to alienate crown lands in favour of the nobility. The king may therefore have thought it politically prudent, as Dias Dinis suggests, to oblige Henry to curtail the further and major alienations in Fernando's favour which would inevitably take place if the 1436 *alvará* was still in force on his death. This view is, however, difficult to reconcile with the fact that the king, ignoring his duty as Henry's executor, almost immediately set about restoring Fernando's inheritance to what it had been before 1460. It therefore seems possible that the reason for the Prince's behaviour was simply that relations between him and his ambitious nephew had cooled. There is, as we have seen in an earlier chapter, some evidence that, despite his leading role in the capture of Alcácer-Ceguer, Fernando was in the process of developing doubts about the wisdom of committing Portugal to a policy of indefinite crusading in Morocco – doubts which certainly would not have pleased his uncle if he knew about them. The real point to be made about all this, though, is that the attempt made by Henry in 1460 to reduce Fernando's earlier expectations entirely failed. The living Fernando's political clout proved far more powerful than that of his dead uncle. Within three weeks of the Prince's death, most of the new provisions of the 1460 will were cast aside by Henry's royal executor so that, in the end, Fernando inherited from his godfather largely as had been planned in 1436.[11] It looks as if the political influence at court of the man described by Zurara as the greatest of princes without a crown faded so rapidly after his death that even his testamentary dispositions were ignored. With the complicated, flesh-and-blood Henry permanently out of the way, the dynasty was now free to set about portraying him in the unsophisticated terms of myth as the heroic visionary genius whose qualities had made him not only the embodiment of Portugal's crusading destiny in North Africa but also, as writers of the next generations were accustomed to put it, the 'inventor' of Portugal's maritime expansion.

The other documents under discussion, if they contribute nothing towards settling the question of the extent of the Prince's knowledge of cosmography and navigation, do provide additional proof, if any were needed, of his religious dedication. In a characteristically medieval way, he saw his devotion to the Church and its institutions as the surest guarantee that his yearning to secure his posthumous fame would be satisfied. Chroniclers might do their best for him but their works were subject to the vicissitudes of fortune. Only by leaving his fame in the hands of the Church and its institutions and rituals could he be really sure it would be secure for ever after his death.

Taken as a whole, the 1460 testamentary documents are overridingly concerned with making sure that, by using the tools offered by the Church, future generations of Portuguese would never be allowed to forget him and his achievements. One of them thus lists the locality of church after church and chapel after chapel in the Atlantic islands, in Morocco and in continental Portugal which he had already caused to be built or orders for whose building he had given. The overt purpose of these lists was to reconfirm that the 'spirituality' of all the religious establishments named in them was vested in the Order of Christ, and to make it the responsibility of the Order to see that prayers for his soul were said in them in the manner he had ordered. But, as already noted, they are more than mere lists of places and churches. In these documents the Prince sometimes adds observations of an autobiographical nature describing his special connection with the locality named. A number of them confirm that his obsession with the conquest and conversion of Morocco continued to occupy his mind on his deathbed. Thus, when describing the establishment of a commandery of the Order of Christ in Ceuta after the city's capture in 1415 or the recent transformation of the main mosque in Alcácer-Ceguer into the church of Santa Maria da Misericórdia, he is careful to draw attention to the fact that he was personally present at the capture of both places.[12] In the same document he also notes that it was he who presented to the church of Santa Maria he had founded in Ceuta the famous image known as Santa Maria de África – it is still there today – which, he remarks with satisfaction, had already wrought many miracles. In another clause he declares that the chief officers of the Order of Christ must see to it that clerics are appointed to serve not only in the two captured Moroccan fortresses mentioned but also in Tangier and Tetuan 'when these two places have been conquered'.

There is, though, a significant omission from the long list of churches and chapels at home and overseas in which prayers for his soul are to be said in perpetuity, using funds designated by him for this purpose in his will. He is unable to refer to any specific location on the African mainland south of Morocco where he claimed to have founded a single church or chapel. He has to content himelf, instead, with the vague injunction that such prayers should be said 'in every religious foundation in those lands [of Guinea].' The absence of any mention of any church or chapel associated with the Portuguese factory permanently established on Arguin Island for some time past is particularly surprising in this respect. Moreover, since the sole justification for Henry's monopoly in the African Atlantic as underwritten by the papacy was the evangelization of Black Africa – a process successive popes had been assured by him was proceeding apace – the vagueness of Henry's allusion to the progress of Christianity there is particularly telling. It was one thing to make such claims to the distant Roman curia but quite another to repeat them without qualification in a testamentary document which would be read by those who knew what the real situation was.

Another feature of these letters is the way they all establish exact rules for the regular celebration in perpetuity of masses and prayers for Henry's soul in all the churches and chapels founded by him anywhere. The Prince was not content with this. As already noted, similar prayers must also be said in any religious establishments founded after his death in any overseas territory that came under Portuguese control so that people there would be reminded that it was thanks to him that Portugal had been enabled to become a power in those new lands. There is evidence that this wish was duly implemented everywhere in Africa or Asia where the Portuguese installed themselves permanently.

Nothing was left to chance about the liturgical form these prayers were to take. The Prince named the kind of Mass and other exact details of the celebrations of his memory which were to take place every Saturday wherever a church or chapel had been built.[13] The officiating priest was admonished always to follow to the letter his directions as he now set them out. The payments to be paid annually to each church or chapel where this office was held were usually to be charged against the various taxes due to the Order of Christ on all income arising from trade, rents etc. originating in the Atlantic islands, or from trade with Guinea.

One item in the will raises directly the much debated question of the Prince's intellectual interests and confirms that, as far as these were concerned, it was for his support of theological studies in Portugal that he wished to be remembered. He directs that twelve silver marks annually, funded by the Order of Christ's income from the island of Madeira, shall be used in perpetuity to pay for the teacher (*lente*) appointed to the chair in theology (*cadeira de prima*) at Lisbon University founded by him. The appointment did not solely embrace academic duties. Part of the *lente's* terms of appointment obliged him regularly to say prayers for the chair's founder (Henry), not only in the University but also in various religious houses in the city of Lisbon. In addition, at the beginning of every academic year, the *lente* must read out in public the Prince's letter setting up the chair.[14] The benefaction was presumably no great surprise to the university authorities as, since about 1431, Henry had enjoyed the title of 'Governor and Protector' of the university. His decision to establish his own chair of theology there is, however, more significant than it might seem. In the later Middle Ages a university could not be considered of the first rank unless it had papal authority to set up a faculty of theology and the graduates of that faculty enjoyed the right to teach theology anywhere in the Christian world (*facultas ubique docendi*). This right had been denied by the curia to Lisbon-trained theologians in the fourteenth century. As late as 1380 it was again refused to any whose training was limited to the Portuguese university. Though it is clear from the 1431 statutes that a faculty of theology existed there then, it seems that, at the time when Henry first became the official protector of the institution, graduates from that faculty may have been few and far between.[15] Henry, perhaps advised by his scholarly confessor, the Dominican Frei Afonso Velho, established his chair to improve the status of theological studies at Lisbon University vis-à-vis the more famous faculties at other European universities of his day.

In his role as governor and protector of the university the Prince had, as was his way, long showed that he had no intention of being a mere royal figurehead. He intervened actively in the university's affairs, sometimes, one imagines, to the annoyance of the members of the academic body. Thus we find him in 1443 complaining that it had been reported to him that some lecturers frequently failed to give the weekly number of classes they were supposed to. He instructed the rector to make sure that the university bedel visited each faculty every Saturday to check up on the number of classes given by each teacher that week and ordered that any delinquent should suffer a deduction from his pay in respect of every class missed.[16] He also took a hand in the architecture of the university's buildings. In 1431 he donated to it some houses he had bought. The purpose was to improve the available teaching accommodation. Far from leaving it to the university body to decide how to use the new accommodation, he laid down detailed rules regarding the allocation of each new room to a particular branch of study and even directed what symbolic portraits were to be painted on the walls of each room to show to which faculty it had been allocated. Thus on the wall of the room assigned to lectures on natural and moral philosophy a portrait of Aristotle was to be painted.[17] The final part of the donation contains more evidence of Henry's life-long concern that his good works should not be forgotten. He directed that a record of his donation should be inscribed on a large stone which was to remain for ever set into the wall above the entrance to the new university houses in question. All this is difficult to reconcile with the opinion sometimes hinted at that Henry, unlike his brothers Duarte and Pedro, can have had little general interest in learning or in matters intellectual. He was clearly concerned that posterity should remember him *inter alia* for his record as an active reforming governor of the university and a patron of theological scholarship.

The Prince's very real interest in theology is indisputable. A copy of Peter Lombard's *Sentences*, the standard theological textbook of the Middle Ages, was one of the very few books recorded as having been with him when he died. It was at his request, too, that a Portuguese Franciscan, André do Prado, a professor of philosophy at Bologna university, wrote a dialogue in Latin on the symbolic meaning of the Apostles' Creed which André entitled *Horologium fidei* (*The Dial of Faith*).[18] This is nominally a dialogue *à deux* in which Henry fictionally participates in person. His role is mostly to ask brief but pertinent questions about the subject matter of the dialogue. Its author then replies at length to each question. In the prologue (*c.* 1448) to this work, whose references to Henry are couched in the most obsequious terms, André do Prado seems to show awareness of the contents of the Prince's horoscope. He thus lauds the Prince's appetite for conquest and his eagerness to take part in battles. More unexpectedly, André, in a flight of rhetoric, also praises the courage with which Henry 'sails' the seas. As we have seen in an earlier chapter, this was not the only occasion on which fifteenth-century ecclesiastics turned the Prince into a practical as well as theoretical practitioner of navigation. The Franciscan theologian also praises him for his determination to explore unknown regions of the world, his understanding of the stars, his wisdom and scholarly vigils, and his dedication to theological studies.[19] All these activities are seen by Fr André as different aspects of Henry's single-minded quest to serve God, an explanation of the underlying motivation behind the Prince's life's work with which the latter no doubt entirely concurred when he read the prologue to the friar's treatise.

There are two surviving official inventories of the possessions found in Henry's palace in Lagos and in his other dwellings and properties in the Algarve at the time of his death. These take the form of quittances requiring the approval of the king as the Prince's executor.[20] They bring us immediately into contact with some of the more everyday realities of his domestic and entrepreneurial life in these final years. Like most Portuguese itemized quittances of the time, the two inventories are somewhat chaotic documents whose compilers only make sporadic efforts to organize their contents into appropriate categories. It would, moreover, be naïve to suppose that these inventories dutifully record everything that was to be found in the Prince's Algarvian establishments shortly after he died. For example, it has been noted that only eight books, six of them liturgical or biblical, are listed in them.[21] One should certainly not conclude that this fact enables any significant conclusions to be drawn about Henry's library at that time or earlier. The list, for example, does not even mention a manuscript of the *Horologiun fidei*, a work of which he surely would have possessed a copy. Nor is there any mention of the astronomical treatises or any of the well-known geographical or travel writings of his age which, as we have seen in earlier chapters, there is every reason to believe he knew. Nor can one suppose that, in his last years, he did not have with him, apart from Peter Lombard's *Sentences*, any of the standard theological, pietistic or improving works in Portuguese a man with his interest in religious matters surely had by him. Missing, too, are any copies of the literary and moralistic writings of his brothers, Duarte I or the former regent, D. Pedro. Also absent is any copy, in Latin or the vernacular, of any textbook on war used by medieval generals, notably, of course, Vegetius's *Epitoma rei militaris*. It seems likely that a number of the books he had in his library in the Algarve had either been given away by him before his death, or had been removed subsequently before the inventories were made. The royal library or the library of the Order of Christ in Tomar were obvious potential destinations but, as far as I am aware, no manuscripts positively identified as having belonged to the Prince have yet been found anywhere. The absence of any maps or of any written reports on Guinea and the Atlantic islands such as those used by Zurara is perhaps less surprising. These were probably held in the offices of the Guinea Agency in Lagos and so automatically became crown property on the Prince's death.

The presence in one of the inventories of two silver seals weighing together one mark four ounces and a small gold signet seal serves as a reminder that his ducal chancery, with its officials and clerks, accompanied him, at least in theory, wherever he went. Under his signet he doubtless validated his private correspondence of which hardly anything survives. As explained in the Introduction, one of the unfortunate consequences of the fact that Henry's Guinea monopoly was personal to him was that documents relating to it were normally issued by his chancery, the contents of which have largely been lost.

Little personal clothing appears in the inventory of his domestic possessions. This does, however, contain a detailed description of one rather unexpected item of uniform. The inventory makers found in one of Henry's Algarvian wardrobes a complete outfit of the robes worn by knights of the Order of the Garter. The whole array of undertunic, mantle, cap, sash and other ceremonial appurtenances in the then Garter colours of crimson, scarlet, gold and blue is individually described. The robes, as was routine, had been brought to Henry from England by the Garter King of Arms after his election to the Order in 1443.[22] Henry perhaps attached more importance to his membership of the famous order of chivalry established by his English great-grandfather than did brothers or his nephew, Afonso V. It was perhaps by Henry's order that the arms of the Garter are also displayed on the tomb made for D. Pedro in Batalha in 1455 after his posthumous rehabilitation and ceremonial reburial there. The reburial was organized and presided over by the Prince who, we are told, appeared for the occasion clad in the deepest mourning.[23] His political posture in 1449 had largely contributed to Pedro's death at Alfarrobeira but, as we saw in the case of D. Fernando, Henry found no difficulty about appearing as chief mourner for a brother for whose death many thought him largely responsible. No doubt on this occasion, too, he considered that he deserved praise rather than blame for having been willing to sacrifice a brother for a principle.[24] It is, of course, tempting to wonder whether he kept the ceremonial robes of the Garter beside him in the Algarve so that he could deck himself out in them on important occasions there, as when, for example, he received foreign knights seeking to enter his service, or when – as Zurara states and documents confirm – chiefs from the Canaries or from Black Africa whom he wanted to impress came to visit him as his household guests.

One of the inventories, as we have already seen, supplies details about the domestic slaves attached to the Prince's personal household at the time of his death. The names of some nine of them, all evidently converts to Christianity, are supplied.[25] One or two may have been slave–interpreters, perhaps Canarian as well as African, whose task was to help the Prince to communicate both with these free visitors from their homelands and with those newly kidnapped in Guinea whom he wished to interrogate.

One of the inventories provides detailed information about the contents of the dockyard and warehouses operated by Henry in Lagos in connection with his monopoly of trade with Guinea and the steadily growing trade with his Atlantic islands. Caravels belonging to him are referred to, unfortunately without any details as to their numbers, names or tonnage. Also partly inventoried is the equipment necessary to fit out them and other types of vessel for sea. Lateen sails for the caravels, anchors, cables, ropes, every sort of ship chandler's goods, as well as stocks of materials like wood, planks, iron and so on needed to build or repair ships are included.[26] It is clear from the document that Henry's shipbuilders in Lagos did not only build caravels for him. Ordinary square-rigged merchant ships (known as *urcas* in Portuguese), also formed part of his fleet of sea-going ships. The latter were probably mainly employed on the Madeira run, though there is some evidence that, already before the Prince's death, it had been found that, contrary to earlier belief, it was possible for square-rigged vessels successfully to make the journey to Guinea and back.

Many items of military equipment – light cannon (Port. *troons*), bombards, gunpowder, crossbows and bolts – as well as all types of armour are listed in the second inventory. Some of them may have been intended for the defence of Lagos castle. We know, however, that Henry's caravels always went to Guinea equipped with cannon and bowmen to help with their defence if they were attacked by tribesmen there. They also needed such armaments to deal with unlicensed foreign interlopers found south of the Canaries as well as with Moorish corsairs operating in the Atlantic out of Moroccan bases. The cost of purchasing much of this material, some of it imported from Flanders and Germany and other countries, helps to flesh out Henry's frequent references to the great expenses he had had to meet to sustain the task of exploring Guinea and supporting the development of the Guinea trades.

On the negative side, these documents have disappointingly little to say about imports from and exports to either Arguin or to the *resgates* in Black Africa. The only commodities mentioned as having been found in the Lagos warehouse are sugar (presumably from Madeira), elephant tusks and orchil.

Henry's debts also figure prominently in the documents under discussion. His 1460 will contains the usual routine instruction to his executor to settle these as a first priority but without naming any individual creditors or amounts. He does, though, recognize that finding the money to pay off all his debtors was not going to be an easy task for his executor. For this reason he requested the king to allow his estate to go on receiving for a period of three years after his death the income which had accrued to him annually in his lifetime from various specified sources. These included Madeira and Guinea as well as the lucrative kingdom-wide soap monopoly.[27] His request was not acceded to by Afonso V, probably as a result of the objections of D. Fernando.

The debts fell into two categories. One involved the salaries, maintenance and other payments due to the officials and other members of his household. These, it seems, were often in arrears. In addition various large loans made to the Prince, some of them long-standing, remained unsettled. The king, in his role as executor, was informed from Lagos that insufficient liquid funds were available in the estate in the Algarve even to pay Henry's personal staff what was due to them. It was therefore necessary, as we have just noted, to dispose of his properties and all of his movable possessions there, including his slaves, by transfer or sale, to satisfy, or partially to satisfy, these household debtors. The will is noteworthy for the more than routine concern Henry showed in it for the future wellbeing of those other than his slaves who had served him in his lifetime. He wrote,

... many of those who serve me depend on me for their subsistence in the form of salaries on which they rely so that, if these were be taken away from them from the hour of my death, they would be left in great need and my conscience burdened. I therefore request my Lord the King and the Prince D. Fernando, my very dear son, and whoever holds the Mastership [of the Order of Christ] after me, to grant, out of their love for God and for me, that each one continue to receive the income that belongs to his office for the rest of his life and be accepted into their own service as if they had been in it [from the start]. Thanks be to God they are persons who will cause any who grant them this favour to consider it well done.[28]

Henry's obvious concern on his deathbed for the future of those who had served him during his lifetime confirms Zurara's statement that he always treated members of his household with kindness even when, the chronicler suggests, they did not deserve it. His request was met, at least in part, by Afonso V. A considerable number of letters patent survive in which the king confirms in their offices various former members of the Prince's personal and extended household. Among them were those who had been responsible for overseeing in Lagos on his behalf the operations of the trade with Arguin and with Guinea in general.

The problem of the Prince's larger creditors could not be met by the sort of appeals to the indulgence of the king or D. Fernando mentioned above. These debts could be both very considerable and sometimes long-standing. When Duarte de Meneses, then the governor of Alcácer-Ceguer, produced documents showing the king that he was owed 444,000 *reais brancos* (1,755 *cruzados*) due to him in repayment of loans made to Henry, the king was forced to grant him a licence to send a caravel to Guinea with permission to continue trading there, free of all taxes, until he had made a profit worth the amount claimed.[29] What is certain is that, fifty-seven years after his death, the descendants of some of those who had lent Henry money were still waiting for it to be repaid. Manuel I, in his will dated 1517, recommended his successor to see to it that an effort be made to settle any of Henry's debts that were then still outstanding. It was only right, said the king, that these should be met by others out of regard for a deceased prince who had done such good service to Portugal.[30] Manuel, it may be noted, does not explain why he, now with the riches of the Orient at his disposal, had evidently not practised what he preached.

Lack of any direct evidence makes it impossible to discover with certainty why the Prince, on paper the wealthiest magnate in Portugal, apparently died as he had lived – substantially in debt. Whether, despite the inroads he made on the revenues of the Order of Christ, the scale of the profits said by traders to be made in Guinea, and the steadily growing income from Madeira, he failed to make the Guinea enterprise pay for itself we cannot tell. Perhaps the main cause of his financial difficulties was the cost of maintaining the great number of retainers and officials who made up his extended and semi-regal household in Portugal. Be that as it may, it is unlikely that a prince of Henry's times and temper was as much troubled by his debts as modern scholars may think he ought to have been. As we saw earlier, in his day a taste for conspicious expenditure was regarded as an essential outward sign of a truly noble and chivalrous spirit. Lavish material generosity nourished knightly fame so that in the world of chivalry prodigality was seen as positively virtuous, and any sign of penny-pinching as ignoble. In the language of Aristotle's *Ethics*, a work known to Zurara amd doubtless at first or second hand to the Prince too, the reputation for magnificence great men should always seek to acquire demanded of them a continuous display of openhandedness.[31] As we have just seen, Henry himself referred with pride to the size and, by implication, to the expense of his household. The chronicler João de Barros, in his sixteenth-century description of Henry's character and achievements, still refers admiringly to the way the Prince showed his magnificence by lavish spending.[32]

Henry's death-bed account of his life's work was not intended to remind God of his good works. It could be assumed that God, by definition, knew about them and the Prince, anyway, felt pretty secure of his place in Heaven. It was the security of his posthumous fame in this world which, as always, troubled him, leading him in these documents to remind posterity of his proudest achievements and to lay down how the liturgical practices of the Church were to be used to keep his memory and achievements green for all time. In fact, as it turned out, he had no need to worry about his posthumous fame. If, as the poet has said, fame is the food that dead men eat, then it must be agreed that Henry himself and his contemporaries had ensured that an ample sufficiency of such provender was ready for him when the time came for him to enter the waiting tomb in Batalha.

Bearing in mind the purposes for which it was intended, it is not surprising this deathbed inspection of Henry's life only came up with reminders of what the Prince regarded as successes pleasing to God. If he allowed himself to feel that there were any occasions in his long life when his behaviour or actions had fallen short of what was required of the dedicated Christian knight he always proclaimed himself to be, such were reserved for the ear of his confessor. These documents are, therefore, of no great help in solving the various uncertainties and enigmas that will always encompass many of Henry's motives and much of his personal life. In particular, his letter to his father in 1428 raises many questions about who the real man was behind the public persona which we cannot answer. In the letter, to be found in the Appendix, Henry shows himself to be a competent and objective reporter of things seen. In particular, and surprisingly, he writes in a matter-of-fact way about an important religious occasion, even to the extent of describing the events associated with his brother's marriage in Coimbra with a certain amount of mild humour. The outstanding feature of the letter is, though, its self-confidence as well as its sheer down-to-earth ordinariness. Henry clearly did not think it appropriate to strike attitudes when writing privately to his father on a family matter. Reading the document now, one may feel that the gap between the persona Henry put on show and the real individual may be even greater than might be supposed. But the letter was written before the Henrican discoveries had begun and before the disaster at Tangier and other setbacks suffered by the Prince, so we can have no idea of what long-term effects, if any, these events had on his character or his behaviour.

Prince Henry died in the Vila do Infante, probably on the night of 13 November 1460.[33] According to the information Diogo Gomes is said to have given to Martin Behaim some decades later, Henry's body was moved to Lagos that same night and, as was the custom then, given temporary burial in the parish church of Santa Maria while, with the aid of lime, it decomposed. The old man claimed that, a year later, he had been personally charged by Afonso V with the task of opening the grave to see if the Prince's body, expected now to consist only of his bones, was ready for transfer to the elaborate late-Gothic wall tomb in the Founder's Chapel at Batalha where his father and mother and his brothers were buried. Gomes declared that he then found the body, clad in a horsehair shirt, to be dry and uncorrupted except for the tip of the nose.[34] He inevitably deduced from his supposed discovery physical proof of the saintly status of the dead Prince. Gomes's story of finding an uncorrupted corpse receives no support from Rui de Pina, the royal chronicler of Afonso V's reign. He states categorically that, in 1461, the Prince's bones were escorted by his adoptive son, with much ceremony, from Lagos to Batalha where the king and 'all the nobility of Portugal and many bishops' waited to receive them in solemn procession'.[35]

That the tomb had been constructed in Henry's lifetime to a design presumably approved by him is established by royal letters patent issued in 1439 and 1449 giving him permission to erect an altar and a tomb in the Founder's Chapel at Batalha. That the tomb was duly built there before 1460 is confirmed by a clause in his second will which reads 'I order that my body shall be deposited in the monument which awaits it where the king my lord and father lies in the monastery of Santa Maria da Vitoria.'[36] Henry gave a characteristic explanation for his concern to ensure that he was interred in the Founder's Chapel. In what is perhaps a reference to the situation that he supposed would arise when the Resurrection of the Dead occurred, he declared that his presence in a tomb there would ensure that he could continue to serve John I and Queen Philippa in seemly fashion after his death as he had always served them in life.

On the top of the sarcophagus there is a full-length recumbent sculpture of the Prince, his head half concealed within an elaborate laterally placed Gothic baldechino. His head rests on a pillow and his hands are raised in an attitude of prayer. According to the custom of those times, the face is clean-shaven. The head above the face is covered by a flat cap with richly decorated brim. The body is clad in armour which is partly covered by a dalmatic. No sword is visible. Within a large panel below the recumbent figure the sarcophagus exhibits three coats-of-arms. The left-hand one is that of the Order of Christ, the right-hand one Henry's own princely escutcheon. Between these, in the centre of the panel, he had caused to be carved the arms of the Order of the Garter with the famous encircling motto 'Honi soit qui mal y pense'.

Since the tomb was made in Henry's lifetime, it might be taken for granted that we have here the oldest and most true-to-life of the surviving sculptures and paintings of the Prince's face and head. In fact, the Prince's face, at least as we see it today, is disappointingly stereotypical, little attempt having been made to define its features with any sense of authenticity or artistry. Its most noticeable features now are the protuberant, blank staring eyes which, though often found in tomb sculptures, here give the unfortunate impression that this is the face of a blind man. Wrinkles across the forehead, extending from the eyes and also affecting the lips and sides of the mouth, though carved in a summary way, make it clear that, though the cheeks are full, we are dealing with a man of some age.

Unfortunately it is by no means certain how close the face we see today actually is to that seen by worshippers at Batalha for three centuries after his death. The fabric of the Founder's Chapel was severely damaged by the great earthquake of 1755 so that for a long time the original stone work of all the royal tombs there is said to have been exposed to rain-water. Neither the drawings of the tombs made by the British architect James Cavanah (sic) Murphy, at Batalha in 1789, nor the accompanying text, refer, to any such exposure.[37] It is quite certain, however, that all the tombs were damaged in 1810 at the hands of Napoleon's troops. Much of Henry's tomb as it appears today, and in particular his face, is perhaps what emerged as a result of extensive restoration work carried out as best they could mostly by nineteenth-century masons and sculptors attached to the monastery staff.[38] Though modern critics inevitably prefer to assume that the artistic shortcomings of the recumbent figure of the Prince as we see it today are largely due to the restorers, there is of course no hard evidence that, in its original fifteenth-century form, the sculpture was a more faithful or refined representation of the living Henry than the restorers have left us with. At all events, despite its history, Henry's tomb still reflects in broad terms the original piece of Gothic funerary sculpture approved by him in his lifetime.[39] Running the whole upper length of the monument, above the shields, is a long and partly damaged Gothic inscription identifying the tomb as his. At the end of the inscription spaces were left in which to insert, when the moment arrived, the day, month and year of his death.[40] Neither the Dominican monks of Batalha nor the chantry priests who regularly said masses for the Prince's soul in the chapel, nor his adopted son, D. Fernando, nor anyone else ever bothered to see that the missing information was duly added to the inscription. One can perhaps deduce from this that no popular cult of Henry centred on the tomb at Batalha ever developed. The process of turning him into a posthumous dynastic cult figure was the work of the court and its chroniclers and other adherents. The failure of anyone to add the missing data to the inscription on the tomb seems to symbolize the flight from the man of flesh and blood whose bones lay within it to a figure fabricated by the requirements of myth, a metamorphosis for which Henry himself in his lifetime had done his best to prepare. Considered as a metaphor for Henry's view of himself when he ordered his tomb to be made, one thing is clear. The Gothic tomb he had designed, its representation of himself and everything else about it belonged wholly to the later Middle Ages. So, when all is said and done, did he and all his works. The Henrican discoveries, as well as the way the Prince explained and justified them, are seen to be an entirely medieval phenomenon in which, uniquely, the doctrines of the crusade and the ideology of chivalry came together to make possible, under Prince Henry's direction, a major scientific contribution to European man's knowledge of the wider world about him.

Appendix

Newsletter written by Prince Henry to his father John I of Portugal from Coimbra on 22 September 1428 reporting on the goings-on at the marriage there of the heir to the throne, D. Duarte, to Leonor of Aragon . . . It is the only strictly private letter written by Henry that has ever been found. The letter was partly written before the day of the marriage, was completed after the ceremony and a last-minute sentence added, still on the day of the ceremony, to inform the king that the marriage had just been consummated.[1]

Most high and most honoured and much esteemed Lord

I your son and servant the Infante D. Henrique, Duke of Viseu and Lord of Covilhã, very humbly send to kiss your hands and to commend myself to your favour and blessing.

Most high and most honoured and much esteemed Lord. May it please you to learn that the things which have happened since I [last] wrote to you are these which follow. My lord the Infante [D. Duarte] duly arrived here as I wrote to Your Grace, and he lodged in the other chamber which is at the end of the palace where are the rooms where My Lady the Infanta [of Aragon] is lodged. Every day he used to go to see her two or three times in her room to enjoy himself in her company. Nevertheless, as far as I have been able to learn, during all that time he never once kissed her.

[Also] during that time he sometimes went hunting and so amused himself as he pleased, but he refused to go far into the lands reserved for the chase. One day he ordered me to go there and I took with me some guards and I killed a boar near the city. The next day I ordered the beaters to cordon off two of them for the archbishop of Lisbon. He asked the Infante's permission to take them and went to where they were. My lads whom I had ordered to go with him mortally wounded one as it was coming out of its lair. However, when it was about to drop, it ran at a peasant living in that place and slashed him four times because it mistook him [for one of his attackers]. When it could not move any further and fell to the ground, those of my lads who were present finished it off. The other boar fled.

When my lord the Infante comes across any dancing or singing or anything else which can provide pleasure, he gladly joins in. Thanks be to God, he is very happy and in good health. He praises greatly the

Appendix

singing of the Infanta and her playing the clavichord and her way of dancing which, they say, is the way she always dances. He ordered Dona Guiomar to arrange for two bulls to be run in honour of the Infanta and we [Duarte and Henry] both together fought them, one in the palace stables and the other where the jousting was to take place, in front of [the monastery of] Santa Clara. Two of my lads waited to finish off the palace one because it was small. They killed it very skilfully.

Other news, my lord, is that my brother the Infante D. Pedro reached Avelãs last Friday, and my lord the Infante and I with him went after dark to visit him in that place. He, when he knew we were coming, came out the distance of a stone's throw [from where he was living] mounted on a palfrey and with torches. When he saw the Infante he dismounted and the Infante and I also did so. Everyone seemed to me very happy from one end to the other of the place. From there we went to his house to drink and take a light supper. The Infante slept there that night and the next day I went to eat with him at Botão where my [half]-brother the count [Afonso, count of Barcelos] had arrived. That day they [all] went to hear Mass at Santa Clara. That night I went to sleep a league away and on Saturday I returned to hear Mass in this monastery where I am now lodged.

After we had eaten I went to receive him [D. Duarte]. With me were the archbishops of Lisbon and Braga and the bishop from here [Coimbra] and the marshal and other knights and plenty of noble people. We journeyed for about a league to a spot where my brother [Pedro] and the count, [also] accompanied by many noble people, came to meet us. When we drew near, my brother the Infante sent the archbishops of Lisbon and Braga to escort the countess Dona Costança. With everyone now gathered together, the bishop of Santiago and the bishop from here were present to receive him. At the entry to the city was waiting the bishop of Ceuta dressed in his pontifical robes. [They all] then walked in procession to Santa Clara, a goodly sight. When my brother caught up with the procession he dismounted and kissed the relics. There were rugs and a damask cushion for him to kneel on.

From there he walked in procession on foot as far as Santa Cruz where he said a prayer. Next he went to see the Infanta and to kiss her hand. She received him very gladly. Before we reached the palace my brother the Infante D. Fernando had joined us and we three, along with my brother the count, spoke with the aforesaid lady and then we went to the house where the Infante D. Pedro was lodged. I had invited him for that day but he insisted that what he wanted was to return to his dwelling. After we had left him there I sent the count my brother to his lodgings too, and took the Infante D. Fernando with me to speak to my lord the Infante [D. Duarte]. That day and the next day he was my guest for dinner. After that, my brother looked after him.

On Monday we went dancing. My brother [Duarte] and his retinue seem to me to be very elegantly dressed. On Tuesday night it was decided to have the wedding on Wednesday. What then took place, in accordance with your blessing which you had given the Infante my lord, is as follows:

First the preparations were like this. Rugs had been placed on a large section of the walls and floor of the cloister of Santa Clara through which my lady the Infanta would have to pass. Inside the door of the church, which is located inside the nuns' cloister, hung a rich cloth of crimson brocade which covered the place where the blessings would be given. A range of hangings ran the whole length of the church and out into the street and also where there is a staircase leading to the choir, where the tomb of Queen Isabel is. The whole route was similarly decorated with hangings and rugs and the walls of the choir were completely covered with tapestries, as was the church inside and outside, the ground being covered by rugs. From the altar as far as the wall and laid on the rugs was a covering of ten cloths, each one a cloth wide and each of blue velvet-like satin.

The altar frontal and canopy was made of rich crimson brocade. The coverlet of the dais [on which the couple were to be married] and the canopy over it were also of very rich crimson brocade. The cushion on which they would have to kneel was all of woven gold without other embellishment. The altar was well equipped with silver [plate], some of it belonging to you and some from here. The bishop performed the offices wearing the mitre and carrying the crozier given by you. Thus, thanks be to God, everything was done in good order.

While the Infanta was waiting in the chapter house, my lord the Infante came from his lodging riding on a well-caparisoned palfrey and wearing a very rich tunic with an emerald clasp. My brothers the Infante D. Pedro and the Infante D. Fernando rode on one side of him and I and my brother the count were on the other side. Also with us were many other knights, all finely dressed. And so we arrived at the doors [of the church]. There the Infante dismounted and walked as far as the choir accompanied by the Infante D. Fernando and the count. Meanwhile the Infante D. Pedro and I went to fetch the Infanta and led her from the place where the blessings had been given. My lord the Infante then joined her. Next the precentor of Évora [cathedral] sang briefly and after that we were [formally] received and the Office began.

The Infanta was very gorgeously dressed. The torches were carried by D. Fernando and D. Sancho and D. Duarte and D. Fernando de Castro and other youthful great lords who were present. Mass was said, not sung, but the deacon and sub-deacon were in their pontificals as for a sung one. The offertory was of two hundred gold *dobras*. When the Office ended the Infanta was so exhausted because of her cape, which was very heavy, and because of the heat caused by the number of good people who were there and the light from the torches that, when we went to conduct her away, she fainted. We threw water on her and she came to. At this point all the men left while the women stayed behind. The count [of Barcelos] acted as groomsman and his countess as matron of honour. Dona Guiomar carried the bride's train.

The Infante returned to his abode in the same way as he had come from it. When night had fallen we went to join the Infanta in the monastery where she had already eaten. It was just as if she had married from the house of Queen Isabel, who also came from Aragon. Every one of us thought that this matter had worked out so well because of the holiness of the said Queen Isabel from whose house [the monastery of Santa Clara] it had started. Next the Infanta mounted a horse. My brother D. Pedro and I went on foot as far as her lodging holding up the boards [honouring the bride and bridegroom]. The Infante D. Fernando and the count and all the other knights came too. She was riding a white palfrey, its accoutrements all of gold, which Your Grace saw and which the Infante sent her. She was escorted by some sixty torches carried by squires. Behind her came the count and Dona Isabel de Taude and other ladies and maidens.

After we had seen her to her chamber we danced and sang a while in the palace and the Infante came there and sat in state with his standard beside him. The chamber was adorned with hangings and he was served with wine and fruit by us. The Infante D. Pedro carried the napkin, I the dish with sweetmeats, the Infante D. Fernando the fruit and the count the wine. After the Infante had taken some wine we all took our leave of him and returned to our several lodgings and, just as I was finishing this letter, I have learnt that a short while since my lady the Infanta became in the full sense your daughter. They, thanks be to God, are in good shape as are all of us who are here, your servants and myself.

Very noble and very honourable and very much esteemed lord. May Almighty God keep you and your affairs in his holy care and at his service leading to the exaltation of your status and honour as your heart desires.

Written in Coimbra, twenty-two September 1428.

Abbreviations

ACA	Archivo de la Corona de Aragón
ACCP	*Arquivos do Centro Cultural Português*
ACCCG	*Arquivos do Centro Cultural Calouste Gulbenkian*
ACL	Academia das Ciências de Lisboa
ADAN	*Alguns Documentos do Archivo Nacional*
AEA	*Anuario de Estudios Atlánticos*
AGC	Agência Geral das Colónias
AGS	Archivo General de Simancas
AGU	Agência Geral do Ultramar
ANTT	Arquivo Nacional da Torre do Tombo
APH	Academia Portuguesa da História
AV	Archivio Segreto Vaticano
BAE	Biblioteca de Autores Españoles
BHS	*Bulletin of Hispanic Studies*
BMLF	Biblioteca Mediceo-Laurenziana (Florence)
BNL	Biblioteca Nacional (Lisbon)
BNM	Biblioteca Nacional (Madrid)
BRABLB	*Boletín de la Real Academia de Buenas Letras de Barcelona*
CCCG	Centre Culturel Calouste Gulbenkian
CEQMDH	Comissão Executiva das Comemorações do Quinto Aniversário da Morte do Infante D. Henrique
CDD	*Crónica de D. Duarte*
CdG	*Chronique de Guinée*
CDDM	*Crónica de D. Duarte de Meneses*
CDPM	*Crónica de D. Pedro de Meneses*
CEGP	Centro de Estudos da Guiné Portuguesa
CEHU	Centro de Estudos Históricos Ultramarinos
CEHCA	Centro de Estudos de História e Cartografia Antiga
CFCG	*Crónica dos Feitos na Conquista de Guiné*
CIHD	Congresso Internacional de História dos Descubrimentos
CLAMPR	Colecção de Legislação Antiga e Moderna do Reino de Portugal
CLIHP	Colecção de Livros Inéditos de História Portugueza
CNCDP	Comissão Nacional para as Comemorações dos Descobrimentos Portugueses
CODOIN	*Colección de Documentos Inéditos para la Historia de España*
CSIC	Consejo Superior de Investigaciones Científicas

CUP	Cambridge University Press
DHP	*Dicionário de História de Portugal*
DP	*Descobrimentos Portugueses*
DP(S)	*Descobrimentos Portugueses (Suplemento)*
DPIG	*De Prima Inuentione Guinee*
EH	*Estudos Henriquinos*
EHESS	École des Hautes Études en Sciences Sociales
ESA–WA	Ethnographic Survey of Africa–Western Africa
Esmeraldo	Duarte Pacheco Pereira, *Esmeraldo de situ orbis*
EWA	*Europeans in West Africa*
HCRP	*História da Casa Real Portuguesa*
IAC	Instituto de Alta Cultura
ICP	Instituto de Cultura Portuguesa
IFAN	Institut Français de l'Afrique Noire
IICT	Instituto de Investigação Tropical
INCM	Imprensa Nacional-Casa da Moeda
INIC	Instituto Nacional de Investigação Científica
JICU	Junta de Investigações Científicas do Ultramar
JIU	Junta de Investigações do Ultramar
MCAA	*Monumenta Cartographica Africae et Aegypti*
MH	*Monumenta Henricina*
MMA	*Monumenta Missionária Africana*
MPV	*Monumenta Portugaliae Vaticana*
OUP	Oxford University Press
PMC	*Portugaliae Monumenta Cartographica*
RAH	Real Academia de la Historia
RFL	*Revista da Faculdade de Letras*
RPH	*Revista Portuguesa de História*
RUC	Revista da Universidade de Coimbra
SEVPEN	Service d'Édition et de Vente des Publications de l'Éducation Nationale
SGL	Sociedade de Geografia de Lisboa
SVCTT	Sociedad V Centenario del Tratado de Tordesillas
VF	*Manuscrito 'Valentim Fernandes'*

Bibliographical Note

In the endnotes the bibliographical references normally consist of the author's last name, date of publication of the work referred to, and page reference; 'p.' or 'pp.' are only used to avoid confusion when preceded by a document number. Full bibliographical references are given when the first endnote to a chapter consists of suggestions for further reading, or when the first reference to a major narrative source is mentioned. In the text and in the endnotes material in a foreign language has been translated into English. The version in the original language is only given when the translation is contentious.

Notes

Introduction

1 Purchas, *Hakluytus Posthumus or Purchas His Pilgrimes*, 1905, 10. This work was first published in 1625.

2 The thesis that Henry has been given undeserved credit for starting the discoveries was first authoritatively emphasized by V. Magalhães Godinho in *Documentos sôbre a expansão portuguesa*, ii (Lisbon, 1945), e.g. 168–9. See also V. Magalhães Godinho, *L'Économie de l'empire portugais aux XVe et XVIe siècles* (Paris, 1969), 41. This thesis, which has had various other supporters, was submitted to close scrutiny by Léon Bourdon (*Chronique*, 27–31) who concluded: 'cette séduisante construction ne repose malheureusement sur rien'(28).

3 *Johnson*, 1825, 218–9.

4 Robertson, 1778, I, 43.

5 *Ibid*, 44.

6 The strongest argument for believing the figure shown on the São Vicente panel to be of Prince Henry was its very close similarity to the alleged portrait of him which appears as an introductory illumination in the Paris manuscript copy of Zurara's *Crónica dos feitos da Guiné*. The latter's existence was first made known in 1840. The manuscript dates from the end of the fifteenth century or the early sixteenth century. The authority of the Paris illumination has recently been effectively undermined. It has been shown that the leaf carrying it was added to the MS after it was first bound. Henry's Anglo-Norman motto shown beneath the portrait is spelt according to usages only normal after the middle of the *sixteenth* century. The marginal ivy leaf decoration used is not found elsewhere in Henrican iconography. It therefore seems probable that the portrait in the Paris manuscript, far from guaranteeing, as has often been supposed, the authenticity of the late fifteenth-century representation of the Prince attributed to Nuno Gonçalves, is itself a sixteenth-century work by an artist familiar with the figure shown on the São Vicente panel or with another lost version of it. It seems nevertheless that the belief that the anomalous figure on the panel was Prince Henry was current long before the nineteenth century. (see, *inter alios*, *O rosto do Infante*, 1994, 21–2).

7 Gomes Eanes de Zurara, *Crónica da Tomada de Ceuta por El Rei Dom João*, ed. Francisco Maria Esteves Pereiras (Lisbon: Academia das Ciências de Lisboa, 1915).

8 Zurara, *Crónica dos feitos notáveis que se passaram na conquista de Guiné por mandado do Infante D. Henrique*, ed. Torquato de Sousa Soares, 2 vols (Lisbon: Academia Portuguesa da História, 1978–81).

9 Zurara, *Chronique de Guinée*, ed. Léon Bourdon, Robert Ricard and others, Mémoires de L'Institut Français d'Afrique Noire, N° 60 (Dakar: IFAN, 1960; repr. (Paris: Éditions Chandeigne, 1994). For the complex manuscript history of the *Chronicle of Guinea*, see particularly *CdG*, 10–26. This chronicle was unknown to scholars in its original form until its rediscovery in Paris in the nineteenth century.

10 João de Barros, *Ásia; Primeira Década*, 1988, 61.

11 Damião de Góis, 1977, 20–22. For a recent scholarly dismissal of the Sagres legend see Luís de Albuquerque, *Vértice*, II Série, 63, (1994), 81–6.

12 Pacheco Pereira, 1975, 68.

13 Las Casas, I (México, 1951), 94–7, 137–9.

14 Las Casas had at one stage

suggested that black slaves from Africa should be brought to America to free the Indians from labouring for the Spaniards. He explains in the *Historia de Las Indias* that he deeply regretted making a proposal which failed to recognize that enslaving black Africans was no less unjust than enslaving Indians (*ibid.*, III, 274–5).

15 The label seems first to have been given general currency by the German geographical statistician J. E. Wappäus who describes the Prince as 'Heinrich der Seefahrer' in the title of a volume he published in 1842 – *Untersuchungen über die geographischen Entdeckungen der Portugiesen unter Heinrich dem Seefahrer*, I (Göttingen, 1842).

16 Major, 1868, vii.

17 Beazley, 1901, xvii.

18 Silva Marques (ed.), *Descobrimentos portugueses*, 3 vols (Lisbon: IAC, 1944–71). The third volume contains documents issued after the Prince's death (1461–1500) but often relevant to his times.

19 A. J. Dias Dinis OFM (ed.) *Monumenta Henricina*, (ed.), 15 vols, (Coimbra: Atlântida, 1960–74). Between them *DP* and *MH* reprint most of the documents previously published in earlier collections. Notable among the latter were José Ramos Coelho (ed.), *Alguns documentos do Archivo Nacional da Torre do Tombo acerca das navegações e conquistas portuguezas*, I, (Lisbon, 1892) and Pedro de Azevedo, *Documentos das chancelarias reais anteriores a 1551 relativos a Marrocos*, 2 vols, Academia das Ciências de Lisboa (Lisbon-Coimbra: Imprensa da Universidade, 1915–34).

20 For a discussion of the part played by Cerveira's narrative in Zurara's chronicle see particularly *CdG*, 26–28 and the article on Zurara in *DHP*, VI, 396–7.

21 Cerveira's text evidently reproduced a number of now lost documents relating to the early voyages to Guinea. Zurara seems to have omitted most of these on the grounds that his courtly readership would find them tedious. Thus referring to the 1446 donation to Henry of a monopoly over navigation to the Canary Islands, he commented 'although we have found the text of this document recorded in the first book written by Afonso Cerveira, which we follow in this present history, we shall not transcribe it here because, as far as any informed person is concerned, the sight of such documents is nothing new and we know that their style is so commonplace that their presence, rather than awakening in the reader any desire to peruse their hackneyed formulas, would bore them' (*CFCG*, II, 473–4).

22 The best text is that edited by Tullia Gasparrini Leporace – *Le navigazioni atlantiche del veneziano Alvise da Mosto* (Rome: Istituto Poligrafico Dello Stato, 1966). It is based on the oldest surviving fifteenth-century MS of Cadamosto's work. There is an English translation and edition by G. R. Crone (*The Voyages of Cadamosto and Other Documents on Western Africa in the Second Half of the Fifteenth Century*, The Hakluyt Society, Second Series, No. LXXX (London: The Hakluyt Society, 1937), 1–84.

23 *De prima inuentione Guynee* in *O manuscrito 'Valentim Fernandes'*, ed. António Baião (Lisbon: Academia Portuguesa da História, 1940). Gomes's reminiscences were taken down verbatim from the Portuguese by the Bohemian cosmographer Martin Behaim who probably turned them into German. Someone, perhaps the Moravian publisher known to the Portuguese as Valentim Fernandes, subsequently turned them into the

crude Latin which is the form in which they have survived. Quite apart from the reliability of Diogo Gomes's memory in his old age and his urge to maximize his importance, the linguistic and editorial permutations the text underwent after Gomes had been questioned reduce its credibility as an eyewitness account. There is an English translation in the Hakluyt Society volume referred to in the previous note.

24 For an account in English of the relevance of the Simancas documents see P. E. Russell, 'Castilian documentary sources for the history of the Portuguese expansion in Guinea in the last years of the reign of D. Afonso V' reprinted in the same author's *Portugal, Spain and the African Atlantic, 1343–1490*, Variorum Collected Studies Series (Variorum, Aldershot, and Brookfield, Vermont, 1995), a study originally printed in Portuguese in 1971. Professor M. A. Ladero Quesada has suggested to me that further information that indirectly casts light on the Guinea controls in the Henrican period may be available in the records of the *Contaduría de Cuentas* and the *Escribanía de Cuentas* in Simancas.

25 See Richard Gray and David Chambers, *Materials for West African History in Italian Archives*, Guides to Materials for West African History (London: The Athlone Press, 1965) – useful though the great majority of the entries recorded are from the state and other official archives and belong to the post-Henrican period.

26 Text in *MH*, III, no. 125, 255–9. See also Appendix A. I am grateful to Professor A. H. de Oliveira Marques for his confirmation that there is no reason to doubt the authenticity of this important Henrican document.

Chapter One

1 Madrid: Editorial Castalia, 1988.

2 'He emerged from the belly of his mother bearing with him in his embrace a semblance of the Cross of our Lord Jesus Christ for whose love and reverence he always had a very great desire to make war on the infidels' ('elle do uemtre de sua madre trouxe comssigo abraçada a semelhamça da cruz de nosso Senhor Jesu Christo, por cujo amor e rreueremça sempre teue muy gramde deseio de guerrear aos jmfiees' (*CTC*, 45).

3 Purchas, 1905, 10.

4 Fernão Lopes, *CDJI (II)*, 306; *MH*, I, no. 115; *MH*, III no. 162.

5 This information is provided by Henry in his will (*EH*, 159); see also Russell, 1992), 4.

6 *CFCG*, II, 65–6; for an analysis of the horoscope see *CdG*, 269–70. I am much indebted to Dr Kristen Lippincott, Director of the Old Royal Observatory, Greenwich, for her advice and guidance about Prince Henry's *nacimento* though the interpretation given here is, of course, entirely my responsibility. For a thorough examination of the renascent role of astrological prediction in late-medieval Europe see particularly Thorndike, *A History of Magic and Experimental Science*, III and IV (New York, 1953), *passim*. A typical series of fourteenth-century royal horoscopes, including the official 'nativities' of the future Charles V of France and his children, survive, together with other contemporary astrological material, in St John's College, Oxford, MS LXVII (at end). See also Thorndike, III, 1953, p. 589, n. 19. The only Portuguese nativity I have seen is that of Sebastian I (b. 1554), a lengthy document preserved in BNL, COD 8920, ff. 39*v*–41*v*.

7 'But I rate as more important than

8 CdG, 269–70.
9 A reminder contained in a letter to the author from Dr Lippincott dated 5 July 1993.
10 Egidio de Colonna, *Regimiento de príncipes* (Seville: Menardo Ungut and Stanislao Polono, 1494, fol. cix v).
11 Jewish doctors (*físicos*) in the service of the king or of princes and noblemen often doubled as astrologers because astrology also played an important part in contemporary medicine. The much-privileged Mestre Guedelha was the personal doctor and astrologer of Duarte I and Afonso V and also enjoyed the title of chief rabbi (*rabi-mor*) – see Tavares, 1982, 258, n. 9 and *passim*.
12 Duarte I, 492–3 (in *Crónicas de Rui de Pina*, ed. M. Lopes de Almeida, Tesouros da Literatura e da História (Oporto, 1977).
13 See CTC, xviii–xx.
14 For a detailed study of the economic and monetary situation of Portugal in Henry's early years see, *inter alia*, Magalhães Godinho, 1984, I, 109–24.
15 MH, I, no. 133 and p. 314, n. 1. This educator was Fernando Alvares de Almeida who can hardly have served as a model of sexual restraint for his charges to emulate. Despite the vows of celibacy then taken by the knights of Aviz, he contrived to father four illegitimate sons. Another candidate for the post of tutor to the royal princes is the head of Queen Philippa's household, Lopo Dias de Sousa, a distinguished soldier and master of the Order of Christ (Silva de Sousa, 1991), 18.
16 Russell, *Traducciones*, 1984, 60.
17 Armindo de Sousa, 1987, II, 596.
18 MH, VIII, no. 103, p. 107.
19 *Horologium fidei*, 1994, 32–4.

20 Frei João Alvares, 1960, 8.
21 MH, V, no. 101, 201–4.
22 CDJI, (II), caps. cxlviii and cxlix.
23 What these were is described (and remedies for them suggested) in a famous letter written from Bruges late in 1425 or early in 1426 by D. Pedro to his elder brother, Duarte, on the woes of the kingdom (MH, III, no. 71). D. Pedro's report that in England the Portuguese determination to remain in occupation of Ceuta was regarded as an act of folly can hardly have been well received by Henry.
24 Legge, 1941, nos. 28, 287, 297, 397 and British Library, MS Cotton, Vesp. F. III, fol. 47 (the latter transcribed with errors in Figanière, 1853, 121).
25 Leal Conselheiro, 1942, 51
26 MH, VI, no. 46, p. 89 and no. 50, p. 104.
27 CTC, 61.
28 CDJI (I), 308.
29 CTC, 129.
30 Keen, 1984, 252.
31 Vale, 1981, 29–3.
32 See EH, 15–24; MH, I, nos. 134 and 150; Silva da Sousa, 1991, 11–12 and *passim*.
33 EH, 30–2.
34 MH, I, no. 149 and EH, 21–3.

Chapter Two

1 Partly quoted in Huizinga, *The Waning of the Middle Ages* (London, 1937), 64–5.
2 CTC, 9.
3 CTC, 45.
4 Original documents in ACA, *registro* 2406, fol. 127v; Cartas Reales, (Fernando I), *caja* 1, no. 3; *registro* 2408, fol. 5r; Cartas Reales, (Fernando I), caja 6, no. 969. For Fernando I's instructions to his agent dated 3 April and 18 May 1415 see MH, II, nos. 56 and 58. For Ruy Diaz's reports see *ibid.*,

no. 57, pp. 132–46 and no. 71, pp. 166–9.

5 *MH*, II, no. 68. The letter to the archbishop of Santiago in Castile was written on John I's direction by his chief standard-bearer (*alferes mor*). According to it, the fleet had a strength of 270 sail and carried 7000–7500 men-at-arms, 5000 bowmen and some 20,000 footmen. These figures are unacceptably higher than those given by Díaz de Vega in April. It was however in the Portuguese interest at this point to make the Aragonese and Castilians believe the expeditionary force to be very large.

6 Silva de Sousa, 1991, 20 and 124–5.

7 Arundel was married to John I's illegitimate daughter, Beatriz. Zurara states that a rich English citizen, called in his text 'Momdo', took part in the Ceuta expedition with four or five ships and 'many archers' (*CTC*, 154). Díaz de Vega confirms that a 'London' corsair 'Mundy de Arcamua [?Dartmouth]' was to supply four merchant ships, but added that Henry V had forbidden any English soldiers to go to Portugal (*MH*, II, no. 57, 141). Esteves Pereira found evidence of 'Mundy's' existence in ANTT, *Chancelaria de D. João I*, livro V, fol. 24*v*.

8 Antoine de La Salle, 1903, especially 142–7.

9 Díaz de Vega at this stage believed an alliance with Catherine of Lancaster against Fernando was the most likely explanation of the Portuguese preparations (*MH*, II, 142–3). The rumour he had heard about an invasion of Morocco involved the entirely implausible story that the Marinid king, Abu Sa'id 'Utman, wished to become a Christian and to join John I in a crusade against his Muslim neighbours!

10 Díaz de Vega wrote to Fernando from Sacavém on 28 July 'My lord,

it is reliably believed that this expedition is against Gibraltar or Ceuta' (*MH*, II, no. 71, 167).

11 *MH*, II, no. 68.

12 The actual bulls of crusade presumably issued by the antipope John XIII have not been traced.

13 *CTC*, 51–9.

14 For the gold trade with trans-Saharan Africa in the later Middle Ages see Bovill, *The Golden Trade of the Moors*, 2nd edn (London: Oxford University Press, 1968). For the economic role of Ceuta in Mediterranean trade in general at the time of the Portuguese conquest see *inter alia*, R. S. Lopez, 'I Genovesi in Africa Occidentale', *Studi sull' economia genovese nel Mediterraneo* (Turin, 1938); J. Heers, 'Le royaume de Grenade et la politique marchande de Gènes en Occident', *Le Moyen Age* 63 (1957), 87–121; *idem*, Gènes au xv siècle. Activité économique et problèmes sociaux, EPHE – VIe section (Paris: SEVPEN, 1961); Vitorino Magalhães-Godinho, *Historia económica e social da expansão portuguesa* (Lisbon, 1947); *idem*, *A economia dos descobrimentos henriquinos* (Lisbon, 1962); *idem*, *Os descobrimentos e a economia mundial*, 2nd edn, 4 vols (Lisbon: Editorial Presença, 1984); M. Arribas Palau, 'Repercusión de la conquista portuguesa de Ceuta en Aragón', *Tamuda*, 3 (1955), 9–21 and 307–22, all give useful accounts of Ceuta at the time of the Portuguese conquest and of the effect of the conquest on European trade in the Maghrib. Still important, though much of its material has been reprinted in other collections of documents, is Pedro Augusto de Azevedo (ed.), *Documentos das chancelarias reais anteriores a 1531 relativos a Marrocos* (Coimbra, 1915–34).

15 *CTC*, 94.

16 Heers, 1961, 68–71.

17 The Moorish mob's sobriquet for

the Christian knights and others in the service of their rulers was *tarjan* (Sp. *farjan* or, more commonly, *farfan*) from the plural of *taraj*, meaning 'low or vile persons'. The term was, however, soon accepted by the Christians serving in the royal bodyguard as an honorific. See Alemany, 1904, 133–69. For the important and now largely forgotten role the Farfanes were to play in the early European expansion in the African Atlantic, see the later chapters of this book. For a study of the political, economic and military activities of the Crown of Aragon in the Maghrib in the two centuries before the Portuguese intervention there, see C.-E. Dufourcq, Paris, 1966.

18 On 10 May 1413 the antipope John XXIII had nominated Aimary de Aurillac, an English Franciscan who is alleged to have come to Portugal with Queen Philippa, as bishop of Morocco in succession to another Franciscan, Fray Diego de Jérez (*MH*, II, no. 15).

19 *CTC*, 73.

20 *MH*, VI, no. 24, p. 49.

21 *CTC*, 258; Alvares, 1969, 18–19, refers to the plans of the Infante D. Fernando to go to England to win military honour and to secure a decent standard of living. The same aims made the count of Arraiolos decide to go to Castile and the count of Ourém to go to seek his fortune anywhere outside the kingdom. The journeys of D. Pedro, Henry's elder brother, to seek knightly honour and material rewards abroad from 1425 to 1428 are well-known.

22 'pera o bom exercício das armas ser praticado por cuja mingoa muytas gentes e regnos se perderom, e tyrarmos nosa gente de vida oçiosa, fora de virtudes' (*MH*, VI, no. 48, p. 94).

23 Zurara's explanation of events was first challenged by António Sérgio as long ago as 1919. Sérgio attrib- uted the attack on Ceuta to the chronic shortage of cereals, especially wheat, in Portugal. He claimed that the real driving force behind the expedition, voiced, he believed, by the royal treasurer, must have been the merchant class's desire to secure access to the wheat fields of Morocco (*Ensaios*, I, 2nd edn, (Coimbra, 1949, 307–29)).

24 *CTC*, 33, 61.

25 See, for example, Magalhães Godinho, 1962, 109. The same scholar writes 'we owe to the excellent essay of António Sérgio 'A conquista de Ceuta' [first published in *Ensaios*, I (Rio de Janeiro, 1920)] irrefutable proof (*sic*) that the Ceuta enterprise was solely the result of an initiative taken by João Afonso [de Alenquer] supported by the king in the name of the economic and financial interests of the cities' (*ibid.*).

26 *CTC*, 154.

27 *CTC*, 30–7.

28 Jorge Faro, *Receitas e despesas da fazenda real de 1384 a 1481: subsídios documentais*, (Lisbon: Publicações do Centro de Estudos Económicos, 1965), 66. In English coinage of the period, the amount concerned represented 15,126 gold nobles – or 7,563 marks.

29 This was done by the device of introducing a new supposedly silver coinage, the *real branco* or 'white' real, which, in fact, contained a great deal of base metal – hence its name. An artificial value of 35 *reais* to the *libra* (well above its actual silver value) was then assigned to the new coin. The debts contracted by the crown in connection with the expedition were to be repaid at their original nominal value in *libras* but that value was now to be calculated at the official rate in the new, depreciated currency (Magalhães Godinho, 1981, I, 118).

30 *CTC*, 267–8.

31 *CTC*, 129.

32 *CTC*, 157.

33 D. Duarte, *Leal Conselheiro*, ed. Joseph M. Piel, cap. XIV.

34 It is extremely difficult to establish the exact course of events from Zurara's lengthy but confused narrative, written without the first-hand knowledge of the topography of the Moroccan port the chronicler later acquired.

35 'combatent la ciutat ab gran multitud de bombardas e altras artelleries, djns spay de xiij hores ha[n] presa la ciutat' ('after attacking the city with a great number of bombards and other artillery, the place was captured in the space of thirteen hours') *MH*, II, no. 105, p. 222. The news had reached Valencia from Seville, confirming earlier information received there via Granada. The *battle general*'s letter spoke in enthusiastic terms of the Christian victory over the infidel; his satisfaction was not, as we shall see, shared by the Aragonese king.

36 La Salle, 145 and 147. La Salle's account helps to explain various passages in Zurara's confused account of the action. He recalls Henry's physique as large and powerful and, like many other contemporaries, remarked on his chastity. This may be evidence that the Prince's reputation in this latter respect was already a subject of public comment in 1415, when he was only twenty-one.

37 See, for example, Thomas Walsingham, I , 1864, 314. The capture of the city is also alluded to in the Venetian chronicle of Antonio Morosini and the *Rufus-Chronicle* of Lübeck (Wylie, 1914 , I, 450–1).

38 'a qual perda era mujto chorada dalgu[n]s daquelles de uill geeraçam, ca os boõs e nobres nom puynham seu cuydado em semelhamtes cousas' (*CTC*, 235).

39 For the attempts of the Genoese to ingratiate themselves with the victors see also *CNAP*, 202.

40 Arribas Palau, 1955, 12–13.

41 *CTC*, 262–3. Zurara claims that Martim Afonso was badly advised by two squires who showed no concern either for his soldierly reputation or for the greatness of the honour the king had offered him. This unlikely explanation plainly represents a retrospective attempt to excuse Martim Afonso's refusal.

42 *CTC*, p. 267; *MH*, II, no. 115. Pedro de Meneses remained as governor and captain of Ceuta until his death there in 1437.

43 *MH*, II, no. 114, p. 238.

44 *MH*, II, no., 108, pp. 227–9.

45 *MH*, II, no. 119, p. 244.

46 *MH*, II, nos. 110 and 111.

47 *CNAP*, 204.

48 *CTC*, 267; *MH*, II, no., 115.

Chapter Three

1 *MH*, II, no. 116.

2 For a modern account of the career of the first governor see António Joaquim Dias Dinis, 'D, Pedro de Meneses, primeiro conde de Vila Real e primeiro capitão e governador de Ceuta', (1974, 517–62).

3 *CFCG*, II, 50.

4 *CDPM* in *Colecção de inéditos de história portuguesa*, II, 1702.

5 *EH*, 306–7.

6 A document of 1473 based on earlier accounts from the time of John I assessed the cost of the capture of Ceuta at 280,000 gold *dobras*. The cost of Prince Henry's relief force in 1418/19 is given as 85,000 *dobras*. The same document offers the instructive information that, by comparison, the cost to the royal treasury of the marriage in 1430 of John's daughter Isabel to the Duke of Burgundy was no less than 250,000 *dobras* (Faro, 1956, *passim*).

7 *MH*, V, no. 147, p. 353. According to the exchange rates fixed by the crown in 1416, a Florentine florin

or a ducat was worth 400 Portuguese *libras*, the *dobla cruzada* 470 and the English gold *noble* 870 (*DCRM*, I, Adenda. no. X, p. 452),

8 *MH*, VI, no. 10, p. 19.
9 *MH*, VII, no. 12.
10 Though accounts involving the royal treasury were kept annually by those responsible for recording receipts and expenditure, it was the custom in Portugal to present them to the king for quittance in groups so that the accounts for a number of past years were discharged together. It was clearly not a system that guaranteed exact accounting. Many quittances relating to Ceutan affairs were published in full in Pedro de Azevedo's invaluable *DCRM*. Material from that source is often reprinted or calendared in *DP* and, less extensively, in *MH*.
11 *MH*, no. 80.
12 'tesoureiro das cousas da nossa cidade de Ceuta' (*DP*, I (S), no. 731).
13 *MH*, IV, no. 121.
14 See *MH*, VI, no. 100. This document contains a detailed account of the duties and powers of the treasurer.
15 The Casa da Guiné was joined in the 1470s by the Casa da Mina, which was mainly concerned with the gold trade after the discovery then of the Mina [Gold] Coast. After the end of the century the royal monopoly of commerce with Asia was managed through the Casa da India.
16 cf. *DP*, I (S), no. 951.
17 *DP*, I (S), no. 1191.
18 *MH*, II, no. 142, p. 280.
19 *CDPM*, I, cap. 80; *DP*, I (S), no. 700.
20 *CDPM*, I, 310 and *passim*.
21 *MH*, II, no. 152.
22 cf. *MH* IV, no. 1.
23 *MH*, II, no. 192.
24 *MH*, VIII, no. 125, p. 198.
25 *MH*, XII, no. 116.
26 *MH*, III, no. 71, p. 148.
27 *MH*, IV, no. 24, p. 125.

28 Pero Tafur, 1874, 7–8.
29 *Historia desponsationis Frederici III cum Eleonora Lusitanica* in RGSV, II, (Strassburg, 1717), 55–80; text reproduced in Caetano da Sousa, *HCRP*, (2nd. ed.), *Provas*, I (III), 349–51. Thankfully there is now a modern edition and translation of the above – Nicolau Lanckman de Valckenstein... *Diário de viagem do embaixador Nicolau Lanckman de Valckenstein*, ed. and trans. by Aires A. Nascimento (Lisbon: Edições Cosmos 1992), 56–61.
30 Hieronymus Münzer, *Itinerarium Hispanicum*, ed. Ludwig Pfandl, *Rhisp.* XLVIII (1920).
31 *MH*, XII, no. 52.
32 *DP*, I (S), no. 342.
33 João de Barros, 1988, 12–13.
34 Zurara, *CDPM*, I, cap. 81 quoted in *MH*, II, no. 171, pp. 351–2.
35 *MH*, II, no. 171, pp. 350–1.
36 See *DP*, I (S), no. 101, p. 128 – document of 1438. For an account of the activities of Portuguese corsairs in the Mediterranean during the fifteenth century see Luis Adão da Fonseca, 1978, *passim*.
37 *MH*, XV (*Suplemento*), nos. 18 and 19.
38 *MH*, X, no. 182.
39 In 1453 the treasurer of the Casa de Ceuta authorized supplies of wheat, barley and other cereals to be loaded on four caravels described as sailing to Guinea 'on our [the king's] service' (*MH*, XII, no. 130, pp. 264–7). Pacheco issued similar authorizations in 1454. This evidence has been taken to mean that, by the mid-1450s, Afonso V himself was engaged in sending numbers of caravels to Guinea despite Henry's monopoly. While this is possible, the phrase 'on the king's service' may have been used in the quittance, with the acquiescence of the king, to cover Henry's use of supplies destined for Ceuta to provision some of his own caravels about to sail for Guinea

from Lisbon. During his lifetime most sailings for Guinea started from Lagos.

40 'for the cost of the people whom the said count had with him in Ceuta during the said year [1450] (*MH*, XI, no. 17, p. 26).

41 *MH*, XI, no. 17, n. 1. For Afonso V's confirmation of the agreement see no. 23. For a more detailed discussion of this matter see *EH*, 313–15.

42 *MH*, II, nos. 179–183.

43 *MH*, II, nos. 179 and 180.

44 At the request of John I, Duarte I and Afonso V, the Curia several times issued bulls directing the Orders of Christ, Santiago and Aviz to build and maintain convents in Ceuta and later in Alcácer-Ceguer. In 1464, however, Paul II revoked the earlier bulls and recognized that these institutions had no statutory obligation to operate outside metropolitan Portugal (*MH*, XIV, no. 133).

45 *Ibid.*, 312–13.

46 For a full account of the background to John I's reform of the military orders and of the history of the Order of Christ under Henry's governance see Silva de Costa, 1991, chap. 5 and *passim*.

47 Henry's public commitment to celibacy must have taken place after 1419 since in that year his father obtained from the pope a number of dispensations that presumed the prince's marriagability (*MH*, II, nos. 156 and 172).

48 *MH*, VIII, no. 1.

Chapter Four

1 *CFCG*, II, 50. Zurara's five islands consist, as he makes plain in chapter 83 of *CFCG*, of Madeira, Porto Santo and Deserta and two in the Azores group, Santa Maria and São Miguel. The chronicler has already described the benefits the produce of the Atlantic islands has brought to Portugal in more hyperbolical terms in *ibid.*, 37.

2 For an account of these legendary Atlantic islands see Albuquerque, 1989, cap. 3.

3 Rubió i Lluch, 1908, I, 25. For this prince's keen interest in maps, charts, astrolabes, compasses, astronomical tables, sextants etc. see *ibid.* I and II, *passim*. For Martin I of Aragon's desire to secure an up-to-date *mappa mundi* in 1399 see *ibid.*, I, 410.

4 Barros, 1988, 47.

5 *CDFG*, II, 49.

6 Contemporary documents about the Madeiran archipelago always define this as consisting of the islands of Madeira, Porto Santo and Deserta. The latter reference is to the modern Deserta Grande – a narrow island some nine miles long and rising to a height of 1,600' lying about twelve miles south-east of Madeira. According to the sixteenth-century island historian Gaspar Frutuoso, Deserta Grande was used for cattle-raising and had a permanent population consisting of a few shepherds, a factor and a priest. It was administered from Funchal. In the fifteenth century Deserta Grande also provided the Prince and his heirs with a good deal of orchil. A ruined chapel on the island dates, it is said, from Henry's time.

7 Luís de Albuquerque, 1989, 159–63.

8 The complete text of John I's charter (*foro*) granted to the settlers has not survived. The text of the 1433 donation will be found in *MH*, IV, no. 81.

9 For a summary of the contents of the best known of these legends, which attributes the discovery of Madeira to a lovelorn Englishman called 'Machim' and his lady who were blown there by contrary winds while sailing from England to France (!) see, *inter alia*, *HDP*, 48–52 and the article 'Lenda de

Machin' in *DHP*, IV, 119–20. This tale in its variant forms has all the characteristics of a 'sentimental romance' – a type of prose fiction popular in Spain and Portugal in the fifteenth century.

10 *MH*, IV, nos. 81 and 82.

11 '... como rrey e senhor da dita ilha e de todo o que nella ha ... lhes faso a dita merçe pera sempre, como de cousa minha propia ... (*MH*, III, no. 72, p. 151).

12 Cadamosto, 1966, 16.

13 Cadamosto puts the amount at 400 'kantari'. The *cantaro* of Genoa weighed 47.65 kg. Magalhães Godinho (*DEEM*, IV, 74–5) calculates Cadamosto's figures to be the equivalent of 1600 *arrobas* (@ 1 *arroba* = 11 kg.).

14 The heyday of sugar exports from Madeira occurred after Henry's time. By 1470 annual production had reached 20,000 *arrobas*.

15 Cadamosto, 1966, 16–17.

16 *CDFG*, II, 37.

17 Gaspar Frutuoso, 1873, 462–71.

18 For an authoritative account of the *sesmaria* system in Portugal see Virgínia Rau, 1982, *passim*.

19 *MH*, III, no. 72, p. 151.

20 *MH*, IV, no. 81.

21 *Ibid.*, no. 81 p. 268, n. 1.

22 *Ibid.*, no. 82.

23 *Ibid.*, no. 138, pp. 354–5.

24 *Ibid* no. 81, n. 2.

25 *MH*, VII, no. 72. 'The two sub-donatories, in documents issued by them, use the phrase 'ruler on behalf of the said lord 'Henry' ('*regedor por ho dicto senhor*') to describe their administrative functions – e.g. *DP*, I, no. 397.

26 *Ibid.*, no. 72, p. 99.

27 Tristâo Vaz, according to Gaspar Frutuoso, died in 1470 aged 79, by which time he had four sons and eight daughters.

28 *MH*,' IX, no. 143.

29 *DP*, I, no. 356.

30 The fee was at the rate of one silver mark annually payable to any one mill, or two standard-sized planks

per week (*DP*, I, no. 353, p. 450 and no. 385, p. 484).

31 *CFCG*, II, 471.

32 See *DP* (*S*), nos. 118, 923, 1072.

33 See Virgínia Rau & Jorge de Macedo, 1962, *passim*: Lúcio de Azevedo, 1973, especially 218–228; Magalhães Godinho, 1987 & n.d., III, 234–5, IV, 73–89 & 171–174.

34 Cadamosto, 1961, 14–18.

35 Cadamosto, 1961, 11–12.

36 As an example of Henry's willingness to allow foreigners to settle on Madeira as cultivators, one may cite his donations of land near Funchal in 1457 to two different German farmers alluded to in a document of 1457 (MH, XIII, no. 56). The document is also of interest because it details the island products which were reserved for the Prince's use – yew logs, furs, *cannas* and any dyestuffs or gums.

37 A summary account of the various theories will be found in *HDP*, 61–77 and *DHP*, I, 18–19.

38 The author of the *Libro del Conoscimiento* names as visited by him, apart from islands in the Canaries and Madeiran group, the following Atlantic islands: Isla del Lobo, Isla de las Cabras, Isla del Brasil, La Colunbaria, Isla de la Ventura, Isla de San Jorge, Isla de los Conejos and Isla de los Cuervos Marines (*LdC*, 50). They can all be found on fourteenth-century charts. Only two of these names were transferred to the actual islands of the Azorean group when they were discovered or rediscovered – São Jorge and Cuervo (Corvo).

39 The name of the Portuguese pilot is difficult to decipher, but he was probably called Diogo de Silves (see *HDP*, 78–87 and plates XIII and XIV).

40 *Ibid.*, plate XV. For Bianco's depiction of the Atlantic islands in his 1448 chart see also *ibid.*, plate XVI.

41 'Secundus modus est quando insule [non] nascuntur de novo sed

reperiuntur vacue sine habitatore ut insula Brasilii que dicitur esse in linea occidentali contra Ulixbonam et non est habitata et raro possunt eam reperire navigantes, (*DP*, I, no. 281, p. 317 – with minor orthographical changes).

42 *MH*, VI, no. 151.

43 From Port. *açor*, 'goshawk'. The birds the Portuguese explorers so identified were probably buzzards (*buteo vulgaris*). The error was probably a conscious one; by a process familiar to students of discoverers' language, it was normal, when a new species of fauna or flora was found, to name it at first by using the nearest term in their own language that the discoverers could hit upon.

44 *MH*, IX, no. 155, p. 225. The tax exemptions are described in the grant as made to D. Pedro 'so as to give him a better opportunity to ensure that his island of São Miguel gets properly settled' ('por teer azo de ell poder milhor encaminhar como a sua jlha de Sam Miguell seia bem pouorada').

45 *MH*, XI, nos. 180 and 242. See also *DP*, I, no. 413. According to an allegation made in the latter document, D. Pedro had *c.* 1444 ordered a girl of ten, accused of murder, to be transported to São Miguel.

46 The House of Bragança originated in 1401 when John I's bastard son Afonso, count of Barcelos, married Brites Pereira, only daughter of the 'Holy Constable', Nun'Alvares Pereira, and received as dowry some of the very large landed possessions of his father-in-law. The territorial aggrandizement of the House of Bragança continued apace thereafter. In 1442 D. Afonso was granted the title of Duke of Bragança despite which he soon became an implacable enemy of his brother, the Regent D. Pedro. He died in 1461.

47 *MH*, XI, no. 170. According to a fairly well-founded tradition, both Corvo and Flores, the westernmost islands of the Azores group, were discovered *c.* 1452 by Diogo de Teive, a sugar-miller and navigator from Madeira, and his son (see *HDP*, 87–92).

48 *MH*, X, no. 134. Jacques de Bruges is described in the donation as 'servidor' of Prince Henry. He is said to have married in Orense, in Galicia.

49 The document attributes to Prince Henry a provision that, if Jacques had no male descendants, the *capitania* of Terceira could pass to his female descendants. Henry obviously had no reason to connive quite unnecessarily in such a flagrant breach of Portuguese laws on inheritance.

50 For documents referring to Jacques of Bruges's *capitania* on Terceira see *DP*, III, nos. 105 and 110. There is a connection between Jacques of Bruges and England. Philippa of Lancaster's English treasurer in Portugal, Thomas Payn, had a son, Edward, who was born there. Edward Payn became a *comendador* of the Portuguese military Order of Santiago and married Jacques's eldest daughter, Antónia. Edward Payn's desire to succeed his father-in-law as *capitão* of Terceira may well have led to the recasting in forged form of the original Henrican donation to Jacques. His attempt to secure the *capitania* failed because he claimed he was unable to produce this original document.

51 Information given in some of the legends on Behaim's globe (*c.* 1491) and quoted in Gama Barros, V, 327–9. Behaim refers to some of the islands as 'Neu Flandern'.

52 *MH*, XIII, no. 172.

53 The document (see above), after referring to attempts to usurp Henry's jurisdiction in Santa Maria and São Miguel, names two individuals whom he orders Gonçalo Velho to arrest if they should arrive

on the islands 'without showing you any licence from me' (278).

54 *MH*, XIII, no. 187, p. 336. This was not D. Fernando's first declaration of interest in the Atlantic islands. In 1457 he had secured from the Crown an irrevocable donation of any islands he might discover (*DP*, I, no. 425).

55 *DP*, I, no. 194. Henry reserved the rights of the Order of Christ to the 'spirituality' of these and all the other islands together with the customary *vintena* due to it in respect of this ecclesiastical jurisdiction. The lost donation to which the document refers was evidently the one by virtue of which Frei Gonçalo Velho had long, at least nominally, governed the islands as captain and *comendador*. The reference to Corvo as among Henry's islands appears to ignore the royal donation of the island to the duke of Bragança in 1452.

56 *MH*, XIV, no. 31, p. 104.

57 *MH*, XIV. no. 86, p. 226. The islands supposedly discovered by Antonio da Noli were Santiago, Maia, Boavista and Sal.

Chapter Five

1 *Africa Pilot*, 1953, I, 206.

2 *CFCG*, II, 72–3.

3 *CFCG*, II, 113–14.

4 The squire concerned, Gil Eanes, is reported to have been rewarded with a knighthood and a rich marriage arranged for him in Lagos by Henry (Pacheco Pereira, 1975, 71).

5 'Et mes[me]ment se partit la saison avant que nous venissons par dessa un bateau avecques XV compaignons dedans d'une de noz isles nommée Erbane et s'en alerent au cap de Bugeder qui scient ou royaume de la Guynoye, à XII lieuez prés de nous' (*Le Canarien*, III, 1965, 105). The French chronicle on other occasions makes it clear that 'cap de Bugeder' is on

the mainland directly opposite the nearest of the Canaries. The Portuguese form of the toponym (connected with *bojar*, 'to stand out') is a popular derivation from the variant forms ('Buyeder', 'Bugeder' etc.) that appear on pre-Henrican portulan charts and world maps. The suggested Arabic origin of the toponym – *bu-zdur*, 'place of tree trunks' – sounds plausible (see Mauny, 1960), 4, n. 10, and 4–7. On modern maps of the former Spanish Sahara, the name of the cape is given as 'Ras Bu-Yeidour'.

6 *CFCG*, II, 440–1.

7 João Fernandes is one of the undersung heroes of the Henrican period of the Portuguese discoveries. For his lone reconnaissance of the Atlantic Sahara starting from the Río de Oro see text and notes in *CdG*, 129–30, 216–19, 252–3, 256 and Chapter 9 of the present work.

8 From the mid-1450s, Henry, instead of continuing simply to describe Cape Bojador in documents as the point where the discoveries associated with his name had begun, now always asserted that they had started at 'Cape Bojador and Cape Noun'. Since Cape Noun is located on the southern border of the Moroccan sultanate some 270 miles to the north of the real Cape Bojador, the order in which the two toponyms appear is, from a cartographer's point of view, illogical. It reflects, however, the sequence in which the Prince acquired his Guinea monopoly.

9 *MH*, VIII, no. 62.

10 *Libro del Conosçimiento de todos los reynos e tierras e señoríos que son por el mundo . . .*, ed. Marcos Jiménez de la Espada (Madrid: T. Fortanet, 1877; repr. Barcelona: El Albir, 1980). No surviving fourteenth-century world map depicts the coast of West Africa as far to the south of Cape Bojador as

the one used by the author of the *LdC* evidently did. This same material appears however in the Catalan chart of Mecià de Viladestes (1413) and other Catalan maps of the early fifteenth century.

11 Henry, like the rest of Philippa's children, may have been able to read his mother's native language, Anglo-Norman French. Given that Jean de Béthencourt soon became a subject of the Castilian crown and that the Canaries passed under the suzerainty of Castile, it is very likely that a now untraced version or compendium of *Le Canarien* in Castilian existed in Henry's time.

12 *Canarien*, III, 105.

13 There are two versions of *Le Canarien*, one, already mentioned, which was prepared by the French chaplains of Gadifer de La Salle under his direction *c.* 1402 (vol. III) and a much later recension worked on by partisans of Jean de Béthencourt. This includes an account of what is said to have happened after Gadifer's departure in disgust from the archipelago. I have usually used the much more reliable Gadifer version when events fall within its purview.

14 *LdC*, 49, 51 etc.

15 *MH*, XIII, no. 62, p. 107. See also *CFCG*, II, 439–43 and 452 for Zurara's important observations about Henry's contributions to the history of cartography. *MH*, XIII, no. 62, p. 107.

16 *CFCG*, II, 63–4.

17 *Canarien*, III, 15.

18 *Ibid.*, III, 99.

19 For a well-informed general account of the way alluvial gold was mined in Guinea and of the West African gold trade at the end of the Middle Ages see Bovill, 1968. Given the dominant role of Genoa in the African gold trade with Europe through its agents in North Africa and in the Iberian Peninsula, essential reading is Jacques Heers's famous study,

Gênes au xve siècle..., 1961. Required reading in Portuguese on these matters is the classical study of Vitorino Magalhães Godinho in *DEM*, I, chapter 1 and the same author's entry under 'Ouro' in *DHP*, IV. The origins of the toponym 'Guinea' are controversial. Bovill suggests plausibly that it has nothing to do with the place names 'Ghana' or 'Jenne' but derives from Berber *aguinaou*, 'negro' (Bovill, 1968, 116, n.). In the fifteenth century the Portuguese give the term 'Guinea' two different senses. Sometimes it refers to the whole western coast of Africa from the southern border of Morocco as far south as that coast might eventually be found to run. After the explorers had reached the estuary of the River Senegal and the start of Black Africa it is more often used simply as a synonym for the latter. The Roman curia often used the classical 'Aethiopia' to refer *any* part of Africa inhabited by black people, a usage sometimes followed by Portuguese writers such as Pacheco Pereira.

20 The exploit of Ferrer is first known from a legend inscribed on Abraham Cresques's world map of 1375. It accompanies an illumination of his *uxer* – a single-masted craft with square sail, low prow, rounded stern and clearly visible rowers' benches. The *uxer* was designed as a kind of cargo-carrying galley, used particularly for the transport of horses. A large door in the stern was used for loading these (see Dufourcq, 1966), 40. Ferrer was not the first European to attempt this voyage in the Middle Ages. In 1291 the brothers Vivaldi had set out from Genoa in two galleys to find the sea-route to 'India'. Unsurprisingly, nothing further was heard from them but stories about their survival or that of their descendants in the jungles

21 of Guinea still circulated in Genoa in the Prince's time.

21 This part of the panel reproduced as a frontispiece in Bovill, 1968.

22 Reproduced in *MCAA*, IV, 1368–9; an accompanying legend describes it as the 'Angelic River of the black Christians' – an evident allusion to the River Gion which, according to the Prester John legends, was one of the rivers flowing from the Earthly Paradise through the Prester's kingdom.

23 *Esmeraldo*, 1975, 98. Jaffuda Cresques, son of the creator of the famous world map of 1375, was already old enough in 1381 to be appointed maker of *mappae mundi* to the heir to the Aragonese throne. As a result of the anti-Jewish pogroms of the 1390s Jaffuda turned Christian and it is as 'Jacme Ribes' that he makes his final documented appearance in Catalan records in Barcelona in 1409. The fact that Jaffuda was already important enough to be appointed as a master map-maker at the Aragonese court in 1381 (thirteen years before Prince Henry's birth) and that he was still in Barcelona in 1409 makes it somewhat unlikely that he was the cartographer called to Portugal in the 1420s or 1430s. For the documentation relating to Abraham and Jaffuda Cresques see mainly A. Rubió i Lluch, *Documents*, I, 241, 245, 295 and 345–6; II, 245, 253, 255. According to J. M. Millás Vallicrosa (Barcelona, 1960, 302–3), at the end of the fourteenth century and early in the fifteenth century the Datini of Prato sought to obtain from 'Jacme Ribes' and other Majorcan cartographers, secretly if necessary, world maps for the kings of Navarre and England.

24 *CFCG*, II, 104. As we have noted, Prester John is referred to in *Le Canarien*. Its authors seem to have taken their information about him

from the account by the author of the *LdC* of his supposed Atlantic journey to the frontiers of the Prester's empire.

25 The Latin text of this most important document reads 'credens [jnfans Henricus] se maximum in hoc Deo prestare obsequium, si eius opera et industria mare ipsium usque ad jndos, qui Christi nomen colere dicuntur, nauigabile fieret sicque cum eis participare et illos in christianorum auxilium, aduersus sarracenos et alios huiusmodi fidei hostes, commuere posset . . .' (*MH*, XII, no. 36, pp. 73–4).

26 Cadamosto, 1937, 90.

27 *MCAE*, IV, fasc. ii, 1223.

28 *Mappamondo di Fra Mauro Camoldolese*, a cura di Tullia Leporace (Rome: Istituto Poligrafico dello Stato, 1956), tavola X, [p. 26].

29 *Ibid.*, tavola XVIII, [p. 32]. Fra Mauro reported that he had often been told that on the southern entrance to the Sinus Aethiopicus, was a column supporting a hand which pointed to a sign reading 'from this point go no further'. He commented that he was not able to confirm the truth of the report.

30 *LdC*, 63.

31 *LdC*, 63.

32 *MH*, XII, no. 99, p. 192.

33 ACA, *Cancillería Real, reg.* 2,680, fol. 165 (as quoted in *MH*, III, no. 100, p. 208. See also *ibid.*, nos. 99 and 10).

34 De Witte, XLIX (1954), 450 *et seq.* The Prester's ambassadors to the Council of Florence in fact came from the Ethiopian Coptic community in Jerusalem. For Eugenius IV's contacts in the 1430s with Prester John see De Witte, 1, *passim* and La Roncière, II, 116–7.

35 *MH*, XII, no. 154, p. 321. For a possible identification of this envoy see also *ibid.*, XI, no. 3, p. 3, n. l.

36 For accounts of such journeys see

particularly Chapters I and II of *Ethiopian Itineraries...*, 1958.

37 *MH*, VIII, no. 62, p. 107. The 1443 privilege was renewed by Afonso V in September 1448 after he had taken over the government. It followed the earlier document for the most part to the letter except that the 'fifteen' voyages of 1443 were now described as 'many voyages' (*MH*, IX, no. 193).

38 Vessels sent by Henry specifically to attempt to round the cape did not, of course, when they failed, simply return profitless to Portugal. Their commanders were expected to do what they could to make good the costs of the expedition. This they did by attacking Moorish shipping, by going on slave razzias in the Canaries or by making lightning raids on the coasts of Islamic-held territory.

39 Cadamosto, 1966, 6–7.

40 *CFCG*, II, 75.

41 For an examination of the complicated system set up by the Portuguese to secure information from speakers of unknown West African languages, and of the trainng and use of native interpreters see, among others, P. E. Russell, 'Some sociolinguistic problems concerning the fifteenth-century Portuguese discoveries in the African Atlantic', reprinted in the same author's *Portugal, Spain and the African Atlantic, 1343–1490*, 1995), article XIV.

42 *CFCG*, II, 79.

43 *MH*, VI, no. 14.

44 It was, though, not unusual in the Middle Ages for squires to show their mettle by participating in naval warfare. The Castilian *Crónica de Don Pedro Niño* makes much of the prowess of the young Castilian squires who took part in the naval actions Pedro Niño's galleys fought at the beginning of the fifteenth century against the English and the Moors (Díez de Games, 1940, *passim*).

Chapter Six

1 Quoted in Wills, 1964, 414–15.

2 *MH*, VI, no. 27, p. 57. Essential reading for the Tangier expedition is Domingos Mauricio Gomes dos Santos, *D. Duarte e as responsabilidades de Tânger (1433–1438)*, 1960, a work which, for the first time, made extensive use of the documents contained in Biblioteca Mediceo-Laurenziana, *Fondo Asburnham*, MS 1792, vols I–II). These consist primarily of a very large collection of private letters addressed to the abbot D. Gomes in Florence, many of them from Portuguese royal personages and written in the 1430s. Most of those relevant to this and the next chapter have been printed in Gomes dos Santos, 1960 and in *MH*, V and VI. D. Gomes Ferreira, much of whose life was spent in Italy and who was Duarte I's chief representative at the council of Basel, and was one of the most influential Portuguese ecclesiastics of the fifteenth century. A further collection of letters to D. Gomes, mostly from Portuguese ecclesiastics (with some copies of his replies) exists in the Biblioteca Nazionale, Florence, MSS *Badia*, 4 and 29 (formerly 28) – not seen. See also Gomes dos Santos, 1960, p. 13, n. 1. When making use of these documents in this and the ensuing chapter, I have normally followed the transcriptions printed in *Monumenta Henricina*, some of which have been checked against the original manuscripts by me for additional codicological information.

3 For the texts of the various *pareceres* see *MH*, IV, nos. 21, 23, 24 and 26.

4 *MH*, IV, no. 23, p. 114.

5 *Ibid.*, p. 117.

6 The Barcelos *parecer* confirms that, in late April or early May 1432, Duarte had, as deputy for his

father, called a meeting of the royal council to discuss Henry's offer to take an army to Morocco (*MH* IV, no. 24, p. 124).

7 *MH*, IV, no. 21, p. 106: '... se se faz por fama, non a uejo aquy tal que aprouete. Porque cousa começada por uangloria, que he pecado mortal, forçado he que a fym seja semelhante a seu começo.'

8 *MH*, IV, no. 26.

9 The general concern of thc counsellors about Henry's competence as a commander of an army was not solely based on awareness of his rash performances at Ceuta in 1415 and 1419. Everyone knew that the ill-fated military expedition against the pagan-held islands in the Canaries in 1425 had been planned and organized by him.

10 *MH*, IV, no. 26, p. 132.

11 Leonor's mischievous attempts to embroil her adopted country in military interventions in Castile on her brothers' behalf took up a great deal of the Portuguese court's time in the early 1430s. Her evident willingness to put family interests before those of her adopted country was one of the reasons why, after D. Duarte's premature death, she seemed to many Portuguese an unacceptable choice as regent.

12 *MH*, IV, no. 21, p. 102.

13 *Ibid.*, p. 102, n. 6.

14 According to the *Crónica de D. Juan II* (BAE, vol. LXVIII: 1431, cap. xxvi), John II's envoy to Portugal in 1431, charged with reconfirming the peace treaty between the two countries, found that military preparations to support the Infantes de Aragón were openly going on there. He protested to the Portuguese king, who duplicitously promised to put a stop to them (*ibid.*, 501).

15 See D. Duarte, 1982, 57–8.

16 In January 1434 a plot by the Infantes de Aragón to seize Seville was uncovered. The Castilian chronicler Carrillo de Huete asserts

that a leading role in the conspiracy was played by a Portuguese Franciscan friar. A. J. Dias Dinis suggested that this friar may have been in Henry's service, the latter wishing to neutralize the militant and successful resistance of the Seville merchants to his plans to seize the Canary Islands (*MH*, IV, p. 347, n. 1). If the Prince was in fact involved at all, one must suspect, in the light of the Arraiolos *parecer*, that it may have been because he had more ambitious plans for himself in Castile itself at this time.

17 *CDD*, 1977, 494–5.

18 The inventory of Duarte's library has recently been republished in the *Livro dos conselhos de el-rei D. Duarte I*, 1982, 206–8.

19 *MH*, V, no. 26.

20 Álvares, 1960, 19–20.

21 Bull dated 9 September 1434 (*MH*, V, no. 30).

22 The evidence is contained in a personal letter in the Ashburnham collection. The document was originally addressed by Leonor to the bishop of Lérida who sent it on to D. Gomes in Florence so that he could make known to the curia the queen's views about the Tangier project (BMLF, *Fondo Ashburnham*, no. 1792, vol. 2, fol. 83 – transcribed in *MH* VI, no. 11).

23 *MH*, IV, no. 134.

24 The fullest study of the debate between 'papalists' and 'antipapalists' at this time remains the classic one of Michael Wilks, 1964. See also, *inter alia*, Walter Ullmann, 1975, *passim*.

25 *MH*, VI, no. 1,

26 *Ibid.*, 5.

27 *MH*, V, no. 101.

28 *Ibid.*, p. 202.

29 *Ibid.*, 202–3

30 *CDD*, 521.

31 *Ibid.*, 521–2 and *MH*, V, no. 104. For a much more detailed listing of the reasons the king gave for authorizing the expedition see also

MH, VI, no. 48. Though the last paragraph of the latter document was written after the Portuguese defeat, most of it seems to have been drawn up before July 1437.

32 '. . . sobre esto [a armada] me conselhey com os do meu conselho e grande parte se acordou em esta temçom, e a meus confesores o dise, os quaes me louuarom e aprouarom . . .' (*MH*, VI, no. 48, p. 96).

33 The *pedido* was assessed on the value of the property of each individual according to a sliding scale and was similar to the French *taille*. It could only be granted by the Cortes and then only once for a particular and temporary purpose. Nobles, royal officials and serving soldiers were exempt. In 1436 the Jewish *comunas* were obliged to contribute an amount equal to two *pedidos* (Faro, 1965, 68 and 163–7).

34 *MH*, V, no. 133.

35 The best texts are now those supplied in *ibid.*, nos. 140 and 141. These documents were first discovered by de Witte, 'Les bulles pontificales . . .' *RHE*, LXVIII (1953) and subsequently studied by António Domingues de Sousa Costa, *O Infante D. Henrique na expansão portuguesa* (Braga, 1960). For a detailed discussion of their contents with particular reference to Castilian and Portuguese designs on the Canary Islands and the relevance of this to the late-medieval debate about the rights of pagan rulers and societies see P. E. Russell. 'El descubrimiento de Canarias y el debate medieval acerca de los derechos de los príncipes y pueblos paganos' in *Revista de Historia Canaria*, XXXVI (1978), 9–32.

36 *MH*, V, no. 140, p. 301.

37 *Ibid.*, 303–4.

38 *Ibid.*, no. 141, p. 329 and *passim*.

39 *CDD*, 535–7.

40 D. Gomes eventually returned to Portugal in the 1440s to become prior of Santa Cruz at Coimbra. A Latin life of him by a Florentine jurist, Thomas Salvetto, with a dedication to the Regent D. Pedro dated February 1442, exists in the BMLF, *Fondo Ashburnham*, MS 885, ff. 1r–10v).

41 *MH*, V, no. 143 (dated 6 November 1436). In a letter to the Portuguese king written on the same day, Eugenius IV warned him not to undertake any actions that infringed the prior rights of the Castilian crown overseas '*cum asserat terre Africe et insularum prefatarum conquestam ad se spectare*' (*ibid.*, no. 144, p. 349).

42 *MH*, VI, no. 16, p. 35.

Chapter Seven

1 Quoted in Southern, 1959, 58.

2 *MH*, V, no. 102.

3 The king confirmed the *alvará* on the same day (*MH*, V, no. 102). The problems arising from this document are discussed in *EH*, 109–14, in Silva de Sousa, 1991, 256–8 and, from a somewhat different standpoint, by Russell, 1992, 1–14.

4 *MH*, VI, no. 52.

5 *Ibid.*, no. 36, pp. 68–9.

6 *Ibid.*, no. 11. The queen may, of course, have been concerned because, if the expedition to Tangier took place, there could be no question of Portuguese military assistance for her brothers, the Infantes de Aragón, in Castile.

7 *Ibid.*, no. 27, p. 57.

8 *Ibid.*, no. 40, p. 77.

9 *Ibid.*, no. 44.

10 *Ibid.*, nos. 46, 47 and 50.

11 *MH*, VI, no. 50, p. 104.

12 *Ibid.*, no. 50, pp. 106–7.

13 *Ibid.*, no. 47.

14 'non ajais as cousas por feitas antes que o sejam' (*ibid.*, 92–3).

15 For Vegetius's text in English see *Vegetius: Epitome of Military Science*, trans. and ed. N. P. Milner,

1993; 2nd ed. 1996; for the fortunes of Vegetius in translation in the Iberian Peninsula see Russell in *Spain and its Literature: Essays in Memory of E. Allison Peers*, 1997, 49–53.

16 MH, VI, no. 46, pp. 88–9.

17 *Ibid.*, 89.

18 João Alvares, 1960, 11–12.

19 The royal secretary's letter (*MH*, VI, no. 61) gives the date as 25 August. João Alvares, who sailed with D. Fernando, gives the date of the fleet's departure from Lisbon as 22 August. Rui de Pina (*CDD*, 537 and 538) suggests the 22nd or the 23rd. These problems probably arise because of confusion between the date of the fleet's departure from before the city of Lisbon and its final departure from the estuary anchorage off Restelo.

20 *MH*, VI, no. 75 and *CDD*, 539. The king's letter to D. Gomes (17 March 1438) was intended to add some additional explanations for the failure of the Tangier expedition to those contained in another letter – not found – which Duarte had evidently sent earlier for the abbot to pass on to the pope and the cardinals. That the Tangier expedition was something of a cut-price affair is suggested by its comparatively low recorded cost to the royal treasury – 57,000 *dobras* – but this probably omits the proceeds of the special subsidy granted by the Cortes. The capture of Ceuta in 1415 was said to have cost 280,000 *dobras* (Faro, 1965, 66–8).

21 *MH*, VI, no. 75.

22 *CDD*, 541.

23 *CDD*, 538.

24 *CDD*, 544 and *MH*, VI, no. 78.

25 *CDD*, 538.

26 *CFCG*, II, 44 and *CDD.*, 550–1.

27 A feature of the siege of Tangier seems to have been that, as at Ceuta twenty-two years before, the Marinids were quite incapable of organizing any naval measures against

the Portuguese fleet anchored for many days off the city, a fact that helped to prevent an even greater catastrophe.

28 *MH*, VI, no. 63 – another letter from the Fondo Ashburnham. Its anonymous author concluded his account of the actions of 1 and 3 October (which he regarded or affected to regard as victories for the Portuguese) by telling his correspondent in Portugal that he should pass on to the king – in case the reports of the two princes and the constable did not arrive before his – 'this good news which it is to be hoped our Lord God will add to'.

29 It fell to Afonso V eleven years after Henry's death, in August 1471.

30 The document, which only survives in a late sixteenth-century copy, is printed in *MH* VI, no. 64. It is in the form of a personal agreement between the Prince and Salah ben Salah. No other Moroccan official is mentioned as party to the capitulation whose full terms are discussed in *CDD*, 553–5 and 558. Rui de Pina seeks to save Henry's reputation by asserting that the capitulation's terms were first proposed by the Moroccans, but this is wishful thinking. Frei João Alvares, who was there, categorically states that the first approach was made from the Portuguese side (João Alvares, 1960, 25).

31 *MH*, VI, no. 64, p. 211. The text of the capitulation was summarized by Rui de Pina in *CDD*, 558.

32 João Alvares, 1960, 27–8.

33 *MH*, VI, no. 75, p. 230.

34 *Ibid.*, no. 72, p. 224.

35 *CFCG*, II, 43.

36 *CDD*, 362.

37 *Ibid.*, 567; João Alvares, 1960, 32, 33–6, 38 etc.

38 *CDD*, 565–70.

39 *MH*, VI, no. 72.

40 Pina puts D. João among those in favour of surrendering Ceuta but the newsletter to D. Gomes (*Ibid.*, VI, no. 72) puts João on the 'no

41 *MH*, VI, no. 72, p. 225; *CDD*, 571.

42 There is evidence that, at this time, Portuguese envoys were indeed sent to England, Castile and Aragon presumably to request those countries to intervene diplomatically in Fez on Fernando's behalf (*MH*, VI, no. 72, p. 225). According to João Alvares, John II of Castile did send envoys to Morocco to demand that D. Fernando should be ransomed and threatened that, if this was not agreed to, all trade between the sultanate and Castile would be embargoed (*ibid.*, p. 226, n. 10). Nothing of course came of this threat. Trade with Morocco was far too important for Castile or the Crown of Aragon to start applying sanctions on behalf of the Portuguese. Nor was it a good time to ask for the help of Henry VI of England beset as he was by problems in France and political in-fighting at home.

43 *CDD*, 571.

44 Dias Dinis, in AP H, *Anais*, 1965, 151–74.

45 Zurara states that he has dealt with the Tangier affair in detail in the lost *Crónica do Reino*. It is generally believed that the account of this episode in Rui de Pina's *Crónica de D. Duarte* was lifted from Zurara's work.

Chapter Eight

1 Known in French times as the Baie du Lévrier.

2 *CFCG*, II, 181.

3 For a detailed account of Arguin Island and the remains of the Portuguese factory and fort there as it was at the beginning of the twentieth century see A. Gruvel and R. Chudeau, *À Travers la Mauritanie occidentale (de Saint-Louis à Port-Étienne)*, 2 vols. (Paris, 1901–11). For an account of the physical and human geography of the Western Sahara in the fifteenth century, largely from contemporary Portuguese sources, see Vitorino Magalhães Godinho, *O 'Mediterrâneo' Saariano e as Caravanas do Ouro: Geografia Económica e Social do Sáara Ocidental e Central do XI ao XVI Século* (São Paulo, 1956), especially 51–69, 120–6, 135–56. The account by João Rodrigues of the castle at Arguin as it was at the end of the fifteenth century (included in the Valentim Fernandes manuscript) is based on the author's reminiscences of his stay there in 1493 and 1494 on the orders of John II.

4 The original Berber form of the Europeanized toponym (Port. *Arguim*) is not certain. In the earliest charts and normally in Zurara's chronicle it is written 'Ergim'. His first reference to it, however, calls it Adegete, perhaps a Lusism for Berber *adkhaïlt* (*CdG*, 93, n. 4).

5 *MH*, VII, no. 228; *CFCG*, II, 100–1.

6 It is immediately followed in Zurara's text by a resumé of the terms of the Regent's grant in the following year of a monopoly over navigation and trade in Guinea.

7 *MH*, VI, no. 63. Port. 'Mouros' as used in Henrican documents and sometimes by Zurara was a collective term embracing all the Muslim peoples and tribes encountered by the Portuguese in the African Sahara. Later on it was frequently used when referring to the pagan inhabitants of Black Africa even south of the Equator.

8 'he asked us as a reward that we should grant him our letters patent stipulating that no person could go to those lands [Guinea] without his permission and licence, whether it be to make war or to trade' (*'nos pedia por merçee que lhe desemos*

nosa carta que nehüu nom fose aquelas terras sem seu mandado e liçença, asy pera guera como pera mercadarias' (*MH*, VIII, no. 62, p. 107).

9 For Zurara's observation see *CFCG*, II, 507. In 1453 a chancery register refers to a *fidalgo* of the royal household going as captain of the ships 'which we [i.e. Afonso V] are now sending to Guinea' (Baquero Moreno, 1973), 177, n. 99.

10 Zurara generally uses the term *mouros* when referring to any of the Saharan tribesmen. To refer to the Ma'qil Arabs of Yemeni origin, Beduins who began moving into the Mauritania in the fourteenth century, he employs the word *alarve* ('Arab'). He and all his successors describe the Berber tribesmen who were the main inhabitants of the region encountered by the Portuguese as *azenegues*. This term derived from *Azenagui*, the singular form of *Zenaga*, the name of the most important of the Mauritanian tribes. Arab writers of the time referred to them as Sanhadjas. I have preferred the latter term in this book. One branch of the Sanhadjas was not nomadic. These were the Imragen fishermen who lived permanently on the coast in crude cabins. The Portuguese knew them as *schimeiros* from Zenaga *sirme*, 'fish'.

11 The first of such wars in the African Atlantic was represented by the French and Castilian attempts at the beginning of the century to conquer the pagan inhabitants of the Canary Islands, a struggle in which the uninvited troops of Prince Henry had soon joined.

12 All vessels sailing to Guinea in Prince Henry's time and later carried a scrivener (Port. *escrivão*) whose duties included not only recording details of sales and purchases of cargo but also of seeing that the exact terms of the Prince's

written sailing orders (*regimentos*) were obeyed. Some observations of Cadamosto in his account of Pedro de Sintra's voyage of exploration to Guinea in 1462 seem to show that it was also the scrivener's duty to maintain a detailed personal log of what happened and what information was secured on a voyage of exploration (Cadamosto, 1966, 117–18).

13 *DP*, I (*S*), no. 218, pp. 338–9. Quittances to royal officials for monies received and disbursements made were often only issued several years after the transaction had taken place. The one mentioned in the text was not issued until September 1450.

14 Zurara's text confirms that the Portuguese in his time still believed the Senegal to be the Western Nile of medieval cartographers.

15 *CDFG*, II, 169–70.

16 Cadamosto, 1966, 28–9.

17 *CFCG*, II, 450.

18 The account of João Fernandes's travels is to be found in Zurara, *CDFG* II, chap. lxxvii and lxviii. *Ibid.*, chap. lxxvi is also concerned, in part, with an account of the western Sahara which may or may not have also formed part of the squire's observations. Since both accounts deal with the same subject-matter, I have treated them as a single entity in the present chapter. It is to be presumed that Zurara, as usual, copied this material, or most of it, from Afonso Cerveira and doubtless followed his usual practice of omitting facts contained in his source which he thought uninteresting. For an English version of Malfante's letter from Tuat see *The Voyages of Cadamosto and Other Documents on Western Africa in the Second Half of the Fifteenth Century*. Trans. and ed. G. R. Crone, 1937, 85–90.

19 'You should know that the aforementioned Lord Prince of Portugal

has leased this island of Arguin to Christians [*for ten years] in this form: that no one may enter the gulf to trade with the said Arabs except those who hold the lease. These [Christians] have constructed a dwelling-place on the said island of Arguin and the leaseholders keep people continually resident on the island as factors who continually buy and sell. Their trade is with the said Arabs who come down to the coasts . . .' ('Anchora è da saper che'l signor Prince de Portogallo predito ha fato de questa ixola d'Argim un apalto per cristiani [*per dieci anni'] in questo modo: che nesun possi intrar in questo colfo per merchantar con i sopraditi Arabi, salvo quelli che hano el dito apalto, i quali hano fato habitation de la dita ixola d'Argim. E tengono questi tal de l'apalto continuamente zente in questa ixola e fatori che comprano e vendeno. Tratano con li sopraditi Arabi che vengono a le marine' (Cadamosto, 1966, 25–26). The reading 'per dieci anni' is not confirmed by the authoritative critical edition of the oldest MS published by Tullia Gasparrini Leporace in 1966. It offers instead the reading 'per cristiani'. Nevertheless, the later reading seems plausible and may well have been that which appeared in Cadamosto's lost autograph manuscript.

20 'questo signor Prince fa lavorar un castello in questa ixola per conserver e multiplicar questo trafego in perpetuo' (ibid., 26).

21 DP, III, no. 30. Soeiro Mendes's stipend took the form of twelve slaves annually or their value in gold, proof that slaves were already then recognized to be the main import from Arguin. These arrangements did not, however, continue for long since, by 1469, we find that the king had relinquished the tratos de Arguim to his heir, Prince João. The latter, in his turn, leased the Arguin trade to Fernão Gomes – the famous Lisbon contractor to whom Afonso V also leased most of the entire Guinea trade.

22 VF, 44.

23 [Thomas Astley], 1745, 5–6; Gruvel et Chudeau, 1909–11, I, 9–19.

24 For a general account of the gold trade of Arguin – never of great importance – in the fifteenth and sixteenth century see Magalhães Godinho, 1991, I, 145–51; for trades in other goods see ibid., II–IV, passim; also see Blake, 1967, 22–7 and, though for a much later period, three bills of lading translated into English (ibid., 32, 33, 34).

25 There is documentary evidence that cogs belonging to the Prince, as well as caravels, were already being used at this time for the Guinea trade – see (DP I (S), no. 221).

26 PIG in VF, 190.

27 Thus, after describing the alleged impact on the Sanhadjas of their first sight of a Portuguese ship off the Saharan coast, he observes 'these can be confirmed by many of the said Sanhadjas who are in Portugal as slaves as well as by many Portuguese who in that time were accustomed to sail to those ports and from whom I received the aforesaid information.' (Cadamosto, 1966, 30).

28 As already noted, Cadamosto does not categorically state that he had personally visited Arguin but there are passages in his narrative which imply this. Thus, when discussing plagues of locusts in the Western Sahara, he remarks 'Anchòra ho visto in questo paexe, che in alguni anni habonda una grande quantità de loquste' (ibid., 38). Some commentators have concluded that he did not call at Arguin in 1455 because, when he resumes his account of his journey to Senegambia after his description of Arguin

and the Sahara, the journey is recommenced at Cape Blanco, instead of at Arguin, as if the whole account of the Sahara and Mali was an interpolation. But this does not necessarily bear the interpretation put on it. To avoid the well-known navigational perils off the Arguin Bank, which the Venetian explorer himself describes, it would be normal for his caravel, after leaving the island, to set a course west for the safer water off Cape Blanco before sailing south to Cape Verde (see Esmeraldo, 78).

29 See among others Rau, 1965 – separata.

30 'Each year from eight hundred to one thousand slaves are brought from Portugal to Arguin' (Cadamosto, 1964, 26–7). The Ramusio text of the *Navigazioni* (1550) reads 'da settecento in ottocento teste'; this figure, understood to mean 700–800 individual slaves annually, has been accepted by most historians of the Portuguese discoveries. It has, however, no authority in either MS version of the *Navigazioni* or in the first published version (Vicenza, 1507). It is quite likely that Ramusio understood that Cadamosto had referred to individual slaves and translated the figure into the standard auction unit (Port. *peça*: Ital. *teste*) subsequently used by Portuguese and other slave-traders. This gave a number lower than would be achieved by counting as individuals all slaves, whatever their age, sex and condition.

31 'To return to my first point; this [gold] is the best thing which comes out of the said land and country of the Sanhadjas or brown-skinned people for, from the quantity which reaches Wadan every year as I have explained, a certain amount is sent to the coast and sold there to the Spaniards [*sic*] who are continuously present on the said island

of Arguin' (*ibid.*, 36). 'Spagnoli' in this passage is probably a copyist's slip for 'Portogallesi' – used when referring to the nationality of the leaseholders on an earlier occasion (*ibid.*, 26). It is of course just possible, for the reasons given earlier in my text, that Henry allowed some Castilian leaseholders to establish themselves at Arguin.

32 Rozmital, 1957, 120, 123.

33 CFCG, II, 551. As far as is known Zurara never made good his promise to continue the history of Henry's affairs up to his death in 1460.

34 For the expeditions beyond the River Senegal, confusingly presented by Zurara, use is recommended of the text and explanatory notes in CdG, 122–5, 147–54, 175–81, 204–9, 210–13, 237–9, 241–3, 241–7, 257–62.

35 For evidence that cannon and culverins were routinely carried by the exploring caravels in the 1440s see CFCG, II, 300 ('armavan seus trons e suas colobretas').

36 CFCG, II, 504.

37 *Ibid.*, 528.

38 *Ibid.*, 527–9.

39 Zurara reports succinctly that João Fernandes had to remain in Massa until 'another ship' picked him up. This is the part of his narrative where the chronicler states without further explanation that Henry sent to a servant of his resident in Galway in Ireland a lion that had been given to him (*ibid.*, II, 529), an observation that has never been elucidated.

40 MH, II, nos. 142, p. 280 and 146.

41 MH, X, no. 6.

42 *Ibid.*, no. 6, p. 12.

43 The crown retained only its rights to the *sisa*, or sales tax, on goods brought from the regions referred to.

44 MH, XI, no. 116. Records of such sailings only survive when some-

thing happened to cause the crown to intervene. The opening of the Moroccan ports to Portuguese shipping meant, of course, that the Italian merchant colony in Lisbon was now able, using Portuguese vessels, to compete with their fellow Italians in Andalusia.

45 *MH*, XII, no. 124.

46 For a biography of Leonel Gil see Baquero Moreno, 1973, 818. He had participated in the 1445 attack on the island of Tider on the Arguin Bank, earning himself a favourable mention in Zurara's chronicle (*CFCG*, 318). In 1449 he had been appointed to take charge of the collection of the sales tax in Lagos, an important royal office secured for him by the Prince and one which he still held in 1462. As happened with many similar royal offices that Henry persuaded the crown to grant to his followers, Leonel Gil evidently treated his as a sinecure not requiring his continuous presence.

47 *MH*, XIII, no. 1.

48 *MH*, IX, no. 95.

49 Juan II's *real cédula* (Valladolid, 8 July 1449) is printed in *CODOIN*, XXXVI (Madrid, 1860), 499–501. The Castilian Crown ceded to Juan de Guzmán all its rights, including fishing rights, in the region specified except 'la suprema jurisdicion e mineros de oro e plata e otros metales'. See also Pérez Embid, 1948, 155–6.

50 *Crónica de D. Juan II*, 1953, 692.

51 See, for example, the wording of a letter of 15 November 1477 sent by Isabel the Catholic to one of her officials: 'Sepades... como agora nuevamente algunas personas, vezinos de la villa de Palos, tomaron çiertas carauelas de portugueses, que venían de la Guinea... las quales auían ydo contra mis defendimientos e liçença ...pertenesçiendo... a mí la conquista de aquellas partes (*DRRP*, I,

no. 65 cited in Russell, 1995, XII, n. 5).

52 Pérez Embid, 1948, 157.

Chapter Nine

1 Cadamosto, 1966, 7.

2 The etymology of *caravela* (Sp. *carabela*; Fr. *carvelle/caravelle*; Eng. *carvel*) has been much discussed. A widely accepted view is that it ultimately derives from Lat. *carabus* ('a small wicker boat covered with hide'), that passed into an Arabic form from which it was reborrowed by the romance languages.

3 'They persuaded themselves that the eyes which are placed on the bows of the ships were really eyes by means of which my ship was able to see its way wherever it sailed at sea' (Cadamosto, 1961, 71). Cadamosto is here describing the reactions of the Wolofs of Senegal to the arrival there of the Portuguese caravels.

4 For an excellent description of the lateen sail and its handling as well as other features of the caravel see Parry, 1963, 65–6 and *passim*.

5 A petition presented in June 1456 by the inhabitants of Viana do Castelo, Ponte de Lima and Vila do Conde – all in northern Portugal – states that the people of those places had recently begun 'to build large caravels for the transport of fish and other merchandise of the region for two reasons: the first is that these vessels draw little water; the second is that, because of their swiftness, they are able to escape if attacked by corsairs' (*DP* I (*S*), no. 138).

6 Fonseca, 1960, 69, n. 1

7 Zurara, *CDFG*, II, 393: 'the Prince granted one Gomes Pires a licence and made ready for him two caravels, one decked [*tilhada*] and the other used for fishing'.

8 Cadamosto, 1966, 13, says his

caravel was 'de portada zercha bote 90'. The Venetian *botta* is reckoned to have the capacity of 0.6 of a *tonelada*. In this book the capacity of ships is given in terms of the local unit in which it is described in the original source. It should be noted that the English 'ton', used at this time when calculating the dead-weight capacity of English ships, was based on the Bordeaux wine tun which, when full, was taken to weigh 2,240 English pounds. The *tonelada* of Seville, on the other hand, represented two pipes of wine in cask weighing 2,000 pounds and holding forty to forty-five cubic feet of wine. The Portuguese *tonel*, used in calculating the capacity of Portuguese ships, was probably slightly larger than the *tonelada* of Seville.

9 AGS, Registro General del Sello: *Inventarios y Catálogos*, II, (1478–80), nos. 12 and 110.

10 Fonseca, 1960, 392.

11 Parry, 1963, 63.

12 João Paulo Aparício, 'O navio num mundo que se descobre (sécs. xv–xvii)' in *Patrimonia*, 2 (February 1997) [*O navio no imaginário português*], 11–39,

13 Fonseca, 1960, 249.

14 See, for example, Zurara, *CDFG*, II, 116–17. A more explicit reference to Henry's *regimentos* issued to captains of ships sailing to Guinea will be found in *MMA*, IV, no. 2, p. 5 where, in a document of 1470, Afonso V recalls 'the *regimentos* that in the time of the 'Infante D. Henrique . . . used to be given to the caravels and [other] ships . . . which sailed to the trading posts and the lands of Guinea to barter there'.

15 cf. the very precise prohibition contained in Nicholas V's bull *Romanus pontifex* of 8 January 1455 (*MH*, XII, no. 36, p. 74) where, after restating the usual prohibition against trading in certain articles with the infidel, the bull

adds that it is forbidden 'aut ipsos Jnfideles nauigandi modum edocerent propter que eis hostes fortiores ac duriores fierent . . .'

16 *CFCG*, II, 300, describes the jubilant scene when caravels newly arrived from Portugal unexpectedly found four Portuguese vessels already lying off the Ilha das Garças, on the Arguin Bank. Zurara writes 'as [the new arrivals] approached the place where the other ships were lying at anchor, they loaded their cannon and culverins and discharged them as a sign of the joy they felt'.

17 Cadamosto, 1961, 70 and 83.

18 Fonseca, 1960, 458.

19 *EH*, 478.

20 There is no reason to believe, as is sometimes suggested, that the Guinea caravels routinely went as far west as the Azores archipelago itself before setting an eastward course.

21 *CFCG*, II, 487–91; *CdG*, 237–41. The account of these events, which appears to be truthful, is so detailed that it does not seem to have been taken from Afonso Cerveira's lost narrative. It may well have come from a lost source specially devoted to the scrivener's remarkable achievement which was available to Zurara.

22 Cited in Albuquerque, 1989, 181.

23 Münzer, 154. The mileage between Lisbon and Cape Verde is wrongly given in Münzer's text as 500.

24 'Item aliud malum nautae habent, nam in mari meridiano naves nostri ligni per quodam genus vermium ita corroduntur, ut paucae ad tres vel quatuor peregrinationes sufficiant, quin perrodantur. Nec hodie huic malo remedium inventum est. Ostenderunt mihi in portu Lisbonensi huiusmodi carabelas, quas hoc genere vermium perforatas vidi' (*O Instituto* LXXXIII (1932), 155–6).

25 Worm and barnacles continued to be a menace to ships sailing to

26 Gomes, 1959, 199.

27 The seamen's quadrant was a relatively simple device. It was in the shape of a quarter segment of a circle with a scale from 1° to 90° marked on the curved edge, and with two pin-hole sights at either end of one of the straight edges. A plumb-line hung from the apex. The sights were aligned on the Pole Star and a reading taken from the point where the plumb-line cut the scale. The altitude of the Pole measured in degrees by this method gave the observer's latitude (Parry, 1963, 91). [photograph of quadrant *ibid.*, no. 31]

28 Lanckman de Valckenstein, 1992, 346.

29 Cadamosto, 1937, 61: '. . . we saw the Pole Star once only; it appeared very low down over the sea . . . about a third of a lance above the horizon. We also had sight of six stars low down over the sea, clear, bright and large. By the compass, they stood due south. . . . this we took to be the southern wain. . . .'

Chapter Ten

1 The basic contemporary narrative texts for the history of the slave trade in Portugal during the Henrican period are Zurara, *CFCG* and Cadamosto, *Navigazioni*. Documentary evidence becomes much more frequent after Henry's monopoly had reverted to the crown in 1460. A major study in English that deals with all aspects of the lives and treatment of black slaves in Portugal between 1441 and 1555 and is notable for its use of unpublished Portuguese archival material is that of A. C. de C. M. Saunders, *A Social History of Black Slaves and Freedmen in Portugal 1441–1555* (Cambridge: CUP, 1982). For a well-stocked general study of the Portuguese slave trade from its beginnings see Magalhães Godinho, IV, [1987], chap. 9, *passim*. A. Teixeira da Mota, 'Alguns aspectos da colonização e do comércio marítimo dos portugueses na África Ocidental nos séculos XV e XVI', Centro de Estudos de Cartografía Antiga: XCVIII (Secção de Lisboa), 1976, also includes a useful summary account of the Portuguese slave trade. The historical literature relating to the slave trade in general is immense. Many works mainly concerned with the transatlantic trade with America contain some account of the Portuguese trade between Africa and Europe. Useful studies of this kind are William D. Phillips, Jr, *Slavery from Roman Times to the Early Transatlantic Trade* (Manchester: Manchester University Press, 1985) and Hugh Thomas, *The Slave Trade* (New York: Simon & Schuster, 1997). For an up-to-date study of the theoretical writings about the institution of slavery from the Ancient World to the early modern period see particularly Anthony Pagden, *The Fall of Natural Man* (Cambridge: CUP, 1982), *passim*. The basic though not always uncontentious study of the European slave trade in general in the Middle Ages is still that of Charles Verlinden, *L'Esclavage dans l'Europe médiévale*, vol. 1 (Bruges, 1955), together with other articles by the same author. For the slave trade in Catalonia at the end of the Middle Ages and the juridical situation of slaves there see the classic study of Joaquín Miret y Sans, 'La esclavitud en Cataluña en los últimos tiempos de la Edad Media', *Rhisp.* XLI (1917), 1–109. Vicenta Cortés, *La esclavitud en Valencia durante el reinado de los Reyes*

Guinea in the sixteenth century. They are referred to in Richard Eden's account of John Lok's voyage to Mina in 1554–5 (*EWA*, II, 345–6).

Católicos *(1479–1516)*, (Valencia 1964), contains some material relevant to the earlier period. For the Genoese involvement in slave trading centred on the Balkans and the eastern Mediterranean see particularly Jacques Heers, *Gênes au XVᵉ siècle* ... (Paris: SEVPEN, 1961), specially 364–72, 402–4.

2 *MH*, XIII, no. 68, p. 115.
3 The account of the expedition occupies chapters 18–23 of *CFCG*.
4 *CdG*, 109, n. 4.
5 *CDFG*, II, 122–30. Zurara explains that he has sometimes deliberately omitted information about the slave trade which he found in Cerveira's text. Thus, when referring to the arrival of another slave-trading expedition at Lisbon in 1445, he comments 'we do not think it necessary to recount the arrival of the caravels in Lisbon, nor to take up space in our story by describing the auction of the 'Moors' as we find it in the writing of Afonso Cerveira from which we have taken this account, for by now in that city they did not think it a novelty to see 'Moors' from those lands [Guinea]' *(ibid.,* 313).
6 Las Casas, I, 1951, 130.
7 This does not necessarily mean equal in number. The value of each individual slave depended on age, sex, health, apparent intelligence, and other factors. The chronicle's account gives some reason to suppose that the division of the slaves was already made by using the *peça* system of quantity which was certainly routinely employed later. A *peça* represented one healthy, male slave in the prime of life. Older men, boys, women and children were liable to be broken up into groups irrespective of any family relationships to make up what the auctioneer considered to be the equivalent of one *peça*. This could thus be made up of two or even three individuals.
8 *CFCG*, II, 145–8.

9 *Ibid.*, 147.
10 *Ibid.*
11 *CFCG*, II, 204–6.
12 Las Casas, I, 1965, 120–44.
13 Heers, 1961, 313 n. 4. For other information about Genoese involvement in the slave trade see particularly *ibid.*, 370–1, 402–4 and *passim*.
14 Alfonso el Sabio, *Las Siete Partidas*, 1807.
15 *Ibid.*, Madrid, 1807, vol. 3, IV, tít. XXII, viii, p. 125.
16 *Ibid.*, vol. 3, IV, tít. XXIII, ii, p. 128.
17 *Ibid.*, vol. 2, III, tít. XVI, xiii, p. 522.
18 *Ibid.*, vol, 2, V, tít. V, xlv–xlvii, pp. 198–9.
19 *Ibid.*, col. 3, IV, tít. XXII, i–xi, pp. 121–8.
20 *MH*, no. 36.
21 For the slave trade in the Peninsular territories of the Crown of Aragon and the juridical situation of slaves there see, among others, Joaquín Miret y Sans, 1917 and Dufourcq, Paris, 1966) – especially 71–92, 473–4, 551, 573–6; M. Grau, 'La esclavitud en "els terms generals dell castell de Morella" (Castellón) (1350–1450) in *Homenaje a Jaime Vicens Vives*, I (Barcelona, 1965), 445–82. See also Charles Verlinden, 1955, *passim* and Heers, 1961, *passim*.
22 Grau, 1965, 446–7.
23 Heers, 1961, 403.
24 See Teixeira da Mota, 1976, 8–9.
25 Miret y Sans, 1917, 38–43.
26 Rubió i Lluch, II, 1921, no. CCCLXVIII, p. 355: 'Nos havem mester dues peces de drap groch qui ve de Granada o de Barberia per vestir ne dos sclaus negres que ensemps ab altres coses havem deliberat trametre a nostre frare lo duch de Burgunya. . . .'
27 Grau, 1965, 449.
28 *Ibid.*, 455.
29 Saunders, 1982, 15.
30 Grau, 1965, 455.
31 *Ibid.*, 480.

32 *CFCG*, II, 97–8.

33 See, among others, Pike, 1972, 170–4.

34 *MH*, VIII, no. 62 and *ibid.*, IX, no. 193.

35 Cadamosto, 1966, 48–9, 62–3.

36 Godinho, IV, [1987], 157.

37 See Phillips, 1985, 86–7 quoting the tentative estimates of Ralph A. Austen.

38 [Nicholas Lanckman de Valkenstein], *Leonor de Portugal, imperatriz da Alemanha, diario de viagem do embaixador Nicolau Lanckman de Valckenstein*, edição do texto latino e tradução de Aires A. Nascimento (Lisbon: Edições Cosmos, 1992).

39 The Portuguese discoverers frequently described the Canarians and the indigenous people of Black Africa as 'nude'. The term must not to be taken to mean totally naked, which they rarely were. Christian prudery then (as much later) regarded exposing the torso and limbs as being in a state of nudity – a state wholly unacceptable to European true believers for whom European clothing was the only acceptable form of dress for Christians from wherever they came.

40 See *ibid.*, 32–3, 34–5, 40–3, 46–7. Lanckman states that Prince Henry was present and took some part in receiving the imperial ambassadors but, despite the attention he gives to the role of 'Moors', blacks and Canarians in the festivities, the imperial chaplain makes no reference to Henry's role as patron of discovery. Rui de Pina's account of these events (*Afonso V*, 1977, chaps. CXXXI–CXXXI) attributes an important role in organizing the festivities to Henry but does not mention the participation of persons from Africa or the Canaries.

41 *CFCG*, II, 368. The gold *dobra* was not, of course, a Portuguese coin. The Castilian gold *dobra de banda* referred to frequently in Portuguese documents at this time was merely a money of account whose value was artificially fixed by the crown at 120 *reais brancos*. The problem for economic historians is, however, that, even after the restoration of a Portuguese gold coinage in the reign of Duarte I (the *escudo*), Portuguese documents sometimes still use the *dobra*, allocating to it its real market value in *reais*. For a summary study of the complicated monetary history of fifteenth-century Portugal see Magalhães Godinho, 1991, I, especially 124–38.

42 One may suspect a copyist's mistake and that Zurara, whose intention here was, after all, to show what a large profit could be made by bartering cheap trade goods for a slave, perhaps originally wrote 'fifteen'.

43 Dias, 1953, 384–5.

44 Saunders, 25–7. By 1451 the gold *escudo* was worth 140 *reais brancos* (Dinis, 1960, no. 447). In 1457 Afonso V replaced the *escudo* by the *cruzado*, which was worth the equivalent of a ducat or a florin and marked the adhesion of Portugal to the Italian rather than as previously the North African monetary system. On its launch, its value was probably fixed at 225 reais but, by 1460, this had risen to 253 *reais* (*ibid.*, 130).

45 *EH*, 297–9, 473–4; *MH*, XIV. no. 127, pp. 296–7. In the king's quittance (5 July 1464) to the liquidator of the Prince's affairs in the Algarve the *dobra* is still used as a unit of account now valued at 200 *reais* (*ibid.*, p. 297). Another quittance referring to the expenses in Rome from 1456 to 1460 of his representative at the papal court values the ducat at 235 *reais* (*ibid.*, no. 73, p. 201).

46 Phillips, 1985, 120.

47 *CFCG*, 76.

48 Cadamosto, 1966, 50.

49 Diogo Gomes in Cadamosto, 1937, 100–1.

50 In a document of 1462 Afonso V insists that the *sisa* be paid 'on all horses embarked to be taken to Guinea' (*DP*, III, no. 14). The document mentions ordinary merchant ships as well as caravels as by now involved in the trade in horses with Senegal. Cadamosto, too, reports that the horses he sold in Senegal came from the Peninsula.

Chapter Eleven

1 Some of the Castilian documents relating to Henry's attempts to seize the Canary Islands have been reprinted in the relevant volumes of *Monumenta Henricina*. When this is the case I have not referred back to the original source in the endnotes. For many of the relevant Castilian documents, however, the reader will still need to turn to G. Chil y Naranjo, *Estudios históricos, climatológicos, y palatológicos de las Islas Canarias*, [3 vols (Las Palmas, 1876–91)], Primera Parte, II (Las Palmas, 1880), and to the indispensible study of Elias Serra y Ràfols, *Los portugueses en Canarias. Discurso inaugural del año académico, 1941–2* (La Laguna, 1941). Pérez Embid, 1948, is still an indispensable work of reference for this topic. For a discussion of fifteenth-century Spanish and Portuguese attempts to conquer the Canaries in terms of contemporary European arguments about the temporal authority and powers of the papacy see P. E. Russell, 'El descubrimiento de Canarias y los debates medievales acerca de los derechos de los príncipes y pueblos paganos', *Revista de Historia Canaria*, 36 (1978). Rafael Torres Campos, *Carácter de la conquista y colonización de las Islas Canarias. Discurso de ingreso en la Real Academia de la Historia* (Madrid: RAH, 1901), contains the full text

of the report (*Información*) of the commission set up by the Catholic Monarchs in 1478 to enquire into the history and legitimacy of competing claims to the lordship of Lanzarote. This traces in detail the history of the whole archipelago from Jean de Béthencourt's time onwards, taking evidence not only from witnesses involved in the diplomatic negotiations with the Portuguese court in Prince Henry's time, but also from surviving settlers on Lanzarote who had experienced at first-hand the impact of his attacks on the Canaries. Sporadic references to the islands are to be found scattered through *CFCG*, II, *passim*. Towards the end of the chronicle Zurara includes a contemporary account of each island which needs to be set alongside the descriptions given in *Le Canarien*. For English-speaking readers, Chapters 6 and 7 of Felipe Fernández-Armesto's *Before Columbus. Exploration and Colonisation from the Mediterranean to the Atlantic, 1229–2492*, New Studies in Medieval History (Basingstoke & London: Macmillan Education, 1987) offer a valuable overview of Castilian–Portuguese rivalry in the Canaries in Henry's time.

2 *MH*, VI, no. 57, pp. 160–1, quoting St Isidore, *Etymologiae*, XIV, vi.

3 *MH*, V, no. 129, pp. 255–6.

4 *CFCG*, II, 48.400

5 It is the custom of many English-speaking writers to refer to the aboriginal inhabitants of the Canaries as 'Guanches'. The usage is to be avoided since the term 'Guanche' was used only as a descriptive term for themselves by the people of Tenerife. It is inapplicable to the various culturally different indigenous peoples who lived on the other islands.

6 Henry's ships were, of course, in no danger of attack at sea by the inhabitants of Grand Canary or any of the islands not in Franco-

7 See Fernández-Armesto, 1982, Chapter 1 and *passim*.

8 *MH*, VI, no. 57, p. 148. Alonso de Cartagena actually gives 1425 as the date of the expedition but other sources suggest 1424. As we have no idea how long Fernando de Castro's force remained there it is possible that both dates are valid.

9 Barros, 1988, 47. A contemporary listing of extraodinary expenditure incurred by the crown in John I's time refers to a subsidy of 34,000 *dobras* towards the expenses of the expedition (Faro, 1975, 66).

10 *MH*, I, no. 89.

11 'On Wednesday, the tenth day of March in the said year [1403], the proclamation of Mosén Johan Vetancorto as king of the Canaries was made' ('en miércoles, diez días de enero deste dicho año [1403] se fizo el pregón de Mosén Iohan Vetancorto, rey de Canarias' (*Canarien*, III. 1968, 251, quoting from an entry for 12 March in the accounts of payments made to various *pregoneros* [town criers] by the municipality of Seville in that year).

12 *MH*, IX, no. 95, p. 122.

13 *MH*, IV, no. 21, pp. 102–3.

14 *DP*, I, no. 281, pp, 296–7, 314, 328, 340.

15 *MH*, XI, no. 138, p. 174.

16 *MH*, V, no. 129.

17 *Ibid.*, p. 256. The Latin reads *veluti pecudes*, literally 'like cattle' but often used figuratively as here in the sense of 'beast', or 'brute'.

18 *Ibid.*, p. 257.

19 At this time Jean de Béthencourt's nephew, Maciot de Béthencourt, ruled Lanzarote for Castile while Fuerteventura was ruled by the Sevillian Guillén de Las Casas.

20 *MH*, V, no. 129, p. 258. The wording of the curia's Latin is worth recording; '*Quamuis enim infidelium loca propria auctoritate plerique debellare et occupare nitantur, nichilominus, quia Domini est terra et plenitudo eius, qui et sanctitati vestre plenariam orbis tocius potestatem reliqui, que, de auctoritate et permissu sanctitatis vestre possidebuntur, de speciali licencia et permissione omnipotentis Dei possidere videntur . . .*'

21 *Ibid.*, no. 137.

22 The best text of Cartagena's *Allegationes* is now the copy of the one sent by him from Basel to the Castilian ambassador at Bologna on 26 August 1437 (*MH*, VI, no. 57).

23 *Ibid.*, no. 143.

24 *Ibid.*, no. 144. The words '*terre Africe*' appear in the text of the pope's letter juxtaposed with a mention of the Canary Islands. Cosmologists and cartographers of the time always assumed that the archipelago was part of Africa but the use of the term in this particular context also implied that the Castilian claims on the continent went beyond the territories of Visigothic Tingitania (Morocco) as Cartagena had argued in his *Allegationes*. The extension was based on the doctrine of territorial propinquity already used by both Portugal and Castile in their attempt to establish their respective claims to the Canaries.

25 *MH*, VI, no. 22.

26 See *CDFG*, II, chapters 68, 69 and 85.

27 European contacts, presumably Castilian, with La Gomera went back to the 1430s. In 1434 Eugenius IV issued a safe-conduct to 'Peter Chymboyo, a "duke" resident in the island of La Gomera' ('*Petro Chymboyo, duci, in jnsula Gomere conmoranti*') and his family and retinue permitting them to travel anywhere. The Gomeran chief is described there as a

28 Torres Campos, 1901, 144–5.

29 Thanks to La Gomera's peculiar physical character, communication by land even in modern times remains difficult and time-consuming; the high mountain ranges which dominate the whole island are continuously broken by narrow, deep ravines so that mountain tops adjacent to each other as the crow flies may be hours away in walking time. Though, like all the native Canarian peoples, the Gomerans were famous for their remarkable prowess as athletes, even they found movement and communication on their island difficult. For this reason they had evolved their famous whistling language which enabled them to communicate with each other from mountain top to mountain top across the ravines.

Christian convert. The approach (*pro parte tua*) to the pope presumably emanated from the Franciscan house in Seville which had oversight of the somewhat desultory work of the Franciscan missions in the archipelago generally (*MH*, V, no. 37).

30 Cadamosto, 1966, 18–19. Cadamosto also states that he had visited the island of Hierro which was also in the hands of the Christians and accepted the lordship of Herrera.

31 *CFCG.*, II, 392–401.

32 *CFCG*, II, 401–2, 403. See also *ibid.*, 42.

33 *Ibid.*, 461–2,

34 Text in *MH*, IX, no. 95.

35 *CdG*, 263, nn. 1 and 2.

36 Maciot was found guilty by a Castilian court in 1454 of rebellion against his territorial lords by selling Lanzarote to Henry (Chil y Naranjo, 1880, 587; Torres Campos, 1901, 160–1). The verdict caused him no inconvenience since by then he had long resided in Madeira as a pensioner of the Prince.

37 *Ibid.*, no. 174 and Torres Campos, 1901, 125. For other information about the sale and about Maciot and his descendants see *ibid.*, p. 273, n. 1.

38 His daughter married Rui Gonçalves da Câmara, who became the first Portuguese *capitão* of the island of São Miguel in the Azores. Rui Gonçalves himself was a son of the first colonizer of Madeira and first captain of Funchal, João Gonçalves Zarco.

39 For an account of the Portuguese occupation of Lanzarote see Zurara, *CDFG*, II, 547–8; *CdG*, 263–4 and footnotes; also Serra y Ràfols, 1941, 30–1.

40 Torres Campos, 1901, 123 and 131.

41 The Castilian king's letters, dated 25 May 1452 and 10 April 1454, survive only in the form in which Bartolomé de Las Casas copied them into his *Historia de las Indias* (end of chapter 18). They are nevertheless undoubtedly authentic. They are fully reproduced and annotated in *MH*, XI, nos. 138 and 236.

42 Serra y Ràfols, 1941, 31.

43 *MH*, XI, no. 138, pp. 175–6.

44 *Ibid.*, 177.

45 *MH*, XI, no. 236, p. 343

46 Serra y Ràfols, 1941, 32.

47 I have made no attempt in this chapter to bewilder the reader with accounts of the various different individuals who paid liege-homage to the king of Castile for the lordship of the Canaries in the Prince's time. Details will be found in Serra Ràfols, 1941, *passim* and Miguel Angel Ladero Quesada, 'Los señores de Canarias en su contexto sevillano (1303–1477)', *AEA*, 23 (1977), 125–64.

48 *Ibid.*, 79–81.

49 *Ibid.*, 81. See also Pérez Embid, 1948, 157.

50 Rui de Pina, 1977, *Afonso V*, 769; João de Barros, I, 48; Chil y Naranjo, 1880, 592–4; Pérez Embid, 1948, 166–8.

51 *Ibid.*, 168.
52 The most up-to-date information about and comment on these permutations is now to be found in *MH*, XIV, no. 145, nn. 1 and 2. The petition of Pedro de Meneses to Pius II admitted the failure of all previous French, Castilian and Portuguese attempts to conquer Grand Canary, Palma and Tenerife. It also declared that the inhabitants of these islands who had been captured, abducted and converted while overseas promptly reverted to their pagan state when they returned to their homes in the archipelago (*ibid.*,331–2).
53 Chil y Naranjo, 1880, 592–5
54 The Portuguese finally abandoned their claims to the Canaries in exchange for a free hand in Guinea in the treaty of Alcaçovas (1479).
55 For details see Fernández-Armesto, 1982, 13–21, and *passim*.

Chapter Twelve

1 Cadamosto, 1966, 5.
2 As already indicated, ambiguity surrounds the question of the exact location of the 'Vila do Infante' ('The Prince's Town'), as Henry with characteristic arrogance immediately baptized it. Nor is it certain whether its much delayed construction was far enough advanced in the 1450s for him actually to reside there. A number of documents issued by his chancery at that time were dated from the Vila but students of the peregrinations of royal chanceries in the Middle Ages will know that that is no guarantee that Henry was then personally in residence there.
3 As early as November 1434 Duarte I granted to the Venetian 'Antonio Valim', at the request of 'the carpenter of the Venetian galleys', exemptions from certain citizens' obligations that otherwise would

fall to him as a resident in the village of Raposeira (*MH*, V, no. 44). Raposeira lies a short distance to the east of Vilar do Bispo, a few miles inland from modern Sagres and about half-way between it and Lagos. It was for a long time the site (now unidentified) of one of Prince Henry's favourite residences in the Algarve.
4 Cadamosto, 1966, 268.
5 In theory Henry, in the first of the circumstances described, was allowed to collect for himself the royal *quinto* (one-fifth) of the value of the cargo, but there is other evidence that, in practice, he actually collected one-quarter.
6 Cadamosto gives the capacity of the caravel as 90 *botte*. The *botta* was originally a large wine cask. Its exact equivalent has been much disputed, but it probably equalled 10 Genoese cantars or 476 kgs, that is, 0.48 metric tons (Mallett, 1967, 179).
7 See the extensive note in Tullia Gasparrini Leporace's 1966 edition, 284, n. 88.
8 cf. Gamble, 1957, 16 and Davidson, 1967, 57.
9 Cadamosto, 1966, xiv.
10 *Ibid.*, xiv and 117.
11 *Ibid.*, 32–6.
12 For a description of the navigational techniques used by Cadamosto see Taylor, 1958, 157–62.
13 Cadamosto's date is at odds with Zurara, who attributes the discovery of the mouth of the Senegal to Dinis Dias in 1445. The Venetian perhaps had been informed that 1450 was the date when a *resgate* had been established in that region.
14 ADAN, 65. The statement occurs in Afonso V's donation, dated 30 May 1489, of the trade and *senhorio* of Guinea from Ponta da Gale to the *resgate* de Gudumel [i.e. Budamel] ('onde foi feito o primeiro resgate de Gudumel por Lourenço Dias').
15 Cadamosto, 1966, 49 and 62.

16 For the activities of the Genoese merchants in fifteenth-century Portugal see, for example, Virgínia Rau, 'Uma família de mercadores italianos em Portugal no século XV – os Lomellini' in *Estudos de História* (Lisbon:Verbo, 1968), 13–58.

17 Cadamosto, 1966, 73 and 282.

18 Antoniotto (b. 1416) had been a director of the Mint in Genoa and a shareholder in the Banco di S. Giorgio but had been obliged to take refuge abroad about 1450 to escape his creditors. He first went to Seville and later to Lisbon, where, in the hope of making enough money in Guinea to settle his debts in Genoa, he secured a licence from the Prince to trade there. He also accompanied Cadamosto on the latter's 1456 journey. His letter to his creditors in Genoa describing the successes he achieved on his 1455 journey in the Venetian's company is an unreliable source for the history of the Henrican expansion (Latin text in Magnaghi, 1935, 24–9). Antoniotto does not mention his association with Cadamosto in his letter. He seems to have achieved, during his 1456 voyage with the latter, the financial success he predicted in his letter for he went back in Genoa in 1458 and then became the agent in Caffa (on the Black Sea) for the house of Marchioni. He died in 1462.

19 For a useful general account of the history and the political and social set-up of the Wolof (or Djoloff) states consult J. F. A. Ajayi and Michael Crowder, *History of West Africa*, I, 2nd edn, (London: Longman, 1976; repr. 1979), 461–79.

20 If Cadamosto uses the Italian *miglia* (equal to 4,100 English feet), his distances must be reduced by one-fifth to arrive at the modern equivalents (Taylor, 1958, 105).

21 C. Barbey, *Notes Africaines*, no. 116 (October, 1967), 122–4 and no. 117 (January, 1968), 22–5.

22 The short life of horses in Senegal is unlikely to have been caused by the tsetse fly as the region even in the fifteenth century was largely outside the forest belt.

23 Cadamosto, 1968, 69.

24 *Esmeraldo*, 79.

25 Cadamosto, 1966, 69 and 72. The text of the *Navigazioni* appears to imply by its silence that the slaves obtained by Cadamosto at Budomel were carried in his caravel on its subsequent voyage of exploration up the River Gambia before it set sail for Portugal. If so, one can understand the hostile reception he received from the local people there.

26 The statement claims that Cadamosto got his information about navigational conditions in the Senegal River 'from our Portuguese who have been inland' – ('da nostri Cristiani Portogallesi che sono stati dentro'), (Cadamosto, 1966, 40, n.).

27 In reality the Senegal is navigable at some seasons of the year for vessels of light draught as far as modern Kayes, 500 miles from the sea.

28 *Ibid.*, 48. Despite all this information, the Venetian navigator still believed, like Zurara, that the Senegal was a branch of the Gion, i.e. one of the rivers that flowed from the Terrestrial Paradise through the dominions of Prester John to become the fabled Western Nile.

29 Cadamosto, 1966, 46.

30 *Ibid.*, 57.

31 *Ibid.*, 52–3.

32 See R. Mauny, 1952, *passim*.

33 Saunders, 1982, 15–16.

34 Cadamosto, 1966, 85.

35 In accordance with their custom, on this portion of the coast the Portuguese applied the name of the ruler – 'Bezeguiche' – to the place where he ruled. The same process

explains the toponym 'Río dos Barbaciis', where *Burba-Sine* is a formation meaning 'chief of the Sine people'. The Portuguese form was also applied to the land of the Sine and to the people themselves. The Rio dos Barbaciis is the modern River Salum.

36 Cadamosto's text (1966, 77) states that the caravels anchored four or five miles from the shore. This statement is not as surprising as might appear since the *Africa Pilot*, 1953, 234–41, makes it clear that, south of Cape Verde, frequent and uncharted off-shore shoals made such caution advisable.

37 Cadamosto, 1966, 76–7.

38 At its western limit the estuary is today seventeen miles wide, eventually narrowing to two and a half miles at the entrance to the river proper. The Gambia is about seven hundred miles long and is comparatively easily navigable for some one hundred-sixty miles. At the right season craft up to a draught of some six feet can sail 112 miles further on without serious difficulty. The Portuguese caravels by the late 1450s routinely managed to cover these distances.

39 Ajayi and Crowder, 483–4.

40 Cadamosto, 1966, 72.

41 *Ibid.*, 85.

42 For a comment on this observation see Cadamosto, 1937, 61, n. 1.

43 Cadamosto, 1966, 86.

44 Parry, 1963, 90–4. For a readable account of the way fifteenth-century sailors navigated and the instruments they had at their disposal see chapter 5 ('Pilotage and Navigation') of this author's *The Age of Reconnaissance*, 1963.

45 Complete text in *MH*, XII, no. 99. The autograph does not survive. The version known to scholars is a copy made in the second half of the fifteenth century (Genoa, Biblioteca Universitaria, MS B. I 36). It is likely that Antoniotto returned to Genoa late in 1456 after his second journey to Gambia with Cadamosto in that year; in 1458 he was already established in Caffa, Genoa's Black Sea outpost.

46 Cadamosto, 1966, 91.

47 Critics of Cadamosto have rightly pointed out that this assertion, categorical though it is, is impossible to reconcile with the Venetian explorer's earlier comment that the caravels, after leaving Lagos early in March, had made an exceptionally rapid journey to Cape Blanco. Cadamosto, who was anxious to place on record in the *Navigazioni* that the 1456 expedition was the first to sight the Cape Verde Islands (though the credit for their discovery had subsequently gone elsewhere), is unlikely to have put his case in jeopardy by so obvious an error as the Marciana text suggests.

48 *Africa Pilot*, I, 1953, 251.

49 Godinho, 1984, I, 151–2.

50 'It was not on this voyage that I saw [all] this, but on another voyage which I afterwards made in [my] caravel up the River Gambia'. ('E sì non fo questo viazo ch'io li vidi, ma un altro viazo, che da poi veni in su la caravella a intrar in questo fiume de Gambra', Cadamosto, 1966, 104). This passage only occurs in *A*, the oldest of the Marciana MSS.

51 Cadamosto, 1966, 106–7.

52 The Marciana MS reads '2 zorni' ('two days') but this is clearly a copyist's error. Later editors of Cadamosto's text either rejected it in favour of longer periods or omitted any attempt to state the duration of the stay in Batimansa's country.

53 The *Navigazioni* is a unique source for our information about the way the slave–interpreter system worked in Henry's time (and later). For a synoptic account of the system see Russell, 1995, XIV, *passim*.

54 Cadamosto, 1966, 113.

Chapter Thirteen

1 Silva de Sousa, 1991, 45–6.
2 *MH*, XIII, no. 68.
3 '. . . from many years past to the present time I have set about enquiring and discovering what lay from the said Cape Noun onwards, not without great labours by me and endless expenditure, specially of the revenues from income and taxes belonging to the said Order [of Christ] with whose government I am charged' (*ibid.* 116).
4 *Ibid.*, 117: 'Dom Afonso, my lord and nephew, twelfth king of these realms and eighth king of the Algarve, third lord of Ceuta and *first lord of the said lands of Guinea* . . . [my italics].'
5 *MH*, XIII, no. 20.
6 The story of Afonso's involvement in this in the end aborted crusade is usefully summarized in Veríssimo Serrão, II, 1978, 81–5. For a view of Alfonso V of Aragon's responses to the papal call for a crusade see Ryder, 1990, 290–7, 412–17.
7 Pina, 1977, 772.
8 *MH*, XIII, no. 55, p. 91.
9 Afonso's obsession with crusading for the faith and for seeking military glory certainly owed much to the example and teachings of his uncle. Afonso was, however, no mere swashbuckling fire-eater. He was a well-educated and cultured prince who, as his private correspondence with the chronicler Zurara shows, enjoyed intellectual discussion.
10 *MH*, XIII, no. 18.
11 A record of these events made by the prior of Santa Maria da Sabonha notes that he had witnessed the final departure of the fleet from Setùbal on 30 September 1458 and had personally counted the number of ships in it. Including the smaller vessels as well as the big ones, the total, he declared, was ninety-three (*MH*, XIII, no. 84).
12 Pina, 1977, 776.

13 Afonso's obsession with the capture of Tangier was to result in a new defeat for Portuguese arms there when an expedition led by him against the city in 1463 failed. Only in 1471 did Tangier at last fall into Portuguese hands.
14 Góis, 1977, 34–5.
15 Accounts of the attack on Alcácer and of the sieges by the Moroccans which immediately followed its capture by the Portuguese are given in the chronicles of Rui de Pina (Pina, 1977, 779–89) and Damião de Góis, *Crónica do principe D João,* 1977, 31–40. The chapters of Zurara's *Crónica de D. Duarte de Meneses* that dealt with the actual capture of Alcácer have been lost. See also Veríssimo Serrão, *História*, II, 82–5. and Ricard, 1955, 64–71.
16 The impressive fortifications that are to be seen at Alcácer today date from the period of Portuguese occupation.
17 Zurara's *CDM* certainly contained a more detailed account of the capture of Alcácer which he secured from Moorish as well as Christian informants during the months he spent in the place in 1467 and 1468 to secure on-the-spot information for the chronicle. Unfortunately the chapters describing the capture (27–33) are missing in the surviving manuscripts. Chapters 35–62 contain a vivid account of the heroic and in the end succesful resistance the Portuguese garrison put up during the two sieges of Alcácer, lasting in all 107 days, that began shortly after the king had left there for Ceuta.
18 The size achieved by some bombards in the fifteenth century was impressive. Mons Meg (1449) was 15′ long and weighed 15,366 lbs. For technical information about fifteenth-century cannon and bombards and their use see particularly Contamine, 1984, 138–50.
19 Pina, 1977, 776–9; Góis. 1977, 37–9.

20 Pina, 1977, 778. The king lost no time in seeking to redress this balance. Within two years he made his first and unsuccessful attempt to seize Tangier.

21 *MH*, XIII, no. 182.

22 Pina mentions by name the presence of only one *comendador* of the Order. He was killed in action.

23 *CDFG*, II, 43–4.

Chapter Fourteen

1 *Esmeraldo*, 1975, 98.

2 Latin text in *VF*, 187–200; partial English translation in Cadamosto, 1937, 91–102. For an excellent summary biographical account of Valentim Fernandes in English see Painter, 1971, lxxiv. See also *DHP*, II, 204–5. The original manuscript of *VF* is in the Bavarian State Library in Munich.

3 For a brief description of this thesis, put forward by José Saraiva, see Zurara, *CDG*, 1960, 32, n. 5.

4 For Hieronymus Münzer's narrative about the history of the discoveries (*De inventione Africae maritimae et occidentalis videlicet Geneae per Infantem Heinricum Portugalliae* see the text, with Portuguese translation, published by Basílio de Vasconcelos in *o Instituto*, 83 (1932), 140–72. The thesis put forward by José Saraiva (n. 3 supra) supposes that Münzer's narrative, too, is a paraphrase of Diogo Gomes also forged by Valentim Fernandes.

5 Diogo Gomes's accounts of his own voyages beyond the Senegal begin at *VF* 193.

6 *Afromomum Melegueta* and its twin species *Afromomum Granum-paradisi* often known as 'grains of Paradise'. Malagueta was imported from Africa into Europe by caravan at least from the thirteenth century. For a detailed account of the exploitation by the Portuguese of

this spice see Magalhães Godinho, 1985, II, particularly 146–51.

7 '180 pondera auri' (VF, 194). This is translated in Cadamosto, 1937, 92 as 180 *arráteis*. Since an *arrátel* = 12.5 ounces or 0.340 kg the figure quoted would represent over 62 kilos or nearly 134 lbs of gold and is therefore obviously wrong.

8 'Et ego ascendi fluuium quantium potui, et inueni Cantor, que est habitatio magna circa flumen illud' (*VF*, 194).

9 It is probable that the Cantor of the Portuguese is recalled by modern Kuntaur, though this is located on the *north* bank of the river downstream from Georgetown.

10 The Mandingo emperor of Mali is called in the *VF* text 'Bormelli'. The use of Wolof-Serer *bur* instead of the Mandinka term *mansa* suggests that Gomes's sources of information were Wolof or Serer rather than Mandinka.

11 '*niumi*' in Mandinka means 'coast'. The Niumi-Mansa's domain was on the right bank of the estuary of the Gambia (Ajayi and Crowder, 484).

12 *VF*, 198. Diogo Gomes goes into some detail about the priest allegedly sent by Henry in 1458 or 1459, to the Niumi-Mansa. Though he did not recall the man's name he described him as a relation of 'the abbot of 'Soto de Cassa' (*sic*). The priest was said to have been escorted by a young man of Henry's household, João Delgado. No identifications of either abbot or priest have proved possible, though a João Delgado of Lisbon, the owner of a caravel, was privileged in 1440 at the Prince's request for his services at Tangier (*MH*, VII, no. 78).

13 Gomes's 'Burbruck' can plausibly be identified with the Brak of Walo, the Wolof state occupying both sides of the lower reaches of the Senegal River. It is less easy to explain the title 'Borgebil, qui fuit rex de Geloffa', the name used by

Gomes to identify the ruler the Brak had ousted.

14 Decades later Duarte Pacheco Pereira complained of a marked decline in the number of slaves which a horse would fetch in the Senegambian anchorages.

15 *VF*, 199–200. The text refers several times to the trading anchorage used by the Portuguese in the region of the Salum estuary as 'Zaza' – a name which seems to appear in no other source.

16 Cadamosto, 1966, 117.

17 *MH*, XIV, no. 117.

18 *Esmeraldo*, 1975, 124 and *Esmeraldo*, 1936, 132. The editor of the latter work suggests that the 'Rio de Pero de Sintra' may be identifiable as the modern Opobo River (lat. 4° 35′ N).

19 Later versions of the *Navigazioni* read 'Besegue'. A. Teixeira da Mota gives a different explanation of the toponym (*VF*, 1951, 168, n. 157), but there seems to be no good reason to doubt that given to Cadamosto by Pedro de Sintra's scrivener.

20 The similarities of appearance which led the Portuguese explorers to name the twin promontories at the south-western end of Île Tombo after the Sagres capes are made clear by a map of Conakry published in *Afrique occidentale française: Togo*, Les Guides Bleus (Paris: Hachette, 1958), facing 312.

21 Cadamosto, 1966, 119.

22 *Ibid.*

23 The origins of the name (Port. 'Lyoa' here is presumably a fem. adjectival form of *leão*, not the nominal form *leoa*, 'lioness') have caused controversy. Some have supposed – improbably – that lions were detected in the mountains by the Portuguese explorers. Others, more plausibly, have concluded that the frequent rumbles of thunder heard coming from the mountains made them think of the roaring of lions. Pedro de Sintra's explorations in this region did take place during the early part of the rainy season. Pacheco Pereira, however, asserts that Pedro de Sintra himself told him that he had coined the toponym because the region looked rugged and desolate [like lion country] (*Esmeraldo*, 96). However, it seems unlikely that Pedro de Sintra, the inventor of the toponym Cape Ledo, can have so described the appearance of the lush mountains of Sierra Leone. It is possible that the region was named because the Portuguese encountered it at the beginning of the entry of Leo into the zodiacal constellation.

24 Since 1510 St Ann's Day has been celebrated by papal decree on 26 July. Assuming that this date was also used in fifteenth-century Portugal, some editors have thought there is a confusion in the text since the Portuguese had given the name 'Our Lady of the Snow' (feast on 5 August) to the Bagru River, further north. There may well be no such confusion. It has to be remembered that Pedro de Sintra was primarily concerned with exploring and fully charting this coast, a duty which weather conditions must sometimes have involved retracking to secure or check data.

25 Cadamosto, 1966, 124.

26 In medieval Portuguese *'mesurado'* meant 'courteous' or 'prudent'. Cadamosto correctly translates the name into Italian as 'Cavo Cortese'. The text gives no hint of the reason for this unexpected choice of toponym.

27 Cadamosto, 1966, 125–6.

28 British Library. *Additional Manuscripts*, 6390. Reproduction in Cadamosto, 1937, (opposite, p. 84). Benincasa's map is the first known one to show the Cape Verde Islands.

29 Barros, I, 1988, 120.

Chapter Fifteen

1 'Anno Domini 1460 Dominus Infans infirmatus in villa quadam sua quae est in Cabo Sancti Vincenti, de quo mortuus est XIII die nouembris anno praedicto in vna quinta feria' (*DPIG*, 198). The material contained in the first part of this chapter follows quite closely that published in Russell, 1992.

2 These documents were studied in detail in Dias Dinis, 1960, 109–316 (see also the appendix of documents in the same work).

3 *MH*, VI, no. 52, pp. 108–32.

4 *Ibid.*, VI, 108–32.

5 *EH*, 113 and 216–17.

6 *MH*, XI, no. 96.

7 *MH*, XIV, no. 3.

8 This was Frei João Martins, M.Th. who describes himself as 'having been confessor of the Infante in this his final ending' (*MH*, XIV, no. 48, p. 136).

9 *EH*, 161–2.

10 *Ibid.*, 162.

11 The circumstances in which the king decided to ignore Henry's last testamentary wishes are explored at length by Dias Dinis (*EH*, 246–67). If some legal grounds were put forward at the time to justify Afonso's action, no trace of them appears in the documents.

12 *EH*, 173–5.

13 *Ibid.*, 165.

14 *EH*, 166 and 184–8.

15 For the fifteenth-century history of Lisbon University an essential source is the splendid collection of documents edited by Arturo Moreira de Sá, *Chartularium Universitatis Portugalensis (1288–1517)*, 6 vols (Lisbon: Instituto de Alta Cultura, 1968–74). The religious orders in Portugal had traditionally sent their Portuguese members to study theology in Paris, at one of the Italian universities, or at Oxford or Cambridge or Salamanca. Paris was the most frequent choice.

16 *MH*, VIII, no. 54, p. 97.

17 Moreira de Sá, IV (1970), no. 955, pp. 28–30.

18 The Latin text of this substantial work, together with a Portuguese translation and an introduction, has recently been published in a scholarly edition by Aires A. Nascimento, *Horologium fidei: Diálogo com o Infante D. Henrique*, CNCDP (Lisbon: INCM, 1994).

19 *Ibid.*, 32–4.

20 *MH*, XIV, nos. 127 and 129.

21 *Ibid.*, no. 127, pp. 293–4 and 298–9.

22 Anstis, 1784, I, 178–93 and II, 180–1. Henry succeeded to the stall in Windsor of Sir Simon Felbridge. Garter King of Arms spent ten months on a journey to Portugal to initiate Prince Henry into the Order (*ibid.*, II, 184). He was not the first Portuguese prince to be elected to the Order of the Garter. This honour had earlier been bestowed on John I, on Duarte I and on the regent D. Pedro as gestures to England's Portuguese ally and to the blood relationship between the two royal houses.

23 Pina, 1977, 770–1 (chap. 137).

24 The sepulchre made for D. Pedro displays the arms of the Order of the Garter on its outward face. Since the tomb Henry had made for himself in his lifetime also does so, it is possible that he had ordered this to be done to remind future generations of Pedro's international reputation as a knight.

25 *EH*, 297–9, 471–4.

26 *EH*, 283 and 478–9.

27 *Ibid.*, 169.

28 *MH*, XIV, no. 11, p. 29.

29 *EH*, 462–3.

30 *MH*, XV, 156.

31 See, for example, Aristotle, *The Nicomachean Ethics*, IV, i–ii, *passim*.

32   *MH*, XIV no. 20, p. 88.

33   'In the year of Our Lord 1460 the Lord Infante was taken ill in a certain town belonging to him which is in [the neighbourhood] of Cape St Vincent and died on 13 November in that year which was a Friday' (*DPIG*, 198). 13 November 1460 actually fell on a Thursday. Henry's death apparently took place during the night which may explain the apparent error.

34   *DPIG*, 199.

35   Pina, 1977, 791.

36   *MH*, XIV, no. 11, pp. 26–7.

37   Murphy, 1795, 33–40.

38   For details see Reis-Santos, 1960, 33–8.

39   The *Primeira Parte* of the *História de São Domingos* attributed to Frei Luís de Sousa (Lisbon, 1623) refers to some then well-preserved paintings attached to the individual altars associated with each princely tomb. He reports that the painting attached to that of Prince Henry was of D. Fernando depicted as saint and martyr.

40   Reis-Santos, 1960, 25. The end of the Portuguese text, translated, reads '[who] died on ... of the era one thousand and ...'. The reference to the 'era' is somewhat unexpected since, in medieval Portuguese documents, this word usually refers to the Julian or Spanish era (thirty-eight years ahead of the Christian era). Portugal adopted the style of the Nativity in 1422 though it was not uncommon, especially in religious documents, for the term 'era' still to be used when the new style is meant.

Appendix

1   Best text in *Monumenta Henricina*, III, no. 125) from BNParis, Fonds Portugais, no. 20, fol. 97 – a fifteenth- or early sixteenth-century copy.

Select Bibliography

Manuscript Sources

Arquivo Nacional da Torre do Tombo*
    Leitura Nova, no. 36, *Livro das Ilhas*
        Livro I de Extras
        Místicos, 4
        Livros de Chancelaria D. João I (4); D. Duarte; D. Afonso V (1 to 5 only)

*Note that most documents relating to D. Henrique in the surviving royal chancery registers and other *Livros* in ANTT have been printed in whole or in part in *Descobrimentos Portugueses* [*DP*] or as complete texts in *Monumenta Henricina* [*MH*].

Archivo de la Corona de Aragón
        Cancillería (Fernando I and Alfonso V): *reg.* 2391 and 2410

Biblioteca Medicea-Laurenziana (Florence)
        Fondo Ashburnham, 1792, *passim*

Biblioteca Nacional, Lisbon
        Fundo Geral, 3776, fols. 195*r*–199*r*
        COD, 8920, fols. 39*v*–41*v* (horoscope of King Sebastian)

St John's College, Oxford
        MS CLXIV

Select Bibliography

[Afonso v], *Ordenaçoens do Senhor Rey D. Affonso*, in *Colecção de Legislação Antiga e Moderna do Reino de Portugal*, Parte I: *Legislação Antiga*, 5 vols (Coimbra: Imprensa da Universidade, 1797; facsimile repr. Lisbon: Fundação Calouste Gulbenkian, 1983)

Afrique Occidentale Française – Togo, Les Guides Bleus (Paris: Librarie Hachette, 1958)

Ajayi, J. F. Ade, and Ian Espie, (eds.), *A Thousand Years of West African History* (Ibadan: Ibadan University Press and Thomas Nelson, 1965; repr. 1976)

——, and Michael Crowder, *History of West Africa*, I (2nd edn, London: Longmans, 1976; repr. 1979)

Albuquerque, Luís [Mendonça] de, 'The Historical Background to the Cartography and Navigational Techniques of the Age of Discovery with Special Reference to the Portuguese' (unpublished public lecture delivered in Oxford in February 1969)

——, *Introdução à História dos Descobrimentos Portugueses*, Forum da História, 3 (4th edn, [Lisbon]: Publicações Europa–América, [1989]; 1st edn (Coimbra: Atlântida, 1962)

Select Bibliography

——, 'Os "Sábios" Henriquinos e a "Escola de Sagres" ', in *Vértice*, LXIII (1994), 81–6

Albuquerque, Luís de, and Maria Emilia Madeira Santos, (eds.), *Portugalia Monumenta Africana*, Instituto de Investigação Científica Tropical (Lisbon: INCM and CNCDP, 1993)

Alemany, José, 'Milicias cristianas al servicio de los sultanes musulmanos del Almagreb', in *Homenaje a D. Francisco Codera* (Zaragoza: M. Escar, 1904), 133–69

Alfonso el Sabio, *Las Siete Partidas del rey Don Alfonso el Sabio,* 3 vols (Madrid: Imprenta Real, 1807)

Almada, André Alvares de, *Tratado breve dos rios de Guiné do Cabo Verde, desde o rio de Sanagá até aos baixos de Sant'Ana,* [1594], ed. Luís Silveira (Lisbon: Oficina Gráfica, 1946)

Almeida, Fortunato de, *História da Igreja em Portugal,* 4 vols (Coimbra: Imprensa da Universidade, 1910–22; 2nd edn, Oporto: Portucalense Editora, 1967–71)

——, *História de Portugal,* 6 vols (Coimbra: Imprensa da Universidade, 1922–9)

Alvares, Francisco, *Verdadeira informação das terras do Preste João das Índias* ([Lisbon]: Publicações Europa–América, 1989)

Alvares, Frei João, *Trautado da vida e feitos do muito vertuoso Sor Infante D. Fernando,* ed. Adelino de Almeida Calado in *Obras,* I, Acta Universitatis Conimbrigensis (Coimbra: Editorial Atlântida, 1960)

Alves, José da Felicidade, *O mosteiro dos Jerónimos;* III: *Para um inventário do recheio do Mosteiro de Santa Maria de Belém,* Colecção Cidade de Lisboa (Lisbon: Livros Horizonte, 1993)

Amaral, Joaquim Ferreira do, *Pedro Reinel me fez: à volta de um mapa dos descobrimentos* (Lisbon: Quetzal Editores, 1995)

Andrade, António Alberto Banha de, *Mundos novos do mundo: panorama de difusão, pela Europa, de notícias dos descobrimentos geográficos portugueses,* 2 vols (Lisbon: JIU, 1972)

[Anon.], *Libro del conosçimiento de todos los reynos y tierras e señoríos que son por el mundo e de las señales e armas que han cada tierra e señorío por sý . . . ,* ed. Marcos Jiménez Espada (Madrid: T. Fortanet, 1877; repr. Barcelona: El Albir, 1980)

——, *Book of the Knowledge of all the Kingdoms, Lands, and Lordships that are in the World,* ed. and transl. Sir Clements Markham, The Hakluyt Society, Second Series, no. XXIX (London: The Hakluyt Society, 1912)

——, *A Thousand Years of Portuguese Art* (London: Royal Academy of Arts, [1955])

Anstis, John, *The Register of the Most Noble Order of the Garter,* 2 vols (London: J. Barber, 1724)

Aparício, João Paulo, 'O navio num mundo que se descobre (sécs. xv–xvi)' in *Patrimonio*, II (February 1977), 11–39

Aragão, Augusto Carlos Teixeira de, *Descripção geral e histórica das moedas cunhadas em nome dos reis, regentes e governadores de Portugal*, 3 vols (Lisbon: Imprensa Nacional, 1874–7; repr. Oporto: Livraria Fernando Machado, [1964]–6)

Archivo General de Simancas: *Catálogo XIII: Registro General del Sello (1454–84)*, ed. Gonzalo Ortiz de Montalbán, 3 vols (Valladolid: CSIC, 1950–3)

Aristotle [Pseudo], *Segredo dos segredos: Tradução portuguesa, segundo um manuscrito inédito do século xv* (Lisbon: Faculdade de Letras da Universidade de Lisboa, 1960)

Arribas Palau, Mariano, 'Reclamaciones cursadas por Fernando I de Aragón a Abu Sa'id 'Utman III de Marruecos', in *BRABLB*, XXX (1963–4), 307–22

——, 'Repercusión de la conquista portuguesa de Ceuta en Aragón' in *Tamuda* [Tetuan], III (1955), 9–21

Ashmole, Elias, *The Institution, Laws and Ceremonies of the Most Noble Order of the Garter* (London: J. Macock for Nathaniel Brooke, 1672)

Astley, Thomas, [John Green (?), (ed.)], *A New General Collection of Voyages and Travels printed for Thomas Astley*, 4 vols (London: Printed for Thomas Astley, 1745–7) [Vol. II contains a description of Arguin fort, island and village in Dutch times.]

Aubin, Jean, *Le Latin et l'astrolabe: Recherches sur le Portugal de la Renaissance, son expansion en Asie et ses relations internationales* (Lisbon and Paris: CCCG and CNCDP, 1996)

Azevedo, J. Lúcio de, *Épocas de Portugal económico: Esboços de história* (3rd edn, Lisbon: Livraria Clássica Editora, 1973)

Azevedo, Pedro Augusto de S. Bartolomeu de, (ed.), *Documentos das chancelarias reais anteriores a 1531 relativos a Marrocos*, 2 vols (Lisbon: Academia das Ciências, 1915–35)

Bagrow, Leo, and R. A. Skelton, *History of Cartography* (London: C.A. Watts and Co., 1964)

Baião, António, Hernani Cidade, and Manuel Múrias, (eds.), *História da expansão portuguesa no mundo*, 3 vols (Lisbon: Editorial Átiea, 1937–40)

Barber, Richard, *The Knight and Chivalry* (London: Longmans, 1970; 2nd edn, Ipswich: Boydell, 1974; rev. edn, Woodbridge, Suffolk: Boydell, 1995)

Barbey, C., 'Le Littoral de Dakar à Saint-Louis, à la lumière de documents anciens', in *Notes Africaines*, CXVI (October 1967), 122–4

Barradas de Carvalho, Joaquim, *As fontes de Duarte Pacheco Pereira no "Esmeraldo de Situ Orbis"* (Lisbon: INCM, 1982)

Barros, Henrique da Gama, *História da administração pública em Portugal nos séculos XII–XV* (1st edn, 4 vols, Lisbon: Imprensa Nacional, 1885–1922; 2nd edn, 11 vols, Lisbon: Sá da Costa, 1945–54)

Select Bibliography

Barros, João de, *Ásia: Décadas I & II*, facsimile of 1932 edition of António Baião (Lisbon: INCM, 1988)

Beaujouan, Guy, *L'Astronomie dans la Péninsule Ibérique à la fin du Moyen Age*. Offprint from *RUC*, XXIV (Coimbra: JIU, 1969)

Beazley, C. Raymond, *Prince Henry the Navigator: The Hero of Portugal and of Modern Discovery, 1394–1460 A.D.* (New York and London: G.P. Putnam's Sons, 1895; repr. London and Haarlem: Frank Cass & Co., 1968)

Beckford of Fonthill, William, *Excursion a Alcobaça et Batalha*, texte de l'édition originale, traduction, introduction, et notes de André Parreaux (Paris: Société d'Editions "Les Belles Lettres"; Lisbon: Livraria Bertrand, 1956) [The English text of Beckford's journey (made in 1794) was first printed London in 1835.]

Bell, William E., and Harry F. Williams, (eds.), *Semeiança del mundo: A Medieval Description of the World*, University of California Publications in Modern Philology (Berkeley and Los Angeles: University of California Press, 1959)

Bensaúde, Joaquim, *L'Astronomie nautique au Portugal à l'époque des grands découvertes* (Bern: Max Drechsel, 1912)

——, *A cruzada do Infante D. Henrique* (Lisbon: AGU, 1960)

Blake, John William, *European Beginnings in West Africa, 1454–1578*, Royal Empire Society Imperial Studies, no. 14 (London: Longmans, Green & Co., 1937)

——, (ed. and trans.), *Europeans in West Africa (1450–1560): Documents to Illustrate the Nature and Scope of Portuguese Enterprise in West Africa*, 2 vols, The Hakluyt Society, Second Series, Nos. LXXXVI & LXXXVII (Cambridge: The Hakluyt Society, 1942; Kraus repr. Nendeln, Liechtenstein, 1967)

Boulegue, Jean, *L'Impact économique et politique des navigations portugaises sur les peuples côtiers: le cas de la Guinée du Cap Vert (XVᵉ–XVIᵉ siècles)* (Lisbon: CEHCA, 1988)

Bovill, E. W., *The Golden Trade of the Moors* (2nd edn, London: OUP, 1968)

Boxer, C. R., 'Faith and Empire: The Cross and the Crown. Portuguese Expansion Fifteenth–Eighteenth Centuries [sic]', in *Terra Incognitae*, VIII (1976), 73–89

——, *The Portuguese Seaborne Empire, 1415–1825* (2nd edn, Manchester: Carcanet Press, 1991)

Bracciolini, Gian Francesco Poggio, *Epistolae selectae*, in Angelo Mai, (ed.), *Spicilegium romanum*, vol. X (Romae: Typis Collegie Urbani, 1844), 225–371

Branco, Theresa Schedel de Castillo, *Os panéis de S. Vicente de Fora: As chaves do mistério* (Lisbon: Quetzal Editores, 1994)

Brásio, António, (ed.), *Monumenta Missionária Africana*; I: *África Ocidental (1471–1531)*, and IV: *África Ocidental (1469–1599)* (Lisbon: AGU, 1952 and 1954)

Brooks, George E., 'Historical Perspectives on the Guinea–Bissau Region, Fifteenth to Nineteenth Centuries', in Carlos Lopes, (ed.), *Manas, escravos, grumetes e* gentio: *Cacheu na encruzilhada de civilizações. Actas do IV Centenário da Fundação da Cidade de Cacheu* (Lisbon: INEP and INCM, 1993)

Bruin, Georgius [Georg Braun] with Franz Hogenberg, *Civitates orbis terrarum*, I and II (Coloniae [Agrippinae]: prostant apud auctores, et Anuerpiae [*sic*], apud Phillipum Gallæum, 1572) [Illustrations of Lisbon waterfront with caravels (fols. 1–2).]. See also *Old European Cities. Thirty-Two 16th-Century City Maps and Texts from the Civitates orbis terrarum of Georg Braun and Franz Hogenberg. With a Description by Ruthardt Oehine of Early Map-Making techniques* (London: Thames and Hudson, 1955; rev. edn, 1965). [This edition does not reproduce the illustrations of Lisbon, Ceuta or Tangier.]

Bryans, Robin, *The Azores* (London: Faber and Faber, 1963)

Burwash, Dorothy, *English Merchant Shipping 1460–1540* (Newton Abbot, Devon: David and Charles Reprints, 1969)

Cà da Mosto, Alvise da [Luigi Cadamosto], *Le navigazioni atlantiche del veneziano Alvise da Mosto* (a cura di Tullia Gasparrini Leporace), Il Novo Ramusio, V (Rome: Istituto Poligrafico dello Stato, 1966)

——, *The Voyages of Cadamosto and Other Documents on Western Africa in the Second Half of the Fifteenth Century*, ed. and translated by G.R. Crone, The Hakluyt Society, Second Series, LXXX (London: The Hakluyt Society, 1937)

Caddeo, Rinaldo, *Le navigazioni atlantiche di Alvise da Cà da Mosto, Antoniotto Usodimare e Niccoloso da Recco* (Milan: Edizioni "Alpes", 1929)

Calado, Adelino de Almeida, 'O Infante D. Fernando e a Restituição de Ceuta', in *RPH*, X (1962), 119–52

Campos, Viriato, *Sobre o descobrimento e povoamento dos Açores* (n.p.: Europress, [*c.* 1980–3])

Carnero Ruiz, Ismael, *Vocabulario geográfico-sahariano* (Madrid: CSIC, 1955)

Carreira, António, *Notas sobre o tráfico português de escravos* (rev. 2nd edn, Lisbon: Universidade Nova de Lisboa, 1983)

Carus-Wilson, Eleanora Mary, *The Overseas Trade of Bristol in the Later Middle Ages*, Bristol Record Society's Publications, VII (Bristol: Bristol Record Society, 1937; 2nd edn, New York: Barnes & Noble, 1968) [Contains information about Portuguese and English cargo-carrying caravels at Bristol in the mid-fifteenth century.]

Castro, Armando, *Portugal na Europa do seu tempo: história socio-económica medieval comparada* (Lisbon: Seara Nova, 1970)

Cenival, Pierre de & Théodore Monod, (eds. and translators), *Description de la côte d'Afrique de Ceuta au Sénégal par Valentim Fernandes (1506–1507)* (Paris: Larousse, 1938)

Chaunu, Pierre, *L'Expansion européenne du xiiie au xve siècle*, Nouvelle Clio (Paris: Presses Universitaires de France, 1969)

Select Bibliography

Chil y Naranjo, Gregorio, *Estudios históricos, climatológicos, y patológicos de las Islas Canarias*, 3 vols (Las Palmas: I. Miranda, 1876–91; Primera Parte, II: 1880)

Cipolla, Carlo M., *Guns and Sails in the Early Phase of European Expansion – 1400–1700* (London: Collins, 1965); Port. translation: *Canhões e velas na primeira fase da expansão europeia (1400–1700)* (Lisbon: Editorial Gradiva, 1989)

Coelho, José Ramos, (ed.), *Alguns documentos do Archivo Nacional da Torre do Tombo acerca das navegações e conquistas portuguezas* (Lisbon: Imprensa Nacional, 1892)

Colección de Documentos Inéditos para la Historia de España, vol. XXXVI (Madrid: Imprenta de la viuda de Calero, 1860), 499–501

Contamine, Philippe, *La Guerre au moyen âge* (Paris: Presses Universitaires de France, c. 1980); Eng. trans. Michael Jones: *War in the Middle Ages* (Oxford: Basil Blackwell, 1984)

Coquery-Vidrovitch, Catherine, *La Découverte de l'Afrique: L'Afrique noire atlantique des origines au XVIIIᵉ siècle*, Collection Archives (Paris: Réné Julliard, 1965)

Corbett, Julian Stafford, (ed.), *Papers Relating to the Navy during the Spanish War, 1585–1587*, Publications of the Navy Records Society, XI (London: Navy Records Society, 1898) [Contains much information about Cape Sagres and its fortress at the end of the sixteenth century.]

——, *Drake and the Tudor Navy*, 2 vols (rev. edn, London: Longmans, Green & Co., 1899; repr. in one vol., Aldershot: Temple Smith, 1988) [More information about Sagres.]

Cornevin, Robert, *Histoire de l'Afrique*; I: *Les origines au xviᵉ siècle*, Bibliothèque Historique (Paris: Payot, 1962)

——, and Marianne Cornevin, *Histoire de l'Afrique des origines à nos jours* (Paris: Payot, 1964)

Cortés Alonso, Vicenta, 'La conquista de las Islas Canarias a través de las ventas de esclavos en Valencia', in *AEA*, I (1955), 479–547

——, *La esclavitud en Valencia durante el reinado de los Reyes Católicos (1479–1516)* (Valencia: Publicaciones del Archivo Municipal de Valencia, 1964)

Cortesão, Armando, *Cartografia e cartógrafos portugueses dos séculos XV e XVI*, 2 vols (Lisbon: Seara Nova, 1935)

——, *História da cartografia portuguesa*, I (Coimbra: JIU, 1969)

——, *Pizzigano's Chart of 1424*, Agrupamento de Estudos de Cartografia Antiga, XL (Coimbra: JIU, 1970)

——, and Avelino Teixeira da Mota, (eds.), *Portugaliae monumenta cartographica*, 6 vols (Coimbra: CMIH, 1958–63)

Costa, Abel Fontoura da, *Marinharia dos descubrimentos* (3rd edn, Lisbon: AGC, 1960)

——, *As navegações atlânticas no século XV*, Biblioteca Breve (Lisbon: ICP, 1979)

Costa, António Domingues de Sousa, OFM, 'O Infante D. Henrique na expansão portuguesa', in *Itinerarium* [Braga], V (1959), 419–68

——, *Estudos sobre Álvaro Pais* (Lisbon: IAC, 1966)

——, (ed.), *Monumenta Portugaliae Vaticana*; IV: *Súplicas do Pontificado de Martinho V* (Braga: Editorial Franciscana, 1970)

Costa Lobo, António de Sousa Silva, *História da sociedade em Portugal no século XV e outros estudos históricos* (Lisbon: Imprensa Nacional, 1903; repr. Lisbon: Cooperativa Editora, 1979)

Coutinho, Carlos Viegas Gago, *A naútica dos descobrimentos*, 2 vols (Lisbon: AGU, 1951–2; 2nd edn, 1969)

Crawford, O. G. S., (ed.), *Ethiopian Itineraries circa 1400–1524*, The Hakluyt Society, 2nd Series, CIX (Cambridge: CUP, 1958)

Crescentio, Bartolommeo, *Nautica mediterranea* (Rome: Bartolomeo Bonfadino, 1602 [1609])

Cresques, Abraham, *L'Atlas català de Cresques Abraham* ([Barcelona]: Diafora S.A., 1975) [Contains introductory essays by various specialists, transcriptions of the legends on the atlas and many plates.]

Crewe, Quentin, *In Search of the Sahara* (London: Michael Joseph, 1983)

Cristo, Ordem de [Christ, Order of], *A regra e diffinçoões da Ordem do mestrado de nosso senhor Iesu christo* ([Lisbon: Valentim Fernandes, c. 1504])

Crone, G. R., *Maps and their Makers: An Introduction to the History of Cartography* (2nd edn, London: Hutchinson University Library, 1962; repr. 1964)

Crónica de D. Juan II, Biblioteca de Autores Españoles 68 (Madrid: Atlas, 1953)

Cunha, Maria Cristina Almeida, & Maria Cristina Gomes Pimenta, 'A casa senhorial do Infante D. Henrique: Organização social e distribuição regional', in *Revista da Faculdade de Letras* [Oporto], *História*, 2da Série, I (1984), 221–84

Cuscoy, Luis Diego, *Paletnología de las Islas Canarias*, Publicaciones del Museo Arqueológico, no. 3 (Santa Cruz de Tenerife: Museo Arqueológico, 1963)

Davidson, Basil, and F. K. Bush, *The Growth of African Civilisation: A History of West Africa 1000–1800* (London: Longmans, 1965; new edn, 1967)

Davis, Ralph, *The Rise of the Atlantic Economies*, World Economic History (London: Weidenfeld and Nicolson, 1973)

Denoix, Commandant L., 'Caractéristiques des navires a l'époque des grandes découvertes', in Michel Mollat & Paul Adam, (eds.), *Les Aspects internationaux de la découverte océanique au XVe et XVIe siècles* (Paris: SEVPEN, 1966), 137–47

De Witte, Charles-Martial, OSB, 'Les Bulles pontificales et l'expansion portugaise au XVe siècle', in *Revue d'histoire ecclésiastique*, XLVIII (1953), XLIX (1954), LI (1956) and LIII (1958).

Dias, J. S. da Silva, *Os descubrimentos e a problemática cultural do século xvi* (Coimbra: Universidade de Coimbra, 1973)

——, *Influencia de los descubrimientos en la vida cultural del siglo XVI* (Mexico: Fondo de Cultura Económica, 1986)

Dias, Manuel Nunes, *O capitalismo monárquico português (1415–1549)*, 2 vols (Coimbra: Faculdade de Letras, 1963–4)

Dicionário de História de Portugal, ed. Joel Serrão, 6 vols (Oporto: Livraria Figueirinhas, 1992)

Díez de Games, Gutierre, *El Victorial: crónica de Don Pedro Niño, conde de Buelna*, ed. Juan de Mata Carriazo, Colección de Crónicas Españolas, 1 (Madrid: Espasa Calpe, 1940)

——, [Díaz de Games, Gutierre], *The Unconquered Knight: A Chronicle of the Deeds of Don Pero Niño*, translated by Joan Evans (London: Routledge and Sons, 1928)

Diffie, Bailey W., & George D. Winius, *Foundations of the Portuguese Empire, 1415–1580: Europe and the World in the Age of Expansion*, I (Oxford: OUP, 1977) [The bibliography, though more than twenty years old, is still essential reading for English-speaking students of the Henrican explorations.]

Dinis, António Joaquim, OFM, *Estudos henriquinos*, I (Coimbra: Acta Universitatis Conimbrigensis, 1960)

——, (ed.), *Monumenta Henricina*, 15 vols (Coimbra: CEQMDH, 1960–74)

——, (ed.), 'Carta do Infante Santo ao Regente D. Pedro, datada da masmorra de Fez a 12 de Junho de 1441', in *Anais da Academia Portuguesa da História*, II Série, XIII (1965), 151–74

——, 'D. Pedro de Meneses, primeiro conde de Vila Real e primeiro capitão e governador de Ceuta', in *Studia*, XXXVIII (1974), 517–62

D. Duarte, *Leal conselheiro*, ed. Joseph M. Piel (Lisbon: Bertrand, 1942); *see also* João Morais Barbosa, (ed.) (Lisbon: INCM, 1982)

Duarte, Luís Miguel, 'Um rei a reinar (algunas questões sobre o desembargo de D. Afonso V na segunda metade do século XV)', in *Revista de História*, VIII (1988), 69–81

——, 'Crimes do mar e justiças da terra', in *Revista da Faculdade de Letras* [Oporto], *História*, 2da Série, VIII (1991), 43–73

——, 'A expansão à descoberta do reino (Quem sabia o quê no Portugal de Quatrocentos?)', unpublished paper '*Crossroads/Encruzilhadas*', given in 1995 in the University of California at Los Angeles as part of the Proceedings there of the XVIII Symposium on Portuguese Traditions.

Select Bibliography

Dufourcq, Charles-Emmanuel, *L'Espagne catalane et le Maghrib au XIIIe et XIVe siècles* (Paris: Presses Universitaires de France, 1966)

Duncan, T. Bentley, *Atlantic Islands: Madeira, the Azores, and the Cape Verdes in Seventeenth-Century Commerce and Navigation*, Studies in the History of Discoveries (Chicago: University of Chicago Press, 1972)

Fage, J. D., *A History of West Africa: An Introductory Survey* (Cambridge: CUP, 1969)

Faro, Jorge, 'Duas expedições à Guiné anteriormente a 1474 e custeadas pela fazenda de D. Afonso V', in *BCGP*, XII (1957), 47–104

——, *Receitas e despesas da fazenda real de 1384 a 1481 (subsídios documentais)* (Lisbon: Instituto Nacional de Estatística, 1965)

Fernandes, Valentim, *De prima inuentione Guynee* in *O manuscrito "Valentim Fernandes"*, ed. António Baião (Lisbon: APH, 1940), 133–86 [*See also* Gomes, Diogo.]

——, *Description de la côte d'Afrique de Ceuta au Sénégal* ... [*See* Pierre de Cenival and Théodore Monod, (eds. and translators).]

Fernández-Armesto, Felipe, *The Canary Islands after the Conquest: The Making of a Colonial Society in the Early Sixteenth Century*, Oxford Historical Monographs (Oxford: Clarendon Press, 1982)

——, *Before Columbus. Exploration and Colonisation from the Mediterranean to the Atlantic, 1229–1492*, New Studies in Medieval History (Basingstoke and London: Macmillan Education, 1987)

Ferrão, José Eduardo Mendes, *The Adventure of Plants and the Portuguese Discoveries* ([Lisbon]: The Institute of Tropical Research, 1994)

Ferreira, J. A. Pinto, 'A cidade que viu nascer o Infante: o Porto na época henriquina', in *Studium Generale*, [Oporto], VII (1960), 185–222

Ferro [Tavares], Maria José Pimenta, *Estudos de história monetária portuguesa (1383–1438)* (Lisbon: Tipografia–Escola, 1974)

——, *Os Judeus em Portugal no século XV*, I (Lisbon: Universidade Nova de Lisboa, 1982)

Ferronha, António Luís, Mariana Bettencourt and Rui Loureiro, *A fauna exótica dos descobrimentos*, Colecção "As Grandes Navegações" ([Lisbon]: Edição Elo, 1993)

Ficalho, Conde de, *Plantas úteis da África portugueza* (Lisbon: Sociedade de Geographia de Lisboa-Imprensa Nacional, 1884; 2nd edn, Lisbon: AGC, 1947)

——, *Memória sobre a malagueta* (2nd rev. edn, Lisbon: AGC, 1945)

——, (ed.), *Viagens de Pêro de Covilhã* (Lisbon: António Maria Pereira, 1898: fascimile edn, Lisbon: INCM, 1988)

Select Bibliography

Figanière, Frederico francisco de la, *Catálogo dos manuscriptos portugueses existentes no Museu Britânico* . . . (Lisbon: Imprensa Nacional, 1853)

Fonseca, Henrique Quirino da, *A caravela portuguesa e a prioridade técnica das navegações henriquinas* (Coimbra: Imprensa da Universidade, 1934)

Fonseca, Luís Adão da, *Navegación y corso en el Mediterráneo occidental: los portugueses a mediados del siglo xv*, Cuadernos de Trabajos de Historia, 8 (Pamplona: Ediciones Universidad de Navarra, 1978)

——, and José Manuel Ruiz Asencio, (eds.), *El tratado de Tordesillas: corpus documental* (Valladolid: SVCTT and CNCDP, 1995)

Freire, Anselmo Braamcamp, *Brasões da Sala de Sintra*, 3 vols, (2nd edn, Coimbra Imprensa da Universidade, 1921–30; repr. Lisbon: INCM, 1973)

Freitas, Jordão de, *A vila e fortaleza de Sagres nos séculos xv a xviii* (Coimbra: IAC, 1938)

Freitas, Paula and Maria de Jesus Gonçalves, *Panéis de S. Vicente de Fora. Uma questão inútil?*, Colecção Arte e Artistas (Lisbon: INCM, 1987)

Frutuoso, Doutor Gaspar, *Saudades da Terra*, ed. Álvaro Rodrigues de Azevedo, Livros V and VI (Funchal: Tipografia de Amigo do Povo, 1873; 2nd edn, Ponta Delgada: Instituto Cultural de Ponta Delgada, 1963–78)

——, *Las Islas Canarias*, Fontes Rerum Canarium XII (La Laguna de Tenerife: Instituto de Estudios Canarios, 1964)

Fyfe, Christopher, *Sierra Leone Inheritance* (London: OUP, 1964)

Galvão, António, *Tratado dos descobrimentos*, ed. Vizconde de Lagoa (3rd edn, Oporto: Livraria Civilização, 1944)

Gamble, David P., *The Wolof of Senegambia: Together with Notes on the Lebu and the Serer*, ESA–WA Part XIV (London: International African Institute, 1957)

Garcia, José Manuel, *Ao encontro dos descobrimentos: temas de história da expansão* (Lisbon: Editorial Presença, 1994)

García Merchante, Eustaquio, *Los tapices de Alfonso V de Portugal que se guardan en la extinguida colegiata de Pastrana* (Toledo: Editorial Católica Toledana, 1929)

García Sánchez, Julián, 'La artillería española en el siglo xv', in *Actas de las II jornadas nacionales de historia militar* (Sevilla:Cátedra General Castaños, Capitanía General de la Región Militar Sur, 1993), 361–4

García Santa María, Alvar and others, *Crónica de D. Juan II*, Biblioteca de Autores Españoles 68 (Madrid: Atlas, 1953)

Garter, Order of the, [*See* John Anstis (ed.).]

Gavetas da Torre do Tombo, As, ed. A. da Silva Rego, 12 vols (Lisbon: CEHU, 1960–77)

Godinho, Vitorino Magalhães, (ed.), *Documentos sôbre a expansão portuguesa*, 3 vols (Lisbon: Editorial Gleba, 1943–56)

——, 'A economia das Canarias nos séculos XIV e XV', in *Revista de História* [São Paulo], X (1952), 311–48

——, *O "Mediterrâneo" saariano e as caravanas do ouro: geografia econômica e social do Sáara Ocidental e Central do XI ao XVI século*, Coleção da Revista de História, XVIII (São Paulo, 1956)

——, *A economia dos descobrimentos henriquinos* (Lisbon: Sá da Costa, 1962)

——, 'Os descobrimentos: inovação e mudança nos séculos XV e XVI', in *Revista de História Económica e Social*, II (1978), 1–28

——, *Os descubrimentos e a economia mundial*, 5 vols (2nd edn, Lisbon: Editorial Presença, 1984–91)

——, 'Comemoração e História (A Descoberta da Guiné)', in *Vértice*, LXIII (1994), 73–9

Goís, Damião de, *Crónica do príncipe D. João*, ed. Graça Almeida Rodrigues (Lisbon: Universidade Nova, 1977)

——, *Crónica do felicíssimo rei D. Manuel*, 4 vols, Acta Universitatis Conimbrigensis (Coimbra: n.p., 1949–55)

Gomes, Diogo, *De la première découverte de la Guinée, récit par Diogo Gomes (fin xve siècle)*, ed. Th. Monod, R. Mauny and G. Duvel (Bissau: CEGP, 1959)

Gonçalves, Iria, 'Físicos e cirurgiões quatrocentistas: as cartas de exame', *Do Tempo e da História*, I (1965), 69–112

[Gonçalves, Nuno], *Nuno Gonçalves: Novos documentos, estudo da pintura portuguesa do século XV* (Lisbon: Instituto Português de Museus, 1994)

Gordillo Osuna, Manuel, *Geografía urbana de Ceuta* (Madrid: CSIC, 1974)

Grau, M., 'La esclavitud en "els terms generals" del castell de Morella (Castellón) (1350–1450)' in *Homenaje a Jaime Vicens Vives*, I (Barcelona: Universidad de Barcelona, 1965), 445–82

Gray, John Milner, *A History of the Gambia* (Cambridge: CUP, 1940)

Gray, Richard and David Chambers, *Materials for West African History in Italian Archives*, Guides to Materials for West African History (London: University of London, Athlone Press, 1965)

Gruvel, A. and R. Chudeau, *À Travers la Mauritanie occidentale (de Saint-Louis à Port-Etienne)*, 2 vols (Paris: E. Larose, 1909–11)

Hair, P. E. H., 'The Use of African Languages in Afro–European Contacts in Guinea: 1440–1560', in *Sierra Leone Language Review*, V (1966), 5–26

——, 'Discovery and Discoveries: The Portuguese in Guinea 1444–1650', in *BHS*, LXIX (1992), 11–28 [The Notes contain an excellent bibliography of books and articles in various languages on the Portuguese in Guinea in the period named.]

——, 'How the South was Won and How Portuguese Discoveries Began', in *BHS*, LXXI (1994), 39–53

Hakluyt, Richard, *The Principall Navigations, Voiages and Discoveries of the English Nation*, 2 vols (London: Bishop and R. Newberie, 1589; repr. Hakluyt Society, Cambridge: CUP, 1965)

Hamann, Günther, *Der Eintritt der Südlichen Hemisphäre in die Europäische Geschichte*, Österreichische Akademie der Wissenschaften (Vienna: Hermann Böhlaus Nachf., 1968)

Heers, Jacques, 'L'Expansion maritime portugaise à la fin du Moyen-Age', in *RFL*, XXII (1956), 84–112

——, 'Le Royaume de Grenade et la politique marchande de Gênes en occident (xv^E siècle)', in *Le Moyen Âge*, LXIII (1957), 87–121

——, *Gênes au XVe siècle: activité économique et problèmes sociaux*, École Pratique des Hautes Études – Centre de Recherches Historiques (Paris: SEVPEN, 1961)

——, *Esclaves et domestiques au moyen âge dans le monde méditerranéen* (Paris: Fayard, *c.* 1981); Portuguese trans. *Escravos e servidão doméstica na idade média no mundo mediterrânico*, Anais, 3 (Lisbon: Publicações Dom Quixote, 1983)

Helms, Mary W., *Ulysses' Sail: An Ethnographic Odyssey of Power, Knowledge and Geographic Distance* (Princeton, N.J.: Princeton University Press, 1988)

Hernández Suárez, Manuel, (ed.), *El museo canário: breve reseña histórica y descriptiva* (Las Palmas de Gran Canaria: Ediciones El Museo Canario, 1967)

Homem, Amadeo Carvalho, (ed.), *Descobrimentos, expansão e identidade nacional*, publications of the *Revista de História das Ideias*, 14 (Universidade de Coimbra: Faculdade de Letras, Instituto de História e Teoria das Ideas, 1992)

Homem, Armando Luís de Carvalho, 'Da vedoria da fazenda ao bispado do Porto – a carreira de D. João Afonso Aranha', in *Humanidades* [Oporto], I (1982), 7–14

Huizinga, Johan, *The Waning of the Middle Ages* (London: Edward Arnold: 1924; 2nd repr., 1937)

Hurry, Jamieson B., *The Woad Plant and its Dye* (London: OUP, 1930)

Hyde, J.K., 'Real and Imaginary Journeys in the Later Middle Ages', in *Bulletin of the John Rylands University Library of Manchester*, LXV (1982–3), 125–47

Iria, Alberto, *O Infante D. Henrique no Algarve (estudos inéditos)*, ed. José Manuel Garcia and Pedro Moreira (Lagos: Centro de Estudos Gil Eannes, 1995)

Jobson, Richard, *The Golden Trade, or a Discovery of the River Gambia, and the Golden Trade of the Aethiopians* (London: Nicholas Okes, 1623)

Kamal, Prince Youssef, *Monumenta cartographica Africae et Aegypti*, 16 vols (Cairo: La Société Royale de Géographie de l'Égypte, 1926–51) [Reproduces in the early volumes all the surviving charts and maps relating to the European exploration of the west coast of Africa known to exist before the year 1939.]

Keen, Maurice, *Chivalry* (New Haven and London: Yale University Press, 1984)

Kimble, George H., (ed.), *The Catalan World Map of the R. Biblioteca Estense at Modena* (London: Royal Geographical Society, 1934)

La Fosse, Eustache de, 'Voyage a la côte occidentale d'Afrique en Portugal et en Espagne 1479–1480', ed. Raymond Foulché-Delbosc, in *Revue Hispanique*, IV (1897), 174–201

——, *Voyage d'Eustache de La Fosse sur la côte de Guinée, au Portugal et en Espagne (1479–1481)*, ed. Denis Escudier (Paris: Editions Chandeigne, 1992)

La Roncière, Charles de, *La Découverte de l'Afrique au moyen âge: cartographes et explorateurs*, 3 vols (Cairo: La Société Royale de Géographie de l'Égypte, 1924–7)

La Salle, Antoine, 'Du Réconfort de Madame du Fresne', in Joseph Nève, (ed.), *Antoine de la Salle: sa vie et ses ouvrages* (Paris–Brussels: Champion, 1903), 101–55)

[La Salle, Gadifer de], vol. 3 of *Le Canarien: crónicas francesas de la conquista de Canarias*, ed. Elías Serra and Alejandro Cioranescu, 3 vols, Fontes Rerum Canariarum (La Laguna de Tenerife: CSIC, 1959–64)

Ladero Quesada, Miguel Ángel, 'Los señores de Canarias en su contexto sevillano (1403–1477)', in *AEA*, XXIII (1977), 125–64

Laguarda Trias, Rolando A., *La aportación científica de mallorquines y portugueses a la cartografía náutica en los siglos XIV y XVI* (Madrid: CSIC, 1964)

[Lanckman von Valckenstein, Nicholas], *Leonor de Portugal, imperatriz da Alemanha: diario de viagem do embaixador Nicolau Lanckman de Valckenstein*, ed. do texto latino e tradução de Aires A. Nascimento (Lisbon: Edições Cosmos, 1992)

Las Casas, Bartolomé de, op, *Historia de las Indias*, ed. Agustín Millares Carlo, 3 vols (México–Buenos Aires: Fondo de Cultura Económica, 1951)

Lawrence, A.W., *Trade Castles and Forts of West Africa* (London: Jonathan Cape, 1963)

Legge, M. Dominica, (ed.), *Anglo–Norman Letters and Petitions from All Souls MS 182*, Anglo–Norman Text Society, vol. 3 (Oxford: Basil Blackwell, 1941), nos. 28, 287, 297 and 397. [Note also British Library, MS Cotton, Vesp. F. III, fol. 47, transcribed, with errors, in Frederico Francisco de la Figanière, *Catálogo dos Manuscriptos Portugueses existentes no Museu Britânico . . .* (Lisbon: Imprensa Nacional, 1853), 121]

Leite, Duarte, *História dos descobrimentos: colectânea de esparsos,* ed. Vitorino Magalhães Godinho, 2 vols (Lisbon: Edições Cosmos, 1959–62)

——, *Acerca da "Cronica dos feitos de Guinea"* (Lisbon: Livraria Bertrand, 1940)

Select Bibliography

Leo Africanus, *The History and Description of Africa; Done into English by John Pory*, 3 vols, The Hakluyt Society, Old Series, vols 92–4 (London: The Hakluyt Society, 1896)

Lévi-Strauss, Claude, *Tristes tropiques*, English trans. by John and Doreen Weightman (Harmondsworth: Penguin Books, 1976)

Libro del conosçimiento, [*See under* Anon.]

Livro dos conselhos de el-rei D. Duarte (livro da Cartuxa), transcription of João José Alves Dias, rev. A. H. de Oliveira Marques and Teresa F. Rodrigues (Lisbon: Editorial Estampa, 1982)

Lopez, Robert Sabatino, *Studi sull' economia genovese nel Medio Evo* (Turin: S. Lattes, 1938)

Luttrell, Anthony, 'Slavery and Slaving in the Portuguese Atlantic (to about 1500)', in Christopher Fyfe, (ed.), *The Transatlantic Slave Trade from West Africa*, Centre of African Studies (Edinburgh: University of Edinburgh, 1965; [mimeograph], 61–80

Ly, Abdoulaye, *Un Navire de commerce sur la côte sénégambienne en 1685*, Catalogues et Documents n° XVII (Dakar: IFAN, 1964)

Magnaghi, Alberto, *Precursori di Colombo? Il tentativo di viaggio dei genovesi fratelli Vivaldi nel 1291* (Rome: Arti Grafiche, 1935)

Major, Richard Henry, *The Life of Prince Henry of Portugal, Surnamed the Navigator* (London: A. Asher, 1868; repr. London: Frank Cass and Co., 1967)

Malfante, Antonio, *The Letter of Antoine Malfante* [from the oasis of Tuat in 1447], ed. and trans. G.R. Crone and included in *The Voyages of Cadamosto and other Documents*, The Hakluyt Society, Second Series, LXXX (London, The Hakluyt Society, 1937)

Mallett, Michael E., *The Florentine Galleys in the Fifteenth Century: with the Diary of Luca di Maso degli Albizzi, Captain of the Galleys, 1429–1430* (Oxford: Clarendon Press, 1967)

Markl, Dagoberto L., *O retábulo de S. Vicente da Sé de Lisboa e os documentos* (Lisbon: Editorial Caminho, 1988)

Marques, A. H. de Oliveira, *A sociedade medieval portuguesa* (5th edn, Lisbon: Sá da Costa, 1987)

——, *Portugal na crise dos séculos XIV e XV*, Nova História de Portugal, IV (Lisbon: Editorial Presença, 1987)

——, *Guia do estudante de história medieval portuguesa*, Imprensa Universitária, 15 (3rd edn, Lisbon: Editorial Estampa, 1988) [Essential reading for any student of medieval Portuguese history.]

Marques, Alfredo Pinheiro, *Origem e desenvolvimento da cartografia portuguesa na época dos descobrimentos*, Descoberta do Mundo (Lisbon: INCM, 1987)

——, *Portugal e o descobrimento do Atlântico: síntese e cronologia. Portugal and the Discovery of the Atlantic: A Summary and a Chronology* (Lisbon: INCM, 1990) [Useful for reproductions of maps, etc.]

——, 'A maldição da memória e a criação do mito: o Infante D. Pedro e o Infante D. Henrique nos descobrimentos', in *Vértice*, LXIV (1995), 63–74

Marques, José, 'Relações luso-castelhanas, no século XV' in *Relações entre Portugal e Castela nos finais da Idade Média*, Textos Universitários de Ciências Sociais e Humanas (Lisbon: Fundação Gulbenkian and Junta Nacional de Investigação Científica e Tecnológica, 1994), 349–73

Martins, Mário, 'Representações teatrais em Lisboa no ano de 1451', in *Brotéria*, LXXI (1960), 422–30

Mascarenhas, Jerónimo de, *Historia de la ciudad de Ceuta [1648]*, ed. Afonso de Dornelas (Lisbon: Academia das Sciências de Lisboa, 1918)

Mauny, Raymond, *Les Navigations mediévales sur les côtes sahariennes antérieures à la découverte portugaise (1434)* (Lisbon: CEHU, 1960)

——, *Tableau géographique de l'ouest africain au moyen âge d'après les sources écrites, la tradition et l'archéologie* (Dakar: IFAN, 1961)

Mauro Camaldolese, Fra, *Il mappamondo di Fra Mauro*, ed. Tullia Gasparrini Leporace (Rome: Istituto Poligrafico del Stato, 1956)

Mendonça, Henrique Lopes de, *Estudos sobre navios portugueses nos séculos XV e XVI* (Lisbon: ACL, 1892)

Mendonça, Manuela, *D. João II: um percurso humano e político nas origens da modernidade em Portugal*, Imprensa Universitária, 87 (Lisbon: Editorial Estampa, 1991)

Millás Vallicrosa, José María, *Estudios sobre historia de la ciencia española* (Barcelona: CSIC, 1949)

——, *Nuevos estudios sobre historia de la ciencia española* (Barcelona: CSIC, 1960)

——, *Las tablas astronómicas del rey Don Pedro el Ceremonioso: edición crítica de los textos hebraico, catalán y latino, con estudio y notas* (Madrid: CSIC, 1962)

Miret y Sans, Joaquín, 'La esclavitud en Cataluña en los últimos tiempos de la Edad Media', in *Rhisp*, XLI, no. 99 (October 1917), 1–109

Mitjá, Marina, 'Abandò de las Illes Canàries per Joan I d'Aragó', in *AEA*, VIII (1962), 325–53

Mollat, Michel, 'Y a-t-l une économie de la Renaissance?' 'in *Etudes sur l'économie et la société de l'Occident médiévale, XIIe–XVe siècles* (London: Variorum Reprints, 1977), 37–54

Mollat, Michel, & Others, *L'Économie européenne aux deux derniers siècles du moyen âge*, in Rendiconti del Xe Congresso Internazionale di Scienze Storiche (Rome, 1955), *Relazioni*, VI

Monod, Th., R. Mauny and G. Duval, *De la première découverte de la Guinée: récit par Diogo Gomes (fin XVe siècle)* (Bissau: CEGP, 1959)

Monod, Th., A. Teixeira da Mota, & R. Mauny, (eds.), *Description de la côte occidentale d'Afrique (Sénégal au Cap de Monte, Archipels): par Valentim Fernandes (1506–1510)* (Bissau: CEGP, 1951)

Monteiro, João Gouveia, *A guerra em Portugal nos finais da idade média* (Lisbon: Editorial Notícias, 1998)

Monteiro, Saturnino, *Batalhas e combates da marinha portuguesa: 1139–1521*, I (Lisbon: Sá da Costa, 1989)

Monumenta Cartographica Vaticana, (ed. R. Almagià), vol. I (Vatican City: Biblioteca Apostolica Vaticana, 1944)

Moreno, Humberto Baquero, (ed.), *A batalha de Alfarrobeira: antecedentes e significado histórico* (Lourenço Marques: Tipografia Minerva Central, 1973)

——, *Itinerários de El-Rei D. Duarte (1433–1438)* (Lisbon: APH, 1976)

——, 'As Cortes de Lisboa de 1448' in *RPH*, XVI (1978), 185–208

Mota, A. Teixeira da, *Topónimos de origem portuguesa na costa occidental de Àfrica desde o Cabo Bojador ao Cabo de Santa Caterina* (Bissau: CEGP, 1950)

——, *Guiné portuguesa*, 2 vols (Lisbon: AGU, 1954)

——, 'As rotas marítimas portuguesas no Atlántico do século XV ao último quartel do século XVI', in *Do Tempo e da História*, III (1970), 13–33

——, *Alguns aspectos da colonização e do comércio marítimo dos portugueses na África Ocidental nos séculos XV e XVI*, Centro de Estudos de Cartografia Antiga, XCVIII (Lisbon: JICU, 1976)

Münzer, Hieronymus, *Itinerarium Hispanicum*, ed. Ludwig Pfandl, in *Rhisp*, XLVIII, no. 13 (February 1920), 1–179

——, *De inventione Africae maritimae et occidentalis videlicet Geneae per Infantem Henricum Portugaliae*, Latin text with Portuguese translation published by Basílio de Vasconcelos in *o Instituto*, LXXXIII (1932), 140–72

Murphy, James Cavanah [sic], *Plans, Elevations, Sections and Views of the Church of Batalha . . . Illustrated with 27 Plates* (London: I. & J. Taylor, 1795). [Murphy, an architect by profession, visited Batalha in 1789. His textual account of the monastery, translated and annotated by him, is taken from Frei Luís de Sousa's *História de S. Domingos* (Bemfica: Giraldo de Vinha, 1623).]

Nascimento, Aires A., (ed. and trans.), *Princesas de Portugal: contratos matrimoniais dos séculos XV e XVI* (Lisbon: Edições Cosmos, 1992)

New Cambridge Medieval History, The, vol. VII (*c.* 1415–*c.* 1500), ed. Christopher Allmand (Cambridge: CUP, 1998)

Newton, Arthur Percival, (ed.), *Travel and Travellers of the Middle Ages* (London: Paul Trench and Trubner, 1926; repr. Freeport, NY: Books for Libraries Press, 1967)

Nordenskiold, Nils A. E., *Periplus: An Essay on the Early History of Charts and Sailing Directions*, translated by Francis A. Bather (Stockholm: P. A. Norstedt and Sönner, 1897)

Oliver, Roland, (ed.), *The Dawn of African History* (London: OUP, 1961; repr. 1963)

Ordenaçõens do Senhor Rey D. Affonso V [*See* Afonso V.]

Origo, Iris, *The Merchant of Prato: Francesco di Marco Datini* (London: Jonathan Cape, 1957)

Painter, George G., *Catalogue of Books Printed in the XVth Century now in the British Museum: Part X: Spain–Portugal* (London: Trustees of the British Museum, 1971)

Pais, Frei Álvaro, *Espelho dos reis (Speculum regis)*, translated by Miguel Pinto de Meneses, 2 vols (Lisbon: IAC, 1955–63)

Palencia, Alfonso de, *Gesta hispaniensia ex annalibvs svorvm diervm collecta*, ed. Brian Tate & Jeremy Lawrance. I: Libri I–V (Madrid: Real Academia de la Historia, 1998)

Park, Mungo, *Travels into the Interior of Africa* (London: Eland, 1983)

Parry, J. H., *The Age of Reconnaissance* (London: Weidenfeld and Nicolson, 1963)

[Paulino, Francisco Faria, (coordinator)], *Catálogo – o rostro do Infante* ([Lisbon]: CNCDP, 1994)

Paviot, Jacques, 'L'Imaginaire géographique des Découvertes au XVᵉ siècle', in Jean Aubin, Alfredo Pinheiro and others, (eds.), *La Découverte, le Portugal et l'Europe: actes du colloque, Paris 26 à 28 mai 1988*, Société Française d'Histoire de Portugal (Paris: Fondation Calouste Gulbenkian, 1990), 141–58

——, (ed.), *Portugal et Bourgogne au xvᵉ siècle* (Paris–Lisbon: CCCG and CNCDP, 1995)

[Pedro, Infante D.], *Actas do congresso comemorativo do 6° centenário do Infante D. Pedro*, in *Biblos*, LXIX (1993)

Pereira, Armando da Câmara, *Ciência e mito nos descobrimentos (ensaio iconológico sobre cosmografia e cartografia)* (n.p: Secretaria Regional de Educação e Cultura [dos Açores], [1990])

Pereira, Duarte Pacheco, *Esmeraldo de situ orbis*, trans. and ed., George H.T. Kimble, The Hakluyt Society, Second Series, no. LXXIX (London: The Hakluyt Society, 1937)

——, *Esmeraldo de situ orbis*, ed. Augusto Epiphánio da Silva Dias (Lisbon: Sociedad de Geografia de Lisboa, 1805; facsimile edn, 1975)

Peres, Damião, (ed.), *Regimento das Cazas das India e Mina* (Coimbra: Imprensa da Universidade, 1947)

——, *História dos descobrimentos portugueses*, (1st edn, Oporto: Portucalense Editora, 1943; 4th edn, Oporto: Vertente, 1992)

——, *O livro de recebimentos de 1470 da Chancelaria da Câmara* (Lisbon: APH, 1974)

Pérez Embid, Florentino, *Los descubrimientos en el Atlántico y la rivalidad castellano-portuguesa hasta el tratado de Tordesillas* (Seville: Escuela de Estudios Hispano-Americanos, Universidad de Sevilla, 1948)

Phillips, J. R. S., *The Medieval Expansion of Europe*, OPUS (Oxford: OUP, 1988; repr. 1990; 2nd edn 1998)

Phillips, William D., Jr., *Slavery from Roman Times to the Early Transatlantic Trade* (Manchester: Manchester University Press, [1985])

Pimpão, Álvaro Júlio da Costa, 'A "Crónica dos feitos de Guiné", as minhas "teses" e as "teses" de Duarte Leite', in *Biblos*, XVII (1941), 665–96

Pina, Rui de, *Chronica do Senhor Rey D. Duarte*, in *Crónicas de Rui de Pina*, ed. M. Lopes de Almeida, Tesouros da Literatura e da História (Oporto: Lello & Irmão, 1977), 487–575

——, *Crónica do Rei D. Duarte*, ed. António Borges Coelho (Lisbon: Editorial Presença, 1966)

——, *Chronica do Senhor Rey D. Affonso V*, in *Crónicas de Rui de Pina*, ed. M. Lopes de Almeida, Tesouros da Literatura e da História (Oporto: Lello and Irmão, 1977), 577–881

——, *Crónica de El-Rei D. João II*, ed. Alberto Martins de Carvalho (Coimbra: Atlântida, 1950)

[Polo, Marco], *Libro de las cosas maravillosas de Marco Polo* [1477] (Madrid: Sociedad de Bibliófilos Españoles, 1947)

——, *Viatges de Marco Polo: versió catalana del segle xiv*, ed. Annamaria Gallina, Els Nostres Clàssics (Barcelona: Editorial Barcino, 1958)

Portugaliae Monumenta Africana, directed by Luís de Albuquerque and Maria Emilia Madeira Santos, Instituto de Investigação Científica Tropical, I (Lisbon: CNCDP and INCM, 1993)

Prado, André do, *Horologium fidei: diálogo com o Infante D. Henrique*, ed. Aires A. Nascimento, Mare Liberum (Lisbon: INCM, 1994)

Prestage, Edgar, *The Portuguese Pioneers* (London: A. & C. Black, 1937; repr. New York: Barnes and Noble, 1967)

Prince Henry the Navigator and Portuguese Maritime Enterprise: Catalogue of an Exhibition at the British Museum, September–October 1960 (London: Trustees of the British Museum, [1960])

Purchas, Samuel, *Hakluytus Posthumus, or Purchas his Pilgrimes*, 2 vols (London: W. Stansby, 1625; repr. Glasgow: J. MacLehose and Sons, 1905–7)

Radulet, Carmen M., *Os descobrimentos portugueses e a Italia*, Colecção Documenta Historica (Lisbon: Vega, 1991)

Randles, W.G.L., 'Sur l'idée de la découverte', in *Les Aspects internationaux de la découverte oceanique au xve et au xvie siècles: Actes du 5e colloque internationale d'histoire maritime* (Paris: SEVPEN, 1966), 17–21

Rau, Virgínia, *Sesmarias medievais portuguesas* (Lisbon: Bertrand, 1946; 2nd edn, Lisbon: Editorial Presença, 1982)

——, *A exploração e o comércio do sal de Setúbal: Estudo de história económica* (Lisbon: IAC, 1951)

——, 'Uma família de mercadores italianos em Portugal no século xv: os Lomellini', in *RFL*, XXII (1956), 56–83; also in *Estudos de História* (Lisbon: Verbo, 1968), 13–58

——, and Jorge de Macedo, *O açucar da Madeira nos fins do século XV* (Funchal: Junta Geral do Distrito Autónomo de Funchal, 1962)

——, 'Cartas de Lisboa no Arquivo Datini de Prato', in *Estudos Italianos em Portugal*, XXI–XXII (1962–3) [*separata*, 1–13]

——, 'Rumos e vicissitudes do comércio do sal português nos séculos xiv a xviii', in *RFL*, III Série, VII (1963), 5–27

——, 'Feitores e feitorias "instrumentos" do comércio internacional português no século XVI, in *Brotéria*, LXXXI (1965) [*separata*, 1–56]. [Also contains information about factories and factors before the sixteenth century.]

Reis-Santos, Luís, *Iconografia Henriquina* (Coimbra: CEQMDH, 1975)

Ribeiro, Manuel Sampayo, *O verdadeiro retrato do Infante D. Henrique*, Colecção Biblioteca de História (Lisbon: Editorial Notícias, 1991)

Ricard, Robert, *Études sur l'histoire des Portugais au Maroc*, Acta Universitatis Conimbrigensis (Coimbra: Atlântida, 1955)

Robertson, William, *The History of America*, 2 vols (London: W. Strahan, T. Cadell and J. Balfour, at Edinburgh, 1777)

Rodrigues, Graça Almeida, *Cinco autores historiais: Fernão Lopes, Gomes Eanes de Zurara, Rui de Pina, João de Barros e Damião de Góis* (Lisbon: Editorial Presença, 1979)

Rodrigues, Maria Teresa Campos, *Aspectos da administração municipal de Lisboa no século XV* [separata dos números 101 a 109 da *Revista Municipal*] (Lisbon, 1968)

Roërie, Guilleux de la, *Navires et marins: de la rame à l'hélice*, 2 vols (2nd edn, Paris: Rombaldi. 1946)

Rogers, Francis M., *The Travels of the Infante Dom Pedro of Portugal*, Harvard Studies in Romance Languages, 26 (Cambridge, Mass.: Harvard University Press, 1961)

Select Bibliography

Rosário, Morais do, *Genoveses na história de Portugal* (Lisbon: Minerva do Comércio, 1977)

Roux, Jean-Paul, *Les Explorateurs au moyen âge* (Paris: Editions du Seuil, 1967)

Rozmital, Leo of, *The Travels of Leo of Rozmital*, trans. and ed. Malcolm Letts, The Hakluyt Society, Second Series, no. CVIII (Cambridge: CUP, 1957)

Rubim, Nuno José Varela, 'Sobre a possibilidade técnica do emprego de artilharia na batalha de Aljubarrota', in *Revista de Artilharia*, nos. 725/726 (Jan. and Feb., 1986), 257–83

Rubió i Lluch, Antoni, *Documents per l'història de la cultura catalana mig-eval*, 2 vols (Barcelona: Institut d'Estudis Catalans, 1908–21)

Ruiz, Juan, Arcipreste de Hita, *Libro de buen amor*, ed. G.B. Gybbon-Monypenny (Madrid: Castalia, 1988)

Rumeu de Armas, A., *Piraterías y ataques navales contra las Islas Canarias*, 3 vols (Madrid: CSIC, 1947–50)

——, 'La torre africana de Santa Cruz de la Mar Pequeña: la segunda fundación', in *AEA*, I (1955), 397–477

——, *España en el África atlántica*, 2 vols (Madrid: CSIC, 1956)

Russell, P. E., *Prince Henry the Navigator*, Canning House Seventh Annual Lecture (London: The Hispanic and Luso–Brazilian Councils, 1960)

——, 'Fontes documentais castelhanas para a história da expansão portuguesa na Guiné nos últimos anos de D. Afonso V', in *Do Tempo e da História*, IV (1971), 5–33

——, 'El descubrimiento de Canarias y el debate medieval acerca de los derechos de los príncipes y pueblos paganos', in *Revista de historia canaria*, XXXVI (1978), 9–32

——, *O Infante D. Henrique e as Ilhas Canarias: uma dimensão mal compreendida da biografia henriquina*, Academia das Ciências de Lisboa, Nova Série, Fasc. V (Lisbon: ACL, 1979)

——, *Prince Henry the Navigator: The Rise and Fall of a Culture Hero*, Taylorian Special Lecture, 10 November 1983 (Oxford: Clarendon Press, 1984)

——, [Russell, Peter], *Traducciones y traductores en la Península Ibérica (1400–1550)* (Bellaterra: Escuela Universitaria de Traductores e Intérpretes, 1984)

——, '*Veni, vidi, vici*: Some Fifteenth-Century Eyewitness Accounts of Travel in the African Atlantic before 1492', in *Historical Research*, LXVI (1993), 115–28

——, 'Prince Henry and the Necessary End', in, T. F. Earle and Stephen Parkinson, (eds.), *Studies in the Portuguese Discoveries*, I (Warminster, Wilts.: Aris and Phillips, 1992), 1–15

——, *Portugal, Spain and the African Atlantic: Chivalry and Crusade from John of Gaunt to Henry the Navigator* (Aldershot and Brookfield, Vermont: Variorum, 1995)

——, 'The Medieval Castilian Translation of Vegetius, *Epitoma de rei militaris*: An Introduction', in Ann L. Mackenzie (ed.) *Spain and its Literature: Essays in Memory of E. Allison Peers* (Liverpool: Liverpool University Press and Modern Humanities Research Association, 1997), 49–63

Russell-Wood, A. J. R., *A World on the Move: The Portuguese in Africa, Asia and America 1415–1808* (Manchester: Carcanet Press, 1992)

——, 'Before Columbus: Portugal's African Prelude to the Middle Passage and Contribution to Discourse on Race and Slavery', in Vera Hyatt and Rex Nettleford, *Discourse and the Origin of the Americas: A New World View of 1492* (Washington, DC: Smithsonian Institution Press, 1994), 134–68

Ryder, A.F.C., *Materials for West African History in Portuguese Archives*, Guides to Materials for West African History (London: University of London, The Athlone Press, 1965)

——, *Alfonso the Magnanimous, King of Aragon, Naples, and Sicily 1396–1458* (Oxford: Clarendon Press, 1990)

Sá, Artur Moreira de (ed.), *Chartularium Universitatis Portugalensis (1288–1537)*, 12 vols (thus far) (Lisbon: IAC, 1966–)

Saldanha, António Vasconcelos de, *As capitanias: o regime senhorial na expansão ultramarina portuguesa* ([Funchal]: Centro de Estudos de História do Atlântico, 1992)

Salgado, Abílio José & Anastásia Salgado Mestrinho (eds.), *Registos dos reinados de D. João II e de D. Manuel I* (facs. edn, Lisbon: Ministério da Saúde, 1996)

Santarém, 2do Visconde de, *Memórias para a História e Teoria das Cortes Geraes*, Partes 1 and 2 (Lisbon: Impressão Regia, 1827–8)

——, *Atlas composé de mappemondes, de portulans et de cartes hydrographiques et historiques depuis le vi^e jusqu'au le xviie siècle*, 3 vols (Paris: Maulde et Renou, 1849–52); *Atlas de Santarém: Facsimile of the Final Edition, 1849*, ed. Helen Wallis and A. H. Sijmons (Amsterdam: R. Muller, 1985)

Santos, Domingo Maurício Gomes DO, SJ, *D. Duarte e as responsabilidades de Tânger (1433–38)* (Lisbon: Editora Gráfica Portuguesa, 1960)

Santos, Reynaldo dos, *Nuno Gonçalves* (London: Phaidon, 1955)

S. José, Frei João de and Henrique Fernandes Sarrão, *Duas descrições do Algarve do século XVI*, ed. Manuel Viegas Guerreiro and Joaquim Romero Magalhães, Cadernos da Revista de História Económica e Social, 3 (Lisbon: Sá da Costa, 1983)

Saunders, A. C. de C. M., *A Social History of Black Slaves and Freedmen in Portugal 1441–1555*, Cambridge Iberian and Latin American Studies (Cambridge: CUP, 1982); Portuguese translation: *História social dos escravos e libertos negros em Portugal (1441–1555)*, Temas Portugueses (Lisbon: INCM, 1994)

Scammell, G. V., *The World Encompassed: The First European Maritime Empires, c. 800–1650* (Berkeley and Los Angeles: University of California Press, 1973)

Seligman, C. G., *Races of Africa*, The Home University Library (3rd edn, London and New York: OUP, 1961; 4th edn 1966)

Sérgio, António, *Ensaios*, I (2nd edn, Lisbon: Sá da Costa, 1976)

Serra y Ràfols, Elias, *Los portugueses en Canarias. Discurso inaugural del año académico 1941–42* (La Laguna: Universidad de La Laguna, 1941)

Serrão, Joaquim Veríssimo, *História de Portugal*, 3 vols (Lisbon: Editorial Verbo, 1977–8)

——, *Cronistas do século XV posteriores a Fernão Lopes*, Biblioteca Breve ([Lisbon]: ICP, 1977)

Serrão, Joel, (ed.), *Dicionário de História de Portugal*, 6 vols (Oporto: Livraria Figueirinhas, 1992)

Singer, Charles and others (eds.), *A History of Technology*, 2 vols (Oxford: Clarendon Press, 1956; corrected repr., 1957)

Skelton, R.A., *Explorers' Maps: Chapters in the Cartographic Record of Geographical Discovery* (London: Routledge and Kegan Paul, 1958; repr. London: Spring Books, 1970)

Smalley, Beryl, *Historians of the Middle Ages* (London: Thames and Hudson, 1974)

Sousa, António Caetano de, *Provas da história genealógica da casa real portuguesa* (1st edn, Lisbon, 1739–48, 2nd edn by Manuel Lopes de Almeida and César Pegado, 12 vols, Coimbra: Atlântida, 1946–54)

Sousa, Armindo, *As cortes medievais portuguesas (1385–1490)*, 2 vols (Oporto: INIC, 1987)

Sousa, Ivo Carneiro de, 'Economia e religião nos descobrimentos henriquinos', in *Catálogo da Exposição 'Henrique, o Navegador'* (Oporto: n.p., 1994) [*separata*, 1–8]

Sousa, João Silva de, *A casa senhorial do Infante D. Henrique* (Lisbon: Livros Horizonte, 1991)

Sousa, Frei Luís de, OP [and Frei Luís Cácegas, OP], *Primeira parte da história de S. Domingos* (Bemfica: Giraldo de Vinha, 1623)

Southern, R. W., *The Making of the Middle Ages* (London: Arrow Books, 1959)

Suárez Fernández, Luis, *Relaciones entre Portugal y Castilla en la época del Infante Don Enrique, 1393–1460* (Madrid: CSIC, 1960)

——, 'La cuestión de Canarias, ante el concilio de Basilea', in CIHD, *Actas*, IV (1961), 505–11

Tafur, Pero, *Andanças e viajes*, ed. M. Jiménez de la Espada (Madrid: Imprenta Ginesta, 1874)

Taylor, E. G. R., *The Haven–Finding Art: A History of Navigation from Odysseus to Captain Cook* (London: Hollis and Carter, 1956; new impr., 1958)

Terrasse, Henri, 'Note sur les contacts artistiques entre le Maroc et le Portugal, du xve au xviie siècle', in *Mélanges d'études luso-marocaines dédiés à la memoire de David Lopes et Pierre de Cenival*, L'Institut Français au Portugal: Collection Portugaise, 6 (Lisbon: Portugalia Editora, 1945)

Tesi, Mario (ed.), *Monumenti di Cartografia a Firenze (sec. X–XVII), IX Conferenza Internazionale di Storia della Cartografia* (Florence: Biblioteca Medicea Laurenziana, 1981)

Thomas, Hugh, *The Slave Trade* (New York: Simon and Schuster, 1997)

Thomaz, Luís Filipe F. R., *De Ceuta a Timor* (Lisbon: Difel, 1994)

Thomson, James, *The Complete Poetical Works of James Thomson*, ed. J. Logie Wilson (Oxford: OUP, 1951)

Thorndike, Lynn, *A History of Magic and Experimental Science*, vols II–IV (New York: Columbia University Press, 1923–34; repr. 1953–8)

Tooley, R. V., *Maps and Map-makers* (7th edn, London: Batsford, 1987)

Torre, Antonio de la and Luis Suárez Fernández (eds.), *Documentos referentes a las relaciones con Portugal durante el reinado de los Reyes Católicos*, 3 vols (Valladolid: CSIC, 1958–63)

Torres Campos, Rafael, *Carácter de la conquista y colonización de las Islas Canarias. Discurso de ingreso en la Real Academia de la Historia* (Madrid: Real Academia de la Historia, 1901)

Trimingham, J. Spencer, *A History of Islam in West Africa*, Glasgow University Publications (Oxford & New York: Oxford University Press, 1962)

Ullman, Walter, *Law and Politics in the Middle Ages* (Bristol: The Sources of History Ltd., 1975)

Ure, John, *Prince Henry the Navigator* (London: Constable, 1977)

Vale, Malcolm, *War and Chivalry: Warfare and Culture in England, France and Burgundy at the End of the Middle Ages* (London: Duckworth, 1981)

Valera, Mossen Diego de, *Crónica de los Reyes Católicos*, ed. Juan de M. Carriazo, *Revista de Filología Española*, anejo VIII (Madrid: J. Molina, 1927)

Vallvé Bermejo, Joaquín, 'Descripción de Ceuta musulmana en el siglo XV', in *Al-Andalus*, XXVII (1962), 398–448

Van Answaarden, Robert, *Les Portugais devant le grand conseil des Pays-Bas (1460–1580)*, EHESS (Paris: Fondation Calouste Gulbenkian, 1991)

Vegetius Renatus, Publius Flavius, *Vegetius: Epitome of Miliary Science*, ed. and trans. N. P. Milner, Translated Texts for Historians, 16 (Liverpool: Liverpool University Press, 1993; 2nd edn, 1996)

Vergé-Franceschi, Michel, *Henri, le Navigateur* (Paris: Editions du Félin, 1994)

Verlinden, Charles, 'La Colonie italienne de Lisbonne et le développement de l'économie métropolitaine et coloniale portugaise', in *Studi in onore de Armando Sapori*, II (Milan: Istituto Editoriale Cisalpino, 1958), 617–28

——, 'Formes féodales et domaniales de la colonisation portugaise dans la zone atlantique aux xive et xve siècles et spécialement sous Henri le Navigateur', in *RPH*, IX (1960), 1–44

——, 'António de Noli e a colonização das Ilhas do Cabo Verde, in *RFL*, série iii, VII (1963), 28–45

Vernet, Joan and David Romano (eds.), *Atlas catalan de 1375* (Barcelona: n.p., 1961)

Vitoria, Francisco de, *Obras: Relecciones teológicas*, ed. Teófilo Urdanoz, OP (Madrid: Biblioteca de Autores Cristianos, 1960)

——, *Political Writings*, ed. Anthony Pagden and Jeremy Lawrance, Cambridge Texts in the History of Political Thought (Cambridge: CUP, 1991)

Walsingham, Thomas, *Historia Anglicana, 1272–1422*, ed. H. T. Riley, 2 vols (London: Rolls Series, 1862–4)

Wappäus, J. E., *Untersuchungen über die geographischen Entdeckungen der Portugiesen unter Heinrich dem Seefahrer: ein Beitrag zur Geschichte des Seehandels und der Geographie im Mittelalter*, I (Göttingen: Dieterichsche Buchh., 1842)

Watson, A. M., 'Back to Gold – and Silver', in *Economic History Review*, Second Series, XX (1967), 1–34

Wilks, Michael, *The Problem of Sovereignty in the Later Middle Ages: The Papal Monarchy with Augustinus Triumphus and the Publicists*, Cambridge Studies in Medieval Life and Thought. New Series, vol. IX (Cambridge: CUP, 1964)

Wood, W. Raymond, 'An Archeological Appraisal of Early European Settlements in the Senegambia', in *Journal of African History*, VIII (1967), 39–60

Wylie, James Hamilton, *The Reign of Henry V*, 3 vols (Cambridge: CUP, 1914–29)

Wyngaert, P. Anastasius van de, OFM, (ed.), *Sinica franciscana: Itinera et relationes fratrum minorum saeculi XIII et XIV*, I (Ad Claras Acquas [Florence]: Queracchi, 1929)

Zurara, Gomes Eanes de, *Crónica da tomada de Ceuta por El Rei Dom João I*, ed. Francisco Maria Esteves Pereira (Lisbon: Academia das Ciências de Lisboa, 1915)

——, *The Chronicle of the Discovery and Conquest of Guinea*, trans. C. Raymond Beazley and Edgar Prestage, 2 vols, Hakluyt Society, Series I, nos. 95 and 100 (London: The Hakluyt Society, 1896–9)

——, *Crónica de Guiné*, ed. José de Bragança (2nd edn, Oporto: Livraria Civilização, 1973)

——, *Chronique de Guinée*, ed. and trans. Léon Bourdon with the collaboration of Robert Ricard, Mémoires de l'Institut Français de l'Afrique Noire, no. 60 (Dakar: IFAN, 1960); repr. (Paris: Éditions Chandeigne, 1994)

——, *Crónica dos feitos notáveis que se passaram na conquista de Guiné por mandado do Infante D. Henrique*, ed. Torquato de Sousa Soares, 2 vols (Lisbon: Academia Portuguesa da História, 1978–81)

——, *Chronica do Conde Dom Pedro de Meneses, see* CLIHP, II (Lisbon: Academia Real das Sciências de Lisboa, 1792), 213–635

——, *Chronica do Conde Dom Duarte de Meneses, see* CLIHP, III (Lisbon: Academia Real das Sciências de Lisboa, 1793), 7–385

——, *Crónica do Conde D. Duarte de Meneses*, ed. diplomática de Larry King (Lisbon: Universidade Nova de Lisboa, 1978)

Index

Subheadings are listed alphabetically. Toponyms: references are normally to current English language forms of the toponym concerned but, if appropriate, the fifteenth-century Portuguese form is shown in parentheses and is also cross-referenced.

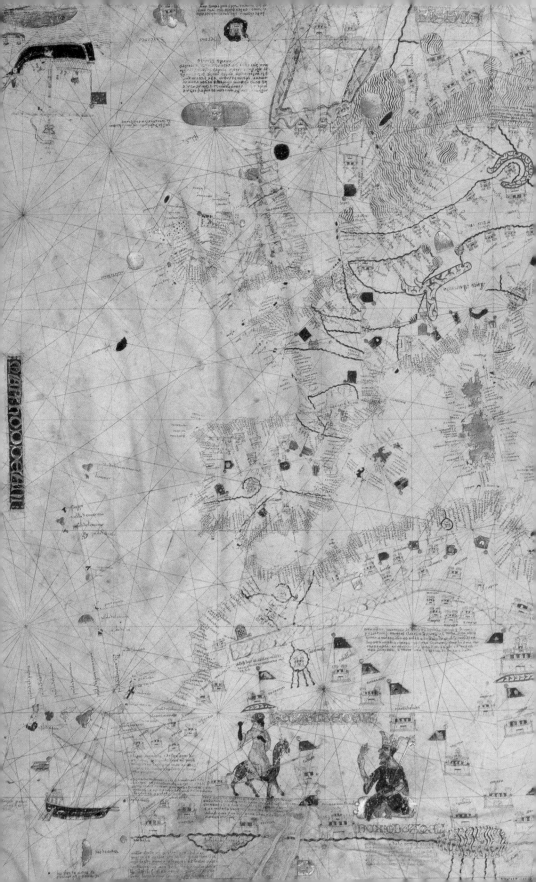